Mastering Active Directory
Second Edition

Deploy and secure infrastructures with Active Directory,
Windows Server 2016, and PowerShell

Dishan Francis

BIRMINGHAM - MUMBAI

Mastering Active Directory
Second Edition

Commissioning Editor: Vijin Boricha
Acquisition Editor: Heramb Bhavsar
Content Development Editor: Nithin George Varghese
Senior Editor: Rahul Dsouza
Technical Editor: Komal Karne
Copy Editor: Safis Editing
Project Coordinator: Vaidehi Sawant
Proofreader: Safis Editing
Indexer: Priyanka Dhadke
Production Designer: Aparna Bhagat

First published: June 2017
Second edition: August 2019

Production reference: 1080819

Published by Packt Publishing Ltd.
Livery Place
35 Livery Street
Birmingham
B3 2PB, UK.

ISBN 978-1-78980-020-3

www.packtpub.com

In memory of my uncles, Douglas Joseph, Norman Joseph, and Colvin Joseph.
You will always be in my heart.

`Packt.com`

Subscribe to our online digital library for full access to over 7,000 books and videos, as well as industry leading tools to help you plan your personal development and advance your career. For more information, please visit our website.

Why subscribe?

- Spend less time learning and more time coding with practical eBooks and Videos from over 4,000 industry professionals

- Improve your learning with Skill Plans built especially for you

- Get a free eBook or video every month

- Fully searchable for easy access to vital information

- Copy and paste, print, and bookmark content

Did you know that Packt offers eBook versions of every book published, with PDF and ePub files available? You can upgrade to the eBook version at `www.packt.com` and as a print book customer, you are entitled to a discount on the eBook copy. Get in touch with us at `customercare@packtpub.com` for more details.

At `www.packt.com`, you can also read a collection of free technical articles, sign up for a range of free newsletters, and receive exclusive discounts and offers on Packt books and eBooks.

Contributors

About the author

Dishan Francis is a technology consultant with over 15 years' experience in IT. He is a dedicated and enthusiastic IT expert who enjoys professional recognition and accreditation from several respected institutions. When it comes to managing innovative identity infrastructure solutions to improve system stability, efficiency, and security, his level of knowledge and experience place him among the very best in the field.

He is a six-time Microsoft MVP in Enterprise Mobility. He is also a Microsoft Wiki Ninja judge. He has maintained the RebelAdmin technology blog over the years, with lots of useful articles that focus on on-premise Active Directory services and Azure Active Directory. He currently works with Frontier Technology Ltd.

Although I wrote this book, there were many other people behind me. Without their support, it would have been an impossible task to complete. So, I take this opportunity to thank my lovely wife, Kanchana, and my children, Selena and Andrew, for their great support. My deepest gratitude goes to my parents and relatives for continuing to encourage me. Also, I'd like to thank the publisher, the reviewers, and my employer, Edwin, for all of their support on this journey.

About the reviewer

Florian Klaffenbach is currently working as a technology solutions professional at Microsoft. He is a well-known expert when it comes to hybrid cloud scenarios, cloud connectivity, and cloud environment optimization. Before he started at Microsoft, he worked at several companies in different roles, including as a technical community manager and solutions expert at Dell, and as a solutions architect at CGI Germany. He is also one of Packt's authors and has worked on books such as *Multi-Cloud for Architects* and *Implementing Azure Solutions*, first and second editions, all available from Packt Publishing. He spends his free time with his wife and his two little sons.

Packt is searching for authors like you

If you're interested in becoming an author for Packt, please visit authors.packtpub.com and apply today. We have worked with thousands of developers and tech professionals, just like you, to help them share their insight with the global tech community. You can make a general application, apply for a specific hot topic that we are recruiting an author for, or submit your own idea.

Table of Contents

Preface

Microsoft Active Directory is the most widely used identity management solution. It can centrally manage identities across its infrastructure. It is equipped with different role services, features, and components that help us handle identities securely and effectively according to business requirements. For the last 20 years, Microsoft has continued improving Active Directory, and Active Directory 2016 further consolidates its approach in terms of rectifying industry requirements and protecting identity infrastructures with emerging security threats. However, a technology-rich product is not simply going to make a productive, reliable, scalable, and secure identity infrastructure. It requires knowledge of Active Directory roles services, components, and features. It also requires knowledge of how to use those effectively to match different operation requirements. Only then can we plan, design, manage, and maintain a robust identity infrastructure.

Over the past few years, more and more organizations have adopted cloud technologies for a variety of reasons. With the growth of the cloud footprint, organizations' identity requirements have also changed. We can no longer limit corporate identities to on-premises infrastructures. By using Microsoft Azure Active Directory, we can extend our on-premises identities to the cloud. The hybrid AD approach provides lots of benefits for modern authentication requirements. However, security-wise, it also opens up a whole new level of challenges. Therefore, the majority of new content in the second edition is related to designing the Azure AD hybrid cloud, securing a hybrid AD environment, and protecting sensitive data.

Who this book is for

If you are an Active Directory administrator, system administrator, or network professional who has basic knowledge of Active Directory and is looking to become an expert in this topic, this book is for you.

What this book covers

Chapter 1, *Active Directory Fundamentals*, explains what Active Directory is and its characteristics. This chapter also explains the main components (physical and logical structure), object types, and role services of Active Directory. Last but not least, this chapter also covers Azure Active Directory and its capabilities in a nutshell.

Chapter 2, *Active Directory Domain Services 2016*, explains what's new in AD DS 2016 and how it will help improve your organization's identity infrastructure.

Chapter 3, *Designing an Active Directory Infrastructure*, talks about what needs to be considered in Active Directory infrastructure design. This chapter discusses how to place the AD DS logical and physical components in the AD DS environment according to best practices. It also covers the approach we need to take in order to move to a hybrid identity.

Chapter 4, *Active Directory Domain Name System*, explains how DNS works in the AD DS infrastructure. This chapter also includes information about the DNS server component, different types of DNS records, zones, and DNS delegation.

Chapter 5, *Placing Operations Master Roles*, talks about the FSMO roles and their responsibilities. This chapter also describes things we need to consider when placing FSMO roles in an Active Directory environment.

Chapter 6, *Migrating to Active Directory 2016*, covers the AD DS installation with different deployment models. This chapter also provides a step-by-step guide to migrating from an older version of AD DS to the new version, AD DS 2016.

Chapter 7, *Managing Active Directory Objects*, discusses how to create objects, find objects, modify objects, and remove objects (small-scale and large-scale) by using built-in Active Directory management tools and PowerShell commands.

Chapter 8, *Managing Users, Groups, and Devices*, further explores the Active Directory objects by deep diving into attributes, managed service accounts, and management of different object types. Last but not least, you will also learn about Active Directory object management best practices.

Chapter 9, *Designing the OU Structure*, teaches you how to design the OU structure properly, using different models to suit business requirements. This chapter also describes how to create, update, and remove OU. Furthermore, this chapter also discusses how we can delegate AD administration by using OU.

Chapter 10, *Managing Group Policies*, mainly discusses Group Policy objects and their capabilities. Group policy processing in an AD environment depends on many different things. In this chapter, we will deep dive into group policy processing to understand the technology behind it. We are also going to look into the different methods we can use for group policy filtering. Last but not least, we will learn about how to use group policies in an infrastructure, according to best practices.

Chapter 11, *Active Directory Services*, walks us through the more advanced Active Directory topics, such as AD LDS, Active Directory replication, Active Directory sites, Active Directory database maintenance, RODC, AD DS backup, and recovery.

Chapter 12, *Active Directory Certificate Services*, discusses the planning, deployment, and maintenance of Active Directory Certificate Services. Furthermore, we will also learn about how signing, encryption, and decryption work in a **public key infrastructure (PKI)**.

Chapter 13, *Active Directory Federation Services*, focuses on AD Federation Services such as planning, designing, deployment, and maintenance. This chapter also covers new features of AD FS 2016, such as built-in Azure MFA support.

Chapter 14, *Active Directory Rights Management Services*, covers the Active Directory Rights Management Service role, which we can use to protect sensitive data in a business. Data is the new oil, and the value of data keeps increasing. Therefore, protection of data is important for every business. In this chapter, we will learn about how AD RMS works and how to configure it.

Chapter 15, *Active Directory Security Best Practices*, covers the protection of the Active Directory environment. Recent attacks and studies prove that adversaries are increasingly targeting identities. So, we need to be mindful of protecting our Active Directory infrastructure at any cost. In this chapter, we will learn about different tools, services, and methods we can use to protect the Active Directory environment. If you are using Azure AD in hybrid mode, then there are different features and services that can be used to protect both environments (cloud and on-premises). In this chapter, we will also learn about some of these solutions, such as Azure AD Privileged Identity Management and Azure Information Protection.

Chapter 16, *Advanced AD Management with PowerShell*, is full of PowerShell scripts that can be used to manage, secure, audit, and monitor our Active Directory environment. We will also learn about the Azure Active Directory PowerShell for Graph module, which we can use to manage, query, and update AD objects in a hybrid AD environment.

Chapter 17, *Azure Active Directory Hybrid Setup*, discusses how we can extend our on-premises AD DS infrastructure to Azure Active Directory. Before we work on the implementation, we will deep dive into the planning process of the Azure AD hybrid setup. In this chapter, we will also learn about different authentication methods for a hybrid environment and the technology behind them.

Chapter 18, *Active Directory Audit and Monitoring*, teaches you how to monitor your on-premises/hybrid AD DS infrastructure using different tools and methods (cloud-based and on-premises). This chapter also demonstrates how to audit an Active Directory environment.

Chapter 19, *Active Directory Troubleshooting*, discusses how to troubleshoot the most common Active Directory infrastructure issues using different tools and methods. Furthermore, we will also look into the most common Azure AD connect errors, which can have a direct impact on the health of the Azure AD hybrid environment.

Appendix A, *Assessments*, covers the *Question and Answer* section chapter wise. It's freely available online for our readers and here is the link: https://static.packt-cdn.com/downloads/Mastering_Active_Directory_Assessments.pdf.

Appendix B, *References*, covers the *Further reading* section chapter wise. It's freely available online for our readers and here is the link: https://static.packt-cdn.com/downloads/Mastering_Active_Directory_References.pdf.

To get the most out of this book

This book is ideal for IT professionals, system engineers, and administrators who have a basic knowledge of Active Directory Domain Services. A basic knowledge of PowerShell is also required, since most of the role deployment, configuration, and management is done by using PowerShell commands and scripts.

Download the color images

We also provide a PDF file that has color images of the screenshots/diagrams used in this book. You can download it here: https://static.packt-cdn.com/downloads/9781789800203_ColorImages.pdf.

Conventions used

There are a number of text conventions used throughout this book.

`CodeInText`: Indicates code words in the text, database table names, folder names, filenames, file extensions, pathnames, dummy URLs, user input, and Twitter handles. Here is an example: "SLDs are domain names that don't have DNS suffixes such as `.com`, `.org`, or `.net`."

Any command-line input or output is written as follows:

```
Get-ADDomain | fl Name,DomainMode
```

Bold: Indicates a new term, an important word, or words that you see on screen. For example, words in menus or dialog boxes appear in the text like this. Here is an example: "Go to **All Services** | **Azure AD Domain Services**."

Get in touch

Feedback from our readers is always welcome.

General feedback: If you have questions about any aspect of this book, mention the book title in the subject of your message and email us at `customercare@packtpub.com`.

Errata: Although we have taken every care to ensure the accuracy of our content, mistakes do happen. If you have found a mistake in this book, we would be grateful if you would report this to us. Please visit `www.packt.com/submit-errata`, selecting your book, clicking on the Errata Submission Form link, and entering the details.

Piracy: If you come across any illegal copies of our works in any form on the internet, we would be grateful if you would provide us with the location address or website name. Please contact us at `copyright@packt.com` with a link to the material.

If you are interested in becoming an author: If there is a topic that you have expertise in, and you are interested in either writing or contributing to a book, please visit `authors.packtpub.com`.

Reviews

Please leave a review. Once you have read and used this book, why not leave a review on the site that you purchased it from? Potential readers can then see and use your unbiased opinion to make purchase decisions, we at Packt can understand what you think about our products, and our authors can see your feedback on their book. Thank you!

For more information about Packt, please visit `packt.com`.

Section 1: Active Directory Planning, Design, and Installation

This section will help you to learn about the physical and logical components of Active Directory, and how those can be used to build an Active Directory environment by considering business requirements, availability, efficiency, and security. Before we dive into the management and advanced functionalities of Active Directory, we still need to learn about the technology behind a directory service, and the chapters in this section will guide you with this. Apart from that, we are also going to look into the new features of Active Directory 2016.

As we all know, organizations are moving into cloud services on an increasingly frequent basis. This changes the authentication and authorization requirements as well. Therefore, we are also going to evaluate the benefits of moving to a hybrid identity with Azure Active Directory.

This section contains the following chapters:

- Chapter 1, *Active Directory Fundamentals*
- Chapter 2, *Active Directory Domain Services 2016*
- Chapter 3, *Designing an Active Directory Infrastructure*
- Chapter 4, *Active Directory Domain Name System*
- Chapter 5, *Placing Operations Master Roles*
- Chapter 6, *Migrating to Active Directory 2016*

1
Active Directory Fundamentals

It has been two years since the release of the first edition of this book, *Mastering Active Directory*. First of all, I would like to thank all my readers for their valuable feedback, which encouraged me to write the second edition so soon after the first. I am sure that you will all benefit from the additional content that has been added to this new edition.

So, the biggest question is, what has changed in Active Directory? Many articles stated that there were no significant changes in Active Directory 2019 soon after its release. Is this true? Does Microsoft not want to do anything more to improve an on-premises Active Directory? Before we look for answers, let's see what has changed in the requirements for identity infrastructure.

Edwin Drake is considered the father of the petroleum industry. Back in 1859, he drilled the first oil well in Titusville, Pennsylvania. Before this, people gathered oil when it naturally rose to the surface, or when they accidentally found it in wells or mines. Nobody drilled wells for the purpose of gathering oil. Therefore, the innovation of the oil well created a whole new industry. It made a huge contribution to the second Industrial Revolution. Oil became the new currency. It created many new opportunities, new businesses, new monopolies, and new politics.

Similarly, we now live in another revolutionary period. This time, **data is the new oil**. More and more data is now being stored and processed using computers:

Regulating the internet giants

The world's most valuable resource is no longer oil, but data

Is data the new oil? How information became the fuel of the future

It's driving new economies, creating new power players and monopolies — and fuelling new conflicts

THE AUSTRALIAN
The new oil: data is the world's most valuable resource

≡ Forbes
Drilling Into The Value Of Data

The following are the links to the articles mentioned in the preceding screenshot:

- **The Economist**: `https://www.economist.com/leaders/2017/05/06/the-worlds-most-valuable-resource-is-no-longer-oil-but-data`
- **Evening Standard**: `https://www.standard.co.uk/lifestyle/esmagazine/is-data-the-new-oil-how-information-became-the-fuel-of-the-future-a3740481.html`
- **The Australian**: `https://www.theaustralian.com.au/news/inquirer/the-new-oil-data-is-the-worlds-most-valuable-resource/news-story/f386217a9c63ac5ee6e1473413e90bda`
- **Forbes**: `https://www.forbes.com/sites/howardbaldwin/2015/03/23/drilling-into-the-value-of-data/#19693a5c65fa`

When we consider identity infrastructures, our digital identities define *what* level of access we have, *how* we access data, and *when* we have access to the data associated with it. Our identities follow data. For over 15 years, Microsoft Active Directory has been helping organizations to store digital identities in a central repository and arrange it according to the needs of the business. When the infrastructure security boundary is smaller, it is easier to manage identities and the associated data.

But with the fast adoption of cloud technologies, our infrastructure security boundaries are expanding. With these new changes, on-premises identity infrastructures are also transforming into cloud-only and hybrid identity infrastructures. It is changing the way we manage our identities. It is changing the way we secure our identities. It is changing the way identities are contributing to data security. So, yes, to fit its purpose, Microsoft is adding more features to **Azure Active Directory** (**Azure AD**) (cloud-based identity and access management). Most of these features also support hybrid identity infrastructure environments.

Therefore, in this second edition, I am going to share more knowledge, which will help you to transform your on-premises identity infrastructure to a hybrid infrastructure. This will allow you to receive the benefits from both the Azure AD and the on-premises Active Directory. It will help you, and your organization, to face the challenges of modern identity infrastructure with confidence.

We are going to start this journey by familiarizing ourselves with the building blocks of the Microsoft Active Directory service. With that in mind, this chapter will cover the following topics:

- Benefits of using Active Directory
- Understanding Active Directory components
- Understanding Active Directory objects
- Active Directory server roles
- Azure AD

Benefits of using Active Directory

A few years ago, I was working on an Active Directory restructuring project for a world-famous pharmaceutical company. According to the company policies, I had to travel to their headquarters to perform the project tasks. So, on a rare sunny English morning, I walked into the company's reception area. After I explained who I was and why I was there, the receptionist handed me a set of forms to fill in. The forms included questions such as my name, phone number, how long I would be there, and in which department. Once I had completed the forms, I handed them over to the receptionist, and she had to make a few calls to verify whether my visit was expected, and then confirm my access to different buildings with the respective department managers. Then, she made a magnetic card with my details on it, and handed it over to me. She instructed me on how to use it and which buildings I was allowed into.

The following diagram outlines this process:

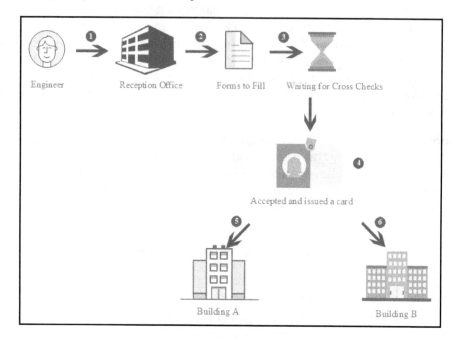

When we think about this process, we find that it contains the functions of a directory service:

- The forms that the receptionist handed over to me contained certain questions to help her understand who I was. They were predefined questions, and I had to answer them in order to register my information in their system. Similar to this form, in a directory service we have to provide values for specific attributes.
- Once I had submitted the forms, she didn't hand over the magnetic card right away. She made a few calls to verify my identity, and also to confirm which buildings I would have access to. Then, my details were registered in the system, and it generated a magnetic card that had my photo and a barcode. With that, I became a part of their system, and that particular card was my unique identity within their organization. There would be no other visitor with the same barcode and identification number at the same time. Similarly, in a directory service, each identity is unique.

- If I needed to get access to buildings, I needed to tap the card at the entrance. Could I use my name or any other card to get through? No! The locking system of the building doors only recognized me if I presented the correct card. So, having a unique identity in their system was not enough; I needed to present it in the correct way to get the required access. Likewise, in an identity infrastructure, you need to validate your identity according to the method that the system had defined. It can be a username and password, a certificate, biometric information, and so on.

- I went to another building and tried to tap the card. Even when I used it correctly, the doors wouldn't open. The guard in the building asked for my card to check. Once I handed it over, he scanned it with a barcode reader and checked some information on his computer screen. Then he informed me that I was not allowed into that building, and he guided me to the correct building. This means that my information can be accessed from any building through their system in order to verify my identity and access permissions. In a similar way, in a directory, identities are saved in a central repository. This data can be accessed and verified from any system or person who has the authority.

- When I used the card in the correct buildings, it allowed me in. In the system, it first verified my identity and then checked whether I was *authorized* to work in that facility. If I was authorized, the system allowed access; if not, it rejected my request to enter.

- When I entered or left the building, I did not have to record my time. But the managers in that department knew how many hours I had worked, as my check-in and check-out times had been recorded in the system every time I tapped the card at the entrance or exit. These points collected the data, and the managers could review the information at any time. Similarly, as identities are unique in a directory, it helps to identify who has done what in a system in a given period (based on authentication and authorization data).

This system acted as an *authentication* and *authorization* system. It used different protocols and standards to manage and protect the identities that were saved in a central database. This is the primary function of a directory service.

Every organization has its own organizational structure. The most common way is to group roles, assets, and responsibilities into different departments; for example, sales, IT, production, and quality assurance. Apart from skills and knowledge, employers use company resources such as applications and hardware devices to reach their goals. In order to use these resources efficiently, it's important to have some kind of access control in place. The resources should be available for the required users at the required time. This is very easy if all the data about users, applications, and resources is recorded in a central repository that uses authentication and authorization in order to manage resources. These are the main characteristics of a directory service.

Different service providers have different directory services; for example, Novell directory services, the Oracle directory service, and the Red Hat directory service. However, the Microsoft Active Directory service is the most commonly used directory service in the industry.

In 1988, the **ITU Telecommunication Standardization Sector** (ITU-T) developed industry standards for directory services, called **X.500**. This was the foundation for Microsoft Active Directory services. In X.500, the **Directory Access Protocol** (DAP) was defined, and many alternatives were made available to enable its use with the TCP/IP networking stack. The most popular alternative was the **Lightweight Directory Access Protocol** (LDAP). The first version of this was released in 1993 with limited features. The University of Michigan released the first **stand-alone LDAP daemon** (**slapd**) server in 1995. The matured version of LDAP, LDAPv3, was released in 1997, and most vendors, including Microsoft, started developing directory services based on LDAP. Microsoft released its first Active Directory version with Windows 2000.

Centralized data repository

Active Directory stores the identity information of users, applications, and resources in a **multi-master** database. This database is a file called `ntds.dit`, and is based on the **Joint Engine Technology** (JET) database engine. The data in this database can be modified using any alternative domain controller. The Active Directory database can store almost 2 billion objects. Users can use the identity data that is stored in Active Directory from anywhere in the network in order to access resources. Administrators can manage the authentication and authorization of the organizational identities from a centralized location. Without directory services, identities would be duplicated across different systems, which would add administrative overheads in order to manage the data.

Replication of data

There are organizations that use a single domain controller. But when it comes to complex business requirements, such as branch offices and redundancies, multiple domain controllers are required (we are going to look at domain controller placement in Chapter 11, *Active Directory Services*). If the identities are managed from a centralized system, it's important that each domain controller is aware of the changes that have been made to the Active Directory database. Say a user, Jane, in the sales department, forgets her password and asks the IT department to reset it. In 30 minutes, she's going to be working from a branch office located in a different city. The IT administrator resets her password from the headquarters' domain controller, DC01. In order to have a successful login from the branch office, this change to the directory needs to be replicated over to the domain controller in the branch office, DC05.

Microsoft Active Directory has two types of replication. If a domain controller advertises the changes made on that particular domain controller to neighboring domain controllers, it is called **outbound replication**. If a domain controller accepts the changes advertised by neighboring domain controllers, it is called **inbound replication**. The replication connections (from who and to whom) and replication schedule can be modified based on the infrastructure requirements.

High availability

High availability is important for any business-critical system in an organization. This is also applicable to domain controllers. On other systems, in order to implement high availability, we need to make software or hardware changes. With built-in fault-tolerance capabilities, Active Directory domain controllers do not need additional changes. A multi-master database, and the replication of domain controllers, allows users to continue with authentication and authorization from any available domain controller at any time.

Security

Data and identity security are very important in modern businesses. We are living in a world where identity is the new perimeter. A significant portion of this book is focused on the features of Active Directory that can secure your identity infrastructures from emerging threats. Active Directory allows you to use different authentication types, group policies, and workflows to protect the resources in your network. Even applications benefit from these technologies and methodologies. They help administrators to build different security rules based on departments and groups, in order to protect data and workloads. It also forces individuals to follow organizational data- and network-security standards.

Auditing capabilities

Setting up advanced security policies will not be enough to protect your identity infrastructure. Periodic audits will help you to understand new security threats. Active Directory allows you to capture and audit events occurring in your identity infrastructure. These could be related to user authentication, directory service modifications, or access violation. It also helps you to collect data from a centralized location, which will help you to troubleshoot authentication and authorization issues in an effective manner.

Single sign-on (SSO)

In an organization, there can be many different applications in use. Each of these applications may have a different authentication mechanism. It will be difficult to maintain different user credentials for authentication on different applications. Most application vendors now support integration with Active Directory for authentication. This means that with Active Directory credentials, you can authenticate on different systems and applications that are used by your organization. You will not need to keep typing your credentials in order to get access. Once you authenticate on a computer, the same session will be used to authenticate other Active Directory-integrated applications.

Schema modification

Any kind of database has its own structure, called the **schema**. This is also applicable to an Active Directory database. This schema describes all the objects in Active Directory. By knowing the schema, you can modify or extend it. This is important for the development of Active Directory-integrated applications. Microsoft publishes **Active Directory Service Interfaces** (**ADSI**) with a set of **Component Object Model** (**COM**) interfaces, and it can be used to access Active Directory service features from different network providers. Application developers can use it to develop their application to be Active Directory-integrated, and publish it to the directory. Users can search for the service through Active Directory, and applications can access Active Directory objects as required.

Querying and indexing

By maintaining a central data repository, Active Directory also allows users and applications to query objects and retrieve accurate data. If I need to find user John's account, I do not need to know which branch he is in, or to which department he belongs. With a simple Active Directory query, I will be provided with information about the user account. In a manner similar to when we add a new object to the directory, objects will publish their attributes and make them available to users and applications for queries.

These are some of the main capabilities of the Active Directory service, and these features will be explained in detail in later chapters, including how to plan, implement, and maintain them within your identity infrastructure.

Understanding Active Directory components

Active Directory components can be divided into two main categories:

- Logical components
- Physical components

When you design your identity infrastructure, you need to consider both components. The logical components of the Active Directory structure can change at any given time according to business requirements. But you won't be able to modify the physical components as easily as the logical components. The placement of these components will define the efficiency, security, reliability, and manageability of your identity infrastructure. So, it's crucial that we get it right at the beginning, before we move on to advanced identity infrastructure planning.

Logical components

Each business has its own hierarchical organization layout. It may contain multiple branch offices, multiple groups of companies, and many different departments. Each of these components in the business carries out different operations. Operations in the sales department are completely different from in the IT department. Everyone is bound to the company by following different operational guidelines and targets. When we design the identity infrastructure, we need to match it with the company hierarchical layout, in order to effectively manage resources and security. The logical components of Active Directory help you to structure the identity infrastructure by considering design, administration, extensibility, security, and scalability.

The Active Directory logical structure contains two types of objects. Objects can be either **container objects** or **leaf objects**. Container objects can be associated with other objects in the logical structure. Leaf objects are the smallest components in the logical structure. They will not have any other child objects associated with them.

In following section, we are going to explore more about logical components in the Active Directory environment.

Forests

The Amazon is the world's largest rainforest. There are many different animal species, and more than 400 tribes live there. Each of these animal species is different from each other. Reptiles, mammals, snakes, and fish all have different characteristics, and we can group each of them by considering their characteristics. The tribes that live in the forest also have their own languages, cultures, and boundaries. But all these animals and tribes share one forest. They use food, water, and other resources from the Amazon rainforest in order to survive. The Amazon rainforest has well-defined boundaries. Another forest 100 miles away from the Amazon is not called the Amazon rainforest. Its name and boundaries are unique.

The Active Directory forest can also be explained in a similar way. It represents a complete Active Directory instance. It is made of one or more domains and domain trees. We will explore what domain and domain trees are in the following sections. Each domain has its own characteristics, boundaries, and resources. But at the same time, it shares a common logical structure, schema, and directory configuration within the forest. Similarly, tribes have a relationship with the forest and other tribes, and domains in the Active Directory forest will have a two-way trust relationship. Different tribes in the Amazon forest aren't named after the *Amazon*; each tribe has its own name. Similarly, domains in a forest can contain any domain name:

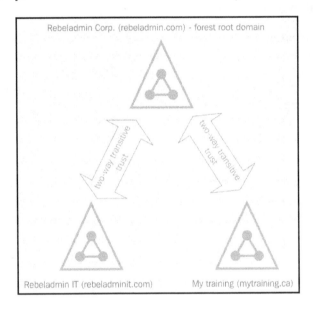

The first domain controller in the Active Directory service deployment is important. When you create the first domain, it will also create the forest. Then, the first domain will become the forest root domain. A domain tree contains its own root domain, but forests can contain multiple root domains.

In the previous diagram, **Rebeladmin Corp.** is an IT solution provider. rebeladmin.com is the forest root domain. It does have another two companies: one is **Rebeladmin IT** with the rebeladminit.com domain name, and it provides managed IT services. The other company is **My training**, with the mytraining.ca domain name, and it provides IT training to professionals. rebeladminit.com and mytraining.ca are both root domains in their own domain trees. Both domains in the forest will trust each other with **two-way transitive trust**.

Two-way transitive trust is a logical link between domains, where the trusting domain honors the logon authentication of the trusted domain. When considering the previous example, users in `rebeladminit.com` can authenticate into `mytraining.ca`, and vice versa. Any object located in a particular domain inherently trusts other objects in other domains in the same forest. This is not the same as when considering authentication between forests. For that, it may (depending on the trust method) require additional login credentials. An organization can have a single forest or multiple forests based on the company's business requirements.

When Microsoft releases a new Active Directory service version, new features are bound to the forest and domain functional levels. If you want to use Active Directory Domain Services 2016 forest-level features, your directory's Active Directory forest should use the Windows Server 2016 forest functional level. Before Windows Server 2012 R2, forest functional-level upgrades were one-way. Now, it is possible to roll back to the lower forest functional level if required. The forest functional level is dependent on the oldest domain controller version in the network.

For example, if the forest functional level is Windows Server 2008, it is allowed to install the domain controller inside the forest with the operating system, Windows Server 2016. But this doesn't mean it can use the features provided by Windows Directory Services 2016 until it upgrades its domain and forest functional levels. If you upgrade the forest functional level to Windows Server 2016, you can only have domain controllers running a minimum of Windows Server 2016.

Domains

Referring back to my example about the Amazon rainforest, we can say that there are more than 400 tribes living there. Each of these tribes is unique in certain ways. Each tribe has a different language and culture. Each tribe has its own territory for hunting, farming, and fishing. Each tribe know its boundaries and does not cross others' boundaries as that can lead to war between tribes. Each tribe has its own tools and methods for hunting and farming. Also, each tribe has different groups assigned to different tasks. Some are good at hunting, some are good at farming, and some are good at cooking. All their contributions help them to survive and grow as a tribe.

The Active Directory domain can also be explained in a similar way. The domain contains the logical components to achieve the administrative goals of the organization. By default, the domain becomes the security boundary for the objects inside it. Each object has its own administrative goals. Individuals in tribes have different identities and responsibilities, but all of them are part of the tribe and the forest. In the same way, all the objects in the domain are part of a common database. Also, everyone in the tribe still needs to follow some of the common rules. Objects in the domain are also controlled by the defined security rules. These security rules are only applicable within that particular domain, and are not valid for any object outside the domain boundaries. A domain also allows you to set smaller administrative boundaries within the organization. In the previous section, I explained that a forest can contain multiple domains.

Managing a forest is difficult, as its administrative boundary is large, but the domain allows you to set smaller administrative targets. Active Directory is divided into multiple partitions in order to improve its efficiency. The domain is also a partition of Active Directory. When I described the Active Directory forest, I mentioned that every domain inside the forest shared the same schema. Each of the domain controllers also has a copy of the domain partition, which is shared only by the domain controllers within the same domain tree. All the information about objects in that particular domain is saved in that domain partition. This ensures that only the required data is replicated across the domain trees and forests:

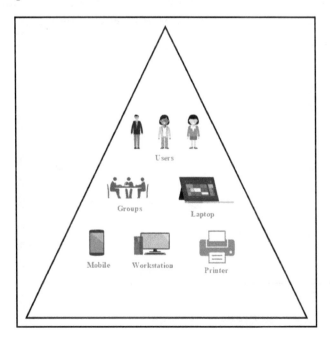

The Active Directory domain's functional levels define the Active Directory capabilities. With every new version of the directory services, new features are added to the domain's functional level. In order to use the features within the domain, the domain functional level needs to be upgraded. The version of the domain function level that you can run on the domain depends on the forest functional level. You cannot have a domain functional level that is higher than the forest functional level.

Domain trees

A **domain tree** is a collection of domains that reflects the organization's structure. My parents and I are bound by a parent-child relationship. It is obviously different from other kinds of relationships. Similarly, domains inside the domain tree have a parent-child relationship. The first domain in the domain tree is called the **parent** domain. This is also the root domain. All other domains in the domain tree are called the **child** domains. There will be only one parent domain in a domain tree.

In some documentation, child domains are also called **subdomains**. When dealing with internet domains, the creation of an additional placeholder, a sub-URL, is sometimes required. For example, `rebeladmin.com` is the domain name that is used for the website and organization needed to host another website, in order to maintain support requests. But it needs to use the same contiguous namespace. To do that, we can create another folder in the domain root, and create a Domain Name System (**DNS**) record for the `support.rebeladmin.com` subdomain:

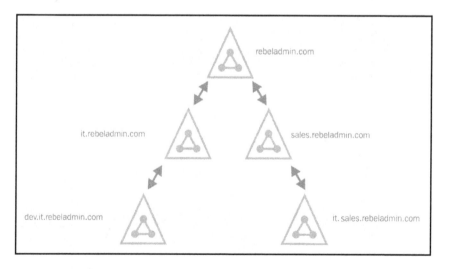

An Active Directory forest can contain non-contiguous domain names. But within the domain tree, it will share the same contiguous namespace. In the previous example, `rebeladmin.com` is the parent domain for the domain tree. It has two child domains, `it.rebeladmin.com` and `sales.rebeladmin.com`. As you can see, it shares the same `rebeladmin.com` namespace. Similarly, when it goes down to the next level in the domain tree, it shares the namespace from the preceding level. Each child domain maintains its own domain partition. This configuration data will be replicated only to the domain controllers of the same child domain. When the child domain is introduced to the domain tree, it will automatically create a trust relationship with the parent domain. If two child domains on different domain trees want to authenticate, authenticated traffic must pass through the forest root domains.

 All domain trusts within the Active Directory forest are two-way transitive trusts. Two-way trust means that the authentication requests can be processed between two domains in both directions. Transitive means it goes beyond the initial two-way trust between domains, and trusts its child domains too, even though there is no direct connection.

Organizational units

In the preceding section, I explained how we can group objects using domains and forests. But within the organization, objects can be categorized into different groups according to operations, organizational structure, geographical locations, or roles and responsibilities. As an example, organizations have multiple departments. We can convert each of these departments into child domains and group each of the department objects. But the child domain needs a separate domain controller, as it will have a separate domain partition.

Isn't there a better way to group these objects within the domain? That's where organizational units come in. Organizational units help group objects on a smaller scale within the domain. The most common way is to group objects that have similar security and administrative requirements together. For example, there are more than 50 users in the sales department. The sales department uses common shared folders and printers. Their security requirements for data and networks are similar. Therefore, we can create an **organizational unit** (**OU**) called *sales* and group all the sales department users into it. We can now apply security policies at the OU level, instead of the user level.

When deploying a domain controller, it creates a default OU structure to segment the most common object types, such as users, computers, and domain controllers. The administrator can add, remove, and delete an OU as required.

 Sometimes, I have seen engineers removing/modifying the default OU structure. All these default OUs have different security policies attached. If it really needs to be changed, it is important to compare the security policies that are applied and reattached to the new OU if required. I highly recommend that you do not modify/remove domain controllers' default OU at least. That said, you are still allowed to add or change security policies applied to default OUs.

Once an object is assigned to an OU, it inherits the security settings and permissions that are applied to the OU level. If the same object is moved to a different OU, then it will apply the settings from the new OU, and discard the settings that were applied from the previous OU. OUs also help to delegate administrative control to individuals for specific tasks. Domain administrators have privileges that allow them to manage any object within the domain. But it's possible to create administrators and assign them to manage objects and resources on an OU level. For these administrators, the OU will be the security boundary. They will not be able to modify any other object outside that particular OU. I will be explaining delegated administration later in this book. OUs are container objects. They can be associated with similar or other objects. Similar to parent-child domains, OUs can also contain child OUs. These are also **nested organization units**.

OUs can also contain object types, such as users, groups, contacts, computers, organizational units, and printers:

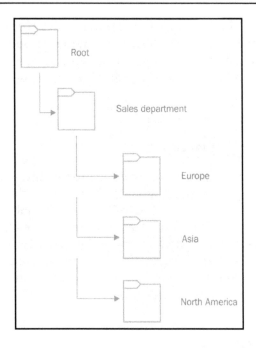

In the previous example, Rebeladmin Corp. has a **Sales department**. In the OU hierarchy, the first thing you need to do is create an OU called **Sales department**. All the regional offices have their own sales department. Most of the security and administrative requirements for objects in the sales department are the same. But creating OUs based on geographical areas will allow domain administrators to delegate control over those objects to individuals or groups in the regional offices. Also, if a specific security policy needs to be applied to a regional office sales department, it can be applied on a relevant OU level, rather than applying it to the entire **Sales department** across the branch offices. All the child OUs inherit the permissions that are applied in its parent OU by default.

In the previous example, individuals or groups who have permission to control **Sales department** objects have control over the objects in the **Europe**, **Asia**, and **North America** OUs by default. The OU hierarchy is independent. It is not going to affect any other domain's OU hierarchy. The OU can also contain objects only from the same domain.

Physical components

In the previous section, I explained the logical components of Active Directory. Now, it's time to look into the physical components. Even though the logical and physical components are equally important in Active Directory Domain Services design, they are independent. Replication is the core feature of the Active Directory Domain Services. If a system has multiple domain controllers, changes made in one domain controller should be replicated to others. Physical component placement can affect Active Directory replications in certain ways. Logical components can easily be rearranged compared to physical components.

Domain controllers

The domain controller is a computer that runs a Windows server operating system, and holds the Active Directory Domain Services role. It can be either a physical server or a virtual server.

The domain controller holds the directory partition that will be replicated to the other domain controllers in the same domain. The domain can have any number of domain controllers. The number of domain controllers is dependent on the enterprise's size, geographical placement, and network segmentation. In Windows NT, it uses multiple domain controllers, but it maintains a single-master schema. This means that directory changes can only be made from a specific domain controller. Since Windows 2000, there has been support for the multi-master mode. Any object-level changes made in one domain controller will be replicated to all other domain controllers (directory service-related). That said, some of the Active Directory-related operational role changes can only be modified by the designated operation master role owner (FSMO roles).

Before Windows 2000 Domain Services, one of the domain controllers acted as the **primary domain controller** (**PDC**), and all other additional domain controllers were called **backup domain controllers** (**BDCs**). Some people still use this terminology to describe the operations of the domain controllers in the infrastructure. But after Windows Server 2000, the only difference between domain controllers was either their **flexible single master operation** (**FSMO**) role holder or the global catalog server.

Global catalog server

The global catalog server holds the full writable copy of objects in its host domain, and the partial copy of the objects in other domains in the same forest. The partial replica contains a copy of every object in the forest and the most commonly used attributes in queries. Applications and users in one domain can query for the objects in another domain (in the same forest) via the global catalog server. All domain controllers in the domain will not be global catalog servers by default. When installing the first domain controller, it will become the global catalog server, and other domain controllers can be promoted as global catalog servers according to the business requirements. Not every domain controller in the domain needs to be a global catalog server.

Active Directory sites

The Active Directory site defines a physical topology of the network. Sites can be separate buildings in a campus network, with the branch office in a separate city or even in a separate country. For example, the head office of Rebeladmin Corp. is located in London, UK. It runs a few domain controllers (**DC01** and **DC02**) within its physical network. It uses IP address allocation for the network with the subnets of 192.168.148.0/24, 10.10.10.0/24, and 172.25.16.0/24. Due to the business requirements, the company opened a branch office in Toronto, Canada. It got its own domain controllers (**DC03** and **DC04**) running, but logically, it is in the same Active Directory forest and domain. Both networks are interconnected with a leased line.

The Canada network uses the IP subnets of `10.11.11.0/24` and `172.0.2.0/24`:

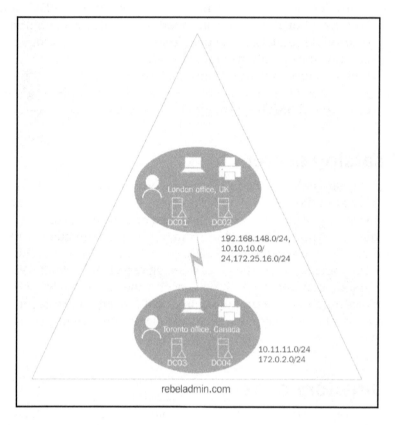

In the preceding diagram, the two offices can be identified as two sites. This is because there are clearly two network segments. The Active Directory logical design does not really consider physical network segmentation. Since they are in the same domain and forest, **DC01** to **DC04** should replicate changes to each other in order to maintain a healthy identity infrastructure.

Mainly, there are three benefits that we can identify:

- **Replication**: In a typical AD DS setup, all domain controllers are set to replicate changes between each other, assuming all are connected via fast network links. But in the real world, they're not. Sometimes, connections between two sites are 256 kbps or 512 kbps. The same links will also be used for other enterprise operations. Using AD DS sites, it's possible to perform bandwidth optimization and replication schedules for reliable replication across domain controllers.

- **Service location**: In an infrastructure, there can be Active Directory-integrated applications/services; for example, Active Directory certificate services and exchange services. Using sites and the subnet setup, we can point users to the nearest server for the services. So, users on the Toronto site are served by the Microsoft Exchange Server (mail server) on the Toronto site when they try to access an email, instead of passing the request to the London site.

- **Authentication**: When a user logs in to the domain, they need to communicate with the domain controller to gain authentication. In the preceding example, a user on the Toronto site does not need to connect to a domain controller on the London site for authentication. AD DS sites will allow you to ensure that users on the Toronto site will use the nearest domain controller for authentication. This will reduce latency and bandwidth through the site links.

Since AD DS sites represent a physical network topology, when changes are made to the physical topology, they also need to be updated on the AD DS site configuration. For example, if a new subnet is added, this information needs to be updated in the AD DS site subnet section too. Sometimes, engineers forget to do this, which prevents infrastructures from having the full benefits of AD DS sites.

Understanding Active Directory objects

If we need to describe a person or thing, we use different adjectives. This can include personality, ethnic background, physical appearance, or other characteristics. Most of these are not unique. For example, when you talk about a 6-foot-tall boy, there can be lots of 6-foot-tall boys in the city. But it still explains that the *person* that we're trying to describe is definitely not a girl. If we need to uniquely identify a person or thing, we need to identify some unique attributes associated with them. If it's a person, then their passport number, telephone number, or social security number will make it easier to uniquely identify them from others. If it's an object, the unique identifier could be the serial number or barcode.

Within an organization, there are many physical entities. These can be either employees or resources. In order to manage these using Active Directory Domain Services, each of these physical entities needs to be presented to Active Directory. Active Directory will understand these entities as objects.

In Active Directory, there are two types of objects. *Container objects* can store other objects in the Active Directory. The domain itself is an example of a container object. The organizational unit is also a container object. *Leaf objects* cannot store other objects in Active Directory. A service account is an example of a leaf object.

In the same way that we use adjectives to describe a person or a thing, Active Directory objects use attributes to describe their nature. For example, the following screenshot shows the wizard you will get when you create a new user account. In the wizard, in the following screenshot (on the left-hand side), **First name**, **Last name**, **Full name**, and **User logon name** are attributes. In the same way, when you create a computer account, it needs a **Computer name** attribute to describe it (on the right-hand side):

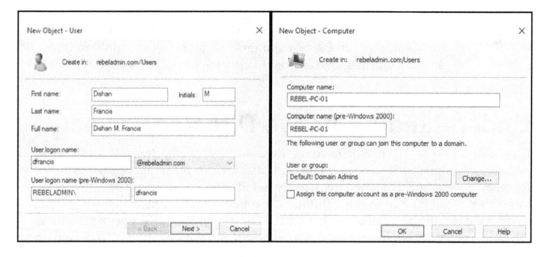

According to the preceding screenshot, depending on the object type, the associated attributes are also changed. Also, it doesn't matter if you create one user object or hundreds of user objects in Active Directory; you still need to use the exact same attributes to describe the object you are creating. This is because each of the objects is attached to an *object class*. Within the Active Directory schema, the attributes that are attached to each object class are defined.

Let's look at a simple scenario to understand this further. When you sign up for an online service for the first time, it will provide you with an online form to fill. At the backend, it is attached to a database. The information you provide will be recorded in the database for future use. If you need to sign up for the service, you must provide the answers to the questions that are asked. You cannot change the questions that you need to answer, because the database will not be able to understand it. The database contains a table designed with columns, rows, and data types to store the data that will be captured from the form. Similarly, object class attributes are defined by a schema. Active Directory does have different types of object classes. Users, groups, computers, printers, and domain controllers are examples of object classes.

Some of these attributes are mandatory for object classes. For example, in user account creation, the **User logon name** must be provided in order to continue. But if we do not provide the **Last name**, we can still proceed with the user account creation. Attribute values also need to be provided with an acceptable data format that is defined by the schema. Sometimes, due to the operational requirements, organizations may require custom attributes. By modifying the Active Directory schema, it is possible to add additional attributes to the object classes. This will be demonstrated further in `Chapter 7`, *Managing Active Directory Objects*.

Globally unique identifiers and security identifiers

In a city or organization, there can be multiple people with the same name. But their passport number or social security number will be unique to them. So, in order to identify a person or thing accurately from a group of similar things, we need to consider the associated unique value.

In an Active Directory database, nearly 2 billion objects can be stored. How will it uniquely identify each and every object? Every time we create an object in Active Directory, it will be assigned with one or two unique values. If it is a user or group object, it will receive a **globally unique identifier (GUID)** and a **security identifier (SID)**. The GUID value will be saved in the `objectGUID` attribute in each object and the SID value will be saved in the `objectSid` attribute in each object.

In order to view the GUID and SID values for the user account, the following PowerShell command can be run from the domain controller:

```
Get-ADUser username
```

username can be replaced by the actual username of the user.

In the following screenshot, ObjectGUID lists the GUID value and SID lists the SID value associated with the user account:

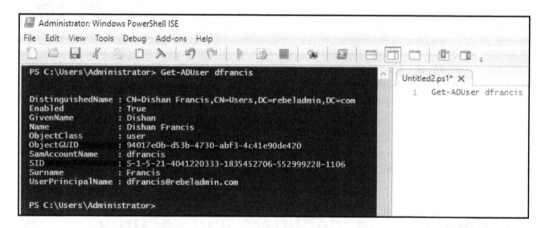

ObjectGUID is a 128-bit value, and is applied to each and every object in Active Directory. This value is not just for the particular Active Directory domain. It is valid globally as well. Once a GUID is assigned to an object, it will be there until the object is deleted from the directory. Modifying or moving objects will not change the value of the GUID. The ObjectGUID attribute value will be published to the global catalog servers. If an application in a domain needs to search for a user object, the best method will be to query using ObjectGUID, as it will give an accurate result.

> There is a misunderstanding that the GUID value is a *unique value*. None of the documentation says that this value is unique. They only say it is quite unlikely to have a duplicated GUID as the method it used to generate it is complex.

The SID value for an object is unique within its domain. The SID values associated with the user will be changed if the user object is migrated to another domain. An SID value assigned by one domain will not be accepted by another domain. As soon as a user object is migrated to another domain, a new SID value will be generated. Then, the old SID value will be saved in the sIDHistory attribute. This attribute can contain multiple values. When the system creates a Kerberos ticket for user authentication, it will consider a new SID value and all other SID values listed in the sIDHistory attribute. sIDHistory is important, especially in Active Directory restructuring. The resources in the domain decide whether to access or deny permission to a user account based on the **access control list** (**ACL**). This ACL uses the SID values. So, if an object moves to a different domain without sIDHistory, it will lose its access to resources until the ACL is modified. But if the system considers sIDHistory when granting an access token, and if the old SID value is moved over to the new domain, the user is still allowed to access the resources they were assigned.

Distinguished names

Distinguished names in Active Directory can also be used to uniquely identify an object. This is very similar to the way your postal address works. A postal address uses a hierarchical path to uniquely identify you. Starting from the country, it goes to province, then to the city, street, and house number. In the same way, using the full path to the object within the directory will help you uniquely identify an object.

There are three types of Active Directory naming attributes that have been used to generate distinguishing names:

- organizationName (O) or organizationalUnitName (OU): Organization represents the root-level domain. The OU is where the object is located.
- domainComponent (DC): This is the naming attribute for the domain and the DNS. If the DNS name for the domain is rebeladmin.com, the domain components for it will be DC=rebeladmin, DC=com.
- commonName (CN): This refers to the objects and containers within the directory.

In the previous screenshot, when the query for the domain user is returned, the distinguishing name for the user is as follows:

```
CN=Dishan Francis,CN=Users,DC=rebeladmin,DC=com
```

Here, `DC=rebeladmin,DC=com` represents the domain name, `CN=Users` represents the user container, and at the end, `CN=Dishan Francis` represents the actual object name.

The **relative distinguished name** (RDN) is a unique value within its parent container. For the preceding example, the RDN for the object is `CN=Dishan Francis`. Active Directory allows you to have the same RDN for multiple objects within the directory, but all of them need to be in separate containers. It is not permitted to have the same RDN for the object within the same container.

In the previous section, you learned that the `SID` value for the object will not be changed unless it's migrated to a different domain controller. Changing values in the object will not modify the `SID` value. But if the hierarchical path was changed for an object, the **Distinguished Name** (DN) will be changed. For example, if you move a user object from one OU to another, the DN value for the user object will be changed.

Active Directory server roles

There are five main Active Directory server roles. These roles are grouped together in the required Active Directory environment, in order to set up and configure Active Directory server roles:

- **Active Directory Domain Services (AD DS)**
- **Active Directory Federation Services (AD FS)**
- **Active Directory Lightweight Directory Services (AD LDS)**
- **Active Directory Rights Management Services (AD RMS)**
- **Active Directory Certificate Services (AD CS)**

Since Windows Server 2008, these roles can be installed and configured using Windows Server Manager. It is the same in Windows Server 2016.

Each of these server roles can also be installed and configured using PowerShell. The following PowerShell cmdlets can be used to install Active Directory server roles:

PowerShell cmdlets	Description
`Install-WindowsFeature AD-Domain-Services`	This cmdlet will install the AD DS role.
`Install-WindowsFeature AD FS-Federation`	This cmdlet will install the AD FS role.
`Install-WindowsFeature ADLDS`	This cmdlet will install AD LDS.
`Install-WindowsFeature ADRMS`	This cmdlet will install AD RMS. This role has two subfeatures, which are AD Rights Management Server and Identity Federation Support. If required, these individual roles can be installed using `Install-WindowsFeature ADRMS, ADRMS-Server, ADRMS-Identity` or `Install-WindowsFeature ADRMS -IncludeAllSubFeature`. It will install all the subfeatures.
`Install-WindowsFeature AD-Certificate`	This cmdlet will install AD CS. This role has six subroles, which are certification authority (`ADCS-Cert-Authority`), Certificate Enrollment Policy Web Service (`ADCS-Enroll-Web-Pol`), Certificate Enrollment Web Service (`ADCS-Enroll-Web-Svc`), Certification Authority Web Enrollment (`ADCS-Web-Enrollment`), Network Device Enrollment Service (`ADCS-Device-Enrollment`), and Online Responder (`ADCS-Online-Cert`). These subfeatures can be added individually or together.

The `Get-WindowsFeature` command will list all the roles and subfeatures that are available, along with the names that can be used with PowerShell to install the roles. When you install the roles, it is important to add `-IncludeManagementTools` as management tools, as the role will not be installed by default.

Active Directory Domain Services

In the previous sections in this chapter, I explained what Active Directory and what its components are. As a recap, I would like to list some key points about AD DS:

- AD DS can manage an organization's resources in a secure, efficient manner, and helps to organize objects in a hierarchical structure.
- The Active Directory forest is an identity infrastructure security boundary, and the forest can contain multiple domains with their own directory partitions.
- The Active Directory domain maintains a multi-master database to store data about objects and replicate it with other domain controllers in the domain. Any writable domain controller in the domain can add, modify, or delete objects from the Active Directory database, and other domain controllers will be aware of these changes.
- The OU will be used to arrange objects in Active Directory in a hierarchical structure. It is also used to delegate permissions for administrative tasks.

Read-only domain controllers

With Windows Server 2008, Microsoft introduced a new type of domain controller called the **read-only domain controller** (**RODC**). It allows organizations to have domain controllers in locations where data security and network security cannot be guaranteed.

Domain controllers contain a writable copy of the AD DS database. It is replicated among all the domain controllers in the same domain, but the read-only domain controller will have a read-only AD DS database.

This feature is useful in a *branch* network. Not every branch office of an organization can afford a fully-blown network with a high-speed leased line, a protected data center facility, and IT staff. If it's an Active Directory environment, and if the branch office needs to be connected to the corporate environment, engineers will need to deploy the domain controller in the branch office network too. But if the branch office has limited connection to a corporate network, fewer IT resources, and poor physical data and network security, deploying a domain controller in that network can be a greater security threat to corporate networks. But deploying an RODC will protect the identity infrastructure security from such threats, and users in the branch office will still be able to use the fast and reliable authentication and authorization provided by AD DS.

The RODC holds a copy of Active Directory objects and attributes from writable domain controllers, except the account passwords. If any changes need to be made to objects, they need to be made in a writable domain controller. Sometimes, the branch office may host applications that need write capabilities to the directory services. These requests will be pointed to the writable domain controller instead of the RODC.

Active Directory Federation Services

AD FS allows you to share identities between trusted identity infrastructures and is based on a **claim-based authorization (CBA)** mechanism. Modern-day organization workloads are complicated. Application service providers have shifted most of their applications to the cloud (**software as a service (SaaS)**). Also, organizations share web-based systems and applications with other organizations for some operations. Almost all of these systems need some kind of authentication and authorization process to allow users to access the applications or systems. This makes the identity infrastructure requirements complicated.

Rebeladmin Corp. is a manufacturing company. Northwood Industrial is a partner company of Rebeladmin Corp. Rebeladmin Corp. has a web-based content management system to track sales leads, orders, and projects. As a partner company, sales users from Northwood Industrial like to access this system. Both companies use their own identity infrastructures. An easy way to do this is to set up an Active Directory forest trust between two organizations. But that is an administrative and security nightmare. If Rebeladmin Corp. has many partners, will it be practical to have a forest trust for each and every organization? It also adds additional operational costs to facilitate secure communications links between organizations. The partner company only wants to access one application, but providing trust will open up additional security threats to the Rebeladmin Corp. infrastructure.

AD FS allows you to provide access to protected applications without any of these hazards. It will trust identities from completely different identity infrastructures, and pass identity information as *claims* to the organization that hosts the applications. Then, the company that hosts the application will map these claims to claims that the application understands, and make the authorization decisions. The important point here is that this process will be done with minimum changes to the infrastructure. Both organizations will maintain their own identity infrastructures. Communication will happen only via an HTTPS protocol, and there will be no need to open up additional firewall ports between the organizations' networks.

In normal scenarios, if you share a web-based system or application between two identity infrastructures, the partner organizations need to provide two credentials. One credential is to authenticate themselves with their own infrastructure, and the second one is to authenticate themselves with the remote infrastructure. AD FS allows users to have a SSO experience with the application.

Organizations today use more and more web-based applications. Some are for their own operations, and some are client-focused. If these are Active Directory-integrated applications, opening them to the public internet can create security threats. AD FS can also be used to provide multi-factor authentication to web-based applications. AD FS can be hosted in a **demilitarized zone** (**DMZ**) in the network, and it will be the only public-facing interface for the applications.

There are four AD FS role services:

- **Federation service**: The federation servers' hosted federation service will route authentication requests from identities in another identity infrastructure using a federated web SSO method, or from clients through the internet using the web SSO design method. These design options will be explained in detail in `Chapter 13`, *Active Directory Federation Services*.
- **Federation Service Proxy**: Federation proxy servers can be places in the DMZ (the perimeter network segment) and can forward claims to the federation service located in a secure network. This adds an additional layer of security for web-based applications.
- **Claims-aware agent**: AD FS uses claims to create trust between two identity infrastructures. The claims-aware agent can be used in the application web server to allow queries for AD FS claims. Then, the application will use claims in the AD FS security token to make the authorization decision.
- **Windows Token-based agent**: This agent is to be installed on a web server that hosts a Windows Token-based application. It will convert the AD FS security token into a Windows access token, and the application will make an authorization decision based on this.

These federation roles can be installed on separate servers based on the organization's federation requirements.

Active Directory Lightweight Directory Services

Some applications require a directory-enabled environment in order to operate. But there is no need to be in a fully-blown Active Directory environment. Microsoft developed AD LDS to enable data storage and retrieval for directory-enabled applications, without the dependencies that are required for AD DS. When we deploy AD DS, it keeps its own directory partition and the schema inherited from the forest. If we need an additional directory partition, you are required to deploy another domain or child domain, but AD LDS allows you to maintain an independent schema with each AD LDS instance. You can also host multiple AD LDS instances on one computer.

AD DS and AD LDS are both builds based on the same core directory service technologies. AD LDS does not need to depend on the Active Directory domain or forest setup. But in an AD DS environment, AD LDS can use AD DS for authentication.

Active Directory Rights Management Services

AD RMS help organizations to protect sensitive data from unauthorized access.

Let's say Peter received a document that contains some sensitive data about company stock prices. Peter sends it to Liam. We know this should be a confidential conversation between Peter and Liam. How can we verify that this data has not been passed on to another user? What if someone gets a printed copy of this document? What if Liam edits this and adds some false information? Using AD RMS, you can prevent this kind of misuse of confidential corporate data. AD RMS can be used to encrypt managed identities and apply authorization policies to your files, emails, and presentations. This will prevent files from being copied, forwarded, or printed by unauthorized people. This also allows file expiration, which will prevent users from viewing the data of a document beyond a specified period of time.

AD RMS contain two roles services:

- **Active Directory Rights Management Server**: This installs the AD RMS server service that requires you to protect the content in an organization.
- **Identity Federation Support**: The AD RMS service also supports integration with AD FS services. It will allow you to protect content shared between two organizations, without setting up AD RMS in both infrastructures. This role service helps integrate AD RMS with AD FS.

Active Directory Certificate Services

AD CS helps organizations build **public key infrastructure (PKI)** in an easy, cost-effective way. Digital certificates issued by the certification authority can be used to authenticate users, computers, and devices. The certification authority is responsible for receiving certificate requests, verifying certificate requests, and issuing, renewing, and revoking certificates.

There are six role services for AD CS:

- **Certification authority (CA)**: Mainly, there are two types of CA. Microsoft named them root and subordinate CA. The placement of these on a network will be dependent on the PKI design. CA is responsible for issuing certificates to users, computers, and devices. It will also manage the validity of certificates.
- **Certification Authority Web Enrollment**: This is a web interface that connects to CA in order to allow users to submit certificate requests, retrieve issued certificates, and download the certificate chain.
- **Online Responder**: This will receive and respond to individual user requests to verify the status of digital certificates.
- **Network Device Enrollment Service**: This service allows non-domain-joined network devices to obtain certificates.
- **Certificate Enrollment Web Service**: This role service works with the Certificate Enrollment Policy Web Service, and allows users and computers to perform certificate enrollment using HTTPS. It also allows certificate enrollment for domain computers or devices that are not connected to the domain, and computers or devices that are not part of the domain.
- **Certificate Enrollment Policy Web Service**: This publishes the certificate enrollment policy information to users and computers.

Azure AD

Microsoft started their Azure journey back in 2008. **Windows Azure** was available to the public from 2010 (it was renamed as **Microsoft Azure** in 2014). Today it is a mature, industry-leading public cloud service. Its **infrastructure as a service (IaaS)**, **platform as a service (PaaS)**, and **SaaS** offerings are well trusted by many different parties such as governments, Fortune 500 companies, militaries, universities, hospitals, service providers, and so on. Now, more than ever, businesses are moving their data, applications, and operations to Microsoft Azure; taking into consideration business growth, efficiency, experience, agility, cost, and assurance.

When businesses are looking to move existing data, applications, or operations to Azure, there are two paths to consider:

- **Lift and shift**: Existing servers and applications can shift to the cloud using methods such as replication.
- **Build in the cloud**: Organizations can directly start using pre-built Azure services and applications, and migrate existing data using methods such as replication, backup, and restore.

Even though there are two different approaches for migration, overall identity needs stay the same. Most corporate applications and services are already using Microsoft Active Directory in their on-premises environments. When you lift and shift, there should be a way to facilitate authentication, authorization, and accounting requirements. Even if we use cloud-only services, the same requirement applies.

Therefore, can't we extend an existing on-premises Active Directory environment to the cloud? Yes, we can do it by using one of the following methods:

- **Site-to-site VPN or ExpressRoute**: By using site-to-site VPN or ExpressRoute, we can extend our infrastructure boundary to the cloud.
- **An additional domain controller in Azure**: We also can set up additional domain controllers in Azure and replicate them from an on-premises Active Directory. Then, Azure will treat it as another Active Directory site.
- **A brand new domain controller**: If it is a cloud-only environment, you can also deploy a brand new domain controller in an Azure virtual machine, and use this.

However, all the preceding options come with additional costs and administrative overheads, which add more dependencies. This is not the only problem. When we introduce more and more cloud services, our identities will appear in different places, such as mobile apps, Microsoft cloud applications, third-party cloud applications, consumer identity providers, and so on. When identity management gets more segregated, it faces more security challenges. Azure AD is a cloud based, managed, **Identity as a Service (IDaaS)** provider, which can provide world-class security, strong authentication, and seamless collaboration. It doesn't matter where your applications or services are running. It also doesn't matter where identities originated from. It can be from an on-premises active directory, or it could be through business partners or consumers. Azure AD can bring all these together and provide secure, trustworthy, and centralized identity and access management.

The latest stats from Microsoft confirms that it stands strong (`https://aka.ms/TechCommunity/Ignite/PPT/BRK2254`):

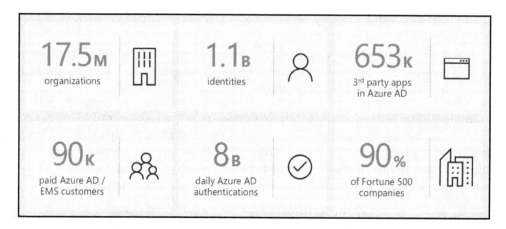

Azure AD is capable of providing the following:

- Identity and access management across Azure service offerings (IaaS, PaaS, and SaaS).
- SSO experience in hybrid environments. It doesn't matter where the service is located. Everyone will have the same unified access experience.
- Identity and access management for third-party applications.
- Secure access to on-premises web-based applications (using **Application Proxy**).
- Easy-access collaboration with business partners (using **Azure AD B2B**).
- Access based on an existing social identity (using **Azure AD B2C**).

Centralized identity and access management

Seamless integration capabilities and centralized management allow Azure AD to apply authentication and security features to different Azure service offerings in equal ways. For example, we can use Azure AD conditional access rules to prevent a risky sign-in to an SaaS application, an Azure resource, or an on-premises web application without worrying about the platform, geolocation, or service.

SSO experience

In an on-premises environment, we usually need to add additional components, such as Microsoft AD FS, in order to enable SSO for applications. But using Azure AD, we can provide SSO experience for SaaS workloads, PaaS workloads, or on-premises workloads, without depending on additional components or complex configurations. Also, if required, we can use additional security features such as Azure **Multi-Factor Authentication** (**MFA**) or conditional access rules, along with SSO, in order to add an additional layer of protection to the sign-in process.

Domain services

When I talk about Azure AD with people, quite often I find that some people think that Azure AD is the *cloud version* of the on-premise Active Directory. This is completely wrong. Azure AD can do certain things that an on-premises Active Directory is not capable of. Although they can be integrated with each other quite easily, they are two completely different products, developed for two different purposes.

Were your cloud workloads to require Windows Active Directory-compatible domain services such as domain join, LDAP, or Kerberos/NTLM authentication, then Azure AD would be fully capable of doing so. You can use these features without deploying domain controllers under your Azure tenant. However, it is a managed service; so, we can't expect a like-for-like service.

Azure AD Application Proxy

If we want to publish a web application from on-premises infrastructure to the public, we have to do a few things. We need to set up the relevant firewall rules and DNS records for it. If SSO is required, we need to configure a service such as AD FS. If it is a cloud-based app, we do not have to do any of these things; the only thing we need to worry about is the sign-on experience and protection. We can use Azure AD for authentication, and Azure MFA for an additional layer of security. However, not every application can be replaced by a cloud version. Azure AD Application Proxy allows us to publish on-premises web applications to the internet, and apply the same authentication and access experiences as in existing SaaS applications. This is done via a lightweight agent installed on an on-premises network. I will be explaining this feature further in Chapter 17, *Azure Active Directory Hybrid Setup*.

Azure AD B2B

If partner businesses want to share access between their infrastructures, and both organizations are using Windows AD, then we can use *AD trusts* to facilitate this. This also requires additional configurations in firewalls and DNS. It also adds management overheads, as partners need to manage additional directories. In Azure, we can use Azure AD B2B to provide secure, smooth access between partners, without additional configurations or management overheads. It is just a matter of sending an automated invitation to the partner organization, and then they can complete the sign-up process in minutes. Also, it is not essential for your partner to have Azure AD in order to perform a B2B connection.

Azure AD B2C

Azure AD B2B allows us to enable secure access between partners. In such a situation, identity management will be still manageable, as it is only between known environments. But what if it were a public-facing web application with thousands of consumers? It would not be practical to force every consumer into B2B connections. Azure AD B2C allows consumers to use their existing social accounts, such as Microsoft, Gmail, or Facebook, to log in to the application. If required, they can also sign in directly with the application.

Azure AD versions

There are five different versions of Azure AD. Each version has a different set of features:

Features	Free	Office 365	Basic	P1	P2
Directory Objects	500,000	No limit	No limit	No limit	No limit
User Management	Yes	Yes	Yes	Yes	Yes
SSO	10 app per user	10 app per user	10 app per user	No limit	No limit
B2B	Yes	Yes	Yes	Yes	Yes
Azure AD Connect	Yes	Yes	Yes	Yes	Yes
Security Reports	Basic	Basic	Basic	Advanced	Advanced

Self-Service Password Reset	Yes	Yes	Yes	Yes	Yes
Group-based access management	-	Yes	Yes	Yes	Yes
Company Branding	-	Yes	Yes	Yes	Yes
Application Proxy	-	Yes	Yes	Yes	Yes
SLA	-	Yes	Yes	Yes	Yes
Self-Service Password reset with on-premises writeback	-	-	-	Yes	Yes
Device writeback	-	-	-	Yes	Yes
Azure MFA	-	Yes	-	Yes	Yes
Microsoft Identity Manager	-	-	-	Yes	Yes
Cloud App Discovery	-	-	-	Yes	Yes
Connect Health	-	-	-	Yes	Yes
Conditional Access	-	-	-	Yes	Yes
Identity Protection	-	-	-	-	Yes
Privileged Identity Management	-	-	-	-	Yes
Microsoft Cloud App Security	-	-	-	Yes	Yes

Summary

This is the end of the introductory chapter on Active Directory fundamentals. I am sure most of you are already aware about most of the functions of AD DS. But refreshing your knowledge about Active Directory components and their operations before we dive deep into the advanced topics wasn't in vain. In this chapter, we also covered Active Directory objects, GUID and SID values, and DN. Later, I explained the Active Directory server roles and their core values. In this chapter, we also touched on an introduction to Azure AD and it is capabilities.

In the next chapter, you will learn about new features and enhancements to AD DS 2016, specifically about the new approach to protect identities from modern security threats.

2
Active Directory Domain Services 2016

Microsoft **Active Directory Domain Services** (**AD DS**) has been in the industry for over 15 years now. The first Microsoft AD version was released with Windows Server 2000. After that, with each and every Microsoft Server release, a new AD DS version was released too. These new versions brought changes that improved the functions, security, manageability, and reliability of identity infrastructures.

Each and every time Microsoft releases a new version of their software, IT engineers, professionals, and administrators rush in to figure out what is *new* in it. It's good practice to be on top of industry trends. However, simply migrating to the latest version of AD DS is not going to solve your identity challenges. In many cases, I have seen people upgrading just for the sake of it. First, we need to evaluate our requirements against the new features and gain an understanding of how upgrading can benefit the existing identity infrastructure. Then, we can introduce new features wisely.

Microsoft released AD DS 2016 at a very interesting point in the technological timeline. As I stated in the previous chapter, today's identity infrastructure requirements for enterprises are challenging. From Fortune 500 companies to small, local businesses, many enterprises already use cloud-based services for their operations, such as **software as a service** (**SaaS**) and **platform as a service** (**PaaS**). These cloud services also require some sort of identity and access management. These new requirements also extend the security boundaries of an enterprise's identity infrastructure. Therefore, legacy protections used for identity infrastructures no longer fall in line with these new changes. Considering these industry trends and requirements, the primary investment in AD DS 2016 was *identity infrastructure security and hybrid cloud collaborations*.

In this chapter, the following AD DS 2016 features will be explained in detail:

- **Privileged Access Management (PAM)**
- Time-based group memberships
- Microsoft Passport
- **Active Directory Federation Services (AD FS)** improvements
- Time sync improvements
- Azure AD join

Features of AD DS 2016

AD DS' improvements apply to its forest and domain functional levels. Upgrading the operating system or adding domain controllers that run Windows Server 2016 to an existing AD infrastructure isn't going to upgrade the forest and domain functional levels. In order to use or test these new AD DS 2016 features, you need to have the forest and domain functional levels set to Windows Server 2016. The minimum forest and domain functional levels you can run on your identity infrastructure depend on the oldest domain controller version that is running.

For example, if you have a Windows Server 2008 domain controller in your infrastructure, even if you add a Windows Server 2016 domain controller, the forest and domain functional levels need to be maintained as Windows Server 2008 until the last Windows Server 2008 domain controller is demoted from the infrastructure.

Deprecation of Windows Server 2003's forest and domain functional levels

Windows Server 2003 is no longer supported by Microsoft. When I talk to customers, I still see organizations (including banks, retailers, and pharmaceutical companies) using Server 2003 on their production networks. There are enough reasons to upgrade from Server 2003. The same holds true even for AD DS. Sometimes, it is not easy to upgrade from one version to another, especially under a limited budget. But it's always important to evaluate the risks an enterprise might face without an upgrade. We need to be mindful of protecting the right things at the right time.

If you haven't yet upgraded from AD DS 2003, then this is the right time to make that decision.

Windows Server 2003's forest and domain functional levels have been deprecated in AD DS 2016. The same happened in Windows Server 2012 R2; if you are creating a new domain, you cannot use the Windows Server 2003 forest or domain functional levels anymore. The following screenshot shows the available forest functional levels for Windows Server 2016:

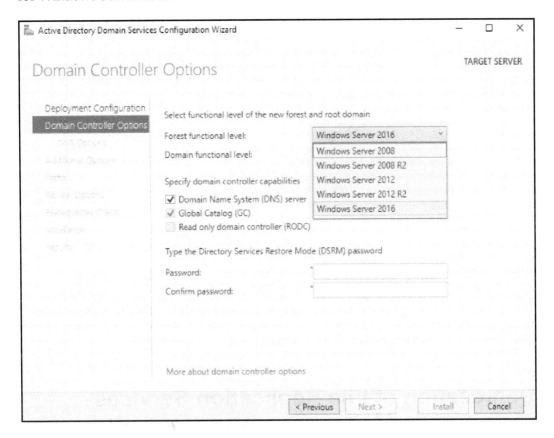

The following screenshot shows the available domain functional levels for Windows Server 2016:

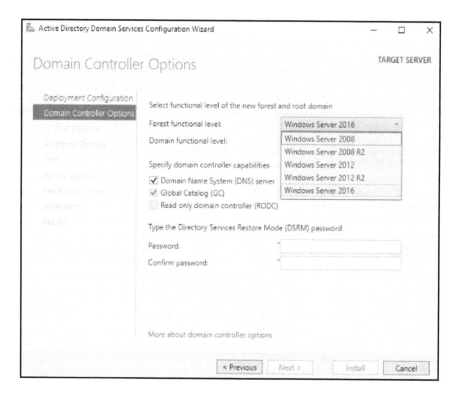

If your domain was originally created using Windows Server 2003 and you need to migrate to Server 2016, you can still do it. You can add a domain controller with Server 2016 and migrate the **flexible single master operations** (**FSMO**) roles across. In some documentations, I have seen people stating that it's not possible to migrate from Server 2003 to 2016 directly, but that's not true.

Deprecation of File Replication Services

In Windows Server 2000, Microsoft introduced the **File Replication Service** (**FRS**); it was used to replicate the SYSVOL AD folder.

 SYSVOL is a folder that contains public files from the domain that needs to be replicated to other domain controllers in the domain. It contains files required for group policies and user login scripts.

FRS has had a lot of issues when it comes to replications, especially performance-wise. FRS always replicates the entire file, no matter what kind of changes you've made. This is an issue for AD sites connected by slow WAN links. FRS does not have API or **Windows Management Instrumentation** (**WMI**) support, which can be used to monitor performance. It also doesn't support any health-reporting mechanisms. FRS was replaced by **Distributed File System Replication** (**DFSR**) in Windows Server 2003 R2 and, since Server 2008, DFSR has been used to replicate the SYSVOL folders.

DFSR supports partial file-change (block-level) replications instead of entire files. This leads to in faster replication and optimized bandwidth usage between AD sites connected by WAN links. It also supports file compression on per-file-type basis. The number of files that can be transferred (either inbound or outbound) has been increased compared to FRS. DFSR also has a self-healing mechanism for filesystem problems.

With Windows Server 2008 R2, FRS has been deprecated, and if you deploy a new domain with a Windows Server 2008 forest functional and domain level at a minimum, it will use DFSR by default to replicate SYSVOL. If you're migrating from a Windows 2003 domain environment, FRS-to-DFSR migration will be manual. This is one of the steps most engineers forget when they do domain migrations from older versions. FRS deprecation remains the same in AD DS 2016. The migration steps from FRS to DFSR work in the same way and will be explained in Chapter 11, *Active Directory Services*. In the next section, we are going to look at the most important improvement in AD 2016.

PAM

PAM has been one of the most-discussed topics in presentations, tech shows, IT forums, IT groups, blogs, and meetings over the past few years (that is, since 2014). It has become a trending topic, especially after the Windows Server 2016 preview releases. In 2016, I found myself involved in many presentations and discussions about PAM.

First of all, this is not a feature you can enable with a few clicks. It is a combination of many technologies and methodologies that come together and make a workflow or, in other words, a *way of living* for administrators. AD DS 2016 includes features and capabilities supporting PAM, but it also requires **Microsoft Identity Manager** (**MIM**). Replacing a product is easy, but changing a process is more complicated and challenging. This is one of the greatest challenges you can encounter when introducing this new way of thinking and working.

I started my career in 2003 with one of the largest North American hosting companies. I was a systems administrator at that time, and one of my tasks was to identify hacking attempts and prevent workloads being compromised. In order to do that, I had to review lots of logs on different systems. However, around that time, the intention of most attackers from individuals or groups was to put their names on websites in order to prove that they could cause damage. The average daily number of hacking attempts per server was around 20 to 50. Some collocation customers were even running their websites and workloads without any protection (even when advised against it). But as time went by, year by year, the number of attempts dramatically increased, and we were beginning to talk about hundreds or thousands of attempts per day. The following graph is from the latest *Symantec Internet Security Threat Report (2018)*, and it confirms that the number of web-based attacks has increased every month in millions:

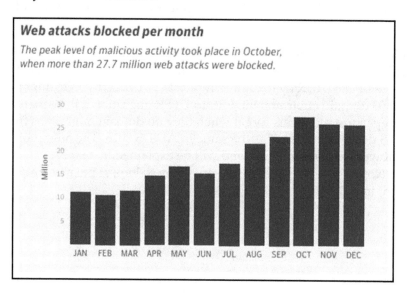

Web attacks blocked per month

The peak level of malicious activity took place in October, when more than 27.7 million web attacks were blocked.

The preceding graph is available at https://www.symantec.com/content/dam/symantec/docs/reports/istr-23-2018-en.pdf on *page 65*.

Not only have the numbers changed but so has the motive behind the attacks. As I said, in the earlier days, it was script kiddies who were after fame. Later, as users started to use more and more online services, the focus of the attacks changed to financial gain. Attackers started to focus on websites that stored credit card information. In the past 10 years, I have had to change my credit card 4 times as my credit card information was exposed due to web attacks. These types of attacks are still happening.

When considering the progression of threats, after the year 2012, a number of things changed. Instead of fame or financial gain, attackers started to target *identities*. In the earlier days, data about a person was stored in different formats. For example, when I walked into my medical center 15 years ago, before I saw the doctor, the administrative staff had to go and find the file with my name on it. They had a number of racks filled with files and papers, which included patient records, treatment history, test reports, and more. But now, things have changed: when I walk into the center, no one in administration needs to worry about my file. The doctor can see all my records from his computer screen with just a few clicks. In this way, data has been transformed into a digital format; more and more data about people is being transformed into digital format. In such a healthcare system, I become an *identity*, and my identity is attached to data, as well as to certain *privileges*. Consider your online banking system; you've got your own username and password to type in when you log in to the portal. This means that you have your own identity in the bank system; once you log in, you can access all your accounts, transfer money, make payments, and more. The bank has granted some *privileges* to your identity. With your privileges, you cannot look into your neighbor's bank account. But your bank manager can view your account and your neighbor's account too. This means that the privileges attached to the bank manager's identity are different. The amount of data that can be retrieved from the system depends on identity and privileges.

In addition to this, some of these identities are integrated with multiple systems. Industries use different systems for different operations; for example, email systems, CMS systems, or billing systems. Each of these systems holds data. To make operations smoother, these systems may be integrated with one identity infrastructure, such as Microsoft AD. This will allow users to have a single sign-on experience instead of using different identities for each and every application. It's making identities more and more powerful within any system. For an attacker, consider what is worth more—focusing on one system, or targeting an identity attached to data and privileges on many different systems? Which one would cause more damage?

Additionally, when it comes to identities, is it all just about usernames and passwords? Well, no, it's not; identities can cause more damage than that. Usernames and passwords just make it easy—just think about recent well-known cyber attacks.

 Back in July 2015, a group called **The Impact Team** threatened to expose the user account information of the *Ashley Madison* dating site if its parent company, *Avid Life Media*, did not shut down the *Ashley Madison* and *Established Men* websites completely.

For example, in the Ashley Madison website hack, was it the financial value that made it dangerous? No, it was the *names* that caused damage to people's lives. The leak of names was enough to humiliate people; it ruined families, and children lost parents to divorce. This proves that it's not only about permissions attached to an identity; individual identities themselves are more important in the modern *big data* environment.

It's been a few years since the last US presidential elections and, by now, we can see how much news can be generated with a single tweet. It isn't necessary to have special privileges to post a tweet; it is the identity that makes that tweet important. On the other hand, if that Twitter account got hacked and someone posted a fake tweet on behalf of the actual person who owns it, what kind of damage could it cause to the whole world? In order to do so, would you need to hack Jack Dorsey's account? The value of an individual identity is more powerful than Twitter's CEO.

According to the following report, the majority of the information exposed by identity attacks includes names, addresses, medical reports, and government identity numbers:

Top 10 Types of Information Exposed

➤ Financial information includes stolen credit card details and other financial credentials.

	2015 Type	2015 %	2014 Type	2014 %
1	Real Names	78%	Real Names	69%
2	Home Addresses	44%	Gov. ID Numbers (e.g., SSN)	45%
3	Birth Dates	41%	Home Addresses	43%
4	Gov. ID Numbers (e.g., SSN)	38%	Financial Information	36%
5	Medical Records	36%	Birth Dates	35%
6	Financial Information	33%	Medical Records	34%
7	Email Addresses	21%	Phone Numbers	21%
8	Phone Numbers	19%	Email Addresses	20%
9	Insurance	13%	User Names & Passwords	13%
10	User Names & Passwords	11%	Insurance	11%

The preceding table is available at `https://www.symantec.com/content/dam/symantec/docs/reports/istr-21-2016-en.pdf` on *page 53*.

Attacks targeting identities are rising every day. The following graph shows the number of identities that have been exposed compared to the total number of incidents:

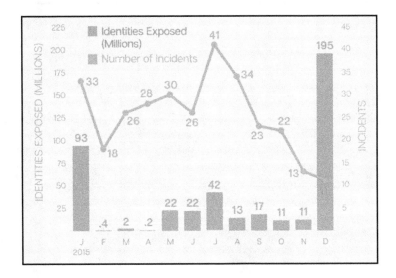

The preceding graph is available at `https://www.symantec.com/content/dam/symantec/docs/reports/istr-21-2016-en.pdf` on *page 49*.

In December 2015, there were only 11 incidents, yet 195 million identities were exposed. This shows how much damage these types of attacks can cause.

Each and every time this type of attack occurs, the most common responses from engineers include "*Those attacks were so sophisticated!*"; "*It was too complex to identify!*"; "*They were so clever!*"; "*It was a zero-day attack*"; and so on. But is that really true?

 Zero-day attacks are based on system bugs and errors unknown to vendors. The latest report shows that the average time it takes to detect a breach is less than 7 days, and 1 day to release a patch (*Symantec Internet Security Threat Report, 2016*).

The *Microsoft Security Intelligence Report Volume 21 (January through June 2016)* report contains the following graph that explains the complexity of these vulnerabilities. It clearly shows that a majority of vulnerabilities are still less complex to exploit. High-complexity vulnerabilities still comprise less than 5% of the total vulnerability disclosures. This proves that attackers are still after low-hanging fruit:

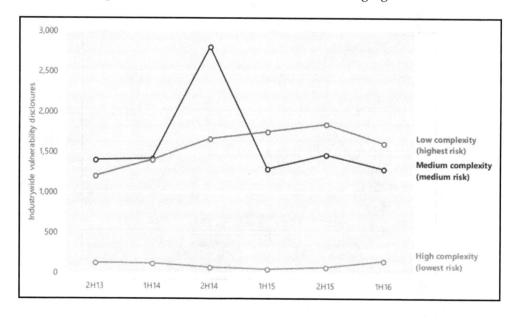

 The preceding graph is available at `https://download.microsoft.` `com/download/E/B/0/EB0F50CC-989C-4B66-B7F6-68CD3DC90DE3/` `Microsoft_Security_Intelligence_Report_Volume_21_English.` `pdf` on *page 46*.

Microsoft AD is a leader in providing identity and access management solutions. In all this constant news about identity breaches, the Microsoft AD name also appears. Interestingly, people start to question why Microsoft can't fix it. But if we evaluate these problems, it's obvious that just providing a technology-rich product is not enough to solve these issues. With each and every new server OS version, Microsoft releases a new AD version. With every release, there are new features to improve identity infrastructure security. However, when I go to work on an AD project, I find that the majority of engineers don't even following security best practices defined by AD versions that were released 10 years ago!

Let's consider a car race: race categories are usually based on engine displacement; for example, 3 L, 5 L, and so on. In a race, most of the time, it's the same models or the same manufacturer's cars racing together. If it's the same manufacturer, and if they have the same engine capacity, how does one driver win and the other lose? Well, it's the car's tuning and the driver's skills that decide the winner. If AD DS 2016 can fix all identity threats, that's really good, but simply providing a product or technology doesn't seem to have worked so far. That's why we need to change the way we think about identity infrastructure security. We should not forget that we are fighting against human adversaries—the tactics, methods, and approaches they use are changing every day. The products we use do not have such frequent updates, but we can change their ability to execute an attack on the infrastructure by understanding the fundamentals and using products, technologies, and workflows to prevent it.

Before we move on to identity-theft prevention mechanisms, let's take a look at a typical identity infrastructure attack:

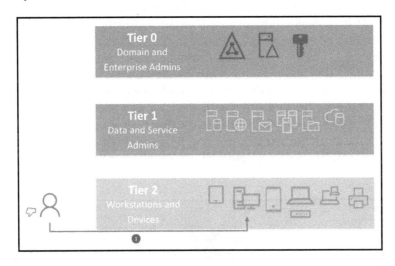

The Microsoft tiered administration model is based on three tiers. All these identity attacks start by gaining some kind of access to the identity infrastructure and then move laterally until they have the keys to the kingdom, that is, the **Domain** or **Enterprise Admin** credentials. Then, they have full ownership of the entire identity infrastructure.

As the preceding diagram shows, the first step of an identity attack is to get some kind of access to the system. They do not target the **Domain Admin** or **Enterprise Admin** account first. Getting access to a typical user account is much easier than a **Domain Admin** account; all they need is some kind of beachhead. For that, even now, the most common attack technique is to send out a phishing email. It's typical that someone will still fall for this and click on it. Then, once they have some sort of access to your identity infrastructure, the next step is to start moving laterally to gain more privileges. How many of you have completely eliminated local administrator accounts in your infrastructure? I'm sure the answer will be almost none. Users keep asking for software installations and system-level modifications to their systems frequently, and most of the time, engineers end up assigning local administrator privileges. If the compromised account is a local administrator, it becomes extremely easy to move to the next level.

If not, then the attacker will make the compromised system misbehave. So, who will come to the rescue? Well, it's the superhero IT help-desk people, of course. In lots of organizations, IT help desk engineers are **Domain Admins**. If not that, they're at least local administrators on systems. So, once they receive the call about a misbehaving computer, they use an **Remote Desktop Protocol** (RDP) or log in locally using a privileged account. RDP always sends your credentials in plain text. If the attacker is running a password-harvesting tool, it's extremely easy to capture the credentials. You may be wondering how a compromised *typical user* account can execute such programs. Well, it so happens that Windows' OSes do not prevent a user from running any application in their user context. They will not allow a user to change any system-level settings, but they will still allow the user to run scripts or user-level executables:

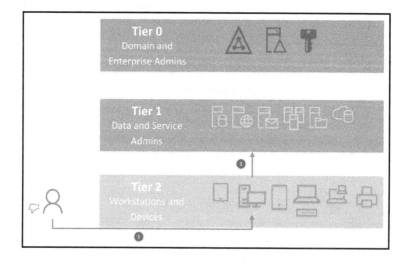

Once an attacker has gained access to an identity in an organization, the next level of privileges to own will be **Tier 1**. This is where the application administrator, data administrator, and SaaS application administrator accounts live. In a typical modern-day infrastructure, we have too many administrators. Primarily, we have domain administrators and enterprise administrators, and then we have local administrators. Different applications running on the infrastructure have their own administrators, such as Exchange administrators, SQL administrators, and SharePoint administrators. Other third-party applications, such as CMS and the billing portal, may have their own administrators. Additionally, if you are using cloud services, SaaS applications have another set of administrators. So, are we really aware of the activities happening in these accounts? Mostly, engineers only worry about protecting Domain Admin accounts but, at the same time, forget about the other kinds of administrators in the infrastructure. Some of these administrator roles can cause more damage to a business than a Domain Admin. These applications and services decentralize management in the organization. In order to move laterally with privileges, these attackers only need to log in to a machine or server where the administrators log in. **Local Security Authority Subsystem Service** (**LSASS**) stores credentials in its memory for active Windows sessions. This avoids the hassle of users entering credentials for each and every service they access. It also stores Kerberos tickets. This allows attackers to perform a pass-the-hash attack and retrieve locally stored credentials. Decentralized management of administrator accounts makes this process easier.

 There are features and security best practices that can be used to prevent pass-the-hash attacks in an identity infrastructure. I will explain them in detail in `Chapter 15`, *Active Directory Security Best Practices*.

Another problem with these types of accounts is that once they become service admin accounts, they can eventually become **Domain** or **Enterprise Admin** accounts. I have seen engineers create service accounts and, when they can't figure out the exact permissions required for the program, add them to the **Domain Admin** group as an easy fix. However, it's not only infrastructure attacks that can expose such credentials. Service admins are attached to the application too, so compromising the application can also expose identities.

In such a scenario, it will be easy for attackers to gain the keys to the kingdom:

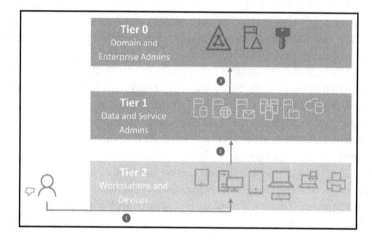

Tier 0 is where the **Domain and Enterprise Admins** operate. This is what the ultimate target of an identity infrastructure attack is; once they obtain access to **Tier 0**, they own your entire identity infrastructure. The latest reports show that, after the initial breach, it only takes less than 48 hours to gain **Tier 0** privileges. According to these reports, once attackers gain access, it takes up to 7-8 months at least to identify the breach. This is because once they have the highest privileges, they can create backdoors, clean up logs, and hide forever if needed. The systems we use always treat administrators as trustworthy people. This is no longer the case in the modern world; how many times do you check your system's logs to see what your Domain Admins are doing? Even though engineers look at the logs of other users, rarely do any of them check Domain Admin accounts. The same thing applies to an internal security breach too: as I said, most people are good, but you never know. Many high-profile identity attacks have proven this already.

When I have a discussion with engineers and customers about identity infrastructure security, these are the common comments I hear:

- We have too many administrator accounts.
- We do not know how many administrator accounts we've got.
- We have fast-changing IT teams, so it's hard to manage permissions.
- We do not have visibility over administrator account activities.
- If there is an identity infrastructure breach or attempt, how do we identify it?

The answer to all these issues is PAM. As I mentioned at the beginning of the chapter, this is not one product; it's a workflow and a new way of working. The main steps and components of this process are as follows:

1. Apply pass-the-hash prevention features to the existing identity infrastructure (for more information, you can refer to `Chapter 15`, *Active Directory Security Best Practices*).
2. Install Microsoft Advanced Threat Analytics to monitor the domain controller traffic to identify potential real-time identity infrastructure threats (refer to `Chapter 15`, *Active Directory Security Best Practices*).
3. Install and configure Microsoft Identity Manager 2016—this product enables us to manage privileged access to an existing AD forest by providing task-based, time-limited privilege access. I will explain this in detail later in this chapter using examples.

What does PAM have to do with AD DS 2016?

AD DS 2016 now allows time-based group membership, which makes this whole process possible. A user is added to a group with a **time-to-live** (TTL) value and, once it expires, the user is removed from the group automatically. For example, let's assume your CRM application has administrator rights assigned to the `CRMAdmin` security group. The users in this group only log in to the system once a month to do some maintenance. But the admin rights for the members in that group remain untouched for the remaining 29 days, 24/7. This provides enough opportunity for attackers to try and gain access to privileged accounts. So, if it's possible to grant access privileges for a shorter time period, isn't that more useful? Then, we can be assured that, for the majority of the days in a month, the CRM application does not run the risk of being compromised by an account in the `CRMAdmin` group.

What is the logic behind PAM?

PAM is based on the **just-in-time** (**JIT**) administration concept. Back in 2014, Microsoft released the PowerShell toolkit, which allows **Just Enough Administration** (**JEA**). Let's assume that you are running a web server in your infrastructure; as part of the operation, you need to collect some logs every month to make a report. You've already set up a PowerShell script for this purpose. Someone in your team needs to log in to the system and run it. In order to do so, you require administrative privileges. Using JEA, it is possible to assign the required permissions for the user to run only that particular program. In this way, there's no need to add the user to the Domain Admin group. The user will not be allowed to run any other program with the permission assigned as it is, and it will not apply for another computer either. JIT administration is bound in *time*. This means that users will have the required privileges only when they need them; they will not hold privileged access rights all the time.

PAM operations can be divided into four major steps, as shown in the following diagram:

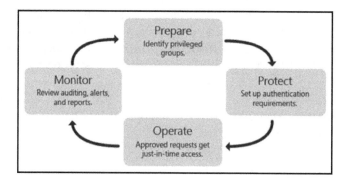

Let's take a look at these four major steps:

- **Prepare**: The first step is to identify the privileged access groups in your existing AD forest and start to remove users from them. You may also need to make certain changes to your application infrastructure to support this setup. For example, if you assign privileged access to user accounts instead of security groups (in applications or services), this will need to change. The next step is to set up equivalent groups in a *bastion forest* without any members.

When setting up MIM, a bastion forest will be used to manage privileged access in an existing AD forest. This is a special forest and cannot be used for other infrastructure operations. This forest runs on a minimum of a Windows Server 2012 R2 AD forest functional level. When an identity infrastructure is compromised and attackers gain access to **Tier 0**, they can hide their activities for months or years. But how can we be sure our existing identity infrastructure has not been compromised already? Well, if we implement this in the same forest, it will not achieve its core targets. Additionally, domain upgrades are painful, requiring time and money. But with a bastion forest, this solution can be applied to your existing identity infrastructure with minimal changes.

- **Protect**: The next step is to set up a workflow for authentication and authorization. We need to define how a user can request privileged access when required. This can be done using a MIM portal or an existing support portal (with an integrated MIM REST API). It is possible to set up a system to use **Multi-Factor Authentication** (**MFA**) during this request process to prevent any unauthorized activity. Additionally, it's important to define how the requests will be handled. It can be either an automatic or manual approval process.

- **Operate**: Once the privileged access request is approved, the user account will be added to the security group in the bastion forest. The group itself has an SID value. In both forests, the group will have the exact same SID value. Therefore, the application or service will not see a difference between the two groups in two different forests. Once the permission is granted, it will only be valid for the time defined by the authorization policy. Once it reaches the time limit, the user account will be removed from the security group automatically.

- **Monitor**: PAM provides visibility over privilege-access requests. On each and every request, events will be recorded, and it is possible to review them and also generate reports for audits. This helps to fine-tune the process and also identify any potential threats.

Let's examine how it really works:

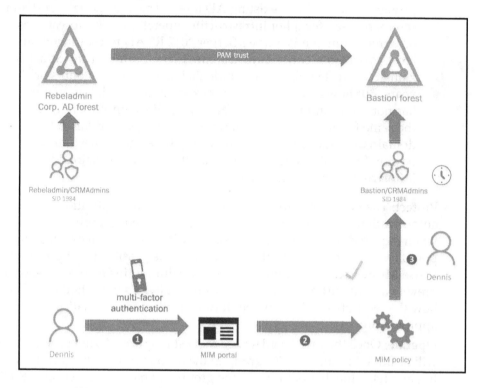

Rebeladmin Corp. uses a CRM system for its operations. The application has the administrator role and **Rebeladmin/CRMAdmins** security group assigned to it. Any member of that group will have administrator privileges to the application. Recently, PAM has been introduced to Rebeladmin Corp. As an engineer, I have identified **Rebeladmin/CRMAdmins** as a privileged group and am going to protect it using PAM. The first step is to remove the members of the **Rebeladmin/CRMAdmins** group. After that, I set up the same group in the bastion forest. It's not just that the name is the same, but both groups have the same SID value: **1984**.

User **Dennis** used to be a member of the **Rebeladmin/CRMAdmins** group and was running monthly reports. At the end of one month, he tried to run it and found that he did not have the required permissions. The next step for him was to request the required permission through the MIM portal.

According to the policies, as part of the request, the system wants **Dennis** to use MFA. Once **Dennis** verifies the PIN, the request is logged in the portal. As an administrator, I receive the alert about the request, and I log in to the system to review the request. It's a legitimate request, so I approve his access to the system for 8 hours. Then, the system automatically adds the user account for Dennis to the **Bastion/CRMAdmins** group. This group has the same SID value as the production group. Therefore, a member of the **Bastion/CRMAdmins** group will be treated as an administrator by the CRM application. This group membership contains the TTL value too. After it passes 8 hours from approval, Dennis's account will be automatically removed from the **Bastion/CRMAdmins** group. In this process, we didn't add any member to the production security group, which is **Rebeladmin/CRMAdmins**. So, the production forest stays untouched and protected.

Here, the most important thing we need to understand is that the legacy approach to identity protection is no longer valid. We are up against human adversaries. Identity is our new perimeter in the infrastructure and, to protect it, we need to understand how our adversaries are attacking it, and stay a step ahead. PAM with AD DS 2016 is a new approach in the right direction.

Time-based group memberships

In the previous section, I explored PAM features in the new AD DS 2016. Time-based group membership is a part of that broader topic. It allows administrators to assign temporary group membership, which is expressed by a TTL value. This value will be added to the Kerberos ticket. It is also called the **expiring links** feature. When a user is assigned to a temporary group membership, their login Kerberos **ticket-granting ticket (TGT)** lifetime will be equal to the lowest TTL value they have. For example, let's assume that you grant temporary group membership to user A to be a member of the Domain Admin group. It is only valid for 60 minutes. But the user logs in 50 minutes after the original assignment and only has 10 minutes left as a member of the Domain Admin group. Based on this, the domain controller will issue a TGT that is only valid for 10 minutes to user A.

This feature is not enabled by default. The reason for this is that, to use this feature, the forest functional level must be Windows Server 2016. Additionally, once this feature is enabled, it cannot be disabled.

Let's examine how it works in the real world:

1. I have a Windows domain controller installed and it is running with the Windows Server 2016 forest functional level. This can be verified using the following PowerShell command:

   ```
   Get-ADForest | fl Name,ForestMode
   ```

2. Then, we need to enable the expiring links feature. This can be enabled using the following command:

   ```
   Enable-ADOptionalFeature 'Privileged Access Management
   Feature' -Scope ForestOrConfigurationSet -Target
   rebeladmin.com
   ```

   The `rebeladmin.com` domain name can be replaced with your **fully qualified domain name (FQDN)**.

3. I have a user called Adam Curtiss who I need to assign Domain Admin group membership to for 60 minutes; take a look at the following command:

   ```
   Get-ADGroupMember "Domain Admins"
   ```

4. It lists the current members of the Domain Admin group:

   ```
   Administrator: Windows PowerShell
   PS C:\Users\Administrator> Get-ADGroupMember "Domain Admins"


   distinguishedName : CN=Administrator,CN=Users,DC=REBELADMIN,DC=COM
   name              : Administrator
   objectClass       : user
   objectGUID        : c804fa0b-8aff-49c6-8b9b-85cf046667d8
   SamAccountName    : Administrator
   SID               : S-1-5-21-4041220333-1835452706-552999228-500


   PS C:\Users\Administrator>
   ```

5. The next step is to add Adam Curtiss to the Domain Admin group for 60 minutes:

   ```
   Add-ADGroupMember -Identity 'Domain Admins' -Members
   'acurtiss' -MemberTimeToLive (New-TimeSpan -Minutes 60)
   ```

6. Once it has run, we can verify the remaining TTL value for the group membership using the following command:

```
Get-ADGroup 'Domain Admins' -Property member -
ShowMemberTimeToLive
```

The following screenshot illustrates the output for the preceding command:

7. Once I log in as the user and list the Kerberos ticket, it shows the renew time as less than 60 minutes. This is because I've logged in a few minutes after being granted permission:

Once the TGT renewal period is crossed, the user will no longer be a member of the Domain Admin group.

Microsoft Passport

The most common way of protecting access to a system or resource is to introduce authentication and authorization processes. This is exactly what AD does as well; when a user logs in to a domain-joined device, AD first authenticates the user to see whether they're the user they claim to be. Once authentication is successful, it then checks what the user is allowed to do (authorization). To do that, we use usernames and passwords. This is what all identity infrastructure attackers are after. They need some kind of username and password to get into the system. Passwords are a rather weak authentication method; they are breakable, it's just a matter of time and the methods used in order to break them. As a solution to this, organizations are tightening password policies, but when they are forcibly made complex, more and more people start to write them down. I have seen a few people who just use sticky notes and stick them on their monitor. So, if it's a weak authentication method, what is the solution?

With Windows 10, Microsoft introduced its new biometric sign-in system. Windows Hello allows us to use face recognition, fingerprints, or PIN numbers for authentication. However, this does not allow the user to use any services or apps; it is an additional layer of security to allow the device to identify its correct user. After the system identifies its user as legitimate, the user still needs to authenticate to be allowed access to resources. Microsoft Passport provides strong two-factor authentication instead of passwords. The user needs a specific device and biometric authentication/PIN to be allowed access.

In the process of the Microsoft Passport setup, it will generate a new public-private key pair and store the private key in the device's **Trusted Platform Module (TPM)**. If the device doesn't have a TPM, it will save this in the software. The private key will stay on the device all the time. The public key can be stored in AD (on-premises) or Azure AD (the cloud). AD DS 2016 supports Microsoft Passport configuration.

In the process of authentication using Microsoft Passport, the user first needs to authenticate to the device using Microsoft Hello. Then, the user needs to prove their identity using MFA, smart cards, or gestures. This information will be passed to AD. Then, the device generates a unique key, attests the key, isolates the public key part, and sends it to AD to register it. Once AD DS registers the public key, it asks the device to log in using the private key. Once the device successfully logs in with the private key, AD DS validates it and generates the authentication token. This token will allow the user and the device to use the resources.

This feature eliminates the traditional method of using a username and password, and provides a robust, secure, and future-proof way of authentication.

AD FS improvements

AD FS allows the sharing of identities between trusted business partners (federated) with minimum identity infrastructure changes. AD FS 2016 added many new features to protect federated environments from rising identity infrastructure threats. In Chapter 13, *Active Directory Federation Services,* I will explain AD FS in detail. Right now, I am going to summarize the shiny new features it has.

In the previous section about Microsoft Passport, I explained why the traditional username/password method is no longer an option against modern identity threats. This is applicable to federated environments as well. Most federated environments use MFA as another layer of security. AD FS 2016 supports three new methods to authenticate without usernames and passwords.

Microsoft Azure provides Azure MFA as a service to protect cloud workloads from unauthorized access. If on-premises AD is federated with Azure AD, it can also be used to protect on-premises workloads. AD FS 2016 supports Azure MFA integration. If you need to set up AD FS 2012 R2 and integrate with Azure MFA, you need an on-premises MFA server. With AD FS 2016, no additional components are required, as it comes with a built-in Azure MFA adapter. If Azure MFA is configured as the primary authentication, then the user needs to provide a username and **one-time password** (**OTP**) from Azure Authenticator for authentication.

AD FS 2016 also supports passwordless access from compliant devices. This is combined with Conditional Access policies, which is another big feature of AD FS 2016. Azure Conditional Access policies can be used with devices registered with Azure AD or Intune (an enterprise mobility suite). AD FS 2016 allows us to use the same conditional policies to manage access to on-premises resources. If the devices are not managed or compliant, we can force use of MFA for access using policies.

AD FS 2016 also supports access using Microsoft Hello and Microsoft Passport. Using these new authentication methods, users can access AD FS protected workloads from an intranet or extranet.

Some organizations use non-Microsoft directory services for operations. AD FS 2016 now supports LDAP v3-based directories. This allows us to federate identities between AD and non-AD environments. This also allows corporations to federate their identities with Azure services even if they use third-party directory services.

In the previous version of AD FS, if you needed to upgrade it to the latest version, you needed to build a separate AD FS farm and then export/import the configuration. But with AD FS 2016, this is no longer needed. You can introduce an AD FS 2016 server to an existing AD FS 2012 R2 farm. Then, it will operate on the AD FS 2012 R2 level. Once the last AD FS 2012 R2 server is removed from the farm, the farm's functional level can be raised to AD FS 2016.

In previous AD FS versions, we only had limited customization options for the login pages. With AD FS 2016, we are able to change text, images, logos, and themes to provide a more personalized GUI experience for organizations.

The rest of the AD FS operational enhancements will be explained in detail in `Chapter 13`, *Active Directory Federation Services*.

Time sync improvements

Time accuracy is important for AD infrastructures to maintain Kerberos authentication between users and domain controllers. Currently, the time accuracy between two parties should be less than 5 minutes. In an AD environment, domain members sync time with domain controllers (that is, the **Primary Domain Controller** (**PDC**), a domain controller in the root forest, or a domain controller with the **good time server**, or `GTIMESERV`, flag) to maintain accurate time across the environment.

However, sometimes, this doesn't work as expected. As an example, virtual servers sync time with their hosts, which can cause accuracy issues. Depending on the network topology, the reply packets for time requests can take longer to reach the requester. This can also cause accuracy issues between the domain controller and the client. Mobile devices and laptops may not connect with the domain very often, which can also lead to time-accuracy issues.

Time accuracy impacts an organization's business and operations in different ways:

- AD replications between domain controllers are the primary requirement of a healthy AD infrastructure. Inaccurate time syncs create replication issues.
- Credit-card processing requires a 1-second accuracy, according to industry standards.
- There are government regulations enforced for stock trades (that is, 50-microseconds accuracy from FINRA).

- It can result in inaccurate data for reports, log analytics and threat analysis, and troubleshooting in infrastructures.
- It impacts distributed systems such as clusters, SQL farms, and database farms.

With Windows Server 2016, Microsoft made several improvements to maintain accurate time synchronization across infrastructures. Its improved algorithms will mitigate the impact of NTP data accuracy, resulting in network congestion and network latency. It also uses an improved API for accurate time references. With these improvements, it can provide a 1-microsecond time accuracy.

The Hyper-V 2016 time sync service has also been improved to provide accurate time for virtual environments. It will provide the initial accurate time for the **virtual machine** (**VM**) to start and then interrupt with corrections for W32Time samples. This allows us to have a time accuracy that is between 10 and 15 microseconds.

With Windows Server 2016, new performance monitor counters have also been implemented to monitor and troubleshoot time-accuracy issues in infrastructures.

Azure AD join

Azure AD is rapidly becoming a unified identity and access management solution for enterprises. More and more new features are being introduced to Azure AD regularly to improve identity management, information protection, device management, experience, and more. Azure AD is a fully supported integration with on-premises AD infrastructure. Most Azure AD features also work well in hybrid environments. I agree that not every business can shift all their identity and access management processes to the cloud, but why not start with the hybrid setup and use the best of both technologies?

Rebeladmin Corp. has two offices—one office is located in Toronto, Canada and the other is located in London, United Kingdom. Both have desktop computers, virtual servers, and physical servers running. All of these devices are already connected to the AD domain. Even with its two locations, it still maintains one identity infrastructure. When devices are located in certain physical locations with proper connectivity, it is easy to control them using AD group policies, login scripts, permissions, and more. It also uses the **System Center Configuration Manager** (**SCCM**) to manage devices. This means that with fixed security boundaries, we know where our devices and users are. While there is nothing wrong about this setup, in the modern world, people are no longer bound to a desk and chair in an office.

More often than not, they work from remote locations. They use laptops, tablets, and smartphones to do their work. Some even use the same device for their personal work and their office work. In such environments, organizations are starting to lose control and visibility over devices and users. So, how we can know where these devices are? How do we know if the corporate data that is saved in those devices is protected? How do we know if the devices are complying with company security policies unless they are those that are connected to the corporate network?

Azure AD join can help to overcome these challenges; with it, we can do the following:

- Keep users and devices connected to the corporate identity infrastructure, wherever and whenever.
- Protect identities and devices from emerging threats.
- Analyze user and device activities, events, logs, and behaviors.

Azure AD joined devices

In an on-premises AD environment, we have different types of objects such as user accounts, groups, and devices. Using AD, we can manage the state of these objects. This can be related to access, security, or management. Similarly, Azure AD can also manage objects from the cloud only, or in the hybrid environment. Using Azure AD join, we can shift control of these device objects to Azure AD. There are two methods that we can use to give device control to Azure AD. Let's go ahead and look at these two methods in details.

Over a year ago, I wanted to enroll my little girl, Selena, in swimming lessons conducted at my local leisure center. When I walked into the reception to query about it, they said there was no space available. However, we were given the opportunity to *register* under a waiting list. It was a matter of filling in a small form with some basic details such as name, contact details, and preferred dates. By registering in their system, I became an identity. The form I filled in contained data that could be used to identify me uniquely from others in the same list. It only provides enough information to contact me when space is available. Similarly, by *registering* a device with Azure AD, we can make it an identity. However, it will only give partial control to Azure AD. Once the device is registered, Azure AD can enable/disable the device, capture sign-in events, and collect assert information. We also can enroll the device with Microsoft Intune; this will give additional control over the device to maintain the organization's security stands and compliance requirements.

After being on the waiting list for a few months, I finally got the opportunity to sign my daughter up for swimming lessons. During the sign-up process, they collected more information, such as my bank details. Additionally, I had to sign a different set of forms to comply with their rules. So, now they have more control over me and my daughter, as we became members of their program. Similarly, by *joining* devices to Azure AD, we will give more granular control over the device state. If users are using their own devices to access corporate resources, it is best to *register* devices with Azure AD rather than AD join as it will not change the state of the device. If it is a corporate device, it should join Azure AD, as it will give more control over the device, its applications, and the data stored in it:

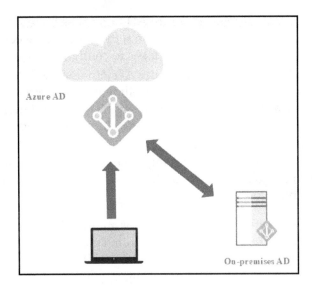

A Windows 10 device can directly register with Azure AD. It doesn't need any on-premises component. This is ideal for an environment that is trying to reduce the on-premises footprint. This also works well in hybrid environments. Even device management has moved to Azure AD; the device will still have access to applications and resources in an on-premises infrastructure seamlessly.

We can enroll the devices using the following:

- **With Windows Autopilot**: This can be done using the built-in Windows Autopilot feature, or by enabling Autopilot through Microsoft Intune. More information about device enrollment using Windows Autopilot is available under my blog post at `http://www.rebeladmin.com/2018/11/step-step-guide-enroll-windows-10-devices-microsoft-intune-using-autopilot/`.

- **During Windows 10 installation**: During a fresh installation, we can connect the device to Azure AD.
- **Using Windows sign-in options**: If the device is already installed, then go to **Accounts** | **Access work or school** to join the device to Azure AD

Azure AD join devices have the following benefits:

- **Single sign-on (SSO)**: Users can log in to Azure AD join devices directly using their corporate accounts. This allows the user to access cloud or on-premises services and resources seamlessly without additional login prompts.
- **Enterprise State Roaming**: Azure AD Enterprise State Roaming allows you to sync user settings and application settings data between Azure AD join devices. This reduces the time it takes to configure devices for the first time.
- **Seamless MDM integration**: Azure AD join devices can easily enroll with Microsoft Intune (by using auto enrollment). This helps to manage the device state according to the organization's security standards (by using device compliance, Conditional Access, and Cloud App Security).
- **Self-services**: Azure AD join device users can reset their passwords themselves through the device login screen using Azure AD self-service. Users also can join their devices to Azure AD without the help of the IT department.

As I mentioned earlier, Azure AD join is ideal for an organization that doesn't have an on-premises AD or is trying to move away from an on-premises AD. If you have systems running that are older than Windows 10, and if you still wish to use Azure AD features with minimum infrastructure changes, you have to use the **hybrid Azure AD join** method.

Hybrid Azure AD join devices

This is the typical setup for most organizations that are starting their cloud journey afresh. In the beginning, it is hard to make big changes to the environment, as this can impact the organization in many different ways. This is not only for cloud migrations, but is also the same with any new technology—it takes time and patience to adopt new changes. If an organization already has an on-premises AD set up, it means that the majority of the devices are already part of the domain. With hybrid Azure AD join, devices can simply *register* with Azure AD without changing their status.

Devices will be still part of the on-premises domain and there will be no upgrade to Windows 10:

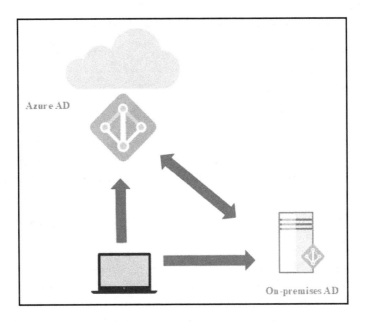

Hybrid Azure AD join supports a wide range of operating systems. Based on the differences in the registering process, we can group these operating systems into two.

Windows' current devices

The following are Windows' current devices:

- Windows 10
- Windows Server 2016
- Windows Server 2019

By using the **Group Policy Object** (**GPO**) or SCCM, we can force Windows' current devices to register with Azure AD automatically. Using these methods, we can also control which devices need to register with Azure AD. The configurations step for this will be explained in more detail in `Chapter 17`, *Azure Active Directory Hybrid Setup*.

Windows' down-level devices

The following are Windows' down-level devices:

- Windows 8.1
- Windows 7
- Windows Server 2012 R2
- Windows Server 2012
- Windows Server 2008 R2

Before registering down-level devices, we need to install an agent (`https://www.microsoft.com/en-us/download/details.aspx?id=53554`). This can be pushed to computers using SCCM or GPOs. We will also explain this further in `Chapter 17,` *Azure Active Directory Hybrid Setup*.

There are a few things you need to bear in mind before you consider the hybrid Azure AD join method:

- If Windows 10 devices are already Azure AD joined, we need to remove those settings before enabling hybrid Azure AD join. Dual registration is not supported.
- When considering down-level devices, hybrid Azure AD join is not going to work if AD Connect is using Azure AD pass-through authentication without seamless SSO.
- Hybrid Azure AD join is not supported for domain controllers.
- If you're using system images, make sure the image doesn't have hybrid Azure AD join settings.

You may be asking yourself why I have added this topic about Azure AD join to this chapter. I agree that this is not a *feature* of AD 2016. However, on-premises AD on its own can't provide answers to the complex identity and access management requirements that today's businesses have. Azure AD is becoming more mature every day; it gets more features regularly. So, we have no choice but to take the good aspects of both technologies to address our requirements. AD 2016 is fully supported to work side by side with Azure AD and make our identity infrastructures solid, secure, and future-proof.

Summary

In this chapter, we looked at the new features and enhancements that come with AD DS 2016. One of the biggest improvements was Microsoft's new approach toward privilege access management. This is not just a feature that can be enabled via AD DS, but is part of a broader solution. It helps protect identity infrastructures from novel adversaries, as traditional techniques and technologies are no longer valid in the face of rising threats. We also saw the new types of advanced authentication methods allowed by AD DS. Typical username/password combinations are the weaker option with current infrastructure-security challenges. AD FS 2016 also has additional security enhancements to protect identities in a federated environment. We also explored the improvements made to time synchronization to maintain time accuracy across the AD domain. When we consider hybrid environments, Azure AD join helps organizations to register domain-joined devices with Azure AD and allows them to use features from both technologies. In this chapter, we learned what Azure AD join is and how it works with on-premises AD.

In the next chapter, we are going to look at designing AD infrastructures. The correct design is key for a productive, highly available, and secure identity infrastructure.

Designing an Active Directory Infrastructure

3

The **Active Directory** (**AD**) deployment process in IT infrastructure has been made easy over the years. Even if you don't have advanced knowledge of Active Directory, with a few wizards, you can install **Active Directory Domain Services** (**AD DS**) on a server. But there is a lot more to think about before you install your first domain controller into an IT infrastructure. We need to evaluate our business requirements, evaluate our security/compliance requirements, and we need to decide what AD features/services to enable and where to place them in the infrastructure. We need to get the blueprint of the identity infrastructure correct before the implementation phase, otherwise it will not deliver what we expect.

In this chapter, we are going to learn how to design on-premises and a Hybrid Identity infrastructure properly. In the design phase, we will be looking at information gathering techniques, risk mitigation, capacity planning, component placement, best practices, and costs.

This chapter covers the following topics:

- Designing a forest structure
- Designing a domain structure
- Designing an OU structure
- Designing the physical topology of Active Directory
- Global catalog server placement
- Designing a Hybrid Identity

What makes a good system?

When I was 15 years old, my dad bought me my first bicycle. It was brand new and I jumped on it and cycled a round the house very quickly a few times before I crashed into my grandmother. Even though it was brand new, the brakes didn't work properly. Luckily, she wasn't hurt. Then, my dad came to me and said even if it was brand new, it hadn't been *tuned* yet.

The same day, my dad took the bike to a shop. The mechanics in there removed the parts of the bicycle one by one and then started to fit them in again after applying oil and grease. While they were doing this, they asked questions about what kind of seat I would like and whether I needed different lights, different pedals, and so on. Based on my answers, some parts were added and some parts were fine-tuned. In this way, from a brand-new bicycle, they made me a bicycle that was fit for my requirements. Although I liked it even before they'd tuned it, I liked it even more after the tuning.

For a few years, I maintained it properly: I washed it, oiled it, changed parts when needed, and upgraded it as new things came into development. When I went to high school, I had to leave it at home, so I didn't have time to take care of it. Within a few years, it wasn't usable at all.

A perfect product doesn't make for a perfect solution. In this story, the bike was much better when it was tuned. Also, it worked as intended when I maintained it properly. When I couldn't maintain it properly, it eventually became unusable. This applies to any system we use.

What makes a good system? Let's take a look:

- A good design – the fundamentals need to be right
- Correct implementation according to the plan
- Monitoring the system to find possible issues
- Maintaining the system by fixing issues and performing upgrades as required
- A **disaster recovery** (**DR**) solution to recover from system failure

This theory applies to an Active Directory infrastructure as well. Design is the key requirement for any identity infrastructure. As engineers, we are rarely assigned to build an identity infrastructure from scratch. We're usually assigned to expand or maintain the existing infrastructure. But it's important to know the foundation of the design; then, even if it has to be extended or changed, you know whether that is possible or not.

When I work on Active Directory projects, one of the common questions I get from customers is *do you think our design is correct?* On most occasions, I can't give a yes or no answer. Instead, it's usually a yes *and* no answer.

The reason for this is that it may not be valid for the current business with respect to the requirements of the organization, but it was a valid design for the same organization some time ago. If I ask their IT managers or engineers questions such as *why did you put this domain controller here?* or *why did you configure this domain controller like this?*, most of the time, they have a valid reason to justify it. It is difficult to draw the line between the right and wrong design unless the design's fundamentals are right or wrong.

If it's not a fresh design, there are occasions in which you may need to revise or redesign the existing Active Directory topology.

New business requirements

When designing an Active Directory infrastructure from the ground up, it would be ideal if management can confirm what it will become in 20 years' time. Then, you know what to do. But this only happens in a perfect world. When organizational changes happen, it may affect the infrastructure too. It can be a change, such as introducing a new department, hiring more people, introducing a new business acquisition, or doing business mergers. Some of these changes may be easy to implement, and some may require larger, organization-wide changes. If we think about it from an identity infrastructure prospect, the most challenging change will be to extend the security boundaries. Your Active Directory forest is your security boundary for the identity infrastructure. If your requirement is beyond that, it always involves a design change.

For example, if Rebeladmin Corp. merges with My-Learning Inc., the management of Rebeladmin Corp. needs a centralized IT administration and sharing of resources between the two organizations. Both organizations maintain their own Active Directory forests. The My-Learning Inc. forest is beyond the Rebeladmin Corp.'s identity infrastructure security boundary. In order to merge them, we need to create a forest trust or domain trust relationship between the two infrastructures. With these changes, the Rebeladmin Corp. identity infrastructure will have new security boundaries. Their operations and security will also change accordingly.

Correcting legacy design mistakes

These kinds of situations are pricier for organizations. Most of the time, they end up restructuring domain infrastructures. Recently, I was talking to a company about a domain restructure. It's a multimillion dollar trading company with offices across the world. The problem was that when they designed the AD infrastructure a long time ago, they used a **single label domain** (**SLD**) name as the primary domain.

SLDs are domain names that don't have DNS suffixes such as .com, .org, or .net. After some time, they realized the limitations of SLDs and didn't fix them as that required some *administrative* changes. No one wanted to have the responsibility, either. The company kept growing, and instead of fixing the fundamental problem, they kept introducing new forests and new domains. In the end, it became almost unmanageable, with multiple domains and forests, which didn't make sense. Therefore, they had no option other than redesigning the whole Active Directory structure since the organization had decided to move a majority of workloads to Azure Cloud. But it was a very costly and painful change. If you can snip off the weeds growing in your garden with your hands, do it right away; don't wait until you have to use a saw.

There can be design mistakes in any system. This can be due to lack of knowledge, lack of resources, or even due to a lack of funding. Sometimes, we recognize things as *mistakes* or *design issues* as they no longer match our business or operational requirements. As an example, we know that it is recommended to use at least two domain controllers in a site for high availability. A startup company only used one domain controller in the beginning as they were able to afford the downtime of a domain controller. After a couple of years, this is recognized as a *design issue* because the growth of the company and the importance of business operations can no longer afford the downtime of a domain controller. The only way we can find this kind of design change requirements are by evaluating the current design and business requirements. I like to propose that I will carry out a similar exercise at least once a year.

Gathering business data

Before we start to figure out how many forests, domains, and domain controllers to create, we need to gather some data to help us make an accurate design that agrees with the core business requirements.

Understanding the organizational structure correctly is vital to designing an identity infrastructure. An organizational chart is a good place to start. It will give you an idea of who you need to ask questions to in order to collect the specific data that will help in your design.

For example, if you need to know what your software development department requires from the directory services, the best person to talk to will be the technical lead or architect of the team. They will be able to give you the exact answer you are looking for. If you ask the same question to the managing director, the answer may not be that accurate. So, before you seek the answers to your questions, you need to find the correct source.

When we gather business data, we need to consider the following:

- Who are these changes applicable to? Is this going to be a company-wide change or it is only going to apply for certain user groups, business units, or departments?
- Who can explain the requirements in detail?
- What are the authentication and authorization requirements?
- What are the security requirements?
- When does the solution need to be in place?
- What is the budget?

Defining security boundaries

The next step in the process is to define the security boundaries. If you purchase empty land to build a house, what will be the first thing you do? You need to clearly identify the plot's boundaries. Your building/development can't go beyond it. What kind of information do we need to gather in order to identify an identity infrastructure's boundaries? Understanding business operations is vital for this.

Rebeladmin Corp. owns a group of companies. The operations of each business are completely different from one to another. One is a hosting company and the other one is an IT training institute. They also have a pharmaceutical company. The operations and business requirements are different for each of those companies. In such scenarios, multiple forests will be ideal as none of the companies depend on each other's resources for its operations.

Sometimes, even if it's a single company, some business units may need logical separation – at least from the directory service point of view. For example, Rebeladmin Corp. has a research and development department. Engineers in that department keep testing new software and services, and most of them are Active Directory-integrated. Their security requirements rapidly change as well. They need to test different group policies for testing purposes. If it's the same Active Directory forest, the activities of these tests will impact the entire directory. Therefore, the best option will be to isolate their activity in a separate forest.

Identifying the physical computer network structure

Once we've identified the organizational structure and security boundaries, the next thing is to identify the physical computer network structure. It's important to identify how many branch networks there are, how they are connected together, and what kind of bandwidth is available between sites. This information helps us design the domain structure. Also, as part of this exercise, it's important to identify potential issues and bottlenecks between physically separated networks. In network diagrams, it may look nice to have links connected between sites, but if these connections have reliability and bandwidth issues, that's also going to impact your design. To overcome this, gather utilization reports and availability reports for three months and review them. It will give you good insights. In Chapter 1, *Active Directory Fundamentals*, I explained **read-only domain controllers** (RODC). These are used on branch networks when they cannot guarantee security and a reliable connection. Even the branch offices that are connected together and linked aren't reliable, and if the links have already been fully utilized, we need to fix that bottleneck first or place RODC instead of the fully blown domain controller. Gathering this information will help you make that call.

It is also important to gather information about the company road map and the company products' road maps, as that will also impact the identity infrastructure design. For example, if a company is in the process of business acquisition or merging, your design should be future-proof to address that requirement. In the same way, if the company is going to downsize, that's also going to impact the design. So, it's best to discuss this with the relevant people and get a better understanding of future changes. As I mentioned previously, identity infrastructure changes are costly and involve a lot of work. By understanding the company's future, you will prevent this kind of awkward situation.

The company IT administration model is also important for identity infrastructure design. It can be either centralized or decentralized. Rebeladmin Corp. has a group of companies. Each of these companies has its own IT department. So, each company's IT teams are responsible for their own infrastructure. In this case, maintaining separate forests is helping to divide the responsibilities for IT operations. Also, some companies may outsource their IT operations to a third-party company. This will change the security requirements in the identity infrastructure from in-house IT operations. Some of the workloads may need to be isolated from them due to data protection and legal requirements. The design will need to match these types of IT operation requirements.

Businesses are subject to specific government regulations. For example, banks and hedge funds need to follow specific rules in their operations to protect customer and trade data. Businesses that process credit cards need to be PCI-compliant and follow specific regulations. Also, if organization operations are aligned with ISO standards, it's another set of rules and best practices to follow. If an organization has branch offices in different countries, the government rules and regulations that are applied to those will be different from the rules that are applied to the headquarters. It is important to gather this data as it can also make an impact on the design.

Modern identity infrastructure requirements are complicated. Some organizations have already extended their identity infrastructures to the cloud. Some organizations have been fully moved to Azure Active Directory-managed domains. Most application vendors have moved their products to the public cloud. So, businesses need to collaborate with technology changes that are happening around them. Some products and services aren't going to continue anymore as in-house services, and customers need to move to the cloud version. The identity infrastructure design should be future-proof as far as possible. Therefore, it's important to research and evaluate new technologies and services that can improve the organization's identity infrastructure and adopt them in the design as required.

In any project, the implementation phase is relatively easy. The design and planning process is complicated and time-consuming, but it is vital for business satisfaction. Once you collect the data as described, go through it a few times and understand it properly. If you have doubts, go and gather more data to clear it. When Jonathan Ive designed the Apple Mac, do you think he designed it in one go? I am sure he must have used an eraser. But, in the end, everyone loved the Apple designs. No one cared about how hard it was or how much time he spent on it. The end result was the ultimate success. Therefore, don't be afraid to use an eraser in the design phase.

Designing the forest structure

The Active Directory design starts with designing the forest structure. The Active Directory forest is the security boundary for the identity infrastructure. When you deploy the first domain controller in your infrastructure, it creates a forest as well. Every Active Directory infrastructure has at least one forest.

There are two types of forest implementations:

- Single forest
- Multiple forest

Single forest

A single forest deployment is the default deployment mode. Most business models fit into the single forest model. The complexity and cost of implementation are low in this model. One of the main things you need to consider in this mode is replication. Domains are used to partition the directory and manage the replication. But forest-wide data, such as schemas, still needs to be replicated across all domains. If replication involves branch offices, you need to make sure forest-wide replications are handled properly.

Multiple forest

The multiple forest model is a complex implementation process. The cost of implementation is also higher as it requires additional resources (hardware, software, and maintenance). There are several reasons why you might need the multiple forest model:

- **Business operations isolations**: Businesses can have groups of companies or departments that are required to operate independently. Their dependence on other departments and partner companies may be minimal. In such scenarios, it is good to create a separate forest for them.
- **Rapid changes in directory services**: Business may have some departments or business units that involve rapid directory changes. For example, R&D, DevOps test environments, and software development departments may require AD schema changes, Active Directory integrations, and group policy changes to test or develop the products and services. It is best to keep them in a separate forest in order to minimize the impact on the entire identity infrastructure.

- **IT operation mode**: Some organizations have decentralized IT operations. Groups of companies are an example for this. Each company may have its own IT staff and be required to operate independently. A separate forest will define the security and operation boundaries for each of those companies.

- **Resource isolation**: This is an ideal solution for service providers or organizations with multiple separate forests that like to share resources. For example, Rebeladmin Corp. has a group of companies with separate AD forests. Each company has its own IT department. But the mother company still likes to share some common systems among all the companies, such as payroll, email, and CMS. Creating a separate forest for these resources will allow the organization to manage them in an efficient, secure way. Other forests can have the forest trust the resource forest and use the services hosted in there. Also, service providers can create resource forests to isolate their products and services.

- **Legal requirements**: Businesses are bound to government rules and regulations. They may also have business agreements with partners and merged companies. Based on that, they may be required to create a separate forest to isolate data, services, and identities.

- **Business acquisitions or divestiture**: Business acquisitions or divestiture will require extended security boundaries or isolated resources and identities. The best way to do that will be to use the multiple forest model. If there is a requirement to share data or resources between forests, cross-forest trust can be established.

Creating the forest structure

Once the forest mode has been decided, the next step is to create the forest structure. In order to do that, we need to decide whether we are going to achieve autonomy or isolation.

Autonomy

Autonomy gives you independent control over resources. The Active Directory environment that is focused on autonomy will help administrators manage the resources independently, but there will be more privileged administrators who can manage the resources and privileges of other administrators.

There are two types of autonomy:

- **Service autonomy**: This will provide privileges to an individual or a group of administrators to control the service level of AD DS fully or partially. For example, it will allow administrators to add or remove domain controllers, modify the Active Directory schema, and modify DNS without the forest owner.
- **Data autonomy**: This will provide privileges to an individual or a group of administrators to control data stored in Active Directory or domain-joined computers. This also allows you to perform any administrative tasks regarding data without approval from a privileged user. This autonomy will not prevent forest service administrators from accessing the data.

Isolation

Isolation gives independent and privileged control over the resources. Administrators can control resources independently, and no other accounts can take control.

There are two types of isolation:

- **Service isolation**: This will prevent any other control or interference with AD DS, other than the administrators defined in it. In other words, it will provide full control over the identity infrastructure. Service isolation happens mainly due to operations or legal requirements. As an example, Rebeladmin Corp. has three different services that are built in-house. Each service has its own customer base. Operations in one product should not impact others. Service isolation will allow the organization to isolate the operation for each service.
- **Data isolation**: This will provide ownership of the data that is stored in Active Directory or domain-joined computers to individuals or groups of administrators. However, data administrators cannot prevent the service administrator from accessing the resource they control. In order to isolate a subset of data completely, they will need to create a separate forest.

The number of forests that are needed for an infrastructure depends on the autonomy or isolation requirements.

Selecting forest design models

Once the forest model and the number of forests have been decided, the next step is to select forest design models. There are three forest design models: organizational, resource, and restricted.

The organizational forest model

In an organizational forest model, resources, data, and identities will stay on separate forests and will be managed independently. This model can be used to provide service autonomy, service isolation, or data isolation:

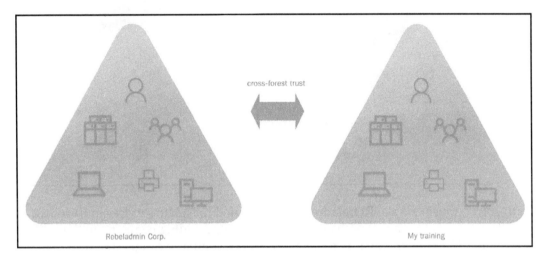

In the preceding example, **Rebeladmin Corp.** and **My training** are two companies under the same mother company. Due to the operation requirements, it needs service isolation. In order to do that, engineers have created two separate forests. Each company has its own IT department and manages resources and identities independently. If resources need to be shared between two forests, that can be done via **cross-forest trust**.

The resource forest model

In a resource forest model, a separate forest is used for resources. A resource forest doesn't contain any user accounts; instead, it contains service accounts and resource forest administration accounts. All of the identities for the organization will be in a separate forest. The cross-forest trust that's created between forests and users for an organization forest can access resources in the resource forest without additional authentication. Resource forest models provide service isolation:

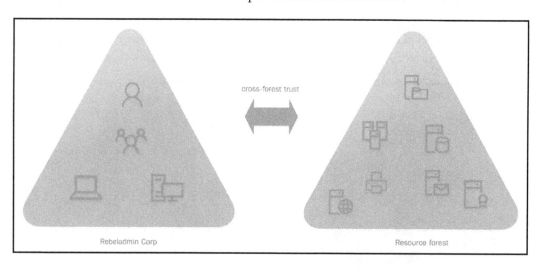

In the preceding example, **Rebeladmin Corp** wanted to isolate services in **Resource forest** as it's about to merge with another IT-service-providing company in the next six months. Once the merge is completed, the other company can use the resource forest to access the services and resources as well. It will only need cross-forest trust to be established between the company forest and **Resource forest**.

The restricted access forest model

In the restricted access forest model, a separate forest is created to isolate identities, and data must be separated from the other organization's data and identities. No trust is created between the two forests, so identities in one forest will not be able to access the resources in another. To access the resources in each forest, we need to have separate user accounts. The **restricted access forest** model provides data isolation:

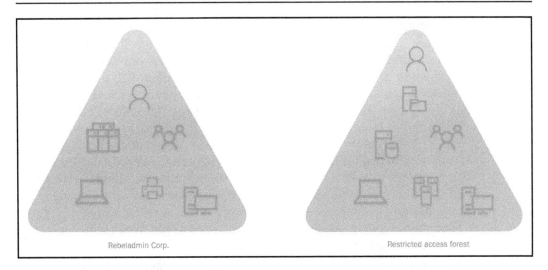

In the preceding example, **Rebeladmin Corp.** is involved with a corporate divestiture process. For some of the assets, data and identities need to be isolated completely there. In order to do that, the company introduced **Restricted access forest**.

Once the forest structure, the number of forests, and the design model have been finalized, the next step will be to design the domain structure.

Designing the domain structure

Every AD DS forest has at least one domain. When you set up your first domain forest, it is also set up as a default domain. There are a few reasons why you will need to consider having multiple domains in a forest:

- **Smaller administrative boundaries**: Active Directory is capable of managing nearly 2 billion objects. Having a large directory creates administrative nightmares. Imagine managing a large herd of sheep. As the herd grows, shepherds need to put in more and more effort to manage it. Predators will also take advantage of it, and, sometimes, shepherds may not notice missing sheep as they are too busy managing the herd. Instead of managing a large number of sheep together, isn't it easy if each shepherd manages smaller herds? Domains will help set smaller administrative boundaries and smaller management targets. This will help manage organization resources efficiently.

- **Replication**: Every domain in the Active Directory forest shares the same schema. It needs to be replicated to all the domain controllers. However, each domain has its own domain partition, which will only need to be replicated to the domain controllers inside the domain. This allows you to control the replication within the Active Directory forest. Rebeladmin Corp. has branches in different countries. These branches are connected together with leased lines. Each of these branches also has domain controllers set up. So, if it's a single-forest-single-domain setup, each and every domain controller will need to be replicated with each other. Leased lines between countries aren't cheap, and they're not always high-speed links. The same bandwidth is also used for the other company operations. If we create different domains to represent each branch office, it will eliminate unnecessary replications as the domain partition only needs to be replicated within domain boundaries.

- **Security**: In the previous section, we talked about data and service isolations based on forests. These are due to operational and legal requirements in the business. Domains help isolate resources and objects based on the security requirements within the forest. My-Learning Inc. is an IT training company. It has mainly two types of students. Some are academic students who are studying the HND program, and others are students who are taking professional exams. Both groups have separate labs, software, and resource access. Both groups have their own data, resources, and identity security requirements. Some of these requirements are only achievable via domain-wide security settings. Therefore, having two separate domains will allow them to apply different security standards without interaction.

There are two models we can use for designing the domain structure: the single domain model and the regional domain model.

Single domain model

A single domain model contains the single-domain-single-forest structure. It is easier to administer and has a lower cost to implement. When we set up the Active Directory infrastructure for the first time, it will be in this single domain model by default. The domain will become the root domain for the forest by default, and all the objects will be stored in there:

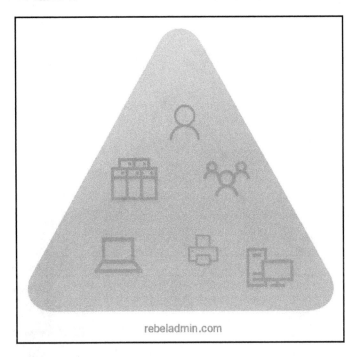

In this mode, all the directory data will need to be replicated to all the available domain controllers. It doesn't matter if it's in a different geographical location. The user can use any available domain controller to authenticate into any system or resources. All domain controllers in the domain can act as global catalog servers. The downside of this model will be the administrative overhead and the less-controlled replication traffic.

The regional domain model

In the regional model, the AD DS forest will contain the forest root domain and the multiple domains that are connected via **wide area networks** (**WANs**). This is mainly applicable to branch offices and subcompanies located in different geographical locations:

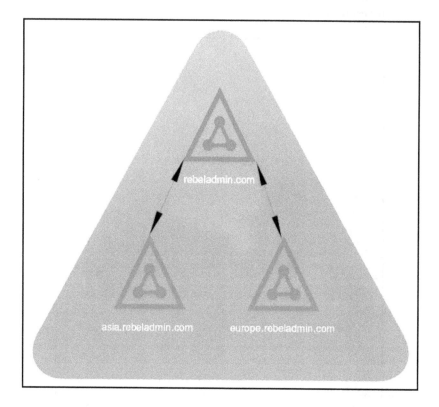

This model is complex to implement compared to the single domain model and will require additional hardware and resources. In this model, the domain partition data will only be replicated to the domain controllers inside the domain, and it will allow you to reduce the replication traffic flow between WAN links. This model will also help you isolate the security requirements. Note that this will not provide data or service isolation. If it's the requirement, it needs to be done at the forest level.

The number of domains

After deciding on the domain structure model, the next step is to identify the number of domains that are required. The number of domains depends on the number of objects that will be managed, the number of geographical locations, administrative requirements, and the bandwidth of links.

In the following table, I have listed the number of users that can be maintained in a domain against the replication bandwidth:

Bandwidth	If 1% of bandwidth is allowed for replication	If 10% of bandwidth is allowed for replication
128 kbps	25,000	100,000
256 kbps	50,000	100,000
512 kbps	80,000	100,000
1.5 Mbps	100,000	100,000

Bandwidth between locations is not the only reason for multiple domains. Administrative requirements and security requirements are also valid reasons for it.

When the number of domains increases, the complexity, cost of implementation and maintenance, and management of diverse security settings increase as well. Therefore, decide on the number of domains in a meaningful manner. I have seen people create domains in places where they can achieve the same thing using an OU or some different group policies.

Deciding on domain names

Every domain in the forest needs to have a unique name. There are mainly two types of names: NetBIOS names are used for Windows (SMB)-based sharing and messaging, whereas DNS names can be resolved by the internet and different systems. When you're promoting the domain, it asks for the DNS name, as well as the NetBIOS name.

When considering the naming, keep the following points in mind:

- Don't use names that you do not legally own; if it's a fully qualified domain name, make sure that you have authority over it with the internet registrar.
- Don't use numbers and special characters that can easily confuse users.

- Don't use names associated with products and operating systems, for example, NT and Windows.
- Avoid using longer domain names or suffixes.
- Be careful with the spelling. I have seen people who deployed the entire domain structure and then realized they made a mistake with the spelling.

 Once the domain name has been assigned, it can't be changed without redeployment, completing a domain rename process, or by performing domain migration. When planning names for the domain tree, try to define a standard. For example, it can be based on a continent, country, product, or service name. You can use the forest root domain name as a prefix, but it isn't a must.

The forest root domain

The first domain that's set up in the forest becomes the forest root domain. This root domain contains two important privileged groups, which are Enterprise Admins and Schema Admins. Members of these security groups can add/remove domains and modify the Active Directory schema.

In the multiple domain model, there are two types that you can use to define the forest root domain:

- **Dedicated forest root domain**: A separate domain to operate as the forest root domain. It will not contain any regular user accounts, objects, or resources. It will only contain the service administrator accounts. All the other domains in the forest will be child domains for this root domain. In a single domain environment, domain administrators can add themselves to the Enterprise Admin or the Schema admin group. But when you have a separate root domain, child domain administrators will not be able to add them to these privileged groups without doing that from the forest root domain level. The dedicated forest root domain shouldn't share a geographical naming convention, and it should stand with a separate name from the rest of the child domains. For example, `rebeladmin.com` can be a root domain name instead of `Europe.rebeladmin.com`.

If you are using a top-level domain (ex-rebeladmin.com) as your AD name, you may face issues if the company is also running a public website under the same name. In such a scenario, you need to adjust the internal DNS records; that is, if users want to browse the website from the local network.

- **Regional forest root domain**: If you're not going to use a separate forest domain, the regional domain can also be selected as the forest root domain. It will be the parent domain for all other regional domain controllers. For example, HQ.rebeladmin.com can be the regional root domain. This domain can contain regular user accounts, groups, and resources.

Now, we have all the required information to design the domain structure. The next step will be to determine the domain and forest functional levels.

Deciding on the domain and forest functional levels

Once the domain and forest designs are ready, the next step is to decide on the forest and domain functional levels. The forest and domain functional levels define the AD DS features that can be used in the identity infrastructure. You cannot have AD DS 2016 features if your organization level is running on the Windows Server 2012 domain and forest functional levels. When you add the domain controller to the existing forest or domain, it will automatically match the existing forest and domain functional level.

There are a few things you need to consider when you're deciding on the forest and domain functional levels:

- **Existing domain controllers**: It is always good to run the latest and greatest functional levels, but it isn't always practical. If you are extending the existing identity infrastructure, the lowest domain controller (the operating system) in the domain decides on the maximum forest and domain functional you can have without an upgrade. As an example, in your domain, if you are running a Windows Server 2008 domain controller, the maximum forest and domain functional level you can have is Windows Server 2008. It will not prevent you from adding a domain controller with Windows Server 2016; however, until you decommission the Windows Server 2008 domain controller, it isn't possible to upgrade the forest and domain functional levels further.

- **Application requirements**: Sometimes, legacy applications support only certain domain and forest functional levels. This happened to me on several occasions when I was planning domain upgrades for customers. Most of the time, it happens when companies have custom-made applications. Therefore, check with your application vendors in terms of whether they're going to be compatible and supported before deciding on the forest and domain functional levels.

Once you have defined the forest and domain functional levels, the lower domain controller version cannot be introduced to the system. If you are running the Windows Server 2016 domain and forest functional levels, you cannot introduce the Windows Server 2012 R2 domain controller to the same forest.

 Before AD DS 2012 R2, if the domain and forest functional levels were raised, they couldn't be downgraded again. After AD DS 2012 R2, you can downgrade forest and domain functional levels if required.

In order to find the current domain and forest functional levels, you can run the following commands from any domain controller:

- To find the domain functional level, run the following command:

  ```
  Get-ADDomain | fl Name,DomainMode
  ```

- To find the forest functional level, run the following command:

  ```
  Get-ADForest | fl Name,ForestMode
  ```

Designing the OU structure

In Active Directory, there are different types of objects, such as user accounts, groups, and devices. It is important to manage them effectively. OUs can group objects that have similar administrative and security requirements within the domain. Organizational units are used to delegate the administration of objects and apply group policies.

OU design changes are less complex compared to domain- and forest-level structure changes. Since OUs are bound to group policies, when you change the structure, you need to make sure that the correct group policies are still applied. When you move objects from one OU to another, they will inherit the security settings and group polices that are applied to the destination OU. It will not move any settings it has in the source OU level.

The forest owner can delegate permission to users to become OU administrators. OU administrators can manage objects and manage policies within the OU. They can also create child OUs and delegate permissions to another user/users to manage child OU objects. OU administrators will not have control over the directory services operations, and it is another way of managing privileged access within the identity infrastructure.

There are two types of organization units:

- **Account OU**: Account OU contains the user, group, and computer objects. It is the forest owner's responsibility to create the OU structure and delegate the administration over the objects.
- **Resource OU**: Resource OU contains the resources and user accounts that are used to manage resources. The forest owner must create the OU structure and delegate permissions as required.

It's important to follow up on some standards when you're defining the OU tree. These standards can be specific for the organization's requirements. In the following list, I have mentioned a few methods that can be used to organize an OU tree:

- **Based on the organization structure**: The OU tree can match the same organization structure; this will be easy to follow in most cases, but it will make the boundaries larger.
- **Based on geographical locations**: This method can be used to build the OU structure if the organization has branch offices. It can be further broken down using departments or teams that exist in each branch office.

- **Based on departments**: This is the most commonly used method for creating the OU structure. It can be further categorized based on geographical location. For example, the sales OU can have child OUs to represent branch offices such as Dallas, London, and Toronto.
- **Based on security requirements**: Group policies can be used to apply security policies and settings to objects in the OU. Depending on the same objective, we can build the OU structure. For example, tier-1 support engineers in the IT team will have a different set of security polices from tier-3 engineers. To accommodate that, we can create a tier-1 OU and a tier-3 OU. This method is suitable for small business.
- **Based on the resource type**: The OU tree can be structured based on server roles, applications, and device types.

It's possible to use a mixture of all of these methods as well. There is no limit to the number of child OUs you can create, but for administration and manageability, Microsoft recommends that you don't have more than 10 levels.

Once you have finalized the OU structure, make sure that you document it properly. Also, provide guidelines so that engineers can follow the method you used to structure it. When I've worked on projects, I've noticed that some OU structures don't make any sense at all as, over time, different engineers used their own methods to structure the OUs. Organizations should have a specific standard to follow.

Designing the physical topology of Active Directory

In the previous sections of this chapter, I explained how we can design the Active Directory logical topology. The next step is to design the physical topology of the Active Directory design.

Physical or virtual domain controllers

Most of the workloads we have in modern infrastructures are virtualized. Domain controllers can also be virtualized; however, depending on the virtualization vendor, the best practices will be different. Therefore, if you plan to deploy virtual domain controllers, refer to your software vendor and find out what the recommendations for virtual domain controllers are. The guidelines in this section will focus on the Microsoft Hyper-V virtualization platform.

It isn't recommended that you use only virtual domain controllers. In fact, it is recommended that you balance it between physical and virtual domain controllers for availability and integrity. This is especially applicable if virtual domain controllers and Hyper-V clusters use the same domain. As an example, Rebeladmin Corp. uses `rebeladmin.com` as its primary domain. When the company started, it was using physical servers to host the server roles. The company was running two physical Active Directory domain controllers. After some time, in the virtualization era, the company created a Hyper-V cluster. This cluster was also joined to the `rebeladmin.com` domain. The company was moving workloads from physical servers to virtual servers. With the new release of Active Directory, they set up virtual domain controllers and moved FSMO roles to virtual domain controllers. The Hyper-V cluster service needs to maintain 50% and more host availability in order to maintain the quorum. In hardware failure, if the system lost quorum, the cluster will go down and workloads will not live migrate properly. Since all the domain controllers are virtualized in such an event, when the Hyper-V host boots up, it will have a problem with cluster authentication since virtualized domain controllers are down. Therefore, make sure that you use physical domain controllers on the appropriate occasions.

 In a virtualized environment, make sure that you distribute the domain controllers among hosts. This will help maintain availability in a disaster.

In the following table, I have listed the dos and don'ts in terms of the virtualized domain controllers:

Dos	Don'ts
Run domain controllers in different virtualized clusters in different data centers in order to avoid a single point of failure.	Don't save the Active Directory database and log files in virtual IDE disks. For durability, save them on a VHD that's attached to a virtual SCSI controller.
Virtual hard disks (**VHDs**) security is important as copied VHDs can map to a computer and read the data inside it. If someone unauthorized gains access to `ntds.dit`, it will expose the identities. Hyper-V 2016 provides the shielded VM feature to encrypt the VHDs and prevent unauthorized access.	In a virtualized environment, engineers use templates to deploy the operating systems faster. Don't install the domain controller on an operating system that hasn't been prepared with sysprep.

Disable time synchronization between the virtual domain controller and the host. This will allow domain controllers to sync time with PDC.	Don't use a copy of the already deployed domain controller's VHD to create additional domain controllers.
N/A	Don't user the Hyper-V export feature to export the virtual domain controller (for rollback or restore purposes).
N/A	Don't pause or stop domain controllers for longer periods of time (longer than the tombstone's lifetime).
N/A	Don't take snapshots of virtual domain controllers.
N/A	Don't use a differencing disk VHD as it decreases the performance.
N/A	Don't copy or clone Active Directory VHDs.

Domain controller placement

Domain controller placement in the infrastructure is dependent on a few things:

- **Network topology**: Organizations can have different buildings, branch offices, and data centers connected together. The services and resources that are hosted in those locations may require domain controller integration. Replication is key for domain controllers. The placement of the domain controllers in the network will depend on whether it's possible to achieve successful replication or not. Network segmentation can prevent relevant traffic from passing through networks, which can impact replications. It is important to adjust the network topology to support the Active Directory design you have in place.

- **Security**: Physical security is important for domain controllers as its holds the identity infrastructure footprint. In places where you cannot guarantee physical security in your network, it is recommended that you don't place the domain controller. In such scenarios, instead of the domain controller, it is possible to deploy a RODC.

- **Link reliability between sites**: As I mentioned previously, replication is key for the health domain controller infrastructure. If the connectivity between sites isn't stable, it isn't possible to place the domain controller and maintain healthy replication. In such scenarios, it's advisable that you use RODC.

- **Active Directory sites**: We covered Active Directory sites in Chapter 1, *Active Directory Fundamentals*. This is important in terms of physical topology design. In later chapters, I will demonstrate how to set up site links and how to manage them.

Global catalog server placement

Global catalog servers are responsible for keeping a fully writable copy of objects in its own domain and a partial copy of all other domains objects in the forest. It facilitates querying about objects in the entire forest. The global catalog service is part of the domain controller services, and it cannot be separated.

In a single-forest-single-domain environment, all the domain controllers can be global catalog servers as it won't be different from domain replication. But in a multidomain environment, global catalog server placement involves planning as it increases the amount of data to be replicated, as well as the bandwidth.

There are certain things that you need to consider when you're placing a global catalog server:

- **Number of users**: It is recommended that you place a global catalog server on any site that has over 100 users. This will help maintain site availability in the event of WAN link failure.
- **WAN link reliability**: If you are struggling with link availability between sites, it's recommended that you place global catalog servers in a remote site, and enable universal membership caching.
- **Roaming users**: Roaming users are required to connect to the global catalog server when they log in for the first time from any location in the infrastructure. Therefore, if users are using roaming profiles in remote sites, it's important that you place the global catalog server.
- **Application requirements**: Applications such as Microsoft Exchange heavily depend on global catalog servers. If similar applications are hosted on remote sites, they will be required to have a global catalog server.

When the universal membership caching feature is enabled in the domain, any domain controller can process any login request locally without going through a global catalog server. This will provide a faster logon experience and reduced traffic when users use it over WAN.

Once the global catalog server placement has been determined, the Active Directory design phase is complete. Now that we have the logical and physical design for the Active Directory infrastructure ready, let's have a look at designing Hybrid Identity.

Designing a Hybrid Identity

There are many reasons why organizations are looking to *extend* their on-premises AD to Azure AD. Let's look into some of those reasons:

- **Using cloud applications (SaaS)**: Organizations use different types of applications for their operations (on-premises). Standalone applications are easy to manage and maintain, but some applications have dependencies. Some require lots of resources. SAP solution is one great example. If it's on premises, it needs different components, such as database servers, application servers, GUI severs, and so on, since all of these components depend on each other. If any of the components fail, the whole application fails too. Therefore, you need to plan for high availability on top of that. Now, more and more vendors are taking away this burden from customers and offer cloud versions of applications instead of on-premises ones. By doing this, organizations don't have to worry about scalability, availability, and maintenance. The application will be available for users whenever it's required. If an organization is moving to cloud applications, it also requires some sort of identity and access management. A majority of these SaaS solutions support Azure AD integration. By extending on-premises AD to Azure AD, organizations can maintain the same identities for authentication.
- **Authentication requirements**: On-premises AD uses Kerberos and NTLM for authentication. However, modern authentication requirements are more complex than that – especially when you consider web-based services. Unlike Windows AD, Azure AD is built for the cloud, and so it supports advanced authentication protocols such as SAML 2.0, OAuth 2.0, OpenID Connect, and WS-Federation. Using Hybrid Identity, we can have both types of authentications under one identity infrastructure.

- **Advanced identity protection**: Identities play a vital role when it comes to data security. Modern day adversaries target identities as it opens up access to valuable data. Microsoft is well aware of this and is continuously investing in order to improve identity and data protection. Conditional access, Azure information protection, Azure RMS, Azure Identity Protection, and Azure Privilege Identity Management were born as a result of this effort. These new features/services only work in cloud-only and Hybrid Identity infrastructures.

- **Moving workloads to Azure IaaS and Azure PaaS**: If an organization has already made decisions to move workloads to the cloud, there is no point in deploying additional domain controllers in Azure in order to extend the on-premises AD. It will only add additional dependencies and management overhead. Instead, the organization can choose a Hybrid Identity path. Once the workloads have been fully moved to the cloud, the organization can cut off connections with on-premises AD.

- **Unified access experience**: Some organizations use cloud applications (SaaS) as well as on-premises (web) applications for their operations. These systems may have different types of authentications and different types of portals to do authentication. But using Azure AD, Application Proxy, and **single sign-on** (**SSO**), they can have unified access experience across all web applications. If the organization is willing to use existing identities for authentication, on-premises AD needs to extend to Azure AD:

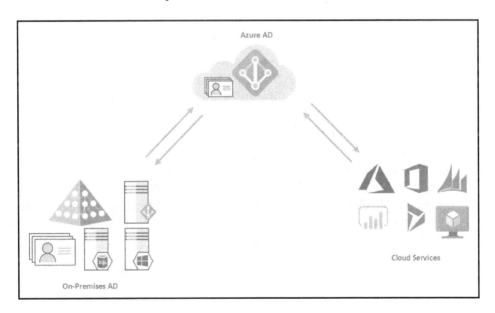

Rebeladmin Corp. runs their applications and services from a data center located in their head office. They are using Microsoft Active Directory to manage their corporate identities and access. Recently, the company replaced some of their on-premises applications and services with cloud versions. Now, these applications and services also require some sort of identity and access management. Due to this, they have decided to extend their on-premises AD to Azure Active Directory. The final solution includes doing the following:

- On-premises identities and password hashes are synced to Azure AD using Azure AD Connect. This allows users to authenticate with on-premises and cloud application/services using the same username and passwords.
- Rebeladmin Corp. is using password writeback and the self-service password reset feature of Azure AD, which allow users to reset their password without the help of an IT helpdesk.
- Azure AD's seamless SSO feature allows users to authenticate into cloud and on-premises applications automatically via corporate devices.
- In Azure AD, objects are stored in a flat structure. Therefore, object management is still done using on-premises AD. Here, engineers can structure AD objects in a hierarchical order. They are still using group policies to manage user and computer settings in the on-premises infrastructure.
- All Windows 10 devices are directly joined to Azure AD, and down-level devices are registered with Azure AD using the hybrid Azure AD join method. Rebeladmin Corp. is managing the state of this device using Microsoft Intune.
- Rebeladmin Corp. published few on-premises web-based applications to the internet using Azure AD's Application Proxy. In this way, users will not feel a difference when they authenticate into cloud or on-premises services.
- Azure MFA is also in place to provide an additional layer of security during the authentication process.
- Sign-in logs, risk events, and log analytics running in Azure help organizations identify identity infrastructure threats in advance.
- Rebeladmin Corp. is using Azure identity protection, Azure information protection, and conditional access in order to implement advanced identity and data protection to both cloud and on-premises resources.

The preceding scenario is a perfect example for corporate Hybrid Identity setup. The solution hat in place is not only extending the identity infrastructure – it's also using Azure AD-related services and features to improve identity and access management, identity protection, and data security across the board. However, every organization has a different budget, different business requirements, and different skills, all of which will affect the Hybrid Identity design. Let's look into a few areas you need to consider when you're designing your Hybrid Identity.

Cloud approach

Businesses are moving to the cloud for many reasons. Based on our intentions, we can group these organizations into four categories:

- **Cloud only**: This typically applies to new businesses. They aren't willing to invest on on-premises solutions at all. They are running their operations completely on the cloud. This model is ideal for businesses who are concerned about availability and scalability. Hybrid Identity is irrelevant for these types of businesses as there is no on-premises footprint.
- **Future cloud only**: There are organizations that already have an on-premises infrastructure, but are willing to move completely to the cloud in coming years. They have already decided there will be no more on-premises infrastructure refreshments and that all the new investments are already going toward the cloud. For them, Hybrid Identity is an intermediate solution. On-premises compatibility is no longer a concern for them when they want to implement a new service or feature.
- **Permanent hybrid**: Due to legal requirements, compliance requirements, or business requirements, some organizations are not going to be cloud only, but they are comfortable with using cloud services, which helps them improve their current operations. Most of these solutions will be hybrid compatible. They are going to continue investing in the improvements of the on-premises infrastructure.
- **Forced to cloud**: On rare occasions, some organizations have to move to cloud services as they have no other option. This could be due to a vendor who no longer provides on-premises solutions and has moved completely to a SaaS solution. Alternatively, it could be due to a partner who moved their services to the cloud. For them, Hybrid Identity is just to get authentication to an app or a service using the same on-premises identities. There will be no additional investments to improve the identity infrastructure using Azure AD or associated services.

So, which category does your organization fall into? We must understand the organization's cloud approach correctly before we propose a design. Most of the time, designs get rejected not because of the technical reasons, but due to a mismatch of interest or budget.

Identifying business needs

If I go to the Auto Trader website and just search for a car, I receive more than 400,000 results. It is impossible to go through all of those to find the car I have in mind. But if I, say, need a BMW 4 series, automatic, 2018 build, it is very easy to find the one I need. As long as we express our requirements correctly and as long as the supplier captures them correctly, we will get the solution we are looking for.

Business needs in organizations come in different forms. It can be in the form of interest, operation improvement, strategy change, or compliance/security requirements. In order to provide the appropriate solution, we need to know the ins and outs of the requirement. This is the most challenging phase of the design process for engineers. This always starts with some sort of communication between engineers and the business owner, director, manager, or department head. Some of them may not be that technical to explain what exactly they need from a Hybrid Identity. Therefore, it is best to use generic questions to gather as much information as possible.

To design Hybrid Identity, we need to gather information from the following areas:

- Cloud services (the ones we are going to use)
- Current on-premises infrastructure
- Authentication requirements
- Security requirements
- Monitoring/reporting/alerting requirements

Here, I have listed a set of generic questions and what we can provide based on the outcome:

- **Cloud services**:
    - Why is the organization looking to move to the cloud? (The answer will help determine the organization's cloud approach.)

- What cloud services is the organization going to use? For example, SaaS, PaaS, IaaS (based on the solution, the Azure AD implementation will change as well. As an example, if the organization is going to use PaaS, the relevant virtual networks and DNS should be associated with the Azure AD setup.)
- How many users are going to use these services? (The answer will help determine the Azure AD license requirements.)
- Who is going to manage these services? (The answer to this will help determine whether staff require additional training, professional support, and so on.)
- How critical is this service going to be? (This helps us decide on the support options for the solution.)

- **Current on-premises infrastructure**:
  - Explain your current identity infrastructure (this is very important as this will help you understand the physical and logical design of the current identity infrastructure).
  - Are you experiencing any issues with user authentication? (Based on the answer, we can decide whether we need to perform on-premises AD health checks before Hybrid Identity implementation).
  - What AD services are currently in use? For example, ADFS, RMS, and ADCS (The answer will help you decide what Azure AD services can replace/improve the operations of these components. As an example, ADFS can be replaced with Azure Pass-through and seamless SSO services. AD RMS can potentially be replaced by Azure RMS).
  - Does the organization have web services published externally? Are you happy to have the same login experience across the board? (If the answer is yes for both, we can use Azure AD Application Proxy to provide the same login experience for both cloud and on-premises web services.)
  - Does the on-premises device state need to be managed by Azure AD? (This will help determine what Azure AD join method to use and decide whether they require a MDM solution such as Intune.)

- **Authentication requirements**:
    - Who will use this cloud service? (Is it the same users who are existing in on-premises AD?)
    - Do any partner organizations wish to access cloud/on-premises services? (If the answer is yes, we can implement Azure AD B2B instead of AD FS.)
    - Do you wish to allow external users to use their existing social identities to authenticate to cloud services? (If the answer is yes, we can use Azure AD B2C for that.)
    - Do users require SSO? (This can be easily achieved using Azure Seamless SSO.)
    - What are the supported authentication technologies for applications? For example, NTLM, OAuth, SAML, Kerberos, and so on (Azure AD support legacy authentication methods as well as advanced methods such as SAML, OAuth, and OpenID).
    - Does the business allow you to sync password hashes to the cloud? Does the password hash sync comply with company compliance and legal requirements? (If the answer is no, we need to either use AD FS or Pass-through authentication.)
- **Security requirements**:
    - Is the organization happy to control access to resources based on device state, location, sign-in-risk? (If the answer is yes, we can implement conditional access to do this.)
    - Does the user require MFA? (This can be done using Azure MFA, for cloud users as well as on-premises users.)
    - Does the organization wish to identify risky activities related to identities? (Azure identity protection can detect potential vulnerabilities of your identity infrastructure.)
    - Does data that's stored/used in the cloud and on-premises applications need protection? (We can use cloud app security and Azure information protection to protect sensitive data.)
    - Does the organization want to protect privileged accounts with advanced security measures? (We can provide just-in-time privilege access using Azure AD privileged identity management.)

- **Monitoring/reporting/alerting requirements**:
    - Does the organization wish to review sign-in logs, error logs, and audit logs from a centralized location? (We can collect and review logs from centralized locations by enabling log analytics for Azure AD.)
    - Does the organization wish to get insight about the overall identity infrastructure's security? (Azure AD's identity secure score, security overview, and Azure security center can provide lots of insight about the health of the current identity infrastructure and even recommend things we can do to improve it.)

Synchronization

Synchronization controls how your identities are appearing in the cloud. In a typical AD environment, engineers do identity-related changes such as password changes, name changes, group membership changes, and add/remove custom attributes. In a hybrid environment, the cloud identity should represent the same characteristics of an on-premises identity. This is why synchronization is crucial. Azure AD Connect is a Microsoft tool that was designed to sync on-premises identity to the cloud.

Azure AD Connect has five main features:

- **Synchronization services**: This service checks whether Azure AD has the same identities and attributes as on-premises AD. If it doesn't match, it will replicate relevant objects and changes to Azure AD (we can decide what data it should consider for the comparison).
- **Federation service**: Azure AD Connect can be used to provide a Hybrid Identity via an on-premises AD FS farm. This is mainly used when organizations don't want to sync password hashes to Azure AD.
- **Password hash synchronization**: Azure AD Connect can sync user password hashes from on-premises AD to Azure AD.
- **Pass-through authentication**: This feature allows users to authenticate to Azure AD using the same password without a password hash sync or federate environment. More information about this feature can be found under `Chapter 17`, *Azure Active Directory Hybrid Setup*.
- **Monitoring**: Azure AD Connect health monitors the health of Azure AD Sync. These stats can be viewed using the Azure portal.

Let's look at a few things you need to consider when you're deciding on synchronization:

- **On-premises AD topology**: Azure AD connect support two types of configurations:
  - **Single AD forest-single Azure AD**: This is the most commonly used deployment topology. When a user has a single AD forest, it can be synced to one Azure AD tenant. Even if it has multiple domains, it can still be used with one AD tenant. The Azure AD Connect express setup only supports this topology. However, at any given time, only one the Azure AD connect server can sync data to the Azure AD tenant. For high availability, staging server support is available.
  - **Multiple AD forest-single Azure AD**: Some organizations have multiple AD forests for various reasons. Azure AD has support for syncing identities from all the forests into one Azure AD tenant. Each AD forest can have multiple domains as well. The AD Connect server should be able to reach all the forests, but this doesn't mean it needs to have AD trust between forests. The Azure AD Connect server can be placed in a perimeter network and then allowed access to different forests from there. A rule of thumb in this model is to represent a user only once in Azure AD. If a user exists in multiple forests, it can be handled in two ways:
    - We can set it to match the user's identity using the mail attribute. If MS Exchange is available in one or more forests, it may also have an on-premises GALsync solution. GALsync is a solution that used to share exchange mail objects between multiple forests. This will allow you to represent each user object as a *contact* in other forests. If a user has a mailbox in one forest, it will be joined with the contacts in the other forests.
    - If users are in an account-resource forest topology that has an extended AD schema with Exchange and Lync, they will be matched using ObjectSID and sExchangeMasterAccountSID.

- **Password hash sync or federated**: If the organization is allowed to use a password hash sync to the cloud, it is the easiest way to get the identities to sync to the cloud. If it isn't, there are two options. If the organization is already using federation, we can use the same method to authenticate to Azure AD. To do this, we need to maintain a highly available AD FS environment. Pass-through authentication, on the other hand, provides similar functionality, but it is all based on Agents. You don't have to maintain different server farms for it. You will learn how to implement this feature in Chapter 17, *Azure Active Directory Hybrid Setup*.

- **Directory extensions**: There are AD integrated applications that require AD schema extensions in order to work. Normally, this initial schema modification happens during the installation process. Also, the required engineers can add custom attributes to the AD schema and use them in their own applications (this is further explained in Chapter 7, *Managing Active Directory Objects*). Azure AD Connect can sync these custom attributes to Azure AD. This allows businesses to build their own applications in the cloud and use values from these custom attributes. This requires additional configuration in Azure AD Connect. Therefore, it is important to gather this information before you finalize design.

- **Password writeback**: In most cases, organizations like to keep control of their passwords for the on-premises AD. So, if a user needs to reset their password, this needs to be done in the on-premises AD and then synced to Azure AD (if password hash sync in use). If required, we also can allow users to reset their passwords in Azure AD and write it back to the on-premises AD. This can also be done via the Azure AD Connect services.

Cost

Last but not least, cost also has an impact on the design of the Hybrid Identity. AD DS services doesn't cost you extra as they come with the Windows Server operating system. Azure AD is a managed service and it comes with a cost. There is a free version of Azure AD, but that has very limited features. Therefore, when you are proposing the design, you need to consider licensing costs as well. Most of the identity protection and data protection features of Azure AD are only available under Azure AD P1 and P2. We can't protect diamonds and paperclips in the same way without them. If the organization wants to drop features because of the cost, make sure that they understand the damage it can do.

In this section, we looked at things we need to consider when we're designing a Hybrid Identity. In Chapter 15, *Active Directory Security Best Practices*, and Chapter 17, *Azure Active Directory Hybrid Setup*, I will be demonstrating how to implement the services/features that were discussed in here.

Summary

Design, implementation, and maintenance are key stages for any successful service deployment. In this chapter, we learned how to design the Active Directory infrastructure according to industry standards and best practices. The Active Directory infrastructure has two types of components: logical and physical. In this chapter, we learned about the design and placement of both types. As part of the design exercise, we also learned how to gather business data, how to identify risks, and how to do sizing.

We also looked into the designing process of Hybrid Identity. Here, we learned why Hybrid Identity is important and what we need to consider during the design phase. We also learned how we can gather required information from businesses using questionnaires.

In the next chapter, we are going to look into the DNS, which is the naming system for infrastructures.

4
Active Directory Domain Name System

We can't talk about **Active Directory Domain Services** (**AD DS**) without mentioning the **Domain Name System** (**DNS**). Since Windows Server 2003, DNS has become the primary name resolution service. Before that, Windows was using NetBIOS and the **Windows Internet Name Service** (**WINS**) for name resolution.

WINS and DNS are both TCP/IP network name resolution services. There are legacy systems that still use WINS instead of DNS.

DNS helps to locate resources via the internet and intranet. DNS can run as an independent server role on the intranet, perimeter network, or public network. There are different vendors who provide DNS solutions other than Microsoft; Linux/Unix **Berkeley Internet Name Domain** (**BIND**) is a good example of that. There are mainly two categories of DNS infrastructure. One category is organizations that host their own DNS servers to facilitate name resolution requirements for their corporate infrastructures. Another category is organizations that sell DNS as a service, such as Azure DNS, **Dynamic DNS** (**DynDNS**), and Amazon Route 53.

In this chapter, our main focus will be to understand how AD-integrated DNS works in the infrastructure. Throughout the chapter, you will learn about the following topics:

- Hierarchical naming structures
- How DNS works
- DNS records
- DNS zones
- Zone transfers
- DNS delegation

What is DNS?

In mobile phones, we have phone books. If we need to save someone's phone number, how we do that? Do we just enter the number and save it? No. We attach the number to a person's name or something we can remember, so the next time we open the contact list, we can easily find it. The same applies when you are dealing with IP addresses. I remember a few of the most commonly used IP addresses in my clients' infrastructure, but I do not remember most others. I remember lots of servers by their hostnames rather than their IP addresses. This is because hostnames are more user friendly and are easier to remember than IP addresses. This is exactly what DNS does: it maps IP addresses to domain names or common terms that are user friendly.

As I stated, there can be no functioning AD domain infrastructure without DNS. There are two main reasons why AD DS needs DNS:

- **Maintaining hierarchical infrastructure design**: In the previous chapters, I talked about designing the AD infrastructure. I mentioned implementing multiple forests, domains, and child domains. We use domain namespaces to separate them with each other and build the AD hierarchy. The only way you can reflect that logical structure infrastructure is by using DNS.
- **Locating domain controllers**: Devices in infrastructure need to communicate with AD domain controllers for authentication. If it's a remote site, it needs to locate its closest domain controller for authentication. This process is done using DNS **service (SRV)** records. Also, if an application or service needs to locate a host or resources, DNS will help resolve that.

Before DNS, systems were using **LAN Manager Hosts (LMHOSTS)** and hosts files to map IP addresses to friendly names. This is still done in small networks. The LMHOSTS file helps find NetBIOS names in TCP/IP networks. The hosts file helps to find domain names in TCP/IP networks. This is also used to override the DNS entries because in name resolution, the host file still gets priority.

The LMHOSTS and hosts files are located at `C:\Windows\System32\drivers\etc`:

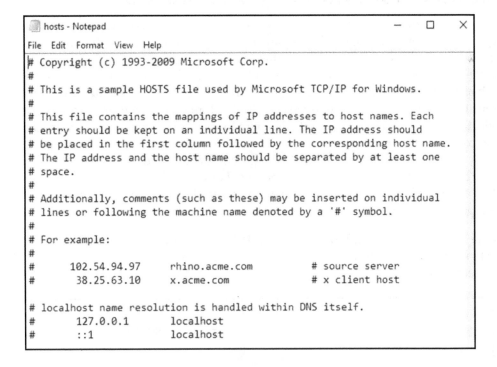

DNS was invented to support email communication in the **Advanced Research Projects Agency Network** (**ARPANET**). In the past, people were using the LMHOSTS and hosts file, and as networks grew, it wasn't a practice to maintain large hosts files. The first conversation to start a better, centralized name resolution system started with RFC 606 in December 1973. It took almost a decade with several RFCs to decide on the technology outline for modern DNS, and the final RFCs were released in November 1983 (RFC 881, 882, 883).

DNS maintains a database that contains various DNS data types (A, MX, SRV, and AAAA). This database can be distributed among multiple servers. This also provides control over the DNS infrastructure and enables administrators to add/edit/delete DNS entries. DNS allows you to delegate administration over the DNS domain. It also allows you to share a read-only copy of the database where we cannot guarantee infrastructure security.

Hierarchical naming structures

In `Chapter 1`, *Active Directory Fundamentals*, we looked into domain trees and explored how they can be used to organize the domain structure in the hierarchical method. DNS allows you to translate that logical structure into the domain namespace. Similar to a tree, it starts from the root and is spread into different layers, such as branches and leaves. In the domain tree, the root is represented by a dot (.). A typical tree branch contains many leaves. In the domain tree, a branch represents a collection of named resources, and a leaf in a branch represents a single named entry. In a tree, branches and leaves depend on each other. Branches or leaves are part of one system until everything is attached together. When we describe a leaf or a branch, we explain it with the relationship to the tree. For example, if I need to show someone a leaf of an apple tree, I will explain that it is an apple leaf. Then, the person knows it's a part of an apple tree.

In the following diagram, **Level 1** represents the **Top-Level Domains** (**TLDs**). These are managed by the internet name registration authority according to international standards:

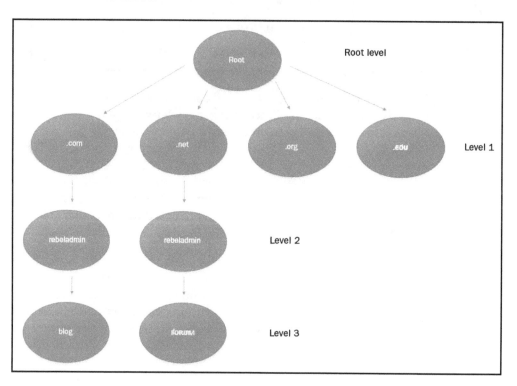

Top-Level Domain Managers (**TLD Managers**)—each and every TLD has its own domain manager organization. These organizations are responsible for the delegation of TLDs. The complete list of TLD managers can be accessed via `https://www.iana.org/domains/root/db`.

The following table describes common TLDs:

TLD name	Description
.com	This is the most commonly used TLD and it is mainly used to register businesses that are focused on profits. This is also used to register sites such as personal websites, blogs, and community websites. It is open for any person to register.
.org	This is mainly used by non-profit organizations and communities. It is open for any person to register.
.net	This is used to represent distributed computer networks. It is open for the public and anyone can register a name under it.
.edu	This is a limited registration for educational institutions.
.gov	This is limited to government entities.
.ca, .co.uk	These are used to represent countries. The registration of a domain under these depend on the rules and regulations of their country's domain name registrar authority.

 The complete list of TLDs can be viewed at `http://data.iana.org/TLD/tlds-alpha-by-domain.txt`.

Level 2 in the hierarchy is controlled by the organization. In my example, I need two domain names called `rebeladmin.com` and `rebeladmin.net` for my organization. I can go to the domain name registrar and register the names (for example, GoDaddy or Dotster).

Once I register it, no-one else can have the same name without my authority, unless the name expires. As the domain owner, I can create any sub-domain (child domain) under `rebeladmin.com` and `rebeladmin.net`. In DNS, there are some records that need to be published on the internet. For example, if I need a website hosted under my domain that people can access via the internet, I need to map my web server IP address to the `www.rebeladmin.com` DNS record. In order to do that, I need an authoritative server. This needs to be highly available as well. When you register the domain name, the domain registrar will use their own DNS servers as authoritative DNS servers by default. But if we need to, we can have our own DNS servers and point to them using **nameserver (NS)** records.

In **Level 3**, domain owners have complete authority to create any sublevel DNS namespace. In my example, they are `blog.rebeladmin.com` and `forum.rebeladmin.net`. Each dot (`.`) represents each level of the domain tree:

The leftmost part represents the lowest level in the domain tree and the rightmost part shows the domain root.

If you own a domain name, you can use the same name to represent your AD domain name, but there are a few things you need to consider doing:

- **Manually set up DNS records to match public DNS records**: As an example, I am going to use `rebeladmin.com` as my AD domain name. I am using domain registrar DNS servers to set up the public DNS records. I have a website, `www.rebeladmin.com`, and it points to the `38.117.80.2` public IP address. I also use AD-integrated DNS servers to maintain local infrastructure DNS records. But when I go to access the `www.rebeladmin.com` website from a domain PC, first I need to make sure it is not trying to resolve the name using a local DNS server. If DNS record is needed to resolve to external IP addresses, we need to create the relevant records manually under a local DNS server.

- **Modify DNS records to use the lowest routing path**: In my previous example, the web server's public address is `38.117.80.2`. This web server can also be accessed via its local IP address, `192.168.0.100`. If I traceroute to `www.rebeladmin.com` with the `38.117.80.2` DNS record, it takes nearly 10 network hops to reach the web server. But if I use the `192.168.0.100` local IP address, it gets resolved with one network hop. Therefore, if your domain name has public and private DNS entries, make sure that you make adjustments and help users use the lowest routing path in order to improve performance and accessibility.

> Maintaining the same domain namespace on two infrastructures is called a split-brain DNS structure. This will require manual record adjustments in both infrastructures in order to maintain service availability and integrity. The recommended setup for a similar infrastructure is a whole-brain DNS structure. Linking both DNS namespaces into one using a standard DNS name resolution mechanism will reduce manual user interaction.

How DNS works

A few days ago, I posted a birthday card to my mother who lives in Sri Lanka. I posted it from the local post office in Kingston upon Thames, England. Once I put it inside the post box, the delivery process started, and now it was the postal service's responsibility to deliver it to the correct person. So, when the local post office worker who picked up my letter, did they know my parents' exact house location? No, they didn't. But at the end of my address, it said the country was Sri Lanka. They then knew that if this letter goes to Sri Lanka, then the postal service there will be able to deliver it. So, the next stop of the mail was Sri Lanka. Once the card reached the main postal sorting facility in Sri Lanka, would the worker who picked up the letter know the exact address location? Maybe not, but if they don't, they could look for the city that it should be delivered to. Then, the post office in that city would know what to do. Once the letter reached the city's mail sorting facility, the worker would know which local post office this letter should be delivered to.

Once it reached the local post office in my parents' city, the postal carrier there would definitely know where my parents' house is located. In the end, even though my local post office did not know where my parents live, the letter got delivered. How did they do it? Even though they did not know the end delivery location, they knew someone who could figure it out in each stage. This is exactly how DNS resolves addresses too. The DNS server in your infrastructure isn't aware of billions of websites on the internet and their IP addresses. When you type a domain name and press *Enter*, your DNS server will try to resolve it, but if it doesn't know how, it will work with other DNS servers that may know about it and work with them to find the correct destination.

In the following example, my friend William is trying to access the `www.rebeladmin.com` website from his laptop. This device is a domain-joined device and the user logs in to the device using the domain username and password.

In order to get the IP address of the `rebeladmin.com` web server, the DNS client in William's PC needs to perform a DNS query from its DNS server.

A DNS query can happen between the DNS client and the DNS server or between DNS servers.

There are two types of DNS queries:

- **Recursive**: A recursive query is usually sent by DNS clients. Once the query is processed, it expects a success or failure response from the DNS server. It is the DNS server's responsibility to work with other DNS servers in order to provide an answer if it cannot process the query by itself.
- **Iterative**: Once the DNS server receives an iterative query, it will respond with the best answer it has by looking at its DNS zones and caching. If it cannot resolve the query, it will respond with a negative answer.

In the following example, a user in an AD environment is trying to access the `www.rebeladmin.com` website. This website is hosted in the external network. Let's go ahead and see how this DNS query works:

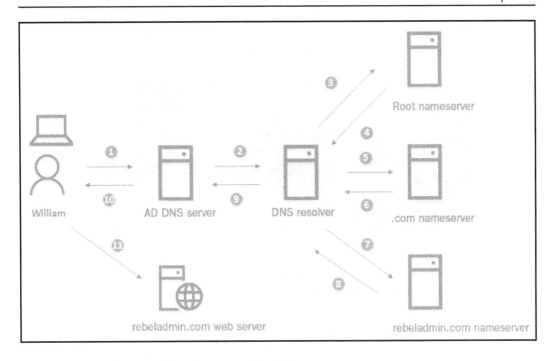

The following steps explain the preceding diagram:

1. William's laptop sends the recursive DNS query to the AD DNS server in order to resolve the IP address for the www.rebeladmin.com website. This DNS server information is defined in the IP configuration of the laptop.

2. The AD-integrated DNS server tries to resolve the name to an IP address, but it cannot. It doesn't have a relevant DNS record configured for it. However, it knows a DNS server that can help resolve this. This is defined as a DNS forwarder in DNS server configuration. Normally, it will be the **Internet Service Provider's (ISP)** DNS server or a public DNS server, such as Google's.

In order to check the DNS forwarder address on your DNS server, you can use the following PowerShell command:

```
Get-DnsServerForwarder
```

The following screenshot shows the output for the preceding command:

```
Administrator: Windows PowerShell

Windows PowerShell
Copyright (C) 2016 Microsoft Corporation. All rights reserved.

PS C:\Users\Administrator> Get-DnsServerForwarder


UseRootHint         : True
Timeout(s)          : 3
EnableReordering    : True
IPAddress           : 8.8.8.8
ReorderedIPAddress  : 8.8.8.8


PS C:\Users\Administrator>
```

3. If the DNS resolver does not have a record in its cache or local zone, then it will send an iterative query to the root NS. There are 13 root servers clustered and operating from different geographical locations. They are controlled by the **Internet Assigned Numbers Authority (IANA)**.

   Microsoft DNS uses an option called root hints. By default, this contains all 13 root servers. If you do not have the forwarder set up in your DNS server, it will use these root servers to resolve DNS queries:

```
PS C:\Users\Administrator> Get-DnsServerRootHint

NameServer            IPAddress
----------            ---------
m.root-servers.net.   2001:dc3::35
l.root-servers.net.   2001:500:9f::42
k.root-servers.net.   2001:7fd::1
j.root-servers.net.   2001:503:c27::2:30
i.root-servers.net.   2001:7fe::53
h.root-servers.net.   2001:500:1::53
g.root-servers.net.   2001:500:12::d0d
f.root-servers.net.   2001:500:2f::f
e.root-servers.net.   2001:500:a8::e
d.root-servers.net.   2001:500:2d::d
c.root-servers.net.   2001:500:2::c
b.root-servers.net.   2001:500:84::b
a.root-servers.net.   2001:503:ba3e::2:30


PS C:\Users\Administrator>
```

4. Since it's an iterative query, the root server will look into it and respond saying, I do not know about `rebeladmin.com`, but I know someone who knows about `.com`, and it attaches the information about the `.com` TLD **nameservers (NSes)** to the response.

5. Based on the response from the root server, the DNS resolver sends an iterative query to the .com TLD NSes.

6. The TLD NSes look into the query and respond by saying, I do not know about the IP address of rebeladmin.com but I know NS information for rebeladmin.com; go and check with them – they may be able to help you.

7. Now, the DNS resolver knows about the rebeladmin.com NS and sends an iterative query to it by asking for the IP address for www.rebeladmin.com (A record).

8. The question finally came to the right person who can answer it. The rebeladmin.com NS responds with the IP address for www.rebeladmin.com.

9. Now, the DNS resolver knows the answer, and it responds to the AD DNS server.

10. Then, the DNS client on William's laptop gets the response for its recursive query with the IP address for www.rebeladmin.com.

11. William's laptop connects to the rebeladmin.com web server and views the website.

This is how the DNS request will be processed from top to bottom in an infrastructure. This will not be exactly the same on each and every request, as DNS servers will cache the data. If DNS servers can find the answer from their cache, the process will be quicker.

DNS essentials

In a Windows Server environment, the DNS service can be run as an individual service or as an AD-integrated service. Either way, core DNS components, technology, and terms will be same for both scenarios.

DNS records

The DNS database holds various types of resource records. In an AD-integrated DNS setup, most of these records will be created automatically when adding resources to the domain, changing settings in resources, or when promoting/demoting domain controllers (SRV records, A records, and AAAA records). However, in an infrastructure, some of resource records may still need to be created manually in DNS servers (static).

Start of authority record

Each DNS zone must have a **start of authority** (**SOA**) record, and it is created when a zone is created for the first time. This record provides lots of general information for the DNS zones, such as the following:

- **Primary server**: The best DNS source for the zone.
- **Responsible person**: The email address of the zone administrator.
- **Serial number**: A number that is used to track the zone changes. If there is a secondary DNS zone on another server, when it checks the updates with the master zone, it will compare this serial number. If the secondary zone has a lower serial number than the master zone, it will update its copy.
- **Refresh interval**: This value is defined when the secondary server should check for zone updates with the master server.
- **Retry interval**: This value defines how long the secondary server should wait to try for updates if the first request is unsuccessful.
- **Expires after**: If the secondary server can't refresh the zone before the value defined here, it will no longer consider the secondary server as self-authoritative.
- **Minimum (default) TTL**: If the **time-to-live** (**TTL**) value is not defined in the resource records, it will use the default TTL value defined in here. This TTL value is attached to the response of DNS-resolved queries.

The following PowerShell command can be used to view the properties of an SOA record:

```
Get-DnsServerResourceRecord -ZoneName "REBELADMIN.COM" -RRType "SOA" |
Select-Object -ExpandProperty RecordData
```

In the preceding command, REBELADMIN.COM can be replaced with any zone. Select-Object -ExpandProperty RecordData is used to expand the output.

A and AAAA records

Host records are used to map a **fully qualified domain name** (**FQDN**) to an IP address. These records are used for IPv4, and AAAA records are used for IPv6. In AD and integrated DNS, every device will have an A or AAAA record when it is added to the domain. If the IP addresses are changed, the system will automatically update its DNS record, too.

To add an A record, run the following command:

```
Add-DnsServerResourceRecordA -Name "blog" -ZoneName "REBELADMIN.COM" -
IPv4Address "192.168.0.200"
```

To remove an A record, run the following command:

```
Remove-DnsServerResourceRecord -ZoneName "REBELADMIN.COM" -RRType "A"
-Name "blog"
```

To list A records in a zone, run the following command:

```
Get-DnsServerResourceRecord -ZoneName "REBELADMIN.COM" -RRType "A"
```

In the preceding commands, REBELADMIN.COM can be replaced with any zone name.

NS records

NS records are used to list authoritative DNS servers for the zone. In an AD-integrated DNS setup, all the domain controllers with the DNS role installed will be added to the NS records in the zone file. Having multiple NSes will add redundancy to the DNS setup.

The following command can list the NS for a zone. REBELADMIN.COM can be replaced with any zone name:

```
Get-DnsServerResourceRecord -ZoneName "REBELADMIN.COM" -RRType "NS"
```

Mail exchanger records

Mail exchanger (**MX**) records specify the MX server for a domain. The MX can be any email server (including Microsoft Exchange, Exim, or Office 365). A domain can have multiple MX records and the mail server priority number will be used to maintain the priority order. The lowest value will get the highest priority.

Canonical name records

Canonical name (**CNAME**) records are aliases for FQDN. They work similar to nicknames. For example, I have an A record set up for `blog.rebeladmin.com`; there is a blog running under it. Some time ago, I used `my.rebeladmin.com` for the same blog. If users still use `my.rebeladmin.com`, I need them to still see my blog at `blog.rebeladmin.com`. To do that, I have to use CNAME records.

Pointer records

Pointer (**PTR**) records are used to map IP addresses to FQDN. Some call it reverse DNS records as well. The reverse lookup zone will not be created when the DNS is set up with AD; instead, it will need to be created manually. If you have multiple address spaces, you will need to create separate reverse lookup zones to represent each address space.

SRV records

SRV records are used to specify the location of a service inside an infrastructure. For example, if you have a web server in the infrastructure, by using an SRV record, you can specify the protocol, service, and domain name and then define the service location. In an AD environment, SRV records are important as they help to locate the nearest domain controllers. In the previous chapters, I explained AD sites: when a user logs in, the system needs to point the user to the site's local domain controller instead of the domain controller in the hub. This is done via SRV records.

In an SRV record, the following information can be specified:

- **Service**: This will define the service that belongs to the SRV record.
- **Protocol**: This will define the protocol it will use. It can be either **Transmission Control Protocol** (**TCP**) or the **User Datagram Protocol** (**UDP**).
- **Priority**: This will define the service priority (only if the service supports this function).
- **Weight**: This will help define the priority of the same type records.
- **Port number**: This will define the service port number.
- **Host offering this service**: This will define the server offering this particular service. It needs to use FQDN.

The AD-integrated DNS environment has a set of default SRV records created.

SRV records can be listed using the following command:

```
Get-DnsServerResourceRecord -ZoneName "REBELADMIN.COM" -RRType "SRV"
```

Detailed output can be viewed using the following command:

```
Get-DnsServerResourceRecord -ZoneName "REBELADMIN.COM" -RRType "SRV" |
Select-Object -ExpandProperty RecordData
```

 In the preceding commands, REBELADMIN.COM can be replaced with any zone name.

Zones

The Microsoft DNS server supports four types of zones explained in the following sections. Each of these zones has different responsibilities and characteristics within the DNS namespace.

Primary zone

A primary zone is a read/write container that contains the DNS records for a domain. When you create the first domain controller with integrated DNS in a domain, it will create a primary zone by default. It holds a master copy of the zone and stores it in AD DS. Primary zones will be the source for secondary zones. Users are allowed to create primary zones and integrate them with AD DS, even though they are not related to the AD DS domain name.

There are two types of primary zone:

- Standard primary zones
- AD-integrated primary zones

Standard primary zones are mostly used in non-AD environments to manage DNS. As an example, if you are hosting a public-facing website, you can also install a DNS role and manage the DNS for it by yourself. But a DNS server doesn't necessarily have to be a domain controller or a member server of an AD environment. A standard primary zone will save its data in a text file located in the c:\windows\system32\DNS folder. The first server to host the standard primary zone becomes the master server. The DNS records under the primary zone can only be updated via the master server.

An AD-integrated primary zone stores data in AD. It uses the multi-master replication method. Therefore, we can update DNS records from any available domain controller and it will be replicated to all other domain controllers. AD-integrated primary zones also have faster replication, as they are part of AD replication. It also can apply security features from AD.

In an AD-integrated DNS setup, a primary zone can be created using the following command:

```
Add-DnsServerPrimaryZone -Name "rebeladmin.net" -ReplicationScope
"Forest" -PassThru
```

This will create an AD-integrated primary DNS zone for the `rebeladmin.net` domain. Its replication scope is set to the forest, which means it will replicate to any DNS servers running on domain controllers in the `rebeladmin.net` forest. If you use the wizard to create the primary zone, the replication scope is set to the `rebeladmin.net` domain by default, which refers to any DNS servers running on domain controllers in the `rebeladmin.net` domain:

Primary zones are the only DNS zones that can be edited. Standard primary zones should have a backup zone for redundancy purposes, and this is called a secondary zone. Let's go ahead and see what a secondary zone is and how it works.

Secondary zone

A secondary zone keeps a read-only copy of a primary zone. It needs to refresh the zone data by contacting the primary zone hosted on another server. Reliable network connectivity and sufficient zone transfer permissions are key to maintaining a healthy secondary zone. Secondary zones cannot be stored in AD DS.

I have an AD-integrated primary zone called `rebeladmin.net`. I have a standalone DNS server, and for application requirements, I need to set up a secondary zone in it.

Before I set up the secondary zone, I need to adjust the permissions for zone transfer. By default, zone transfer is not allowed in AD DS-integrated zones:

```
Set-DnsServerPrimaryZone -Name "rebeladmin.net" -SecureSecondaries
TransferToSecureServers -SecondaryServers 192.168.0.106
```

In the preceding command, `rebeladmin.net` is my zone and `TransferToSecureServers` defines that the transfer will be allowed only for the listed secondary server, `192.168.0.106`.

If needed, configuration can be modified with `-TransferAnyServer` to allow transference to any server and `-TransferToZoneNameServer` to allow transference only to NS:

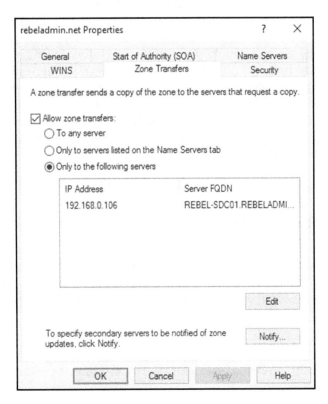

Now, I can set up a secondary zone from the `192.168.0.106` server.

In the following command, `-MasterServers` defines the IP address of the master server. The `-ZoneFile` parameter is there, but only for file-backed DNS servers:

```
Add-DnsServerSecondaryZone -Name "rebeladmin.net" -ZoneFile
"rebeladmin.net.dns" -MasterServers 192.168.0.105
```

Stub zones

A stub zone is a read-only copy of a master zone but contains only SOA and NS records. It is not an authoritative DNS server for that zone. Stub zones are not a replacement for secondary zones, and they cannot be used for load sharing or redundancy purposes. Some think stub zones and conditional forwarders do the same thing, but they are completely different. A conditional forwarder has a list of DNS servers that can help your DNS server to resolve DNS queries for a specific domain. Once your DNS server receives a query for that domain, it forwards the query to the servers list in the conditional forwarder. This may or may not include all the authoritative DNS servers for the domain. A stub zone is aware of all the authoritative DNS servers for its domain. When your DNS server receives a query for a stub zone, it goes ahead and queries directly from the servers listed on the zone and retrieves the result.

Reverse lookup zones

Reverse lookup zones hold PTR records. A reverse lookup zone can also be a primary zone, a secondary zone, or a stub zone. Reverse lookup zones will need to match the organization network segment. Even if it is AD DS-integrated, the system will not create a default reverse lookup zone. It needs to be created manually.

As an example, I need to create a reverse lookup zone for my `10.10.10.0/24` network. I can use the following command to do that:

```
Add-DnsServerPrimaryZone -NetworkID "10.10.10.0/24" -ReplicationScope
"Domain"
```

In the preceding command, `-ReplicationScope` is set to `Domain`. This means that it will be replicated to all domain controllers with integrated DNS in the domain.

We have now gone through all four types of DNS zones. We learned the different characteristics of each zone and also looked into the roles of each zone.

DNS server operation modes

There are three types of DNS server operation modes. These modes are not something we can choose during the setup process. They are listed based on their characteristics:

- **Dynamic**: AD DS-directory-integrated DNS uses DynDNS by default. DynDNS allows hosts and users to register, update, and remove DNS records from DNS servers. Let's assume we have an AD environment with 200 computers. It uses **Dynamic Host Configuration Protocol (DHCP)** to maintain the IP assignment; so every three days, each device will renew its IP allocation. Some may have the same IP address, but some may receive a new one. But if the system uses static DNS every three days, administrators will need to update the DNS list to match IP allocations. Also, AD will not be able to find the devices to establish authentication or handle resource access requests. However, thanks to DynDNS, this is no longer manual work, and it allows the environment to maintain up-to-date DNS information without user interaction.
- **Read/write**: This is applicable when DNS zones run without AD DS integration. For example, one of the Rebeladmin Corp. clients wants to host their own web server. Therefore, as a service provider, we need to provide a solution, which DNS design is part of. The client likes to keep the cost to a minimum, and since it's a testing environment, they aren't worried about high availability. For their web server DNS requirements, we can set up a standalone DNS server in the same web server and use it as an authoritative DNS server. Records there are not going to change often, so there is no need for DynDNS. If records need to be updated, an authorized user can update them manually.
- **Read-only**: If the DNS server only keeps a read-only copy of a master zone, it operates in read-only mode. Some DNS servers keep only secondary zones for security, load balancing, or disaster recovery purposes. This can typically be seen in web-server farms. Read-only DNS servers will check with master DNS servers for DNS updates periodically.

With Windows Server 2008, Microsoft introduced **read-only domain controllers (RODCs)**. RODCs can be used in infrastructures where physical security and connectivity cannot be guaranteed. RODCs run AD DS-integrated primary DNS zones in read-only mode.

These operation modes can be used in infrastructures in order to meet their DNS requirements. It is possible to mix DNS servers with different operation modes. But it's important to clearly understand the capability of each operation mode for DNS troubleshooting.

Zone transfers

Healthy DNS replication is a key requirement for service and infrastructure integrity. In the previous section, I explained the different zones. I also mentioned how to set the zone transfer permissions. Now, it is time to look into DNS replications.

There are two types of zone file replications:

- **Asynchronous Full Transfer Zone** (**AXFR**): When setting up a new secondary zone, the system will replicate a full copy of the zone file from the master server. It is not just for the secondary zone; it's applicable to other zones, too. In the event of DNS replication issues, the administrator may need to request a full zone transfer from its master server from time to time.
- **Incremental Zone Transfer** (**IXFR**): After the initial full zone transfer, the system will only replicate the records that have been modified. It reduces the replication traffic as well as providing faster replication.

When there is a change in the master DNS zone, the system will send a notification to secondary servers about the change. Then, the secondary servers will request for a zone update. If secondary servers lose connection to the primary server, or after the service is restarted, the system will still query (based on SOA refresh intervals) from master DNS servers for zone updates.

DNS delegation

In the previous chapter, when we were looking at the AD DS design, I explained child domain controllers and how they can be used to organize the company's AD hierarchy. When you create a child domain in a forest, it also creates its own DNS namespace. In a DNS infrastructure, sometimes, it is required that you divide the DNS namespace to create additional zones. DNS delegation allows organizations to achieve this without the need to change the domain structure.

In AD-integrated DNS, you are allowed to create any DNS zone, and it will be replicated to other domain controllers. But there are situations where this can lead to administrative overhead. Rebeladmin Corp. uses `rebeladmin.com` as its AD DS domain name. They have a software development department that develops web-based applications.

In order to test their applications, they have to use a web URL. Every time they need to test something, they open a support ticket and the IT team creates A records for it in the DNS server. Of late, these requests have become too frequent, and sometimes due to the workload, the IT team faces delays in processing these requests. This starts to affect software release deadlines. What can we do in order to overcome this situation and provide a better solution? If there was a way to allow the software development team to create A records when they are required, they would not need to wait for the IT team. But at the same time, it shouldn't be complex, as it will still create additional administration tasks for the IT team. With the help of the DNS delegation feature, we can deploy a DNS server and create a DNS zone called `dev.rebeladmin.com`. Then, we can allow the software development team to manage the DNS record under it. They can create A records for apps such as `app1.dev.rebeladmin.com` and `app2.dev.rebeladmin.com`. Also, all the users under `rebeladmin.com` will still be able to access these URLs without additional changes, as the `rebeladmin.com` DNS zone knows which DNS server has authority over the `dev.rebeladmin.com` DNS entries.

DNS delegation can also be used to divide the DNS workloads into additional zones in order to improve the performance and create a fault-tolerant setup.

Before we start the delegation process, we need a second DNS server with an active primary DNS zone.

In my example, I have a new DNS server called `REBEL-SDC01.rebeladmin.com`. I have installed the DNS role in it and created a primary DNS zone called `dev.rebeladmin.com`:

```
Add-DnsServerPrimaryZone -Name "dev.rebeladmin.com" -ZoneFile
"dev.rebeladmin.com.dns"
```

I have also created an A record in the zone called `app1`:

```
Add-DnsServerResourceRecordA -Name "app1" -ZoneName
"dev.rebeladmin.com" -AllowUpdateAny -IPv4Address "192.168.0.110"
```

In order to set up the DNS delegation, I log in to the `REBEL-PDC-01.rebeladmin.com` domain controller and run the following command:

```
Add-DnsServerZoneDelegation -Name "rebeladmin.com" -ChildZoneName
"dev" -NameServer "REBEL-SDC-01.rebeladmin.com" -IPAddress
192.168.0.110
```

In the preceding command, `ChildZoneName` defines the zone name in the other DNS server.

Now, when I go to **DNS Manager** and expand the tree, I can see the delegated zone entry for `dev.rebeladmin.com`:

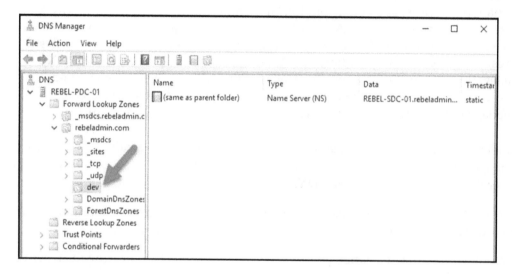

When I ping `app1.dev.rebeladmin.com` from a PC in `rebeladmin.com`, I can successfully reach it:

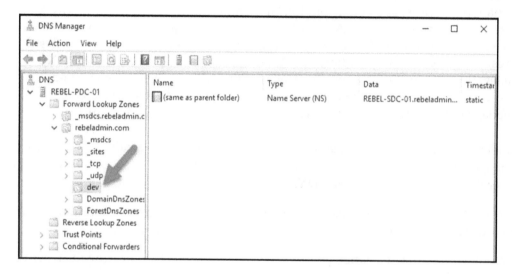

DNS service providers

In this chapter, we mainly talked about how DNS works in AD environments. However, this is not the only way to use DNS. If we need to manage DNS for external URLs such as websites, we need to configure DNS servers in a different way. This type of DNS server mainly works with public IP addresses. In order to set up an external-facing DNS server, first we need to register NS records. Then, via NS domain registrar, we need to point the domain DNS to this newly created NS. After that, we can set up the required DNS records for the domain using our own DNS server. As with any other server role, DNS also requires maintenance from time to time. Also, we need to maintain the high availability of the DNS servers. Instead of all this additional maintenance overhead, we can also use a DNS service provider to do the same thing. Godaddy, Dotster, 1&1, and DynDNS are some of the most well-known DNS service providers. All we need is a valid subscription and within minutes, we can start adding the relevant DNS records. This doesn't require firewall changes, servers, or any other resources. DNS record management is also very easy to implement through the web interface. We also do not need to worry about backup, replication, or high availability as they are all handled by the service providers.

Summary

In an infrastructure, we can't talk about AD DS without mentioning DNS. In this chapter, we covered the basics of DNS and you learned why it's important. Then, we moved on to the hierarchical naming structure and saw how it helps translate an organization's logical structure to the domain namespace. We also learned exactly how DNS works behind the scenes. Then, we looked at DNS records and DNS zones. This also included some explanation of how to create different zones. At the end of the chapter, you learned about different DNS operation modes and replications. I hope this information helps you understand the importance of DNS in an infrastructure and how to use it properly.

In next chapter, we will look at the AD FSMO roles and explore how to place them correctly in an infrastructure.

5
Placing Operations Master Roles

Rebeladmin Corp. is a managed IT service provider. They have introduced a new client management system, where clients can open service tickets, check their invoices, track project progress, and so on. Every customer and every employee gets an account in this system. Each of these user accounts gets certain privileges based on their roles and responsibilities. Support engineers are allowed to open tickets, edit tickets, and close tickets. But they are not allowed to change the schedules, delete tickets, change the appearance of the portal, or change the system database settings. Only the operations manager, Sean, can do similar system-level changes. What if everyone is allowed to do these kinds of system-level changes? Will the system be able to maintain its integrity for long? Keeping system-level change permissions to certain roles will prevent unnecessary design and configuration changes.

Active Directory infrastructures are built upon multi-master databases. This means that any writable domain controller in the domain can update the database values. But there are some operations that need to be controlled in a sensible manner in order to maintain the integrity of **Active Directory Domain Services** (**AD DS**). These operations are better managed in a single-master mode rather than a multi-master mode. These special roles are called **Flexible Single Master Operation** (**FSMO**) roles. These roles can run from one domain controller or be distributed among multiple domain controllers (according to guidelines). But each role can appear only once in a domain or forest. It makes the operations master role holder important in an AD DS infrastructure. If the domain controller that holds the operations master role fails and can't recover, another domain controller will have to forcefully regain control over its operations master roles.

In this chapter, we are going to look into the following topics:

- FSMO roles and duties
- FSMO role placement
- Moving FSMO roles
- Seizing FSMO roles

FSMO roles

There are five flexible single master operations roles in the Active Directory infrastructure. Each of them perform specific Active Directory tasks that other domain controllers in the infrastructure are not permitted to perform. These five FSMO roles are divided into two categories based on their operation boundaries:

Forest level	Domain level
Schema operations master	The **primary domain controller (PDC)** emulator operations master
Domain-naming operations master	The **relative identifier (RID)** operations master
N/A	The infrastructure operations master

When we create the first Active Directory forest and the first Active Directory domain, all these FSMO roles will be installed in the domain's first domain controller (obviously; there's no other place). A majority of the Active Directory infrastructures leave the default configuration as it is, even though they keep adding domain controllers. Keeping them in one domain controller is not a failure, but if you want to get best out of it, there are certain guidelines to follow.

However, there are many different reasons that can have a negative impact on FSMO role placements, such as size of the organization, network topology, and infrastructure resources. We are going to look into these as well, so we know both sides of the story.

Schema operations master

This role boundary is the forest. This means that an Active Directory forest can have only one schema master. The owner of this role is the only domain controller in the forest who can update the Active Directory schema. In order to make schema changes in the forest, it also needs to have a user account that is a member of the Schema Admins group. Once the schema changes are done from the schema master role owner, those changes will be replicated to other domain controllers in the forest.

In an Active Directory forest, the schema master role owner can be found using the following command:

```
Get-ADForest | select SchemaMaster
```

 When you add a new version of Active Directory to the domain for the first time, it will need a schema modification. If you run the Active Directory configuration wizard with a user account that has the Domain Admin permission, it will fail. You need an account with Schema Admin privileges.

Domain-naming operations master

The domain-naming operations master role holder is responsible for adding and removing domains controllers to and from the Active Directory forest. In the Active Directory forest, the domain-naming operations master role owner can be found using the following command:

```
Get-ADForest | select DomainNamingMaster
```

When you add or remove a domain controller, it will contact the domain-naming operations master role holder via the **Remote Procedure Call** (**RPC**) connection, and if it fails, it will not allow you to add or remove the domain controller from the forest. This is a forest-wide role, and only one domain-naming operations master role holder can exist in one forest.

Primary domain controller emulator operations master

The **primary domain controller** (PDC) operations master role is a domain-wide setting, which means each domain in the forest will have a PDC operations master role holder. One of the most common Active Directory-related interview questions is: *which FSMO role is responsible for time synchronization?* The answer is *PDC!* In an Active Directory environment, it allows a maximum of a 5-minute time difference (time skew) between server and client to maintain successful authentication. If it's more than 5 minutes, devices will not be able to be added to the domain, users will not be able to authenticate, and the Active Directory-integrated application will start throwing authentication-related errors.

It is important that domain controllers, computers, and servers in the Active Directory domain controller agree on one clock:

Computers in a domain will sync their time with the domain controller they are authenticated with. Then, all of the domain controllers will sync their time with the **domain PDC** role holder. All the **domain PDC** role holders will sync the time with the forest **root domain PDC** role holder. Finally, the **root domain PDC** role holder will sync the time with an **external time source**.

Apart from time synchronization, the PDC role holder is also responsible for maintaining password change replications. Also, in the event of authentication failures, PDC is responsible for locking down the account. All the passwords changed in other domain controllers will be reported back to the PDC role holder. If any authentication failure occurs in a domain controller before it passes the authentication failure message to the user, it will check the password saved in the PDC, as that will prevent errors that can occur due to password replication issues.

In the Active Directory domain, the PDC role owner can be found using the following command:

```
Get-ADDomain | select PDCEmulator
```

The PDC is also responsible for managing the **Group Policy Object** (GPO) edit. Every time a GPO is viewed or updated, it will be done from the copy stored in the PDC's SYSVOL folder.

Relative ID operations master role

The **relative identifier** (**RID**) master role is a domain-wide setting, and each domain in the forest can have RID role owners. It is responsible for maintaining a pool of relative identifiers that will be used when creating objects in the domain. Each and every object in a domain has a unique **security identifier** (**SID**). The RID value is used in the process of SID value creation. The SID is a unique value to represent an object in Active Directory. The RID is the incremental portion of the SID value. Once the RID value is being used to generate a SID, it will not be used again. Even after deleting an object from AD, it will not able to reclaim the RID value back. This ensure the uniqueness of the SID value. The RID role owner maintains a pool of RIDs. When the domain has multiple domain controllers, it will assign a block of 500 RID values for each domain controller. When they are used more than 50%, domain controllers will request another block of RIDs for the RID role owner.

In the Active Directory domain, the RID role owner can be found using the following command:

```
Get-ADDomain | select RIDMaster
```

In the event of an RID role owner failure, its impact will be almost unnoticeable until all domain controllers run out of allocated RID values. It will also not allow you to move objects between domains.

Infrastructure operations master

This role is also a domain-wide setting, and it is responsible for replicating SID and **distinguished name** (**DN**) value changes to cross-domains. SID and DN values get changed based on their location in the forest. So, if objects are moved, their new values need to be updated in groups and ACLs located in different domains. This is taken care of by the infrastructure operations master. This will ensure that the changed objects have access to their resources without interruptions.

In the Active Directory domain, the infrastructure operations master role owner can be found using the following command:

```
Get-ADDomain | select InfrastructureMaster
```

The infrastructure operations master role owner checks its database periodically for foreign group members (from other domains), and once it finds those objects, it checks its SID and DN values with the global catalog server. If the value in the global catalog is different from the local value, it will replace its value with the global catalog server's value. Then, it will replicate it to other domain controllers in the domain.

By design, the global catalog server holds a partial copy of every object in the forest. It does not have the need to keep a reference of cross-domain objects. If the infrastructure master is in place in a global catalog server, it will not know about any cross-domain objects. Therefore, the infrastructure operations master role owner should not be a global catalog server. However, this is not applicable when all the domain controllers are global catalogs in a domain because, that way, all the domain controllers will have up-to-date information.

FSMO role placement

The first domain controller in the first Active Directory forest will hold all five FSMO roles. All these roles are critical in the Active Directory infrastructure. Some of them are heavily used and some roles are only used on specific occasions. Some role owners will not be able to afford any downtime, and some role will still be able to have downtime. So, based on features, impact, and responsibilities, these can be placed on different domain controllers. However, FSMO roles placement is heavily dependent on characteristics of the infrastructure. Let's go ahead and look into few of those in detail.

Active Directory's logical and physical topology

If it's a single forest-single domain environment, it is not wrong to keep all the FSMO roles in one domain controller. According to the best practices infrastructure, the master role should not be held by the global catalog server. But, it is only if the environment has multiple domains. In single forest-single domain environment, on most occasions, all servers are global catalog servers.

In the following example, in the `rebeladmin.com` single forest-single domain environment, there are three domain controllers in the infrastructure:

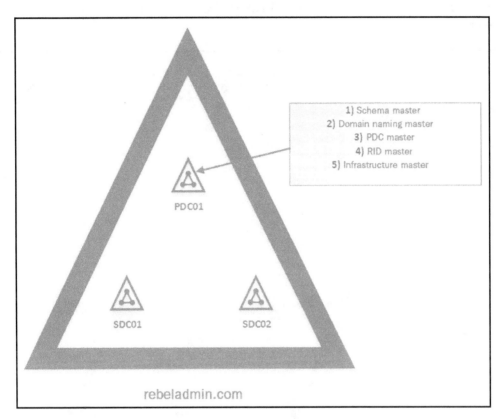

PDC01 is recognized as the most powerful (capacity) and most reliable domain controller. Therefore, **PDC01** holds all five FSMO roles. **SDC01** and **SDC02** are also two global catalog servers. In this case, just moving the infrastructure master role to one of the domain controllers will not make a significant impact. In the event of a **PDC01** failure, secondary domain controllers will be able to claim ownership of FSMO roles (this process is called **seizing FSMO roles** and will be described later in the chapter).

In a multiple-domain environment, this will change. Forest-wide roles and domain-wide roles will need to be placed properly in order to maintain high availability and performance.

In the following example, Rebeladmin Corp. has three domains. The
rebeladmin.net domain is the forest root domain. The rebeladmin.com domain is
used at its headquarters in the USA and rebeladmin.ca is used at its Canadian
branch:

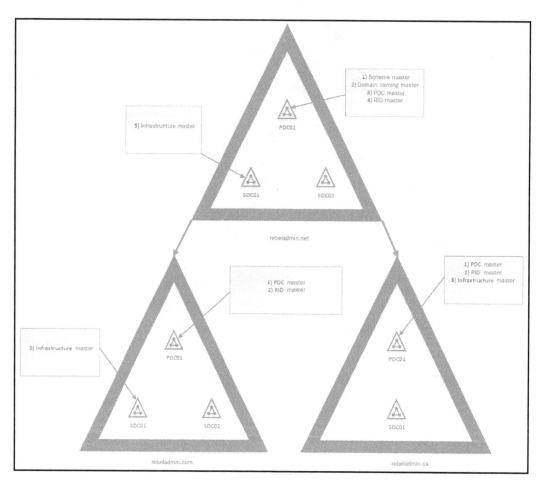

All these three domains share one forest. Therefore, forest-wide roles, which are the
Schema master and the **Domain naming master**, will be placed in the forest root
domain, rebeladmin.net. It has three domain controllers. **PDC01** is identified as the
most reliable domain controller.

The **Schema master** and the **Domain name master** roles use relatively lower amounts of processing power, as forest-wide changes will not happen frequently. But high availability is a must, as other domain activities will depend on it. PDC is the most consumed FSMO role, as it will replicate password changes, control time synchronization, and manage GPO edits. So, it's important for PDC to run on the domain controller that has the most processing power. The PDC role holder is the biggest customer of the **RID master**. Therefore, reliable communication between two role holders is crucial.

It is advised that you keep PDC and RID together in one domain controller in order to avoid network-latency-related issues. So, in the end, we can place four FSMO roles in **PDC01**. In a multi-domain environment, cross-domain referencing is important. If the user account in the forest root domain changes its name, it will immediately be replicated to all the domain controllers in the forest root domain. But, if the user is a part of group in the other domains, they also need to know about these new values. Therefore, **SDC01** is made as a non-global catalog server and it holds the **Infrastructure master** role. **SDC02** is kept as a backup domain controller; if any of the FSMO role holders are dead, it can claim role ownership. In some infrastructures, the forest root domain is not used for active operations. In such situations, keeping multiple domain controllers is a management overhead.

When considering the `rebeladmin.com` domain, it only holds domain-wide FSMO roles. The PDC and RID masters run from **PDC01** and **SDC01** runs the **Infrastructure master** role. It is also not a global catalog server. **SDC02** is the domain controller that can be used as an FSMO role holder in the event of an existing role owner failure.

The `rebeladmin.ca` domain is used in a regional office infrastructure. It has less than 25 users, and most of them are sales people. Therefore, keeping multiple domain controllers cannot be justified based on capacity or reliability facts. The setup is limited to two domain controllers, and **PDC01** hosts all three domain-wide **FSMO** roles. **SDC01** is kept as a backup domain controller, to be used in a DR scenario.

Connectivity

Healthy replication between domain controllers is a must for the Active Directory infrastructure. FSMO role holders are designated to do specific tasks in the infrastructure. Other domain controllers, devices, and resources should have a reliable communication channel with FSMO role holders in order to get these specific tasks done when required.

In Active Directory infrastructures, there can be regional offices and remote sites that are connected using WAN links. Most of the time, these WAN links have limited bandwidth. These remote sites can host domain controllers, too. If replication traffic between sites is not handled in an optimized way, it can turn into a bottleneck. Rebeladmin Corp. is a managed services provider and it has two offices. The HQ is located in Toronto and the operation center is based in Seattle, USA. It is connected via a 512 KB WAN link. In the Toronto office, there are 20 users and in the Seattle office, there are 500 users. It runs on a single-domain Active Directory infrastructure.

As I mentioned earlier, among all these FSMO roles, the PDC is the most highly used FSMO role. Devices and users keep communicating with PDC more frequently than other FSMO role holders. In this scenario, if we place the PDC in the Toronto office, 500 users and associated devices will need to go through the WAN link in order to communicate with the PDC. But if we place it in the Seattle site, then the traffic that will pass through the WAN link will be lower. In a regional office scenario, make sure you always place the PDC near the site that hosts the greatest number of users, devices, and resources.

Network topology use for inter-site connectivity also makes an impact on the FSMO role placement. In the following example, the Active Directory setup has three Active Directory sites with a single domain infrastructure. **Site Canada** connects to **Site USA** and **Site USA** connects to **Site Europe**. But **Site Canada** does not have a direct connection with **Site Europe**:

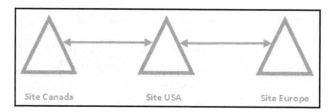

Now, if the FSMO roles are placed in **Site Canada**, **Site Europe** will have issues communicating with it. **Site Europe** will not be able to perform any FSMO-related tasks. According to the network topology, the best option will be to place the FSMO roles in **Site USA**, as both sites have a direct connection to it.

The number of domain controllers

The number of domain controllers that can be deployed on an Active Directory infrastructure depends on the budget and available resources (computer resources, space, power, and connectivity).

Based on the number of domain controllers, engineers will need to decide to either run all FSMO roles together or distribute them among domains controllers. It is recommended that you have at least two domain controllers in a site. One will be holding the FSMO roles, and the other one will be kept as a standby domain controller. In the event of a primary server failure, FSMO roles can be hosted on standby domain controller.

Capacity

The capacity of the Active Directory infrastructure also affects the FSMO roles placement. When the number of users, devices, and other resources increases, it also increases FSMO role-related activities. If it's a multi-site environment, it's recommended that you place FSMO roles on sites that run with a high capacity of Active Directory objects in order to lower the impact of replication and latency issues.

FSMO role holders are also involved in typical Active Directory tasks, such as user authentication. In large Active Directory environments (10,000+ objects), it is important to prioritize FSMO-related tasks over regular Active Directory tasks. This mainly impacts the PDC emulator, as it is the most active FSMO role. It is possible to prioritize domain controller operations by editing the *weight* value of the DNS SRV record. The default value is `100`, and reducing it will reduce the number of user authentication requests. The recommended value is `50`.

This can be done by adding a new registry key under `HKLM\SYSTEM\CurrentControlSet\Services\Netlogon\Parameters`. The key should have a `DWORD` value with the entry name, `LdapSrvWeight`.

Moving FSMO roles

In the Active Directory infrastructure, on certain occasions, FSMO roles will need to be moved from one domain controller to another. Here, I have listed a few scenarios where it will be necessary to consider FSMO roles transfers:

- **Active Directory upgrades**: When the infrastructure needs to be upgraded from one Active Directory version to another, first we need to introduce the new domain controllers to the existing infrastructure and then move the FSMO roles. After that, the domain controllers that run older versions can decommissioned, and then we can increase the forest and domain functional levels to the latest (Windows server 2016).

- **Active Directory logical and physical topology**: When installing the first domain controller in the infrastructure, it will automatically hold all five FSMO roles. But, based on the Active Directory topology design, the roles can be transferred to ideal locations, as discussed in the previous section. This can be based on the initial design or an extended design.
- **Performance and reliability issues**: FSMO role owners are responsible for specific tasks in an Active Directory infrastructure. Each role can appear in only one domain controller in a domain. Some of these roles are focused on more processing power, and other roles are more concerned about the uptime. Therefore, in general, FSMO roles should be running on the most reliable domain controllers in the infrastructure. If the allocated resources are not enough for the FSMO role operations or if the servers have reliability issues, it will be necessary to move on to another host. This happens mainly when these roles are running on physical servers. If it's a virtual server, it will just be a matter of increasing the allocated resources. Some businesses also have infrastructure refreshment plans, which will kick off every 3 or 5 years. In such situations, the FSMO roles will need to move into the new hardware.

Let's look at how we can transfer the FSMO roles.

Before we start, we need to check the current FSMO role holder. This can be done by running the following command:

```
netdom query fsmo
```

In the infrastructure, there is a new domain controller added with the name REBEL-SDC02, and I'd like to move the domain-wide FSMO roles, which are the PDC, RID, and infrastructure roles, to the new server:

```
Move-ADDirectoryServerOperationMasterRole -Identity REBEL-SDC02 -OperationMasterRole PDCEmulator, RIDMaster, InfrastructureMaster
```

FSMO role transfer commands need to be run with the required privileges. If you need to move domain-wide roles, the minimum you need to have are Domain Admin privileges. If they are forest-wide roles, they need to be Enterprise Admin privileges. To move the schema master role, Schema Admin privileges are the minimum requirement.

Once the move is completed, we can check the role owners again:

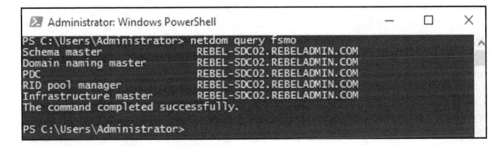

If we need to move all five FSMO roles to a new host, we can use the following command:

```
Move-ADDirectoryServerOperationMasterRole –Identity REBEL-SDC02 –
OperationMasterRole SchemaMaster, DomainNamingMaster, PDCEmulator,
RIDMaster, InfrastructureMaster
```

The following screenshot shows the output for the netdom query fsmo command:

If we need to move a single FSMO role, the Move-ADDirectoryServerOperationMasterRole command can be used with the individual role.

Once the transfer is completed, the system will create an event in the event viewer under the directory service log with the event ID 1458.

Seizing FSMO roles

In the previous section, I explained how to transfer FSMO roles from one domain controller to another. But there are certain situations where we will not be able to transfer the FSMO roles, such as the following:

- **Hardware failures**: If the domain controller that holds the FSMO roles failed due to hardware issues and there is no other way to bring it back online using a backup/DR solution, we need to use seize method to recover FSMO roles.
- **System operation issues**: If the domain controller has issues, such as operating system corruptions, viruses, malware, or file corruptions, it may not be allowed to transfer the FSMO role to another domain controller, which will also lead to a FSMO role seize.
- **Forcefully removed domain controller**: If the FSMO role holder is forcefully decommissioned using the `/forceremoval` command, we need to use the seize method from any other available domain controller to recover FSMO roles.

The FSMO role seize process should be used only in a disaster where you cannot recover the FSMO role holder. Some of the FSMO roles (RID, domain naming master, and schema master) can still afford a few hours of downtime with minimum business impact. Therefore, we do not use the seize option as the first option if the FSMO role holder can still be recovered or fixed.

Once the seize process is completed, the old FSMO role holder should not be brought online again. It is recommended that you format and remove it from the network. At any given time, it is not possible to have the same FSMO role appear in two servers on the same domain.

In the following example, there are two domain controllers in the infrastructure. REBEL-SDC02 is the FSMO role holder and REBEL-PDC-01 is the additional domain controller. Due to hardware failure, I cannot bring REBEL-SDC02 online and I need to seize the FSMO roles:

```
Administrator: Windows PowerShell                                    —    □    ×
PS C:\Users\Administrator> netdom query fsmo
Schema master                    REBEL-SDC02.REBELADMIN.COM
Domain naming master             REBEL-SDC02.REBELADMIN.COM
PDC                              REBEL-SDC02.REBELADMIN.COM
RID pool manager                 REBEL-SDC02.REBELADMIN.COM
Infrastructure master            REBEL-SDC02.REBELADMIN.COM
The command completed successfully.

PS C:\Users\Administrator> ping REBEL-SDC02 -t

Pinging rebel-sdc02.rebeladmin.com [192.168.0.110] with 32 bytes of data:
Request timed out.
Request timed out.
Reply from 192.168.0.105: Destination host unreachable.
Request timed out.
Request timed out.
Reply from 192.168.0.105: Destination host unreachable.
Request timed out.
Request timed out.
Request timed out.
Request timed out.
Request timed out.
Request timed out.

Ping statistics for 192.168.0.110:
     Packets: Sent = 12, Received = 2, Lost = 10 (83% loss),
Control-C
PS C:\Users\Administrator>
```

In order to seize the roles, the following command can be used:

```
Move-ADDirectoryServerOperationMasterRole -Identity REBEL-PDC-01 -
OperationMasterRole SchemaMaster, DomainNamingMaster, PDCEmulator,
RIDMaster, InfrastructureMaster -Force
```

This command will take a few minutes to complete in the background, and it will try to connect to the original FSMO role holder.

The only change in the command from the FSMO role transfer is the `-Force` parameter at the end. Otherwise, it's the exact same command. You also can seize the individual role using `Move-ADDirectoryServerOperationMasterRole -Identity REBEL-PDC-01 -OperationMasterRole <FSMO Role> -Force`.

`<FSMO Role>` can be replaced with the actual FSMO role value.

Once the command is completed, we can check the status of new FSMO role holder:

```
Administrator: Windows PowerShell
PS C:\Users\Administrator> netdom query fsmo
Schema master                     REBEL-PDC-01.REBELADMIN.COM
Domain naming master              REBEL-PDC-01.REBELADMIN.COM
PDC                               REBEL-PDC-01.REBELADMIN.COM
RID pool manager                  REBEL-PDC-01.REBELADMIN.COM
Infrastructure master            REBEL-PDC-01.REBELADMIN.COM
The command completed successfully.

PS C:\Users\Administrator>
```

As we can see, `REBEL-PDC-01` becomes the new FSMO role holder.

Summary

This is the end of another Active Directory infrastructure design chapter that was focused on FSMO role placements. FSMO roles are designated to do specific tasks in an Active Directory infrastructure in order to maintain integrity. In this chapter, you learned about FSMO roles and their responsibilities. Then, we moved on to FSMO role placement in the infrastructure, where you learned about techniques and best practices that need to be followed in order to maintain the best performance and availability. After that, we looked at how to transfer the FSMO roles from one domain controller to another using PowerShell, followed by a guide for seizing FSMO roles in the event of a disaster where you cannot recover the original FSMO role holder.

In the next chapter, we will look at actual Active Directory deployment scenarios and explore how to migrate from older versions of Active Directory to AD DS 2016.

6
Migrating to Active Directory 2016

In previous chapters, we looked at **Active Directory** (**AD**) infrastructure components and learned how to design an identity infrastructure using them. We also learned about the new features and enhancements of Active Directory 2016. Now, it's time to look at installing **Active Directory Domain Services** (**AD DS**), as well as its migrations. It would be perfect if we could design and implement an identity infrastructure from scratch, but the majority of organizations already have an Active Directory environment. Due to this, most of the time, they will be looking to migrate from one version of Active Directory to a newer one so that they can use that version's new features and enhancements.

This chapter is mainly focused on gaining hands-on experience with the different deployment scenarios of AD DS. Because of this, we will cover the following topics:

- AD DS installation prerequisites
- AD DS deployment scenarios
- How to plan an Active Directory migrations
- How to migrate to AD DS 2016
- How to confirm a successful installation and migration

AD DS installation prerequisites

Before we look at installing AD DS, there are certain prerequisites that need to be fulfilled. Without these, even if we have a good design, we will not have healthy AD DS environment.

Hardware requirements

In modern infrastructures, most workloads run as virtualized environments. AD DS can also be deployed in virtualized platforms, but there are certain scenarios where physical domain controllers should be used. For AD DS 2016, the following are the minimum hardware requirements:

- 1.4 GHz 64-bit processor
- 2 GB RAM
- A storage adapter that supports the PCI Express architecture (Windows Server 2016 does not support IDE/ATA/PATA/EIDE for boot, data or page drives)
- 32 GB of free space
- 1 x network adapter
- DVD drive or support for a network USB boot

 These are the minimum requirements for installing the AD DS 2016; however, this doesn't mean it can accommodate an organization's identity infrastructure requirements. The system needs to be size based on the AD DS roles, the number of objects, and operation requirements.

Virtualized environment requirements

Today, virtualization solutions allow organizations to build their own private cloud or use public cloud providers such as Microsoft Azure and Amazon AWS. AD DS 2016 supports both scenarios. If it's a private cloud, it will allow you to have more control over resource allocation, but in the public cloud, this will depend on the subscription and the amount the organization is capable of spending.

The minimum requirements for a virtualized environment are as follows:

- 1.4 GHz 64-bit processor
- 2 GB RAM
- Virtual SCSI storage controller
- 32 GB of free space
- 1 x virtual network adapter

Depending on your virtualization service provider, there will be specific guidelines for virtualized domain controllers. Always follow these recommendations to get the most out of them.

In Chapter 3, *Designing an Active Directory Infrastructure*, we looked at the dos and don'ts for when we're deploying virtualized domain controllers. Refer to this chapter for more details.

Microsoft **Advanced Threat Analytics (ATA)** is an application that allows administrators to find Active Directory infrastructure security threats. This will be covered in more detail in Chapter 15, *Active Directory Security Best Practices*. As part of that solution, you will require a standalone gateway, or the ATA Lightweight Gateway, which can be installed on domain controllers. To install it on a domain controller, you will need the minimum RAM requirements for the service, which is 6 GB. Therefore, if you are going to use ATA in your infrastructure, domain controllers need to have at least 8 GB of RAM allocated to them.

Additional requirements

Apart from the physical or virtual resource requirements, there are other factors to consider before installing your first domain controller:

- **Operating system version and installation mode**: Windows Server 2016 has standard and data center versions. AD DS roles are available under both versions, but it is important to decide and arrange the required licenses in advance. Windows Server 2016 supports three installation modes. A server with desktop experience is the standard installation method. Server roles and operations can also be managed by using GUIs or commands. The Server Core method also supports AD DS. Server Core doesn't have a GUI, and it reduces the operating system footprint. It also reduces the attack surface of the identity infrastructure.

Nano Server mode was introduced with Windows Server 2016. It is similar to Server Core, but is optimized for private clouds. Its OS footprint is lower than Windows Server Core and only allows 64-bit applications. It also only allows remote administration. At the time of writing this book, Microsoft Nano Server doesn't support AD DS. Before installing the domain controller, it's important to decide on the server's operating system version and installation mode. Depending on this, the system's prerequisites and licensing will change as well.

- **Design document**: Documentation is crucial in any system implementation. Before starting the installation process, produce a document that includes the Active Directory physical and logical topology, risks, technologies in use, and so on.

> It is recommended to get the documentation approved by authorized people before deployment. This helps everyone agree on one design and refer to it when required. It also creates a starting point for future identity infrastructure changes.

- **Domain and forest names**: During the AD DS installation, we need to specify the domain name and the forest name. In an organization, it's important to agree about these names with management before starting the installation process. This information can be added to your Active Directory design document and submitted for approval. Back in 2015, I wrote an article on my blog about the Active Directory domain rename process. Engineers write to me if they require any further guidance regarding the renaming process, and I am always curious to find out the reason for a domain rename as it's not *normal*. One of the instances was very interesting. It was a large organization, with nearly 500 users. They changed their business name and wanted to create a separate forest and domain structure and move users over to it, along with resources in a merged company. They hired an engineer to do so. The engineer created a new Active Directory structure and moved more than 400 users and devices over to the new structure.

After a few weeks, management came back and said that instead of using `.com` in the primary domain, they would prefer to use the `.ca` domain name. Even after long discussions, the company still didn't change its mind and wanted to remove the `.com` domain name. Some organizations use `.local` (**non-routable domain**) for their domain names. If we extend the on-premises AD infrastructure with a non-routable domain to Azure AD, we have to add additional **User Principle Names** (**UPNs**) with a routable domain name and force users to use it. Therefore, it's good practice to use routable domain names in the first place.

- **Dedicated IP address**: Domain controllers are recommended if you wish to operate with static IP addresses. Before installation begins, assign static IP addresses to domain controllers and test their connectivity. Active Directory domain controller IP addresses can be changed later if required, but it is recommended to avoid that as much as possible.

- **Monitoring**: Once AD DS is installed, we need to monitor system performance, replication health, and integrity component and services to identify potential service impacts and bottlenecks. Microsoft **System Center Operations Manager** (**SCOM**) and Microsoft **Operations Management Suite** (**OMS**) are the recommended monitoring tools since they include modules that have been specially designed to identify both service-level and security-level issues.

- **Backup/disaster recovery**: The high availability of identity infrastructure is a must for organizational operations as many services, applications, and other business components depend on it. Therefore, we need to plan on how to keep the identity infrastructure functioning in a disaster, with minimal operations being impacted. There are different technologies and services that can be used to back up Active Directory domain controllers, and some of these will be evaluated in `Chapter 11`, *Active Directory Services*. After deciding on the solution you're going to use, you also need to plan for periodic DR tests in order to verify the solution's validity.

- **Virus protection in domain controllers**: As with any other system, domain controllers can also get infected by malicious code. There is debate about whether an Active Directory domain controller should have antivirus software installed or not, but in the Microsoft documentation, I have never found anything saying it shouldn't have antivirus software. Always refer to your antivirus solution provider and check whether the solution supports protecting Active Directory domain controllers.

Once, I was working on an Active Directory upgrade project for a world-leading bank. Everything went smoothly, and one morning, after project closure, I received a call from their support team about the domain controller's replications. When I checked them, I found out that they had installed antivirus software on the domain controllers and that it was preventing DFS `SYSVOL` replication between domain controllers.

AD DS installation methods

There are two methods we can use to install the Active Directory domain controllers:

- **Using the Windows GUI**: After Microsoft introduced Server Manager with Windows Server 2008, the installation process of AD DS was simplified. In order to install the AD DS using Windows GUI, we need to install the AD DS role using Server Manager. Once this has been completed, we can run the AD DS configuration wizard:

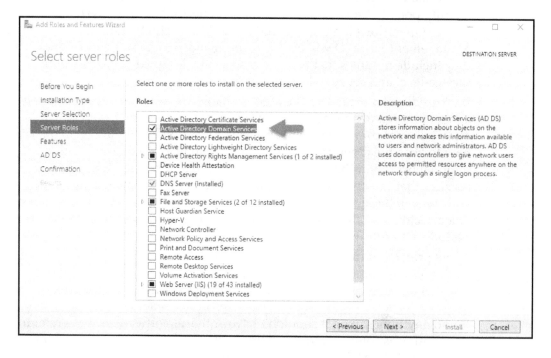

The following screenshot shows the **Active Directory Domain Services Configuration Wizard**:

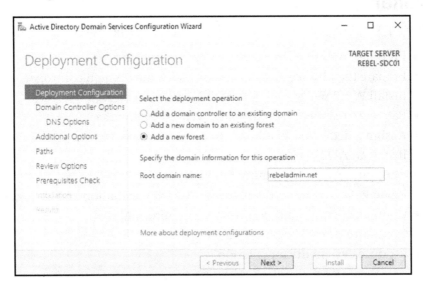

- **Using PowerShell**: Before Windows Server 2012, AD DS could be configured using *Dcpromo unattended* files. The Dcpromo tool was used to configure AD DS, and, using a text file, it was possible to pass the configuration values that were required. It removed user interaction for the AD DS configuration. With Windows Server 2012, Dcpromo was replaced with PowerShell. Now, we can use a PowerShell script to install and configure AD DS. In this chapter, we will be using PowerShell for deployments.

AD DS deployment scenarios

In this section, we are going to look into different installation scenarios for AD DS.

Setting up a new forest root domain

For the first scenario, I am going to demonstrate how to set up the new Active Directory forest. This will be the first domain controller of a new identity infrastructure. You can use the following checklist to make sure you have done your homework before clicking on the installation button.

AD DS installation checklist for the first domain controller

The following checklist can be used for a fresh AD DS installation:

- Produce an Active Directory design document.
- Prepare the physical/virtual resources for the domain controller.
- Install Windows Server 2016 Standard/Datacenter.
- Patch your servers with the latest Windows updates.
- Assign a dedicated IP address to the domain controller.
- Install an AD DS role.
- Configure AD DS according to the design.
- Review the logs to verify a healthy AD DS installation and configuration.
- Configure service and performance monitoring.
- Configure AD DS backup/DR.
- Produce system documentation.

Design topology

As we can see from the following diagram, in this scenario, `rebeladmin.com` will be the forest root domain:

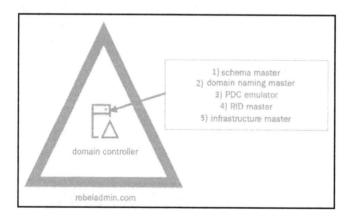

The first domain controller that's installed on the forest will hold all five **Flexible Single Master Operation** (**FSMO**) roles. In the previous chapter, we learned about FSMO role placement, and how, once additional domain controllers are added to the domain, these roles can be migrated to the best location.

Installation steps

Here, I will be demonstrating how to install the first domain controller in the forest. These demonstration steps are based on Windows Server 2016:

1. Log in to the server as a member of the local administrator's group.
2. From here, verify the static IP address' allocation by using `ipconfig /all`.
3. Launch the PowerShell console as an administrator.
4. Before the configuration process, we need to install the AD DS role in the given server. In order to do that, we can use the following command:

    ```
    Install-WindowsFeature -Name AD-Domain-Services
      -IncludeManagementTools
    ```

    We don't need to reboot to complete the role service installations.

5. Now that we have the AD DS role installed, the next step is to proceed with the configuration:

    ```
    Install-ADDSForest
    -DomainName "rebeladmin.com"
    -CreateDnsDelegation:$false
    -DatabasePath "C:\Windows\NTDS"
    -DomainMode "7"
    -DomainNetbiosName "REBELADMIN"
    -ForestMode "7"
    -InstallDns:$true
    -LogPath "C:\Windows\NTDS"
    -NoRebootOnCompletion:$True
    -SysvolPath "C:\Windows\SYSVOL"
    -Force:$true
    ```

There are no line breaks for the preceding command; I have listed it like this to allow you to see the parameters clearly. In the preceding command, the -DomainName and -DomainNetbiosNames values can be replaced with the domain and NetBIOS names for your environment.

6. The following table explains the PowerShell commands and what they do:

Cmdlet	Description
Install-WindowsFeature	This cmdlet allows us to install Windows roles, role services, or Windows features in a local server or remote server. It is similar to using Windows Server Manager to install them.
Install-ADDSForest	This cmdlet allows us to set up a new Active Directory forest.

7. The following table explains the arguments for the commands and what they do:

Argument	Description
-IncludeManagementTools	This installs the management tools for the selected role service.
-DomainName	This parameter defines the FQDN for the Active Directory domain.
-CreateDnsDelegation	Using this parameter, we can define whether we will create a DNS delegation that references Active Directory's integrated DNS.
-DatabasePath	This parameter defines the folder path for storing the Active Directory database file (ntds.dit).
-DomainMode	This parameter will specify the Active Directory domain's functional level. In the previous example, I used mode 7, which is Windows Server 2016.
-DomainNetbiosName	This defines the NetBIOS name for the forest root domain.
-ForestMode	This parameter will specify the Active Directory forest's functional level. In the previous example, I used mode 7, which is Windows Server 2016.

-InstallDns	Using this, you can specify whether a DNS role needs to be installed with the Active Directory domain controller. For a new forest, it is required that you set it to $true.
-LogPath	A log path can be used to specify the location that you save domain log files to.
-SysvolPath	This is used to define the SYSVOL folder path. The default location for it will be C:\Windows.
-NoRebootOnCompletion	By default, the system restarts the server after domain controller configuration. Using this command can prevent an automatic system restart.
-Force	This parameter will force a command to execute by ignoring the given warning. It is typical for the system to pass warnings about best practices and recommendations.

8. Once executed, the command will prompt you for
   the **SafeModeAdministratorPassword**. This is used in **Directory Services
   Restore Mode** (**DSRM**). Make sure that you use a complex password
   (according to Windows' password complexity recommendations). The
   failure to do so will stop the configuration:

9. Once the configuration is complete, reboot the domain controller and log
   back in as the domain administrator.

10. Let's do a further check to confirm the successful installation of the services:

```
Get-Service adws,kdc,netlogon,dns
```

The preceding command will list the status of the Active Directory-related
services running on the domain controller:

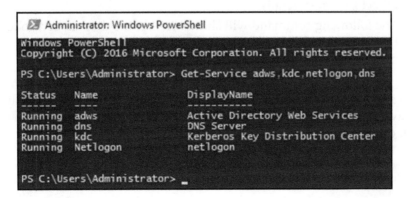

11. The following command will list all the configuration details of the domain controller:

```
Get-ADDomainController
```

The following screenshot shows the output for the preceding command:

12. The following command will list the details of the Active Directory domain:

```
Get-ADDomain rebeladmin.com
```

13. In the same way, `Get-ADForest rebeladmin.com` will list the Active Directory forest details.

14. The following command will show whether the domain controller shares the SYSVOL folder:

```
Get-smbshare SYSVOL
```

As we can see, AD DS components are installed and configured successfully. Now that we have a new root domain installed, we will extend this further and set up an additional domain controller.

Setting up an additional domain controller

In this scenario, we are going to look into installing an additional domain controller in an existing Active Directory domain. Before we look into this, there are a few prerequisites that need to be fulfilled:

- **Environment setup**: Before we promote the physical server or VM that's going to be used as the additional domain controller, it needs to be added to the existing Active Directory domain. If the additional domain controller is going to be a DNS server, set its own IP address as the primary DNS server in the NIC settings and the existing domain controller IP address as the secondary DNS server. During the installation process, it needs to have connectivity to existing domain controllers (via LAN or WAN) in order to replicate the Active Directory data.

  By default, during the installation process, the system will try to replicate the Active Directory partitions from any available domain controller. If this is via a slow WAN link, it is going to affect the installation process. Therefore, in such a scenario, Active Directory can be installed using installation media. This is similar to an Active Directory backup from an existing domain controller. Then, the system will use local media to replicate the initial Active Directory data. This will be explained in detail in `Chapter 11`, *Active Directory Services*.

- **Existing infrastructure information**: In order to add an additional domain controller, we need to know about certain information regarding the existing Active Directory infrastructure, such as the following:
    - The Active Directory domain name
    - The Active Directory site
    - Whether the additional domain controller needs to be a global catalog server, DNS server, or **read-only domain controller (RODC)**
    - The initial Active Directory data sync source (a specific Active Directory domain controller or media installation)

- **Schema preparation and domain preparation**: Let's assume that we have an Active Directory infrastructure based on Windows Server 2012 R2. Here, we need to add a domain controller, but we need it to use Windows Server 2016. Each version of Active Directory has a different schema. By default, the AD DS 2012 R2 schema will not recognize the domain controller running on Windows Server 2016. Before the actual configuration begins, the existing schema needs to be modified to support this new requirement. This is done by using the `adprep.exe` file, which comes with the *operating system source files*. Before Windows Server 2012, this file had to be copied to the schema master, and we needed to run `/domainprep` and `/forestprep` to prepare the domain and forest. However, at the time of writing, it comes as part of the AD DS configuration, and it will run these commands in the background. In order to do that, the configuration process of the domain should be run as a Schema Admin or Enterprise Admin.

AD DS installation checklist for an additional domain controller

The following checklist can be used if you wish to install an additional domain controller:

- Prepare the physical/virtual resources for the domain controller.
- Install Windows Server 2016 Standard/Datacenter.
- Patch the servers with the latest Windows updates.
- Assign a dedicated IP address to the domain controller.
- Add the domain controller to the existing Active Directory domain as a domain member.
- Find information about existing domain sites and the initial replication method.
- Log in to the server with a privileged account (such as Schema Admin or Enterprise Admin).
- Install the AD DS role.
- Configure AD DS.
- Review the logs to verify healthy AD DS installation and configuration.
- Configure service and performance monitoring.
- Configure AD DS backup/DR.

Design topology

As per the following diagram, we are going to add an **additional domain controller** to the rebeladmin.com domain:

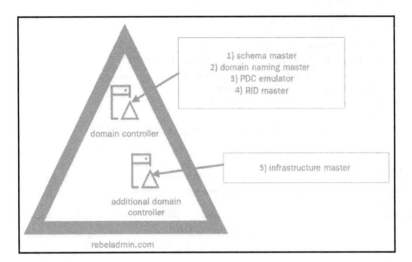

This domain controller isn't going to be a global catalog server, and so we will move the infrastructure master FSMO role over to new domain controller at the end of the configuration.

Installation steps

The following steps demonstrate how to add an additional domain controller to an existing domain:

1. Log in to the server as a member of the Schema or Enterprise Admins group.
2. Here, verify the static IP address' allocation by using ipconfig /all.
3. Launch the PowerShell console as an administrator.
4. Install the AD DS role service:

```
Install-WindowsFeature -Name AD-Domain-Services
 -IncludeManagementTools
```

5. After successful installation of role service, the next step is to configure the domain controller:

```
Install-ADDSDomainController
-CreateDnsDelegation:$false
-NoGlobalCatalog:$true
-InstallDns:$true
-DomainName "rebeladmin.com"
-SiteName "Default-First-Site-Name"
-ReplicationSourceDC "REBEL-SDC01.rebeladmin.com"
-DatabasePath "C:\Windows\NTDS"
-LogPath "C:\Windows\NTDS"
-NoRebootOnCompletion:$true
-SysvolPath "C:\Windows\SYSVOL"
-Force:$true
```

There are no line breaks for the preceding command. The following table contains the parameters that were used here:

Argument	Description
Install-ADDSDomainController	This cmdlet will install the domain controller in the Active Directory infrastructure.
-NoGlobalCatalog	If you don't want to create the domain controller as a global catalog server, this parameter can be used. By default, the system will enable the global catalog feature.
-SiteName	This parameter can be used to define the Active Directory site name. The default value is Default-First-Site-Name.
-DomainName	This parameter defines the FQDN for the Active Directory domain.
-ReplicationSourceDC	You can use this parameter to define the Active Directory replication source. By default, it uses any available domain controller, though you can specify one if you wish.

6. Once executed, the command will ask for the **SafeModeAdministratorPassword**. Use a complex password to proceed. This will be used for DSRM.

7. After the configuration has completed, restart the system and log back in as an administrator to check the AD DS status.

8. The following command will confirm the status of the AD DS service:

```
Get-Service adws,kdc,netlogon,dns
```

9. The following command will list the domain controllers, along with their IP addresses and the sites they belong to:

```
Get-ADDomainController -Filter * |  Format-Table Name,
   IPv4Address, Site
```

10. The following command will list the global catalog servers that are available in the domain and confirm that this new domain controller server isn't a global catalog server:

```
Get-ADDomainController -Discover -Service "GlobalCatalog"
```

11. As per our plan, the next step is to move the infrastructure master role to the new additional domain controller:

```
Move-ADDirectoryServerOperationMasterRole
   -Identity REBEL-SDC-02
   -OperationMasterRole InfrastructureMaster
```

12. By using the `netdom query fsmo` command, we can confirm this change:

```
PS C:\Users\administrator.REBELADMIN> netdom query fsmo
Schema master                    REBEL-SDC01.rebeladmin.com
Domain naming master             REBEL-SDC01.rebeladmin.com
PDC                              REBEL-SDC01.rebeladmin.com
RID pool manager                 REBEL-SDC01.rebeladmin.com
Infrastructure master            REBEL-SDC-02.rebeladmin.com
The command completed successfully.

PS C:\Users\administrator.REBELADMIN>
```

This is the end of this scenario. The next step will be to extend the domain further by adding an additional domain.

Setting up a new domain tree

An Active Directory **domain tree** is a collection of domains that share a contiguous namespace. An Active Directory forest can have multiple domain trees that use different namespaces. In one forest, each of these domain trees have explicit trust among them by default. In this scenario, we are going to create a new domain tree in an existing Active Directory forest.

Before we start with the installation, we need to consider a few things:

- **Environment setup**: The new physical server or the VM that is going to be promoted as the domain controller. This should have network reachability to the existing forest root domain. It can be in different network segments, but in order to add it to the existing forest, a connection is required. We also need local administrator privileges to be set for the new server and a Schema Admin (if schema modification is required) or Enterprise Admin account's login details for the existing forest.
- **Information**: In order to set up the new domain tree, we need to gather the following information:
    - FQDN for the new domain
    - Forest name
    - Schema Admin or Enterprise Admin credentials for the existing *forest root domain*
- **Schema preparation**: If the new domain controller is going to be a newer version than the existing AD DS version, it needs the forest schema modified with `adprep /forestprep` to support the new version. As I explained in the previous scenario, this is now a part of the Active Directory configuration process. However, we need Schema Admin privileges to do this.

AD DS installation checklist for a new domain tree

The following checklist covers all the steps that need to considered for a new domain tree deployment:

- Prepare the physical/virtual resources for the domain controller.
- Install Windows Server 2016 Standard/Datacenter.
- Patch the servers with the latest Windows updates.
- Assign a dedicated IP address to the domain controller.
- Find information about the AD forest and Schema Admin/Enterprise Admin login details for the existing forest root domain.
- Log in to the server as a local administrator.
- Install the AD DS role.
- Configure the AD DS new domain tree.
- Review the logs to verify healthy AD DS installation and configuration.

- Configure service and performance monitoring.
- AD DS backup/DR configuration.

Design topology

As per the following diagram, in this scenario, we are going to add `rebeladmin.net`, which is a new domain tree:

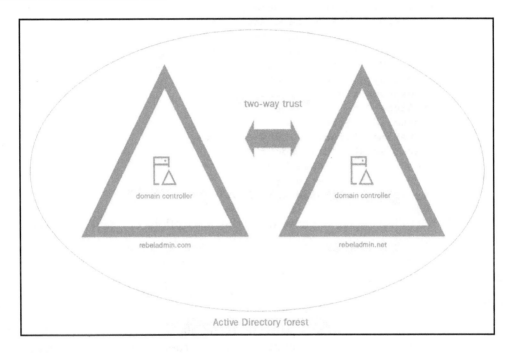

The `rebeladmin.com` domain is the forest tree that was created in the first scenario. Both domain trees will be under one **Active Directory forest**. The system will automatically create **two-way trust** between the two domain trees. Let's get started.

Installation steps

The following steps demonstrate how to add a new domain tree to an existing Active Directory forest:

1. Log in to the server as a local administrator.
2. Here, verify the static IP address' allocation by using `ipconfig /all`.
3. Launch the PowerShell console as an administrator.

4. Install the AD DS role service:

```
Install-WindowsFeature -Name AD-Domain-Services
 -IncludeManagementTools
```

5. After successful role service installation, the next step is to set up the new domain tree:

```
Install-ADDSDomain
-Credential (Get-Credential)
-ParentDomainName "rebeladmin.com"
-NewDomainName "rebeladmin.net"
-NewDomainNetbiosName "REBELNET"
-DomainMode "WinThreshold"
-DomainType "TreeDomain"
-CreateDnsDelegation:$false
-NoGlobalCatalog:$false
-InstallDns:$true
-SiteName "Default-First-Site-Name"
-DatabasePath "C:\Windows\NTDS"
-LogPath "C:\Windows\NTDS"
-NoRebootOnCompletion:$true
-SysvolPath "C:\Windows\SYSVOL"
```

6. In the following table, I have listed the descriptions of new PowerShell arguments:

Argument	Description
Install-ADDSDomain	This cmdlet installs the new Active Directory domain.
-Credential (Get-Credential)	This parameter allows us to pass the credentials that we need in order to connect to the parent domain.
-ParentDomainName	This parameter defines the existing parent domain in the AD forest.
-NewDomainName	This defines the FQDN for the new AD domain name.
-NewDomainNetbiosName	This parameter defines the NetBIOS name for the new domain.
-DomainType	Using this parameter defines the type of the domain. The options will be child domain or domain tree. The default value for the parameter is Child Domain.

7. Once this has been processed, system will prompt you to provide the credentials for the Schema Admin/Enterprise Admin so that it can connect to the parent domain. If this is not defined in the command, it will use the account of the user that's already logged in:

8. It will also ask for the **SafeModeAdministratorPassword**. Use a complex password to proceed. This will be used for DSRM.

9. Once the configuration is complete, reboot the domain controller and log in as the new Domain Admin.

10. After logging in, we can do some testing to confirm that the configuration was a success.

11. The following command will list the FSMO role holders. As we can see, the forest root domain controller is the forest-wide FSMO role holder:

```
netdom query fsmo
```

12. The following command lists the AD trust information between the two domain trees:

```
Get-ADTrust -Filter *
```

The following screenshot shows the output for the preceding command:

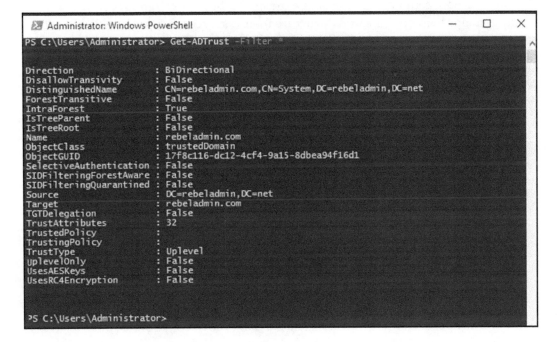

13. The following command confirms the domain controllers under the new domain tree:

```
Get-ADDomainController -Filter * | Format-Table Name,
    IPv4Address
```

14. The following command lists the details about the new Active Directory domain:

```
Get-ADDomain
```

The commands that we used in the previous two scenarios can be used to test the domain's setup further. In the next scenario, you will learn how to extend the domain trees further using child domains.

Setting up a new child domain

In a domain tree, domains maintain a contiguous namespace. The domains in a domain tree have a parent domain, and all other domains under it are called **child domains**. Just like children use their parents' surname, child domains also use the name of their parent domain. For example, if the parent domain is rebeladmin.com, the child domain could be europe.rebeladmin.com or asia.rebeladmin.com. Child domains help organizations structure their resources and provide flexible IT management.

Before we start the installation process, let's look into a few prerequisites, which are as follows:

- **Information**: In order to set up a child domain, we need to gather the following information:
    - FQDN for the child domain
    - Forest name
    - Schema Admin or Enterprise Admin credentials for the existing forest root domain

- **Environment setup**: The resource requirements for the installation are similar to creating a new domain tree. The server shouldn't connect to the existing domain but, during the installation process, it needs connectivity to the parent domain. It also needs the credentials for the Schema Admin or Enterprise Admin account from the parent domain.
- **Schema preparation**: As we explained in the previous scenarios, if the new domain controller is going to be newer than the existing AD DS version, it needs the forest schema modified with `adprep.exe /forestprep` and `adprep.exe /domainprep` to support the new version. This action is now part of the Active Directory configuration process. However, we need Schema Admin/Enterprise Admin privileges to do this.

AD DS installation checklist for a new child domain

The following checklist covers all the steps you need to follow when deploying a new child domain:

- Prepare the physical/virtual resources for the domain controller.
- Install Windows Server 2016 Standard/Datacenter.
- Patch the servers with the latest Windows updates.
- Assign a dedicated IP address to the domain controller.
- Find information about the AD forest and Schema Admin/Enterprise Admin login details for the existing forest root domain.
- Log in to the server as a local administrator.
- Install the AD DS role.
- Configure the AD DS new child domain.
- Review the logs to verify healthy AD DS installation and configuration.
- Configure service and performance monitoring.
- Configure AD DS backup/DR.

Design topology

As per the following diagram, we are going to add a new child domain to the `rebeladmin.com` domain tree:

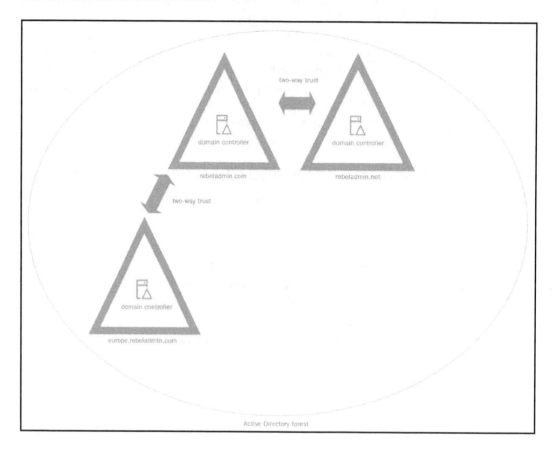

The name of the new child domain will be `europe.rebeladmin.com`. This will still be under the same **Active Directory forest**. Similar to a new domain tree, the child domain and parent domain will have two-way domain trust created automatically. This domain controller is going to be the first domain controller on the child domain, so it cannot be a RODC.

Installation steps

The following steps demonstrate how we can add a new child domain to the existing domain:

1. Log in to the server as a local administrator.
2. Here, verify the static IP address' allocation by using `ipconfig /all`.
3. Launch the PowerShell console as an administrator.
4. Install the AD DS role service:

```
Install-WindowsFeature -Name AD-Domain-Services
  -IncludeManagementTools
```

5. After successful role service installation, the next step is to set up the new child domain:

```
Install-ADDSDomain
-Credential (Get-Credential)
-ParentDomainName "rebeladmin.com"
-NewDomainName "europe"
-NewDomainNetbiosName "EUROPE"
-DomainMode "WinThreshold"
-DomainType "ChildDomain"
-CreateDnsDelegation:$true
-NoGlobalCatalog:$false
-InstallDns:$true
-SiteName "Default-First-Site-Name"
-DatabasePath "C:\Windows\NTDS"
-LogPath "C:\Windows\NTDS"
-NoRebootOnCompletion:$true
-SysvolPath "C:\Windows\SYSVOL"
```

6. In the following table, I have listed the descriptions of some PowerShell arguments:

Argument	Description
-DomainType	You can use this parameter the define the type of the domain. The options will be for the child domain or domain tree. For this scenario, the default `ChildDomain` type is selected.
-CreateDnsDelegation	When a child domain is set up, DNS delegation is a must with its parent domain. Delegation records must be created in the parent domain's DNS zone so that it can provide correct referrals to the DNS servers of the server client's DNS queries.

7. After executing the preceding commands, you will be prompted for credentials. We need to provide Schema Admin/Enterprise Admin account details for the parent domain.

8. It will also ask for the **SafeModeAdministratorPassword**. Use a complex password to proceed. This will be used for DSRM.

9. Once the configuration is complete, reboot the domain controller and log in as the new Domain Admin.

10. Let's do some tests to verify the configuration. Here, I have logged in to the parent domain controller. In the DNS, I can see that the new zone delegation is set up for the child domain:

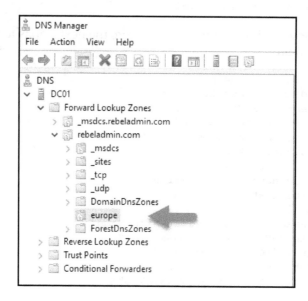

11. We can use the following command to verify the FSMO role placement for the new child domain:

```
netdom query fsmo
```

It is recommended that the preceding command is executed on the child domain controller.

12. I ran the following command to verify the two-way trust between the parent domain and the child domain. This is processed from the parent domain controller:

```
Get-ADTrust -Identity europe.rebeladmin.com
```

13. The following command will list the details about the new subdomain:

```
Get-ADDomain europe
```

The following screenshot shows the output for the preceding command:

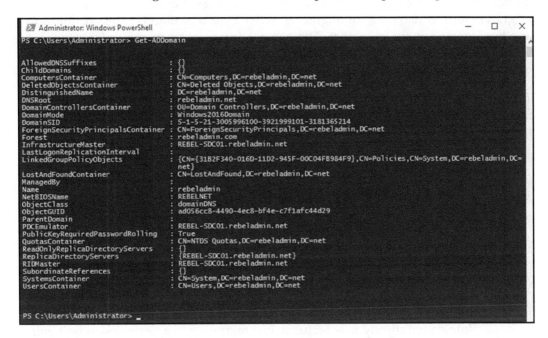

14. We can use the following command to verify the status of the AD DS:

```
Get-Service adws,kdc,netlogon,dns
```

According to the test results, the child domain is functioning properly. This is the end of the AD DS installation scenarios. In the next section, we are going to look into AD DS migration.

How to plan Active Directory migrations

Active Directory migration from an older version to a newer one is a common challenge for any identity infrastructure. In some documentation, this is called **Active Directory upgrades**, but I prefer to call it **Active Directory migration**. In this process, a new AD DS version will be installed on a new server. Then, the FSMO roles will migrate to the new domain controllers.

Once this is completed, the older version of AD DS will be decommissioned. Afterward, the domain and forest function levels will be raised to match the new AD DS version. Even though each AD DS version has core functions that are the same, newer versions always have new features and enhancements that apply to the domain or forest level. Therefore, it's more of a *migration* than an *upgrade*. The **migration** term is also used for migrating Active Directory objects from one forest to another, or one domain to another. There may or may not be an Active Directory version change. In this section, we are only going to look at migrating from one version to another.

There can be many reasons why an organization may consider an Active Directory migration. I have listed a few main reasons that have occurred in my projects as follows:

- **To implement new features in the identity infrastructure**: Every new version of Active Directory comes with new features and enhancements. Some of these changes are game changers. As an example, AD DS 2016 privilege management is a turning point for identity infrastructures. In order to implement these new features, companies look for AD DS migrations. At the time of writing, it's only been a few months since the AD DS 2019 release, and I have already finished a few large projects to migrate to the new version, which is a good trend. I am a geek and I always prefer to run the latest and the greatest. At the same time, I have seen that some organizations just like to run the latest but don't worry much about implementing any new features. Just migrating to a new version isn't going to give you any benefits if it's not used properly. There's no point buying a Ferrari just to drop your kids to school. Therefore, as organizations, it's important to evaluate our objectives thoroughly before Active Directory migration.

- **To address support issues and compliance issues**: Back in 2015, Microsoft ended its support for Windows Server 2003. At that time, organizations that were running AD DS 2003 had no choice but to migrate to a new version. Some businesses needed to comply in order to run their operations. Businesses in the financial sector are a good example of this. These compliances have standards related to IT systems. As an example, the businesses that were subject to **Payment Card Industry** (**PCI**) compliance had rules stating that it couldn't use end-of-life OSes for operations. These types of business requirements force organizations to migrate from one AD DS version to another.

- **To fix existing issues**: The good health of identity infrastructure is key for an organization's operations and security. Like any other system, it is possible for the identity infrastructure to have issues. These could be due to bad design, configuration issues, system corruptions, and so on. Fixes for these problems may lead to migrations as well. When I get my car serviced, sometimes they tell me that some parts need to be replaced. But before these parts are replaced, the mechanic normally gives me a few options. Some parts are of the same make and model, while others are for a new version. Therefore, the mechanic makes sure to explain the advantages of the new model and what it can provide me, rather than just fix the problem. Most of the time, I end up using the new model, as it doesn't just fix the existing issue, it fixes it in a better way. So, if existing identity infrastructure issues can be fixed in a *better way* by migrating to a new version, don't hesitate to go for it. But at the same time, there are some basic AD health requirements that need to be fulfilled before performing the migration. This will be covered later in this chapter.

- **Operation requirements**: In business, there can be different operational requirements that can lead to AD migrations. New application implementations are a good example of this. Some applications only support certain AD DS schema versions. In such situations, businesses have no other option but to upgrade. There is another scenario that applies to organizations that run AD forest with multiple domain trees. As an example, Rebeladmin Corp. has three domain trees with one forest. Each domain tree represents a separate subsidiary with its own IT department. One company has business requirements to upgrade its domain and forest function levels to a newer version. However, in order to do that, the other two domains also need to upgrade their AD DS versions. Although this isn't an operational requirement for two of the companies, in order to support the forest level upgrade, there is no option but to upgrade their AD DS.

Migration life cycle

Based on the steps in the AD DS migration process, I have come up with the following life cycle:

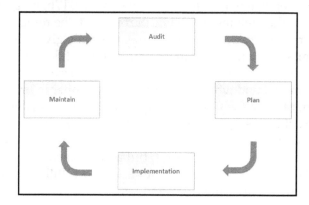

Following this will ensure that every aspect of the migration process is covered.

Auditing

In the migration process, auditing and planning are the most important stages. When you have proper auditing and a plan, the implementation process is quite easy. It minimizes the post-implementation issues. In the audit stage, we review the current Active Directory infrastructure and get a clear understanding of the logical and physical topology, as well as its health status. This also helps us to identify potential risks in the migration process.

Active Directory logical and physical topology

A few years ago, I needed to add an additional room in my house, so I went to meet an architect and explained my requirements. When I explained it to them, I mentioned the structure of the house, where it's located, why I needed this extension, and where I thought it was best suited. Even though I explained the structure, one of the initial requests from the architect was to show him the current house plan. My verbal explanation about the house wasn't enough for him to provide me with a new plan. This was because my explanation was still missing some critical information, such as length, width, door and window locations, and more. However, the current house plan indicates all of this information, which helped him to make a new, accurate plan.

Similarly, in Active Directory migration projects, one of my initial requests to customers is to provide an Active Directory topology diagram. However, most of the time, I only get basic information back, such as the number of domain controllers, the number of sites, and so on. This isn't enough to get an understanding of the domain trees, replication topology, site links, and FSMO role placements. In most cases, I have to create an Active Directory topology diagram from scratch as part of the exercise. The Microsoft Active Directory Topology Diagrammer is a tool that can be used to automatically generate a diagram with a lot of important data, such as domain trees, sites, server system information, and organizational units. It connects to the Active Directory using an LDAP connection and generates a Visio diagram. In order to run this, we need a domain-joined computer with Microsoft Visio installed. This tool doesn't have many updates, but it can do the job. It can be downloaded from `https:/ /www.microsoft.com/en-gb/download/details.aspx?id=13380`. The diagram it generates can be modified as per other requirements.

Apart from the topology diagram, network diagrams also help the engineers understand the physical placement of the Active Directory components. The topology diagram includes data about its physical structure, such as site links, the number of domain controllers, and the number of sites, but it doesn't give much of an overview of how traffic flows (network segments) and what kind of connections and bandwidth each site has. Network diagrams provide help so that it can gather this data.

Some organizations always keep these diagrams up to date with all the required changes, but this isn't the same for the majority. Lots of companies either don't have any of these diagrams or, even if they have them, they may not be up to date. Depending on the project scope, it may not be your responsibility to create a topology diagram and network diagram, but you need to collect the data that is vital for the AD DS migration project at the very least. If you are dealing with fragmented data, you can use other techniques, such as interviews and questionnaires with engineers, managers, and team leaders to clear up doubts. You can also refer to the asset changes if your company has a change-tracking system.

The following are the types of data we need to gather during this exercise:

- Active Directory logical topology
- Active Directory physical topology
- The organization's network topology
- Links between Active Directory sites
- Bandwidth between Active Directory sites

Active Directory health check

My first car was a white 2004 Honda Civic model (I loved that little beast). After I bought the car, I saw little rust spots on the bonnet. I took it to a paint shop and the man who checked it said that it needed a fresh coat of paint. I agreed and got it done. After a few months, I started to see some bubbles again on the bonnet. I took it back to the shop since I had 6 months warranty for the job they had done. They said they would redo the paint job. But guess what – after a few months, the same issue occurred. I didn't want to waste any more of my time, and so I took it to another place that specialized in paint jobs. When I explained the issues I was having, the engineers there performed some tests and said that they needed to remove the whole paint and apply anti-rust first, which they did. After that, there were no more bubbles on the bonnet. Just applying a new coat of paint didn't fix the issue. It was only a waste of time and money.

If the Active Directory infrastructure has got existing issues related to its core operations (such as replications, DNS, and site links), then those need to be identified and fixed before migration. There is no specific, predefined sequence for Active Directory health checks. You can have your own checklist. The following are some key areas that need to be covered in any Active Directory health check:

- **Replication health**: A healthy replication is critical for any Active Directory infrastructure. All domain controllers in the infrastructure need to be aware of every change to the Active Directory database. There are tools and techniques we can use to identify the replication issues between Active Directory domain controllers. `Repadmin.exe` is a Microsoft-built tool that can be used to diagnose Active Directory replication issues. Since Windows Server 2008, it has come built into the operating system, and it can be used if the AD DS role is installed. This tool needs to be run as an Enterprise Admin. If it runs as a Domain Admin, it can only be used to review domain-level replications:

  ```
  Repadmin /showrepl
  ```

  The preceding command will display the status of the last inbound replication of the Active Directory partition. This will only list the replication status of the domain controller this command executes from.

  If you need to check the replication status of a specific domain controller, you can use a command similar to the following. `REBEL-SDC-03` can be replaced with the name of the domain controller:

  ```
  Repadmin /showrepl REBEL-SDC-03
  ```

The /replicate parameter can be used to trigger a replication between the domain controllers so that you can see the results in real time:

Repadmin /replicate REBEL-SDC-03.rebeladmin.com REBEL-PDC-01.rebeladmin.com DC=rebeladmin,DC=com

The preceding command will initiate replication of the rebeladmin naming context from REBEL-PDC-01 to REBEL-SDC-03.

The following commands will initiate the full replication of all the changes from REBEL-PDC-01 to REBEL-SDC-03:

Repadmin /replicate REBEL-SDC-03.rebeladmin.com REBEL-PDC-01.rebeladmin.com DC=rebeladmin,DC=com /full

The /replsummary parameter can be used so that you can view the summary of the replication status of all the domain controllers:

Repadmin /replsummary

The preceding command will provide a summary of all the domain controllers in the infrastructure:

```
PS C:\Users\Administrator> repadmin /replsummary
Replication Summary Start Time: 2017-02-05 14:53:08

Beginning data collection for replication summary, this may take awhile:
.......

Source DSA          largest delta    fails/total %%    error
  REBEL-PDC-01            54m:10s       0 /   6    0
  REBEL-SDC-02      02d.15h:05m:56s     4 /   4  100   (1908) Could not find the domain controller for this domain.
  REBEL-SDC-03           58m:42s       0 /   6    0

Destination DSA     largest delta    fails/total %%    error
  REBEL-PDC-01      02d.15h:05m:56s     4 /  10   40   (1908) Could not find the domain controller for this domain.
  REBEL-SDC-03           54m:10s       0 /   6    0

Experienced the following operational errors trying to retrieve replication information:
        58 - 9a145fff-4ea2-4595-ba37-1df8ddaf98ba._msdcs.rebeladmin.com
      8341 - REBEL-SDC-02.europe.rebeladmin.com
PS C:\Users\Administrator>
```

The following command will only list the domain controllers that have replication issues with other domain controllers:

Repadmin /replsummary /errorsonly

- **Event Viewer**: **Event Viewer** can also be used to evaluate the replication health of the Active Directory environment. There are certain event IDs you can use to filter this data. You can find these events under **Event Viewer** | **Application and Service Logs** | **Directory Services**.

Here, I have listed some key event IDs that will show the replication problems:

Event ID	Cause
1925	The attempt to establish a replication link for a writable directory partition failed. This can be caused by network issues, domain controller failures, or DNS issues.
1988	The local domain controller has attempted to replicate an object from a source domain controller that isn't present on the local domain controller because it may have been deleted and already garbage-collected. Replication will not proceed for this directory partition with this partner until the situation is resolved. This happens when a domain controller is down for a long time (more than the tombstone's lifetime) before being brought back online. After this, however, it could have non-existing objects (lingering objects). They need to be cleaned to initiate replication again.
2087	AD DS could not resolve the DNS hostname of the source domain controller to an IP address, and replication failed. This will show up in the destination domain controller when it cannot resolve the DNS name for its source domain controller. If DNS lookup fails in the first place, it will also try FQDN and NetBIOS to resolve the name. It will prevent replication until it's been resolved.
2088	AD DS could not resolve the DNS hostname of the source domain controller to an IP address, but replication succeeded. In this situation, the destination domain controller failed to resolve the source name using DNS lookup, but it was able to connect to it using the FQDN or NetBIOS name.
1311	The replication configuration information in AD DS doesn't accurately reflect the physical topology of the network. This usually occurs due to the misconfiguration of Active Directory site links. It may have the wrong subnets assigned to it.

Once an object is deleted from the Directory, it will not be deleted from the Active Directory database right away. It will be removed by the garbage collector once it passes the tombstone lifetime value. The default value is `180` days.

- **Domain controller health**: In the previous section, we learned how to evaluate the replication's health. The next step is to check the health of the domain controllers. Similar to `Repadmin`, Microsoft has tools that can be used for this task.

  The `Dcdiag.exe` tool can be used to run predefined tests to evaluate the health of the domain controllers:

  ```
  Dcdiag /e
  ```

  The preceding command will test the domain controllers in the forest:

  ```
  Dcdiag /s:REBEL-SDC-03
  ```

  The preceding command will run the test on the `REBEL-SDC-03` domain controller.

  Instead of running all the tests, the following command will only run a replication test on `REBEL-SDC-03`:

  ```
  Dcdiag /test:replications /s:REBEL-SDC-03
  ```

  The following command can be used to check Active Directory services on the local domain controller:

  ```
  Dcdiag /test:Services
  ```

- **DNS health**: We can't talk about Active Directory health without talking about a healthy DNS infrastructure. Active Directory heavily depends on DNS functionalities.

  To start with, I prefer to review the DNS server-related events in the domain controllers. We can access the DNS logs by going to **Event Viewer** | **Application and Service Logs** | **DNS Server**:

  The `Dcdiag` utility can also be used to test DNS health:

  ```
  Dcdiag /test:DNS /DNSBasic
  ```

  The preceding command will run a basic DNS check to ensure that the DNS services are running, the resource records are registered, and that the DNS zones are presented.

The following command will test whether the DNS forwarders are functioning properly:

```
Dcdiag /test:DNS /DnsForwarders
```

The following command will test the registration of DC locator records:

```
Dcdiag /test:DNS /DnsRecordRegistration
```

In this section, I have mentioned the most common things we need to check during an Active Directory health check. However, based on the findings from our testing, we will need to perform an additional test. The whole point of an Active Directory health check is to verify the state of the Active Directory environment and make sure it is ready for an upgrade.

SCOM and Azure Monitor

SCOM has Active Directory Management Packs and DNS Management Packs that monitor the application-level health events. Azure Monitor includes modules that evaluate the health and security of the Active Directory environment, as well as the replication of its health. If organizations have these tools configured, they can provide real-time data about AD health. If any issues are detected, they provide guidelines on how to fix them (Azure Monitor AD assessment).

Here, I have listed the Active Directory health checklist I use with projects:

- Review the connection status between domain controllers.
- If the organization has a monitoring system, review the reports and latest events about domain controllers, AD DS roles, replication health, and DNS services.
- Review the latest backup reports.
- Review DNS issues and events.
- Review the Active Directory domain controller's health.
- Test Active Directory replications.
- Review Active Directory logs to find any recurring issues.
- Review the existing domain controller's performance.
- Review bandwidth utilization between site links.

Application auditing

If organizations are running AD DS, it's obvious they have Active Directory integrated applications. Some of those may use it just for LDAP authentication, while some may use advanced integration with a modified Active Directory schema. With Active Directory migration, some of these applications may require modifications or upgrades to match the new AD DS version.

Therefore, before the implementation process, it is important to recognize these Active Directory integrated applications and evaluate their impact on the migration:

- **LDAP connection string modifications**: In order to use **single sign-on** (**SSO**) with applications, it may use LDAP connections to the domain controllers. Sometimes, applications use hardcoded hostnames or the IP addresses of domain controllers to define the connections. If domain migration involves IP address changes and hostname changes, alternation between these records will need to be planned.

- **Schema version changes**: Some legacy applications only support certain versions of the Active Directory schema. This is specific to custom-made Active Directory-integrated applications. This is very rare, but I have faced these issues in my Active Directory migration projects. Therefore, if it's not a well-known application, check whether it supports the new AD DS schema version with the application vendor.

- **Application migrations**: Some organizations have legacy application versions that are no longer supported or developed by their vendors. Once, I was working on an AD DS 2003 to AD DS 2012 R2 migration project. The organization had a legacy application that ran on the Windows Server 2000 system. AD DS 2012 R2 doesn't support Windows Server 2000-member servers. The vendor who created the application was no longer in business. As a result, we had to migrate users to a similar type of application that supported the new OSes before we started with the actual Active Directory migrations.

- **Server roles/applications installed on domain controllers**: In the majority of cases, once the FSMO roles are migrated to new domain controllers, the old domain controllers are decommissioned. Even though Microsoft recommends that you don't install applications or other server roles in domain controllers, people still do it. Some of the common roles that are installed in domain controllers are DHCP, RADIUS, and licensing servers.

If existing domain controllers are subject to decommissioning, these applications and server roles need to migrate to new servers. Some of these roles or application versions may not be on the market anymore. For example, the Windows **Internet Authentication Service (IAS)** in Windows Server 2003 was replaced by the **Network Policy Server (NPS)** in Windows Server 2008. If you cannot use the same versions in migration, you will need to plan for upgrades or replace it with an equivalent application.

Planning

After a successful auditing phase, we have a lot of data and insight about the existing Active Directory infrastructure. In the planning process, I usually reevaluate the collected data and make a blueprint to follow in the implementation process. This can be presented as a document so that each party that's involved in the project is aware of it.

The following information needs to be covered in the plan:

Data	Description
Overview of the existing AD DS infrastructure	Based on the data that was collected from the audit, you need to provide an overview of the existing infrastructure. This should include information about the logical and physical topology of Active Directory.
Overview of the proposed solution	Based on the data that was collected from the audit and business requirements, we can provide a detailed design of the proposed solution. This should include data about the topology changes, new domain controller placements, FSMO role placements, new site links, IP addresses, hostnames, required hardware or virtual machine resources, required firewall rule changes, and more.
Risks	One main objective of the audit exercise is to identify the potential risks that can impact the AD DS migration. These can be due to wrong design, the bad health of the Active Directory services, or other infrastructure or application issues. The recognized risks can be categorized based on impact (for example, high, medium, and low).
Risk mitigation plan	Once the risks have been identified, we need to provide a plan to describe what action can be taken to address them. If possible, include a task list, estimated time frame, and budget in the plan.

Service interruptions	During the implementation process, there can be service interruptions. This can be due to events such as application migrations or server IP changes. In this section, make a list of these service interruptions, along with the expected time range, so that the relevant parties can be informed prior to the migration process.
Recommendations	During the audit process, you may have found things that you could do to improve AD DS performance, security, or manageability. What wasn't covered in the initial business requirements can be listed as recommendations. Note that these shouldn't make any direct impact on the AD DS migration process. If this is done, it should be listed in the proposed solution section.
Task list and schedule	The plan should have a detailed task list and schedule for the AD DS migration implementation process. It should also include roles and responsibilities for completing each task.
Test plan	It is also required that you have a detailed test plan in order to test the Active Directory functions after the AD DS migration process so that you can verify its health and integrity. This must be used during the implementation process and should include evidence to prove the successful completion of each test (such as screenshots, events, reports, and more).
Recovery plan	After a successful audit and planning process, there is a very low possibility of project failure. However, the plan still needs to provide a recovery plan that will be used in the event of a failure. It also should include a process for testing the existing DR or backup solution that will be used in the recovery, prior to starting the project.

Once the plan has been produced, explain it to everyone involved in the project. You will need to explain their roles and responsibilities in the project. You also need to get the plan approved by the management before implementation.

Implementation

After a successful audit and planning process, the next step is to perform the implementation. If you did your homework correctly in the previous phases, this process will be straightforward and will end with a successful result.

Active Directory migration checklist

Based on the previous phases, I have created the following checklist that you can use for the Active Directory migration process:

- Evaluate the business requirements for Active Directory migration.
- Perform an audit on the existing Active Directory infrastructure.
- Provide an implementation plan.
- Prepare the physical/virtual resources for the domain controller.
- Install Windows Server 2016 Standard/Datacenter.
- Patch the servers with the latest Windows updates.
- Assign a dedicated IP address to the domain controller.
- Install the AD DS role.
- Migrate the application and server roles from the existing domain controllers.
- Migrate the FSMO roles to the new domain controllers.
- Add new domain controllers to the existing monitoring system.
- Add new domain controllers to the existing DR solution.
- Decommission the old domain controllers (all).
- Raise the domain and forest functional levels.
- Perform ongoing maintenance (Group Policy review, new-feature implementations, identifying and fixing Active Directory infrastructure issues, and more).

As part of this exercise, I am going to demonstrate how to perform migration from AD DS 2012 R2 to AD DS 2016.

Design topology

As per the following diagram, the `rebeladmin.com` domain has two domain controllers:

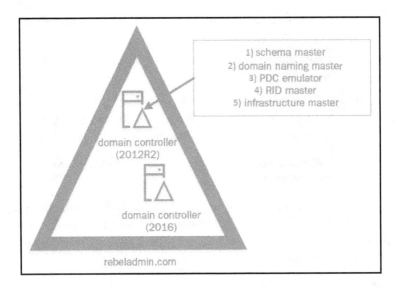

The FSMO role holder is running a domain controller based on Windows Server 2012 R2. The domain and forest functional levels currently operate in Windows Server 2012 R2. A new domain controller with Windows Server 2016 will be introduced and will be the new FSMO role holder for the domain. Once the FSMO role migration is complete, the domain controller running Windows Server 2012 R2 will be decommissioned. After that, the forest and domain function levels will be raised to Windows Server 2016.

Here, `REBEL-WIN-DC01` is the domain controller with Windows Server 2012 R2, while `REBEL-SDC01` is the domain controller with Windows Server 2016.

 When you introduce new domain controllers to an existing infrastructure, it is recommended that you introduce the forest root level first and then go to the domain tree levels.

Installation steps

Using the following steps, we can install the new domain controller and migrate FSMO roles to it:

1. Log in to the server as a member of the local administrator's group.
2. Add the server to the existing domain as a member.
3. Log in to the domain controller as an Enterprise Admin.
4. Verify the static IP address' allocation by using `ipconfig /all`.
5. Launch the PowerShell console as an administrator.
6. Before the configuration process, we need to install the AD DS role in the given server. In order to do that, we can use the following command:

   ```
   Install-WindowsFeature -Name AD-Domain-Services
   -IncludeManagementTools
   ```

7. Configure the new server as an additional domain controller (these steps were covered under *Setting up an additional domain controller* section).
8. Migrate all five FSMO roles to the new domain controller by using the following command:

   ```
   Move-ADDirectoryServerOperationMasterRole -Identity
   REBEL-SDC01 -OperationMasterRole SchemaMaster,
   DomainNamingMaster, PDCEmulator, RIDMaster,
   InfrastructureMaster
   ```

   In the preceding command, `REBEL-SDC01` is the domain controller running Windows Server 2016.

9. Once we're done, we can verify the new FSMO role holder using the following command:

   ```
   netdom query fsmo
   ```

10. The next step is to decommission the old Windows domain controllers running on Windows Server 2012 R2. To do that, execute the following command as an Enterprise Admin from the relevant domain controller:

    ```
    Uninstall-ADDSDomainController -DemoteOperationMasterRole
    -RemoveApplicationPartition
    ```

11. After executing the preceding command, you will be asked to define a password for the local administrator account:

```
Administrator: Windows PowerShell                                    _ □ X
Windows PowerShell
Copyright (C) 2013 Microsoft Corporation. All rights reserved.

PS C:\Users\Administrator> Uninstall-ADDSDomainController -DemoteOperationMasterRole -RemoveApplicationPartition
LocalAdministratorPassword: *********_
```

Once this has been completed, new server will be a member server of the `rebeladmin.com` domain.

12. The next step is to raise the domain and forest functional levels to Windows Server 2016. To do that, you can use the following commands. To upgrade domain functional levels, use the following command:

```
Set-ADDomainMode -identity rebeladmin.com
 -DomainMode Windows2016Domain
```

To upgrade forest functional levels, use the following command:

```
Set-ADForestMode -Identity rebeladmin.com
 -ForestMode Windows2016Forest
```

Now, we have completed the migration from AD DS 2012 R2 to AD DS 2016. The same steps apply when you're migrating from Windows Server 2008, Windows Server 2008 R2, and Windows Server 2012.

Verification

Although the migration is complete, we still need to verify whether it's completed successfully. The following command will show the current domain functional level of the domain after the migration:

```
Get-ADDomain | fl Name,DomainMode
```

The following command will show the current forest functional level of the domain after migration:

```
Get-ADForest | fl Name,ForestMode
```

You can also use the following command to verify the forest & domain functional level updates:

```
Get-EventLog -LogName 'Directory Service' | where {$_.eventID -eq 2039
-or $_.eventID -eq 2040} | Format-List
```

The following screenshot shows events `2039` and `2040` in the `Directory Service` log, which verify the forest and domain functional level updates:

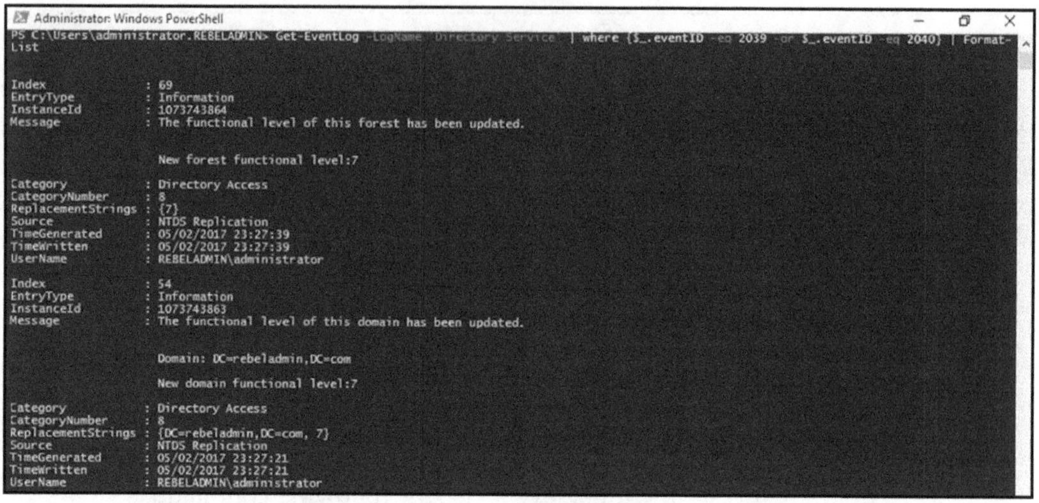

Event ID `1458` verifies the transfer of the FSMO roles:

```
Get-EventLog -LogName 'Directory Service' | where {$_.eventID -eq
1458} | Format-List
```

You can use the following command to verify the list of domain controllers and make sure that the old domain controller is gone:

```
Get-ADDomainController -Filter * | Format-Table Name, IPv4Address
```

Apart from these, you can also go through the directory service and DNS logs to see whether any issues have been recorded.

Maintenance

I am a petrol head; I love the smell of burning fuel. I always service my car at the right time, wash it regularly, put in the best oil, and do all the tune-ups when required. Because of that, my little beast never gets me into trouble when I'm on the go – touch wood!

Likewise, it doesn't matter how good your Active Directory infrastructure is today; if you don't maintain and tune it, you aren't going to get much out of it. Here, I have listed things you need to do after Active Directory migration to get the most out of it:

- **Add to the monitoring system**: The new domain controllers now hold the responsibilities of your identity infrastructure. It is important to be notified if a part of the hardware or system service has failed that will affect company operations. For that task, I prefer to use an advanced application layer monitoring system, such as SCOM or OMS, which not only alerts you about service and system failures, but also predicts issues in advance and allows engineers to rectify them. OMS also provides guidance based on Microsoft's best practices to improve performance and security in the identity infrastructure.

- **Add to the DR solution**: In the event of a hardware failure or natural disaster, the company should be able to recover its workloads to continue its operations. There are many different solutions out there that we can use as DR solutions for an AD environment. My preference for this is to keep additional domain controllers in DR sites, along with a backup. In a disaster, this will allow other applications to continue their operations with minimum impact. Once you add new domain controllers to the backup or DR solution, make sure to test them periodically to verify their validity.

- **Implement new features**: Once the domain and forest functional levels have been updated, you can start using the new features of AD DS 2016, which I described in `Chapter 2`, *Active Directory Domain Services 2016*. Applying new features is one of the main objectives of any AD DS migration project. When you're applying features, try to apply them to test devices or a group of test users first before applying them organization-wide. This will minimize their impact if you need to alter or completely remove them. The features you can use for your organization depend on the organization's business model and operations.

- **Group Policy reviews**: Group policies can be used to manage systems, application and security settings for users, devices, and other resources in the Active Directory infrastructure. As the system migrates from one AD DS version to another, Group Policy capabilities change too. In an infrastructure, there can be group policies that contain legacy settings that are no longer valid for the organization's operations. Otherwise, the newer AD DS version may have a *better way* of doing things. Therefore, after AD DS migrations, review your group policies and make any required amendments or implementations. For Group Policy testing, always try it against a test group and test devices before applying it to production.

- **Documentation**: Documentation is required for any system implementation. Once the migration process is complete, prepare a document that includes data about the design, implementation steps, configuration changes, test results, the resources that have been used, Group Policy changes, new feature configurations, and more. It will be a good starting point for engineers and management so that they can plan future AD DS migrations. It will also help engineers when they do system troubleshooting.

Summary

The first few chapters of this book were focused on understanding AD DS and its capabilities. This chapter is different from those as it is more focused on the *implementation* of AD DS. In the first part of this chapter, we learned about the implementation of domain controllers in different scenarios. The second part of this chapter was focused on AD DS migration from an older version of AD DS to AD DS 2016. Here, we learned how to plan AD migration properly. As part of this learning experience, we looked at how to perform Active Directory health checks, application audits, information gathering, and AD design reviews. Last but not least, we learned how to migrate from AD DS 2012 R2 to AD DS 2016.

In the next chapter, we are going to learn about managing Active Directory objects.

Section 2: Active Directory Administration

In an Active Directory environment, we use objects and attributes to represent users, teams, roles, and devices. In this section, we are going to take a detailed look at different object types and how to manage them using different tools. When the number of objects grows in Active Directory, we need a way to group similar types of objects together (based on role or operation requirements). This will make it easier for engineers to manage them. In an Active Directory environment, we can do this by using groups and organization units. You will learn about both of these methods through the chapters in this section.

In an organization, we use policies to standardize the operations and state of assets. Similarly, we use group policies in an Active Directory environment to standardize the state of objects, environments, and the use of resources. In this section of the book, we will also go through group policy capabilities and management in detail.

This section contains the following chapters:

- Chapter 7, *Managing Active Directory Objects*
- Chapter 8, *Managing Users, Groups, and Devices*
- Chapter 9, *Designing the OU Structure*
- Chapter 10, *Managing Group Policies*

7
Managing Active Directory Objects

I started my career as a web developer. I still remember my first day at work. It was at a software development company with 20 engineers. I didn't know anything about **Active Directory** (**AD**) back then as I was too focused on being a software engineer. So, I turned on the computer and typed in my username and password to log in. Then, it said I needed to set a new password. I typed the most complex password I could think of. After that, I logged in and started working. It was a pretty busy morning, learning new things. After a quick break in the late afternoon, I came back to my seat to continue my work. I typed my complex password to log in but failed. I tried it again but had the same result. I kept on trying, and after a few attempts came the famous account lockout message. I walked into the server room and mentioned my account situation to the administrator. He gave me the typical admin look and opened up a type of console on his screen. Then, he expanded some folders in a folder tree and selected something that had my name on it. After a few clicks, he opened a small box and asked me to type in a new password. What magic! After a few years (when I changed careers), I realized that was the **Active Directory Users and Computers** (**ADUC**) **Microsoft Management Console** (**MMC**), which can manage AD objects. I am sure all of you felt a similar sense of excitement when you saw this AD console for the first time. It is impossible to explain AD without these tools, which manage AD objects as visual components of the AD infrastructure.

As explained in `Chapter 1`, *Active Directory Fundamentals*, the things we need to represent in AD are created and saved as objects. These can be users, computers, printers, or groups. Attributes are used to describe these objects. It's similar to the way we use characteristics to describe a person or things. There are different tools and methods we can use to add, modify, or remove objects from the AD database.

AD object management is one of the basic skills requirements for AD administrations. Adding/removing objects and modifying attributes of objects are tasks that engineers work on more often than other AD administration tasks. If you are already working on an AD environment, you may be already using the methods described here for AD object management, but going through this chapter, you will learn different tools and techniques you can use to improve the AD object management experience.

In this chapter, we will cover the following:

- Tools and methods for managing AD objects
- Creating, modifying, and removing objects in AD
- Finding objects in AD

Tools and methods for managing objects

There are different tools and methods we can use to manage AD objects. When you install AD DS on a server, it will also enable access to these management tools. There are other third-party vendors who build AD management tools as well. But in this chapter, we will only be using built-in tools on Windows Server systems.

 Windows Admin Center is the latest Microsoft server management tool. This is the recommended management tool from Windows Server 2019. It is a web-based management tool. It can be installed in a separate server and can be used to manage multiple systems. It also has AD management capabilities similar to its predecessor, Server Manager. More information about Windows Admin Center is available at `https://docs.microsoft.com/en-us/windows-server/manage/windows-admin-center/overview`.

Active Directory Administrative Center

The ADUC MMC is the most commonly used tool to manage AD environments. This tool has been built into the system since early versions of AD and has continued to the latest. With AD DS 2008 R2, Microsoft introduced the **Active Directory Administrative Center** (**ADAC**), which is a built-in PowerShell command-line interface technology. It provides an enhanced GUI that can be used to manage AD objects in an efficient way. With AD DS 2012, Microsoft introduced the PowerShell History Viewer, which helps administrators to learn about PowerShell commands associated with AD objects. I do not see a majority of engineers use this interface compared to the ADUC MMC. This tool comes with the AD DS role. Once you complete the role installation, it will be available for operations without any additional configuration.

To access the ADAC console, you can type `dsac.exe` in a PowerShell command line or the **Run** box:

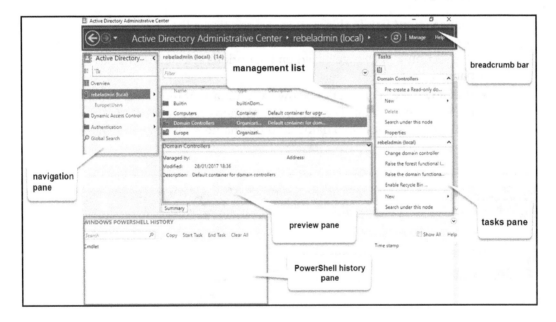

The preceding screenshot shows the default interface for ADAC and its components, which can be used to manage AD objects:

- **Breadcrumb bar**: This can be used to navigate to different containers directly. In order to navigate to a specific container, you need to use its distinguished name. It can also be used the other way round, to find out the distinguished name of a container:

Using the **Manage** option allows us to add navigation nodes to the navigation pane. Basically, it's similar to adding a shortcut to specific containers.

- **Management list**: In this section, we can find a list of containers, objects contained in the containers, object search results, and more. Data display in this section will change based on the options selected in the navigation pane.

- **Preview pane**: This section shows a summary of the object you selected in the management list. The summary contains certain attribute values, such as the description, DNS name, and username, as well as the time the object was modified:

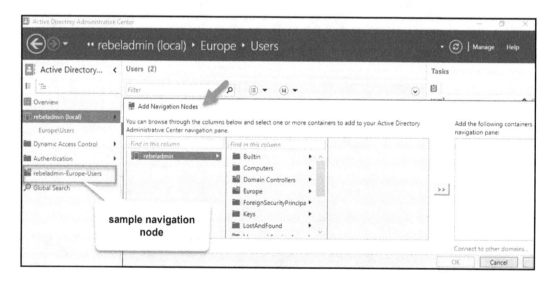

- **Navigation pane**: This is similar to the navigation pane in the ADUC MMC. By using it, you can navigate to different containers in your domain. This can also be used to upgrade the domain and forest functional levels and enable the AD recycle bin. Using the navigation pane, we can add objects such as **User**, **Group**, **Organizational Unit**, or **Computer** to the directory:

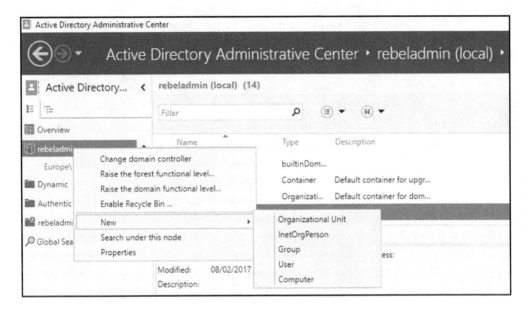

The navigation pane also lists the **Global Search** option, which can be used to locate AD objects in the directory. Once the search returns an object, it also provides options to perform administrative tasks:

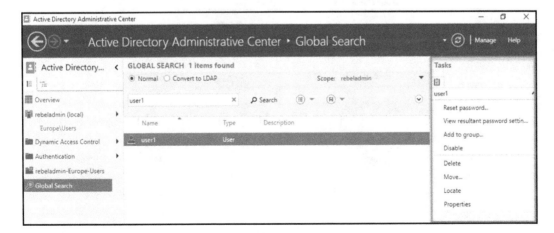

- **Tasks pane**: The tasks pane lists down the administrative tasks associated with the objects you select, such as moving objects, password resets, properties, and deletion. The list of administrative tasks will change based on the object type.

- **PowerShell history pane**: ADAC is built based on PowerShell command-line interface technology, so each and every task performed in ADAC is executed as a PowerShell command. In this pane, it will list all executed PowerShell commands. Engineers can copy these commands and reuse or develop them further to manage AD objects via PowerShell directly. It also allows us to search for commands, if required.

When you open ADAC for the first time, you will not see the PowerShell history pane in expanded mode, as shown in the following screenshot. You need to click on the **WINDOWS POWERSHELL HISTORY** bar to expand it:

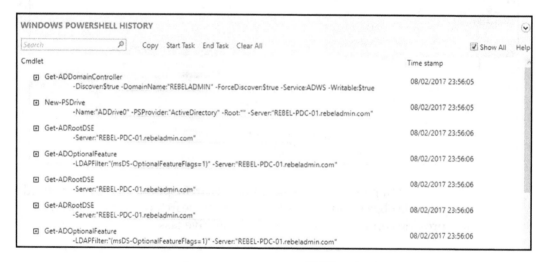

ADAC also allows us to manage objects from other domains. It can also be opened using **Server Manager** | **Tools** | **Active Directory Administrative Center**. If domains have one-way or two-way trust between them, it will allow us to add them to the same ADAC console. In order to do that, you need to go to the breadcrumb bar and click on **Manage** | **Add Navigation Nodes**, and then click on **Connect to other domains...** in the window:

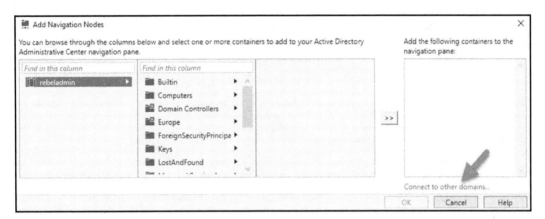

Another advantage of ADAC is the advanced object property window. If you've used the ADUC MMC before, you may already know that, in order to view an object's properties, we need to go through lots of different tabs. But with the ADAC advanced object properties window, we can view a lot of data in one window. If required, you can easily navigate to different sections.

Using the same window, you can run administrative tasks related to the objects. Not only that, it also allows us to modify the sections in the properties page as we want:

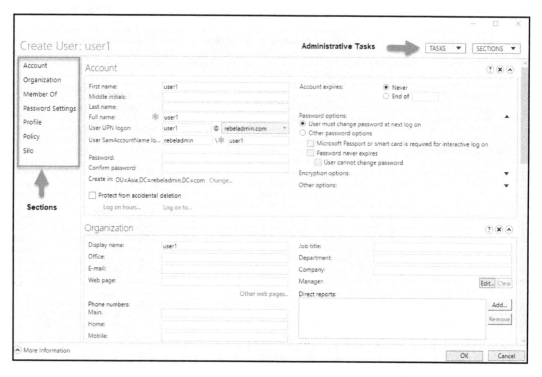

ADAC capabilities can be summarized as follows:

- Creating users, groups, computer accounts, and **organizational units (OUs)**
- Managing users, groups, computer accounts, and OUs
- Removing users, groups, computer accounts, and OUs
- Managing AD objects from other trusted domains
- Filtering AD objects using queries

The ADUC MMC

The ADUC MMC is the most commonly used tool to manage AD objects. This tool is available from AD DS 2000 onward and, over the years, hasn't changed much in terms of its look and feel. This MMC comes with the AD DS role, and it can also be installed using **Remote Server Administration Tools** (**RSAT**) on domain-joined computers.

It can be opened using dsa.msc in PowerShell Command Prompt or the **Run** box from the Start menu:

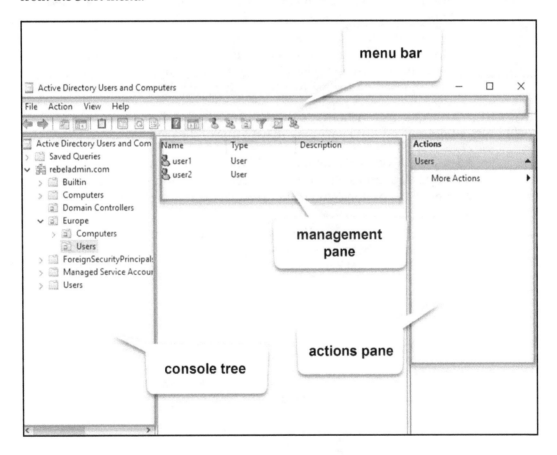

Let's go through the main sections of the console:

- **Menu bar**: This contains menus with different options. Most of the options mentioned in the menus can also be executed using icons beneath the menu bar or actions pane.
- **Console tree**: The console tree lists the structure of AD components and helps us to navigate through containers and find objects.
- **Management pane**: This displays the objects inside the selected container in the console tree. It can display different objects' **Type**, such as **User**, **Group**, and **Device**. The content will change depending on the selected container.
- **Actions pane**: The **Actions** pane contains the administrative tasks related to selected AD objects. As an example, if a user object is selected, the actions pane will list administrative tasks, such as moving the object, deleting it, resetting the password, and disabling the account.

We won't be looking at its functions too much here as it's the most commonly used tool by any administrator. But I am going to list some of the main features:

- **Advanced features**: By default, the MMC will not list all of the containers and object properties related to advanced system administration. In order to access these options, you need to enable them using **View** | **Advanced Features**.
- **Saved queries**: Using the MMC, we can create custom queries to filter AD objects and save these queries to rerun at a later time. This saves time as administrators do not need to spend time navigating through containers to find objects.

To create a query, right-click on **Saved Queries** and select **New Query**. In this window, we can build a query using the **Define Query...** option:

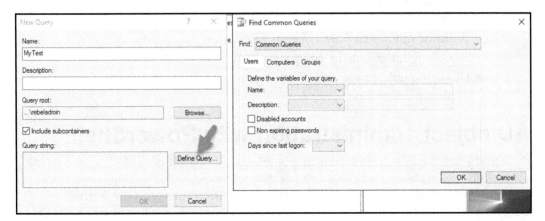

- **Access different domains**: If a domain has relationships of trust with other domains, the same console can be used to access them and manage the objects:

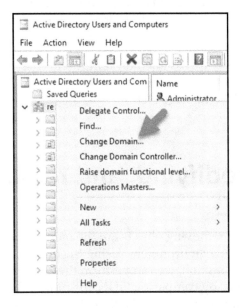

The capabilities of the ADUC MMC can be summarized as follows:

- Adding, editing, and removing users, groups, computers, and OUs
- Managing objects in different domains (needs two-way or one-way trust)
- Building queries to filter objects
- Searching for objects in directories
- Changing object properties

AD object administration with PowerShell

By introducing the PowerShell scripting language, Microsoft provided more control over Windows' system functions and operations. PowerShell also allows engineers to use extra features that cannot be used via GUI. AD DS comes with the **Active Directory Module for Windows PowerShell**, which can be used to manage AD DS, **Active Directory Lightweight Directory Services** (**AD LDS**), and objects. AD objects can still be managed using Command Prompt, but PowerShell provides advanced, centralized control over AD components and services.

Any server that runs AD DS or AD LDS role services has the AD PowerShell module by default. It can also be enabled on a desktop computer or member server by installing RSAT.

If RSAT tools are installed on computers running PowerShell 2, you need to run `Import-Module ActiveDirectory` before using commands to manage AD.

Creating, modifying, and removing objects in AD

Creating, modifying, and removing objects are the most commonly performed management tasks in an AD environment. Using the different tools and methods described in the previous section, we can perform these tasks. Each tool and method has its own pros and cons. By comparing GUI capabilities, the complexity of performing an administrative task, and the time it takes to execute a task, you can choose the tool that is best for you. My recommendation is to use a mix of tools as not every tool is good for every administrative task.

Creating AD objects

Each and every object type has a different set of attributes. When you create objects, you need to provide values for those attributes. Some of these are mandatory and some are not. Based on the company's operations and preferences, some custom attributes may need to be added to the object types.

Creating user objects

In order to create a user object in AD, we can use the `New-ADUser` PowerShell cmdlet. You can view the full syntax of the command along with the accepted data types using the following command:

```
Get-Command New-ADUser -Syntax
```

In order to create a new user account using PowerShell, the minimum value you need to pass is `-Name`. It will create a disabled user account, and you can define values for other attributes later.

Here is an example that can be used to create a user account:

```
New-ADUser -Name "Talib Idris" -GivenName "Talib" -Surname "Idris" -
SamAccountName "tidris" -UserPrincipalName "tidris@rebeladmin.com" -
Path "OU=Users,OU=Europe,DC=rebeladmin,DC=com" -AccountPassword(Read-
Host -AsSecureString "Type Password for User") -Enabled $true
```

This command has the following parameters:

- `-Name`: This parameter defines the full name.
- `-GivenName`: This parameter defines the first name.
- `-Surname`: This parameter defines the surname.
- `-SamAccountName`: This parameter defines the username.
- `-UserPrincipalName`: This parameter defines the **User Principal Name (UPN)** for the user account.
- `-Path`: This defines the OU path. The default location is `CN=Users,DC=rebeladmin,DC=com`. If you do not define the `-Path` value, it will create the object under the default container.
- `-AccountPassword`: This will allow the user to input a password for the user, and the system will convert it into the relevant data type.
- `-Enabled`: This defines whether the user account status is enabled or disabled.

You can create a user account with the minimum attributes, such as name and UPN. Later, you can define a password and enable the account. A user account cannot be enabled without a password. To define a password, you can use the `Set-ADAccountPassword -Identity` cmdlet, and to enable an account, you can use the `Enable-ADAccount -Identity` cmdlet.

Instead of executing multiple commands to create multiple user objects, we can create a **Comma-Separated Values** (**CSV**) file that includes data for attributes and use it to create accounts in one go.

For demonstration, I am using the following CSV file:

	A	B	C	D	E	F	G		attributes
1	Name	GivenName	Surname	SamAccountName	UserPrincipalName	Path			
2	Test1 User1	Test1	User1	tuser1	tuser1@rebeladmin.com	OU=Users,OU=Europe,DC=rebeladmin,DC=com			
3	Test2 User2	Test2	User2	tuser2	tuser2@rebeladmin.com	OU=Users,OU=Europe,DC=rebeladmin,DC=com			
4	Test3 User3	Test3	User3	tuser3	tuser3@rebeladmin.com	OU=Users,OU=Europe,DC=rebeladmin,DC=com			
5	Test4 User4	Test4	User4	tuser4	tuser4@rebeladmin.com	OU=Users,OU=Europe,DC=rebeladmin,DC=com			
6	Test5 User5	Test5	User5	tuser5	tuser5@rebeladmin.com	OU=Users,OU=Europe,DC=rebeladmin,DC=com			
7	Test6 User6	Test6	User6	tuser6	tuser6@rebeladmin.com	OU=Users,OU=Europe,DC=rebeladmin,DC=com			
8	Test7 User7	Test7	User7	tuser7	tuser7@rebeladmin.com	OU=Users,OU=Europe,DC=rebeladmin,DC=com			
9	Test8 User8	Test8	User8	tuser8	tuser8@rebeladmin.com	OU=Users,OU=Europe,DC=rebeladmin,DC=com			
10	Test9 User9	Test9	User9	tuser9	tuser9@rebeladmin.com	OU=Users,OU=Europe,DC=rebeladmin,DC=com			
11	Test10 User10	Test10	User10	tuser10	tuser10@rebeladmin.com	OU=Users,OU=Europe,DC=rebeladmin,DC=com			

I have used data for some of the attributes via the CSV file, and some common values will be passed through the following script:

```
Import-Csv "C:\ADUsers.csv" | ForEach-Object {
$upn = $_.SamAccountName + "@rebeladmin.com"
New-ADUser -Name $_.Name `
 -GivenName $_."GivenName" `
 -Surname $_."Surname" `
 -SamAccountName $_."samAccountName" `
 -UserPrincipalName $upn `
 -Path $_."Path" `
 -AccountPassword (ConvertTo-SecureString "Pa$$w0rd" -AsPlainText -force) -Enabled $true
}
```

In this script, the `Import-Csv` cmdlet is used to import the CSV file that I created in the previous step. I also defined the UPN value, `-UserPrincipalName`, using `$upn = $_.SamAccountName + "@rebeladmin.com"`. At the end, I defined a common password for all of the accounts using `-AccountPassword (ConvertTo-SecureString "Toronto@1234" -AsPlainText -force)`:

By following this section, now we know how to create user objects using PowerShell. In the next section, we are going to learn how to create computer objects in AD using PowerShell and GUI tools.

Creating computer objects

When a desktop computer or member server is joined to a domain, it will create a computer object in AD.

This computer object can be created before being added to the domain. This will not add the device to the domain, but it can be used with offline domain joins and RODC domain joins.

In order to create a computer object, we can use the `New-ADComputer` cmdlet. To view the complete syntax of the command, use this:

```
Get-Command New-ADComputer -Syntax
```

The minimum attribute you need to create a computer object is `-Name`:

```
New-ADComputer -Name "REBEL-PC-01" -SamAccountName "REBEL-PC-01" -Path
"OU=Computers,OU=Europe,DC=rebeladmin,DC=com"
```

In the preceding example, the command will create the `REBEL-PC01` computer object in the OU=Computers,OU=Europe,DC=rebeladmin,DC=com OU. If you do not define the path, it will create the object under the default computer container, `CN=Computers,DC=rebeladmin,DC=com`.

We very rarely need mass computer-object creation in an organization. If it's required, we can do it using a CSV method similar to user-object creation.

I am not going to explain group object administration here, as it will be covered in detail in Chapter 8, *Managing Users, Groups, and Devices*.

User and **Computer** objects can also be created using ADAC or ADUC. In there, we have to follow a wizard to define values for attributes:

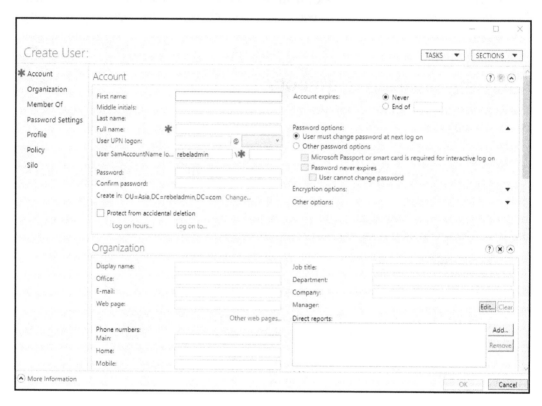

The following screenshot shows the wizard to create a **Computer** object using ADUC:

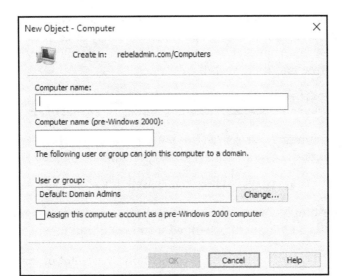

In this section, we learned how to create computer objects using different tools (ADAC, ADUC, and PowerShell). When it comes to AD object management, we also have to modify object attributes from time to time. In the next section, we are going to look into AD object modification using PowerShell.

Modifying AD objects

When we create objects, we define values for attributes. After we've created the objects, there may be situations where we need to edit the values of those attributes or add values to empty attributes.

We can use the Set-ADUser cmdlet to change and add attribute values to existing AD user objects:

```
Set-ADUser tidris -OfficePhone "0912291120" -City "London"
```

In the preceding sample command, we're adding values for the -OfficePhone and -City attributes for the tidris user.

There are occasions where you may need to change the existing value of an attribute:

```
Set-ADUser tidris -OfficePhone "0112291120"
```

In the preceding command, I'm replacing an existing value with a new one.

In the aforementioned commands, I defined the exact user account, but it's not practical if you need to do this for a large number of accounts. To do that, we need to combine the `Set-ADUser` cmdlet with the `Get-ADuser` cmdlet. It will allow us to search for objects first and then push the changes:

```
Get-ADUser -Filter * -SearchBase
'OU=Users,OU=Europe,DC=rebeladmin,DC=com' | Set-ADUser -City "London"
```

In the preceding command, we search for all of the user objects located in `OU=Users,OU=Europe,DC=rebeladmin,DC=com` and set the `City` value to `London`:

```
Get-ADUser -Filter {City -like "London"} | Set-ADUser -City "Kingston"
```

In the preceding example, I searched for all of the users in the directory who have the `City` value defined as `London` and changed it to `Kingston`.

Combining a search query with object modification saves a lot of manual work, and it's not something we can do easily using other GUI tools.

Computer object values can also be added/changed using a similar method. In order to do so, we need to use the `Set-ADComputer` cmdlet:

```
Set-ADComputer REBEL-PC-01 -Description "Sales Computer"
```

The preceding command sets the `Description` object value of the computer named `REBEL-PC-01`.

This cmdlet can also be combined with a search query using the `Get-ADComputer` cmdlet:

```
Get-ADComputer -Filter {Name -like "REBEL-PC-*"} | Set-ADComputer -
Location "M35 Building"
```

In the preceding command, it searches for computers with the name `REBEL-PC` and sets the location value to `M35 Building`.

In the ADAC and ADUC GUI tools, it's just a matter of double-clicking and editing the attribute values. This also allows us to select multiple objects and edit a particular attribute value in one go.

Removing AD objects

In order to remove AD user objects, we can use the `Remove-ADUser` cmdlet. We can find the complete syntax information using the following command:

```
Get-Command Remove-ADUser -Syntax
```

When using the cmdlet, we need to use a value for the `-Identity` parameter to specify the account. We can use a distinguished name, GUID, SID, or the `SamAccountName` value to identify the account. If it is an LDS environment, we need to define the object partition parameter too:

```
Remove-ADUser -Identity "dzhang"
```

The preceding command will remove the AD user object called `dzhang` from the directory. It will ask for confirmation before it removes the object.

This cmdlet can also be combined with the search query to find objects before removing them:

```
Get-ADUser -Filter {Name -like "Test1*"} | Remove-ADUser
```

In the preceding command, we search for the user whose name starts with `Test1` in the entire directory and then remove it.

The `Remove-ADComputer` cmdlet can be used to remove computer objects from the directory:

```
Remove-ADComputer -Identity "REBEL-PC-01"
```

The preceding command will remove the `REBEL-PC-01` computer object from the directory. We can also combine it with a search query:

```
Get-ADComputer -Filter * -SearchBase
'OU=Computers,OU=Europe,DC=rebeladmin,DC=com' | Remove-ADComputer
```

In the preceding command, we search for the computer objects in the given OU and then remove the findings from the directory.

ADAC and ADUC tools can also be used to remove objects from a directory. They can also be used with a search function to locate specific objects and then delete them.

Finding objects in AD

AD holds different types of objects in its database. The most common way to locate an object in AD is to use ADAC or ADUC and browse through the containers. As the number of objects increases, so does the difficulty of locating objects in AD. In this section, we are going to look into more efficient ways of locating objects in an AD environment.

ADAC has enhanced query and filter capabilities. Since it's used via a GUI, it helps us to retrieve results faster compared to PowerShell.

In its management list, there is a filter box in the top section (once you click on the domain name in the navigation pane). It doesn't change the view as you navigate through the containers. It helps you to filter the data displayed in the management list quickly. However, it doesn't search for objects at multiple levels (child containers):

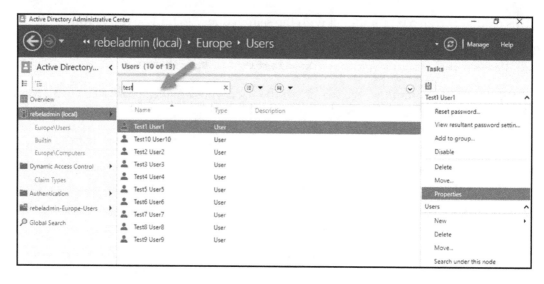

ADAC has a feature called **Global Search**, which can be used to search for objects in the entire directory. This allows a typical text-based search or advanced **Lightweight Directory Access Protocol** (**LDAP**)-based queries:

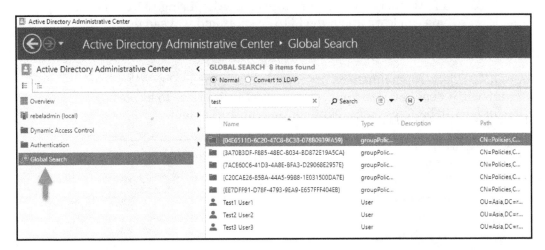

Let's now look at how to perform LDAP-based searches. The method also allows us to define the search **Scope**:

In a **Normal** search, you can use any text pattern. This can be a complete or partial value. In an LDAP search, we need to use exact syntax. Using the **Convert to LDAP** option, we can generate an LDAP query from a **Normal** search. Also, using **LDAP syntax help**, you can learn about the LDAP syntax and ways to use it.

This **Global Search** function can also be accessed from the **Overview** page.

In ADUC, object search functions are very limited compared to ADAC and PowerShell. It does have the **Find...** option, which allows us to locate objects in the directory. It can be accessed by right-clicking on any container:

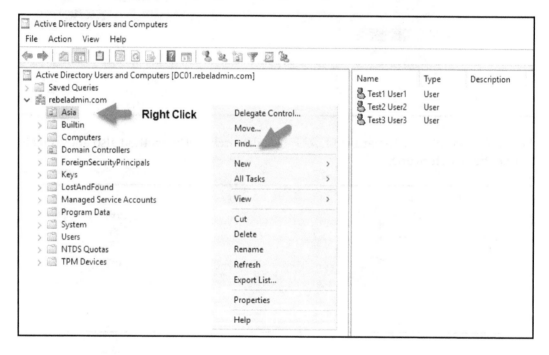

It allows us to do a text-based search as well as an advanced search based on attributes and their values. It also allows us to define the search scope:

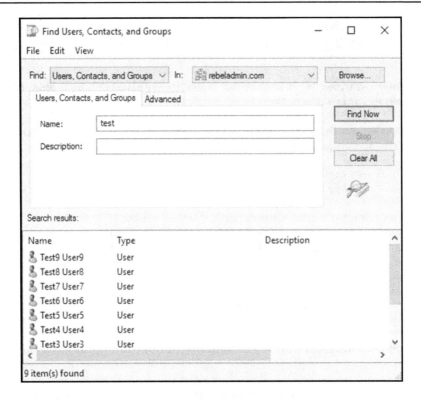

ADUC and ADAC tools are the easiest way to search for an object in AD. The PowerShell method not only allows us to search objects but also combines searching with additional tasks such as the CSV file export of search results, object value modification, and moving and removing AD objects. In the next section, we are going to learn how to find objects using PowerShell.

Finding objects using PowerShell

In the previous section, we learned about the Get-ADUser and Get-ADComputer cmdlets and how they can be used with other commands to filter out objects from AD. They can also be used to retrieve specific attribute values from filtered objects:

```
Get-ADUser -Identity user1 -Properties *
```

The preceding command will list all of the attributes and values associated with user1. This helps us to find the exact attribute names and common values, which can be used for further filtering.

I need to know the values for `Name`, `UserPrincipalName`, and `Modified` for all of the users. The following command will create a table with relevant attributes and their values:

```
Get-ADUser -Filter * -Properties Name,UserPrincipalName,Modified | ft
Name,UserPrincipalName,Modified
```

I can see some accounts in the list that are service and administrator accounts. I only want to see the accounts in the `Kingston` office:

```
Get-ADUser -Filter {City -like "Kingston"} -Properties
Name,UserPrincipalName,Modified | ft Name,UserPrincipalName,Modified
```

The preceding command filters users further based on the `City` value.

Now, I have the list of data I need, and I'd like to export it to a CSV file for future use, like so:

```
Get-ADUser -Filter {City -like "Kingston"} -Properties
Name,UserPrincipalName,Modified | select-object
Name,UserPrincipalName,Modified | Export-csv -path C:\ADUSerList.csv
```

This example demonstrates how a search query can be built up to gather the required information.

The `Search-ADAccount` cmdlet can also be used to search for AD objects based on the account and password status. The full syntax of the cmdlet can be retrieved using the following command:

```
Get-Command Search-ADAccount -Syntax
```

As an example, it can be used to filter accounts that are locked out:

```
Search-ADAccount -LockedOut | FT Name,UserPrincipalName
```

This command will list all of the locked-out accounts with a name and UPN.

Unlike the graphical tools, PowerShell queries can be built to filter exact objects and data from AD.

Summary

There are lots of different tools out there for managing AD objects. In this chapter, we looked into tools built by Microsoft for managing AD objects. Each and every tool has different characteristics, and we learned how we can use them to add, edit, and remove AD objects effectively. We also learned how we can use different tools and technologies to search for specific AD objects and attribute values.

In the next chapter, we will dive deep into AD objects and attributes, evaluating different types of objects and their roles in an AD environment.

8
Managing Users, Groups, and Devices

In the previous chapter, we learned about the main **Active Directory** (**AD**) object types and how we can add, edit, and remove them. We also learned about the different management tools that help us to do these tasks. Last but not least, we learned how we can locate AD objects or the value of an attribute when required, using different tools and methods. This chapter is an extension to that, as here we are going to talk about objects and attributes further.

The characteristics of an object are described using attributes. Some of these attributes are common across different types of objects and some are unique. If required, we can also add our own attributes. In this chapter, you will learn about object attributes and how we can manage them. You will also learn how to add custom attributes. In the previous chapter, we learned how to add/remove user objects. User objects usually represent people. But in an AD environment, we also use user objects to represent service accounts. Microsoft recommends that you use **Managed Service Accounts** (**MSAs**) and **Group Managed Service Accounts** (**gMSAs**) for services and applications instead of typical user accounts. In this chapter, you will learn about the characteristics of these different service account types and how to use them. In an AD environment, we group objects together using AD groups. These groups have different categories. In this chapter, you will learn about these different types of AD groups and how to use them effectively. Apart from users, computers, and groups, AD also supports the registration of devices such as printers as objects. Later on in this chapter, we will look into that as well. Last but not least, we will go through object management best practices, which will help you to improve your object management experience.

In this chapter, we will explore the following areas:

- Object attributes
- Different types of user accounts and their actions
- Different types of groups and their actions
- Different types of devices and other objects that can be managed via AD
- Object management best practices

Object attributes

My daughter, Selena, loves Julia Donaldson's books, especially the books about *The Gruffalo*. So, every time I take her to the library, she picks at least one of her books. Some time ago, I was reading her one of the Gruffalo series books, Th*e Gruffalo's Child*. In that book, the Gruffalo's child asks about the big bad mouse who lives in the snowy forest. The Gruffalo describes the mouse, saying he is strong, his eyes are big, his tail is very long, and he has got whiskers thicker than wires. Then, the Gruffalo's child goes out to find this mouse on a snowy night.

During his journey, he finds animals that match one or a few of the characteristics that his father had described, but none matches all of them. At the end, only a shadow of a small mouse matches the characteristics of the animal he was looking for. Not a real living creature. Transposing this idea to the world of objects, the big bad mouse is an object. The Gruffalo describes it to his kid using characteristics, which are similar to the attributes of an object. When the Gruffalo's kid goes to find it, he also finds other animals that have similar characteristics. Similarly, objects can have attributes that apply to other objects in the same class. At the end, he finds the best match for all the characteristics because some of them couldn't match with the characteristics of any other animal. Similarly, some attributes have unique values that make objects unique, even under the same class.

In the following screenshot, I have opened a user object via the **Active Directory Users and Computers (ADUC) Microsoft Management Console (MMC)**. In there, under **Attribute Editor**, we can see all the attributes associated with this object, including the values:

Using this window, we can add, edit, or remove values from some attributes. Most of these attribute names do not match with the names in the wizard you get when you create the object. As an example, the `givenName` attribute (the **Lightweight Directory Access Protocol** or **LDAP** name) maps to the first name (the display name) in the user account creation wizard.

All the user accounts in AD will have the same set of attributes. This is defined by a class in the AD schema:

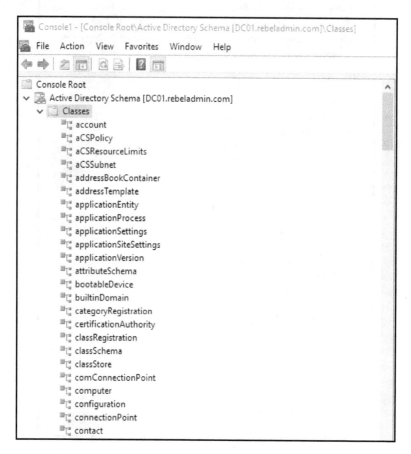

 In order to open the AD schema snap-in, you need to run the `regsvr32 schmmgmt.dll` command from the domain controller. After that, you can use MMC and add the AD schema as a snap-in.

In the preceding screenshot, I have opened an AD schema snap-in and have opened the **user** class. In order to open a snap-in, go to **Run | MMC | File | Add/Remove Snap-in**, and then select **Active Directory Schema** from the list. After that, click **Add** and then click **OK** to complete the wizard. In the object properties window, we can see the list of attributes that associate with objects under the **user** class. The same attributes can be part of different classes, too. As an example, the **mail** attribute is part of the **user** and **group** classes:

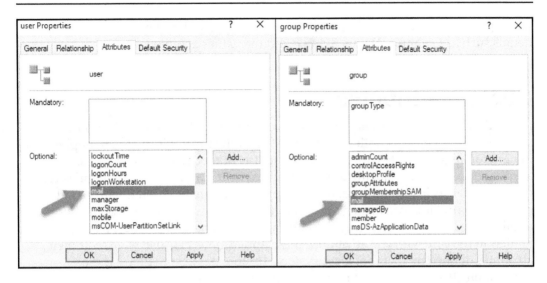

We can review the attribute details by opening attributes from the `Attributes` container:

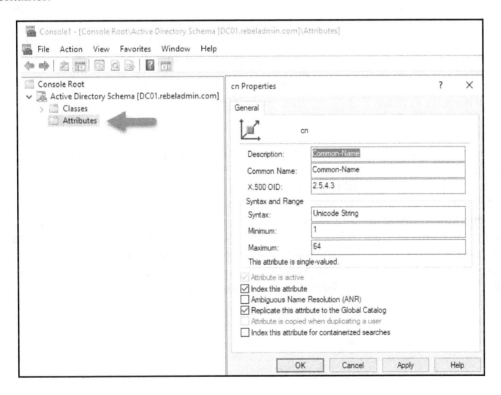

In the preceding screenshot, I opened the **cn** attribute, and in the window it shows details such as **Common Name, Syntax**, and the values accepted.

Custom attributes

In an AD schema, you are allowed to add custom attributes. In organizations, there are situations where this option is useful. Most of the time, it is related to application integration requirements with AD infrastructure. In modern infrastructures, applications are decentralizing identity management. Organizations' identities can sit on AD as well as in applications. If these applications are integrated with AD, it still provides central identity management, but that's not always the case. Some applications have their own way of handling their user accounts and privileges. Similar to the case with AD attributes, these applications can also have their own attributes defined by their database systems to store data. Sometimes, these application attributes may not match the attributes on AD.

As an example, let's assume an HR system uses employee IDs to identify employee records. But AD uses usernames to identify unique records. Each system's attributes holds some data about the objects, even if attributes are referring to the same user or device. If there is another application that requires you to retrieve data from both systems' attributes, how can we facilitate that without data duplication?

I was once working on a similar project. The customer already had an AD infrastructure in place. They were also maintaining an HR system that was not integrated with AD. They had a new requirement for an employee collaboration application, which required data to be input in a specific way. It had defined its fields in the database and we needed to match the data in the order that the fields dictated. Some of these fields required data about users that could be retrieved from AD and some of the user data could be retrieved from the HR system. Instead of using two data feeds, we decided to treat AD as the trustworthy data source for this new system. If AD needed to hold all the required data, we also needed to store the data that came from the HR system. The solution was to add custom attributes to the AD schema and associate it with the **user** class. Instead of both systems operating as data feeds, now the HR system could pass the filtered values to AD, which would export all the required data in CSV format to the application.

In order to create custom attributes, go to the **Active Directory Schema** snap-in, right-click on the `Attributes` container, and select the **Create Attribute...** option.

Then, the system will give a warning about schema object creation. Click **OK** to continue and the following screen will open:

As shown in the preceding screenshot, a form will open up and this is where you need to define the details about the custom attribute:

- **Common Name**: This is the name of the object. You can only use letters, numbers, and hyphens for the **common name (CN)**.
- **LDAP Display Name**: When an object is referring to a script, program, or command-line utility, it needs to be called using the LDAP display name instead of the CN. When you define the CN, it will automatically create an LDAP Display Name.

- **Unique X500 Object ID**: Each and every attribute in an AD schema has a unique **object ID (OID)** value. There is a script developed by Microsoft to generate these unique OID values. It can be found at `https://gallery.technet.microsoft.com/scriptcenter/Generate-an-Object-4c9be66a#content`. It includes the following script, which will generate the OID:

```
#---
$Prefix="1.2.840.113556.1.8000.2554"
$GUID=[System.Guid]::NewGuid().ToString()
$Parts=@()
$Parts+=[UInt64]::Parse($guid.SubString(0,4),
"AllowHexSpecifier")
$Parts+=[UInt64]::Parse($guid.SubString(4,4),
"AllowHexSpecifier")
$Parts+=[UInt64]::Parse($guid.SubString(9,4),
"AllowHexSpecifier")
$Parts+=[UInt64]::Parse($guid.SubString(14,4),
"AllowHexSpecifier")
$Parts+=[UInt64]::Parse($guid.SubString(19,4),
"AllowHexSpecifier")
$Parts+=[UInt64]::Parse($guid.SubString(24,6),
"AllowHexSpecifier")
$Parts+=[UInt64]::Parse($guid.SubString(30,6),
"AllowHexSpecifier")
$OID=[String]::Format("{0}.{1}.{2}.{3}.{4}.{5}.{6}.{7}",
$prefix,$Parts[0],$Parts[1],$Parts[2],$Parts[3],$Parts[4],
$Parts[5],$Parts[6])
$oid
#---
```

- **Syntax**: This defines the storage representation for the object. You are only allowed to use a syntax defined by Microsoft. One attribute can only associate with one syntax. In the following table, I have listed a few commonly used syntaxes:

Syntax	Description
Boolean	True or false
Unicode String	A large string
Numeric String	String of digits

Integer	32-bit numeric value
Large Integer	64-bit numeric value
SID	Security identifier value
Distinguished Name	String value to uniquely identify object in AD

Along with the syntax, we can also define the minimum or maximum number of values. If they're not defined, the custom attribute will take the default values.

As an example, I would like to add a new attribute called nINumber and add it to the **user** class:

As the next step, we need to add it to the **user** class. In order to do that, go to the `Classes` container, double-click on the **user** class, and click on the **Attributes** tab. In there, by clicking the **Add** button, we can browse and select the newly added attribute from the list:

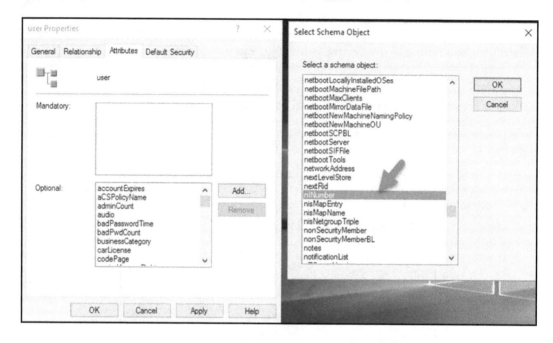

Now when we open a user account, we can see the new attribute:

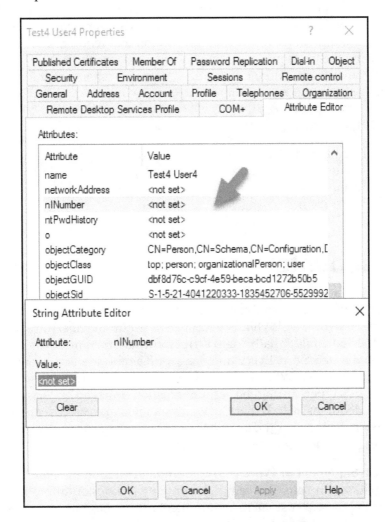

Once the data has been added, we can filter out the information as required:

```
Get-ADuser "tuser4" -Properties nINumber | ft nINumber
```

Here, we learned how to add a custom attribute manually. Sometimes, AD-integrated applications also require certain attributes to be in place in order to store additional data. This is mostly done via an automated schema extension process. Microsoft Exchange Server is a great example of an application that requires an AD schema extension. During the Exchange Server installation process, the AD schema will be extended with new classes. More information about AD schema changes for Microsoft Exchange Server can be found at `https://docs.microsoft.com/en-us/exchange/plan-and-deploy/active-directory/ad-schema-changes?view=exchserver-2016`.

 To add attributes to the schema, you need to have Schema Admin privileges or Enterprise Admin privileges. After adding new attributes, it's recommended that you reboot the system in order to reflect the new changes to the schema.

User accounts

In an AD infrastructure, what is the most common administrative task? Obviously, it's creating and managing user accounts. A user account does not only hold a username and password; it also holds data such as group memberships, the roaming profile path, the home folder path, login script information, remote dial-in permissions, and much more. Every time we set up a new account, we need to define values for these attributes. When the number of attributes increases, the number of mistakes that can happen during the account creation process also increases. An organization's identity is at stake here; even a small mistake can cost an organization a lot. As an example, if you add a user to the wrong user group accidentally, he/she will have access to some resources that they are not supposed to have.

When I create a **Statement of Work (SoW)** or implementation plan for a customer, I always start with a template. This template contains sections outlining what I need to change according to each customer's requirements, but it has lots more information that is common for all customers. When I use a template, it not only saves me time, but also eliminates any risk of mistakes that can happen during document formatting. Similarly, in an AD environment, user accounts may have common attributes and privilege levels. As an example, all users in a sales department will be members of the same security groups. They will also have the same log on scripts to map network shares. Therefore, instead of creating a sales user account from scratch, I can create a template with all the common attribute values and use it to create a new account. From Windows NT onward, Microsoft supports the creation of user account templates.

Even though there are attribute values that are common across user accounts, some attributes still need to have unique values or not a null value.

There are a few things to consider when creating user templates:

- **Do not copy user accounts as templates**: I've seen a lot of engineers just randomly select a user under the same **Organizational Unit (OU)** and use it as template for a new user account. Templates should be a baseline. Other user accounts may have some unique privileges and attribute values, even if they are all under the same OU. Therefore, always keep user account templates separate.
- **Disable accounts**: No one should use template accounts to authenticate. When creating templates, make sure to set them as disabled accounts. During the new user creation process, the status of the account can be changed.

To demonstrate, I am going to create a user template for Technical Department users. The command I will use is as follows:

```
New-ADUser -Name "_TechSupport_Template" -GivenName "_TechSupport" -
Surname "_Template" -SamAccountName "techtemplate" -UserPrincipalName
"techtemplate@rebeladmin.com" -Path "OU=Users,OU=Europe
Office,DC=rebeladmin,DC=com" -AccountPassword(Read-Host -
AsSecureString "Type Password for User") -Enabled $false
```

The preceding command creates a user account called _TechSupport_Template. It also sets the new user account as a disabled account.

I'm also going to add the account to the Technical Department security group:

```
Add-ADGroupMember "Technical Department" "techtemplate"
```

Now, when we go to ADUC, we can see the new template. In order to create a new account from it, right-click and click **Copy...**:

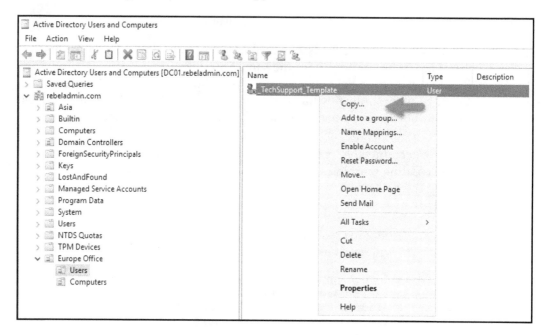

Then, go and fill the information in the wizard and complete the user account creation process.

In this section, we learned how to create user templates and how to use them in an AD environment. Adopting user templates is a great way to maintain the consistency of user permissions in an AD environment. In the next section, we are going to learn about the different types of service accounts and how we can use them correctly in an AD environment.

MSAs

Service accounts are recommended to use when installing applications or services in an infrastructure. A service account is a dedicated account with specific privileges that is used to run services, batch jobs, and management tasks. In most infrastructures, service accounts are typical user accounts with the **Password never expire** option. Since these service accounts are not used regularly, administrators have to keep track of these accounts and their credentials. I have witnessed many occasions where engineers face issues due to outdated or misplaced service account credential details. The trouble is, if you reset the password of service accounts, you will need to update the services, databases, and application settings with a new password. Apart from that, engineers also have to manage the **service principal name** (**SPN**), which helps to identify service instances uniquely.

After considering all these challenges, Microsoft has introduced MSAs with Windows Server 2008 R2. Microsoft's MSAs have the following:

- There is no more password management. MSAs use a complex and random, 240-character password that changes automatically when it reaches the domain or computer password expiry date.
- An MSA cannot be locked out or used for interactive login.
- Only one MSA can be used in one computer. It cannot be shared between multiple computers.
- An MSA provides simplified SPN management; the system will automatically change the SPN value if the `SamAccountName` details of the computer change or DNS name property changes.

In order to create an MSA, we can use the following command. I am running this from the domain controller:

```
New-ADServiceAccount -Name "MyAcc1" -RestrictToSingleComputer
```

In the preceding command, I have created a service account called `MyAcc1` and I have restricted it to one computer.

The next step is to associate the service account with the host `REBEL-SRV01` server, where I am going to use this service account:

```
Add-ADComputerServiceAccount -Identity REBEL-SRV01 -ServiceAccount
"MyAcc1"
```

The next step is to install the service account in the REBEL-SRV01 server. We need the AD PowerShell module for this. We can install it using **Remote Server Administration Tools** (**RSAT**). This can be done by running the Install-WindowsFeature RSAT-AD-Tools command. Once it's ready, run the following command:

```
Install-ADServiceAccount -Identity "MyAcc1"
```

We can test the service account using the following command:

```
Test-ADServiceAccount "MyAcc1"
```

It returns True, which means the test was successful.

From the AD server, we can verify the service account by running the following command:

```
Get-ADServiceAccount "MyAcc1"
```

 When configuring an MSA in service, be sure to leave the password empty. You do not need to define a password as the system auto generates the password.

gMSAs

In the previous section, we talked about MSAs. One MSA can be used with one computer only. But there are operational requirements that require the same service account to be shared in multiple hosts. Microsoft's **Network Load Balancing** (**NLB**) feature and **Internet Information Services** (**IIS**) server farms are good examples of this. All the hosts in these server groups are required to use the same service principal for authentication. gMSAs provide the same functionalities as MSAs, but they extend the higher AD forest level. This was first introduced with Windows Server 2012.

The gMSA has the following capabilities:

- No password management
- Supports sharing across multiple hosts
- Can be used to run scheduled tasks (MSAs do not support the running of scheduled tasks)
- Uses Microsoft's **Key Distribution Center** (**KDC**) to create and manage passwords for the gMSA

Key Distribution Service (**KDS**) was introduced with Windows Server 2012. KDS shares a secret (root key ID) among all the KDS instances in the domain. This value changes periodically. When a gMSA requires a password, a Windows Server 2012 domain controller generates a password based on a common algorithm that includes a root key ID. Then, all the hosts that share the gMSA will query from the domain controllers to retrieve the latest password.

These are the requirements for a gMSA:

- Windows Server 2012 or higher AD forest level
- Windows Server 2012 or higher domain member servers (Windows 8 or higher domain-joined computers are also supported)
- 64-bit architecture to run PowerShell commands to manage the gMSA

 gMSAs are not supported for failover clustering setups. But gMSAs are supported for services that run on failover clusters.

In order to start the configuration process, we need to create a KDS root key. This needs to be run from the domain controller with Domain Admin or Enterprise Admin privileges:

```
Add-KdsRootKey -EffectiveImmediately
```

Once this is executed, there is a default 10-hour time limit to replicate the root key to all the domain controllers and start processing gMSA requests. In a testing environment with one domain controller, you can forcibly remove this waiting time and start responding to gMSA requests immediately. This is not recommended for a production environment. We can remove the 10-hour replication time limit by using the following command:

```
Add-KdsRootKey -EffectiveTime ((get-date).addhours(-10))
```

After that, we can create the first gMSA account. I have created an AD group, IISFARM, and have added all my IIS servers to it. This farm will be using the new gMSA:

```
New-ADServiceAccount "Mygmsa1" -DNSHostName "web.rebeladmin.com"
-PrincipalsAllowedToRetrieveManagedPassword "IISFARM"
```

In the preceding command, Mygmsa1 is the service account and web.rebeladmin.com is the **fully qualified domain name** (**FQDN**) of the service. Once it's processed, we can verify the new account using the following command:

```
Get-ADServiceAccount "Mygmsa1"
```

The next step is to install Mygmsa1 on the server in the IIS farm. Mygmsa1 needs the AD PowerShell module to run. Mygmsa1 can be installed using RSAT:

```
Install-ADServiceAccount -Identity "Mygmsa1"
```

 If you created the server group recently and added the host, you need to restart the host computer to reflect the group membership. Otherwise, the aforementioned command will fail.

Once that's executed, we can test the service account by running the following command:

```
Test-ADServiceAccount " Mygmsa1"
```

Similar to the case with MSAs, when you configure a gMSA with any service, leave the password blank.

Uninstalling MSAs

You'll sometimes need to remove MSAs. This can be done by executing the following command:

```
Remove-ADServiceAccount –identity "Mygmsa1"
```

The preceding command will remove `Mygmsa1`. This applies to both types of MSAs.

Groups

In general, a **group** is a collection of individuals or resources that share the same characteristics and responsibilities. In an organization, individual identities get added and deleted, but roles and responsibilities do not change much. Therefore, the best way to manage privileges in organizations is based on roles and responsibilities rather than individuals. For example, in a sales department, salespersons will change quite often but their operational requirements will not change frequently. They all will access the same file shares, have the same permissions to the **customer relationship management** (**CRM**) application, and have the same privileges to access each other's calendars. AD groups allow you to isolate identities based on the privilege requirements.

In an AD environment, there are two categories of groups:

- **Security groups**: This type is used to assign permissions to the resources. As an example, Rebeladmin Corp. has a team of 10 salespersons. They use a shared folder called `Sales` in the file server. Everyone in the sales team has the same access permissions to it. If the permissions were managed at the user level, the **Access Control List** (**ACL**) for the `Sales` folder would have 10 entries to represent the users. If a new salesperson joins the team, their account will need to be added to the ACL and match with the permissions manually by comparison with existing users in the ACL. Since this is a manual process, there is a possibility of the wrong privileges being applied by mistake. If it's based on security groups, we can create a group for the sales department and then add that to the `Sales` folder ACL with the relevant permissions. After that, we can remove individual entries for each sales user from the ACL. Thereafter, access to the `Sales` folder will be decided based on group membership.

- **Distribution group**: This is to be used with an email system, such as Microsoft Exchange. It is used to distribute one email to a group. These groups are not security enabled, so you cannot use them to assign permissions.

Group scope

Group scope helps to define the operation boundaries within the AD forest. There are three predefined scopes to choose from when creating AD groups:

- **Domain Local**: Domain Local groups can be used to manage privileges to resources in a single domain. This doesn't mean that the group can only have members within the same domain. It can have the following types of members:
  - User accounts from any trusted domain
  - Computer accounts from any trusted domain
  - Universal groups from any trusted forest
  - Domain Local groups from the same domain
  - Global groups from any trusted domain

Domain Local group objects and their membership data will be replicated to every domain controller in the same domain.

- **Global**: Global groups can be used to manage privileges to resources in any domain under the same forest. Global groups can contain the following types of members:
  - User accounts from the same domain
  - Computer accounts from the same domain
  - Global groups from the same domain

Global group objects and membership data will be replicated to every domain controller in the same domain. This group has limited membership and no high availability as group not going to be available for other domains in the forest. This is ideal when categorizing privileges based on roles and responsibilities.

- **Universal**: Similar to Global groups, Universal groups can be used to manage privileges in any domain in the forest. However, it allows you to have members from any domain. As an example, the `rebeladmin.com` and `rebeladmin.net` domains under the same forest can have one universal group called **Sales Managers**, with members from both the domains. Then, I can use it to assign permissions to the folder in `rebeladmin.org` in the same forest. A Universal group can have the following types of members:
  - User accounts from any trusted domain
  - Computer accounts from any trusted domain
  - Global groups from any trusted domain
  - Universal groups from any domain in the same forest

Universal group objects and membership data will be replicated to all the global catalog servers. Universal groups give the flexibility to apply permissions to any resource in any domain under the same forest.

 Groups are supported to have other groups as members. These are called **nested groups**. This reduces the ACL changes further. In the preceding points, we have listed what types of groups are allowed to be added as nested groups under each scope.

Converting groups

Group scope needs to be defined during the group setup process. But with operational requirement or infrastructure changes, there can be occasions where the existing scope is not valid anymore. In such a situation, instead of setting up a new group, we can change the group scope. However, it doesn't mean you can change the existing group scope to any. There are some rules to follow. The following table explains supported ways to convert a group:

Group scope	Domain Local	Global	Universal
Domain Local	N/A	X	Yes (only if there are no other Domain Local groups as members)
Global	X	N/A	Yes (only if it's not a member of other Global groups)
Universal	Yes	Yes (only if there are no other Universal groups as members)	N/A

Setting up groups

Similar to user accounts, there are several methods we can use to create and manage groups:

- **Active Directory Administrative Center (ADAC)**
- ADUC MMC
- PowerShell cmdlets

In this section, I am going to use PowerShell cmdlets to set up and manage AD groups.

The `New-ADGroup` cmdlet can be used to add a new group to an AD environment. We can review the full syntax for the command using this:

```
Get-Command New-ADGroup -Syntax
```

As an example, I am going to create a new security group called `Sales Team`:

```
New-ADGroup -Name "Sales Team" -GroupCategory Security -GroupScope
Global -Path "OU=Users,OU=Europe,DC=rebeladmin,DC=com"
```

In the preceding command, the following is true:

- `-GroupCategory`: This defines the type of the group (security or distribution).
- `-GroupScope`: This defines the scope of the group.
- `-Path`: This defines the path for the group object. If the `-Path` option is not used, the default container will be used, `Users`.

Due to the importance of the group, I want to protect this group object from accidental deletion:

```
Get-ADGroup "Sales Team" | Set-ADObject -
ProtectedFromAccidentalDeletion:$true
```

This can also be set using the group properties window:

Now the group is ready for new members. To add new members, we can use the following:

```
Add-ADGroupMember "Sales Team" tuser3,tuser4,tuser5
```

The previous command will add the `tuser3`, `tuser4`, and `tuser5` users to the group.

If we need to remove a user from the group, we can use the following command:

```
Remove-ADGroupMember "Sales Team" tuser4
```

We can review the group properties using the `Get-ADGroup` cmdlet:

```
Get-ADGroup "Sales Team"
```

By using the following command, we can retrieve specific values from the group:

```
Get-ADGroup "Sales Team" -Properties DistinguishedName,Members | fl
DistinguishedName,Members
```

The preceding command will list the `DistinguishedName` and `Members` values of the `Sales Team` security group:

```
Administrator: Windows PowerShell                                          —    □    ×
PS C:\Users\Administrator> Get-ADGroup 'Sales Team' -Properties DistinguishedName,Members | fl DistinguishedName,Members

DistinguishedName : CN=Sales Team,OU=Users,OU=Europe,DC=rebeladmin,DC=com
Members           : {CN=Test8 User8,OU=Users,OU=Europe,DC=rebeladmin,DC=com, CN=Test7
                    User7,OU=Users,OU=Europe,DC=rebeladmin,DC=com, CN=Test5
                    User5,OU=Users,OU=Europe,DC=rebeladmin,DC=com, CN=Test4
                    User4,OU=Users,OU=Europe,DC=rebeladmin,DC=com...}

PS C:\Users\Administrator>
```

If we need to change the scope of the group, that can be done using the following command:

```
Set-ADGroup "Sales Team" -GroupScope Universal
```

This will change the group scope from `Global` to `Universal`:

```
Administrator: Windows PowerShell
Windows PowerShell
Copyright (C) Microsoft Corporation. All rights reserved.

PS C:\Users\dfrancis> Set-ADGroup "Sales Team" -GroupScope Universal
PS C:\Users\dfrancis> Get-ADGroup "Sales Team"

DistinguishedName : CN=Sales Team,DC=rebeladmin,DC=com
GroupCategory     : Security
GroupScope        : Universal   ⬅
Name              : Sales Team
ObjectClass       : group
ObjectGUID        : 4e0c7040-c4aa-48b5-808b-2e10c372f1fe
SamAccountName    : Sales Team
SID               : S-1-5-21-2210686053-2049469170-776893977-1601
```

Last but not least, a group can be removed using the `Remove-ADGroup` cmdlet:

```
Remove-ADGroup "Sales Team"
```

The preceding command will remove the `Sales Team` group.

 If you have the accidental deletion option enabled in the group, you need to remove it before executing the `Remove-ADGroup` command. Otherwise, it will fail to execute. To remove the accidental deletion option, we can use the `Get-ADGroup "Sales Team" | Set-ADObject -ProtectedFromAccidentalDeletion:$false` command.

TIP

Devices and other objects

Apart from the computers, AD supports a few other devices and object types as well. In this section, we will look into these different object types:

- **Printers**: Printers are one of the most commonly shared resources in office networks. We can use several methods to configure shared printers in user computers. We can set them up using the printer setup wizard in Windows and connect to a printer via an IP address. We can also use logon scripts to map and install printers in workstations. If an organization uses printer servers, we can connect to it and install the printers, too. In an AD environment, we can register the printer as an object in AD. This will allow the users to browse AD, find the relevant printer, and then install it to the workstation.

  To register a printer with AD, go to **Printer properties** and then to the **Sharing** tab. There you can check the **List in the directory** checkbox to list the printer on AD.

  On the workstation, during the printer setup, we need to select the option to list printers from the directory in order to see the AD-integrated printers:

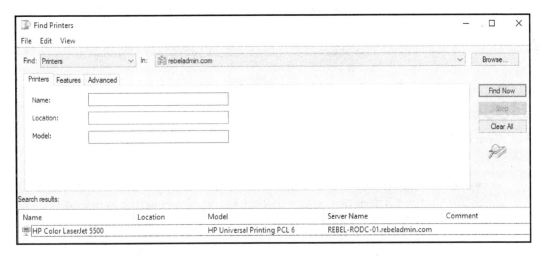

- **iNetOrgPerson**: This object is defined in RFC 2798. This object type is used by other directory services that are based on LDAP and X.500. This object type exists in AD in order to support migration from non-Microsoft directory services and to support applications that require `iNetOrgPerson` objects. This object can be converted into a regular user if required.
  In order to add this object, we can use ADAC, ADUC, or PowerShell. In PowerShell, you would use the same `New-ADUser` cmdlet:

  ```
  New-ADUser -Name "Inet User1" -GivenName "Inet"
   -Surname "User1" -SamAccountName "inetuser1"
   -UserPrincipalName "isuer1@rebeladmin.com"
   -AccountPassword (Read-Host -AsSecureString
   "Type Password for User")
   -Enabled $true -Path
  "OU=Users,OU=Europe,DC=rebeladmin,DC=com"
   -Type iNetOrgPerson
  ```

  The preceding command will add an `iNetOrgPerson` object called `Inet User1`. The only difference in the command from that for a regular AD user is `-Type iNetOrgPerson`, which defines the account type as `iNetOrgPerson`.

  We can convert the `inetOrgPerson` object to a regular AD user object using the following command:

  ```
  Set-ADUser "inetuser1" -Remove @{objectClass='inetOrgPerson'}
  ```

Best practices

Here, we will look into some of the best practices that can be used to manage AD objects:

- **Housekeeping**: It is important to review the validity of AD objects from time to time. There can be objects that are no longer active in operations. There are several ways to handle these objects:
  - If it's possible to confirm that objects are not in use for 100% of the time, objects can be completely deleted from AD.
  - If it's not possible to confirm, the object can be disabled and monitored for events. If there are no events, the object can be removed from AD.

In order to manage disabled objects, it is advised to create a different OU and move the disabled objects to that. This will allow us to keep track of them and allow easy access when required.

In AD, there can be objects that are only used for a limited time. As an example, there can be contractors who only work on certain projects. The user accounts for these contractors are only used during a project. These types of objects can be kept disabled and only enabled when required. Past employee accounts also fall into the same category.

- **Adding description**: In AD objects, there is an attribute where you can add a description about the object. It is recommended that you add a description to an object if it cannot be described with its given name. This mostly applies to service accounts and group objects. Object description allows engineers to locate an object quickly and understand the purpose of it.
- **Protecting objects from accidental deletion**: This feature was introduced with AD DS 2008. It can be enabled on user, computer, and group objects. This prevents objects from being accidentally deleted. It can be enabled at an individual object level or the OU/directory level. This feature needs to be disabled if you want to delete an object.
- **Object naming conversion**: When defining values for objects, always follow a standard. As an example, some organizations prefer to use the first few letters of the first name and last name as a username. Some may prefer the `firstname.lastname` format. These standards can differ from business to business. It is recommended to document these standards so other team members can also follow the same processes. If there is no such document, go and review similar types of objects to understand the standards being used.

Summary

In this chapter, we learned about AD objects and attributes, and how they are defined in the AD schema. We also learned how to add custom attributes to the AD schema. Then, we looked into creating user account templates and the different types of service accounts. In an AD environment, sometimes we need to manage permissions for groups of users who have similar operation requirements (to do with their department, job role, and so on). This is done using AD groups. There are different group categories to choose from. In this chapter, we also looked into these group types and learned how to use them appropriately. In this chapter, we also went through object management best practices to help improve your AD object management experience.

In the next chapter, we will be learning about designing and managing the OU.

Designing the OU Structure

9

The local library in Kingston, London has a collection of nearly 10,000 books. These books cover many different subjects. When I walk into the library, I can see that there are signs hanging from the ceiling, which help to identify the different book categories, such as novels, history, arts, technology, and cooking. So, if I know the type of book I am looking for, I can easily go to the relevant section. Each of these sections has multiple bookshelves. These bookshelves are further categorized into subcategories. At the top of each bookshelf, there is a sign describing which subcategory it belongs to. As an example, the history section has bookshelves with categories such as History of Europe, History of Asia, and World History. This makes book selection even easier—telling me exactly which bookshelves to look for. When I go to a bookshelf, the books are usually organized in alphabetical order. Each book has a small label indicating the first character of the book title. If I am looking for a book on British history, I can look at the books with a *B* label. So, out of 10,000 books, within a few minutes, I can locate a book I need. If it wasn't structured, I would have to spend hours finding books I wanted. This doesn't only benefit the members; when the library receives new books, employees know exactly where to rack those up, as there is a defined system in place for everyone to follow.

But Kingston children's library is different—children do not follow the same rules, as they are too young to understand them. Therefore, books end on up the wrong shelves.

In the main library, it is easier to locate a book than in the children's library. Just having a structured system will not result in the same output. It depends on the way the system is designed and, more importantly, the way it is maintained.

In **Active Directory** (**AD**), there can be hundreds or thousands of objects based on organization's size. Each of these objects has different operational and security requirements. We do not manage a user object in the same way as we manage computer objects. In the preceding library example, the structured environment helps library users to locate a book easily from lots of similar types of objects. It also helps the administrators to maintain the library service with integrity. In an AD environment, **Organizational Units** (**OUs**) allow engineers to categorize objects into smaller administrative boundaries based on the object class and administrative requirements.

OUs can also be used to delegate control and manage the Group Policy processing order. In this chapter, we are going to discuss these in detail. We are also going to learn about different OU design models along with their advantages and disadvantages. Last but not least, we are also going to look into OU management using PowerShell.

In this chapter, we are going to look into the following topics:

- What needs to be considered when designing the OU structure?
- How to choose the OU structure model that is required for a business
- How to manage the OU structure

OUs in operations

In Chapter 3, *Designing an Active Directory Infrastructure,* we learned how we can represent an organization based on domains. But this hierarchical design has border boundaries. There, we do not consider object class requirements. OUs help us to define the hierarchical structure for objects within the domain boundaries based on company requirements.

There are three main reasons for creating an OU:

- Organizing objects
- Delegating control
- Applying group policies

Organizing objects

An AD domain controller supports holding nearly two billion objects. As the number of objects increases in the infrastructure, the effort we need to put in to manage them also increases. If we have a proper structure to group these objects into smaller groups, then we have more control over it and we know at a glance where we can find the specific object:

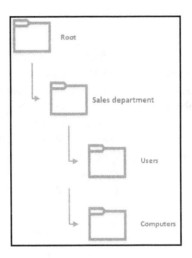

In the preceding diagram, Rebeladmin Corp. has nearly 100 salespersons. They are also using nearly 150 desktops and laptops. There is no problem putting all of those objects into the **Root** of the hierarchy (under default containers). But it will not be easy to identify **Sales department** objects from other AD objects. Instead, we can create the OU for **Sales department**. It can be further categorized into two OUs: **Users** and **Computers**. Both of these OUs will be in the same hierarchical level. Now, if we need to locate a user object in **Sales department** in AD, we definitely know it should be under the **Users** OU of the **Sales department** OU. In the same way, if we need to add a new AD object under **Sales department**, we now have a predefined structure in which we can place it. Every engineer in the IT department should follow the same structure when managing objects, and this will not change based on the individual's preferences.

Delegating control

OUs can be used to delegate administration of a set of objects to individuals or groups. These individuals will have control over managing objects in that OU, and these privileges are usually defined by the Domain Admins or Enterprise Admins. Later on in this chapter, we will look into the configuration steps.

Group policies

We cannot think of AD without group policies. Using group policies, we can apply rules to manage application settings, security settings, and system settings of AD objects. Each and every object in AD has different operation and security requirements. As an example, sales computer security requirements are different from a server that hosts the database system. Group policies can be bound to OUs. Therefore, objects that have different Group Policy requirements can be placed into different OUs and assign corresponding policies to it. Even though this is the most common reason for OUs, this is where things mostly go wrong as well. If you do not consider Group Policy inheritance and Group Policy precedence, it will be difficult to target the relevant objects:

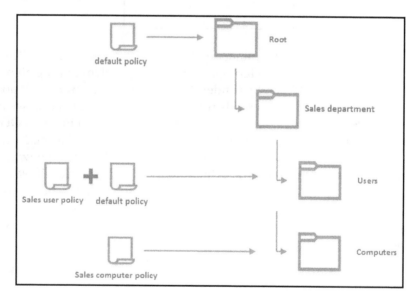

In the preceding example, the structure has a **default policy**, which applies to the majority of the objects in the AD structure. Therefore, it is created at the top of the hierarchy. It is inherited by the child OU levels by default. Therefore, the **Sales department** and **Users** under the **Sales department** will have the **default policy** inherited by default. But the organization would like to add specific sales user settings via a Group Policy. For that, a new Group Policy is created with the name **Sales user policy** and is mapped to the **Users** OU of **Sales department**. By default, the **Computers** OU under **Sales department** will also have inherited the **default policy**, but due to operational requirements, it should block that policy and should only have **Sales computer policy**, which is linked to the **Computers** OU. In order to do that, we have to block the inheritance. Once it is blocked, it will no longer apply any inherited policy from the parent OUs and will only apply the policies that are linked to the OU directly. This explains how we can use OUs to apply group policies to relevant objects.

Before we implement the OU structure, we need to decide why we need each of these OUs. This needs to be evaluated based on the preceding three points which is organizing objects, delegating control and applying group policies; if the requirement does not fall under these three points, we should not set up an OU. Most engineers do not pay attention to designing the OU structure because these structures are easy to change compared to domain structures. If the OU structure does not match your needs, it can be replaced with a completely new structure. But it is followed by moving objects and the Group Policy hierarchy restructure. Even though OUs have the flexibility to adopt structural changes, it's important to get the initial requirements correct.

Containers versus OUs

When you open the **Active Directory Users and Computers** (**ADUC**) **Microsoft Management Console** (**MMC**) with the advanced view, there will be pre-setup folders. But not all of these are OUs. They are mostly **containers**:

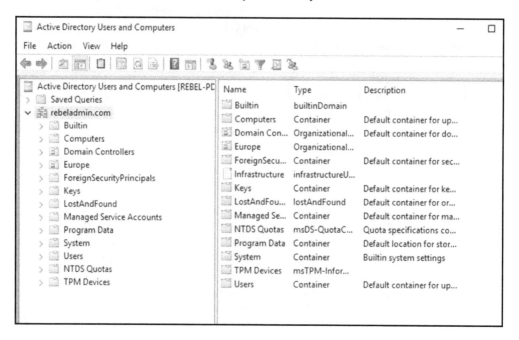

The only default OU in the AD environment is the `Domain Controllers` OU. All other folders in the tree are containers. Containers can also contain objects. The `Computers` and `Users` containers are good examples of that. By default, any computer object will be stored in the `Computers` container. All of the default user accounts and security groups are stored in the `Users` container. Similar to OUs, containers can also be used to delegate administrative control. The only difference between containers and OUs is that group policies cannot apply to containers. Group policies can be assigned only to OUs. The system also does not allow you to create new containers other than the containers that are created by the system.

OU design models

In this section, we are going to look into different OU design models. This doesn't mean every design should be one of these. Modern infrastructure requirements are complex and challenging. These models will guide you to create a design that suits your organization's requirements.

The container model

In *Containers versus OUs* section, I mentioned about default containers in AD environment. One of the characteristics of this default container is that it has large administrative boundaries. As an example, the Computers container will contain any computers added to the AD by default. It can be a physical server, virtual server, desktop computer, or laptop. The container model is based on a similar concept. This is mainly suited for small businesses where you have limited administrative and security requirements with AD objects. When OU boundaries are large, it is not possible to apply tailored group policies or precise delegated controls as each OU can contain different classes of objects:

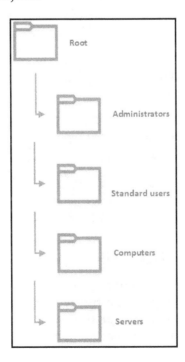

In the preceding diagram, the organization has four main OUs. In the container model, there will not be any child OUs. As we can see, each OU covers a large boundary. As an example, the **Standard users** OU will contain objects from each and every department. This is not going to apply different policies or delegate control based on each department. Here, the user object's OU will be decided based on its privileges. If a user object has administrator privileges, it will be in the **Administrators** OU, and if not, it will be in the **Standard users** OU.

The following table discusses the advantages and disadvantages of the container model:

Advantages	Disadvantages
Easy to implement: There are no child OUs and there are no granular-level security and administrative boundary designs required.	**Less control**: It will not categorize objects in detail. Therefore, administrators will have less control over the objects. Since administrative boundaries are large, it is not practical to implement delegated controls either.
Fewer group policies: When OUs contain a large number of objects from different classes, it's hard to be specific about the system or security settings. Therefore, each OU will have a smaller number of group policies. Even on those, the settings will be more high level than complex tune-ups.	**Less security**: It is difficult to apply different group policies to match the security requirements of objects and workloads as the OU structure doesn't help in grouping the relevant objects together.
Easy to change: Since each OU doesn't contain many group policies and complex inheritance, if needed, the structure can be changed completely with minimum impact.	**Less extensibility**: This is not a future-proof design. As the business grows, object management requirements will change as well. If further categorization is required, it will be difficult to implement without a complete structural change.

The object type model

As we are aware, AD contains different types of objects, such as users, groups, and computers. It is possible to group these different types of objects into separate OUs and manage them. Each of these types can be further categorized into child OUs based on geographical location or roles and responsibilities:

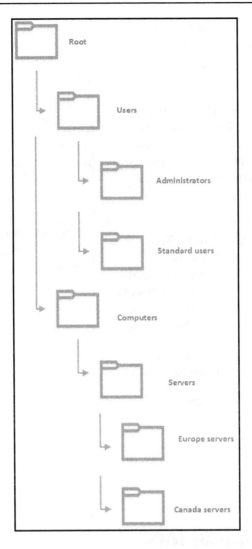

In the preceding diagram, OUs are mainly categorized based on the **Users** and **Computers** object types. The **Users** OU is further categorized into **Administrators** and **Standard users**. These were based on the privilege level and each object's responsibilities within the organization. The **Computers** OU got the child OU for **Servers**. It plays a different role than other computer objects, such as desktops/laptops. It was further categorized based on workloads' geographical locations.

The following table lists the advantages and disadvantages of the object type model:

Advantages	Disadvantages
Flexibility: It gives greater flexibility when it comes to categorizing objects. Under each object type, you can categorize objects further based on roles, responsibilities, geographical locations, teams, departments, and more.	**Complexity**: As this model gives freedom to engineers to categorize objects using many options, the structure can get complex to maintain. There is no limit to the number of levels OUs can break into, but when the number of levels increases, management gets complex too.
Easy management of AD objects: The core value behind this model is the easy manageability. That's why it can use many methods to categorize objects. When objects are categorized into small administrative boundaries, it's easy to manage the objects in every aspect.	**Structural changes are difficult**: If there is a requirement to change the structure of OUs, it will be difficult as more tailored settings and delegated controls are applied to the objects. In structural changes, these specific settings will need to move with objects as well.
Extensibility: Since the model allows you to use a large number of options for categorized objects, it has greater extensibility to implement future organizational requirements with minimum impact.	N/A
Use of group policies: More tailored group policies can be applied to objects as categorization is more granular.	N/A

The geographical model

This is one of the most commonly used model for large organizations. The OU structure will be based on the geographical location of the branch offices. Each of these branch offices may also have its own IT team. So, the main idea behind this model is to delegate administrative control:

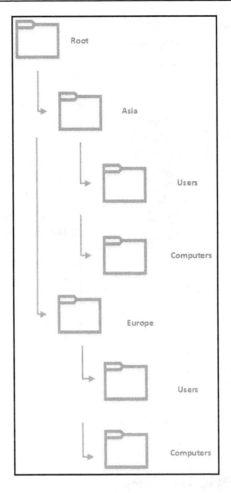

In the preceding diagram, the organization has two branches in Asia and Europe. The first level of the OUs was created based on geographical location and then it was further categorized based on the object types. **Asia** and **Europe** both have **Users** and **Computers** child OUs in their second level. In this model, on most occasions, each geographical location will follow the same structure in its child OUs. This allows you to delegate control for a group of administrators to manage branch office objects easily. This will improve infrastructure management and the productivity of IT operations.

The advantages and disadvantages of the geographical model are listed as follows:

Advantages	Disadvantages
Delegated control: As explained earlier, the core value of this model is *easy delegated control.* Each object related to each branch is located in one structure, and it provides more control for administrators to delegate control.	**Extensibility**: Limited extensibility compared to the object type model. Most of the time, each branch structure should follow predefined standards. Therefore, if structural changes are required, it will have limitations based on these standards.
Repetitive: Most of the time in this model, each branch office will have similar administrative, operational, and security requirements. Therefore, most of the Group Policy settings used in one branch will apply to another branch too.	**Operation limitations**: Each branch office IT team will have delegated control to manage the branch office's objects. But these privileges are limited. It is possible that in order to perform certain tasks, they still need to depend on the HQ IT team.
Maintaining standards: This model allows you to maintain administrative and security standards across the organization even if it has different branches. Even though branch IT teams have delegated control to perform certain tasks. privileged administrators can change or revoke these delegated controls.	N/A

The department model

Departments represent the hierarchical order of organization as well as the categorization of responsibilities. We can also use departments to categorize objects in AD environments:

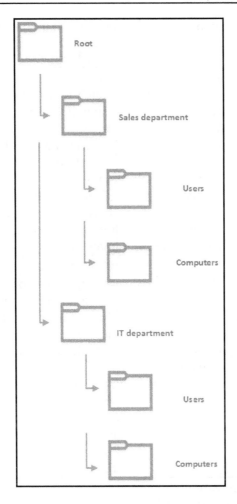

In the preceding diagram, the OU structure starts with the departments. Each department has its own OU, and its objects are further categorized based on the class and responsibilities. This allows us to delegate control to objects in each department easily. As an example, managers in each department can be set up with delegated control to add or modify objects under their own departments.

The advantages and disadvantages of the department model are listed as follows:

Advantages	Disadvantages
Distributed delegated control: Under the department, objects are grouped together based on object classes and responsibilities. This allows administrators to delegate control to individuals or groups in order to manage objects in their own department's operation boundaries. Administrators do not need to change the structure based on delegation requirements as the model will group it the way it is needed by default.	**Object locations will be difficult to match with the structure**: Not all objects can match with this structure. In organizations, there are asserts and services that are shared by different departments. As an example, printers, file servers, and mail servers are shared by all of the departments in the organization. This will need to be represented under the common OU, which is not going to match the organizational structure.
Minimum structural changes: Since the model matches the company's operational and structural designs, the changes to the OU structure will be minimal compared to other models.	**Limitation of applying company-wide settings**: In an organization, there are operational and security requirements that are not dependent on the departments. For example, an organization's data security policies, network security policies, and identity protection measures are common for every department and every user in the organization. Since objects are grouped based on department levels, we will have limitations of targeting objects to apply these different policies.
Less complex: The organization's operational structures (departments) are not complex usually. Departments have a well-defined structure to manage their asserts and responsibilities. Since the OU structure is going to be almost a replica of that model, the OU structure will also be less complex to manage.	N/A

These different types of models can be used as guidelines for designing your OU structure. Maybe none of these models match your business requirements. It is absolutely fine to create a mixed model using all of these, but make sure that you validate the design by considering easy object management, GPO requirements, and appropriate delegated control.

There is no limitation to how many sublevels OUs can have. Having more sublevels helps to categorize objects on a granular level, but at the same time, it will add to the complexity of managing the structure. This is especially effective in Group Policy management. Therefore, try to keep it under three sublevels.

Managing the OU structure

Similar to any other Active Directory object, the OU structure can be managed using **Active Directory Administrative Center** (**ADAC**), **ADUC** MMC, and PowerShell. In this section, I am going to demonstrate how to manage the OU structure using PowerShell.

Let's start this with new OU. We can use the `New-ADOrganizationalUnit` cmdlet to create a new OU. The complete syntax can be reviewed using the following command:

```
Get-Command New-ADOrganizationalUnit -Syntax
```

As the first step, I am going to create a new OU called `Asia` to represent the Asia branch:

```
New-ADOrganizationalUnit -Name "Asia" -Description "Asia Branch"
```

In the preceding command, `-Description` defines the description for the new OU. When there is no path defined, it will create the OU under the root. We can review the details of the new OU using the following command:

```
Get-ADOrganizationalUnit -Identity "OU=Asia,DC=rebeladmin,DC=com"
```

We can add/change the values of OU attributes using the following command:

```
Get-ADOrganizationalUnit -Identity "OU=Asia,DC=rebeladmin,DC=com" |
Set-ADOrganizationalUnit -ManagedBy "Asia IT Team"
```

The preceding command will set the `ManagedBy` attribute to `Asia IT Team`.

When you use the `ManagedBy` attribute, make sure that you use an existing Active Directory object for the value. It can be an individual user object or a group object. If you don't use an existing object, the command will fail.

`ProtectedFromAccidentalDeletion` for the OU object is a nice safeguard we can apply. It will prevent accidental OU object deletion. This will be applied by default if you create an OU using ADAC or ADUC:

```
Get-ADOrganizationalUnit -Identity "OU=Asia,DC=rebeladmin,DC=com" |
Set-ADOrganizationalUnit -ProtectedFromAccidentalDeletion $true
```

As the next step, I am going to create a sub-OU under the `Asia` OU called `Users`:

```
New-ADOrganizationalUnit -Name "Users" -Path
"OU=Asia,DC=rebeladmin,DC=com" -Description "Users in Asia Branch" -
ProtectedFromAccidentalDeletion $true
```

The preceding command will create an OU called `Users` under the `OU=Asia,DC=rebeladmin,DC=com` path. It is also protected from accidental deletion.

Now, we have the OU structure. The next step is to move objects to it. For that, we can use the `Move-ADObject` cmdlet:

```
Get-ADUser "tuser3" | Move-ADObject -TargetPath
"OU=Users,OU=Asia,DC=rebeladmin,DC=com"
```

The preceding command will find the `tuser3` user and move the object to `OU=Users,OU=Asia,DC=rebeladmin,DC=com`.

We can also move multiple objects to the new OU:

```
Get-ADUser -Filter 'Name -like "Test*"' -SearchBase
"OU=Users,OU=Europe,DC=rebeladmin,DC=com" | Move-ADObject -TargetPath
"OU=Users,OU=Asia,DC=rebeladmin,DC=com"
```

The preceding command will first search all of the user accounts that start with `Test` in `OU=Users,OU=Europe,DC=rebeladmin,DC=com` and then move all of the objects it found to the new OU path.

If you have `ProtectedFromAccidentalDeletion` enabled on the objects, it will not allow you to move the objects to a different OU. It needs to be disabled before the object is moved.

If we need to remove the OU object, it can be done using the `Remove-ADOrganizationalUnit` cmdlet:

```
Remove-ADOrganizationalUnit
"OU=Laptops,OU=Europe,DC=rebeladmin,DC=com"
```

The preceding command will remove the
`OU=Laptops,OU=Europe,DC=rebeladmin,DC=com` OU.

Delegating control

Administrators can delegate control based on OUs. This will provide control to individuals or groups to manage objects within OUs.

In my demonstration, I am going to provide delegated control for `Asia IT Team` members to manage objects under the `Asia` OU:

1. To do that, log in to the domain controller as the Domain Admin and open ADUC. Then, right-click on the relevant OU and click on **Delegate Control...**:

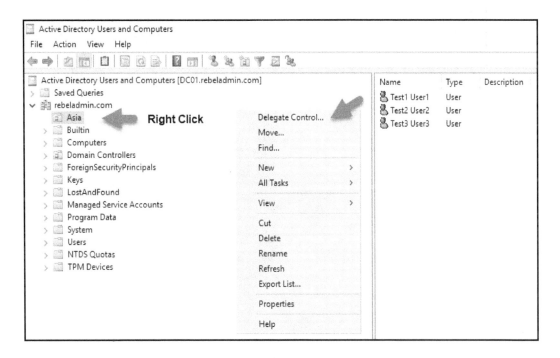

2. Then, it will open up the wizard; there, select the individuals or groups that you'd like to provide delegated controls to. In this demonstration, this is **Asia IT Team (REBELADMIN\Asia IT Team)**:

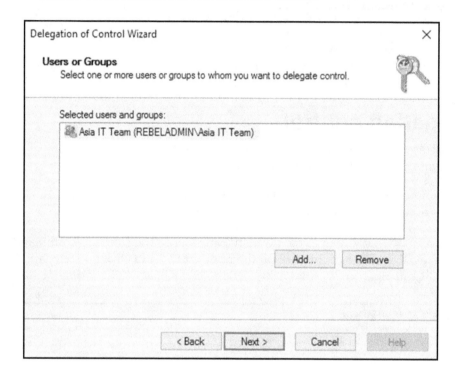

3. In the next window, the system will provide the option to select what kind of control to provide. These are sets of permissions predefined by Microsoft, and they cannot be changed. However, it provides the option to create custom tasks. After selecting the options you need, click **Next** to proceed:

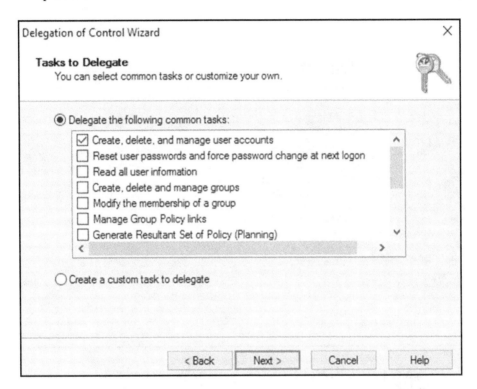

4. After the wizard completes the configuration, the team will have delegated control over the objects under `OU=Asia,DC=rebeladmin,DC=com`. We can review the delegated permission under the OU security settings:

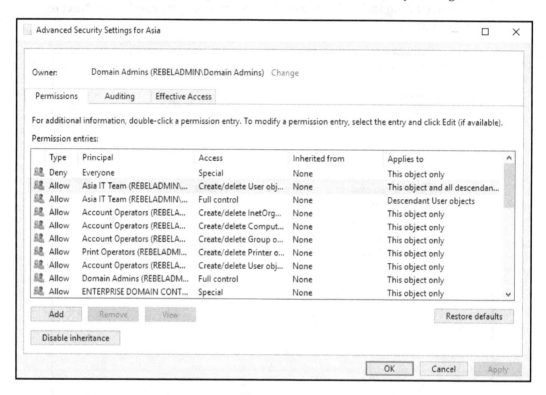

When required, delegated permission can be removed using the same window.

Summary

OUs play a crucial role in AD by allowing engineers to create a hierarchical structure within domain boundaries. This hierarchical structure should be created considering object management, delegating control, and applying group policies to manage applications, services, and security settings. In this chapter, we learned why OU design is important and what needs to be considered when designing the OU structure. After that, we moved on to different OU models that can be used as guidelines to design OU structures. By the end of the chapter, we learned how to manage OUs in the Active Directory infrastructure and how to delegate control for OUs.

In the next chapter, we will look at group policies, which are one of the core features of Active Directory.

10
Managing Group Policies

When I started preparing for this chapter, many things about this topic were going through my head because there's a lot of things to cover in just one chapter. Group policies is a broad topic to discuss, and it's possible to even write a whole book about it. It will be challenging, but I will make sure that I cover a majority of it.

My council tax increased by 8% in April, 2019. It is a rule and whether I like it or not, I have to pay it every month. If not, I will have to face the consequences. This particular rule has a clear audience: it will only apply to houses under the Kingston council. We can consider Group Policy as an authority that executes a rule or set of rules against a clearly identified audience. This is similar to the council in my example.

It is impossible to describe the benefits of **Active Directory** (**AD**) without mentioning group policies. Group policies is one of the main reasons why AD is so important in infrastructure management. Group policies are a double-edged sword. They have lots of advantages as they help to manage various types of security, application, and system settings. But at the same time, if they have not been configured or used properly, according to best practices, it can cost you a lot in many ways. Group Policy troubleshooting is one of the most common types of support calls for IT helpdesks.

That said, in this chapter, we will cover the following topics:

- Benefits of group policies
- Understanding group policies and their capabilities
- Group Policy processing
- Group Policy inheritance
- Group Policy conflicts
- Group Policy filtering
- Loopback processing
- Guidelines for using group policies appropriately in the infrastructure

Benefits of group policies

A Group Policy has two types of settings: computer settings and user settings. Depending on the requirements, rules, configurations, and scripts will fall under these two categories. These will provide non-tangible, but more valued benefits for businesses. Let's review some of these benefits in detail.

Maintaining standards

I assume most of you have heard about **International Organization for Standardization** (**ISO**) standards. They allow organizations to run their operations as per industry standards. In return, a certification will be provided to prove the organization's commitment to maintain standards. Even though organizations pass the ISO certification, the relevant authority will perform a yearly evaluation to make sure they *maintain* the standards. Most companies follow these standards throughout the year, but for some, they come to attention only when the evaluation is due. This is because the implementation of these standards is easy but maintaining them is challenging.

Our infrastructures are also subject to many standards. These standards can be based on the nature of the business, application and service best practices, business preferences, and industry standards. Defining these standards within the organization is relatively easy when compared to the efforts required to maintain them. The best way to maintain the standards is to enforce them. As an example, a common security standard for a password is to use *complex* passwords. But whenever you're asked to define a password, by nature, people go for the easiest password they can remember. But in the system, if we can *enforce* the practice of not accepting a non-complex password, users do not have a choice. They must comply with the password standards in order to define a password.

Group Policy allows us to enforce the infrastructure standards. Group Policy can be based on either user standards or computer standards. This ensures that companies will follow these standards with minimum maintenance efforts because once a policy setting is applied, the target group of users or devices will have to comply with it and are not allowed to opt out. It's almost like converting a standard into a *rule*.

Automating administration tasks

I started my career as a web developer and later moved on to system administration. My job title at that time was *associate system administrator*. One of the common service requests from the development team manager was to deploy software to the software engineer's computers. There were around 20 people in the company, and since I was a *junior* person, I always had to go and install the software on all 20 computers. It was painful, but since it was just 20 computers, it was somewhat manageable. But imagine if it was hundreds of computers; I would be spending days doing boring and repetitive tasks. From a company point of view, this is still at the cost of operations. This was just an example, but a regular helpdesk usually gets requests that are small but repetitive, such as mapping shared folders, printer installations, and customized application settings. Group policies allow engineers to automate these types of common and repetitive administration tasks. As an example, group policies can be used to push application installations, push new printer deployments, and map drives when the user logs in. This reduces the cost of operations and allows us to allocate IT resources for more important tasks.

Preventing users from changing system settings

By default, the Windows system has a software firewall to protect machines from threats, but sometimes, this prevents access to certain application traffic. Most of the time, the reaction to this will be either to disable the firewall or to allow application traffic via the custom rule. But if someone change the firewall settings without the IT team's knowledge, it can possibly put the entire infrastructure at risk. Group policies allow you to force these types of sensitive settings and prevent users from modifying them. As well as firewall settings, group policies can also be used to prevent the modification of services, prevent access to control panel features, prevent changes to applications, and much more.

Flexible targeting

At the beginning of this section, we learned about how group policies can be used to enforce standards. In a business, some of these standards apply to the entire organization, and others can be specific to departments, business units, or users/device groups. Group policies allow us to apply different policies based on AD sites, domains, organization units, or groups. As an example, devices in the IT department can have different firewall settings to the sales department.

We can create two group policies to cover the previous requirements and link them to a relevant organization unit. As well as the standards, this flexible targeting also allows us to apply different system settings for specific audiences. As an example, the sales department's map drive requirements can be different from those of the HR department. Group policies also have *item-level targeting,* which can be used to go granular in finding the exact target and applying the necessary group policies to it.

No modifications to target

Group Policy also uses the server-client architecture. AD domain controllers hold the group policies and process them on a client device's start up or a user log in. In order to apply Group Policy to a client, we do not need to do any system or profile modifications. If the target meets the Group Policy criteria, it will process the Group Policy settings. This architecture simplifies the Group Policy processing as there are fewer dependencies.

Group Policy capabilities

Group Policy can be used to perform many different tasks in an infrastructure. Here, I have listed some of these capabilities:

- Group Policy can be linked to sites, domains, and organization units. This allows us to match the Group Policy requirements with the AD structure.
- Group Policy allow us to use security filtering to target specific groups, users, or computers.
- **Windows Management Instrumentation** (**WMI**) filters are capable of filtering the AD objects based on criteria such as the OS version, roles, and system configuration. Group Policy allows us to use WMI filters for targeting.
- The **Group Policy Object** (**GPO**) status can change based on the operational requirements. If required, group policies can disable group policies completely, or disable user or computer settings individually.
- Group Policy management tasks can be delegated to individuals or groups.
- Group Policy can be used to install, redeploy, or remove programs from computers.

- Group Policy can be used to publish scripts to be executed on computer startup, or to shut down a process.
- Group Policy can be used to deploy printers to computers.
- Group Policy is capable of applying different security policies, such as password policies, lock-out policies, Kerberos policies, firewall policies, and public key policies.
- Group Policy can be used to define system audit settings and enable/manage advanced system audit capabilities, which allow you to capture more data about the roles and their activities.
- Group Policy can be used to add registry keys to systems.
- Group Policy can be used to define software restriction policies and application control policies to control the application behaviors in computer systems.
- Group Policy can be used to set up policy-based QoS rules to define **Differentiated Services Code Point** (**DSCP**) and throttle values for the outgoing network traffic. It will allow you to prioritize/manage network traffic in a system.
- Group Policy administrative templates can be used to define the registry-based policies' targeting system, applications, and service settings.
- Group Policy can be used to apply preference settings to computers and users. For example, it can be used to define mapped drives, printers, power options, Internet Explorer settings, regional settings, local users and groups, and so on.
- Using Group Policy, it is possible to manage end user roaming profile settings, including folder redirection. It will automatically save user data to a network location instead of a local computer. It allows you to access the same profile data from any workstation in the domain.

Group Policy objects

When new AD objects are added, the system saves the object data inside the AD database. But the GPO store procedure is different from the typical AD object; GPO object contents are stored in two locations (the AD database and SYSVOL folder) in the AD infrastructure.

The Group Policy container

As with any other object, the AD database also holds GPO information. This information is more related to system settings and the path reference for the other dataset. When a GPO is created, as with any other AD object, it will also have the **Globally Unique Identifier** (**GUID**) value; this is important as this value is used by both datasets to refer to each other. This value is used in the **Common Name** (**CN**) too. Before we look into datasets, we need to find the GUID value for the GPO. This can be done using the following command:

```
Get-GPO -name "Test Users"
```

The preceding PowerShell command will list the default properties of the Test Users GPO:

```
Windows PowerShell
Copyright (C) Microsoft Corporation. All rights reserved.

PS C:\Users\dfrancis> Get-GPO "Test Users"

DisplayName        : Test Users
DomainName         : rebeladmin.com
Owner              : REBELADMIN\Domain Admins
Id                 : c20cae26-85ba-44a5-9988-1e031500da7e  <---
GpoStatus          : AllSettingsEnabled
Description        :
CreationTime       : 8/3/2019 8:33:41 AM
ModificationTime   : 8/3/2019 8:33:42 AM
UserVersion        : AD Version: 0, SysVol Version: 0
ComputerVersion    : AD Version: 0, SysVol Version: 0
WmiFilter          :
```

In the preceding screenshot, the Id attribute represents the GUID value of the Test Users GPO.

Now that we have the GUID information, the next step is to review the **Group Policy Container** (**GPC**) information for the given GPO. This information can be accessed using **ADSI Edit** MMC or Ldp.exe. On this occasion, let's use Ldp.exe to review the data.

In order to open Ldp.exe, type Ldp.exe into the domain controller's **Run** box. Then, go to the **Connection** menu and select **Bind**. Select the default options if the logged in account has relevant privileges (such as schema or Enterprise Admin). In the next step, click on **Tree** under **View** and select the **DN** domain. As an example, in my demonstration, the **DN** value is DC=rebeladmin,DC=com. GPC values are located under CN=Policies,CN=System,DC=rebeladmin,DC=com:

```
⊟· CN=System,DC=rebeladmin,DC=com
    ··· CN=AdminSDHolder,CN=System,DC=rebeladmin,DC=com
    ··· CN=ComPartitions,CN=System,DC=rebeladmin,DC=com
    ··· CN=ComPartitionSets,CN=System,DC=rebeladmin,DC=com
    ··· CN=Default Domain Policy,CN=System,DC=rebeladmin,DC=com
    ··· CN=Dfs-Configuration,CN=System,DC=rebeladmin,DC=com
    ··· CN=DFSR-GlobalSettings,CN=System,DC=rebeladmin,DC=com
    ··· CN=DomainUpdates,CN=System,DC=rebeladmin,DC=com
    ··· CN=File Replication Service,CN=System,DC=rebeladmin,DC=com
    ··· CN=FileLinks,CN=System,DC=rebeladmin,DC=com
    ··· CN=IP Security,CN=System,DC=rebeladmin,DC=com
    ··· CN=Meetings,CN=System,DC=rebeladmin,DC=com
    ··· CN=MicrosoftDNS,CN=System,DC=rebeladmin,DC=com
    ··· CN=Password Settings Container,CN=System,DC=rebeladmin,DC=com
  ⊟· CN=Policies,CN=System,DC=rebeladmin,DC=com
        ··· CN={31B2F340-016D-11D2-945F-00C04FB984F9},CN=Policies,CN=System,DC=rebeladmin,DC=com
        ··· CN={6AC1786C-016F-11D2-945F-00C04fB984F9},CN=Policies,CN=System,DC=rebeladmin,DC=com
        ··· CN={7ACE60C6-41D3-4A8E-BFA3-D29068E2957E},CN=Policies,CN=System,DC=rebeladmin,DC=com
      ⊟· CN={C20CAE26-85BA-44A5-9988-1E031500DA7E},CN=Policies,CN=System,DC=rebeladmin,DC=com  ⇐
            ··· CN=Machine,CN={C20CAE26-85BA-44A5-9988-1E031500DA7E},CN=Policies,CN=System,DC=rebeladmin,DC=com
            ··· CN=User,CN={C20CAE26-85BA-44A5-9988-1E031500DA7E},CN=Policies,CN=System,DC=rebeladmin,DC=com
    ··· CN=PSPs,CN=System,DC=rebeladmin,DC=com
    ··· CN=RAS and IAS Servers Access Check,CN=System,DC=rebeladmin,DC=com
```

The policy object is further divided into two sections, which represent the computer configuration (machine) and the user configuration (user):

```
Expanding base 'CN={C20CAE26-85BA-44A5-9988-1E031500DA7E},CN=Policies,CN=System,DC=rebeladmin,DC=com'...
Getting 1 entries:
Dn: CN={C20CAE26-85BA-44A5-9988-1E031500DA7E},CN=Policies,CN=System,DC=rebeladmin,DC=com
    cn: {C20CAE26-85BA-44A5-9988-1E031500DA7E};
    displayName: Test Users;
    distinguishedName: CN={C20CAE26-85BA-44A5-9988-1E031500DA7E},CN=Policies,CN=System,DC=rebeladmin,DC=com;
    dSCorePropagationData: 0x0 = ( );
    flags: 0;
    gPCFileSysPath: \\rebeladmin.com\SysVol\rebeladmin.com\Policies\{C20CAE26-85BA-44A5-9988-1E031500DA7E};
    gPCFunctionalityVersion: 2;
    instanceType: 0x4 = ( WRITE );
    name: {C20CAE26-85BA-44A5-9988-1E031500DA7E};
    objectCategory: CN=Group-Policy-Container,CN=Schema,CN=Configuration,DC=rebeladmin,DC=com;
    objectClass (3): top; container; groupPolicyContainer;
    objectGUID: 0bdadc8e-8ae9-404c-b0ae-f701c7e79001;
    showInAdvancedViewOnly: TRUE;
    uSNChanged: 28733;
    uSNCreated: 28728;
    versionNumber: 0;
    whenChanged: 8/3/2019 8:33:42 AM Coordinated Universal Time;
    whenCreated: 8/3/2019 8:33:41 AM Coordinated Universal Time;
```

The preceding screenshot shows details about the GPO we selected, including certain attribute values:

- `displayName`: This attribute contains the name of the Group Policy, which is defined during the GPO setup process.
- `gPCFileSysPath`: This attribute value represents the path to the other dataset of the GPO. This is called the Group Policy template path. It is always under the `SYSVOL` folder.
- `gPCMachineExtensionNames`: This attribute lists all of the **client-side extensions** (**CSEs**) that need to process the GPO computer settings. These are all listed with GUIDs, and `https://blogs.technet.microsoft.com/mempson/2010/12/01/group-policy-client-side-extension-list/` can be used as a reference to most of the known CSEs.

The Group Policy template

When we looked at the Group Policy capabilities, we saw that they can be used to publish applications, run startup/shutdown scripts, and more. From the AD object's point of view, all of these settings are attributes and all of these files and scripts need to be saved in a centralized location. Instead of saving them in an AD database, the system saves all of these policy-related files and settings in the `SYSVOL` folder. The default path for the **Group Policy template** (**GPT**) data is `\\rebeladmin.com\SYSVOL\rebeladmin.com\Policies`. Here, `rebeladmin.com` can be replaced with your domain's **fully qualified domain name** (**FQDN**).

Inside the policy folder, there are two subfolders called `Machine` and `User`. These folders contain files and settings related to the GPO's computer configuration and user configuration. There is another file called `GPT.INI`, which contains the version number of the Group Policy. In every Group Policy edition, the version number will increase automatically and it will be used as a reference to sync the Group Policy changes from one domain controller to another:

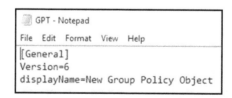

Inside the `Machine` and `User` folders, there are a number of folders that will include the data according to whichever configuration the GPO is set to perform. As an example, the `Applications` folder will contain the software installation files if the GPO is set to publish applications. The `Scripts` folder will contain any startup/shutdown scripts that are published via the GPO:

```
PS Microsoft.PowerShell.Core\FileSystem::\\rebeladmin.com\SYSVOL\rebeladmin.com\Policies\{721DA008-AB1B-4DA1-A456-5C0BED
0B45A5}\Machine> dir

    Directory: \\rebeladmin.com\SYSVOL\rebeladmin.com\Policies\{721DA008-AB1B-4DA1-A456-5C0BED0B45A5}\Machine

Mode                LastWriteTime         Length Name
----                -------------         ------ ----
d-----        25/02/2017     09:52                Applications
d-----        25/02/2017     09:53                Microsoft
d-----        25/02/2017     09:52                Scripts
-a----        25/02/2017     11:55           8046 Registry.pol

PS Microsoft.PowerShell.Core\FileSystem::\\rebeladmin.com\SYSVOL\rebeladmin.com\Policies\{721DA008-AB1B-4DA1-A456-5C0BED
0B45A5}\Machine> cd ..
PS Microsoft.PowerShell.Core\FileSystem::\\rebeladmin.com\SYSVOL\rebeladmin.com\Policies\{721DA008-AB1B-4DA1-A456-5C0BED
0B45A5}> cd User
PS Microsoft.PowerShell.Core\FileSystem::\\rebeladmin.com\SYSVOL\rebeladmin.com\Policies\{721DA008-AB1B-4DA1-A456-5C0BED
0B45A5}\User> dir

    Directory: \\rebeladmin.com\SYSVOL\rebeladmin.com\Policies\{721DA008-AB1B-4DA1-A456-5C0BED0B45A5}\User

Mode                LastWriteTime         Length Name
----                -------------         ------ ----
d-----        25/02/2017     12:35                Applications
d-----        25/02/2017     12:17                Documents & Settings
d-----        25/02/2017     12:17                Scripts
```

In order to process a Group Policy successfully, GPT data synchronization between domain controllers is crucial. `SYSVOL` replication issues will impact GPO policy processing. Before Windows Server 2008 domain services, `SYSVOL` replication used **File Replication Service (FRS)**. After AD DS 2008, this was replaced by **Distributed File System (DFS)**, which provides more efficiency and redundancy in replication.

Group Policy processing

When evaluating Group Policy requirements for an organization, we can identify some settings that are common for objects in the entire domain. But at the same time, some settings are unique to specific departments or groups. Any Group Policy that is applied at the root level will be inherited by other organization units by default. Therefore, organization units can have inherited group policies as well as directly linked group policies.

If multiple group policies are applying to an organization unit, in which order will it be processed? Will it prevent the processing of any Group Policy? If the same setting is applied to different policies, which one will be applied? To answer all of these questions, it's important to understand how Group Policy processing works.

There are two main types of policies in the AD environment:

- **Local policies**: Windows systems are supported to set up local security policies. These policies are different from domain GPOs, and they contain limited features that are more focused on security settings. These are applied to any user who logs in to the system.
- **Non-local policies**: These policies are AD-based policies that we will discuss throughout this chapter. These policies only apply to domain-joined computers and AD users. These policies are feature-rich compared to local policies.

Group Policy can be applied to three levels in the AD environment:

- **Site**: Group Policy can be linked to an AD site. Any site-level Group Policy will apply to all domains in that site.
- **Domain**: Any Group Policy that is applied at the domain level will apply to all users' and computers' AD objects under that domain. By default, the system creates a Group Policy called **Default Domain Policy** at the domain level. Most of the time, domain-level policies will be used to publish security settings that are applicable to the entire infrastructure.
- **Organization units (OUs)**: Group Policy at the OU level is applied to any user or computer object under it. By default, the system creates an OU-level Group Policy called **Default Domain Controllers Policy**, which is applied to the domain controller's OU. Group Policy settings applied at the OU level are more specific as the target audience is smaller compare to site or domain.

The following diagram illustrates the policy levels in AD:

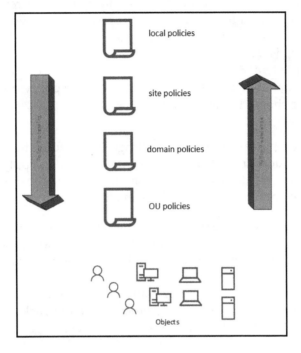

In the AD environment, group policies will be processed in this order:

- **Local policies**
- **Site policies**
- **Domain policies**
- **OU policies**

In general, this order is called **LSDOU**. The first policy to be processed is the local policy, and the last one to be processed is the OU policy. This doesn't mean that the most preferred policy is the local policy. Of all four policies, the policy that holds the lowest precedence value will be the winning GPO, which is the OU policy. This processing order is important when policies have conflicting values because the policy that is closest to the object will be the winning policy. The policy at the OU level will be the *closest* policy to the object. As I said earlier, OU-level policy settings are more specific according to organizational requirements. Therefore, they hold the most accurate policy settings for the targeted objects. This order is the default processing order, and based on the requirements, it is possible to change the precedence order. We will look into this later on in this chapter.

The processing of local policies can be completely turned off if required. This will prevent the application of non-recommended settings that administrators do not have control over or awareness of. This can be disabled by using a Group Policy setting. The policy setting is located at `Computer Configuration\Administrative Templates\System\Group Policy\Turn off Local Group Policy Objects Processing`; to disable policy processing, the value should be set to `Enable`.

In order to apply computer Group Policy settings successfully, the device should have a valid communication with a domain controller, and to apply user Group Policy settings, a user (the domain account) should log in to the domain-joined computer that can communicate with a domain controller.

Group policies are mainly processed in two different modes. By default, a Group Policy's computer settings will start to process during the startup process, before the user login box prompts. Once the user enters their username and credentials, the Group Policy's user settings start to process. This pre-processing mode is called **foreground processing**. During the foreground process, some policies will finish processing but some will not. They will be processed in the **background** after login and network connection are initialized. Also, once the user logs in, every 90 minutes, the group policies will run in the *background* by default. This is the second mode of Group Policy processing.

Foreground processing can be further divided into two sub-modes. Before Windows XP was introduced, all of the policy settings that ran in foreground mode finished before the user saw the desktop after the login process. This is called **synchronous** mode. But after Windows XP, the default mode of processing is **asynchronous**, which means that operating system does not wait until the Group Policy process finishes or before the user starts to use the computer. When the computer is presented with the login screen, in the background, the computer settings that are part of the policies will still be processing. After the user logs in, the system will start to process the user settings as part of the policies. By the time the initial home screen is loaded, the group policies may still be processing in the background. There are four policy settings that are defined by Microsoft, which are always processed in asynchronous mode. If any policy has folder redirection, software installation, disk quota, and drive mapping enabled, it will be processed in synchronous mode. Not only that, all of the startup scripts will also run in the foreground in synchronous mode.

This default processing behavior provides a faster login time for users, but at the same time, some policy settings can take up to two login cycles to apply the changes fully. This behavior impacts the security settings. As an example, if we want to block access to control panel settings, and if the policy settings are not processed in synchronous mode, when the user logs in, there is a possibility for them to have access to the **Control Panel**. Then, it is not going to give the expected results. This default mode is useful when users are connected through a *slow link*. If they aren't connected, it can take an awfully long time to finish the Group Policy processing. If there is no specific reason to use asynchronous mode, it is recommended that you always use synchronous mode. We can force this using Group Policy; the policy settings are located at `Computer Configuration\Administrative Templates\System\Logon\Always wait for the network at computer startup and logon`.

As we saw earlier, there are four Group Policy settings defined by Microsoft that always run in synchronous mode. Even if systems are connected via a slow link, they will process these Group Policy settings in synchronous mode. Therefore, it is recommended that you enable the following two Group Policy settings to force asynchronous mode when you log in via slow link and remote desktop services. Asynchronous mode for slow links can be enabled via `Computer Configuration\Administrative Templates\System\Group Policy\Change Group Policy Processing to run asynchronously when a slow link is detected`. Asynchronous mode for remote desktop services can be enabled via `Computer Configuration\Administrative Templates\System\Group Policy\Allow asynchronous user Group Policy processing when logging on through Remote Desktop Services`.

Group Policy inheritance

Any Group Policy that is applied to the upper level of the structure is inherited in the lower level. The order of the inherited policies is decided by the LSDOU model that we looked at in the *Group Policy processing* section. Group Policy inheritance for each OU can be reviewed using the **Group Policy Management MMC**.

To view the inheritance data, first click on the OU and then click on the **Group Policy Inheritance** tab:

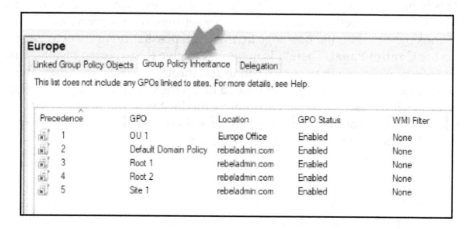

The Group Policy inheritance details can also be viewed by using the `Get-GPInheritance` PowerShell cmdlet. As an example, the same information listed in the preceding screenshot can be viewed using the following command:

```
Get-GPInheritance -Target "OU=Users,OU=Europe,DC=rebeladmin,DC=com"
```

In this example, I have one site-linked Group Policy called **Site 1**. There are two domain-linked group policies called **Root 1** and **Root 2**. I also have an OU-linked Group Policy called **Test Users**:

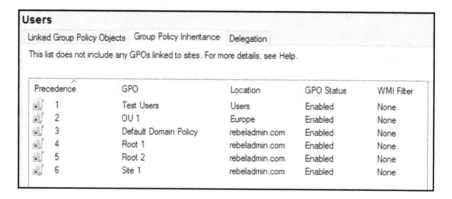

In the list, the first precedence goes to the **Test Users** Group Policy that is closest to the OU—it is the OU-linked Group Policy. Then, precedence order **2** goes to the Group Policy linked to the parent OU. Precedence orders **3**, **4**, and **5** go to the domain-linked group policies. The last in the order is the **Site 1** Group Policy, which is linked to the AD site.

This inheritance is not useful in every scenario. There can be situations where the OU needs to have very specific settings and should not be disturbed by any other inherited policy. When the number of group policies increases, the time they need for processing also increases. If my requirements can be achieved using one Group Policy that is linked to the OU, why should I still apply inherited policies that are not going to help me anyway? In a similar scenario, Group Policy inheritance can be blocked at the OU level. This can be done by using the **Group Policy Management MMC** or the `Set-GPinheritance` PowerShell cmdlet:

```
Set-GPInheritance -Target "OU=Users,OU=Europe,DC=rebeladmin,DC=com" -
IsBlocked Yes
```

The preceding command will block the Group Policy inheritance in `OU=Users,OU=Europe,DC=rebeladmin,DC=com`:

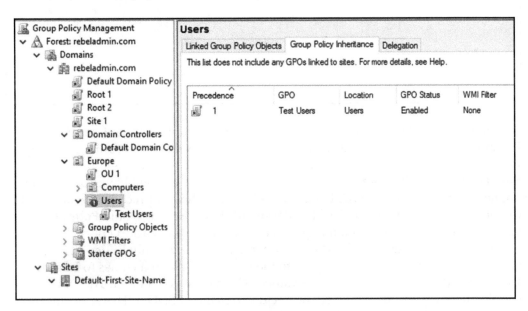

After the Group Policy inheritance block, the only policy in the inheritance list is the policy that is linked to the OU.

Group Policy conflicts

The precedence order of group policies in LSDOU and Group Policy inheritance also decide which policy will win when we have some conflicting settings. Let's look at this further with an example:

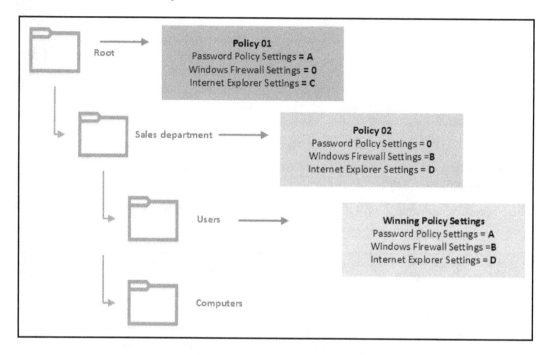

As per the preceding diagram, we have two policies inherited by the **Users** OU. **Policy 01** is the domain-linked Group Policy, and **Policy 02** is the OU-linked Group Policy. Each Group Policy has its own values defined for the three selected settings. Based on the default Group Policy inheritance, the **Users** OU will have both policies applied. According to LSDOU, **Policy 02** will have the lowest precedence value as it is the closest policy is the **Users** OU. For **Password Policy Settings**, only **Policy 01** has a value defined. Therefore, even though it's the least preferred Group Policy, that value will apply to the **Users** OU. For **Windows Firewall Settings**, only **Policy 02** has a value. The same policy will also apply to the **Users** OU. When it comes to **Internet Explorer Settings**, both policies have values, which creates a conflict. The winning conflicting policy setting value will be decided based on LSDOU. Therefore, the winning value will be from **Policy 02**.

Microsoft allows you to change this default policy winning procedure by *enforcing* policies. When a Group Policy has been enforced, it will have the lowest precedence value regardless of where it's been linked. Another advantage of the enforced policy is that it will apply even though the OU has blocked inheritance. If the domain-linked policy is enforced, it will apply to any OU under the domain, and it will hold the lowest precedence. If multiple policies are enforced, all of them will take the lowest precedence numbers in order.

To enforce a policy, load **Group Policy Management Console (GPMC)**, right-click on the selected Group Policy, and then select the **Enforced** option. This will enforce the policy and change the policy icon with a small padlock mark. This allows you to identify enforced policies quickly from the policy list:

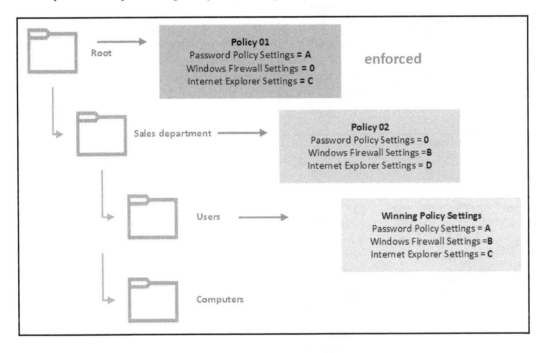

In the preceding example, **Policy 01** was **enforced**. It is the domain-linked Group Policy. Under normal circumstances, **Policy 02** would get the lowest precedence value when it's applied to the **Users** OU. But when the policy is **enforced**, **Policy 01** will have the lowest precedence value. When we look into the winning policy values of the **Users** OU, for **Password Policy Settings**, the system will process the **Policy 01** value as it is the only one with any value defined. For **Windows Firewall Settings**, **Policy 01** does not have any value defined. So, even if a policy has been **enforced**, the winning policy setting will be from **Policy 02** as it's the only one with a value defined. **Policy 01** and **Policy 02** both have values for **Internet Explorer Settings**, but the **enforced Policy 01** is on top of the policy list and the winning policy setting will be from it.

So far, we have talked about conflicting policy settings from different levels in the domain structure. How will it work if it's at the same level? Policies at the same level also apply according to the precedence order. When policies are at the same level, the LSDOU process is applicable. The winning policy will be decided based on its position in the policy list. The order of the list is decided based on the **Linked Group Policy Objects** list. This list can be viewed using the **Linked Group Policy Objects** tab in the OU detail window in GPMC:

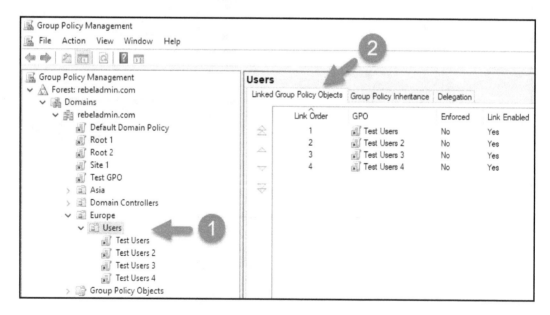

The order of policies in the same level can be changed by using two methods. One method is to enforce the policy. When the policy is enforced, it will take priority over the other policies in the same level, but it will not change the **Link Order** of the policy. The order of the list can be changed using the up and down buttons in the **Linked Group Policy Objects** tab. The link order will match the precedence order of the group policies:

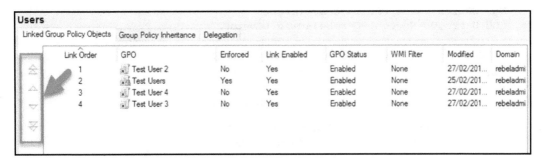

Group Policy conflicts that occur in AD environments do so mostly due to unplanned GPO implementations and lack of knowledge on group policy processing order. Throughout this chapter, you can find relevant information that will help you to organize group policies properly and avoid conflicts.

Group Policy mapping and status

There are a few things we need to consider when we create and link a Group Policy object to a site, domain, or OU:

- If it's a new GPO, it can be created directly under the relevant OU or domain using GMPC.
- In sites, it's only allowed to link to an existing GPO; therefore, if the new GPO needs to link to the site, it needs to add a new GPO using GPMC or a PowerShell cmdlet.
- An already added GPO can link to any OU, domain, or site. As an example, if policy A is created and linked under OU A, it can be reused in any other OU, domain, or site.

A new GPO object can be created using the New-GPO PowerShell cmdlet:

```
New-GPO -Name GPO-Test-A
```

The preceding command will create a GPO called `GPO-Test-A`. By default, it will not link to any OU, domain, or site. In GPMC, it can be viewed under the `Group Policy Objects` container.

After an object is created, it can be linked to an OU, domain, or site by using the `New-GPLink` cmdlet:

```
New-GPLink -Name GPO-Test-A -Target
"OU=Users,OU=Europe,DC=rebeladmin,DC=com"
```

The preceding command links a GPO called `GPO-Test-A` to `OU=Users,OU=Europe,DC=rebeladmin,DC=com`.

Both cmdlets can be combined to create and link a GPO at the same time:

```
New-GPO -Name GPO-Test-B | New-GPLink -Target
"OU=Users,OU=Europe,DC=rebeladmin,DC=com"
```

The preceding command will create a new GPO called `GPO-Test-B` and link it to `OU=Users,OU=Europe,DC=rebeladmin,DC=com` at the same time.

There are occasions when the link to the group policies needs to be disabled. This is useful when you do Group Policy troubleshooting. When the link to the Group Policy is disabled, Group Policy will removed from the Group Policy precedence list; however, it will not remove Group Policy from the **Link Order** list or from its location. This can be done via GMPC or by using the `Set-GPLink` PowerShell cmdlet:

```
Set-GPLink -Name GPO-Test-B -Target
"OU=Users,OU=Europe,DC=rebeladmin,DC=com" -LinkEnabled No
```

The preceding command will disable the link between the `GPO-Test-B` GPO and `OU=Users,OU=Europe,DC=rebeladmin,DC=com`. This is usually used to temporarily disable a policy. It can be enabled at any time by using the `-LinkEnabled Yes` option.

But if this requirement is permanent, this GPO link can be completely removed by using the `Remove-GPLink` cmdlet. This will remove the link, but it will not delete the GPO. It will also not affect any other existing links in the GPO:

```
Remove-GPLink -Name GPO-Test-B -Target
"OU=Users,OU=Europe,DC=rebeladmin,DC=com"
```

This command will remove the `GPO-Test-B` policy from
`OU=Users,OU=Europe,DC=rebeladmin,DC=com`. It will remove the GPO from the
Precedence list, as well as the **Link Order** list.

If the GPO needs to be deleted completely, we can use the `Remove-GPO` cmdlet for
that:

```
Remove-GPO -Name GPO-Test-A
```

The preceding command will delete the mentioned GPO completely from the system.
If the GPO was linked, it will forcefully remove it at the same time.

Without disabling links, removing links, or deleting the GPO, it is also possible to
disable GPO settings only. This feature provides options to disable computer settings,
user settings, or both. Once the settings are disabled, it will not remove them from the
Link Order or **Precedence** list. It will only disable the applied settings:

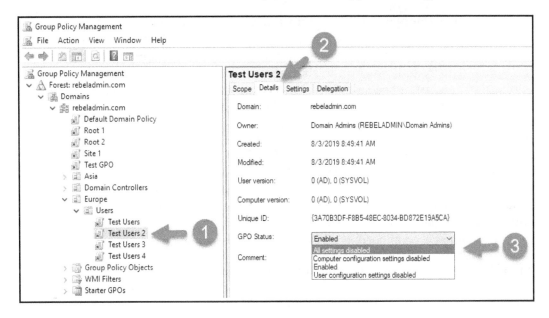

Administrative templates

Group policies allow us to manage computer settings and user settings in many ways. However, infrastructure operation requirements often change due to several reasons. As an example, they can be based on new application versions, new security requirements, new business policy requirements, and more. We know that group policies can be used to manage organization-wide settings, but not all of the requirements will be supported by default. As an example, by the time AD DS 2008 was released, it was not possible to have group policies that could manage settings in the Office 2016 application. Application vendors and developers can develop administrative templates and publish them via group policies to customize, manage, and optimize their products and services. Administrative templates contain registry-based changes to the system. **Administrative Templates**, under **Computer Configuration** in the GPO, can be used to modify the registry entries under the HKEY_LOCAL_MACHINE key.

Administrative Templates, under **User Configuration** in the GPO, can be used to modify registry entries under the HKEY_CURRENT_USER key. Microsoft also has predeployed administrative templates that can be used to edit more than 1,000 individual registry settings. Administrative templates are not just from the application vendors; if needed, we can also create custom administrative templates to address unique requirements.

Before Windows Server 2008, administrative templates came as Unicode-formatted text files with the .adm file extension. But they does have some drawbacks. It saves the .adm file as part of the Group Policy inside SYSVOL. If it is used in different GPOs, it will save a copy of .adm with each and every GPO. It increases the size of SYSVOL. Also, if you need to change a setting in the .adm file, it needs to be edited in each copy of .adm. One .adm file has support for only one language; if you need to use multiple languages, you need a copy of .adm for each language.

After Windows Server 2008, administrative templates were presented as two XML files. The file with the .admx extension is responsible for publishing registry settings and the file with the .adml extension is responsible for providing language-specific interface settings. This allows administrators to edit and manage policies in multiple languages. Unlike .adm files, if you need to edit the .admx file, it needs to be edited in one place only, and it will map the relevant .adml file to provide multi-language support if required.

The .adm file is part of the GPO, so it's always stored in the SYSVOL folder. But by default, for ADMX/ADML, Group Policy holds the settings only for the policy, and when it needs editing, it will pull the ADMX and ADML files from the local workstation. It is possible to change this behavior and save these files in a central location where everyone can pull the templates files when required. This provides easy access and better management for administrative templates.

We can move administrative templates to the SYSVOL folder by using the following steps:

1. Log in to the domain controller as the **Domain Admin** or higher.
2. Create a folder called PolicyDefinitions under \\rebeladmin.com\SYSVOL\rebeladmin.com\Policies. The rebeladmin.com domain can be replaced by your own domain FQDN:

   mkdir \\rebeladmin.com\SYSVOL\rebeladmin.com\Policies\PolicyDefinitions

3. After that, copy the policy definition data into this new folder:

   Copy-Item C:\Windows\PolicyDefinitions*\\rebeladmin.com\SYSVOL\rebeladmin.com\Policies\PolicyDefinitions -Recurse -Force

This will also move ADML files into \\rebeladmin.com\SYSVOL\rebeladmin.com\Policies\PolicyDefinitions with their language name. As an example, US English will be in \rebeladmin.com\SYSVOL\rebeladmin.com\Policies\PolicyDefinitions\en-US. The language to use in policy editing will be decided based on the language used in the workstation.

Group Policy filtering

As we looked at earlier, a Group Policy can map to sites, domains, and OUs. If a Group Policy is mapped to the OU, by default, it will apply to any object under it. But within an OU, domain, or site, there are lots of objects. The security, system, or application settings requirements covered by group policies are not always applied to broader target groups. Group Policy filtering capabilities allow us to further narrow down the Group Policy targets to security groups or individual objects.

There are a few different ways to perform filtering in Group Policy:

- Security filtering
- WMI filtering

Security filtering

Before you apply security filtering, the first thing to check is whether the Group Policy is mapped correctly to the site, domain, or OU. The security group or the objects you are going to target should be at the same level as where the Group Policy is mapped.

We can use the GMPC or PowerShell cmdlets to add security filtering to our GPO:

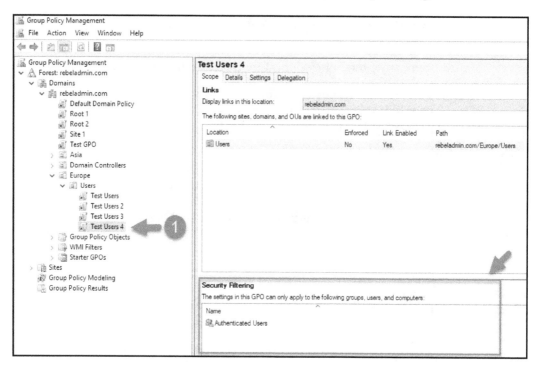

As you can see, by default, any policy that has an **Authenticated Users** group is added to the **Security Filtering** section. This means that, by default, the policy will apply to any authenticated user in that OU. When we add any group or object to security filtering, it also creates an entry under delegation. In order to apply a Group Policy to an object, it needs a minimum of the following:

- **Read**
- **Apply group policy**

Any object added to the **Security Filtering** section will have both of these permissions set by default. In the same way, if an object is added directly to the delegation section and applies both permissions, it will list those objects in the **Security Filtering** section.

Now, before we add custom objects to the **Security Filtering** section, we need to change the default behavior of the security filtering with **Authenticated Users**. Otherwise, it doesn't matter what security group or object you add—Group Policy settings will still be applied to any authenticated user. Before Microsoft released security patch MS16-072 in 2016, we could simply remove the **Authenticated Users** group and add the required objects to it. With these new security patch changes, group policies will now run within the computer's security context. Earlier, group policies were executed within the user's security context. In order to accommodate these new security requirements, one of the following permissions must be available on the Group Policy's **Delegation** tab:

- **Authenticated Users**: Read
- **Domain Computers**: Read

In order to edit these changes, go to the Group Policy and then go to the **Delegation** tab. Click on **Advanced**, select **Authenticated Users**, and then remove the **Apply group policy** permissions:

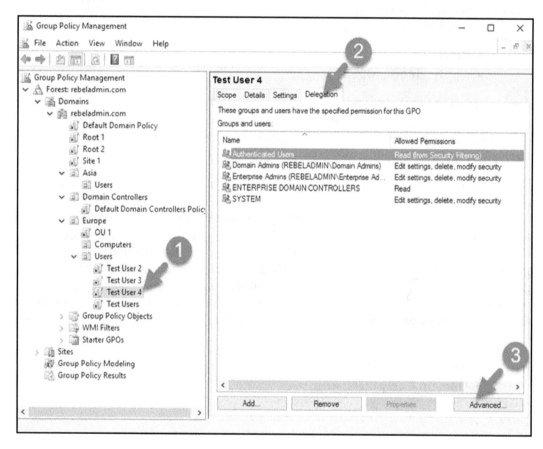

Now, we can go back to the **Scope** tab and add the required security group or objects to the **Security Filtering** section. It will automatically add the relevant **Read** and **Apply group policy** permissions:

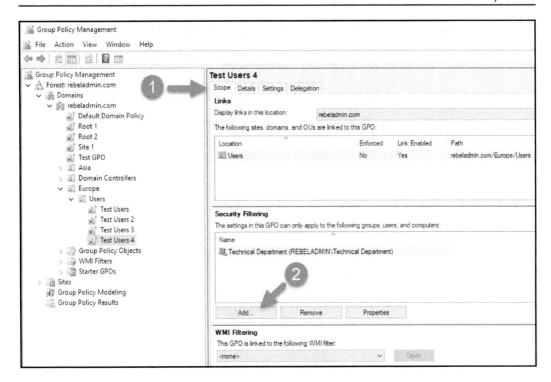

Here, although we are looking at how to apply group policies to a specific target, we are also allowed to explicitly apply policies to a large number of objects and then *block* groups or objects. As an example, let's assume we have an OU with a few hundred objects from different classes. From all of these, we have 10 computer objects that we do not need to apply to a given Group Policy. Which one is the easiest? Go and add each and every security group and object to **Security Filtering**, or allow the Group Policy for everyone and only block access for one security group.

Microsoft allows you to use the second method in filtering too. In order to do that, Group Policy should have default security filtering, which is **Authenticated Users** with **Read** and the **Apply group policy** permissions. Then, go to the **Delegation** tab and click on the **Advanced** option. In the next window, click on the **Add** button and select the group or object that you need to block access to:

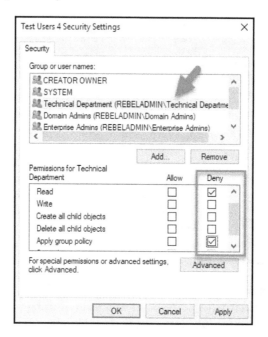

Here, we are denying **Read** and **Apply group policy** permissions to an object so as to prevent it from applying the Group Policy, while all other objects under that OU will still be able to read and apply the Group Policy. Easy, huh?

WMI filtering

WMI filters is another method that we can use to filter the Group Policy target. This method can be used to filter the computer objects only, and it is based on computer attribute values. As an example, WMI filters can be used to filter different OS versions, processor architecture (32 bit/64 bit), Windows Server roles, registry settings, event ID, and more. WMI filters run against the WMI data of the computer and decide whether it should apply the policy or not. If it matches the WMI query, it will process the Group Policy, and if it's false, it will not process the Group Policy. This method was first introduced with Windows Server 2003.

We can use GPMC to create/manage WMI filters. Before applying a filter to a GPO, first, we need to create it. A single WMI filter can be attached to many GPOs, but a GPO can have only a single WMI filter attached.

To create a WMI filter, open GPMC, right-click on **WMI Filters**, and click on **New...**:

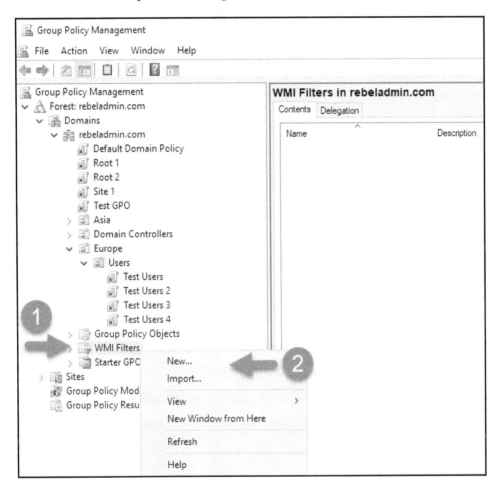

It will open up a new window, where we can define the WMI query:

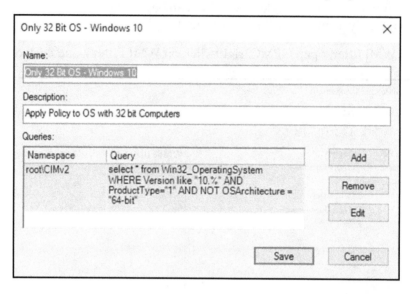

By clicking on the **Add** button, we can define **Namespace** and WMI **Query**. As an example, I have created a WMI query to filter the Windows 10 OS that is running the 32-bit version:

```
select * from Win32_OperatingSystem WHERE Version like "10.%" AND
ProductType="1" AND NOT OSArchitecture = "64-bit"
```

In the following commands, you can find a few examples of commonly used WMI queries:

- To filter OS—Windows 8—64 bit, use the following command:

```
select * from Win32_OperatingSystem WHERE Version like "6.2%"
AND ProductType="1" AND OSArchitecture = "64-bit"
```

- To filter OS—Windows 8—32 bit, use the following command:

```
select * from Win32_OperatingSystem WHERE Version like "6.2%"
AND ProductType="1" AND NOT OSArchitecture = "64-bit"
```

- To filter any Windows Server OS—64 bit, use the following command:

```
select * from Win32_OperatingSystem where (ProductType = "2")
OR (ProductType = "3") AND  OSArchitecture = "64-bit"
```

- To apply a policy to a selected day of the week, use the following command:

```
select DayOfWeek from Win32_LocalTime where DayOfWeek = 1
```

In the previous command, day 1 is Monday.

Once a WMI filter is created, it needs to be attached to the GPO. To do that, go to GPMC and select the required GPO. Then, in the **WMI Filtering** section, select the required WMI filter from the drop-down box:

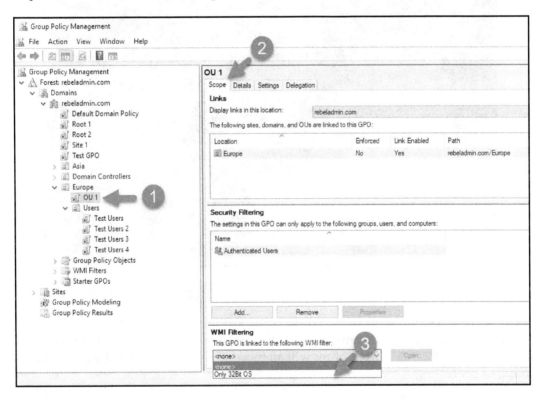

Now, it is time for testing. Our test query is to target 32-bit Windows 10 OSes. If we try to run the query over a 64-bit OS, it will not apply. We can check this by running `gpupdate /force` to apply a new Group Policy and `gpresult /r` to check the results:

```
Administrator: Windows PowerShell
ite Name:                       Default-First-Site-Name
oaming Profile:                 N/A
ocal Profile:                   C:\Users\administrator
onnected over a slow link?:  No

OMPUTER SETTINGS
----------------
    CN=REBEL-PC01,OU=Europe,DC=rebeladmin,DC=com
    Last time Group Policy was applied: 02/03/2017 at 23:52:28
    Group Policy was applied from:      REBEL-PDC-01.rebeladmin.com
    Group Policy slow link threshold:   500 kbps
    Domain Name:                        REBELADMIN
    Domain Type:                        Windows 2008 or later

    Applied Group Policy Objects
    ----------------------------
        Default Domain Policy

    The following GPOs were not applied because they were filtered out
    ------------------------------------------------------------------
        OU 1
            Filtering:  Denied (WMI Filter)
            WMI Filter: Only 32 Bit OS - Windows 10

        Local Group Policy
            Filtering:  Not Applied (Empty)

    The computer is a part of the following security groups
    -------------------------------------------------------
        BUILTIN\Administrators
        Everyone
        BUILTIN\Users
        NT AUTHORITY\NETWORK
        NT AUTHORITY\Authenticated Users
        This Organization
        REBEL-PC01$
        Domain Computers
        Authentication authority asserted identity
        System Mandatory Level
```

The test was successful and the policy was blocked as we were running Windows 10—64-bit OS.

Now, we know how we can apply these different filtering options to target specific objects for a GPO. But in what order will all these apply? Following list explains the order of processing:

1. **LSDOU**: The first filtering option will be based on the order in which policies are placed in the domain structure. This has been covered in detail in an earlier section of this chapter.

2. **WMI filters**: The next filtering it will look for is the WMI filtering, which we looked at in this section. If the result is true, the Group Policy will go to the next step. If the result is false, the Group Policy does not apply.

3. **Security settings**: As a last step, it will look into security filtering and check whether the given security criteria has been met. If they have been met, it will process the Group Policy.

Group Policy preferences

Group Policy preferences were introduced with Windows 2008 to publish administrative preference settings to Windows desktop OSes and server OSes. These preference settings can apply only to domain-join computers. Group Policy preferences provide granular-level targeting and provide easy management via enhanced GUI. Group Policy preferences have replaced many Group Policy settings that required registry edits or complex logon scripts. Group Policy preferences are capable of adding, updating, and removing settings such as the following:

- Drive maps
- Internet Explorer settings
- Registry entries
- Printer deployment
- Start menu items
- Power management
- Local users and groups
- File replication
- Managing VPN connections
- Schedule tasks

Group Policy settings and Group Policy preferences are processed in two different ways. Group Policy settings are applied during the boot-up process and the user logon process. After that, settings are refreshed every 90 minutes (default). Once the Group Policy setting is applied, its values cannot change easily. It is required to push new values via Group Policy. Otherwise, even if it's changed, it will be overwritten in the next policy refresh cycle. But Group Policy preferences will not be enforced. They allow users to alter them if required. This also allows you to configure applications that are not Group Policy-aware.

Group Policy preferences are also divided into **Computer Configuration** and **User Configuration**. We can use GPMC to manage preference settings. To access preference settings, select the Group Policy, right-click on **Edit...**, and expand **Computer Configuration** or **User Configuration**. There, we can see the `Preferences` container:

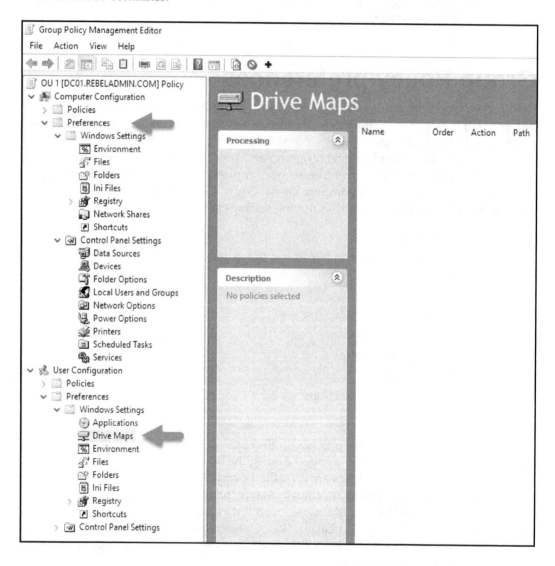

As an example, we can see how we can configure Internet Explorer settings. This is one of the most commonly used preference settings in organizations, specifically to publish proxy settings. Before Internet Explorer 10, Internet Explorer settings were managed by using **Internet Explorer Maintenance (IEM)** in their Group Policy. If your organization has IE settings published using IEM, it will not be applicable to IE 10 and IE 11 anymore. Internet Explorer settings can also be applied via registry edits; Group Policy preferences made this easy as it can use a GUI similar to an actual IE settings window.

In order to configure the settings, open the Group Policy settings and then go to **User Configuration** | **Preferences** | **Control Panel Settings** | **Internet Settings**. Then, right-click and select **New**. There, we can select the settings based on the IE version. There is no option for IE 11, but any setting that applies to IE 10 will apply to IE 11 too:

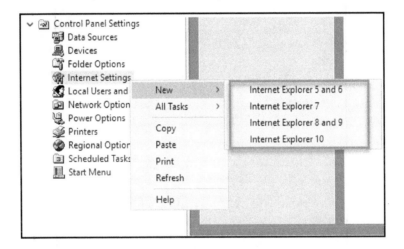

Once you open the relevant configuration, you will see that it is very similar to the settings window we see in the application itself. Complex registry entries to configure IE settings are no longer needed.

One thing you need to make sure is that once you input the changes, press the *F6* key to apply the changes. If they work fine, the *red* dotted line will change to a *green* dotted line. It doesn't matter what changes you make; if you do not activate them by pressing the *F6* key, they will not publish:

These preference settings will not prevent users from changing them. If it is necessary to prevent users from changing preference settings, then we need to use Group Policy settings for it.

Item-level targeting

In the previous section, we looked at how we can use WMI filters for granular-level Group Policy targets. In a similar way, item-level targeting can be used to target Group Policy preference settings based on application settings and properties of users and computers at the granular level.

We can use multiple targeting items in preference settings and make selections based on logical operators (such as *AND*, *OR*, *IS*, and *IS NOT*).

Item-level targeting in Group Policy preferences can be set up/managed using GPMC. To do that, open the Group Policy settings, go to the relevant preference settings, and right-click and select **Properties**.

 As per the previous example (IE 10 settings), the path should be **User Configuration** | **Preferences** | **Internet Settings** | **Internet Explorer 10**. Then, right-click and select **Properties**.

From the **Properties** window, select the **Common** tab, tick **Item-level targeting**, and then click on the **Targeting...** button:

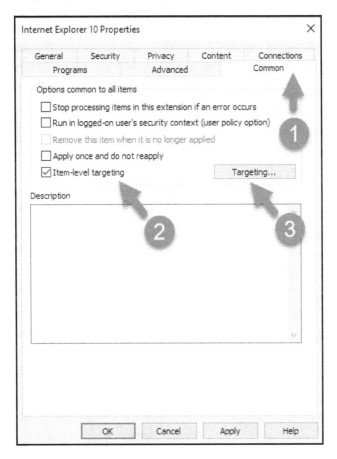

In the next window, we can build granular-level targeting based on one item or multiple items with logical operators:

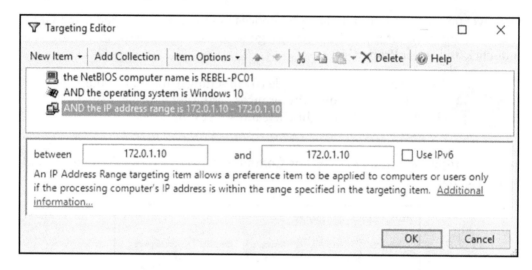

In the preceding example, I built a query based on three settings, which are the NetBIOS name, the OS, and the IP address. In order to apply the preference settings, all three statements should provide the `true` value as a result as I used the *AND* logical operator. If it's the *OR* logical operator, the result can have either `true` or `false` values.

In the previous screenshot, the **New Item** menu contains items we can use for targeting. **Add Collection** allows you to create a parenthetical grouping. The **Item Options** menu is responsible for defining logical operators.

Loopback processing

Group Policy has two main configurations. One is targeted computer settings, and the other is targeted user configuration settings. When we apply user configuration to a user located in OU, it doesn't matter which computer they log in to—their policy settings will follow them. As an example, let's assume user Liam is located under the Sales OU. The computer he usually logs in to is also located under the same OU. But he occasionally logs in to the meeting room laptop that is located under the IT operations OU. The IT operations OU has its own **Computer Configuration** and **User Configuration** policies assigned. But when Liam logs in to it, he still has the same settings he had in the Sales OU PC. This is the normal behavior of group policies. However, there are situations where it needs to apply user policy settings based on the computer the user logs in to. **Remote Desktop Services** (**RDS**) and Citrix Xenapp/XenDesktop solutions are one of the greatest examples of this scenario. These solutions are mostly open for login from remote networks. Therefore, their security and operation requirements are different from a computer in LAN. If users who log in from different OUs are going to have different settings, it's hard to maintain the system with the required level of protection. Using *loopback processing*, we can force users to only have user policy settings that are linked to the OU where computers are located.

There are two modes of loopback processing:

- **Replace mode**: In replace mode, user settings attached to the user from the original OU will be replaced by the user settings attached to the destination OU. If loopback processing replaces the mode enabled, when Liam logs in to the meeting room laptop, he will get the same settings as the user in the IT operations OU.
- **Merge mode**: If merge mode is enabled, in my example, Liam's sales user settings will apply when he logs in to the meeting room laptop first. After Group Policy settings is processed, it will also add the user settings from the IT operations OU. If there are any conflicting settings, the IT operations OU user policy settings will win.

To enable loopback processing for Group Policy, go to the Group Policy edit mode and browse to **Computer Configuration| Policies| Administrative Templates | System | Group Policy | Configure user Group Policy loopback processing mode**:

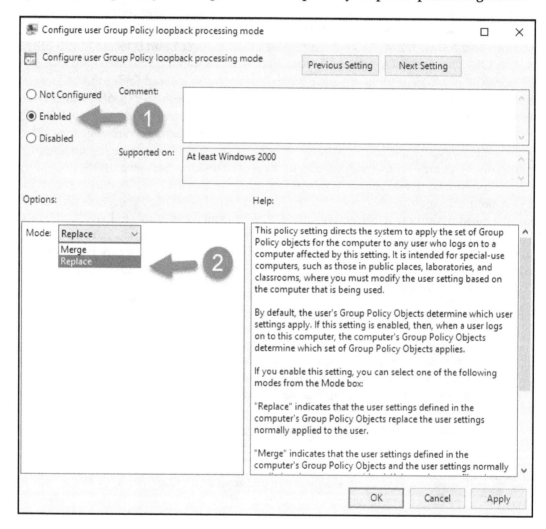

Group Policy best practices

In Sri Lanka, there is a common saying to explain risky action: *eating curd from a knife*. Curd with honey is amazing, but if you have to eat it using a sharpened knife, there is a risk that you may cut your tongue if you're not careful. But it's still worth taking the risk (if you have ever tasted curd and honey before). Group policies are also like that; they can do so many useful things, but only if you use them correctly. In the AD environment, Group Policy-related issues are the most painful and time-consuming troubleshooting task as there are so many things that can go wrong.

Here, I have listed a few tips that will be useful for designing group policies:

- **Identify the best place to link the Group Policy**: The Group Policy can be linked to the site, domain, or OU. Organizations have different Group Policy requirements that can also map with the aforementioned components. It is important to understand the best place in the hierarchy to publish each Group Policy setting. This will prevent repetition and Group Policy conflicts. As an example, password complexity settings are common for all of the objects under the domain, so the best place to link the policy for the password settings is the domain root, not the OU.

- **Standardize settings**: Today, infrastructure requirements are complex. Each business unit has its own operation and security requirements to address via group policies. When designing group policies, always try to summarize the changes as much as possible. If two business units have almost the same user settings requirements, discuss it with the relevant authorized people (such as the line manager and team leads) and try to use the standard settings. This will allow you to use one Group Policy and link it to two business units instead of creating two separate group policies. Always try to reduce the number of group policies that will be used in the system, since when the number of group policies increases, it also increases the time taken for the login process.

- **Use meaningful names**: This is a small suggestion, but I have seen people use Group Policy with names that don't explain anything. In such a scenario, when you go for troubleshooting, it can take an awfully long time to find the relevant Group Policy. Make sure that you name the Group Policy to reflect the settings in there. It doesn't need to have details, but at least have something that you and your colleagues can understand.

- **Avoid mixing user settings and computer settings**: Group Policy has two main configuration sets that will apply to users and computers. Always try to avoid mixing these settings in the same Group Policy. Try to use separate group policies for computer settings and user settings. This will make it easy to organize policies. After that, disable the unused configuration section in the Group Policy to avoid processing. This can be done by using GPMC:

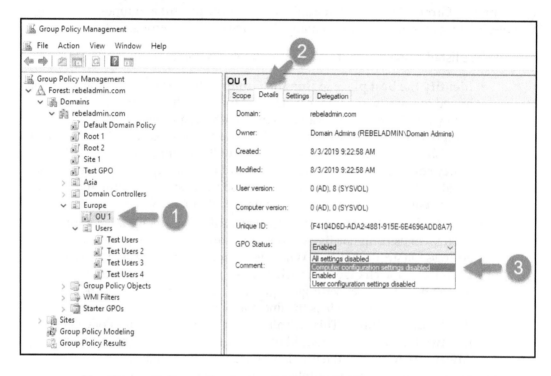

- **Use Group Policy enforcing and block inheritance appropriately**: These features are a good way to manage the default Group Policy inheritance, but use them carefully as they can prevent users/systems from applying critical policy settings from the top of the hierarchy. In the same way, by enforcing policies, you may enforce settings to users and computers that should not be targets. Therefore, always measure the impact before using enforce or blocking inheritance features.

- **Never edit default policies**: There are two default group policies: **Default Domain Policy** and **Default Domain Controllers Policy**. It is highly recommended that you do not use these to publish the Group Policy settings. These can be used as the baseline when you design the group policies, and they allow you to revert to the original settings with minimum effect. These can also be used as a reference to troubleshoot inheritance issues and replication issues.

- **Be careful when using loopback processing**: Issues related to loopback processing are due to lack of knowledge, especially when they involve replace and merge modes. In this chapter, we covered both of these modes. If you are enabling loopback processing, always use separate Group Policy and name it correctly so that everyone understands it when it comes to troubleshooting. My recommendation is that you use it in a situation where you can use the *replace* mode. Merge mode can create lots of hassles with combined group policies plus conflicted settings. Loopback settings are also recommended to use only with **Virtual Desktop Infrastructure (VDI)** solutions such as Citrix and RDS, as they help to maintain the consistency.

- **Win or lose**: Earlier in this chapter, we looked at which policy settings will win when there is a settings conflict. But in theory, there should not be any conflicts at all if the design is done correctly. Therefore, in design, always avoid repeating values in a hierarchical structure. If different values are used for the same setting, use filtering options and block inheritance to prevent the policy conflicts.

- **Housekeeping:** Last but not least, it is important that you review the group policies periodically and remove the policies that have not been used. Also, remove the legacy policy settings if they have been replaced by new policies or methods. Audit and make sure that the hierarchical order is maintained and objects are getting the expected group policies applied to them.

Summary

Group policies are one of the core values of the AD environment. As long as they are designed and maintained properly, they can be used to manage computer and user settings effectively. In this chapter, we learned about Group Policy components and their capabilities. This was followed by explaining features that can be used to design and maintain a healthy Group Policy structure. Last but not least, we learned about Group Policy designing best practices.

In the next chapter, we are moving on to the third part of this book, which will focus on AD server roles. In this part, you will learn about AD DS's advanced features, including schema, replication, **read-only domain controller** (**RODC**), and AD recovery.

Section 3: Active Directory Service Management

3

In this section of the book, we will deep dive into Active Directory role services, such as Active Directory Domain Services, Active Directory Certificate Services, Active Directory Federation Services, and Active Directory Rights Management Services. Throughout the chapters, we will look into the technology behind these role services, evaluate their benefits, and learn how to configure them.

This section contains the following chapters:

11
Active Directory Services

In this chapter, we are moving into the third part of this book, which focuses on the **Active Directory (AD)** server roles. There are five main Active Directory server roles:

- **Active Directory Domain Services (AD DS)**
- **Active Directory Lightweight Directory Services (AD LDS)**
- **Active Directory Federation Services (AD FS)**
- **Active Directory Rights Management Services (AD RMS)**
- **Active Directory Certificate Services (AD CS)**

We have already looked into many AD components, features, and capabilities, but we are not quite done yet. AD services are attached to many different components, such as **Domain Name System (DNS)**, **Distributed File System (DFS)** replication, and group policies. To maintain a healthy AD environment, we need to manage each of these components properly and make sure they do what they are supposed to do. However, in some scenarios, IT professionals and software developers are only interested in AD authentication and authorization capabilities. This can be due to application developments, directory migrations, application authentication requirements, and other reasons. In such situations, we can use AD LDS to provide **Lightweight Directory Access Protocol (LDAP)** services. As the name suggests, it's a cut-down version of AD DS and is not dependent on many other components. It also has fewer management requirements. In this chapter, we will learn about AD LDS in detail.

There are no healthy AD environments without healthy AD replication. With Windows Server 2008, Microsoft introduced a DFS for `SYSVOL` folder replication. It is better than its predecessor, **File Replication Service** (**FRS**), in many ways. In this chapter, we will learn about the differences between FRS and **Distributed File System Replication** (**DFSR**). After that, I will demonstrate how to migrate `SYSVOL` folder replication from FRS to DFSR. Apart from replication technologies, AD sites also have an impact on AD replication. In this chapter, we will learn about AD sites, site links, subnets, and replication intervals in detail. Later on, we will learn about how intra-site and inter-site AD replication work.

In an AD environment, each and every domain controller holds sensitive information about identities. Therefore, the security of domain controllers is crucial. With Windows Server 2008, Microsoft introduced **read-only domain controllers** (**RODCs**), which are ideal for sites where we can't guarantee physical security. In this chapter, we will learn about how RODCs work and how to configure them. Last but not least, we will learn about AD database maintenance, including database defragmentation, backup, and recovery.

In this chapter, we will cover the following topics:

- Overview of AD LDS
- AD replication
- AD sites
- AD database maintenance
- RODCs in action
- AD DS backup and recovery

Overview of AD LDS

When we talk about AD, we refer to it as a single service; however, AD DS is a collection of many other components such as DNS, group policies, and `SYSVOL` folder replication. Each of these components needs to operate well in order to run a healthy AD environment. Managing these components isn't easy; it requires investments in resources, time, and skills. As we can see, the success of identity infrastructure depends on these components. It is not just about service uptime and performance; security also plays a crucial role in this. The failure or compromise of these components/services can have a potential impact on the entire AD infrastructure.

Microsoft Windows Core and Nano Server also count as OSes. They don't have fancy GUIs or lots of defaults running, but they still do the job of an OS. They allow users to build systems from scratch according to their requirements. This also increases the server uptime (fewer updates), reliability, performance, and security. Soon after Microsoft released the first AD version, IT engineers, application developers, and IT professionals started requesting a cut-down version of AD DS with pure LDAP capabilities. They wanted to eliminate all these dependencies and management requirements so they could focus on application development upon core AD functions. After Windows Server 2003, Microsoft released **Active Directory Application Mode** (**ADAM**), which allowed administrators to run a cut-down version of AD without things such as group policies and file replication. It can run on a desktop computer or a member server similar to any other Windows service. With Windows Server 2008, Microsoft renamed it as AD LDS and allowed users to install this role using Server Manager. This version provided administrators with more control and visibility to deploy and manage LDS instances. This was continued with all the AD DS releases after that version, and was included in Windows Server 2016 too.

Where to use LDS?

Few dependencies and management requirements have extended LDS' operational capabilities. In the following section, we will look at several scenarios where we can use LDS.

Application developments

This is the area that has benefited most from AD LDS capabilities. Application developments involve lots of research and testing. If these applications are AD-integrated, it is obvious that they need to be developed and tested within an AD environment. During the process, you may be required to build many test environments. If they're full-blown AD DS instances, it will take resources, time, and effort to deploy and maintain them. AD LDS allows you to run multiple instances of it within the same environment, independently. Each instance will have its own schema, and engineers can maintain the instance for each application test environment. Even if it looks like a cut-down version, it provides the same AD DS authentication and management capabilities, allowing engineers to easily adopt it.

Since AD LDS instances can be run on a desktop or server version of the OS, they do have fewer prerequisites. Therefore, applications can also be released with integrated LDS. For example, not every business runs AD. Even though application functions are based on AD features, it is still not easy to convince everyone that they should have an AD environment in order to run the application. Instead of this, the application installation can have an integrated LDS instance that can installed in the guest system as part of the installation process.

Hosted applications

Nowadays, hosted applications—such as **software-as-a-service (SaaS)** applications—are a common business operation model for lots of businesses. These applications are normally deployed in the perimeter or in a public network. These applications can also have authentication requirements, but it is not recommended to install AD DS in the perimeter or on a public network. In such a situation, the most common method is to deploy AD FS to provide federated access; however, additional resources and skills are still needed to deploy and maintain it. However, if complete isolation is required for the application, we can set up the AD LDS instance inside the perimeter/public network and provide the directory-enabled authentication service to applications. This will ensure the application doesn't have any connection with a LAN or the other LDS instances in the perimeter network, and provides a secure environment by design.

Distributed data stores for AD-integrated applications

Most of the AD-integrated applications also require schema modifications. With schema modifications, the application will store certain datasets in the AD database. For multiple applications, AD's schema and data will continue to grow, which will result in a significant impact on AD replication, especially if this is via slow links. Instead of storing data in the AD database, additional datasets of applications can be stored in the LDS instance. LDS instance will still use AD DS for authentication. Additional datasets stored in the LDS instance will not replicate to any other domain controllers.

Migrating from other directory services

There are environments and applications that use legacy X500-based directory services that like to migrate to AD DS. In such scenarios, AD LDS can be used as a middleman that can also support X500-based applications. It also cleans up the junk and only moves filtered data to AD DS. AD LDS allows the instances to run alongside AD DS, and privileged identity solutions such as MIM can sync data between LDS and AD DS instances if required.

> Azure AD Connect is a Microsoft tool that allows us to synchronize user identities from on-premises AD to Azure AD. Even though AD LDS has directory service capabilities, Azure AD Connect does not support synchronization from AD LDS instances to Azure AD.

The LDS installation

In the Windows Server 2016 OS, LDS can be installed using Server Manager. In order to install LDS, a user needs to log in to the selected systems with *local administrator* privileges.

Once logged in, launch **Server Manager** and click on **Add Roles and Features**. Then, follow the wizard, select **Active Directory Lightweight Directory Services** under **Server Roles**, and proceed with enabling the role:

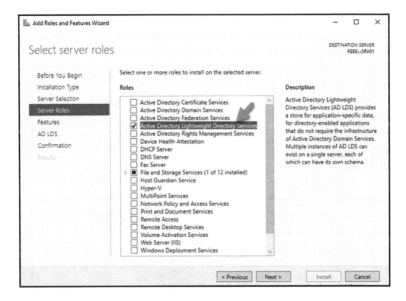

Once the role is installed, click on the **Post-Deployment Configuration** wizard in
Server Manager. LDS can be set up in two ways: one is by using **A unique instance**
and the other one is by using **A replica of an existing instance**. The replica option is
similar to the cloned copy of an existing instance. This is useful, especially in an
application development environment where engineers need to maintain a number of
application versions:

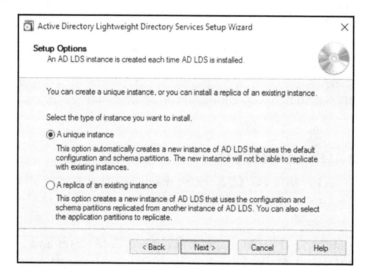

In the next window, we can define the name and description of the LDS instance:

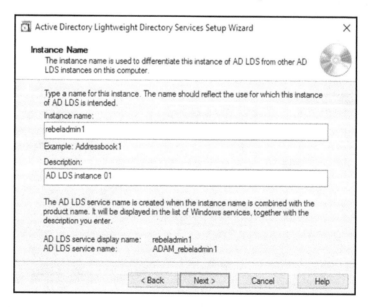

In the next window that appears, we can define the LDS port. By default, the LDAP port is set to 389 and the SSL port is set to 636. If you run multiple instances, these need to be changed accordingly.

After this, we can create the application directory partition. This allows applications to use this partition as a data repository to store the application-related data. If the application is capable of creating a partition, this step is not necessary and we can create a relevant partition during the application deployment process. When defining the application's **Partition name**, we need to provide it in a distinguished name format:

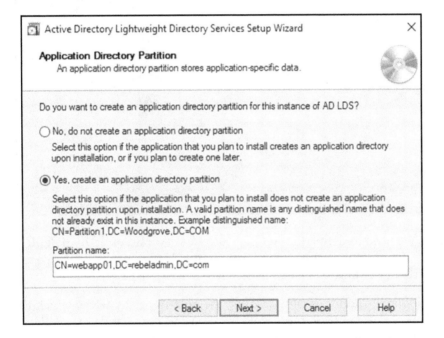

The next step is to define a location in which to store the LDS data files. After this, it gives us the option to specify a service account for LDS. If it's a workgroup environment, you can use the **Network service account** or a local user account for it. If it's a domain environment, it can be any AD user account:

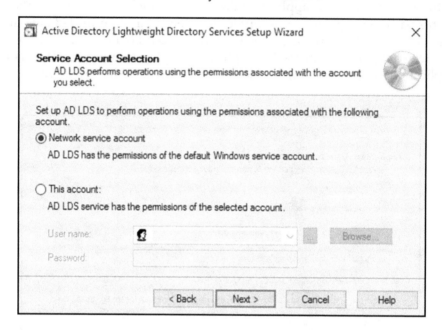

After that, we need to define the AD LDS administrator account. By default, it selects the user account that was used for the installation. If required, it can be changed to a different account or group.

Once we define the administrator account, the next step is to define which LDIF file to import. This is a text file that represents the data and commands that will be used by the LDAP instance. It can contain one or more LDIF files; these files depend on application requirements. For example, for user account functionalities, the relevant LDIF file will be `MSUser`:

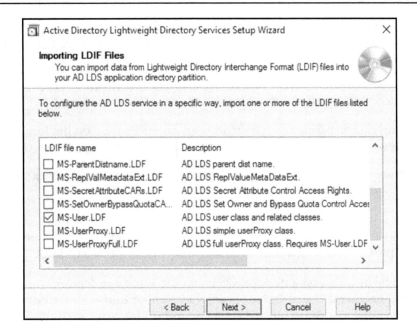

This step completes the AD LDS installation, and once it is completed, we can create the relevant objects and manage them. There are two methods we can use to connect to it. One way is to connect using the **ADSI Edit** tool:

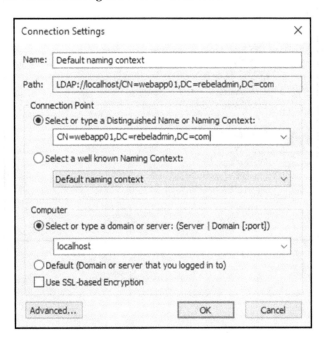

The other method is by using PowerShell cmdlets. These are the same commands that we use for AD DS user object management, with the only difference being the need to define the **Distinguished Name** (**DN**) and server:

```
New-ADUser -name "tidris" -Displayname "Talib Idris" -server
'localhost:389' -path "CN=webapp01,DC=rebeladmin,DC=com"
```

The preceding command creates a user account called `tidris` on the local LDS instance that runs on `389`. Its DNS path is `CN=webapp01,DC=rebeladmin,DC=com`.

```
Get-ADUser -Filter * -SearchBase "CN=webapp01,DC=rebeladmin,DC=com" -
server 'localhost:389'
```

The preceding command lists all the user accounts in the LDS instance, `CN=webapp01,DC=rebeladmin,DC=com`. If you'd like to learn about more commands, please refer to `Chapter 7`, *Managing Active Directory Objects*.

AD LDS can be installed on a desktop OS using the Windows features option under **Program and Features**. The installation steps are similar to the server version. Once AD LDS is enabled, the setup wizard can be found under **Administrative Tools**:

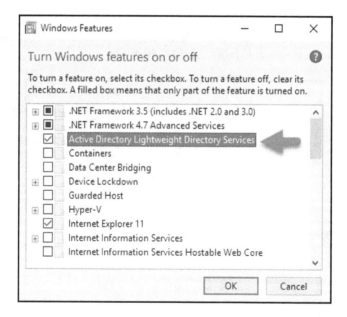

This option is available on all desktop OSes after Windows Vista. If it's Windows 7, it needs to be downloaded from the Microsoft site. In order to manage objects, you need to install **Remote Server Administration Tools** (**RSAT**) or use PowerShell to manage them.

AD replication

Healthy replication is a must for an AD environment. AD uses a multi-master database, so every domain controller in the environment should be aware of every change in an AD database. As well as this, they should also know about changes in group policies, startup scripts, preference setting, and more. When it comes to replication, it is not only the replication service that is responsible for it. There should be an uninterrupted *communication* between domain controllers.

This communication media can be copper cables, fiber cables, or even a **Software-Defined Network** (**SDN**). In this section, we are going to look at how we can use the AD-integrated features to maintain healthy replication.

FRS versus DFSR

Windows Server 2000 and 2003 use FRS to replicate the SYSVOL folder content between domain controllers. With Windows Server 2008, FRS was deprecated and Microsoft introduced DFS for SYSVOL folder replication:

FRS	DFSR
FRS is an outdated protocol and no development or investment was made into it after the release of Windows Server 2003 R2. No bug fixes or updates were released. Outdated protocols can lead to security threats to systems, as they cannot be tested against modern security threats.	Continuous improvements and investments were made toward the DFSR protocol and it was continuously tested against emerging threats.

FRS uses the last write wins algorithm. When the system detects a file change in one of the SYSVOL folders, it becomes the authoritative server and will replicate the *entire* file to other domain controllers. It will not merge the changes. It doesn't matter how small the change is, it always copies the entire file, which can cause performance issues, especially if the domain controllers are connected via slow links.	DFSR allows you to replicate partial file changes using block-level replication. It also supports asynchronous file replication via slow links. If you are running Enterprise Edition, it can use cross-file **Remote Differential Compression (RDC)** to create files on the client side using common blocks used by similar files. It will reduce the amount of data that needs to be transferred via the links.
FRS uses NTFS file compression in the staging folder.	File compression can be controlled based on the file type.
There is no interface for monitoring (API or WMI), and the GUI tools for managing services are very limited. These GUI tools are no longer available after Windows Server 2003. They do not support monitoring using the System Center Operation Manager.	There is an enhanced GUI tool for managing related services, and GUI can use WMI to monitor the health of the service. It also has management packs developed for monitoring through the System Center Operation Manager.
FRS does not have a reporting system to generate diagnostic reports if required. Diagnostic will only be based on events. It also has limited counters to review performances using PerfMon.	DFSR provides support for generating health reports in XML or HTML format. It also includes many counters to review the performance stats using PerfMon.
FRS does not have a system for auto-healing if there is file corruption.	DFSR is capable of auto-healing when it detects data corruption.
FRS does not fully support the RODC environment, and it can have data synchronization issues.	DFSR is fully supported for RODC replication.
FRS does not have advanced audit capabilities, as it only contains limited event logs and debug logs.	DFSR generates data-rich events and logs that can be used to audit, troubleshoot, and debug service failures.

Even though FRS is deprecated with Windows Server 2008 OSes, it can still be used for replication if you have migrated from Windows Server 2000 or 2003. Most of the time, engineers forget to migrate to DFSR as part of the upgrade projects. FRS to DFSR migration cannot migrate automatically and a few manual steps are involved. This can be done using the Dfsrmig.exe utility. In order to perform the migration from FRS to DFSR, your domain and forest functional levels should be at a minimum of Windows Server 2008.

Before we start, we can check the current replication method using the following command:

dfsrmig /getglobalstate

If it passes the status as Eliminated, it is using DFRS for replication. If it passes the status as Start, that means it is still using FRS for replication:

FRS to DFRS migration has four states:

- **state 0** (Start): By initiating this state, FRS will replicate the SYSVOL folder among the domain controllers. It is important to have an up-to-date copy of the SYSVOL folder before beginning the migration process.
- **state 1** (Prepared): In this state, while FRS continues replicating the SYSVOL folder, DFSR will also replicate a copy of the SYSVOL folder. It will be located in %SystemRoot%SYSVOL_DFRS. But this SYSVOL folder will not respond to any other domain controller service requests.
- **state 2** (Redirected): In this state, the DFSR copy of SYSVOL starts to respond to the SYSVOL folder service requests. FRS will continue the replication of its own SYSVOL copy but will not be involved with the replication of production SYSVOL (DFRS) folders.
- **state 3** (Eliminated): In this state, DFS will continue its replication and serve the SYSVOL folder requests. Windows will delete the original SYSVOL folder used by FRS replication and stop FRS replication.

In order to migrate from FRS to DFSR, the migration must go from state 0 to state 3.

Prepared state

The following steps demonstrate how to start migration by setting the system to the prepared state:

1. Log in to the domain controller as the Domain Admin or Enterprise Admin.
2. Launch the PowerShell console.
3. Type `dfsrmig /setglobalstate 1`.
4. Type `dfsrmig /getmigrationstate` to confirm that all the domain controllers have reached the `Prepared` state.

Redirected state

The following steps demonstrate how to move into the redirected state:

1. Type `dfsrmig /setglobalstate 2` and press the *Enter* key.
2. Type `dfsrmig /getmigrationstate` to confirm all the domain controllers have reached the `Redirected` state.

Eliminated state

Using the following steps, we can move into the eliminated state:

1. Type `dfsrmig /setglobalstate 3` and press the *Enter* key.

   If you need to revert back to FRS, you need to do so before this state. When the migration status is in the eliminated state, it will not be possible to go back.

2. Type `dfsrmig /getmigrationstate` to confirm that all the domain controllers have reached the `Eliminated` state.

   This confirms the successful migration from FRS to DFSR. To verify this, we can run *net share*. It will list the shares, and we should be able to see the `SYSVOL_DFSR` share.

Once all is confirmed, we need to *stop* the FRS service and *disable* it:

Once DFSR is enabled, the related firewall ports also need to open for successful DFS replication. TCP ports 137, 139, 389, 135, and 445, and UDP ports 137, 138, 389, and 445 need to be allowed. On some occasions, antivirus software will also block DFS traffic. Therefore, make sure the traffic is not interrupted.

AD sites and replication

AD components represent the physical and logical structure of a business. AD forests, domains, organization units, and AD objects, such as computers and users, represent the logical structure of the business. AD roles and features, such as AD CS, AD RMS, and AD FS, can be used to represent the organization's operational and security requirements. In an infrastructure, all these components are connected together using physical connections such as copper or fiber. Without the physical connection, there is no possibility for these AD components to communicate with each other and perform a logical structure. Based on the business requirements, connectivity may have to be extended to remote geographical locations. This can vary from different buildings in the same location to locations on different continents. These remote networks may use various connection methods to maintain connectivity with each other. It can be VPN, copper leased lines, fiber connections, or even satellite connections. By default, AD will not understand the network topology underneath it. If we consider the **Open Systems Interconnection** (**OSI**) model, AD is operated in the Application layer and physical connections are represented by the Network layer. There are three main reasons why AD should also be aware of this physical network topology, which are as follows:

- Replication
- Authentication
- Service location

Replication

The success of the AD infrastructure largely depends on healthy replication. Every domain controller in the network should be aware of every change in configuration. When a domain controller triggers a sync, it passes the data through the physical network to the destination. It consumes the *bandwidth* of the wire for the data. Depending on the used media and available bandwidth, the impact made by this replication traffic will vary. If it has high-speed links, such as 40 Gbps, 10 Gbps, 1 Gbps, or 100 Mbps, then the impact made by replication traffic will be very low. But in slow links, such as 128 Kbps or 256 Kbps, the impact will be significantly higher.

Most of the time, links between remote networks are slow links and come with a big bill. Therefore, there should be a way to control the replication based on the available bandwidth and AD should be aware of it.

Authentication

When an identity tries to authenticate, the request should be processed by a domain controller. If all the domain controllers are located in one geographical location, it doesn't matter which available domain controller processes the request. But if it's between remote networks, the time it takes to process the request will depend on the available link bandwidth and the number of hops it needs to travel through.

As an example, let's assume that Rebeladmin Corp. has an AD infrastructure and it is stretched between two offices in London and Seattle. It has domain controllers located in both locations. If a user logs in to a PC in the London office, it doesn't make sense to have the authentication request processed by a domain controller in the Seattle office. This is because the request needs to pass through a few network hops and a slow link. If large numbers of requests are processed, the majority of the slow link bandwidth will be used by these requests. Ideally, it should be processed by the closest domain controller, which is located at the same location. Then, there are no additional hops to pass and no bandwidth limitations. Also, it will not depend on the availability of the link between two locations in order to process the requests. Therefore, AD should force identities located in remote networks to authenticate via its closest domain controllers.

Service locations

This is the extension for the things I explained in the previous section. In a remote network, there can be different server roles and AD-integrated applications running. Similar to authentication requests, when users or computers try to use a service or application, it should be processed by the closest application server. It will improve the user experience and the reliability of the application or the services. When it's via a slow link, it does have lots of dependencies and performance-related limitations. In order to do this, there should be a way to process these service requests and point users to the closest servers.

The answer to all the aforementioned requirements is the AD site and related components. These allow us to represent the physical network topology within the AD infrastructure. Then, AD will be aware of where its components are located and how they're connected with each other. Based on this data, AD will allow you to control the replication over slow links and point the authentication and service requests to the closest servers.

So, let's go ahead and look further into AD sites and their related components.

Sites

Sites can be explained as physical locations that contain various AD objects. We should be able to describe these objects using their boundaries. As an example, users, computers, and network devices located in an office location in London can be treated as a site, and these can be identified as unique from similar objects located in the Seattle office. The AD site topology can be divided into four different main designs:

- **Single domain-single sites**: This is the most common setup for small- and medium-sized businesses. In this setup, there is one site and one domain. When we set up the first domain controller in the infrastructure, it is set up as a single domain-single site by default. This is easy to maintain.
- **Single domain-multiple sites**: In this setup, the infrastructure has only one domain, and it's extended to multiple sites. It can be based on different buildings, data centers, or geographical locations. Sites are interconnected using physical network links. This can be via VPN, leased lines, or satellite connections.
- **Multiple domain-single sites**: In one physical site, there can be multiple domain setups. Replications between domains will depend on the logical topology. The replication bandwidth impact is minimal, as domain controllers communicate with each other using fast LAN connections.
- **Multiple domain-multiple sites**: In this setup, multiple domains will be placed in multiple sites. In such a setup, replication will depend on the logical topology as well as the physical topology. In some setups, domains will be limited to certain sites, and in others, domains will be extended to multiple sites.

Subnets

Subnets represent associated IP address ranges in each site. These are equal to the subnets allocated in network devices, but do not need to be exactly the same. For example, if a site uses 10-20 class C subnets, then instead of adding all these to the AD site's subnet, we can summarize them all into a class B subnet and use them. Based on this subnet information, AD allows objects to locate the closest domain controller. When physical subnets are added or removed, they should be updated in the AD site configuration as well, otherwise, they will pass unmanaged traffic via slow links.

Site links

Site links represent the physical connection between sites; however, they don't control the network level routing or connectivity between sites. It's still being handled by the underlying WAN links and network devices. Site links allow for replication jobs to be scheduled and for bandwidth to be controlled (link cost).

Site link bridges

Site link bridges contain multiple site links. These allow transitive communication between each site link under the bridge. By default, all site links are treated as bridges. In some cases, not all site links need to talk to each other. They are controlled by the routing rules in the network devices; if they're set up that way, the default behavior of the link bridges needs to be modified, and make sure to disable **Bridge all site links**:

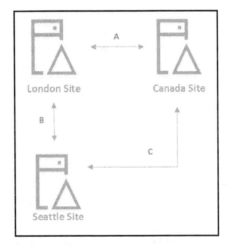

The best way to explain site link bridges is to use this simple example. According to the preceding diagram, for **London Site** to reach **Canada Site**, there are two paths: one is using **A** and the other one is using **B** and **C**. Therefore, on **Seattle Site**, we can create a site link bridge that includes site links **B** and **C**, and present it as an alternative path for reaching **Canada Site**.

Managing AD sites and other components

There are two ways to manage AD sites and related components. One option is to use the AD Sites and Services MMC, and the other one is to use PowerShell cmdlets. In order to add/edit/remove sites and related configurations, we need to have Domain Admin/Enterprise Admin privileges.

The AD Sites and Services MMC will be available in any server that has AD DS service enabled or any server/computer that has RSAT installed. The AD PowerShell module will also be available in any server that has the AD DS role enabled or has the RSAT tools installed.

Managing sites

When the first domain controller is introduced into the infrastructure, the system creates its first site as `Default-First-Site-Name`. This can be changed based on the given requirements. We can review the existing site's configuration using the following PowerShell cmdlet:

```
Get-ADReplicationSite -Filter *
```

It will list the site's information for the AD infrastructure.

Our example only has the default AD site. As this is the first step, we need to change it to a meaningful name so we can assign objects and configurations accordingly. In order to do that, we can use the `Rename-ADObject` cmdlet:

```
Rename-ADObject -Identity "CN=Default-First-Site-
Name,CN=Sites,CN=Configuration,DC=rebeladmin,DC=com" -NewName
"LondonSite"
```

The preceding command renames the `Default-First-Site-Name` site to `LondonSite`. In the existing site, we can change the values using the `Set-ADReplicationSite` cmdlet:

```
Get-ADReplicationSite -Identity LondonSite | Set-ADReplicationSite -
Description "UK AD Site"
```

The preceding command changed the site description to `UK AD Site`.

We can create a new AD site using the `New-ADReplicationSite` cmdlet. The full description of the command can be viewed using `Get-Command New-ADReplicationSite -Syntax`:

```
New-ADReplicationSite -Name "CanadaSite" -Description "Canada AD Site"
```

The preceding command creates a new AD site called `CanadaSite`.

Once the sites are created, we need to move the domain controllers to the relevant sites. By default, all the domain controllers are placed under the default site, `Default-First-Site-Name`.

Even if you do not want to place a domain controller in a site, it can be assigned to the site-aware services, such as DFS and exchange services. Placing a domain controller on a site depends on the number of users and link reliability.

In the following command, we are listing all the domain controllers in the AD infrastructure with filtered data to show the `Name`, `ComputerObjectDN`, `Site` attribute values:

```
Get-ADDomainController -Filter * | select Name,ComputerObjectDN,Site |
fl
```

Now we have the list of domain controllers; in the next step, we can move the domain controller to the relevant site:

```
Move-ADDirectoryServer -Identity "REBEL-SDC-02" -Site "CanadaSite"
```

The preceding command will move the `REBEL-SDC-02` domain controller to `CanadaSite`.

During the additional domain controller setup, we can define which site it will be assigned to. If the site already has domain controllers, it will do the initial replication from those. If it doesn't, it will replicate from any selected domain controller or, if not, from any available domain controller. If the link bandwidth is an issue, it's recommended to promote the domain controller from a site that has fast links, and then move the domain controller to the relevant site.

Managing site links

Now that we have the sites set up, the next step is to create site links. Using site links, we can manage the replication schedule and the bandwidth.

The site link cost

The site link cost defines the nearest resources if the on-site resource are not available. In the network topology, the site link is mainly based on the link's bandwidth. But here, a site link cost is decided based on the bandwidth, latency, and reliability. For example, let's assume site A and site B are connected via a 100 Mbps link. Site A and site C are connected via the 512 Kbps link. If we only consider the bandwidth, site A will prefer site B as the closest site. But this link had a few failures last month, and so 512 Kbps is more reliable. By changing the site link cost, I can force site A to use site C as the preferred closest resource site.

In the following example, we have three sites, and each site has two site links to connect to each other:

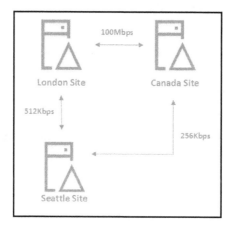

If the line latency and availability are not a problem, then for **London Site**, the first preferred site should be **Canada Site**. If that link fails, it still uses **Seattle Site**. For **Canada Site**, **London Site** is the first preference and the next is **Seattle Site**. For **Seattle Site**, the first preference is **London Site** and the next is **Canada Site**. But here, we are only considering the bandwidth. The link preferences can be modified by changing the site cost. By default, every site link gets the cost of 100.

The site link that holds the lowest site cost value will be the first preference. When the system determines the code to a destination, it does not consider the direct links. In the same way, a network topology will find its best route. In the preceding example, if **London Site** wants to reach **Canada Site**, there are two paths: one is the direct link and the other one is via **Seattle Site**. So, when it considers the best path, it will calculate the cost value of the direct link against the cost value of **London Site** | **Seattle Site** | **Canada Site**.

The following list includes the preferred site cost value based on the bandwidth:

Available bandwidth	Cost
9.6 Kbps	1,042
19.2 Kbps	798
38.4 Kbps	644
56 Kbps	586
64 Kbps	567
128 Kbps	486
256 Kbps	425
512 Kbps	378
1,024 Kbps	340
2,048 Kbps	309
4,096 Kbps	283
10 Mbps	257
100 Mbps	205
1,000 Mbps	171

Inter-site transport protocols

There are two transport protocols that can be used for replication via site links. The default protocol used in site link is IP, and it performs synchronous replication between available domain controllers. The SMTP method can be used when the link between sites is not reliable. It will use mail messages to replicate AD partition data, including the schema changes between domain controllers. If it uses the SMTP method, there should be a certification authority to encrypt the traffic.

Replication intervals

By default, in a default site link, a replication occurs *every 180 minutes*. Based on the requirements, this can be changed to the value we need. If required, it also allows us to disable the replication schedules completely and rely on manually triggered replications.

Replication schedules

By default, site replication is happening 24/7. Based on the site bandwidth considerations, this can be changed. For example, if it's a slow link, it is best to set the replication after operation hours and during lunch hours. It will control the replication traffic impact on slow links and allow the organization to use the link bandwidth for other mission-critical traffic. It's important to evaluate the consequences of changing the replication schedule. If you add/modify objects and policies, those will not replicate between sites unless they match the replication schedule.

In order to set up the site links, we can use the `New-ADReplicationSiteLink` cmdlet:

```
New-ADReplicationSiteLink -Name "London-Canada" -SitesIncluded
LondonSite,CanadaSite -Cost 205 -ReplicationFrequencyInMinutes 30 -
InterSiteTransportProtocol IP
```

The preceding command creates a new site link called `London-Canada`, which includes `LondonSite` and `CanadaSite`. The site cost is set to `205`, and the replication intervals are set to every `30` minutes. Its transport protocol is set to `IP`.

We can do the same configuration by using the **Active Directory Sites and Services** MMC:

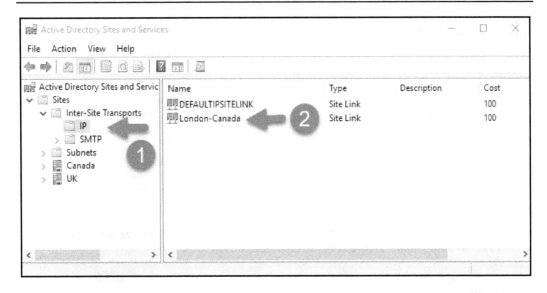

We can change the replication schedule using the `-ReplicationSchedule` option or GUI. In order to change it using GUI, click on the **Change Schedule...** button. Then, in the window, you can change the replication schedule. In this demonstration, I changed the replication to happen from Monday to Friday, from 6:00 a.m. to 10:00 a.m.:

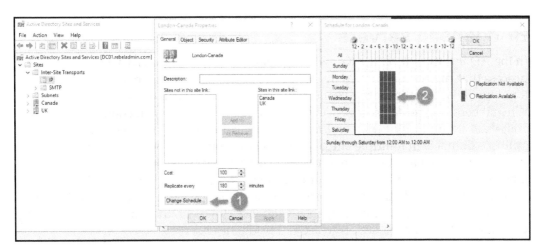

The site link bridge

We can create the site link bridge using the `New-ADReplicationSiteLinkBridge` cmdlet:

```
New-ADReplicationSiteLinkBridge -Name "London-Canada-Bridge" -
SiteLinksIncluded "London-Canada","London-CanadaDRLink"
```

The preceding command creates a new site link bridge called `London-Canada-Bridge` using two site links: `London-Canada` and `London-CanadaDRLink`.

Using the `Set-ADReplicationSiteLinkBridge` cmdlet, the existing site link bridge value can change:

```
Set-ADReplicationSiteLinkBridge -Identity "London-Canada-Bridge" -
SiteLinksIncluded @{Remove='London-CanadaDRLink'}
```

The preceding command removes the `London-CanadaDRLink` site link from the existing site link bridge, `London-Canada-Bridge`:

```
Set-ADReplicationSiteLinkBridge -Identity "London-Canada-Bridge" -
SiteLinksIncluded @{Add='London-CanadaDRLink'}
```

The preceding command adds the given site link to the existing site link bridge.

Bridgehead servers

In the AD infrastructure, the **Knowledge Consistency Checker** (**KCC**) is a built-in process that runs on domain controllers and is responsible for generating replication topology. It will configure the replication connection between domain controllers. When it comes to replication between sites, KCC selects a domain controller as a *bridgehead server,* which sends and receives replication traffic for its site. If you have multiple domains in multiple sites, each domain should have its own bridgehead server. A site can have multiple bridgehead servers for the same domain, but at a given time, only one will be active. It is decided based on the domain controller's lowest GUID value. In the AD environment, if AD involves an intra-site replication, AD automatically selects the bridgehead servers. However, there are situations where you may prefer a specific server to act as a bridgehead server.

By opening the properties of the domain controller, you can choose what you want to set as a bridgehead server. The best practice is to set the most reliable domain controller as the bridgehead server:

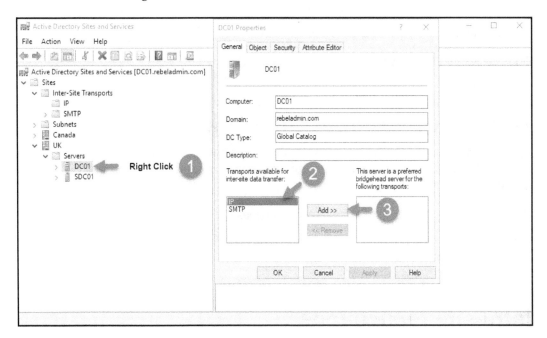

Managing subnets

Now that we have the sites and site links set up, the next step is to assign the subnets to each site. These can be set up using the New-ADReplicationSubnet cmdlet:

```
New-ADReplicationSubnet -Name "192.168.0.0/24" -Site LondonSite
```

The preceding PowerShell command creates a new subnet, 192.168.0.0/24, and assigns it to LondonSite.

Using Set-ADReplicationSubnet, we can change value of the existing subnet:

```
Set-ADReplicationSubnet -Identity "192.168.0.0/24" -Site CanadaSite
```

The preceding command changes the site of the `192.168.0.0/24` subnet to `CanadaSite`.

We can use the `Get-ADReplicationSubnet` cmdlet to find the subnet data:

```
Get-ADReplicationSubnet -Filter {Site -Eq "CanadaSite"}
```

The preceding command lists all the subnets under `CanadaSite`.

How does replication work?

By now, we know the logical and physical components involved in the AD replication process. Now, it's time to put all these together and understand exactly how AD replications happen.

In the AD environment, there are two main types of replications:

- Intra-site replications
- Inter-site replications

Intra-site replications

As the name implies, this covers the replications happening within the AD site. By default, (according to Microsoft) any domain controller will be aware of any directory update within 15 seconds. Within the site, despite the number of domain controllers, any directory update will be replicated in less than a minute:

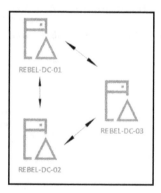

Within the site, the replication connections are being performed in a ring topology, which means that any given domain controllers have two replication links (of course, if there are a minimum of three domain controllers). This architecture will prevent domain controllers from having endless replication loops.

For example, if there are five domain controllers and if all are connected to each other with one-to-one connections, each domain controller will have four connections, and when there is an update to one of the domain controllers, it will need to advertise this to four domain controllers. Then, the first one to receive the update will advertise to its four connected domain controllers, and it goes on and on. There are too many replication processes to advertise, listen, and sort out the conflicts.

But in a ring topology, despite the number of domain controllers in the site, any given domain controller only needs to advertise or listen to two domain controllers at any given time. With this replication topology, there is no need for manual configuration, and AD will automatically determine the connections it needs to make. When the number of domain controllers grows, the replication time can grow as well as it's in a ring topology. But to avoid latency, AD creates additional connections. This is also determined automatically, and we do not need to worry about these replication connections.

Inter-site replications

If the AD infrastructure contains more than one site, a change in one site needs to be replicated over to the other sites. This is called an **inter-site replication**, and its topology is different from intra-site replication. Replication within the site always benefits from high-speed links. But when it comes to the connection between sites, facts such as bandwidth, latency, and reliability all have an impact.

In the previous section, we discussed site links, site costs, and replication schedules, which we can use to control intra-site replications:

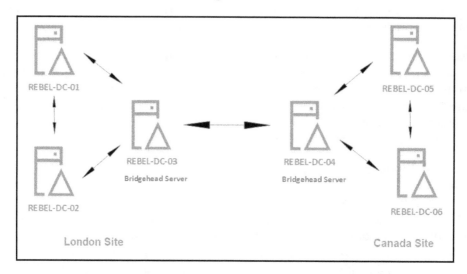

When it comes to inter-site replications, these happen via *site links*. The replication within each site still uses the ring topology. In the preceding example, let's assume an object has been added to **REBEL-DC-02** in **London Site**. Now, based on the topology, it will be advertised to **REBEL-DC-03** too. But apart from being the domain controller, this particular domain controller is a bridgehead server as well. So, it is this server's responsibility to advertise the updates it received into the bridge server in **Canada Site**, which is **REBEL-DC-04**. Once it receives the update, it will advertise to the other domain controllers in the site. The replication between sites still needs to follow the replication schedules.

AD DS automatically selects the bridgehead server for a site. But there are situations where engineers want to select a server they prefer to be the bridgehead server. In the previous section, we looked at how we can force a domain controller to become the *preferred bridgehead server*.

The KCC

When I discussed the Active Directory Replication, I mentioned that AD performs functions such as automatically creating replication links and selecting bridgehead servers. But how does it really do it? The KCC is the one responsible for all these.

The KCC is a built-in service in AD domain controllers and it is responsible for generating and maintaining the replication topology for intra- and inter-site replications. Every 15 minutes, the KCC will revalidate its existing replication topology and make the topology changes if required. It gives enough time for domain controllers to replicate the changes if the existing replication topology is valid.

When it comes to inter-site replication, the KCC selects a single KCC holder in a remote site to act as the **Intersite Topology Generator** (**ISTG**), and the ISTG's responsibility is to select the bridgehead servers for replication. The ISTG creates the view of replication topology for all the sites it is connected to. The ISTG is responsible for deciding the topology for the site, and individual domain controllers (such as the KCC) are responsible for making topology decisions locally.

The best way to understand the KCC is to compare it with a network routing protocol. A network routing protocol is responsible for maintaining a routing path for connected networks. If network A needs to communicate with network B, the routing table will tell it what path to go to. In the same way, the topology created by the KCC will tell us how domain controller A can replicate the changes in domain controller B. When I have worked on AD projects, I have seen engineers create manual replication links between domain controllers. But I really doubt whether someone can be smarter than the KCC when it comes to deciding replication topology.

How do updates occur?

We now know how the replication topology works, but how exactly does a domain controller know when an update has occurred? And how do the connected domain controllers know when to trigger replications? Let's go ahead and explore the technology behind it in further depth.

The Update Sequence Number (USN)

The USN is a 64-bit number, which is allocated to the domain controller during the **DCPromo** process. When there is any object update, the USN allocated to the domain controller will be increased. As an example, let's assume that domain controller A had an initial USN value of 2,000 assigned to it. If we add 5 user objects, the new USN will be 2,005. This number can only increase; it cannot decrease. The USN is only valid for its own domain controller. It is not technically possible for two domain controllers in the site to have the same USN assigned.

The Directory Service Agent (DSA) GUID and invocation ID

Domain controllers involved in the replication process are identified using two unique identifiers. The first one is the DSA GUID. It is generated during the **Dcpromo** process, and it will never change during the lifetime of the domain controller. The next one is the invocation ID. In a restore process, it will change, otherwise, the existing domain controllers will identify it as an existing domain controller and will not replicate data over.

The High Watermark Vector (HWMV) table

The HWMV table is maintained locally by each domain controller in order to keep track of the last change from its replication partner for the given **naming context (NC)**. As you are aware, domain controllers have three NCs: schema NCs, configuration NCs, and domain NCs. There is an HWMV table for each NC. The table contains the latest USN value it received from its replication partner for a given NC. Based on that, the domain controller decides where to start the replication process.

The Up-To-Dateness Vector (UTDV) table

The UTDV table is maintained locally by each domain controller to prevent unnecessary replications. UTDV also—per NC and domain controller—has a minimum of three UTDV tables. The UTDV table contains the highest UPN value it learned from any connected domain controller per NC basis. This prevents domain controllers from replicating the same changes over and over. For example, if domain controller A received a domain NC from domain controller B, it would update the UTDV table and update the UPN value for it. Based on that, it would not retrieve the same update from the other connected domain controllers. Because of UTDV, domain controllers will not send any data to their replication partners if they have already received it from someone else. This is called **propagation dampening**:

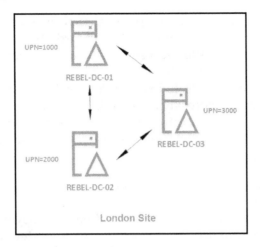

In order to summarize the replication, let's follow a scenario. In the preceding example, we have three connected domain controllers. Each has an initial UPN value assigned. Now, let's assume, using **REBEL-DC-01**, that a new user object has been added. So now, its UPN has increased to **1,001**. At this point, the domain controller knows about its connected replication partners based on the DSA GUID and invocation ID. **REBEL-DC-02** is already aware of the last UPN value it received from **REBEL-DC-01** as it is stored on the HWMV table. Before it updates, it checks the UTDV table to make sure it didn't receive the same update via **REBEL-DC-03**. If not, then it replicates and increases its UPN and the values in the HWMV and UTDV tables. I hope this explains exactly what is happening with the AD replication.

RODCs

RODCs are a great role introduced with Windows Server 2008, which can be used to maintain a domain controller in locations where it cannot guarantee physical security and regular maintenance. Throughout this chapter, we have discussed possible scenarios where we have required a domain controller in a remote site. When considering a domain controller in a remote site, the link between sites is not the only thing we need to consider. A domain controller, by default, will be aware of any changes in the AD structure. Once an update triggers, it updates its own copy of the AD database. This `ntds.dit` file contains everything about the AD infrastructure, including the identity data of the user objects. If this file falls into wrong hands, they can retrieve data related to identities and compromise the identity infrastructure.

When considering information security, physical security is also important. That's why the data centers have all sorts of security standards. So, when deploying a domain controller in a remote site, we also need to take physical security into consideration as we do not want to have loose ends. If you have a requirement for a domain controller in a remote site, but you cannot confirm its security, then RODC is the answer. RODC does not store any passwords in its database. All the authentication requests against an object will be processed by the closest writable domain controller. Therefore, even if someone manages to get a copy of the database, they will not be able to do much.

In a virtual environment, Windows allows you to map the **Virtual Hard Disk** (**VHD**) file to any computer and view the data on it. So, even if you are not the Domain Admin you may have privileges in the virtual environment which can use to retrieve database files. In order to prevent this, Microsoft has introduced the *shielded VMs* with Hyper-V 2016. This allows you to encrypt the virtual machine using BitLocker, and no one will be able to use the copied VHD.

Another advantage of RODCs is that they only do one-way replications. When considering remote sites, you also need to consider how systems will be maintained. Not every organization can maintain IT teams for remote offices. Most of the maintenance tasks can still be carried out remotely, but there are certain situations where you will need to delegate some permissions to people in remote sites. Most of the time, these people are less experienced in IT, so any simple mistakes made by them can be replicated to other domain controllers and make a mess. RODC's one-way replication will prevent this and no change will be replicated over to other domain controllers. Nice, huh?

By default, RODCs do not save any passwords (except RODC objects) for AD objects. Every time an authentication happens, RODC needs to retrieve the data from the closest domain controller. Using **Password Replication Policy** (**PRP**), we can allow certain passwords for objects to be cached. If the connection between a remote site and the closest domain controller is interrupted, our RODC will be able to process the request. One thing to remember is, in order to process a Kerberos request, RODC needs to cache the password for the user object as well as the computer object.

Azure AD Connect does not support RODCs. The domain controller used by Azure AD must be writable as Azure AD Connect does not know how to work with write redirects.

The RODC deployment process involves the following stages. In this process, we can use a preselected account and promote the RODC, using it instead of using a Domain Admin or an Enterprise Admin account:

1. Set up a computer account for the RODC domain controller.
2. Attach that account to the RODC during the promotion process.

In order to create an RODC computer account, we can use the Add–ADDSReadOnlyDomainControllerAccount cmdlet:

```
Add-ADDSReadOnlyDomainControllerAccount -DomainControllerAccountName
REBEL-RODC-01 -DomainName rebeladmin.com -
DelegatedAdministratorAccountName "rebeladmindfrancis" -SiteName
LondonSite
```

The preceding command will create the RODC domain controller account for REBEL–RODC-01. The domain name is defined using -DomainName, and -DelegatedAdministratorAccountName defines which account to delegate the RODC installation. The new RODC will be placed in LondonSite.

Now, we can see the newly added object under the AD domain controllers:

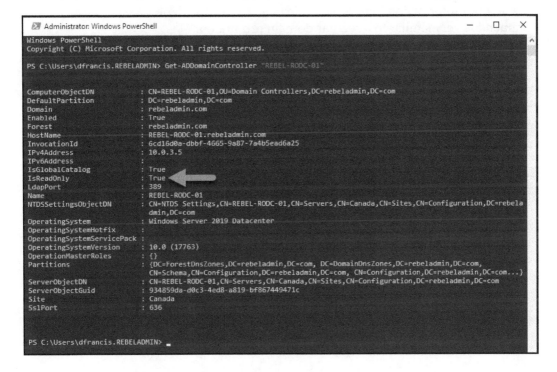

Now, we have things ready for the new RODC and the next step is to install the relevant role service:

```
Install-WindowsFeature -Name AD-Domain-Services -
IncludeManagementTools
```

The preceding command installs the AD DS role in the RODC. Once it's completed, we can promote it using the following command:

```
Import-Module ADDSDeployment
Install-ADDSDomainController `
-Credential (Get-Credential) `
-CriticalReplicationOnly:$false `
-DatabasePath "C:WindowsNTDS" `
-DomainName "rebeladmin.com" `
-LogPath "C:WindowsNTDS" `
-ReplicationSourceDC "REBEL-PDC-01.rebeladmin.com" `
-SYSVOLPath "C:WindowsSYSVOL" `
-UseExistingAccount:$true `
-Norebootoncompletion:$false `
-Force:$true
```

Once this is executed, it prompts us for the user account, and we need to input the user account information, which was delegated for RODC deployment. The command is very similar to a regular domain promotion.

Now that we have the RODC, the next step is to look into PRP.

The default policy is already in place, and we can view the Allowed and Denied lists using the following command:

```
Get-ADDomainControllerPasswordReplicationPolicy -Identity REBEL-
RODC-01 -Allowed
```

The preceding command lists the Allowed objects for password caching. By default, a security group called **Allowed RODC Password Replication Group** is allowed for the replication. This doesn't contain any members by default. If we need caching, we can add an object to the same group:

```
Get-ADDomainControllerPasswordReplicationPolicy -Identity REBEL-
RODC-01 -Denied
```

The preceding command lists the `Denied` objects for password caching. By default, the following security groups are in the `Denied` list:

- **Denied RODC Password Replication Group**
- **Account Operators**
- **Server Operators**
- **Backup Operators**
- **Administrators**

These are high-privileged accounts in the AD infrastructure; these should not be cached at all. By adding objects to **Denied RODC Password Replication Group**, we can simply block the replication.

Apart from the use of predefined security groups, we can add objects to the `Allowed` and `Denied` lists using the `Add-ADDomainControllerPasswordReplicationPolicy` cmdlet:

```
Add-ADDomainControllerPasswordReplicationPolicy -Identity REBEL-
RODC-01 -AllowedList "user1"
```

The preceding command will add the user object named `user1` to the `Allowed` list.

The following command will add the user object named `user2` to the `Denied` list:

```
Add-ADDomainControllerPasswordReplicationPolicy -Identity REBEL-
RODC-01 -DeniedList "user2"
```

 To improve the security further, it is recommended to install an RODC in the Windows Core operating system. Nano Servers introduced with Windows Server 2016 are not yet supported for RODCs.

AD database maintenance

AD maintains a multi-master database to store schema information, configuration information, and domain information. Normally, when we say *database*, the first thing that comes to our mind is software such as Microsoft SQL, MySQL, or Oracle. But here, it's quite different. AD databases use the **Extensible Storage Engine** (ESE), which is an **Indexed and Sequential Access Method** (ISAM) technology.

Here, a single system works as the client and server. It uses record-oriented database architecture, which provides extremely fast access to records. The ESE indexes the data in the database file, which can grow to up to 16 terabytes and hold over 2 billion records. Typically, the ESE is used for applications that require fast and structured data storage. The ESE is used for many other Microsoft applications, including Microsoft Exchange, DHCP, and FRS.

As the database creation process is part of the domain controller installation process, it creates the database under `C:\Windows\NTDS` unless we select a custom path. It is recommended to use a separate partition/disk with a higher speed, in order to increase the database performance as well as the data protection:

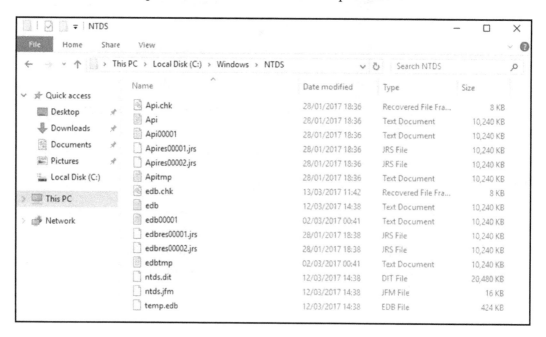

In this folder, we can see a few different files. Out of those, the following files are important.

The ntds.dit file

This is the actual AD database file. This database contains three main tables. The **schema** table includes data regarding the object classes, attributes, and the relationship between them. The **link** table includes data about values referring to another object. Group membership details are a good example of this. The **data** table includes all the data about users, groups, and any other data integrated with AD. In the table, rows represent the objects and columns represent the attributes.

The edb.log file

Here, we can see that a few log files start with edb*, all of which are 10 MB or less in size. This is the transaction log maintained by the system to store the directory transaction before writing data into the database file.

The edb.chk file

This file is responsible for keeping track of the data transaction committed into the database from log files (edb*.log).

The temp.edb file

This file is used during the AD database maintenance to hold data and, also, to store information about AD data transactions that are in progress.

Every domain controller in the AD infrastructure needs to be aware of the changes made in each domain controller. When this happens, you may think that the database is being synced. But it is not the database; only the changes are being synced. Therefore, each domain controller in the domain will not be the same size.

Most of the database systems have their own automatic data grooming techniques to maintain the efficiency of the system. This also gives administrators a chance to perform custom maintenance tasks and granular maintenance. AD database is a self-maintained system. It does not require daily maintenance. However, there are some situations where it requires manual intervention:

- If the default database partition is running out of space or notices a potential hardware failure
- To free up unused space in AD database after mass object deletion

If required, we can move the AD database from its default location. To do that, we can use a command-line tool called `ntdsutil`. When moving the database files, it is also recommended to move the log files so the log files will not need to refer to two different disks. The minimum space requirement for the database file is 500 MB, or the database file size along with 20% of the database file size (whichever is greater). The log file space requirement is also the same.

The database and log files cannot be moved while AD DS is running. Therefore, the first step of the action is to stop the service:

```
net stop ntds
```

This will also stop the associated services, including KDC, DNS, and DFS.

The AD database and log files cannot be moved to a non-existent folder. So before we move the files, the folder needs to be created.

In my demonstration, I will move it to a folder called ADDB in a different partition:

```
ntdsutil
activate instance ntds
files
move db to E:\ADDB
move logs to E:\ADDB
integrityquit
quit
```

In the preceding command, `ntdsutil` initiates the utility, `move db to E:ADDB` moves the database files to the new location, and `move logs to E:ADDB` moves the log files to the new directory. The `integrity` part verifies the integrity of the database and logs files in the new location:

```
PS E:\> ntdsutil
C:\Windows\system32\ntdsutil.exe: activate instance ntds
Active instance set to "ntds".
C:\Windows\system32\ntdsutil.exe: files
File maintenance: move db to E:\ADDB

Successfully updated the backup exclusion key.
Copying NTFS security from C:\Windows\NTDS to E:\ADDB...
The previous NTDS database location C:\Windows\NTDS\dsadata.bak is unavailable. The default NTFS security will be applie
d to NTDS folders.
Default NTFS security on NTDS folders will be set on reboot.
Copying NTFS security from C:\Windows\NTDS to E:\ADDB...

Drive Information:

        C:\ NTFS (Fixed Drive ) free(28.8 Gb) total(39.4 Gb)
        E:\ NTFS (Fixed Drive ) free(1.9 Gb) total(1.9 Gb)

DS Path Information:

        Database    : E:\ADDB\ntds.dit - 20.0 Mb
        Backup dir  : E:\ADDB\DSADATA.BAK
        Working dir: E:\ADDB
        Log dir     : C:\Windows\NTDS - 50.0 Mb total
                        edbtmp.log - 10.0 Mb
                        edbres00002.jrs - 10.0 Mb
                        edbres00001.jrs - 10.0 Mb
                        edb00001.log - 10.0 Mb
                        edb.log - 10.0 Mb

Move database is successful.
Please make a backup immediately else restore will not retain the new file
location.
File maintenance: move logs to E:\ADDB
Successfully updated the backup exclusion key.

Copying NTFS security from C:\Windows\NTDS to E:\ADDB...

Drive Information:

        C:\ NTFS (Fixed Drive ) free(28.9 Gb) total(39.4 Gb)
        E:\ NTFS (Fixed Drive ) free(1.8 Gb) total(1.9 Gb)

DS Path Information:

        Database    : E:\ADDB\ntds.dit - 20.0 Mb
        Backup dir  : E:\ADDB\DSADATA.BAK
        Working dir: E:\ADDB
        Log dir     : E:\ADDB - 50.0 Mb total
                        edbtmp.log - 10.0 Mb
                        edbres00002.jrs - 10.0 Mb
                        edbres00001.jrs - 10.0 Mb
                        edb00001.log - 10.0 Mb
                        edb.log - 10.0 Mb

If move log files was successful,
 please make a backup immediately else restore
will not retain the new file location.
```

Once it's completed, we need to start AD DS using the following command:

```
net start ntds
```

As soon as this process is completed, it is recommended that you make a full backup of AD as the path changes. The previous backup, which was taken, will not be valid anymore.

Offline defragmentation

In any database system, the data will be added, modified, and deleted as it goes. When new data is added, it requires *new* space inside the database. When the data is removed, it *releases* space to the database. When the database is modified, it either needs new space or releases space. In the AD database, once an object has been deleted, it releases the space it used to the database, and not to the filesystem. Therefore, that free space will be used for new objects. This process is called **online defragmentation** because it does not need to stop the AD services. By default, it runs every 12 hours.

However, when a large number of objects or a global catalog server are removed, it is worth releasing this free space to the filesystem. In order to do that, we need to perform **offline defragmentation**. To do so, it is required that we stop the AD services.

Once the service stops (`net stop ntds`), we can run the defragmentation using the following commands:

```
ntdsutil
activate instance ntds
files
compact to E:\CompactDB
quit
quit
```

In the preceding process, we need a temporary folder location in which to save the compact `ntds.dit` file. In my demonstration, I created a folder named `E:\CompactDB` for this:

```
PS E:\> ntdsutil
C:\Windows\system32\ntdsutil.exe: activate instance ntds
Active instance set to "ntds".
C:\Windows\system32\ntdsutil.exe: files
file maintenance: compact to E:\CompactDB
Initiating DEFRAGMENTATION mode...
    Source Database: E:\ADDB\ntds.dit
    Target Database: E:\CompactDB\ntds.dit

              Defragmentation  Status (% complete)

    0    10   20   30   40   50   60   70   80   90  100
    |----|----|----|----|----|----|----|----|----|----|
    ..................................................

It is recommended that you immediately perform a full backup
of this database. If you restore a backup made before the
defragmentation, the database will be rolled back to the state
it was in at the time of that backup.

Compaction is successful. You need to:
    copy "E:\CompactDB\ntds.dit" "E:\ADDB\ntds.dit"
and delete the old log files:
    del E:\ADDB\*.log

file maintenance: quit
C:\Windows\system32\ntdsutil.exe: quit
PS E:\>
```

Once this is completed, the compact database should be copied to the original `ntds.dit` location. This can be done by using the following command:

```
copy "E:\CompactDB\ntds.dit" "E:\ADDB\ntds.dit"
```

After that, we also need to delete the old log file:

```
del E:\ADDB\*.log
```

After that, we can start AD DS using `net start ntds`.

This completes the two scenarios (database path change and defragmentation) where we will need to use manual intervention for AD database maintenance.

AD backup and recovery

AD domain controllers are the main components responsible for the organization's identity infrastructure. Failure of the domain controllers or the services will impact the entire identity infrastructure. Therefore, as with any other critical system, the AD server's high availability is crucial. There are two types of disasters related to AD domain controllers that can occur.

The first type of disaster is when there is a complete system crash due to faulty hardware. Apart from the AD backup, maintaining multiple domain controllers helps organizations to recover from such situations easily without a backup restore. If it's not the **flexible single master operation (FSMO)** role holder, we can forcefully remove the crashed domain controller's related records and introduce a new domain controller. If it's the FSMO role holder, we can *seize* the FSMO roles and make them available from any other live domain controller. On the other hand, most of the workloads are operating in a virtualized environment today, including domain controllers. These virtualized environments usually have solutions in place to recover from failures. As an example, virtualization solutions may use a clustered environment or advanced recovery solution such as the Azure site recovery. Therefore, in modern infrastructures, I rarely see anyone who has had to restore a domain controller from backup.

The second type of disaster is due to the deletion or configuration alternations of AD objects. Restoring a system from backup is not always a *no-impact* disaster recovery. It can take *time* to recover your system to a working condition. The recovery process can be followed by some data loss or operation impacts due to the time taken. If you want to recover an object you deleted in AD, it doesn't make sense to restore the whole domain controller itself from a backup. Therefore, Microsoft uses different tools and methodologies to recover from both situations. In the following sections, we are going to look into these in detail.

Preventing the accidental deletion of objects

With AD DS 2008, Microsoft introduced a small but important feature to prevent accidental AD object deletion. This is not a solution to recover from disasters, but it is a solution to prevent disasters. In every AD object under the **Object** tab, there is a small checkbox to enable this feature. This can be enabled when we create objects using PowerShell. Even if we're not using PowerShell, this can still be enabled using the **Object** properties window at any time. When creating an **Organizational Unit** (**OU**) using GUI, it allows us to enable this option, and it's the only object that's allowed to do so during the setup:

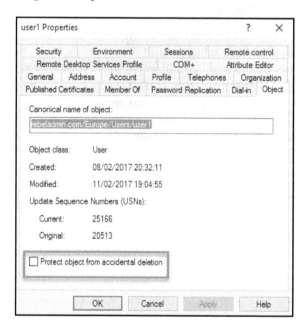

When this option is enabled, it will not allow you to delete the object unless you disable this option:

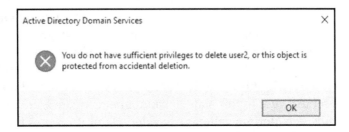

In PowerShell, this can be done using the -ProtectedFromAccidentalDeletion $true parameter.

AD Recycle Bin

The most common AD-related disasters are due to accidentally deleting objects. Once an object is deleted from AD, it is not permanently deleted. As soon as an object is deleted, it will set the isDeleted attribute value to True and move the object under CN=Deleted Objects:

Then, it stays there until the system reaches the *tombstone lifetime* value. By default, this is 180 days, and it can be changed if required. As soon as the object passes the tombstone lifetime value, it is available for permanent deletion. When we discussed the AD database in the *AD database maintenance* section, we discussed online defragmentation. The process uses the garbage collector service to remove the deleted objects from AD database and release that space to the database. This service runs every 12 hours. Once the deleted object exceeds the tombstone lifetime value, it will be permanently removed in the next garbage collector service cycle. The problem with this is that during the tombstone process, most of the object values are stripped off. So, even if you were able to recover objects values would need to be re-entered.

With Windows Server 2008 R2, Microsoft introduced the *Active Directory Recycle Bin* feature. When this feature is enabled, once the object is deleted, it still sets the isDeleted object value to True and moves the object under CN=Deleted Object. But, instead of the tombstone lifetime, it's now controlled by **Deleted Object Lifetime** (**DOL**) values. Object attributes will remain the same in this stage, and they are easily recoverable. By default, the DOL value is equal to the tombstone lifetime. This value can be changed by modifying the msDS-deletedObjectLifetime attribute value. Once it's exceeded the DOL, it is moved into the Recycled state and the isRecycled attribute value is set to True. In this state, it cannot be recovered, and it will be in this state until the tombstone lifetime value is exceeded. After it reaches the value, it will be permanently deleted from AD.

 The AD Recycle Bin feature requires a minimum of a Windows Server 2008 R2 domain and a forest functional level. Once this feature is enabled, it cannot be disabled.

This feature can be enabled using the following command:

```
Enable-ADOptionalFeature 'Recycle Bin Feature' -Scope
ForestOrConfigurationSet -Target rebeladmin.com
```

In the preceding command, -Target can be changed with your domain name.

Once Recycle Bin Feature is enabled, we can revive the objects, which are deleted using the following command:

```
Get-ADObject -filter 'isdeleted -eq $true' -includeDeletedObjects
```

The preceding command searches for the objects where the isdeleted attributes are set to true.

Now, we know the deleted object and it can be restored using the following command:

```
Get-ADObject -Filter 'samaccountname -eq "dfrancis"' -
IncludeDeletedObjects | Restore-ADObject
```

The preceding command restores the user object, dfrancis.

AD snapshots

When we work with virtual servers, we must understand how *snapshots* are important for a faster recovery process. Snapshots allow us to revert the system to a previous working state with minimum impact.

It is not recommended to take snapshots and restore domain controllers using this method, as it will create integrity issues with other existing domain controllers and their data.

With Windows Server 2008, Microsoft introduced the AD snapshot feature, which takes a snapshot of an AD database at a given time. Later, it can be used to compare object value changes and export and import objects that have been deleted or modified. Do not mistake this for a typical snapshot. This happens inside AD, and we cannot use it to completely recover a domain controller. It allows us to mount a snapshot while the existing AD DS configuration is running. However, it does not allow us to move or copy objects between snapshots and a working AD DS instance.

We can create the AD DS snapshot using `ntdsutil`. In order to run this, we need to have domain administrator privileges:

```
ntdsutil
snapshot
activate instance ntds
create
quit
quit
```

Now, we have a snapshot, and at a later time, it can be mounted. To mount it, we need to use the following command:

```
ntdsutil
snapshot
activate instance ntds
list all
mount 1
quit
quit
```

The preceding command mounts a snapshot called 1 from the list, which is listed under the given mount points:

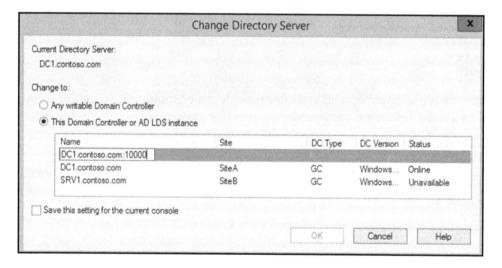

The next step is to mount the snapshot, which can be done using the following command:

```
dsamain –dbpath C:$SNAP_201703152333_VOLUMEE$ADDBntds.dit –ldapport
10000
```

In the preceding command, -dbpath defines the AD DS database path, and -ldapport defines the port used for the snapshot. It can be any available TCP port.

Once the snapshot is mounted, we can connect to it using the server name and the LDAP port, 10000:

Once the work is finished, it needs to be unmounted as well. To do that, we can use the following command:

```
ntdsutil
snapshot
activate instance ntds
list all
unmount 1
quit
quit
```

 If you need to move an object from a snapshot, first you need to export the object, and then import it over.

AD system state backup

An AD system-state backup is required in order to restore AD in the event of a disaster where the database cannot be recovered using the previously explained object-level recovery options. Windows backup is supported for performing system state backups. Also, there are many third-party backup tools that use similar technology to do the AD system state backup.

In a system state backup, the following files are included:

- AD DS database file (`ntds.dit`)
- The `SYSVOL` folder and its files
- The certificate store
- User profiles
- **Internet Information Services (IIS)** Metabase
- Boot files
- **Dynamic-link library (DLL)** cache folder
- Registry info
- COM+ and WMI info
- Cluster service info
- Windows Resource Protection system files

After Windows Server 2008, the system state backup also included Windows system files, so the system state backup is larger than Windows Server 2003 system states backups. It is recommended that you take a system state backup for every domain controller.

The first step to proceed with configuration is to install the Windows backup feature in AD server:

```
Install-WindowsFeature -Name Windows-Server-Backup
-IncludeAllSubFeature
```

Next, let's create a backup policy using the following command:

```
$BKPolicy = New-WBPolicy
```

Then, let's go ahead and add a system state to the policy:

```
Add-WBSystemState -Policy $BKPolicy
```

It also needs the backup volume path:

```
$Bkpath = New-WBBackupTarget -VolumePath "F:"
```

Now, we need to map the policy with the path:

```
Add-WBBackupTarget -Policy $BKPolicy -Target $Bkpath
```

Finally, we can run the backup using the following command:

```
Start-WBBackup -Policy $BKPolicy
```

AD recovery from system state backup

When the system needs to recover from the system state backup, it needs to be done via **Directory Services Restore Mode (DSRM)**.

The first system needs to be rebooted; press the *F8* key and select **Directory Services Restore Mode**.

Once it's loaded to safe mode, we can use the following commands:

```
$ADBackup = Get-WBBackupSet | select -Last 1
Start-WBSystemStateRecovery -BackupSet $ADBackup
```

This will restore the most recent backup the system has taken.

 If you are using AD backup software other than Windows, the recovery options will be different from the aforementioned options and you should refer to the vendor guidelines.

Summary

We started the chapter by looking into AD LDS and its capabilities. Then, we moved on to AD replication. In that section, we focused on the physical and logical components involved in AD replication and how they can be used to optimize complex replication requirements. More importantly, we also looked into how AD replication happens behind the scenes. Then, we moved on to RODCs and looked into their features and deployment scenarios. Later, we looked into AD database maintenance, which included different tools and techniques used to optimize AD database performance. Last but not least, we looked at the AD recovery options.

In the next chapter, we are going to look into another important AD role service: AD CS.

12
Active Directory Certificate Services

The two-man rule in security is used to secure high-valued assets and operations. As an example, many banks provide safe deposit box facilities. People can rent safe deposit boxes to store valuable assets. Most of these safe deposit boxes are designed to support a two-man rule. This means each safe deposit box has two locks. One key to the lock is held by the bank and another key for a second lock is issued to the customer. In order to open it, customers and bank agents need to use their keys at the same time. As soon as a customer shows up at the bank, they can't just go to the place where the safe deposit boxes are located; there is a process to follow. Banks will verify the customer's *identity* first. They will ask for a passport or driving license to verify the customer's identity. After successful verification, the bank will assign a member of staff to go with the customer and open the box using the bank's and the customer's keys. The end goal of these layers of security is to verify that the customer is the person they *claims to be* in order to allow access to the high-valued assets in the safe deposit box.

The **public key infrastructure (PKI)** works in a similar way. The PKI is responsible for verifying objects and services by using digital certificates. When we apply for visas or jobs, sometimes we are asked to verify our identity using police certificates. We may have already provided a copy of our passport and identity card with the application forms. However, the police are a well-known authority that anyone can trust. Therefore, a police certificate that verifies our identity will confirm that we are the person we claim to be. The police department is responsible for the certificate they issued for us. Before providing certificates, it's their responsibility to verify our identity using different procedures.

Modern businesses are increasingly using PKI to counter modern infrastructure threats. As an example, people use digital certificates to certify web services, as well as to authenticate their web applications, such as billing systems, service URLs, and so on. Some use digital certificates to encrypt network traffic between networks and hosts so that no unauthorized party can decrypt them. **Active Directory Certificate Services** (**AD CS**) allows organizations to set up and maintain their own PKI in their own infrastructure boundaries to create, manage, store, renew, and revoke digital certificates. In this chapter, we are going to look at the following topics:

- What is a certificate service and how does a PKI work?
- How to design your PKI
- Different PKI deployment models in action

PKI in action

Sometimes, when I talk to customers and engineers about encrypted traffic, I find that they know that **Secure Sockets Layer** (**SSL**) is *more secure* and works with the TCP port, 443. But most of them do not really know what the role of a certificate is and how this encryption and decryption works. It is very important to know how it works, as it makes deployment and management of PKI easy. Most of the PKI-related issues I have worked on are to do with the misunderstandings of core technologies and components related to it, rather than service-level issues.

Symmetric keys versus asymmetric keys

There are two types of cryptographic methods used to encrypt data:

- **Symmetric keys**: Symmetric methods work in exactly the same way that your door lock works. You have one key to lock or open the door. This is also called a **shared secret** or **private key**. **Virtual private network** (**VPN**) connections and backup software are a couple of examples that still use symmetric keys to encrypt data.

- **Asymmetric keys**: This method, on the other hand, uses a **key pair** to do the encryption and decryption. It includes two keys: one is a **public key** and the other one is a **private key**. Public keys are always distributed to the public and anyone can have them. Private keys are unique to the object in question and are not distributed to others. Any message encrypted using a public key can be decrypted only using its private key. Any message encrypted using a private key can be decrypted only using a public key. PKI uses the asymmetric key method for digital encryption and digital signatures.

Digital encryption

Digital encryption means that data transfer between two parties will be encrypted, and the sender will ensure that the transfer can only be opened by the intended recipient. Even if an unauthorized party gains access to that encrypted data, it will not be able to decrypt the data. The best way to explain it is through the following example:

We have an employee in an organization called **Sean**. In the PKI environment, he owns two keys: a public key and a private key. **Sean** can use these keys for encryption and the signature process. Now, he needs to receive a set of confidential data from the company account manager, **Chris**. He doesn't want anyone else to have this confidential data.

The best way to do this is to encrypt the data that is going to be sent from **Chris** to **Sean**:

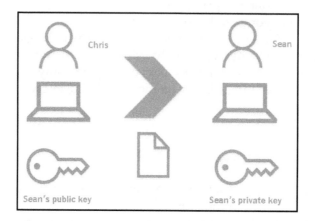

In order to encrypt the data, **Sean** sends his public key to **Chris**. There is no issue with providing the public key to any party. Then, **Chris** uses this public key to encrypt the data that will be sent over to **Sean**. This encrypted data can only be opened using **Sean**'s private key. He is the only one who has this private key. This verifies the recipient and their authority over the data.

Digital signatures

A digital signature verifies the authenticity of a service or data. It is similar to signing a document to prove its authenticity. As an example, before buying anything from a website, we can check its digital certificate and verify the authenticity of the website and confirm that it's not a phishing website. Let's look into this further with a use case. In the previous scenario, **Sean** successfully decrypted the data he received from **Chris**. Now, **Sean** wants to send some confidential data back to **Chris**. It can be encrypted using the same method of using Chris's public key. But the issue is that **Chris** is not part of the PKI setup, and he does not have a key pair. The only thing **Chris** needs to verify is that the sender is legitimate and that he's the same user that he claims to be. If **Sean** can certify this using a digital signature, and if **Chris** can verify it, the problem is solved:

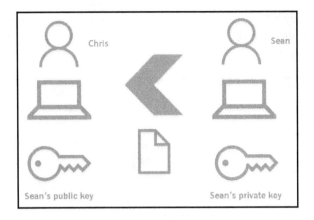

Now, here, **Sean** encrypts the data using his private key. The only key the data can be decrypted with is the public key of **Sean's**. **Chris** already has the public key. When **Chris** receives the data, he decrypts it using **Sean's public key**, and it confirms that the sender is definitely **Sean**.

Signing, encryption, and decryption

In the previous two scenarios, I have explained how digital encryption and digital signatures work with PKI. But these scenarios can be combined to provide encryption and signing at the same time. In order to do that, we use two additional techniques:

- **Symmetric keys**: A one-time symmetric key will be used for the message encryption process, as it is faster than asymmetric key encryption algorithms. This key needs to be available for the receiver, but to improve security, it will still be encrypted using the receiver's public key.
- **Hashing**: During the signing process, the system will generate a one-way hash value to represent the original data. Even if someone manages to get that hash value, it will not be possible to reverse engineer to get the original data. If any modification is done to the data, the hash value will be changed, and the receiver will know this straight away. These hashing algorithms are faster than encryption algorithms, and also, the hashed data will be smaller than the actual data values.

Let's look into this with the aid of a scenario. Let's assume that we have two employees, **Simran** and **Brian**, and both are using a PKI setup. Both have their private and public keys assigned:

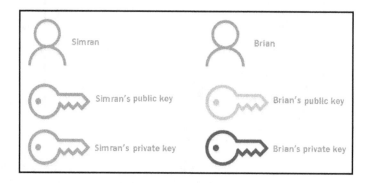

Simran wants to send an encrypted and signed data segment to **Brian**. This process can be divided into two stages: **data signing** and **data encryption**. The data will go through both stages before being sent to **Brian**:

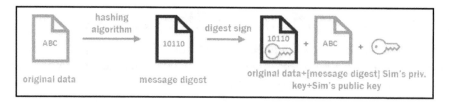

The first stage of the process is the signing of the data segment. The system receives the data from **Simran**, and the first task is to generate a **message digest** using a **hashing algorithm**. This will ensure data integrity; if it's altered, the receiver can easily identify it using the decryption process. This is a one-way process. Once a **message digest** is generated, the **message digest** will be encrypted using **Simran's private key** in order to digitally sign it. It will also include **Simran's public key**, so **Brian** will be able to decrypt and verify the authenticity of the message. Once the encryption process finishes, it will be attached with the **original data** value.

This process will ensure data was not altered and was sent from the expected sender (that is, it is genuine):

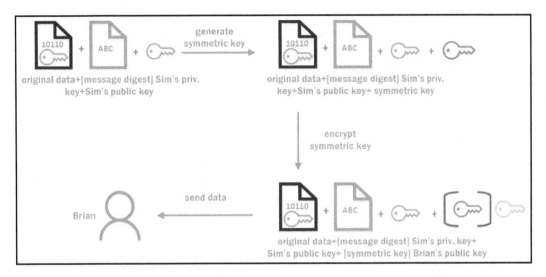

The next stage of the process is to encrypt the data. The first task in the process is to generate a one-time symmetric key to encrypt the data. An asymmetric algorithm is less efficient than symmetric algorithms for use with long data segments. Once a symmetric key is generated, the data will be encrypted using it (including the **message digest** and signature). This symmetric key will be used by **Brian** to decrypt the message. Therefore, we need to ensure that it is only available to **Brian**. The best way to do this is to encrypt the symmetric key using **Brian's public key**. So, once he receives it, he will be able to decrypt it using his private key. This process only encrypts the symmetric key in itself, and the rest of the message will stay the same. Once this is complete, the data can be sent to **Brian**.

The next step of the process is to see how the decryption process will happen on Brian's side:

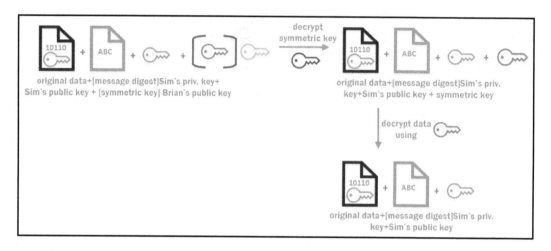

The message decryption process starts with decrypting the symmetric key. **Brian** needs the symmetric key to go further with the decryption process. It can only be decrypted using **Brian's private key**. Once it's decrypted, the symmetric key can be used to decrypt the **message digest** along with the signature. However, once the decryption is done, the same key information cannot be used to decrypt similar messages, as it's a one-time key:

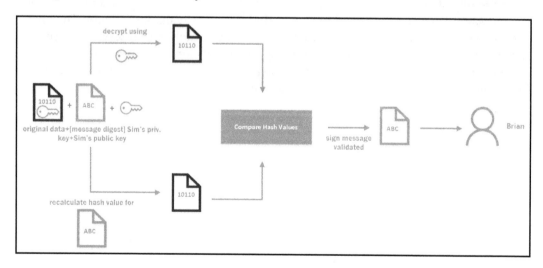

Now we have the decrypted data, the next step is to verify the signature. At this point, we have the **message digest**, which is encrypted using **Simran's private key**. It can be decrypted using **Simran's public key**, which is attached to the encrypted message. Once it's decrypted, we can retrieve the **message digest**. This digest value is one-way. We cannot reverse engineer it. Therefore, the retrieved original data digest value will be recalculated using the exact same algorithm used by the sender. After that, this newly generated digest value will be compared with the digest value attached to the message. If the values are the same, it will confirm that the data wasn't modified during the communication process. When the values are equal, the signature will be verified and the original data will be issued to Brian. If the digest values are different, the message will be discarded, as it's been altered or not signed by **Simran**.

This explains how the PKI environment works with the encryption/decryption process, as well as the digital signing/verification process.

SSL certificates

So far, we have talked about how asymmetric key pairs and symmetric keys work in PKI. But when we talk about PKI, we talk about SSL certificates. So, what is the role of the certificates?

I travel regularly between London and Seattle. When I reach Seattle-Tacoma International Airport, border security officers ask for my passport to verify my identity. They do not know me personally, but the passport I hold is issued by an authority that operates under international migration laws, and they certify that the person who owns the passport is Dishan Francis. If they want to check the authenticity of it, they can confirm with the authority that issued it. So, they have proof of identity, and they can further check the visa status to decide on my entry to the country.

Similarly, when looking at public key cryptography, we know a public key can be used by many applications and services. But how exactly can it be published, and how can the receiver confirm the authenticity of it? This is done using *digital certificates* issued by a **certification authority (CA)**, which can be trusted by the receiver. This digital certificate will include the public key of the object it was issued. The receiver can retrieve the public key of the object or the service it accesses via a digital certificate, and it can be verified by the *trusted* authority.

These digital certificates follow a similar structure, so everyone can understand it. It is similar to the way the passport works; folks with the border agency know where to look, even if it's a passport they have never seen before. These certificates are also time-bound, being only valid for a certain period of time. Once it has exceeded the validity period, it needs to be reissued, similar to a passport renewal.

 The validity period is defined by the certificate template used by the object or service. In the event of exceeding the validity period, you need to contact the CA and request a renewal. It can either be an automatic renewal process or a manual renewal process.

The certificate includes the following data:

- **Version**: X.509 standards define the format of the certificate. It was first introduced in 1988, and currently, it uses version 3.
- **Serial number**: A unique identifier used by the CA to identify the certificate.
- **Signature algorithm**: The type of the algorithm used by the CA to sign the digital certificate.
- **Signature hash algorithm**: The type of hash algorithm used by the CA.
- **Issuer**: The name of the CA who issued the certificate.
- **Valid from**: The day the certificate was issued by the CA.
- **Valid to**: The day the certificate will expire.
- **Subject**: To whom the certificate was issued.
- **Public key**: The public key of the certificate owner. This will be the object or the service it was issued to.

The following screenshot shows a sample certificate:

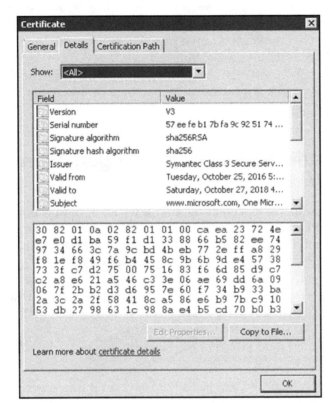

Types of certification authorities

There are two types of certification authorities:

- **Private CAs**: This is what we are covering in this chapter. This type of CA is mainly for internal infrastructures, and it can be used to issue, manage, renew, and revoke certificates for internal objects and services. It doesn't cost anything to issue certificates. **AD CS** is usually installed in an AD environment. However, if necessary, AD CS components can also be installed in a workgroup environment (a standalone CA). If objects in the external network still want to use certificates from the internal CA, the certificate must first be requested within the internal network, and once it's issued, it needs to export and import the certificate into the external network along with the *root certificate,* which certifies the issuer.

- **Public CAs**: Public CAs are available for anyone, and users can pay the associated fees and generate certificates. Most certificate vendors provide insurance along with certificates to ensure a certain level of protection. Internal CAs can trust internal objects, as they are internal and known to the CAs. But for internet-facing services, it doesn't make sense to use internal CA-issued certificates, as not everyone will trust the issuer. Instead of that, we can use a certificate issued by a well-known CA that everyone can trust.

How do certificates work with digital signatures and encryption?

In the previous section, we looked at a scenario where Simran was sending encrypted and digitally signed data to Brian. During the process, we saw how Simran and Brian used each other's private and public keys. A public key has to be shared between two parties. Now, the problem we have is to work out how exactly the system knows that Brian's public key is his, and not from someone that is pretending to be Brian? In order to overcome this challenge, we can use certificates to verify whether shared public keys are from their purported source. Let's introduce certificates to the previous example and see how things would work.

The digital signature process works as follows:

- Simran's private key will be used to encrypt the message digest. This private key will be retrieved from Simran's digital certificate. The private key verifies that the certificate is issued from a valid authority and that it's authentic.
- Simran's public key is also attached to the message, as it can be used by Brian to verify the signature. This will be available to Brain via Simran's digital signature.

The data encryption process works as follows:

- A one-time symmetric key is used to encrypt the whole message, and after that, the key itself will be encrypted using Brian's public key. This public key will be retrieved using Brian's digital certificate, as it confirms that it is from Brian. It is certified by a CA that Simran also trusts.

 During the certificate validation process, the system will verify the certificates using the CA's public key as it will confirm the authenticity of the CA. It also checks the validity period of the certificates using the **Valid to** value in the certificate.

The data decryption process works as follows:

- The first step is to decrypt the one-time symmetric key using Brian's private key. This symmetric key will be retrieved using Brian's digital certificate. Once the key is retrieved, the key will be decrypted, and it will be used to decrypt the entire message.

The signature verification process works as follows:

- The message digest (hash) is encrypted using Simran's private key. It can be decrypted using Simran's public key. This public key can be retrieved from Simran's digital certificate. This certificate is issued by a CA that is trusted by Brian.

The rest of the steps are exactly the same as I explained in the *Signing, encryption, and decryption* section.

What can we do with certificates?

The previously explained scenarios are not the only ways in which we can use a certificate. Let's look into some of the scenarios where we can use certificates:

- When networks extend their network boundaries to allow remote VPNs, it is important to protect the data transfer between two networks. Intercepted network traffic can cause serious infrastructure security issues. **IPSEC** is a network protocol used to encrypt network traffic using cryptographic keys. Using this, we can use certificates to encrypt traffic between two peers.

- The physical security of the data also matters when considering data security. More and more people are moving into mobile computing, and we need a way to protect the data inside these laptops and mobiles if they are stolen. **Encrypted File System** (**EFS**), which is based on certificates, can be used to encrypt and decrypt files. It will prevent any unauthorized access to data even if it is physically available.

- Wireless networks have less control over connections compared to physical cable connections. Anyone who knows a wireless password can connect to the network. Instead of using passwords, we can use certificates to authenticate into a wireless network, and communication will only be allowed from trusted devices.

- In an Active Directory environment, the main authentication method is the username and password. In addition to that, certificates can be used to verify the authenticity of the users' or computers' authentication requests.

- Some services and applications have multiple roles and subservices integrated in order to provide one integrated solution. The communication between these role services or subservices is unique and crucial for system operations. Therefore, those services can use certificates to verify the connectivity to each component and encrypt the communication between them to ensure the protection of application-related traffic.

- The **Secure/Multipurpose Internet Mail Extensions** (**S/MIME**) protocol can be used to encrypt and digitally sign email messages. When it digitally signs emails, it ensures the authenticity of the message and checks that no alteration has been made after it leaves the sender. This is done based on certificates. If you have Exchange Server 2013 SP1 or later, you can use S/MIME. Office 365 also supports this protocol.

- When we search for applications or drivers on the internet, sometimes we can notice fake installation files that pretend to be from the original vendor, but really hold malware or viruses that can harm an infrastructure. Therefore, application vendors and manufacturers use certificates to digitally sign their applications, drivers, and code to confirm their authenticity, so, as users, we know an installation file is definitely from the genuine vendor.

- The most common use of certificates is with websites. The certificate of a website proves a couple of things. One thing it proves is the website's authenticity and that it is not a phishing site. The other thing is that the user of the website knows that the communication between the user and the web server is secure and that any information passed between is encrypted. This is important when online transactions are involved. I will never use my credit cards with a website that doesn't have a certificate. If it's an internet-facing website, it is recommended to use a public CA to maintain visibility and trust.
- Non-repudiation is another benefit of certificates. If an object or service has signed a set of data, they cannot deny that they are the private key holder. The data is signed using a private key, and the public key is attached to the data segment. These keys were retrieved from the certificate, which was issued by a trusted CA. This is why a public CA provides assurance, and they are bound to pay a fee to customers if there is any key compromise. This is important for online businesses that accept internet payments.

AD CS components

AD CS is a collection of role services, and they can be used to design the PKI for your organization. Let's look into each of these role services and their responsibilities.

The CA

CA role service holders are responsible for issuing, storing, managing, and revoking certificates. The PKI setup can have multiple CAs. There are two main types of CA that can be identified in a PKI:

- **The root CA**: The root CA is the most trusted CA in the PKI environment. A compromised root CA will compromise an entire PKI. Therefore, the security of the root CA is crucial. Best practice is to bring the root CA online only when required. By considering the security and hierarchy of the PKI, it is recommended to use the root CA only to issue certificates to subordinate CAs.

- **Subordinate CAs**: In PKI, subordinate CAs are responsible for issuing, storing, managing, and revoking certificates for objects or services. Once a CA receives a request, it will process it and issue the certificate. A PKI can have multiple subordinate CAs. Each subordinate server should have its own certificate from the root CA. The validity period of these certificates is normally longer than that for ordinary certificates. It also needs to renew its certificate from the root CA when it reaches the end of the validity period:

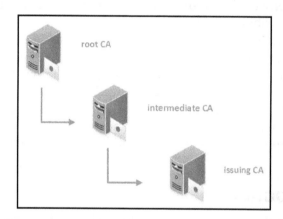

Subordinate CAs can have more subordinate CAs under them. In such situations, subordinate CAs are also responsible for issuing certificates for their own subordinate CAs. Subordinate CAs have more subordinate CAs are called **intermediate CAs**. These will not be responsible for issuing certificates to users, devices, or services. Subordinate servers that issue certificates to objects or services are called **issuing CAs**.

Certificate Enrollment Web Service

Certificate Enrollment Web Service allows users, computers, or services to request a certificate or renew a certificate via a web browser, even it is not domain-joined or is temporarily out of the corporate network. If it is domain-joined and in the corporate network, then auto enrollment or a template-based request process can be used to retrieve the certificate.

Certificate Enrollment Policy Web Service

This role service works with Certificate Enrollment Web Service and allows users, computers, and services to perform policy-based certificate enrollment. Similar to Certificate Enrollment Web Service, client computers can be non-domain-joined devices, or domain-joined devices that are outside the company's network boundaries. When a client requests policy information, the Enrollment Policy Web Service queries the AD DS using **Lightweight Directory Access Protocol (LDAP)** for the policy information, and then delivers it to the client via HTTPS. This information will be cached and used for similar requests. Once the user has the policy information, then they can request the certificate using Certificate Enrollment Web Service.

Certification Authority Web Enrollment

This is similar to a web interface for a CA. Users, computers, or services can request certificates using a web interface. Using the interface, users also can download the root certificates and intermediate certificates in order to validate a certificate. This can be used to request the **certificate revocation list (CRL)**. This list includes all the certificates that have expired or been revoked within the PKI. If any presented certificate matches an entry in the CRL, it will be automatically refused.

Network Device Enrollment Service

Network devices such as routers, switches, and firewalls can have device certificates to verify the authenticity of the traffic that passes through them. The majority of these devices are not domain-joined, and their operation systems are also very unique and do not support typical Windows computer functions. In order to request or retrieve certificates, network devices use **Simple Certificate Enrollment Protocol (SCEP)**. It allows network devices to have X.509 version 3 certificates similar to other domain-joined devices. This is important as if a device is going to use IPSEC, it must have an X.509 version 3 certificate.

Online Responder

Online Responder is responsible for producing information about certificate status. When I talked about Certification Authority Web Enrollment, I explained how the CRL includes the entire list of certificates that are expired or have been revoked within the PKI. The list will keep growing based on the number of certificates it manages.

Instead of using bulk data, Online Responder will respond to individual requests from users to verify the status of a particular certificate. This is more efficient than the CRL method as the request is focused on finding out the status of a certificate at a given time.

The types of CA

Based on the installation mode, CAs can be divided into two types: the **Standalone CA** and the **Enterprise CA**. The best way to explain the capabilities of both types is to compare them:

Feature	Standalone CA	Enterprise CA
AD DS dependency	Does not depend on AD DS; can be installed on a member server or standalone server in a workgroup	Can only be installed on a member server
Operate offline	Can stay offline	Cannot be offline
Customized certificate templates	Does not support; only supports standard templates	Supported
Supported enrollment methods	Manual or web enrollment	Auto, manual, or web enrollment
Certificate approval process	Manual	Manual or automatic based on the policy
User input for certificate fields	Manual	Retrieved from AD DS
Certificate issuing and managing using AD DS	N/A	Supported

Standalone CAs are mostly used as the root CA. In the previous section, I explained how important root CA security is. The standalone CA supports keeping the server offline and brings it online when it needs to issue a certificate or renew a certificate. Root CAs are only used to issue certificates to a subordinate CA. So, manual processing and approval is manageable, as this may only have to be done every few years. This type is also valid for public CAs. Issuing CAs comes under day-to-day CA-related tasks such as issuing, managing, storing, renewing, and revoking certificates. Depending on the infrastructure size, there can be hundreds or thousands of users using these issued CAs. If the request and approval process is manual, it may take a lot of manpower to maintain it. Therefore, in corporate networks, it is always recommended to use an enterprise-type CA.

Enterprise CAs allow engineers to create certificate templates with specific requirements and publish them via AD DS. End users can request certificates based on these templates. Enterprise CAs can only be installed on the Windows Server Enterprise Edition or the Datacenter Edition.

Planning PKI

By now, we understand what PKI is and how it works. You also learned about AD CS components and their capabilities. The next thing is to plan the deployment of the PKI. In this section, we will look into the things we need to consider during the PKI planning process.

Internal or public CAs

AD CS is not just a role that we can install on a server and leave to run. It take knowledge to set up and operate. It needs to be maintained as any other IT system is. It also needs backup and high availability. All this comes with a cost. Public CA certificates need to be purchased through a service provider. Each provider has many different types of certificates with different price ranges. It is important to evaluate these associated costs against your company's requirements. If the company is looking for a few web service certificates, there is no point in maintaining a few servers internally just for that. If a public CA can offer the same thing for $15, it makes sense to invest in that rather than wasting resources and money by maintaining an internal CA. However, it's not only the cost that we need to evaluate. An internal CA provides greater flexibility when it comes to administration. It allows the creation of templates and policies according to organizational requirements. Public CAs give only limited control. All you can do is pay for the certificate, submit the signing request, and then download the certificate once it's issued. Public CAs do have a reputation. If a user outside the corporate network needs to trust a certificate issued by the internal CA, the user needs to trust the issuing CA and the rest of the CAs in the chain, but not everyone would like to do that. However, if the certificate is from a reputable CA, it gives users confidence in the certificate and the content protected by it. When you use a public CA, customers can get professional support via the vendor whenever required – there is no need to have advanced knowledge to request and retrieve a digital certificate – whereas an internal CA requires skill to deploy, manage, and maintain. Considering all these pros and cons, we need to decide which CA model is best suited for the organization's requirements.

Identifying the correct object types

Certificates can be issued to users, computers, services, or network devices. User certificates are mainly used for the authentication process. Certificates can also be used with an application or service. User certificates will be installed in a user certificate store. Computer certificates allow you to uniquely identify a device. Computer certificates will be stored in a computer certificate store. Network devices are allowed to use X.509 certificates, and they can be used to certify a device and encrypt the traffic passing through it. Services such as web and email can use certificates to authenticate or encrypt data. A service itself will not have a certificate, but it will use a computer certificate or user certificate that is associated with the service. It is important to understand what types of objects will have certificates, as the configuration of the CA will be based on it. As an example, if network devices need certificates, we need to install Network Device Enrollment Service and configure it. Certificate templates should be modified to support the object type.

With a CA, we can use Microsoft's default cryptographic provider, which is the **RSA Microsoft Software Key Storage Provider**, or other advanced providers, such as ECDSA_P256, ECDSA_P521, or ECDSA_P384. Based on the provider used, the length of the cryptography key and hash algorithm will also change. Unless there are specific reasons to do otherwise, it is always recommended to use Microsoft RSA.

The cryptographic key length

When the size of the cryptographic key is increased, security is increased further. The minimum recommended key size is 2048 bits and this size can change based on the cryptographic provider. When the key size is increased, the encryption/decryption process takes more system resources.

Hash algorithms

During CA deployment, we can choose the hash algorithm standard. By default, it is SHA256, and it can change into SHA384, SHA512, or MD5. SHA1 is no longer recommended for use as it has been proven to be a weaker hash algorithm than the others.

The certificate validity period

Certificates are time-bound. Using certificate templates, we can specify the validity period of a certificate. It can be months or years. Before a certificate expires, it will need to be renewed (the certificate template will define how many days or weeks in advance it can be renewed). The expiry date of an issued certificate cannot be changed unless there is a renewal or reprocess.

The CA hierarchy

The root CA in a PKI can have more subordinate CAs. It will create a PKI hierarchy and the number of subordinate CAs is based on the organization requirements. There are two main types of hierarchical design: two-tier and three-tier. These will be explained in the next section in detail, but here, what I want to emphasize is that selecting the correct hierarchy model will reduce operational costs and resource waste.

High availability

Based on the organization's requirements, we have to decide what the best solution to maintain high availability is. If it's a heavily used PKI, the availability of the CA role services is important. Service uptime can be guaranteed by running the service in a clustered environment or using advanced site recovery solutions such as Azure Site Recovery. Based on the maximum downtime an organization can afford, the investment in high availability products, the technologies used, and the general approach taken will also change.

Deciding certificate templates

Not every user, computer, or service needs the same type of certificate. If you purchase certificates from a public CA, there are lots of different types of certificates available, all with different prices. Each of these certificates has different options and value-added services. Certificate templates allow you to create custom templates that can match different certificate requirements. As an example, user certificates may need to be renewed every year due to staff changes, while computer certificates may be renewed every five years. As part of the planning process, we need to evaluate certificate requirements so we can create new templates to match them.

The CA boundary

Before starting a deployment, it is important to decide on the operation boundaries that the PKI design will reflect. We need to decide under which domain, forest, or network segment the deployment will operate. Once the boundaries are defined, it can be hard to extend it later without any physical or logical network layer changes. As an example, if you have a CA in the perimeter network and you need to extend the boundary to the corporate network, that will require some network boundary changes. In another example, if a partner company or third party wants to use the corporate CA, that will require AD CS role changes, firewall changes, network routing changes, DNS changes, and more. Therefore, it's important to evaluate these types of operation requirements in the planning process.

PKI deployment models

At several points in this chapter, I have mentioned the PKI hierarchy and components such as root CAs, intermediate CAs, and issuing CAs. Based on the business and operational requirements, the PKI topology will also change. There are three deployment models that we can use to address the PKI requirements. In this section, we will look into these models and their characteristics.

The single-tier model

The single-tier model is also called the **one-tier model**, and it is the simplest deployment model for a PKI. This is not recommended for use in any production network, as it's a single point of failure for the entire PKI:

In this model, a single CA will act as **root CA and issuing CA**. As I explained before, the root CA is the most trusted CA in the PKI hierarchy. A compromised root CA will compromise the entire PKI. In this model, it's a single server, so any breach of the server will easily compromise the entire PKI, as it doesn't need to spread through different hierarchical levels. This model is easy to implement and easy to manage.

Some CA-aware applications require certificates in order to function. **System Center Operations Manager** (**SCOM**) is one of those examples. It uses certificates to secure web interfaces, authenticate management servers, and more. If the organization doesn't have an internal CA, you can either purchase certificates from the vendor or deploy a new CA. Engineers usually use this single-tier model, as it's only used for a specific application or task:

Advantages	Disadvantages
Fewer resources are needed to manage it, as it's all running from a single server.	There is a high possibility of being compromised, as the root CA is online and running all the PKI-related roles from one single server. If someone gets access to a private key of the root CA, they have complete ownership over the PKI.
Deployment is faster and it is possible to get the CA running in a short period of time.	There is a lack of redundancy, as certificate issuing and management all depend on a single server; the server's availability will decide the availability of the PKI.
N/A.	It is not scalable, and the hierarchy will need to be restructured if more role servers need to be added.

The two-tier model

This is the most commonly used PKI deployment model in corporate networks. In this design, the root CA is kept offline. It will help to protect the private key of the root certificate from being compromised.

Root CAs will issue certificates for subordinate CAs, and subordinate CAs are responsible for issuing certificates for objects and services:

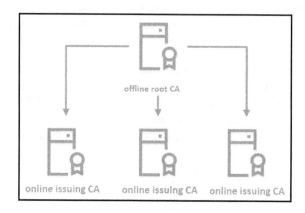

If a subordinate CA's certificate expires, the **offline root CA** will need to be brought online to renew the certificate. The root CA doesn't need to be a domain member, and it should be operating at the workgroup level (a standalone CA). Therefore, the certificate enrollment, approval, and renewal will be a manual process. This is a scalable solution and the number of issuing CAs can be increased based on workload. This allows you to extend the CA boundaries to multiple sites, too. In a single-tier model, if the PKI was compromised, in order to recover all the issued certificates, you would need to manually remove them from the respective devices. In a two-tier model, though, we just need to revoke the certificates issued by the CA, publish the CRL, and then reissue the certificates:

Advantages	Disadvantages
It provides improved PKI security, as in this model, the root CA should stay offline. It will protect the private key from being compromised.	High maintenance – it requires the maintenance of multiple systems and skills to process the manual certificate request/approval/renewal process between the root and subordinate CAs.
Flexible scalability – can start small and expand by adding additional subordinate CAs when required.	Cost – the cost of resources and licenses is high compared to those for a single-tier model.
You can restrict the issuing CA's impact on the CA hierarchy by controlling the certificates scope. It will prevent the issuing of *rogue* certificates.	The manual certificate renewal process between the root CA and subordinate CAs adds more risks; if administrators forget to renew a certificate on time, it can bring the whole PKI down.

Improved performance, as workloads can be shared among multiple subordinate CAs.	N/A.
Flexible maintenance capabilities, as there are fewer dependencies.	N/A.

Three-tier models

The three-tier model is the most advanced model in the list, and it operates with greater security, scalability, and control. Similar to a two-tier model, it also has an offline root CA and online issuing CAs. In addition to that, there are offline intermediate CAs, which operate between the root and subordinate CAs. The role of the intermediate CAs is to operate as policy CAs. In larger organizations, different departments, different sites, and different operation units can have different certificate requirements. As an example, a certificate issued to a perimeter network will require a manual approval process, while users in the corporate network will prefer auto approval. IT teams prefer to have large keys and advanced cryptographic providers for their certificates, while other users operate with the default RSA algorithms. All these different requirements are defined by the policy CA, and it publishes relevant templates and procedures to the other CAs:

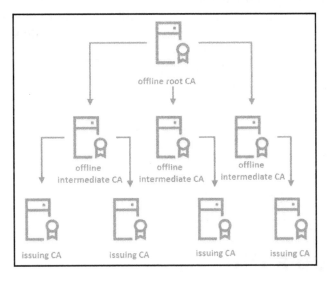

This model adds another layer of security to the hierarchy. However, if you are not using CA policies, the intermediate tier will not be useful. It can be a waste of money and resources. Therefore, most organizations prefer a two-tier model to start with, and then expand as required.

In this model, both the root CA and intermediate CAs operate as standalone CAs. The root CA will only issue certificates to intermediate CAs, and those will only issue certificates to issuing CAs:

Advantages	Disadvantage
Improved security, as it adds another layer of CAs to the certificate verification.	Cost – the cost of resources and licenses is high, as three layers need to be maintained. This also increases the operation cost.
Greater scalability, as each tier can extend horizontally.	High maintenance – when the number of servers increases, the efforts needed to maintain them also increases. Both the tiers that operate standalone CAs require additional maintenance, as automatic certificate request/approval/renewal is not supported.
In the event of the compromise of the issuing CA, the intermediate CA can revoke the compromised CA with minimum impact to the existing setup.	The implementation complexity is high compared to other models.
High-performance setup, as workloads are distributed and administrative boundaries are well defined by intermediate CAs.	N/A.
Improved control over certificate policies, allowing enterprises to have tailored certificates.	N/A.
High availability, as dependencies are further reduced.	N/A.

Setting up a PKI

Now we have finished the theory part of this chapter and are moving on to the deployment part. In this section, I am going to demonstrate how we can set up a PKI using the two-tier model. I have used this model as it is the most commonly used model for medium and large organizations:

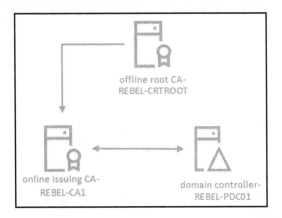

The preceding diagram explains the setup I am going to configure. In it, I have one domain controller, one standalone root CA, and one issuing CA. All are running with Windows Server 2016 with the latest patch level.

Setting up a standalone root CA

The first step is to set up the standalone root CA. This is not a domain member server, and is operating on the workgroup level. Configuring it on a separate VLAN will add additional security to the root CA.

Once the server is ready, log into the server as a member of the local administrator group. The first task is to install the AD CS role service. This can be done using the following command:

```
Add-WindowsFeature ADCS-Cert-Authority –IncludeManagementTools
```

Once the role service is installed, the next step is to configure the role and get the CA up and running:

```
Install-ADcsCertificationAuthority –CACommonName "REBELAdmin Root CA"
–CAType StandaloneRootCA –CryptoProviderName "RSA#Microsoft Software
Key Storage Provider" –HashAlgorithmName SHA256 –KeyLength 2048 –
ValidityPeriod Years –ValidityPeriodUnits 20
```

In the preceding code, `-CACommonName` defines the common name for the CA. Then, `-CAType` defines the CA operation type. In our case, it is `-StandaloneRootCA`. The other available types for CA type are `EnterpriseRootCA`, `EnterpriseSubordinateCA`, and `StandaloneSubordinateCA`. Now, `-CryptoProviderName` specifies the cryptographic service provider. In the demonstration, I am using the Microsoft default service provider. `-HashAlgorithmName` defines the hashing algorithm used by the CA. The option for it will be changed, based on the **Cryptographic Service Provider** (**CSP**) we choose. SHA1 is no longer counted as a secure algorithm; it is recommended to use SHA256 or above. `-KeyLength` specifies the key size for the algorithm. In this demonstration, I am using the 2048 key. `-ValidityPeriod` defines the validity period of CA certificates. It can be hours, days, weeks, months, or years. `-ValidityPeriodUnits` is followed by `-ValidityPeriod` and specifies how many hours, days, weeks, months, or years it will be valid for. In our demonstration, we are using 20 years:

```
Select Administrator: Windows PowerShell                                    –   □   ×

Windows PowerShell
Copyright (C) 2016 Microsoft Corporation. All rights reserved.

PS C:\Users\Administrator> Install-ADcsCertificationAuthority -CACommonName "REBELAdmin Root CA" -CAType StandaloneRootC
A -CryptoProviderName "RSA#Microsoft Software Key Storage Provider" -HashAlgorithmName SHA256 -KeyLength 2048 -ValidityP
eriod Years -ValidityPeriodUnits 20

Confirm
Are you sure you want to perform this action?
Performing the operation "Install-AdcsCertificationAuthority" on target "REBEL-CRTROOT".
[Y] Yes  [A] Yes to All  [N] No  [L] No to All  [S] Suspend  [?] Help (default is "Y"): A

ErrorId ErrorString
------- -----------
      0

PS C:\Users\Administrator>
```

Now we have the root CA up and running. But before we use it, we need to do certain configuration changes.

DSConfigDN

As I mentioned earlier, this is a standalone root CA, and is not part of the domain. However, **CRL Distribution Points** (**CDP**) and **authority information access** (**AIA**) locations, which are required by the CA, will be stored in DC. Since they use **Distinguished Names** (**DN**) with a domain, the root CA needs to be aware of the domain information to publish it properly. It will retrieve this information via a registry key:

```
certutil.exe -setreg ca\DSConfigDN
CN=Configuration,DC=rebeladmin,DC=com
```

CDP locations

CDPs define the location where the CRL can be retrieved from. This is a web-based location and should be accessible via HTTP. This list will be used by the certificate validator to verify the given certificate against the revocation list.

Before we do this, we need to prepare the web server. It should be a domain member, as the issuing CA is also in a domain.

In my demonstration, I am going to use the same issuing CA as the CDP location.

The web server can be installed using the following command:

```
Install-WindowsFeature Web-WebServer -IncludeManagementTools
```

Next, create a folder and create a share so that it can be used as the virtual directory:

```
mkdir C:\CertEnroll
New-smbshare -name CertEnroll C:\CertEnroll -FullAccess
SYSTEM,"rebeladmin\Domain Admins" -ChangeAccess "rebeladmin\Cert
Publishers"
```

As part of the exercise, it will set the share permissions to `rebeladmin\Domain Admins` (full access) and `rebeladmin\Cert Publishers` (change access).

After that, load the **Internet Information Services (IIS)** manager and add a virtual directory, `CertEnroll`, with the aforementioned path:

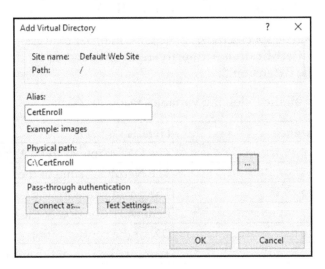

Last but not least, we need to create a DNS record for the service URL. In this demonstration, I am using `crt.rebeladmin.com`. This will allow us to access the new distribution point using `http://crt.rebeladmin.com/CertEnroll`.

Now everything is ready, and we can publish the CDP settings using the following command:

```
certutil -setreg CA\CRLPublicationURLs
"1:C:\Windows\system32\CertSrv\CertEnroll\%3%8%9.crl
\n10:ldap:///CN=%7%8,CN=%2,CN=CDP,CN=Public Key
Services,CN=Services,%6%10\n2:http://crt.rebeladmin.com/CertEnroll/%3%
8%9.crl"
```

The single numbers in the command refer to the options, and numbers with `%` refer to the variables:

Option	Details
0	No changes.
1	Publish the CRL to the given location.
2	Attach the CDP extensions of issued certificates.
4	Include in the CRL to find the delta CRL locations.
8	Specify whether there is a need to publish all CRL information to AD when publishing manually.
64	Delta CRL location.
128	Include the **Issuing Distribution Point** (IDP) extension of the issued CRL.

All these settings can be specified using the GUI. In order to access it, go to **Server Manager** | **Tools** | **Certification Authority**, right-click and select **Properties** of the server, and go to the **Extension** tab.

There, you can add all the following variables using the GUI:

Variable	GUI reference	Details
%1	<ServerDNSName>	The DNS name of the CA server
%2	<ServerShortName>	The NetBIOS name of the CA server
%3	<CAName>	The given name for the CA
%4	<CertificateName>	Renewal extension of the CA
%6	<ConfigurationContainer>	DN of the configuration container in AD
%7	<CATruncatedName>	Truncated name of the CA (32 characters)

%8	`<CRLNameSuffix>`	Inserts a name suffix at the end of the filename before publishing a CRL
%9	`<DeltaCRLAllowed>`	Replaces `CRLNameSuffix` with a separate suffix to use the delta CRL
%10	`<CDPObjectClass>`	The object class identifier for the CDP
%11	`<CAObjectClass>`	The object class identifier for a CA

AIA locations

AIA is an extension that is in the certificate and defines the location where the application or the service can retrieve the issuing CA's certificate. This is also a web-based path, and we can use the same location we used for the CDP.

AIA location can be set using the following command:

```
certutil -setreg CA\CACertPublicationURLs
"1:C:\Windows\system32\CertSrv\CertEnroll\%1_%3%4.crt\n2:ldap:///CN=%7
,CN=AIA,CN=Public Key
Services,CN=Services,%6%11\n2:http://crt.rebeladmin.com/CertEnroll/%1_
%3%4.crt"
```

The options are very much similar to those for the CDP, with a few small changes:

Option	Details
0	No changes.
1	Publish CA certificate to a given location.
2	Attach AIA extensions of issued certificates.
32	Attach **Online Certificate Status Protocol** (**OCSP**) extensions.

CA time limits

When we set up the CA, we defined the CA validity period as 20 years. But that doesn't mean every certificate it issues will have a 20-year validity period. Root CAs will issue certificates only to issuing CAs. The certificate request, approval, and renewal processes are manual. Therefore, these certificates will have longer validity periods. For this demonstration, I will set it for 10 years:

```
certutil -setreg ca\ValidityPeriod "Years"
certutil -setreg ca\ValidityPeriodUnits 10
```

CRL time limits

The CRL also has some time limits associated:

```
Certutil -setreg CA\CRLPeriodUnits 13
Certutil -setreg CA\CRLPeriod "Weeks"
Certutil -setreg CA\CRLDeltaPeriodUnits 0
Certutil -setreg CA\CRLOverlapPeriodUnits 6
Certutil -setreg CA\CRLOverlapPeriod "Hours"
```

In the preceding commands, the following is true:

- CRLPeriodUnits: This specifies the number of days, weeks, months, or years for which the CRL will be valid.
- CRLPeriod: This specifies whether the CRL validity period is measured by days, weeks, months, or years.
- CRLDeltaPeriodUnit: This specifies the number of days, weeks, months, or years that the delta CRL is valid for. Offline CAs should disable this.
- CRLOverlapPeriodUnits: This specifies the number of days, weeks, months, or years that the CRL can overlap.
- CRLOverlapPeriod: This specifies whether the CRL overlapping validity period is measured by days, weeks, months, or years.

Now we have all the settings submitted; in order to apply the changes, the certificate service needs to be restarted:

```
restart-service certsvc
```

The new CRL

The next step is to create a new CRL, which can be generated using the following command:

```
certutil -crl
```

Once that's done, there will be two files under
`C:\Windows\System32\CertSrv\CertEnroll`:

```
PS C:\Users\Administrator> cd C:\Windows\System32\CertSrv\CertEnroll
PS C:\Windows\System32\CertSrv\CertEnroll> dir


    Directory: C:\Windows\System32\CertSrv\CertEnroll


Mode                LastWriteTime         Length Name
----                -------------         ------ ----
-a----        22/03/2017     21:05            793 REBEL-CRTROOT_REBELAdmin Root CA.crt
-a----        22/03/2017     23:00            694 REBELAdmin Root CA.crl


PS C:\Windows\System32\CertSrv\CertEnroll>
```

This completes the initial configuration of a standalone root CA. As a next step, we need to publish the root CA data to AD. This way, AD-joined computers will have the root CA certificates under the computer's Trusted Root Certification Authorities certificates.

Publishing the root CA data to AD

In the preceding screenshot, we see that we have two files. One ends with `.crt`. This is the root CA certificate. In order to distribute it to other clients in the domain, it first needs to be published to AD. To do that, go ahead and copy this file from the root CA to the AD server. Then, log into the domain controller as Domain Admin or Enterprise Admin and run the following command:

```
certutil -f -dspublish "REBEL-CRTROOT_REBELAdmin Root CA.crt" RootCA
```

The next file ends with `.crl`. This is the root CA's CRL. This also needs to be published to AD, so that everyone in the domain is aware of it, too. In order to do that, copy the file from the root CA to the domain controller and run the following command:

```
certutil -f -dspublish "REBELAdmin Root CA.crl"
```

Setting up the issuing CA

Now that we're done with the root CA setup, the next step is to set up the issuing CA. Issuing CAs will be run from a domain member server and will be AD-integrated. In order to perform the installation, log into the server as the Domain Admin or Enterprise Admin.

The first task will be to install the AD CS role:

```
Add-WindowsFeature ADCS-Cert-Authority -IncludeManagementTools
```

I will use the same server for the Web Enrollment Role Service. This can be added using the following command:

```
Add-WindowsFeature ADCS-web-enrollment
```

After that, we can configure the role service using the following command:

```
Install-ADcsCertificationAuthority -CACommonName "REBELAdmin
IssuingCA" -CAType EnterpriseSubordinateCA -CryptoProviderName
"RSA#Microsoft Software Key Storage Provider" -HashAlgorithmName
SHA256 -KeyLength 2048
```

In order to configure the Web Enrollment Role Service, use the following command:

```
Install-ADCSwebenrollment
```

Issuing a certificate for the issuing CA

In order to get AD CS running on the issuing CA, it needs the certificate issued from the parent CA, which is the root CA we just deployed. During the role configuration process, it automatically creates the certificate request under C:\, and the exact filename will be listed in the command output from the previous command:

```
PS C:\Users\administrator.REBELADMIN> Install-ADcsCertificationAuthority -CACommonName "REBELAdmin IssuingCA" -CAType En
terpriseSubordinateCA -CryptoProviderName "RSA#Microsoft Software Key Storage Provider" -HashAlgorithmName SHA256 -KeyLe
ngth 2048

Confirm
Are you sure you want to perform this action?
Performing the operation "Install-AdcsCertificationAuthority" on target "REBEL-CA1".
[Y] Yes  [A] Yes to All  [N] No  [L] No to All  [S] Suspend  [?] Help (default is "Y"): A
WARNING: The Active Directory Certificate Services installation is incomplete. To complete the installation, use the
request file "C:\REBEL-CA1.rebeladmin.com_REBELAdmin IssuingCA.req" to obtain a certificate from the parent CA. Then,
use the Certification Authority snap-in to install the certificate. To complete this procedure, right-click the node
with the name of the CA, and then click Install CA Certificate. The operation completed successfully. 0x0 (WIN32: 0)

ErrorId ErrorString
------- -----------
    398 The Active Directory Certificate Services installation is incomplete. To complete the installation, use the ...
```

The file needs to be copied from the issuing CA to the root CA, then you need to execute the following command:

```
certreq -submit "REBEL-CA1.rebeladmin.com_REBELAdmin IssuingCA.req"
```

As I explained before, any request to the root CA will be processed manually, so this request will be waiting for manual approval. In order to approve the certificate, go to **Server Manager** | **Tools** | **Certification Authority** | `Pending Requests`; right-click on the certificate and select **All Tasks** | **Issue.**

Once it has been issued, it needs to be exported and imported into the issuing CA:

```
certreq -retrieve 2 "C:\REBEL-
CA1.rebeladmin.com_REBELAdmin_IssuingCA.crt"
```

The preceding command will export the certificate. The number 2 is the **request ID** in the CA **Microsoft Management Console** (**MMC**).

Once the export is complete, move the file to the issuing CA, and from there, run the following command. This will import the certificate and start the service:

```
Certutil -installcert "C:\REBEL-
CA1.rebeladmin.com_REBELAdmin_IssuingCA.crt"
start-service certsvc
```

Post-configuration tasks

Similar to the case with the root CA, after the initial service setup, we need to define some configuration values.

CDP locations

The CDP location configuration is similar to the root CA's, and I am going to use the already-created web location for it:

```
certutil -setreg CA\CRLPublicationURLs
"1:%WINDIR%\system32\CertSrv\CertEnroll\%3%8%9.crl\n2:http://crt.rebel
admin.com/CertEnroll/%3%8%9.crl\n3:ldap:///CN=%7%8,CN=%2,CN=CDP,CN=Pub
lic Key Services,CN=Services,%6%10"
```

AIA locations

The AIA locations also can be specified using the following command:

```
certutil -setreg CA\CACertPublicationURLs
"1:%WINDIR%\system32\CertSrv\CertEnroll\%1_%3%4.crt\n2:http://crt.rebe
ladmin.com/CertEnroll/%1_%3%4.crt\n3:ldap:///CN=%7,CN=AIA,CN=Public
Key Services,CN=Services,%6%11"
```

CA and CRL time limits

The CA and CRL time limits also need to be adjusted. This can be done using the following commands:

```
certutil -setreg CA\CRLPeriodUnits 7
certutil -setreg CA\CRLPeriod "Days"
certutil -setreg CA\CRLOverlapPeriodUnits 3
certutil -setreg CA\CRLOverlapPeriod "Days"
certutil -setreg CA\CRLDeltaPeriodUnits 0
certutil -setreg ca\ValidityPeriodUnits 3
certutil -setreg ca\ValidityPeriod "Years"
```

Once all this is done, in order to complete the configuration, restart the certificate service using the following command:

```
restart-service certsvc
```

Last but not least, run the following command to generate the CRLs:

```
certutil -crl
```

Once all of this is done, we can run `PKIView.msc` to verify the configuration:

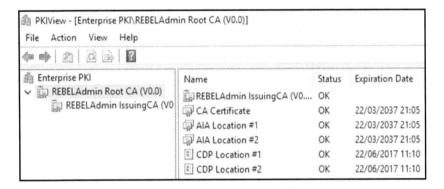

 `PKIView.msc` was first introduced with Windows Server 2003, and it gives visibility on enterprise PKI configuration. It also verifies the certificates and CRL for each CA.

Certificate templates

Now we have a working PKI, and we can turn off the standalone root CA. It should only be brought online if the issuing CA certificates are expired or the PKI is compromised.

The CA comes with predefined **Certificates Templates**. These can be used to build custom certificate templates according to the organization's requirements and can be published to AD.

CA certificate templates are available under the **Certificate Templates** MMC. They can be accessed using **Run** | **MMC** | **File** | **Add/Remove Snap-in...** | **Certificate Templates**.

To create a custom template, right-click on a template and click on **Duplicate Template**:

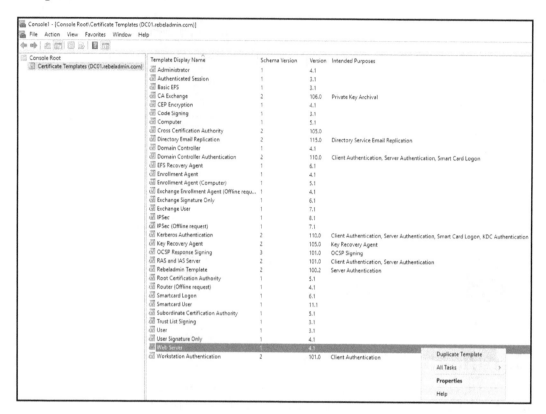

This will open up the **Properties** window, where you can change the settings of the certificate template to match the requirements. Some common settings to change in templates are listed here:

- **Template display name** (the **General** tab): The display name of the template.
- **Template name** (the **General** tab): The common name of the template.
- **Validity period** (the **General** tab): The certificate validity period.
- **Security**: Authenticated users or groups must have **Enroll** permission to request certificates:

Once the template is ready, we need to issue it. Then, the members of the domain can request certificates based on that.

To do so, go to the **Certification Authority** MMC | **Certificate Templates**, then right-click and select **New** | **Certificate Template to Issue**.

Then, from the list, select the template to issue and click on **OK**:

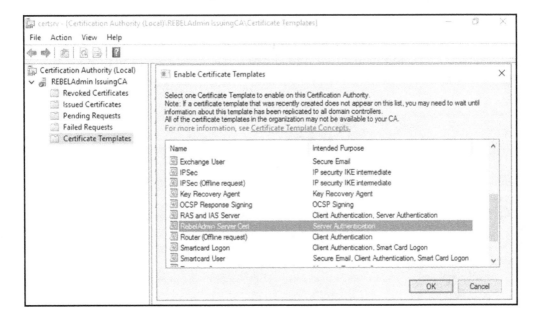

Now we have the new certificate template. The next step is to request a certificate based on the new template we created.

Requesting certificates

Based on the published certificate templates, users can request certificates from the issuing CA. I have logged into an end user PC and I am going to request a certificate based on the template we created in the previous step.

In order to do that, go to **Run**, type MMC | **Add/Remove Snap-in...** | **Certificates**, and click on the **Add** button.

From the list, select the computer account with which you manage certificates for the computer object. This is dependent on the template. Once selected, in the next window, select **Local computer** as the target.

 If the user is not an administrator and only has default permissions, the user will only be allowed to open the **Current User** snap-in. To open the computer account, MMC needs to be **Run as administrator**.

Once MMC is loaded, go to the Personal container, right-click, and then follow **All Tasks** | **Request New Certificate**.

This will open a new window; click **Next** until you reach the **Request Certificates** window. In there, we can see the new template. Click on the checkbox to select the certificate template, and then click on the link with a warning sign to provide the additional details that are required for the certificate:

Then, provide values for the required fields and click on **OK** to proceed. Most of the time, **Common name** is what's required:

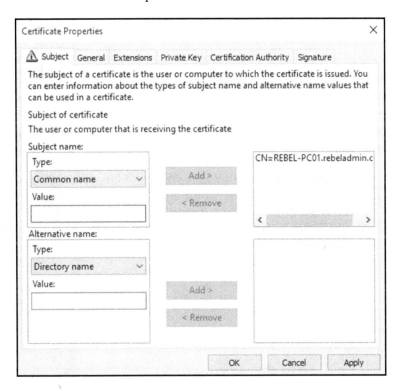

Once that's done, click on **Enroll** to request the certificate. Then, it will automatically process the certificate request and issue the certificate. Once it's issued, it can be found under the `Personal | Certificate` container:

As expected, we can see that a valid certificate has been issued. Information about this issued certificate can be found under the issuing CA's **Certification Authority** MMC | **Issued Certificate**.

In this exercise, you learned how to set up a two-tier PKI from the ground up. After the setup, as with any other system, regular maintenance is required to maintain the health of the system. Also, it is important to have proper documentation about the setup, along with certificate templates and procedures in order to issue, renew, and revoke certificates successfully.

Summary

Digital certificates are used more and more in modern infrastructure as additional layers of security to prove that objects and services are genuine. In this chapter, you learned what a PKI is and how exactly it works. Then, we looked into AD CS components and their roles. After that, we moved into the planning of a PKI and discussed what needs to be considered when building a PKI. Then, we further looked into PKI deployment models and evaluated their advantages and disadvantages. Last but not least, we went through a step-by-step guide to setting up a two-tier PKI.

In the next chapter, you are going to learn about another AD role service—AD Federation Service—and see how identities are handled in a federated environment.

13
Active Directory Federation Services

The days of castles are gone now; we no longer live in a small world. We live in a society where everyone is connected. In cities, we no longer see walls like in the castles from before. This well-connected society provides a lot of benefits to human beings, but it's not the only outcome. Great and strong cities in a connected society can also be vulnerable from time to time.

Modern business operation boundaries are also no longer in a closed or isolated mode. As an example, from on-premises applications, organizations are moving into cloud-based versions. Computer workloads are moving to public or hybrid cloud infrastructures.

In an **Active Directory** (**AD**) environment, most of the systems or applications can be integrated with it, and they use one username and password to access systems (**single sign-on** (**SSO**)). When we extend the identity infrastructure boundaries, we may start to lose control over them, as these system identities are managed by vendors or other organizations.

Therefore, we usually end up having different user accounts and passwords to log in to different systems. From the end user's perspective, it's just different accounts for different systems, but from the service provider's perspective, it's more than that.

Imagine that we have an application developed in house, and we want to sell it as a service. External users need to access it in order to authenticate, and we have to create a username and password for every one of them. Setting an account is not the only thing we need to consider; when we create an account, it becomes a part of our identity infrastructure. We need to make sure it's secured and only has access to that particular application. All of a sudden, new challenges arose for identity management, and if this isn't handled appropriately, it can make the whole system vulnerable. Instead of mixing identities in such scenarios, **Active Directory Federation Services** (**AD FS**) allows businesses to manage their own identity infrastructures and use claims-based authentication on their resources. So, users do not need to use a separate login to access systems, and the resource owners do not need to keep managing identities for external users. In this chapter, we are going to learn about the following:

- What is AD FS and how does it work?
- AD FS components and how to use them in the AD FS setup
- AD FS deployment and management
- **Multi-Factor Authentication** (**MFA**) in action
- Integration with Microsoft Azure

How does AD FS work?

Rebeladmin Inc. is an IT service provider. There are many customers who use different IT and cloud-based services from the company. Recently, the company introduced a new web-based control panel where customers can access their resources. The same application is also used by internal staff to manage the infrastructure services. Rebeladmin Inc. uses **Active Directory Domain Service** (**AD DS**) to manage identities. When a member of internal IT staff logs in to the portal, it doesn't ask for any login details. This is because the web application uses **Integrated Windows Authentication** (**IWA**) to allow access. This is also called **NTLM authentication** or **domain authentication**. It doesn't prompt for the login information initially, or transfer hashed data about the currently logged-in user to the web server to check whether it's allowed. This web server is domain joined and the application in itself is AD integrated. Now, users from the Depache solution also like to get access to the same portal to manage their workloads, which is hosted with Rebeladmin Inc.

There are two ways to facilitate this:

- **Using a user account in Rebeladmin Inc. AD**: When external users try to access the web portal, the initial IWF will fail as the application doesn't understand the external users' accounts. Then, it will prompt them for their login details. If a user has an account in Rebeladmin Inc., AD instance, it can be used to authenticate into the portal. This involves several security-related issues. When users have an account in AD, by default, AD allows users to access any resources, which have *everyone* or *authenticated users*. In the internal network, it is possible to force users to follow policies and best practices to protect their identities. However, it is not possible to apply the same standards to an external party. So, these accounts have a high likelihood of getting compromised. As an example, if an internal user resigns, then normally, their AD user login will be reset and disabled. But if it's an account that is shared with external users, then even if the relevant user resigns, they may still have access to the portal (until it is informed). Some vendors use **Active Directory Lightweight Directory Services** (**AD LDS**) for each customer to minimize the security impact. But this still adds management overhead to keep different instances running.

- **AD trust between two infrastructures**: When there is AD trust, resource access can be allowed from remote infrastructures. In order to have successful trust, there should be a connection between two infrastructures, which is based on TCP/UDP ports such as 389 (**Lightweight Directory Access Protocol** (**LDAP**)) and 53 (**Domain Name System** (**DNS**)). These ports need to be allowed via firewalls in both infrastructures. This additional security task adds additional management tasks for both the infrastructures to protect their confidential data from being exposed to each other.

As we can see, even though both the options can allow *access* from the external infrastructures, both struggle with security and management-related challenges.

Federation trust is the answer to all these concerns. In simple English, the federation service is a web service that authenticates users from the **Identity Provider (IdP)** and provides access to claim-based applications from the **Service Provider (SP)**. There are many federation service providers and the Microsoft federation service is called **Active Directory Federation Service (AD FS)**:

In the preceding example, Rebeladmin Inc. is using AD DS to manage the identities. Its users are using a hosted web application (**MyHostedApp1**) from a cloud service provider. Rebeladmin Inc. uses AD FS in order to create federation trust between Rebeladmin Inc. and the SP. This allows the Rebeladmin Inc. users to launch **MyHostedApp1** using their own Windows credentials. In this setup, the federation service is hosted in the Rebeladmin Inc. infrastructure and it becomes the IdP. From AD FS' point of view, it is also called the **Claims Provider (CP)**. This is because that's where the actual authentication happens. The vendors who host the application also have their own identity infrastructure. The application vendor becomes the SP, also known as the **Relying Party (RP)**, in federation trust, and this depends on the claims provided by the federation service to allow/deny access to the application from the Rebeladmin Inc. users. This setup does not need to open additional firewall rules either. This is based on a secure connection via TCP port 443.

Even if the connection is called trust, it cannot be used to replace AD domains or forest trusts. If the AD trust is in place, then administrators can manage access to resources from remote users in the exact same way it was done for internal users. Users can be allowed to access folders and files based on **New Technology File System (NTFS)** permissions. Users can be given permission to log in to devices. Any application's work with internal users can be allowed for remote users too. But in a federated environment, the access can only be allowed to *claims-aware* applications. A claim is simply an attribute and a relative value. As an example, a claim can have a username attribute and its value, dfrancis. The federation service will request access from the SP based on the claims. If the SP's application doesn't understand *claims*, it cannot decide whether to allow or deny access:

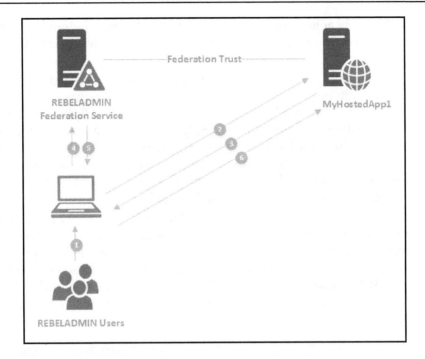

Let's revisit the previous example with a detailed explanation, in order to show you exactly how it works behind the scenes:

1. In the first step, the Rebeladmin Inc. user logs in to a computer in the Rebeladmin Inc. infrastructure. This is a domain-joined device. The user uses their domain credentials to log in to the device.

2. Once the user is logged into the device successfully, they launch their web browser and type the URL for **MyHostedApp1**. This application is hosted in the remote infrastructure.

3. As soon as the application receives the access request from the Rebeladmin Inc. user, it first checks the data passing through the browser (IWF). Then, it realizes it is not from the internal infrastructure, but it's an account from the identity infrastructure, which the SP has a federated relationship with. If it's from a federated environment, the user access rights need to be decided based on claims. Therefore, the SP sends a redirect response to redirect users to the Rebeladmin Inc. federation service web interface.

4. Then, the user is automatically redirected to the Rebeladmin Inc. federation service web interface. In the web interface, the user has to type in their login details.

5. Once the user provides their credentials, it will be validated with the Rebeladmin Inc. AD DS and will retrieve its access rights. Then, the federation service will create a security token that includes user claims, such as name, group memberships, **User Principal Name** (**UPN**), and email address. This security token will be signed by the issuer's digital certificate. At the end of the process, federation services send responses back to the user with a generated security token, plus a `redirect` command to redirect the user's browser session back to **MyHostedApp1**.

6. The user browser session is redirected to the hosted application, and this time, it is the session presented with the security token it received from the federation service. Then, the web server's claims-aware agent decrypts the security token and looks into the claims it provided. Based on the claims, it will decide whether the user is allowed to access the application or not. If the claims are accepted, the user will be able to see the initial page of the application successfully.

In the preceding scenario, the federation trust is made directly with the application. But in some scenarios, the SP will also have the federation service environment on its end. This is mainly when the service provider has multiple clients with federation trusts. In such a situation, the following will happen:

1. When the application finds out that the user needs to log in via the federation, the user will initially be redirected to the SP's federation service.

2. Then, the SP's federation service will redirect the user to Rebeladmin's federation service.

3. Once the user receives the security token, security tokens will present it to the SP's federation service. It will decrypt the token and retrieve the claims inside it. Then, it will map claim to the SP's claims and filter them to match with application claims requirements.

4. Based on the filtered claims, the SP's federation service will create a new security token, which will be signed using the SP's federation service digital certificate. This new security token is the one that will be forwarded to the application server.

What is a claim?

A few times in the preceding example, we have discussed *claims*. But what is exactly a claim, and how is it generated?

A claim is simply a statement about a user that is used for authorization purposes of claim-aware applications. Each claim contains a value about a user such as their UPN, email address, and **Common Name (CN)**.

AD FS supports many different claim types. Claim types are used to show what sort of value will be included in the claim. The following table contains the most commonly used claim types:

Claim type	Description
UPN	UPN of the user
Email	RFC 5322-type email address
Given name	Given name of the user
CN	CN value of the user account
Name	Name of the user
Surname	Surname of the user
Windows Account Name	Domain account in domain/user format
Group	Group the user belongs to
Role	Role of the user
AD FS 1.x UPN	UPN of the user when interacting with AD FS 1.x
AD FS 1.x email address	RFC 5322-type email address of the user when interacting with AD FS 1.x

Claims retrieve values from the attribute store. The attribute store is a directory or database that contains user accounts and associated attributes. Therefore, AD can also play the role of an attribute store. As an example, in an AD environment, if the claim type is UPN, the claim will retrieve the value through users' attributes.

AD FS also supports many industry standards, which are used to build third-party claim-based solutions. It guarantees the interoperability of many cloud-based or hosted applications in the market today.

Security Assertion Markup Language (SAML)

In the federated environment, the **IdP** and the **SP** need to exchange authentication and authorization data. SAML is an XML-based standard format that is used to present the data. This standard was first introduced in 2001 by **OASIS Security Services Technical Committee** and the latest version available is 2.0. This is a commonly used standard by many federation service providers and application developers to provide an SSO experience. The requesting and processing of claims are exactly the same as the example used in the previous section, with the only difference being the format of the token request and response. SAML uses signed XML files as the token. In SAML terminology, the security tokens generated at the IdP end are called **asserts**, and the decryption and processing of asserts at the SP end is called **assertion**.

WS-Trust

This is part of many WS* standards, including WS-Security, WS-Federation, and the WS-Security policy. **WS** stands for **Web Services**. WS-Trust defines the protocols used in requesting and issuing security tokens by WS-Security. **Security Token Service (STS)** is a big feature of WS-Trust, and it can be used to convert locally issued security tokens into other security token formats that can be understood by the application. It can also convert incoming security tokens into supported token formats.

WS-Federation

WS-Federation is also a part of WS* standards. While SAML only works with SAML tokens, WS-Federation supports the use of many token types, including SAML. Basically, WS-Federation provides a mechanism to simplify the communication between an IdP and an SP. The fundamental goal of WS-Federation is to simplify the development of federated services through cross-realm communication and management of federation services by reusing the WS-Trust STS model and protocol. More information about WS-Federation can be found at `http://download.boulder.ibm.com/ibmdl/pub/software/dw/specs/ws-fed/WS-FederationSpec05282007.pdf?S_TACT=105AGX04S_CMP=LP`.

AD FS components

When the AD FS role is installed, there are a few related components we need to be aware of. Before Windows Server 2012 R2, there were four AD FS roles services: the federation service, the federation service proxy, the claim-aware agent, and the Windows token-based agent (which supports the AD FS 1.x interoperability). These are no longer available as role services, and when we go to install AD FS, it will only have the federation service role.

Federation service

This is the main role service for AD FS, and it can work at the IdP end as well as the SP end. In order to install the AD FS role service, the system needs to be a member server of an AD domain. Depending on the workload, multiple federation servers can be installed under the same domain, and this is called an **AD FS farm**. The federation server is responsible for generating security tokens and signing them with its signing certificate. Let's look into the AD FS versions that have been released so far.

AD FS 1.0

AD FS was first introduced with Windows Server 2003 R2. This version of AD FS is no longer available as Windows Server 2003 is end of life. This provided basic SSO capabilities, but it mainly suffered because it had less compatibility with other federation service providers in the market.

AD FS 1.1

This was introduced with Windows 2008, and it did continue with Windows Server 2008 R2. It hasn't been changed much since 1.0. It also suffered from providing limited support to other federation services. It only supported the WS-Federation passive requester profile and SAML 1.0.

AD FS 2.0

This version was released after Windows Server 2008 R2 but as a separate installation (download this via the web: `https://www.microsoft.com/en-gb/download/details.aspx?id=10909`). All other versions came as part of the OS. Before version 2.0, it was supported to use AD LDS as the authentication store. This means users can authenticate with AD LDS, similar to AD. With version 2.0, it no longer supports LDS as the account store. It can work as the attribute store, which can store AD FS data but cannot be used for authentication. AD FS 2.0 also supports a parent-child domain environment, so users in a child domain can use AD FS in another domain for the federation. It reduces the management overhead. It also improved support for federation trusts with the use of industry-standard metadata formats. It allows organizations to create trust between federation partners quickly. Systems that run with version 1.x can have an in-place upgrade to 2.0.

AD FS 2.1

This version comes with Windows Server 2012 and no major changes from the 2.0 version were made.

AD FS 3.0

This version was introduced with Windows Server 2012 R2. This removed a few role services from the AD FS 2.0, such as AD FS Proxy service, and provided an interface between the internet and AD FS servers. It operates from the **Demilitarized Zone (DMZ)** and doesn't need to be domain joined. The idea of it is to protect the identity infrastructure with a bogus token. This was replaced by the Web Application Proxy, which comes under a remote access role. This is not used by AD FS anymore. It also removed the AD FS web agents 1.x, which provided connections with other systems.

Workspace Join is one of the greatest features that came with this. It allows us to register mobile devices (even non-Windows) with corporate to access applications and data with SSO. AD FS 3.0 does not require **Internet Information Services (IIS)** anymore and is installed as a separate role. It also supports **group Managed Service Account (gMSA)**. This is a new type of service account, which supports automatic password changes. The creation and management of this account is explained in `Chapter 8`, *Managing Users, Groups, and Devices*. This version also supports OAuth 2.0 standard access tokens. Those are JSON format tokens and are easy to use with modern applications.

AD FS 4.0

AD FS 4.0 is the latest version available with Windows Server 2016. This is what we will use throughout this chapter. This version is supported by modern hybrid cloud requirements. If you are already using Azure AD, this version allows you to use Microsoft Azure MFA without installing and configuring additional components. With previous AD FS versions, it needed an additional server to configure. With the new version, AD FS has a built-in Azure MFA adapter. Similar to AD FS 3.0, the new version also supports mobile device registration to maintain an organization's compliance requirements. If it's in an Azure AD environment, then by using AD FS 4.0, you can apply conditional access policies to on-premises components.

This version also supports modern authentication standards, such as OpenID Connect and OAuth 2.0. It provides an enhanced user experience with Windows 10 and the latest Android and iOS apps. AD FS 4.0 also supports authentication with LDAP v3.0-compliant directories. It allows people to use AD FS more and more, even when they are not running AD DS. Windows 10 introduced the new password-less log in methods: Windows Hello and Microsoft Passport. These are based on PIN and biometric input, such as fingerprint or facial recognition. AD FS 4.0 supports these new sign-in methods.

Migration from AD FS 2012 R2 has been simplified as well. Before, if we needed to migrate from one version to another, then we needed to build a farm parallel to a production AD FS farm, and then migrate the configuration over. But, with the new version, we can introduce the AD FS 2016 server to the existing Windows Server 2012 R2 farm, and it will start to work in Windows Server 2012 R2 operation level. Once all the Windows Server 2012 R2 servers are removed from the farm, the operation level can upgrade to Windows Server 2016.

What is new in AD FS 2019?

At the time this book was written, Windows Server 2019 had already been on the market for a few months. Even though this book is not about AD 2019, I decided to list down new features introduced by AD FS 2019 as there are a significant amount of changes from AD FS 2016:

- **Primary authentication via third-party authentication providers**: When authenticating via AD FS, so far, we have only been able to use built-in AD authentication methods such as form authentication, certificate authentication, or Azure MFA as primary authentication. Then, as a secondary authentication, we were able to use any other external authentication methods.

With AD FS 2019, we can now use any third-party authentication provider's login method as primary authentication (the provider needs to register with AD FS farm first).

- **Password-less authentication**: AD FS 2019 is fully supported to use password-less authentication as a primary authentication method. With AD FS 2016, it required additional components and additional configurations in order to do the same.
- **Risk Assessment Model**: Engineers can now build their own plugins to block or assign risk scores to authentication requests during the pre-authentication stage by using the AD FS 2019 Risk Assessment Module. More information about this module is available at `https://docs.microsoft.com/en-us/windows-server/identity/ad-fs/development/ad-fs-risk-assessment-model`.
- **Extranet Smart Lockout (ESL) is built into AD FS 2019**: ESL protects user accounts from extranet account lockout when they log in from familiar locations. From a familiar location, if we detect multiple login failures for a particular user account, that means it can be more of an error rather than malicious activity. By using ESL, we can define different lockout thresholds for familiar and unfamiliar locations. AD FS 2019 also allows us to use audit mode to learn about familiar locations while the environment is still protected by classic extranet lockout functionality. With AD FS 2016, you do not have protection if you are using audit mode.

More information about other features and bug fixes are available at `https://docs.microsoft.com/en-us/windows-server/identity/ad-fs/overview/whats-new-active-directory-federation-services-windows-server`.

The Web Application Proxy

We use proxy servers to access the internet because they perform the required communication with the internet on behalf of the internal users and protect them from external threats. The Web Application Proxy allows us to publish web applications (including AD FS) to the public without exposing the backend of it. This role is no longer a part of AD FS, and it comes as a part of the remote access role. AD FS does not require the Web Application Proxy to work, but it is recommended to use it if users log in from external networks. It also provides basic **Denial-of-Service (DoS)** protection by throttling and quieting connections.

The communications between proxy servers and web clients are encrypted (based on SSL). The Web Application Proxy is not supported for installing on the same AD FS server. It doesn't have built-in load balancing capabilities. If load balancing is required, it can be done using any supported software-/hardware-based load balancer.

AD FS configuration database

AD FS configuration settings needs to save in a database. AD FS supports two types of databases. The simplest method is to use the **Windows Internal Database** (**WID**), which comes with the AD FS installation. This is not a standalone database installation, and it is capable of providing high availability by copying databases to other servers in the AD FS farm. When we go for the AD FS configuration, it gives two deployment options:

- Create the first federation server in a federation server farm.
- Add the federation server to a federation server farm.

If WID is used with the first option, then WID will be deployed with scalability, which allows servers to be added to the farm later and replicate WID. The first server in the farm will be the primary server and it hosts the read/write copy of the database.

When we use the second option, the newly added server will replicate the copy of WID from the primary server, and it is maintained as a read-only copy. Any configuration change should be replicated from the primary server. In the event of a primary server failure, other servers in the farm continue to process requests as normal, but no configuration changes will be possible until the primary server is brought online. If it's not possible to bring it online, then a secondary server can be forcefully nominated as a primary server.

AD FS can store configuration data in Microsoft SQL. This enhances the performance of the AD FS farm, especially if it deals with larger processing as it can read and write data faster. Unlike WID, we can add high availability to the SQL instance by using the SQL cluster method or the Always On method. If AD FS uses MS SQL, then every server in the farm has read/write access to the database. It also enables support for features such as SAML artifact resolution and SAML/WS-Federation token replay detection. Both the features require a configuration that is stored in the shared SQL database instead of WID.

AD FS deployment topologies

There are few different deployment models we can use for AD FS deployment. In this section, we are going to look into these different topologies and their characteristics.

Single federation server

This is the simplest AD FS deployment model available. It contains a single AD FS server. It doesn't have high availability (unless in the host level). This is ideal for a lab environment or staging environment:

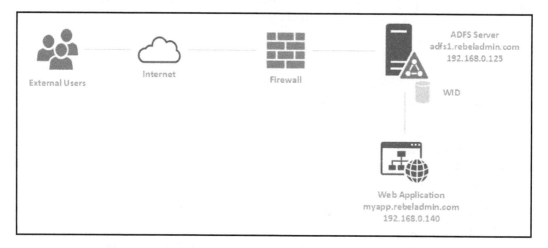

In the preceding example, we have a web application, `myapp.rebeladmin.com`, that needs to allow access via AD FS. We have one AD FS server in the setup with WID. It is behind the corporate firewall and there are **Network Address Translation** (**NAT**) and access rules in place to do the following:

- Map the external IP address to `myapp.rebeladmin.com`, so users can make initial requests from external networks. It is recommended to use TCP `443`.
- Map the external IP address to `secure.rebeladmin.com`, map it to the IP address of `adfs1.rebeladmin.com`, and open TCP `443` from the external networks to allow access.

The application should also have the relevant external and internal DNS records set up. If the request is coming from an external network, it should resolve to a public IP address and if the request is coming from an internal network, DNS should resolve to the internal IP addresses. This is also called a split-brain DNS setup.

My recommendation for this setup is to configure the AD FS server with a **Network Load Balancer** (**NLB**). It is only going to cost you one additional IP address for the NLB cluster IP, but when we need to expand the AD FS farm, all we need to do is configure another server and add it to the NLB. The cluster IP will map to the external IP, and it will be used with an external DNS entry for AD FS.

In this setup, the Web Application Proxy hasn't been used:

Advantages	Disadvantages
Low cost to implement. Only one server required for AD FS and no SQL licenses have been used as it uses WID.	No redundancy. Single point of failure.
Easy to manage.	Poor performance as there is no way to share workloads.
No additional service role integration and therefore fewer dependencies.	Less secure as it is not possible to relay the requests to the AD FS server, and this method uses a direct connection point to process the requests (no Web Application Proxy).
Still can configure to support future expansions and can add servers to the AD FS farm whenever required.	N/A.

Single federation server and single Web Application Proxy server

This is an ideal setup to start with. This removes the security concerns we had with the single federation server. The Web Application Proxy server will be the initial connection point from the external network and it will relay requests into and out of the internal AD FS server.

This is still not going to provide high availability as each role holder only has one instance:

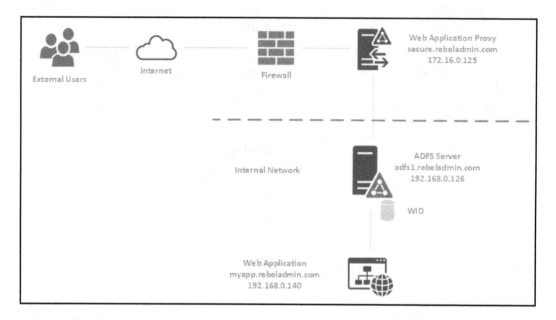

In this setup, we can separate the network functionality between perimeter and corporate networks. The preceding setup needs NAT and access to accomplish the following communication requirements:

- Map the external IP address to `myapp.rebeladmin.com` so users can make initial requests from external networks. It is recommended to use TCP port `443`.
- Map the external IP address to `secure.rebeladmin.com`, map it to the IP address of the Web Application Proxy server, and open TCP port `443` from external to allow access.
- Allow access from the Web Application Proxy server to the AD FS server in TCP port `443`.

In the preceding example, once the external user accesses the application's URL, it will redirect to the Web Application Proxy server. This doesn't need to be domain joined as it operates from the perimeter network. Proxy servers should be able to resolve the DNS name for the AD FS servers from the perimeter network. This can be done by using a DNS server or a host file.

Similar to the previous model, this can be implemented with NLB to allow future expansions with minimum impact. We need two NLB clusters for that. The first NLB cluster is for the Web Application Proxy and the second NLB cluster is for AD FS servers. The only change is in the DNS records. Instead of pointing DNS and firewall rules to the server IP addresses, DNS record needs to point to NLB cluster IP addresses:

Advantages	Disadvantages
Improved security as the Web Application Proxy acts as an intermediate layer between external users and corporate networks.	No redundancy and a single point of failure.
Basic DoS protection by throttling and queuing connections.	The implementation cost is high compared to the single server model as additional servers need to be added.
This setup supports future expansions. It can easily add servers to the AD FS farm and the Web Application Proxy group when required.	Adding more roles also means more dependencies. Both roles need to function correctly to complete the process.

Multiple federation servers and multiple Web Application Proxy servers with SQL Server

So far, we have looked into models that benefit from easy implementation and improved security. But this model is focused on high availability. Each role will be configured with NLB clusters. The AD FS database will be hosted in the SQL Always On cluster environment for high availability. This model is ideal for SPs and other businesses that work with high volumes of AD FS requests.

The NLB cluster is a software-based load balancing solution that comes with the Microsoft server OS. It is easy to implement with no additional licenses. However, hardware load balancers provide higher performance and fewer dependencies.

The following diagram provides a sample design for the given topology:

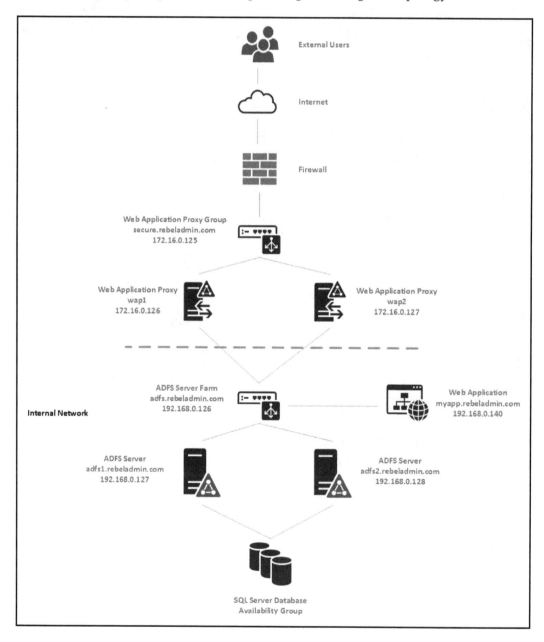

Similar to the previous model, this model's operations are clearly divided into two network segments: perimeter and corporate. A corporate firewall has NAT and access rules to support the following requirements:

- Map the external IP address to `myapp.rebeladmin.com` so that users can make initial requests from external networks. It is recommended to use TCP `443`.
- Map the external IP address to `secure.rebeladmin.com`, map it to the IP address of the Web Application Proxy server group's NLB cluster IP, and open TCP port `443` from the external networks to allow access.
- Allow access from Web Application Proxy servers to AD FS farm NLB cluster IP in TCP port `443`.

For both NLB clusters, the initial connection point will be NLB cluster IP. Apart from the application's external URL, the only external published URL will be the Web Application Proxy's URL. In the preceding example, `secure.rebeladmin.com` is a map to the Web Application Proxy NLB cluster IP.

AD FS servers use the Microsoft SQL Always On availability group to host the AD FS database. This is a read/write database for both the hosts.

 SQL Always On is a high-availability solution that runs on top of the Windows cluster. Windows Server 2016 supports a two-node cluster with Azure Cloud Witness. It reduces the number of servers that need to be used in a SQL Always On setup.

Advantages	Disadvantages
High availability: Each component hosts multiple servers with load balancers. AD FS databases also use an SQL high-availability environment.	**High cost**: It needs multiple servers and licenses (OS, SQL Servers). This also increases the management cost.
High performance: Workloads are distributed between multiple hosts using load balancers.	**Complex setup**: The implementation is time-consuming and requires advanced skills for planning and configuration.
Support for features such as SAML artifact resolution and SAML/WS-Federation token replay detection.	Troubleshooting an issue is time-consuming and complex as there are many systems and application dependencies.

AD FS deployment

In this section, we are going to look into AD FS deployment using a single federation server and a single Web Application Proxy server model. Before we move on to configuration, we need to sort out the following prerequisites:

- DNS records
- SSL certificates

DNS records

We need to have a few DNS records (internal and external) set up prior to starting the deployment:

DNS Record	External	Internal
Application URL	Yes	Yes
WAP URL	Yes	N/A
AD FS URL	N/A	Yes

In the demo environment, the following URLs will be used:

- `myapp.rebeladmin.com` will be the application, and it will have the external DNS record created and mapped to the external IP address. It will NAT to the application server IP address using a firewall. It will also have the internal DNS entry and point to the internal IP address of the application server.
- `secure.rebeladmin.com` will be the WAP URL from the external. WAP servers are in the perimeter network. It is not necessary to have the internal DNS record unless there are multiple WAP servers.
- `adfs.rebeladmin.com` will be the AD FS server DNS entry, and it does not need to have an external DNS entry. However, WAP servers need to connect to AD FS servers via the SSL certificate. Since it's one server, there is no point deploying a DNS server in the perimeter network, and it can be done using the `hosts` file entry.

SSL certificates

AD FS deployment requires a few SSL certificates. In this demonstration, we will use the following:

- `*.rebeladmin.com`: This is a wildcard SSL certificate for external URLs. This is used for the application and WAP.
- `rebeladmin.com`: This SSL is for AD FS service communication.

 In the lab environment, we can create these certificates using internal **Certification Authority** (**CA**). If the domain name is the same, then wildcard certificates are used internally and externally as well. Wildcard certificates simplify certificate management.

Installing the AD FS role

Before installation, the SSL certificate for `adfs.rebeladmin.com` needs to be installed in the computer account as it is required during the AD FS installation. This can be checked using the following command:

```
dir Cert:\LocalMachine\My
```

The following screenshot displays the output of the preceding command:

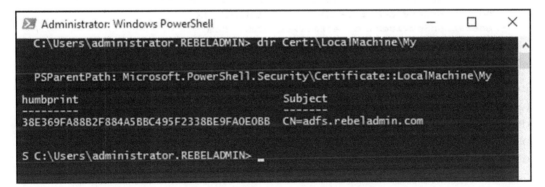

The AD FS server should be a member server of the domain and should log in as the domain administrator or the Enterprise Admin to do the installation.

The next step is to install the AD FS role service, which can be done by using the following PowerShell command:

```
Install-WindowsFeature ADFS-Federation -IncludeManagementTools
```

The following screenshot displays the output of the preceding command:

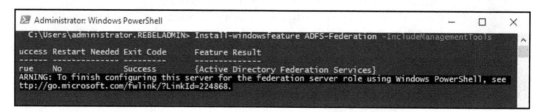

Once this is completed, we need to configure the AD FS server. Let's use the following configuration for the demo setup:

```
Import-Module ADFS
$credentials = Get-Credential
Install-AdfsFarm `
-CertificateThumbprint:"938E369FA88B2F884A5BBC495F2338BE9FA0E0BB" `
-FederationServiceDisplayName:"REBELADMIN INC" `
-FederationServiceName:"adfs.rebeladmin.com" `
-ServiceAccountCredential $credentials
```

In this setup, we are using WID for AD FS, so there is no need for SQL configuration. In the preceding command, `CertificateThumbprint` specifies the SSL certificate (`adfs.rebeladmin.com`), and `FederationServiceDisplayName` specifies the display name of the federation service. `FederationServiceName` is the service name, and it should match the SSL we used. `ServiceAccountCredential` is used to define the service account details for the AD FS setup. In the end, the system needs to be restarted to apply the configuration:

```
PS C:\Windows\system32> Import-Module ADFS
$credentials = Get-Credential
Install-AdfsFarm `
-CertificateThumbprint:"938E369FA88B2F884A5BBC495F2338BE9FA0E0BB" `
-FederationServiceDisplayName:"REBELADMIN INC" `
-FederationServiceName:"adfs.rebeladmin.com" `
-ServiceAccountCredential $credentials
cmdlet Get-Credential at command pipeline position 1
Supply values for the following parameters:
WARNING: A machine restart is required to complete ADFS service configuration. F
or more information, see: http://go.microsoft.com/fwlink/?LinkId=798725
WARNING: The SSL certificate subject alternative names do not support host name
'certauth.adfs.rebeladmin.com'. Configuring certificate authentication binding o
n port '49443' and hostname 'adfs.rebeladmin.com'.
WARNING: The SSL certificate does not contain all UPN suffix values that exist i
n the enterprise.  Users with UPN suffix values not represented in the certifica
te will not be able to Workplace-Join their devices.  For more information, see
http://go.microsoft.com/fwlink/?LinkId=311954.

Message                           Context              Status
-------                           -------              ------
The configuration completed successfully. DeploymentSucceeded Success

PS C:\Windows\system32> |
```

The error about the alternative SSL name, `certauth.adfs.rebeladmin.com`, regards the certificate authentication. Before Windows Server 2016, this was an issue as the system didn't support different bindings for certificate authentication and device authentication on the same host. The default port `443` was used by the device authentication and couldn't have multiple bindings on the same channel. In Windows Server 2016, this is possible and now, it supports two methods. The first option is to use the same host (`adfs.rebeladmin.com`) with different ports (`443` and `49443`). The second option is to use different hosts (`adfs.rebeladmin.com` and `certauth.adfs.rebeladmin.com`) with the same port (`443`). This requires an SSL certificate to support `certauth.adfs.rebeladmin.com` as an alternate subject name.

Once the reboot completes, we can check whether the installation was successful by using the following command:

```
Get-WinEvent "AD FS/Admin" | Where-Object {$_.ID -eq "100"} | fl
```

This will print the content of event `100`, which confirms the successful AD FS installation.

Installing WAP

The next step of the configuration is to install WAP. This doesn't need to be a domain-joined server and should be placed on the perimeter network. Before the installation process, install the required SSL certificates. In my demo, it is for `*.rebeladmin.com`. We can verify this by using this:

```
dir Cert:\LocalMachine\My
```

The following screenshot displays the output of the preceding command:

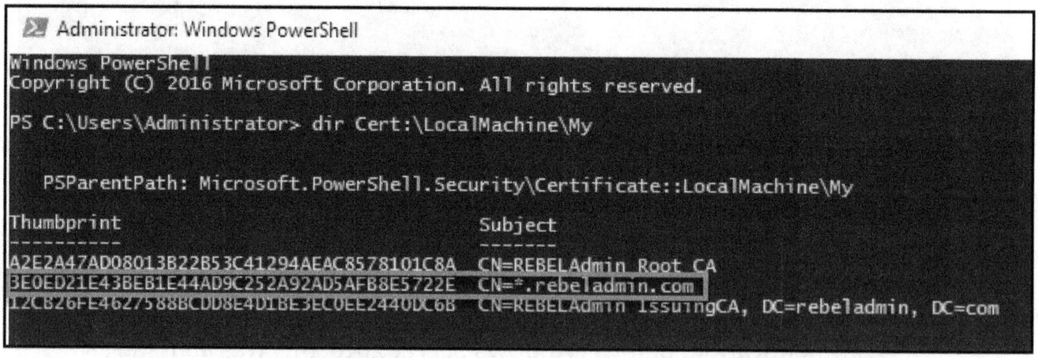

Before proceeding, we also need to check whether a server can resolve to `adfs.rebeladmin.com` as WAP needs to connect to AD FS.

Once everything is confirmed, we can install the WAP role:

```
Install-WindowsFeature Web-Application-Proxy -IncludeManagementTools
```

The following screenshot displays the output of the preceding command:

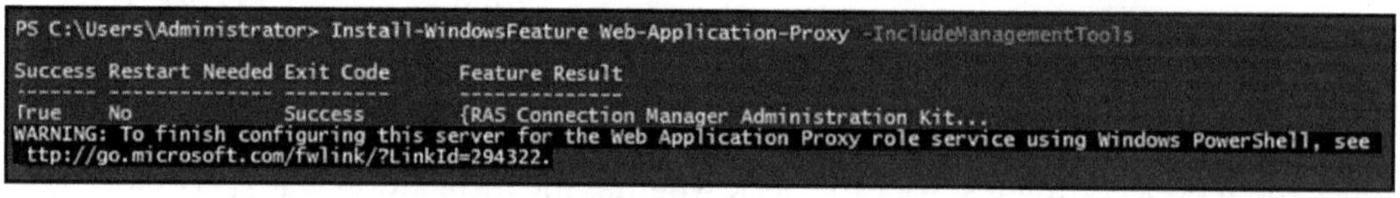

Once it's completed, we can proceed with the configuration by using the following:

```
$credentials = Get-Credential
Install-WebApplicationProxy
-FederationServiceName "adfs.rebeladmin.com"
-FederationServiceTrustCredential $credentials
-CertificateThumbprint "3E0ED21E43BEB1E44AD9C252A92AD5AFB8E5722E"
```

In the preceding commands, `FederationServiceName` is used to define the AD FS service name, and it needs to match the name provided on the AD FS setup. `FederationServiceTrustCredential` is used to provide an account, which is authorized to register a new proxy server with AD FS. The account that is used here should have permissions to manage AD FS. The `CertificateThumbprint` parameter is used to define the certificate for WAP. In our demo, it's the `*.rebeladmin.com` certificate. At the end of the configuration, we need to restart the system to apply the changes:

```
PS C:\Windows\system32> $credentials = Get-Credential
Install-WebApplicationProxy -FederationServiceName "adfs.rebeladmin.com" -FederationServiceTrustCredential $credentials -Certificate
cmdlet Get-Credential at command pipeline position 1
Supply values for the following parameters:
WARNING: Given SSL certificate does not match the STS certificate. Requests doin
g NTLM authentication over the proxy will fail.
WARNING: A machine restart is required to complete ADFS service configuration. F
or more information, see: http://go.microsoft.com/fwlink/?LinkId=798725

Message                              Context              Status
-------                              -------              ------
The configuration completed successfully. DeploymentSucceeded Success
```

Once the reboot is completed, we can confirm the health of the configuration using the following event log in the AD FS server:

```
Get-WinEvent "AD FS/Admin" | Where-Object {$_.ID -eq "396"} | fl
```

The following screenshot displays the output of the preceding command:

```
PS C:\Users\administrator.REBELADMIN> Get-WinEvent "AD FS/Admin" | Where-Object {$_.ID -eq "396"} | fl

TimeCreated  : 30/03/2017 00:37:38
ProviderName : AD FS
Id           : 396
Message      : The trust between the federation server proxy and the Federation Service was renewed successfully.

               Proxy trust certificate subject: CN=ADFS ProxyTrust - REBEL-CRTROOT.
               Proxy trust certificate old thumbprint: 0A191B3E42B8B9B826F8ED1AE6BEC2C142B0CABA.
               Proxy trust certificate new thumbprint: D0CA59939D1427A95FA1EEEO9DAD2B950040E4A0.

TimeCreated  : 30/03/2017 00:36:37
ProviderName : AD FS
Id           : 396
Message      : The trust between the federation server proxy and the Federation Service was renewed successfully.

               Proxy trust certificate subject: CN=ADFS ProxyTrust - REBEL-CRTROOT.
               Proxy trust certificate old thumbprint: 0A191B3E42B8B9B826F8ED1AE6BEC2C142B0CABA.
               Proxy trust certificate new thumbprint: D465695A3D4BE6137903645177E2569ADB8411BE.

TimeCreated  : 30/03/2017 00:27:56
ProviderName : AD FS
Id           : 396
Message      : The trust between the federation server proxy and the Federation Service was renewed successfully.

               Proxy trust certificate subject: CN=ADFS ProxyTrust - REBEL-CRTROOT.
               Proxy trust certificate old thumbprint: 0A191B3E42B8B9B826F8ED1AE6BEC2C142B0CABA.
               Proxy trust certificate new thumbprint: F4C1680F09C36C278B2FB981BFD5FC2415C8E06E.

TimeCreated  : 30/03/2017 00:26:55
ProviderName : AD FS
Id           : 396
Message      : The trust between the federation server proxy and the Federation Service was renewed successfully.

               Proxy trust certificate subject: CN=ADFS ProxyTrust - REBEL-CRTROOT.
               Proxy trust certificate old thumbprint: 0A191B3E42B8B9B826F8ED1AE6BEC2C142B0CABA.
               Proxy trust certificate new thumbprint: FA394B73302BD662407A374FCADC18306964B3B2.
```

Configuring the claims-aware application with new federation servers

At the start of this chapter, I explained that not every application can use AD FS for authorization. It should be a claims-aware application. I have an application called myapp.rebeladmin.com that is already set up. In the configuration, I set it up to use the existing STS and added new AD FS server's metadata URL, which is https://adfs.rebeladmin.com/federationmetadata/2007-06/ federationmetadata.xml.

 If configuration is successful, AD FS installs the metadata XML, and you should be able to view this using the web browser. If it cannot load, then you need to check it before this step.

Once the application is configured, when I go to my application, which is https://myapp.rebeladmin.com/myapp (internally), I can see the following error. This was expected as the AD FS setup does not know about my application yet:

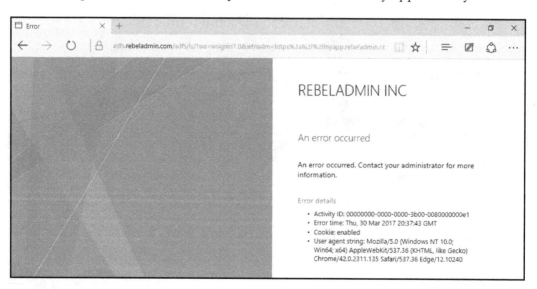

Creating a relying party trust

In order to get our application working, we need to create a relying party trust between our application and the AD FS setup. Then, only the AD FS setup will know about the application.

In order to do that, perform the following steps:

1. Log in to the AD FS server as an administrator.
2. Go to **Server Manager** | **Tools** | **AD FS Management**.
3. Go to **Relying Party Trusts**, and then click on **Add Relying Party Trust**:

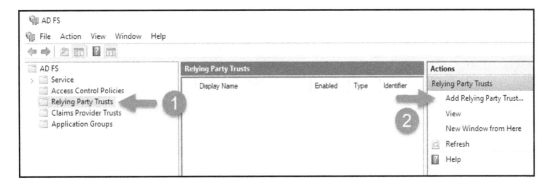

4. The system will open the **Add Relay Party Trust Wizard**. Select **Claims Aware** and click **Start**.

5. In the **Select Data Source** page, select **Import data about the relying party published online or on a local network** and enter the metadata URL for the application. For my application, I have created the metadata file under `https://myapp.rebeladmin.com/myapp/federationmetadata /2007-06/federationmetadata.xml`:

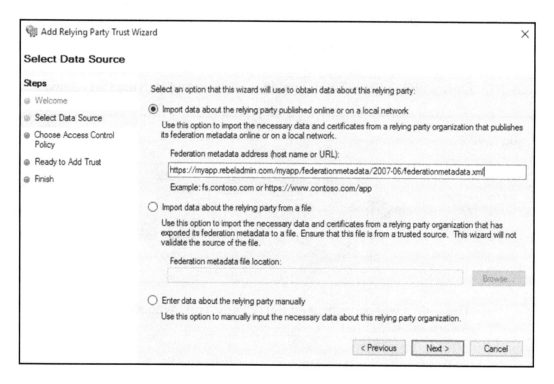

 When we establish a trust, we need to provide certain information to match the SP's application configuration. This is painful as even a small mistake can cause issues. Also, if these settings are changed on the SP's side, we will not know until they inform us of what to modify on the AD FS side. Therefore, service providers use metadata XML files to publish these required settings. This simplifies the configuration. If there is no metadata file, we still can create the trust using the required custom settings.

6. On the next page, go to **Specify Display Name** for the claim and click on **Next**.

7. On the **Choose an access control policy** page, select **Permit Everyone**, and click on **Next**. This is a new feature of AD FS 2016, and it allows us to create access policies easily. It is possible to add customer access policies as well. In this demo, I am not going to use any MFA as it's a test lab:

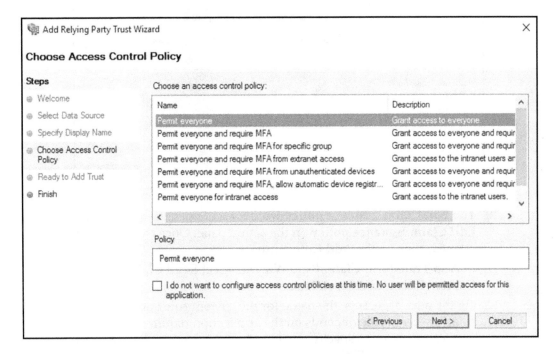

8. In the next window, we can review the settings and click on **Next** to continue.

9. In the **Finish** page, keep the check for **Configure claims issuance policy for this application** and click on **Close**:

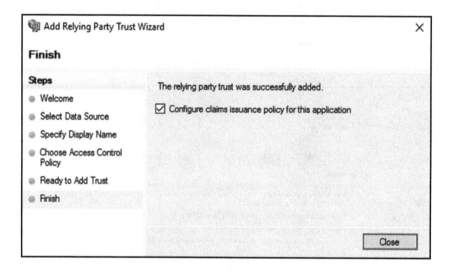

10. The **Edit Claim Issuance policy** window will open. If it does not, click on **Edit Claim Issuance policy** on the action pane. Once the window is opened, click on the **Add Rule** button.

11. In **Add Transform Claim Rule Wizard,** select **Send Claims Using a Custom Rule** and click on **Next**.

12. On the next page, type the name for the custom rule and input the claim rule. The claim rule depends on the application requirements. Most application vendors specify what kind of claim rule you need to have. Once complete, click on **Finish**.

13. Once finished, click **OK** to exit from the wizard.

Configuring the Web Application Proxy

Now, we have the application configured with AD FS. But our requirement is to use the Web Application Proxy to publish the application to the public.

In order to do that, log in to the Web Application Proxy server as an administrator and execute the following command:

```
Add-WebApplicationProxyApplication
-BackendServerUrl 'https://myapp.rebeladmin.com/myapp/'
-ExternalCertificateThumbprint
```

```
'3E0ED21E43BEB1E44AD9C252A92AD5AFB8E5722E'
-ExternalUrl 'https://myapp.rebeladmin.com/myapp/'
-Name 'MyApp'
-ExternalPreAuthentication AD FS
-ADFSRelyingPartyName 'myapp.rebeladmin.com'
```

In the preceding command, `ExternalUrl` specifies the external URL for the application. `BackendServerUrl` specifies the internal URL for the application. `ExternalCertificateThumbprint` is the certificate to use from external networks. The `Name` parameter specifies the custom name for the app, which will be displayed on the proxy page. `ExternalPreAuthentication` defines the authentication mode. On our setup, we're using AD FS mode. It also supports pass-through mode. `ADFSRelyingPartyName` specifies the AD FS relying party name, which will be used for this application.

 The Web Application Proxy can translate hostnames used in the external URL and the backend URL. However, it cannot translate paths.

Once all is done, when we access the application from the external `https://myapp.rebeladmin.com/myapp/`, it successfully proxies to AD FS, and after successful authentication, the application page is displayed:

| | https://myapp.rebeladmin.com/default.asp | Windows Identity Foundati... | |

Welcome : REBELADMIN\dfrancis
Values from IIdentity

| IsAuthenticated:True | Name:REBELADMIN\dfrancis |

Claims from IClaimsIdentity

Claim Type	Claim Value	Value Type
http://schemas.microsoft.com/ws/2014/01/identity/claims/anchorclaimtype	http://schemas.microsoft.com/ws/2008/06/identity/claims/windowsaccountname	string
http://schemas.xmlsoap.org/ws/2005/05/identity/claims/implicitupn	dfrancis@rebeladmin.com	string
http://schemas.microsoft.com/claims/authnmethodsproviders	WindowsAuthentication	string
http://schemas.xmlsoap.org/ws/2005/05/identity/claims/upn	dfrancis@rebeladmin.com	string
http://schemas.microsoft.com/ws/2008/06/identity/claims/primarygroupsid	S-1-5-21-4041220333-1835452706-552999228-513	string
http://schemas.microsoft.com/ws/2008/06/identity/claims/groupsid	S-1-5-21-4041220333-1835452706-552999228-513	string
http://schemas.microsoft.com/ws/2008/06/identity/claims/groupsid	S-1-1-0	string
http://schemas.microsoft.com/ws/2008/06/identity/claims/groupsid	S-1-5-32-545	string
http://schemas.microsoft.com/ws/2008/06/identity/claims/groupsid	S-1-5-2	string
http://schemas.microsoft.com/ws/2008/06/identity/claims/groupsid	S-1-5-11	string
http://schemas.microsoft.com/ws/2008/06/identity/claims/groupsid	S-1-5-15	string
http://schemas.microsoft.com/ws/2008/06/identity/claims/groupsid	S-1-18-1	string
http://schemas.microsoft.com/ws/2008/06/identity/claims/primarysid	S-1-5-21-4041220333-1835452706-552999228-1186	string
http://schemas.xmlsoap.org/ws/2005/05/identity/claims/name	REBELADMIN\dfrancis	string
http://schemas.microsoft.com/ws/2008/06/identity/claims/windowsaccountname	REBELADMIN\dfrancis	string

Integrating with Azure MFA

MFA is a common requirement today for online services. It can be for any hosted solution in organizations such as Citrix, RDS, or other web applications. MFA is also used in hybrid cloud environments to provide the same level of protection to on-premises and cloud. In both the scenarios, AD FS can be used to integrate the traditional authentication with MFA.

There are many MFA service providers in the market. Some of those are on-premises solutions, where we can install an appliance and use MFA services. Others are cloud-based solution providers and sell MFA services as subscriptions. Customers can simply install an agent on-premises and connect it to these cloud-based solutions. Azure MFA was first introduced to be used with Azure services and later developed further to support on-premises workload protections too. Users can use mobile texts, calls, or a PIN on the Microsoft Authenticator application to authenticate. Most of the MFA SPs have a separate agent, which needs to be installed in the AD FS servers in order to connect it with the MFA services.

The Azure MFA integration was complicated in Windows Server 2012 R2 environments. It needed an agent as well as an on-premises Azure MFA server. A big change with AD FS 2016 was the Azure MFA integration enhancement. With AD FS 2016, we no longer need to install these components. The AD FS Azure adapter allows integration with Azure AD in order to pull the configuration. In this section, we are going to look at how we can integrate the AD FS setup with Azure MFA.

Prerequisites

In order to configure Azure MFA, we need a few things:

- A valid Azure subscription.
- Azure Global Administrator privileges.
- The Azure AD Federated setup. Azure AD needs to integrate with AD FS on-premises and synchronize identities to Azure. This will be covered in Chapter 17, *Azure Active Directory for Hybrid Setup*.
- Windows Server 2016 AD FS in local infrastructure.
- Enterprise Admin privileges for AD FS servers to configure MFA.

- Azure MFA needs to be enabled. The users that sync from on-premises AD need to have MFA enabled. I wrote an article about this before, and you can access it via `http://www.rebeladmin.com/2016/01/step-by-step-guide-to-configure-mfa-multi-factor-authentication-for-azure-users/`.
- The Windows Azure AD module for Windows PowerShell in AD FS servers. This can be downloaded from `http://go.microsoft.com/fwlink/p/?linkid=236297`.

Before installing the Azure PowerShell module, the system needs to have the Microsoft online services sign-in assistant installed. It can be downloaded from `https://www.microsoft.com/en-us/download/details.aspx?displaylang=enid=28177`. Once it is installed, we need to install the Azure Resource Manager cmdlet by using `Install-Module AzureRM`. This allows us to manage Azure resources using PowerShell.

Creating a certificate in an AD FS farm to connect to Azure MFA

First, we need to create a certificate, which will be used by the AD FS farm. This needs to run from the AD FS server:

```
$certbase64 = New-AdfsAzureMfaTenantCertificate -TenantID
05c6f80c-61d9-44df-bd2d-4414a983c1d4
```

The preceding command generates the new certificate. TenantID is the subscription ID you have from Azure. This can be found by running this:

```
Login-AzureRmAccount
```

The preceding command will ask for the credentials for Azure and once we provide them, it will list `TenantId`:

```
Environment          : AzureCloud
Account              : dcadmin@REBELADMIN.onmicrosoft.com
TenantId             : 05c6f80c-61d9-44df-bd2d-4414a983c1d4
SubscriptionId       :
SubscriptionName     :
CurrentStorageAccount :
```

This will create a certificate under **Certificates (Local Computer)**:

Enabling AD FS servers to connect with the Azure Multi-Factor Authentication client

Now, we have the certificate, but we need to tell Azure Multi-Factor Auth Client to use it as a credential to connect with AD FS.

Before that, we need to connect to Azure AD by using Azure PowerShell. We can do that by using the following command:

```
Connect-MsolService
```

Then, it will prompt for your login and use your Azure Global Administrator account to connect.

After that, we can pass the credentials by using the following command:

```
New-MsolServicePrincipalCredential -AppPrincipalId 981f26a1-7f43-403b-
a875-f8b09b8cd720 -Type asymmetric -Usage verify -Value $certbase64
```

In the preceding command, `AppPrincipalId` defines the **Globally Unique Identifier** (**GUID**) for Azure Multi-Factor Auth Client.

Enabling the AD FS farm to use Azure MFA

The next step of the configuration is to enable the AD FS farm to use Azure MFA. This can be done by using the following command:

```
Set-AdfsAzureMfaTenant -TenantId 05c6f80c-61d9-44df-bd2d-4414a983c1d4
-ClientId 981f26a1-7f43-403b-a875-f8b09b8cd720
```

In the preceding command, `TenantId` refers to the Azure Tenant ID and `ClientId` represents the Azure Multi-Factor Auth Client's GUID.

Once the command successfully runs, we need to restart the AD FS service on each server in the farm:

```
PS C:\Users\administrator.REBELADMIN\Desktop> Set-AdfsAzureMfaTenant -TenantId 05c6f80c-61d9-44df-bd2d-4414a983c1d4
entId 981f26a1-7f43-403b-a875-f8b09b8cd720
WARNING: PS0177: The authentication provider configuration data was successfully updated.  Before your changes take
effect, you must restart the AD FS Windows Service on each server in the farm.
PS C:\Users\administrator.REBELADMIN\Desktop> _
```

Enabling Azure MFA for authentication

The last step of the configuration is to enable Azure MFA globally for the AD FS server.

In order to do that, log in to the AD FS server as the Enterprise Admin. Then, go to **Server Manager | Tools | AD FS Management**.

Then, in the console, navigate to **Service | Authentication Methods**. Then, in the **Actions** panel, click on **Edit Primary Authentication Method**:

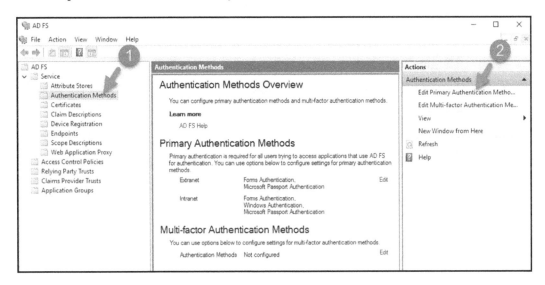

This opens up the window to configure global authentication methods. It has two tabs, and we can see Azure MFA on both. If Azure MFA is used as a primary method by removing other options, then AD FS will not ask for logins and will use MFA as the only authentication method.

Its operation boundaries can be set to intranet or extranet:

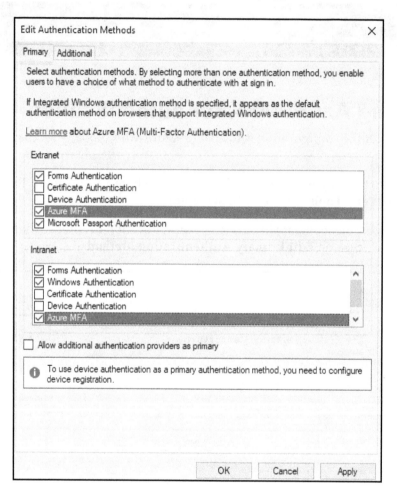

Another option is to select MFA as the secondary authentication method:

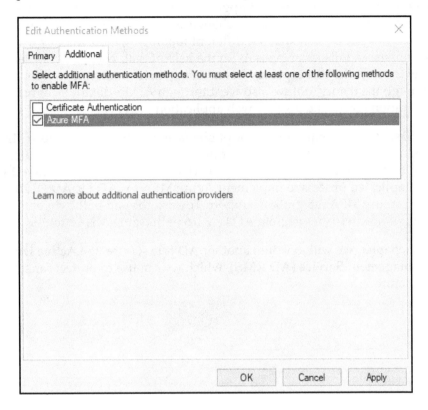

This finishes the Azure MFA integration, and users can use MFA based on the options selected in the preceding wizards. There is still lots to talk about regarding AD FS, and it is hard to cover everything in a chapter.

Summary

We are living in a connected world. Businesses are using cloud-based applications and B2B connections more and more. Microsoft AD FS allows engineers to handle identity requirements for such scenarios in an effective and secure manner, which we cannot get from traditional authorization methods.

In this chapter, we learned about the characteristics of each of these AD FS versions. This allows us to plan for the version upgrades and get the benefits from the new features. AD FS deployment topologies change according to business requirements. In this chapter, we also learned about different topologies, their characteristics, and their advantages and disadvantages. With the help of that, you have now learned about how to select the best topology based on business requirements. Not only did we go through the theory, but we also went through AD FS deployment using a single federation server and a single web application proxy server model.

MFA is a basic security requirement for public-facing web services. Azure MFA was first introduced to provide multi-factor protection to Azure services and later developed further to support on-premises workload protections. Prior to AD FS 2016, it was a complicated process to implement Azure MFA for AD FS. AD FS 2016 now has built-in Azure MFA integration support. Toward the end of the chapter, we learned about how we can integrate AD FS 2016 with Azure MFA successfully.

In the next chapter, we will look into another AD role service, the **Active Directory Rights Management Service** (**AD RMS**), which we can use to protect sensitive data in infrastructure.

14

Active Directory Rights Management Services

Following the invention of the computer, people started to transform analogue data into digital formats. It also transformed the way that people *accessed* data. If someone is in possession of valuable documents, they can put it in a safe, or in any other secure place. In order to access this valuable data, someone needs to physically be there. Digital data is completely different. Even without physically being there, someone could steal valuable data from a computer infrastructure. This is why data security and data governance are so important when it comes to digital data. When the wrong people have access to the wrong data, the consequences can have an impact on people, organizations, or even on countries.

The famous WikiLeaks phenomenon is a good example of this. WikiLeaks got access to state secrets, and some of that data was in digital format, such as emails and scanned files. Someone with authority over that data had passed it to WikiLeaks, or they stole the data illegally. Either way, it's obvious that WikiLeaks should not have had access to that data in first place. Even now, they keep releasing data to the public, and some of that data is even powerful enough to have a negative impact on foreign affairs between countries.

The other concern about data security is related to intellectual property. For example, let's consider a software vendor. They spend a lot of money and time on developing a product, and they release it to market with the hope of making a profit. After a month, someone publishes the software with valid license keys on torrent sites. So, what would happen to the expected revenue?

We all know that there are laws in place to protect companies from similar situations, but companies still have to constantly fight to protect their products from illegal distribution. The same theory is applicable to films, music tracks, box sets, and so on. I've been maintaining my own technical blog (`http://www.rebeladmin.com`) for the last seven years, and I have written more than 400 articles. I also write for Microsoft TechNet. I maintain this blog just to share my experience and knowledge with the public. I do not make money from it in any form. Over the years, I have seen people using my articles on their own websites without saying a word to me. So far, I have never written a single email to any of those people, as I do not maintain my blog to make money.

Two months ago, a gentleman sent me a very interesting email. In his email, he complained that I was copying other people's blog posts. He even said I was copying posts by including the same text as in other blog posts. If I include anything from a website, a white paper, or a book, I always reference the source. So, I was very interested to investigate the complaint further. I asked him for more details, and he sent me links to a post from a website. When I checked, yes, it was exactly the same, but the gentlemen who made the complaint didn't check the published dates. This site had copied my articles and published it as their own work. These articles even included the same screenshots that I used. In the end, I explained and proved that I was the original author. But that wouldn't be necessary if other people didn't use my posts without my permission. It's just another example of the misuse of digital data.

Governments, data security agencies, application vendors, IT communities, and professionals came up with laws, rules, applications, services, methodologies, and best practices to protect digital data, but one thing we need to understand is that none of these solutions are going to completely protect the data in an infrastructure. We need to expect a breach somewhere. But these solutions will help improve data security and prevent breaches as much as possible. **Active Directory Rights Management Services (AD RMS)** is a server role that helps to protect sensitive data from forwarding, printing, or copying. It also allows us to enforce these rules using corporate policies, in order to ensure that data governance is carried out effectively. In this chapter, we are going to cover the following topics:

- What is AD RMS?
- AD RMS components
- How does AD RMS work?
- How do we deploy AD RMS?

What is AD RMS?

Microsoft took its first compliant with **Federal Information Processing Standard** (**FIPS**) 140-1. The updated version of Windows RMS was renamed as AD RMS, and reintroduced with Windows Server 2008. It continued to grow with features, and was included version after that. Microsoft also released Azure RMS (included in Azure Information Protection), which can be used in a hybrid cloud environment to protect data.

As I stated earlier, AD RMS is not the solution for all data security requirements. In an infrastructure, there are other things attached to data security. The first step in protection is to decide who has access to corporate networks and resources. This falls under the perimeter of defense, and hardware/software firewalls can be used to define rules to manage traffic both coming into, and going out of, the corporate network. Modern layer-7 firewalls and next-generation firewalls allow not only the management of connections, but they also go further into analyzing traffic based on applications and user accounts (AD-integrated). If users are allowed to use the internet, this can threaten the security of corporate data. This can happen via viruses, malware, phishing emails, and so on.

Similar threats can be eliminated using layer-7 firewalls or proxies. The next step in data protection is to control data access for users and groups in the corporate network. This is done using **New Technology File System** (**NTFS**) and **access control lists** (**ACLs**). These control *who* has access to *what* data and resources. The challenge is to protect data once users and groups have access to it.

For example, Rebeladmin Inc. has a sales department. The CEO creates a Word document, which includes the previous year's total sales, and saves it in a network folder. The only people who have access to it are the CEO and sales manager. The CEO sends an email to the sales manager, informing him about the file. Access to the network share is protected by ACLs. However, if the sales manager can access it, what will prevent him from emailing it to a person in the technical department, or bringing it home with him and sharing it with a third party? AD RMS controls the behavior of data once users have access to it. But this will not prevent data leakage via digital photographs, third-party screen capturing, hard copies, or viruses and malware.

AD RMS can do the following:

- **Follow data with policies (persistent usage rights and conditions)**: NTFS permission and ACLs can only manage data within their operation boundaries. In my previous example, when the report is inside the `Sales` folder, it can be accessed only by the CEO and the sales manager. However, if it's copied to a local disk and forwarded as an email, it will bypass the NTFS permissions and ACLs. AD RMS uses persistent usage policies that follow the data. Even when it's moved or forwarded, the policies will follow it.

- **Prevent confidential emails from getting into the wrong hands**: Emails are commonly involved in data leakages. Constant news about data leakages confirms the extent to which emails are involved. Once an email has left the outbox, we do not have control over the data, and we do not have any guarantee that it will only be accessed by the intended recipient. AD RMS can prevent the recipient from forwarding, modifying, copying, or printing the content of confidential emails.

- **Prevent data from being accessed by unauthorized people**: Similar to emails, AD RMS can also protect confidential files and reports from being modified, copied, forwarded, or printed by unauthorized users.

- **Prevent users from capturing content using the Windows print screen feature**: Even if users do not use forwarding or copying methods to send data, they can still use the **print screen** option to capture the data in another form. AD RMS can prevent users from using the Windows print screen tool to capture data.

- **File expiration**: AD RMS allows you to set a validity period for the files. When the time is up, the content of the file will not be able to be accessed.

- **Protect data on mobile devices and macOS**: People use mobile devices to access corporate services and data. AD RMS' mobile extension allows you to extend its data protection capabilities to mobile devices. It supports any mobile device that runs Windows, Android, or iOS. In order to do this, the device should have the latest RMS clients and RMS-aware apps installed. This also applies to macOS devices with Office 2016/2019 for macOS, and RMS-aware applications.

- **Integration with applications**: AD RMS not only supports Microsoft Office files. It also supports a wide range of applications and file types. For example, AD RMS can directly integrate with SharePoint (version 2007 onward), in order to protect the documents published on an intranet site. AD RMS supports many other third-party applications and file types such as .pdf, .jpg, .txt, and .xml. This allows a corporate network to protect more and more data types in the infrastructure.

AD RMS operation is supported in three different operation boundaries:

- **Internal**: In this scenario, AD RMS is used only to protect data in an internal network. Policies are applied to internal applications, files, and users. It will not consider how the data will be protected when it leaves the company premises. This will not support corporate data on mobile devices. This mode is suitable for a testing environment or small businesses.

- **Partner networks**: Some businesses have partnerships with other companies. Based on the nature of the business requirements, there can be Active Directory trusts between multiple forests. In this scenario, the company will focus on protecting data that is exchanged between partners. This can be one way or both ways. If it's both ways, both infrastructures will have to have their own AD RMS servers.

- **External**: In this scenario, AD RMS operations are focused on protecting the company's data, which is shared across infrastructures. It can either be a completely remote infrastructure, or a federated infrastructure. Corporate data protection on mobile devices also needs this type of AD RMS deployment. In this mode, certain AD RMS components will need to be hosted in the perimeter network, and allow service URLs to be accessed via the internet.

> Even though there are three main AD RMS deployment modes, it doesn't prevent organizations from setting up AD RMS environments to cover two, or all three, deployment modes. It is easily possible to extend AD RMS operation boundaries based on the organization's requirements. This means that organizations can start with protecting internal data, and then extend it to protect data in a partner environment, or external environments, when required.

The following table lists the applications, file types, and scenarios we can use to protect data using AD RMS:

Requirements	Application	Protected file types
Protect confidential files	Microsoft Outlook Windows (Version 2003 onward) Office for macOS 2016: • Word • Excel • PowerPoint • PDF • Image processing • XPS Viewer • Gaaiho Doc • GigaTrust Desktop PDF Client for Adobe • Foxit PDF Reader • Nitro PDF Reader • Siemens JT2Go	`.doc, .docm, .docx, .dot, .dotm, .dotx, .potm, .potx, .pps, .ppsm, .ppsx, .ppt, .pptm, .txt, .xml, .jpg, .jpeg, .pdf, .png, .tif, .tiff, .bmp, .gif, .jpe, .jfif, .jt, .xps`
Protect confidential emails	• Microsoft Outlook Windows (Version 2003 and newer) • Office for macOS 2016 • Microsoft Exchange 2007 SP1	`.msg`
Protect content on the intranet	Microsoft SharePoint 2007 and newer	`.doc, .docm, .docx, .dot, .dotm, .dotx, .potm, .potx, .pps, .ppsm, .ppsx, .ppt, .pptm, .txt, .xml, .jpg, .jpeg, .pdf, .png, .tif, .tiff, .bmp, .gif, .jpe, .jfif, .jt, .xps`
Protect mobile data	• Microsoft Word • Microsoft Word app • Microsoft Excel app • Microsoft Outlook app • Microsoft PowerPoint app • WordPad • Office for macOS 2016 • Word Online • TITUS Docs • Foxit Reader	`.doc, .docm, .docx, .dot, .dotm, .dotx, .potm, .potx, .pps, .ppsm, .ppsx, .ppt, .pptm, .txt, .xml, .jpg, .jpeg, .pdf, .png, .tif, .tiff, .bmp, .gif, .jpe, .jfif, .jt, .msg, .xps`

AD RMS components

AD RMS has its own role services and related components that need to work together in order to maintain a healthy AD RMS environment. Let's look at these components in detail.

Active Directory Domain Services (AD DS)

AD RMS is one of the Active Directory role services. AD RMS can be installed only in an AD DS environment. As a part of the setup, a **service connection point** (**SCP**) will need to be published via AD. It will help users to discover the service URLs for the AD RMS environment.

The AD RMS cluster

The AD RMS cluster is a single RMS server, or a group of servers that share certificates and licensing requests from their clients. Even though it is named as a *cluster*, it is different from a typical Windows failover cluster. The failover cluster needs at least two nodes. However, with RMS, even though it has a single server, it is called a **cluster**. But there is one requirement for the AD RMS cluster if there are multiple servers involved. AD RMS supports two types of database similar to **Active Directory Federation Services** (**AD FS**). By default, it uses the **Windows Internal Database** (**WID**), and it also supports the Microsoft SQL Server database. If the AD RMS cluster is going to have multiple servers, it must use MS SQL.

There are two types of cluster in AD RMS:

- **The root cluster**: When we first deploy the AD RMS server in the infrastructure, it becomes the root cluster. By default, it responds to both licensing and certificate requests from clients. When required, additional RMS servers can be added to the cluster. Only one root cluster can exist in one AD DS forest.
- **The licensing cluster**: If an organization has multiple sites, it is always best to use local services, especially if the sites are connected through slow links. It improves service performance, as well as reliability. In such scenarios, organizations can deploy licensing-only clusters on remote sites to serve licensing requests.

It is recommended that the root cluster is used whenever possible, as it will automatically load balance both certificates and licensing requests. When a system has two clusters, load balancing is handled by each cluster separately, even though they are components of one system.

Web server

AD RMS requires **internet information services** (**IIS**) with the following role services:

- Web server (IIS)
- Web server:
  - Common HTTP features:
    - Static content
    - Directory browsing
    - HTTP errors
    - HTTP redirection
  - Performance:
    - Static content compression
  - Health and diagnostics:
    - HTTP logging
    - Logging tools
    - Request monitor
    - Tracing
  - Security:
    - Windows authentication
- Management tools:
  - IIS Management Console
  - IIS 6 Management Compatibility:
    - IIS 6 Metabase Compatibility
    - IIS 6 WMI Compatibility

SQL Server

AD RMS supports the WID and Microsoft SQL Server databases (SQL Server 2005 onward). If an AD RMS cluster is going to use multiple servers, the database must be running on MS SQL. AD RMS uses three databases:

- **Configuration database**: This includes configuration data that is related to the AD RMS cluster, Windows users' identities, and the AD RMS certificate key pair that is used to create a cluster.
- **Logging database**: This contains the logging data for the AD RMS setup. By default, it will install it in the same SQL Server instance that hosts the configuration database.
- **Directory service database**: This database maintains cached data about users, SID values, group membership, and related identifiers. This data is collected by the AD RMS licensing service through **Lightweight Directory Access Protocol** (**LDAP**) queries that run against the global catalog server. By default, it's refreshed every 12 hours.

AD RMS supports SQL high-availability solutions, including SQL failover clustering, database mirroring, and log shipping. However, it *does not* support SQL Server AlwaysOn.

Earlier in this chapter, I mentioned that mobile device extensions can be used to extend AD RMS in order to manage corporate data in mobile devices. If you are going to use this feature, AD RMS databases must run on top of MS SQL.

The AD RMS client

We need AD RMS client to communicate with the AD RMS cluster. This is included in all recent operating systems that were released after Windows XP. However, it still needs to be installed manually on macOS and mobile devices in order to use AD RMS.

Active Directory Certificate Service (AD CS)

AD RMS uses several certificates to protect communication between AD RMS components and clients. Most of these can be issued using a corporate trusted **Certificate Authority** (**CA**). For example, the AD RMS cluster can be built using the SSL certificate to protect communication between servers in a cluster. If the AD RMS setup is required to externally publish service URLs, then it will require a certificate from the public CA.

AD RMS itself uses various **eXtensible rights Markup Language (XrML)**-based certificates to protect communication between components and data. These certificates are different from AD CS certificates.

How does AD RMS work?

By now, we know the components of the AD RMS and their responsibilities. In this section, we are going to learn in detail how all these components work together in order to protect corporate data.

Before we start the data protection process, we need a healthy AD RMS cluster, AD RMS clients (author and recipient), and a reliable connection between these components. Once these prerequisites are fulfilled, the data protection process will go through three main stages: protecting the author's content, publishing the protected content, and accessing the protected content on the part of the recipient.

Let's assume Peter is trying to protect a document using AD RMS. He is going to send it to Adam, but he does not want him to edit or print it. This is the first time he is going to use AD RMS. In an AD RMS environment, the user, Peter, will be referred to as an **information author**. In his first authentication into the AD RMS cluster, a **rights account certificate** (**RAC**) is created, which will be the user's identity in AD RMS. This is a one-time process. This certificate contains Peter's public key and private key, which is encrypted by his computer's public key. When Peter registers with the AD RMS cluster, another certificate called the **client licensor certificate** (**CLC**) is also created. The CLC includes the CLC's public key and private key, which are protected by Peter's public key. It also includes the AD RMS cluster's public key, which is signed by the AD RMS private key.

Peter decides what data needs to be protected first. Then, a symmetric key (random) is generated, which encrypts the data that needs to be protected. It uses AES-256 standards to encrypt the data. When the first AD RMS server is added to the cluster, it creates another certificate called the **server licensor certificate** (**SLC**). This represents the identity element of the AD RMS server. This is shared with clients so that they can use it to exchange confidential data in a secure way. The SLC includes the public key of the AD RMS server. In the next step, the system will encrypt the symmetric key that is used for the encryption of the data using the AD RMS server public key. Therefore, only the AD RMS cluster can open it.

After that, the RMS client creates the **publishing license** (**PL**). The PL is used to indicate to the allowed recipients what rights they have, and what conditions will apply toward the protected data. The PL includes an encrypted symmetric key that can be used to decrypt the protected data. All this data is then encrypted with the SLC's public key. Apart from that, the AD RMS client will also sign the encrypted data with the private key of the SLC. In the end, this protected data will be attached to the PL. It also includes the copy of the symmetric key that is encrypted with the SLC public key. This confirms Peter's authority over the protected document, so he can decrypt the document without using another license. Once all these encryptions and signings are done, the document is ready to be sent over to Adam.

Once Adam receives the document, his AD RMS-aware application tries to open it, and finds out that it is a protected document. Similar to Peter, Adam already has his RAC and CLC from the AD RMS cluster. In order to open the protected document at once, does it need to be decrypted or signed with any of Adam's certificates? No, it does not. But his AD RMS client knows who needs to be contacted in order to sort it out for him. To open the protected document, Adam should have a **use license** (**UL**). This is issued by the RMS cluster. So, the AD RMS client request for the license also includes the encrypted PL, the encrypted symmetric key, Peter's CLC, and the public key of Adam's RAC. The protected document will not be sent over with this request to the RMS cluster.

To decrypt the protected document, Adam needs the symmetric key that was used by Peter to encrypt the document. As a first step, the server needs to know whether Adam is permitted to access the document; if he is permitted, what sort of conditions and rights will apply? This information is in the PL. It is encrypted using the public key of the SLC. The AD RMS server is the private key owner for it, and they can easily extract it. If Adam is not allowed in the PL, he will be declined access to it. If it's allowed, it creates a list that states Adam's rights over the document.

The most important part of the decryption process is to retrieve the symmetric key. This is also encrypted by the SLC's public key. Once it is extracted, it will be re-encrypted using Adam's RAC public key. This was a part of the UL request, and it ensures that only Adam's system can see the key. Since the server has all the required information, it generates the UL, including the permission list and the encrypted symmetric key. Then, it sends it over to Adam's RMS client. Once it reaches Adam's system, it can decrypt the symmetric key using the RAC's private key. Then, the RMS-aware application will decrypt the document and attach the rights information retrieved from the UL. In the end, voila! Adam can see the content of the document.

In the preceding example, we saw different certificates, licenses, data encryption, and decryption. I thought it was still better to explain it on a higher level, in order to recap the things you learned:

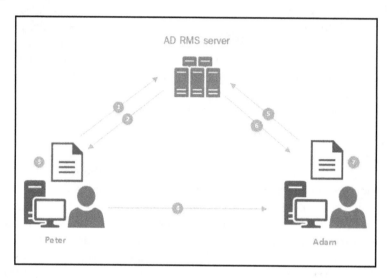

Peter wants to send the protected document to **Adam**. **Adam** should have read-only permissions for the document; he should not be able to modify or print it:

- This is the first time that **Peter** is going to use the **AD RMS server**. As soon as he tries to protect the document, the RMS client initiates a connection to the **AD RMS server** (cluster).
- The **AD RMS server** replies with the RAC and the CLC. This is a one-time process.
- In **Peter**'s system, a random symmetric key is generated, which is used to encrypt the document. Then, this symmetric key is encrypted using SLC's public key. After that, it is attached to a PL, which includes **Adam**'s rights for the protected document. After that, the PL is attached to the encrypted document.
- **Peter** sends the protected document (along with this additional info) to **Adam**.
- **Adam**'s RMS-aware application tries to open it, and finds that it needs the UL from the **AD RMS server**. Then, the RMS client requests it from the RMS server.

- The RMS server decrypts the symmetric key and the PL. After that, the server checks whether the requester matches the PL. In our scenario, it matches, so it goes ahead and creates the UL. This includes the symmetric key (it re-encrypts using **Adam**'s RAC public key), and a list that contains the rights describes in the PL. Then, it delivers it to **Adam**'s system.
- Once **Adam**'s system receives the UL, it retrieves the symmetric key and decrypts the document. Then, **Adam** opens the document and uses it according to the rights described in the PL.

How do we deploy AD RMS?

AD RMS deployment topologies are bit different from other AD role service deployments. Other AD role service deployment topologies are mostly focused on high availability or scalability. But AD RMS deployments are more about addressing different types of business requirements. Let's look in to these topologies in detail.

Single forest–single cluster

This is the most commonly used deployment topology. In this setup, AD RMS operations will be limited to an AD forest. The deployment will only have one AD RMS cluster to process certificates and licensing requirements. The cluster can contain any number of servers, and load balancing is handled at the cluster level. If it has multiple servers, the AD RMS cluster should use the MS SQL Server database, instead of the WID. This deployment model will not consider extending data protection to non-corporate networks.

The following table lists the advantages and disadvantages of a single forest-single cluster:

Advantages	Disadvantages
Easy to implement. Fewer resources (servers and licenses) are used.	Can protect data only within a limited environment.
System maintenance and management is easy due to a smaller operation boundary.	N/A.
Support for extending into any other deployment topologies.	N/A.

Single forest–multiple clusters

This is the extended configuration of a single forest-single cluster topology. There are two types of AD RMS clusters. The AD RMS root cluster is the default cluster, and it answers both certificates and licensing requests. The licensing-only cluster can also be deployed in the same forest, and it will respond to licensing requests only. This suits infrastructures that have sites in different geographical locations. Then, it will rule out the requirement of contacting RMS clusters via slow links. Instead, it will use a license-only cluster on each site for licenses. There is only one root cluster for the forest. But it can have multiple licensing-only clusters.

Based on the role installed in the AD RMS server, it will decide which cluster it will be a part of. However, unless there is a special requirement, it is recommended that you use the root cluster only. Load balancing between member servers is handled at the cluster level, and its configurations are independent. They cannot be shared between different clusters. In this topology, it is important to also have MS SQL high availability.

The following table lists the advantages and disadvantages of this topology:

Advantages	Disadvantages
Remote sites do not need to depend on the site links and bandwidth. The local RMS license-only cluster will process the license requests.	Complexity – deployment requires advanced planning and conflagration.
Complies with government rules to use localized encryption tools and technologies.	High cost – need to use additional resources and licenses for deployment. Also increases the maintenance cost.
N/A.	Distributed management – when placing clusters on remote sites, it may also need to grant privileges to the site's IT team in order to manage and maintain the system. This can have an impact on security and system integrity.

AD RMS in multiple forests

If the organization has multiple AD forests, and if AD RMS needs to be used between them in order to protect data, this deployment method can be used. Each forest can only have one RMS root cluster. Therefore, in multiple forest environments, each domain should have its own AD RMS cluster. The AD RMS cluster uses AD DS to query an object's identity. When there are multiple forests, it needs to have contact objects of users and groups for the remote forest. The following elements are required for AD RMS deployment in multiple forests:

- AD RMS root cluster in each forest.
- Contact objects for remote users and groups (from the different forests) need to be set up.
- Schema extensions need to be in place to trace back to the mother forest of the contact objects.
- Attribute values of contact objects are needed to sync with the mother forest, so that when required, it can be used to trace back to the original object.

Active Directory trust between forests is not a must. It can have two-way trust, one-way trust, or no trust at all. If there is trust, it will simplify the process of managing the permissions and validations of cross-forest objects.

The following table lists the advantages and disadvantages of this:

Advantages	Disadvantages
Extended data protection boundaries	Complexity – deployment requires advanced planning and conflagration.
Standardized data protection with partners in order to protect confidential data	Dependencies – the success of the solution depends on the system configuration and the availability of the AD RMS components of the partner's forest. It can also have dependencies where the primary forest does not have control.

In this topology, AD RMS trust policies control how licensing requests and data protection between different AD RMS clusters are handled. There are two types of trust policies:

- **Trusted AD RMS domains**: This allows the AD RMS root cluster to process requests for the CLC or the UL from users who have an RAC issued by a different AD RMS root cluster. We can add a trusted AD RMS domain by importing the SLC of the AD RMS cluster to be trusted.

- **Trusted publishing domains**: This allows one AD RMS cluster to issue ULs for PLs that were issued by a different AD RMS cluster. We can add a trusted publishing domain by importing the SLC and the private key of the server to be trusted.

AD RMS with AD FS

AD RMS in a multiple-forest topology needs an AD RMS root cluster in each forest. This topology doesn't require trust between forests but if there is trust, it makes it easier to manage permissions. But, not every partner or business wants trust between forests. They may want to use AD RMS, but they may not want to maintain the AD RMS cluster, or create trust between forests. AD FS allows an organization to use the already-deployed AD RMS cluster in a remote forest. AD FS allows user accounts to use their own credentials, established by a federated trust relationship.

Before we set it up, we need to fulfill certain prerequisites, which are required between federated infrastructures. Refer to `https://technet.microsoft.com/en-us/library/dn758110(v=ws.11).aspx` for more details on the configuration.

The following table lists the advantages and disadvantages of this:

Advantages	Disadvantages
No need to maintain multiple AD RMS clusters between organizations. It can use an already-existing federation trust to use AD RMS in other forests.	There are security concerns, as it's possible to spoof someone's user account and access protected data through a federation proxy.
Extended data protection boundaries, and implementation is less complex.	If an internal CA is used to make SSL-based trusts (AD RMS and AD FMS), the federated domain should be configured to trust the root CA (using GPO to publish the root cert). Otherwise, they may need to invest in using public certificates.
Fewer system dependencies between infrastructures.	N/A.

 If it is a hybrid environment, the use of Azure RMS and Azure Information Protection on corporate data is recommended. These can be used to protect data in both environments. Since it is a hosted service, we do not need to worry about resources, maintenance, and dependencies.

AD RMS configuration

In this section, we are going to look in to the configuration of AD RMS 2016, and see how it really works. The demonstration environment that it uses was built using Windows Server 2016 with the latest updates. The AD DS forest and domain function levels are also set to Windows Server 2016.

Setting up an AD RMS root cluster

AD RMS can only be installed on a domain member server. I have a demonstration server, which is already a member server of the domain. The first AD RMS server that is added to the forest creates the AD RMS cluster.

Installing the AD RMS role

The following are the steps that are needed in order to install the AD RMS role:

1. Log in to the server as Enterprise Admin.
2. Install the AD RMS role and related management tools using the following command:

```
Install-WindowsFeature ADRMS -IncludeManagementTools
```

The following screenshot shows the output for the preceding command:

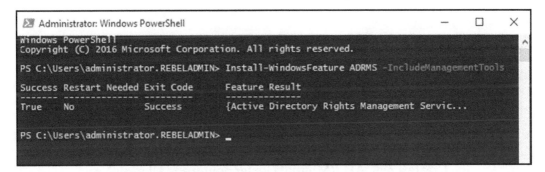

```
Windows PowerShell
Copyright (C) 2016 Microsoft Corporation. All rights reserved.

PS C:\Users\administrator.REBELADMIN> Install-WindowsFeature ADRMS -IncludeManagementTools

Success Restart Needed Exit Code     Feature Result
------- -------------- ---------     --------------
True    No             Success       {Active Directory Rights Management Servic...

PS C:\Users\administrator.REBELADMIN> _
```

Configuring the AD RMS role

The following are the steps that are needed in order to configure the AD RMS role:

1. Launch **Server Manager** and go to the notifications icon by navigating to **Configuration required for Active Directory Rights Management Services** | **Perform additional configuration**; this will open the AD RMS configuration wizard. Click on **Next** to start the configuration:

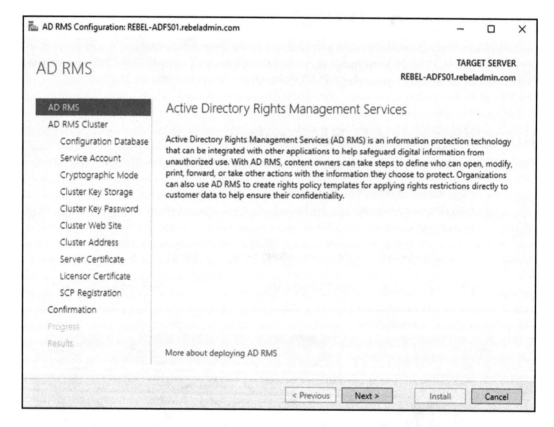

2. On the next screen, there is the option to create a new AD RMS root cluster, or to join it to the existing AD RMS cluster. Since it is a new cluster, select the **Create a new AD RMS root cluster** option and click on **Next**.

3. The next screen defines the AD RMS database configuration. If it's going to use the MS SQL Server, select **Specify a database server and a database instance**, or else select **Use Windows Internal Database on this server**. Note that if the **Windows Internal Database (WID)** is used, it cannot have any more AD RMS servers, and it cannot have the AD RMS mobile extension, either. Since it's a demonstration, I am going to use the WID. Once the selection has been made, click on **Next** to move to the next step:

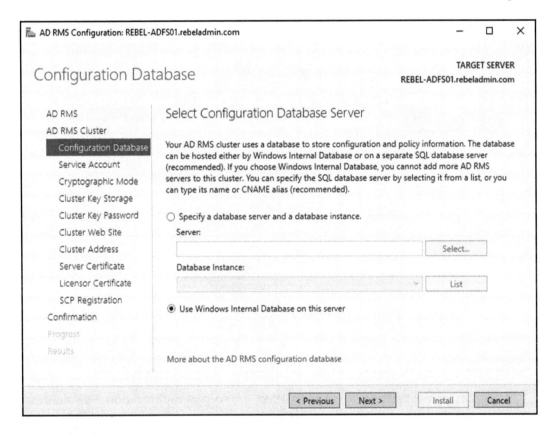

4. In the next window, we need to define the service account. It is used to communicate with other services and computers. This doesn't need to have Domain or Enterprise Admin rights. Click on **Specify...** and provide the username and password for the account. Then, click on **Next** to proceed to the next window:

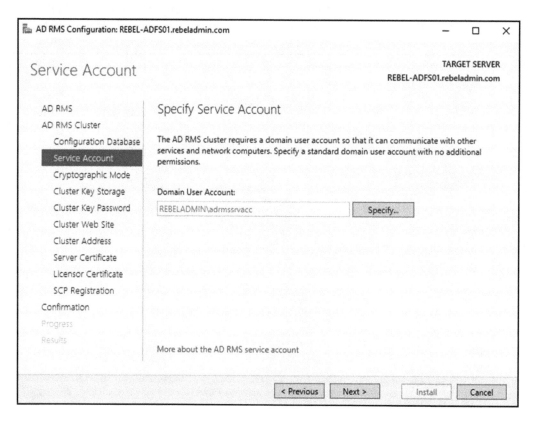

5. On the next screen, we need to select the cryptographic mode. This defines the strength of the hashes. This supports two modes, which are SHA-1 and SHA-256. It is highly recommended that you use **Cryptographic Mode 2 (RSA 2048-bit keys/SHA-256 hashes)**, which uses SHA-256 for stronger hashing. However, this needs to be matched with the other RMS cluster that it deals with. In our setup, I am going to use the default SHA-256. Once the selection is made, click on **Next** to proceed:

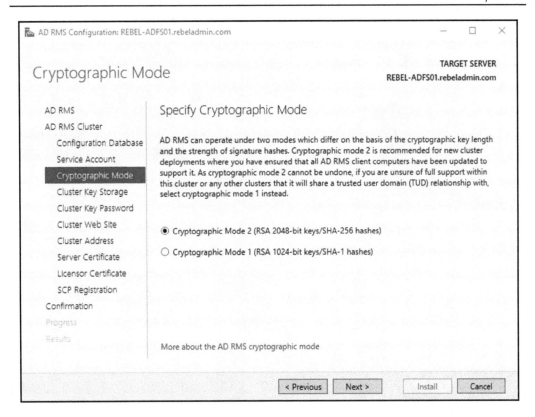

6. AD RMS uses the cluster key to sign the certificate and licenses that it issues. This is also required when AD RMS is restored, or when the new AD RMS server is added to the same cluster. It can be saved in two places. The default method is to use AD RMS in a centrally managed key store. Therefore, it doesn't need any additional configurations. It also supports the use of the **cryptographic service provider (CSP)** as storage, but this requires the manual distribution of a key when adding another AD RMS server to the cluster. In this demonstration, we will use the **Use AD RMS centrally managed key storage** option. Once the selection is made, click on **Next** to proceed.

7. AD RMS also uses a password to encrypt the cluster key described earlier. This needs to be provided when adding another AD RMS server to the cluster, or when restoring AD RMS from the backup. This key cannot be reset. Therefore, it is recommended that you keep it recorded in a secure place. Once you define the AD RMS cluster key password, click on **Next** to proceed.

8. In the next step, we need to define the IIS virtual directory for the AD RMS website. Unless there is a specific requirement, always use the default, and click on **Next**:

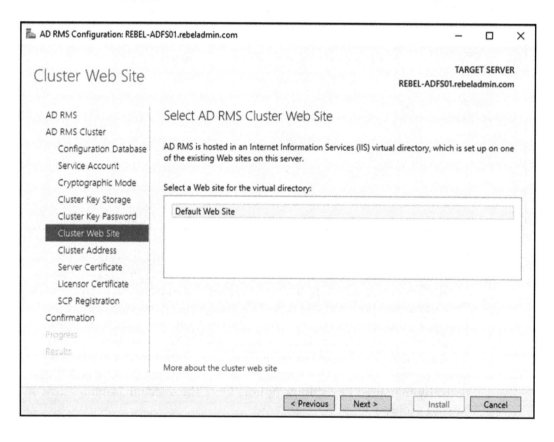

9. In the next step, we need to define an AD RMS cluster URL. This will be used by AD RMS clients to communicate with the AD RMS cluster. It is highly recommended that you use SSL for this, even if it allows it to be used with the HTTP-only method. The related DNS records and firewall rules need to be adjusted in order to provide a connection between AD RMS clients and this URL (internally or externally). Once the configuration values are provided, click on **Next** to proceed. One thing you need to note is that once this URL is specified, it cannot be changed. In this demonstration, I used `https://rms.rebeladmin.com` as the RMS URL:

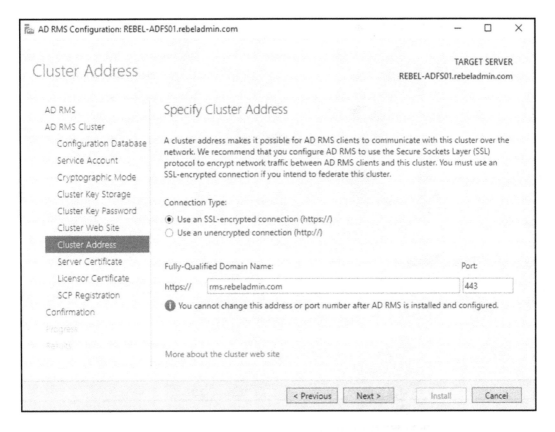

10. In the next step, we need to define a server authentication certificate. This certificate will be used to encrypt the network traffic between RMS clients and the AD RMS cluster. For testing, it can use a self-signed certificate, but this is not recommended for production. If it uses an internal CA, client computers should be aware of the root certificate. In the wizard, it automatically takes the list of the SSL certificates that are installed on the computer, and we can select the certificate from there. It is also possible to configure this setting at a later time. Once the settings are defined, click on **Next** to proceed:

11. On the next window, it asks you to provide a **Name** for the SLC. This certificate is used to define the identity of the AD RMS cluster, and it is used in the data protection process between clients to encrypt/decrypt symmetric keys. Once you've defined a meaningful name, click on **Next** to proceed.

12. The last step of the configuration is to register a AD RMS SCP with AD DS. If needed, this can also be configured later. You need Enterprise Admin privileges to register it with AD DS. In this demonstration, I have already logged in as the Enterprise Admin, so I am using the **Register the SCP now** option. Once this option is selected, click on **Next**:

13. After the confirmation, the installation will begin; wait for the result. If all is successful, log out and log back in to the AD RMS server.

14. Once logged back in, select **Server Manager** and navigate to **Tools | Active Directory Rights Management Service** in order to access the AD RMS cluster:

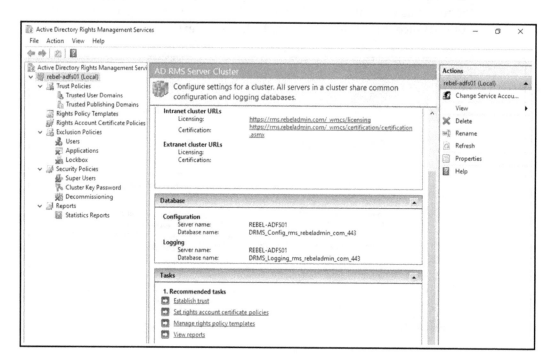

Testing – protecting data using the AD RMS cluster

The next step of the demonstration is to test the functionality of the AD RMS cluster by protecting the data. For that, I use two user accounts, as shown in the following table:

User	Email address	Role
Peter	peter@rebeladmin.com	Author
Adam	adam@rebeladmin.com	Recipient

The email address field is a must, and if the user doesn't have an email address defined, they will not be allowed to protect the document.

The end user computers must add the `https://rms.rebeladmin.com` RMS service URL to Internet Explorer's local intranet trusted site lists. This can also be done via GPO. If it's not added, when you go to protect the document, you will get the following error:

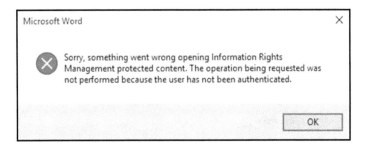

In this demonstration, Peter is going to create a protected document using Word 2013. He wants Adam to have read-only access to the file. At the same time, he wants to make sure no one else has access to the content of the document.

Testing – applying permissions to the document

The following steps need to be performed in order to protect the document:

1. Log in to the Windows 10 (domain member) computer as the user, Peter.
2. Open Word 2013 and type some text.

3. Then, go to **File** | **Protect Document** | **Restrict Access** | **Connect to Digital Rights Management Servers and get templates**:

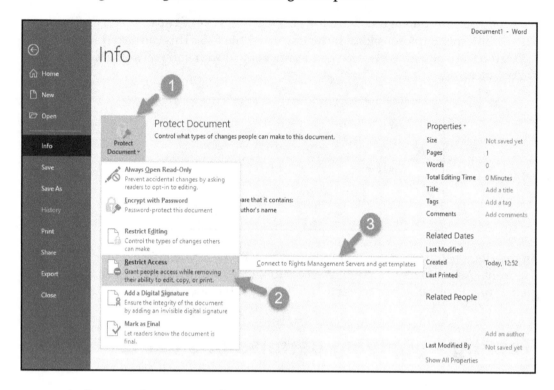

4. Once you have successfully retrieved the templates, go back to the same option and select **Restricted Access**:

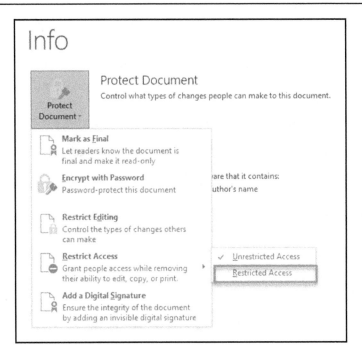

5. Then, it will open a new window. Once there, for the read permissions, type `adam@rebeladmin.com` to provide a read-only permission to the user, Adam. Then, click on **OK**:

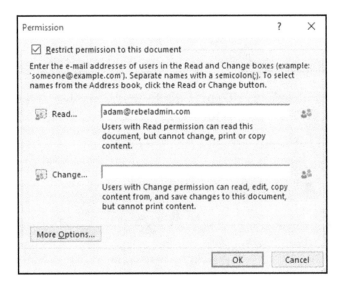

6. After that, save the document. In the demonstration, I used a network share that the user, Adam, also has access to.

7. Now log in to another Windows 10 computer as the user, Adam.

8. Then, browse to the path where the document was saved, and open it using Word 2013.

9. In the opening process, it asks for authentication for the RMS in order to retrieve the licenses. After that, it opens the document. At the top of the document, it says the document has limited access. When you click on **View Permission...**, it lists down the allowed permissions, and matches what we set on the author side:

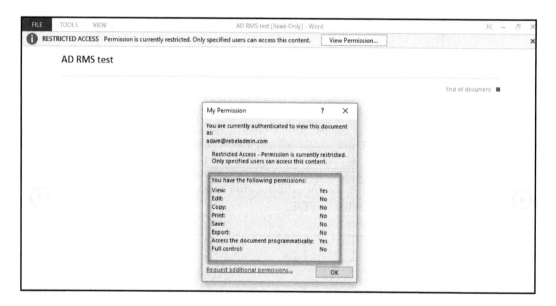

10. Further into testing, I log in to the system as another user (Liam), and when I access the file, I get the following prompt:

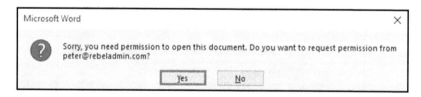

This ends the configuration and the testing of the AD RMS cluster. In this demonstration, I explained how we can set up the AD RMS cluster using minimum resources and configuration. I only used the default configuration of the AD RMS cluster, and no custom policies were applied. Understanding the core functions allows you to customize your setup to meet your organization's requirements.

Summary

Data protection is crucial in modern infrastructures, as more and more analogue data is being transformed into digital data. There are different laws, products, technologies, and methodologies to improve data protection in infrastructures. AD RMS is Microsoft's solution, which can be used to manage the operational behavior of confidential data in an infrastructure.

In this chapter, we learned about AD RMS and its related characteristics. Then, we moved on to understanding how AD RMS works, and how it protects data. After that, we looked at different AD RMS deployment topologies. Last but not least, we worked on AD RMS installation, configuration, and testing.

This ends the third part of this book. The fourth part of the book is going to start with a chapter that is focused on Active Directory security best practices.

4

Section 4: Best Practices and Troubleshooting

This section of the book will cover various areas in the Active Directory environment. Modern security threats are more focused on identities as they open up lots of potential opportunities for attackers. Therefore, the majority of the content in this section will focus on tools and methods that we can use to secure the Active Directory environment. Not only that, but we are also going to learn about services that we can use to protect identities and data in a hybrid AD environment.

In the first section of the book, we learned about the benefits of using a hybrid AD environment. In this section, we are going to take another step forward and learn about how to plan and implement a hybrid AD environment successfully.

The last chapters of this section will focus on steps that we need to implement in order to maintain a healthy Active Directory environment. This includes Active Directory health monitoring, auditing, and troubleshooting (to recover from common issues).

This section contains the following chapters:

- Chapter 15, *Active Directory Security Best Practices*
- Chapter 16, *Advanced Active Directory Management with PowerShell*
- Chapter 17, *Azure Active Directory Hybrid Setup*
- Chapter 18, *Active Directory Audit and Monitoring*
- Chapter 19, *Active Directory Troubleshooting*

15
Active Directory Security Best Practices

AD Security is a very broad topic. 2000-2010, administrators just had to deal with *script kiddies* chasing fame, but today, things are way more complicated. Attacks are performed on far more valuable targets, such as identities, state secrets, and intellectual property. It is no longer about taking full control of a computer infrastructure either; even having access to certain pieces of data is sufficient to do significant damage. In the final days of the last US presidential election, certain emails had been released to the public, and that was enough to change a lot of votes. Stories about WikiLeaks are also a great example of this. Also, in computer infrastructure, we no longer can identify *good* or *bad* people. Most of the recent security breaches have involved some sort of support from *inside*. This is why people are starting to talk about *zero-trust* security. We can no longer say that anything *inside* the perimeter is trustworthy and anything *outside* is a risk. In an infrastructure, **Active Directory** (**AD**) is mainly responsible for managing identities. The protection of identities is crucial when it comes to security. However, there are so many other things that we need to secure, such as network, storage, and data, in order to protect identities. If you need to maintain a car properly, then you can't just only pay attention to the engine. It is the heart of the car, but if you really need it to be a good car, you need to equally take care of, as well as invest in, every other component of the car.

The complexity of modern authentication and authorization requirements also creates further opportunities for intruders. The rise of cloud services forces organizations to extend their identity infrastructure boundaries up to the cloud. If the cloud services are from Azure, we must use Azure AD to provide authentication and authorization services. Azure AD is a managed service, so we can't apply the same methods and techniques that we use in the on-premises AD environment to protect identities in a hybrid or cloud-only environment.

In this chapter, we are going to discuss many different AD features that can be used to improve the security of the AD infrastructure. Also, we are going to look into services and features that we can use to protect identities in Azure AD (a hybrid or cloud-only environment). This chapter will cover the following topics:

- How does AD authentication work?
- Delegating permissions
- The AD Protected Users security group
- Restricted RDP mode
- Authentication policies and authentication policy silos
- **Just-in-time** (**JIT**) administration and **Just Enough Administration** (**JEA**)
- Azure AD **Privileged Identity Management** (**PIM**)
- **Azure Information Protection** (**AIP**)

AD authentication

AD uses Kerberos version 5 as the authentication protocol in order to provide authentication between the server and the client. Kerberos v5 became the default authentication protocol for Windows Server from Windows Server 2003 onward. It is not a proprietary protocol; it is an open standard. Therefore, AD can work with any application or service that supports the same standard. Before we look into improvements in **Active Directory Domain Service** (**AD DS**) security, it is important for us to learn about how AD authentication works.

The Kerberos protocol

The Kerberos protocol is built to protect authentication between the server and the client in an open network. The main concept behind authentication is that two parties first agree on a password (secret) and then use it to both identify and verify their genuineness:

In the preceding example, **Dave** and **server A** have regular communications. They often exchange confidential data. In order to protect this communication, they agree to use a common secret code (**1234**) to verify their identities before exchanging data. When **Dave** makes initial communication, he passes his secret to **server A** and says **Hey! I'm Dave**. Then, **server A** checks the secret to see whether it's true. If it's correct, it identifies him as **Dave** and allows further communication:

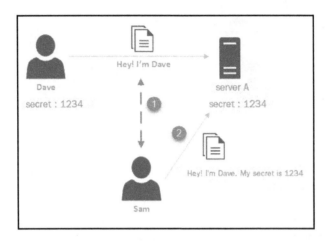

Communication between **Dave** and **server A** happens in an open network, which means that other systems and users exist in it as well. **Sam** is another user in the same infrastructure. He is aware of the communication that happens between **Dave** and **server A**. The data that is exchanged between the two parties has a high value and Sam is trying to get his hands on it. He started sniffing in the network to find out the secret they use. Once he has found it, he can communicate with **server A** and pretend to be **Dave** by providing the secret code, **1234**. However, **server A** doesn't see any difference between requests from **Dave** and **Sam**, as both provide the correct secret.

Kerberos solves this security challenge using the shared symmetric cryptographic key instead of secrets. It also uses this key for encryption and decryption. The name *Kerberos* comes from a powerful three-headed dog in Greek mythology. Just like the mythical three-headed dog, the Kerberos protocol has three main components:

- A client
- A server
- A trusted authority to issue secret keys

This trusted authority is called the **Key Distribution Center** (**KDC**). Before we look into Kerberos in detail, let's first look at how a typical key exchange works:

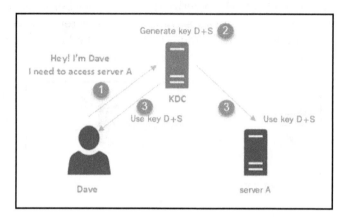

If we revisit our scenario, we now have a **KDC** in place. Instead of communicating with **Server A** directly, **Dave** goes to the **KDC** and says he needs to access **server A**. Dave needs a symmetric key to start communication with **server A**. This key should only be used by **Dave** and **server A**. The **KDC** accepts the request, generates a key (**Key D+S**), and then issues it to **Dave** and **server A**. By the looks of it, this seems quite straightforward, but from the server A point of view, there are a few challenges.

In order to accept a connection from **Dave**, **server A** should have a record regarding **Key D+S**. The easiest way to do this is to store the key in **server A**. We are considering storing only one connection in **server A**, but if there were a hundred connections, **server A** would need to store all the keys involved. This doesn't seem to be practical. As well as the resources, if the server were to be compromised, attackers would have access to all the keys. So, is there a better way of doing this?

In an AD environment, the **KDC** is installed as part of the domain controller. The **KDC** is responsible for two main services: one is the **Authentication Service** (**AS**) and the other is the **Ticket-Granting Service** (**TGS**).

In the preceding example, when **Dave** logs in to the system, it needs to be proved to the KDC that he is the exact person who he claims to be. When he logs in, it sends the username to the **KDC** along with a *long-time key*. The long-time key is generated based on **Dave**'s password. The Kerberos client on **Dave**'s PC accepts his password and generates the cryptographic key. The KDC also maintains a copy of this key in its database. Once the **KDC** receives the request, it checks its username and the long-term key with its records. If it's all good, the **KDC** responds to **Dave** with a *session key*. This is called a **ticket-granting ticket** (**TGT**).

The TGT contains two things:

- A copy of a session key that the **KDC** uses to communicate with **Dave**. This is encrypted with the **KDC**'s long-term key.
- A copy of a session key that **Dave** can use to communicate with the KDC. This is encrypted with **Dave**'s long-term key, so only **Dave** can decrypt it.

Once **Dave** receives this key, he can use his long-term key to decrypt the session key. After that, all future communication with the **KDC** will be based on this session key. This session key is temporary and has a **time-to-live** (TTL) value.

This session key is saved in **Dave**'s computer's volatile memory. Now, it's time to request access to **server A**. **Dave** has to contact the **KDC** again, but this time, he uses the session key provided by the **KDC**. This request includes the TGT and the timestamp encrypted by the session key and the service ID (the service that is running on **server A**). Once the **KDC** receives it, it uses its long-term key to decrypt the TGT and retrieve the session key. Then, using the session key, it decrypts the timestamp. If the time difference is less than 5 minutes, then it proves that it came from Dave.

Once the **KDC** confirms it as a legitimate request, it creates another ticket, and this is called a **service ticket**. It contains two keys: one for **Dave** and one for **server A**. Both keys include the requester's name (**Dave**), the recipient, the timestamp, the TTL value, and a new session key (that will be shared between **Dave** and **server A**). One of these keys is encrypted using **Dave**'s long-term key. The other key is encrypted using **server A**'s long-term key. In the end, both are encrypted together using the session key between the **KDC** and **Dave**. Finally, the ticket is ready and sent over to **Dave**. **Dave** decrypts the ticket using the session key. He also finds *his* key and decrypts it using his long-term key.

This process reveals the new session key that needs to be shared between **Dave** and **server A**. Then, **Dave** creates a new request, which includes **server A**'s key that was retrieved from the service ticket, and the timestamp that was encrypted using the new session key created by the **KDC**. Once **Dave** sends the key over to **server A**, it decrypts its key using its long-term key and retrieves the session key. Using the session key, it can decrypt the timestamp to verify the authenticity of the request. As we can see, in this process, it is not **server A**'s responsibility to keep track of the key used by the client and it's not the client's responsibility to keep the relevant keys.

Authentication in an AD environment

Let's go ahead and revisit our previous example, in order to see how authentication improves in an AD environment:

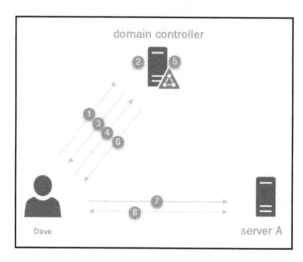

Following list summaries steps involved in the authentication process.

1. **Dave** sends the username and his long-term key to the KDC (**Domain Controller**).
2. The KDC checks the username and long-term key with its database and verifies the identity. Then, it generates a TGT. It includes a copy of a session key, which the KDC uses to communicate with **Dave**. This is encrypted using the KDC's long-term key. It also includes a copy of a session key that **Dave** can use to communicate with the KDC.
3. The KDC responds to Dave with its TGT.
4. **Dave** decrypts his key using his long-term key and the retrieved session key. His system creates a new request, which includes the TGT and the timestamp encrypted by the session key and service ID. Once the request is generated, it is sent to the KDC.
5. The KDC uses its long-term key to decrypt the TGT and retrieve the session key. Then, the session key can be used to decrypt the timestamp. Next, it creates a service ticket. This ticket includes two keys: one for **server A** and one for **Dave**. **Dave**'s key is encrypted using his long-term key and **server A**'s key is encrypted using its long-term key. In the end, both are encrypted using the session key that is used by the KDC and **Dave**.
6. The KDC sends the service ticket to **Dave**.

7. **Dave** decrypts the ticket using the session key and retrieves his key. Then, he decrypts it in order to get a new key, which can be used to establish a connection with **server A**. In the end, the system creates another request, including **server A**'s key (which was created earlier) and the timestamp that is encrypted by the session key that **Dave** decrypted earlier in this step. Once everything is ready, the system sends the request to **server A**.

8. **Server A** goes ahead and decrypts Dave's key using its long-term key and the retrieved session key. Then, using it, **server A** can decrypt the timestamp to verify the request's authenticity. Once everything is green, a connection between **Dave** and **server A** is allowed.

There are a few other things that need to be fulfilled in order to complete this process:

- **Connectivity**: The server, client, and KDC need to have a reliable connection between them in order to process requests and responses.
- **DNS**: Clients use DNS to locate the KDC and servers. Therefore, a functioning DNS with the correct records is required.
- **Time synchronization**: As we can see, the process uses the timestamp to verify the authenticity of the requests. It allows up to 5 minutes' time difference. Therefore, it's a must to have accurate time synchronization with the domain controllers.
- **Service Principal Names (SPNs)**: Clients use SPNs to locate services in the AD environment. If there is no SPN for the services, the clients and the KDC cannot locate them when required. When setting up services, make sure that you set up SPNs as well.

In this section, we have learned about what the Kerberos protocol is and how it works with AD authentication. Kerberos has built-in security features to protect user identities during the authentication process, but this is not enough to protect identities from emerging threats. Therefore, in the next section, we are going to look into the different methods, tools, and features that we can use to improve the security of our AD environment further.

Delegating permissions

In the previous section, we learned about how AD authentication works. As we saw, the Kerberos protocol itself was built to prevent identity compromise. This is all good on paper, but in reality, attackers use many methods and tools to attack AD environments. Therefore, it is important to know the features, techniques, and tools that we can use to protect AD environments further.

In an AD environment, there are different types of management tasks. Managing domain controllers, adding/managing/removing users, adding/managing/removing groups, resetting passwords, and adding devices to computers are just some examples. In a structured IT department, these management tasks can be bound to different job roles.

As an example, let's assume that Rebeladmin Corp.'s IT department has first-line (first support contact), second-line (intermediate), and third-line (senior) IT teams. When considering the AD management tasks, first-line engineers are usually involved with tasks such as user password resets, setting up new user accounts and groups, and adding devices to domains.

Second-line engineers are involved with additional tasks such as Group Policy setup and Group Policy troubleshooting. Third-line engineers usually work on tasks such as advanced troubleshooting, domain controller installations, schema changes, and physical and logical design changes.

In this way, we can group AD management tasks according to the responsibilities of different engineers' roles. This allows different job roles to take *ownership* of different AD management tasks. At the same time, if a certain job role is assigned the ownership of a task, there should be a mechanism to prevent other teams from interfering with that particular task. As an example, if third-line engineers are responsible for AD schema changes, then there should be a way to prevent first-line and second-line engineers from also doing them. If we need to prevent/allow users or groups from entering/to access a folder in a file server (respectively), we can do so using *permissions*. In the same way, AD also allows you to manage users' and groups' authority over objects or management tasks based on permissions. Managing permissions for the IT team is a difficult task, as it is not just about permission. It has a social aspect too. In general, we accept that administrators are trustworthy people; while most of them are, you can't always know. Therefore, it is best to take precautions and manage permissions sensibly. There are a few ways to manage permissions for AD management tasks:

- By using predefined AD administrator roles
- By using object **Access Control Lists** (**ACLs**)
- By using the delegate control method in AD

Predefined AD administrator roles

AD has predefined administrator roles. Each of these roles has predefined permissions attached to them. If a user needs these role permissions, their account needs to be added to the relevant security group. These security groups are predefined groups:

- **Enterprise Admins**: This is the highest AD role permission that can be applied in the AD forest. The accounts that are part of this group can modify the logical and physical topology of the AD infrastructure. This also allows you to perform schema changes. This role is capable of managing other role memberships (Enterprise Admins, Schema Admins, and Domain Admins).
- **Schema Admins**: Members of this group can modify the AD schema. This is only included in the forest root domain as the schema is handled on the forest level.
- **Domain Admins**: This is the highest AD role permission that can be applied in AD domain. When adding the first domain controller to the forest, the default administrator account will be part of the Domain Admin and Enterprise Admin groups. Domain Admins have permission to add/remove other user accounts from the Domain Admin security group.

 These roles are considered to be privileged roles in the AD environment. Therefore, rather than keeping permanent memberships, it's recommended that you use **Privileged Access Management** (**PAM**) to provide time-based group memberships. This was described in detail in Chapter 2, *Active Directory Domain Services 2016*.

Using object ACLs

User or group access permissions to a shared folder are managed by the ACL. Similarly, we can define permissions to AD objects. This can be applied to individual objects or to the AD site/domain/OU, and then the same permissions can be forced onto lower-level objects.

As an example, I have a security group called `First Line Engineers`, and Liam is a member of this group. Liam is an engineer in the Europe office. In the AD environment, Liam should be allowed to add user objects under any sub-OU that is under the `Europe` OU. However, he should not be allowed to delete any objects that are under it. Let's see how we can do this using ACLs:

1. Log in to the domain controller as Domain Admin/Enterprise Admin.
2. Review the group membership using the following command:

   ```
   Get-ADGroupMember "First Line Engineers"
   ```

3. Go to **Active Directory Users and Computers** (**ADUC**), right-click on the `Europe` OU, and click on **Properties**. Then, go to **Security**.
4. In the **Security** tab, click on **Add**.
5. In the new window, type `First Line Engineers` and click on **OK**. Afterward, in the **Security** tab, select **First Line Engineers** and click on **Advanced**:

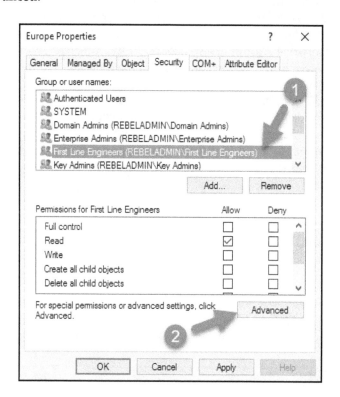

6. In the next window that appears, select **First Line Engineers** from the list and click on **Edit**.

7. From the **Applies to** list, select **This object and all descendant objects** to apply the permission to all child objects:

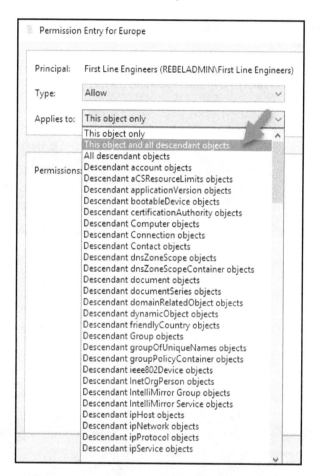

8. Under the **Permissions** section, check **Create all child objects** and click **OK**.

9. Then, keep clicking on **OK** until all permission windows are closed.

10. Then, I log in to a Windows 10 computer as user `Liam`. This computer already has RSAT tools (`https://www.microsoft.com/en-gb/download/details.aspx?id=45520`) installed.

11. According to the permissions, we should be able to add the user account under the `Europe` OU:

```
New-ADUser -Name "Dale"
-Path "OU=Users,OU=Europe,DC=rebeladmin,DC=com"
```

12. This successfully adds the user. Let's see whether we can add another user on a different OU:

```
New-ADUser -Name "Simon"
-Path "OU=Users,OU=Asia,DC=rebeladmin,DC=com"
```

13. As soon as I run the preceding code, I get an `Access is denied` error:

```
PS C:\Users\liam> New-ADUser -Name "Simon" -Path "OU=Users,OU=Asia,DC=rebeladmin,DC=com"
New-ADUser : Access is denied
At line:1 char:1
+ New-ADUser -Name "Simon" -Path "OU=Users,OU=Asia,DC=rebeladmin,DC=com ...
+ ~~~~~~~~~~~~~~~~~~~~~~~~~~~~~~~~~~~~~~~~~~~~~~~~~~~~~~~~~~~~~~~~~~~~~~~~
    + CategoryInfo          : PermissionDenied: (CN=Simon,OU=Use...beladmin,DC=com:String) [New-ADUser], UnauthorizedA
   ccessException
    + FullyQualifiedErrorId : ActiveDirectoryCmdlet:System.UnauthorizedAccessException,Microsoft.ActiveDirectory.Manag
   ement.Commands.NewADUser

PS C:\Users\liam> _
```

14. According to the applied permissions, Liam should not be able to delete any object under `OU=Users,OU=Europe,DC=rebeladmin,DC=com` either. Let's check this using the following command:

```
Remove-ADUser -Identity "CN=Dishan Francis,
OU=Users,OU= Europe,DC=rebeladmin,DC=com"
```

15. As soon as I run the preceding command, I get an `Access is denied` error:

```
PS C:\Users\liam> Remove-ADUser -Identity "CN=Dishan Francis,OU=Users,OU=Europe,DC=rebeladmin,DC=com"

Confirm
Are you sure you want to perform this action?
Performing the operation "Remove" on target "CN=Dishan Francis,OU=Users,OU=Europe,DC=rebeladmin,DC=com".
[Y] Yes  [A] Yes to All  [N] No  [L] No to All  [S] Suspend  [?] Help (default is "Y"): A
Remove-ADUser : Access is denied
At line:1 char:1
+ Remove-ADUser -Identity "CN=Dishan Francis,OU=Users,OU=Europe,DC=rebe ...
+ ~~~~~~~~~~~~~~~~~~~~~~~~~~~~~~~~~~~~~~~~~~~~~~~~~~~~~~~~~~~~~~~~~~~~~~~~
    + CategoryInfo          : PermissionDenied: (CN=Dishan Franc...beladmin,DC=com:ADUser) [Remove-ADUser], Unauthoriz
   edAccessException
    + FullyQualifiedErrorId : ActiveDirectoryCmdlet:System.UnauthorizedAccessException,Microsoft.ActiveDirectory.Manag
   ement.Commands.RemoveADUser

PS C:\Users\liam> 
```

This confirms that we can manage permissions for AD management tasks using ACLs.

Using the delegate control method in AD

The delegate control method also works similarly to ACLs, but it simplifies privilege management as it uses the following:

- The **Delegation of Control Wizard** can be used to apply delegated permissions.
- A predefined task list is available via the wizard and we can easily map permissions to these tasks.

This wizard contains the following predefined tasks, which can be used to assign permissions:

- Create, delete, and manage user accounts.
- Reset user passwords and force a password to change at the next logon.
- Read all user information.
- Create, delete, and manage groups.
- Modify the membership of a group.
- Manage Group Policy links.
- Generate Resultant Set of Policy (Planning).
- Generate Resultant Set of Policy (Logging).
- Create, delete, and manage **inetOrgPerson** accounts.
- Reset **inetOrgPerson** passwords and force a password change at the next logon.
- Read all the **inetOrgPerson** information.

These also allows you to create a custom task to delegate permissions if it's not covered in the common tasks list.

Similar to ACLs, permissions can be applied at the following levels:

- **Site**: Delegated permissions will be valid for all the objects under the given AD site.
- **Domain**: Delegated permissions will be valid for all the objects under the given AD domain.
- **OU**: Delegated permissions will be valid for all the objects under the given **Active Directory Organisational Unit** (**AD OU**).

As an example, I have a security group called `Second Line Engineers`, and Scott is a member of it. I need to allow members of this group to reset passwords for objects in `OU=Users,OU=Europe,DC=rebeladmin,DC`.

In order to do that we need to do the following:

1. Log in to the domain controller as Domain Admin/Enterprise Admin.
2. Review the group membership using the following command:

   ```
   Get-ADGroupMember "Second Line Engineers"
   ```

3. Go to ADUC, right-click on the `Europe` OU, and then from the list, click on the **Delegate Control...** option.
4. This opens a new wizard on the initial page; click on **Next** to proceed.
5. On the next page, click on the **Add** button and add the `Second Line Engineers` group to it. Then, click on **Next** to proceed:

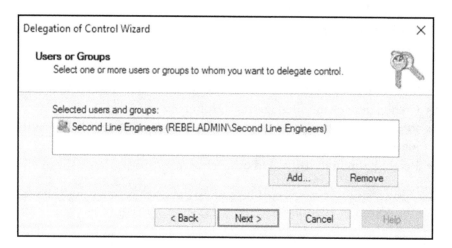

6. From the **Tasks to Delegate** window, select the **Delegate the following common tasks** option, and from the list, select **Reset user passwords and force password change at next logon**. On this page, we can select multiple tasks. If none of those work, we can still select **Create a custom task to delegate**. Once you have completed the selection, click on **Next** to proceed:

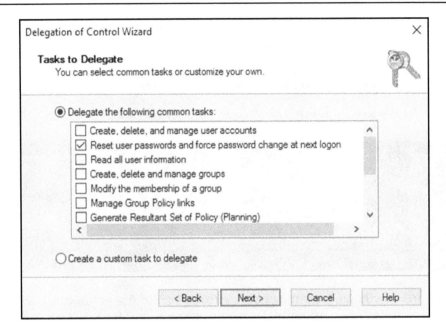

7. This completes the wizard. Click on **Finish** to complete.

8. Now, it's time for testing. I log in to a Windows 10 computer, as user Scott that has RSAT tools (`https://www.microsoft.com/en-gb/download/details.aspx?id=45520`) installed.

9. According to the permissions, Scott should be able to reset the password of an object under `OU=Users,OU=Europe,DC=rebeladmin,DC:`

   `Set-ADAccountPassword -Identity dfrancis`

10. This allows you to change the password successfully:

```
PS C:\Users\sbrewer> Set-ADAccountPassword -Identity dfrancis
Please enter the current password for 'CN=Dishan Francis,OU=Users,OU=Europe,DC=rebeladmin,DC=com'
Password: *********
Please enter the desired password for 'CN=Dishan Francis,OU=Users,OU=Europe,DC=rebeladmin,DC=com'
Password: ************
Repeat Password: ************
PS C:\Users\sbrewer>
```

11. However, it should not allow Scott to delete any objects. We can test it using the following command:

```
Remove-ADUser -Identity "CN=Dishan Francis,
OU=Users,OU=Europe,DC=rebeladmin,DC=com"
```

12. As expected, it returns an `Access is denied` error:

```
PS C:\Users\sbrewer> Remove-ADUser -Identity "CN=Dishan Francis,OU=Users,OU=Europe,DC=rebeladmin,DC=com"

Confirm
Are you sure you want to perform this action?
Performing the operation "Remove" on target "CN=Dishan Francis,OU=Users,OU=Europe,DC=rebeladmin,DC=com".
[Y] Yes  [A] Yes to All  [N] No  [L] No to All  [S] Suspend  [?] Help (default is "Y"): A
Remove-ADUser : Access is denied
At line:1 char:1
+ Remove-ADUser -Identity "CN=Dishan Francis,OU=Users,OU=Europe,DC=rebe ...
+ ~~~~~~~~~~~~~~~~~~~~~~~~~~~~~~~~~~~~~~~~~~~~~~~~~~~~~~~~~~~~~~~~~~~~~~~~
    + CategoryInfo          : PermissionDenied: (CN=Dishan Franc...beladmin,DC=com:ADUser) [Remove-ADUser], Unauthoriz
   edAccessException
    + FullyQualifiedErrorId : ActiveDirectoryCmdlet:System.UnauthorizedAccessException,Microsoft.ActiveDirectory.Manag
   ement.Commands.RemoveADUser

PS C:\Users\sbrewer> _
```

Using all three methods, we can delegate permissions for AD administrative tasks. This helps us assign responsibilities to users or groups in order to keep the AD environment healthy and secure.

Implementing fine-grained password policies

Complex passwords are a basic security setting that any administrator uses. In the AD environment, password complexity settings and account lockout settings can be configured by using GPO settings, which are located at **Computer Configuration | Policies | Windows Settings | Security Settings | Account Policies**. Before Windows Server 2008, there was only one password policy and account lockout policy setting that could be applied to the users. With Windows Server 2008, Microsoft introduced fine-grained password policies, which allow administrators to apply different password and account lockout policy settings to individual users or groups. This allows you to protect privileged accounts using stronger policies than regular user accounts. This feature continued with every AD DS version after 2008 and is available with AD DS 2016 as well.

Once, I was working on an AD audit for a hedge fund. As part of the report, I recommended that they use password policies with greater complexity, as they were not doing so. After I explained things, the IT manager there agreed and I configured the password policy and the account lockout policy. After a few days, I went to the same site, and the IT manager showed me that after forcing the policy, the end users started to write down their complex passwords on sticky notes and papers. So, even though it was a security setting, in the end, it led to bigger security issues as the users could see each other's passwords on sticky notes. However, by using fine-grained password policies, administrators can apply different settings based on the situation. As an example, while using 5-character complex passwords for sales department users, you can use 12-character complex passwords for Domain Admins.

Limitations

Fine-grained password policies have the following limitations:

- Fine-grained password policies can only be applied to users and global security groups. They can't be applied to OUs.
- By default, only Domain Admins/Enterprise Admins can set up/manage/delete fine-grained password policies. It is possible to delegate permission to other users if required.
- The minimum domain functional level is Windows Server 2008.

Resultant Set of Policy (RSoP)

When you use fine-grained password policies, some objects may have multiple fine-grained password policies applied. However, only one password policy can be applied to an object at a given time. It is not possible to merge multiple policies either.

RSoP uses the attribute value of `msDS-PasswordSettingsPrecedence`, which is associated with each password policy in order to decide the winning policy. A precedence value is an integer value an administrator can define. A lower precedence value means higher priority. If multiple password policies are applied to the same object, the password policy with the lower precedence value wins.

The following list further explains how password policies work in an infrastructure:

- There are two ways to link an object to a password policy. The first method is via a directly linked policy. The second method is via group membership. If the policy targets a security group, its members will automatically link to the password policy. However, if a fine-grained password policy is linked to an object, it will be the winning policy.
- If there's no directly linked policy, the object will consider the lowest policy precedence. These policies are inherited from the security groups that they belong to.
- If neither of the settings is applicable, the default GPO password policy setting is applied.

Configuration

There are two ways to apply fine-grained password policies. The first option is to use **Active Directory Administrative Center** (**ADAC**), and the second option is to use PowerShell cmdlets.

In ADAC, browse to **System | Password Settings Container**. Then, right-click and go to **New | Password Settings**. It will open up the window where we can define the policy settings:

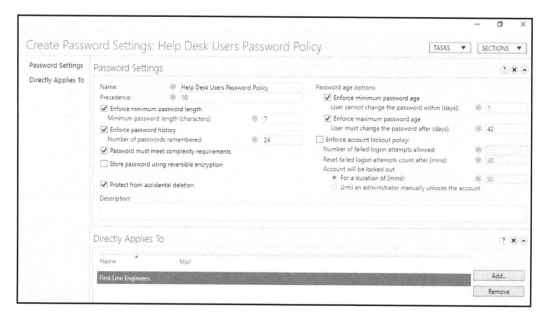

In the policy window, we can define the policy name, precedence, and account lockout policy settings. **Directly Applies To** is the place where we can define the users or security groups this new policy should target. In the preceding example, I added the `First Line Engineers` security group as the target.

Fine-grained password policies can also be created using PowerShell:

```
New-ADFineGrainedPasswordPolicy -Name "Domain Admin Password Policy" -
Precedence 1 `
-MinPasswordLength 12 -MaxPasswordAge "30" -MinPasswordAge "7" `
-PasswordHistoryCount 50 -ComplexityEnabled:$true `
-LockoutDuration "8:00" `
-LockoutObservationWindow "8:00" -LockoutThreshold 3 `
-ReversibleEncryptionEnabled:$false
```

In the preceding command, `New-ADFineGrainedPasswordPolicy` is the cmdlet that is used to create a new policy. `-Precedence` defines the policy precedence. The `-LockoutDuration` and `-LockoutObservationWindow` values are defined in hours. The `-LockoutThreshold` value defines the number of login attempts allowed.

The policy settings can be viewed using ADAC or PowerShell:

```
Get-ADFineGrainedPasswordPolicy - Identity "Domain Admin Password
Policy"
```

The preceding command retrieves the following settings for the given password policy:

```
PS C:\Users\Administrator> Get-ADFineGrainedPasswordPolicy -Identity "Domain Admin Password Policy"

AppliesTo                     : {}
ComplexityEnabled             : True
DistinguishedName             : CN=Domain Admin Password Policy,CN=Password Settings
                                Container,CN=System,DC=rebeladmin,DC=com
LockoutDuration               : 08:00:00
LockoutObservationWindow      : 08:00:00
LockoutThreshold              : 3
MaxPasswordAge                : 30.00:00:00
MinPasswordAge                : 7.00:00:00
MinPasswordLength             : 12
Name                          : Domain Admin Password Policy
ObjectClass                   : msDS-PasswordSettings
ObjectGUID                    : 81b80dc3-4243-41b2-8e2f-0fb54c24df74
PasswordHistoryCount          : 50
Precedence                    : 1
ReversibleEncryptionEnabled   : True
```

We now have a new policy, and the next step is to assign objects to it. We need to add the Domain Admins security group to it:

```
Add-ADFineGrainedPasswordPolicySubject -Identity "Domain Admin
Password Policy" -Subjects "Domain Admins"
```

The preceding command adds the `Domain Admins` group to `Domain Admin Password Policy`. This can be verified using the following command:

```
Get-ADFineGrainedPasswordPolicy -Identity "Domain Admin Password
Policy" | Format-Table AppliesTo -AutoSize
```

This confirms what the policy target is. This value is saved under the `AppliesTo` attribute.

The following command is also useful to list down filtered password policy details:

```
Get-ADFineGrainedPasswordPolicy -Filter * | Format-Table
Name,Precedence,AppliesTo -AutoSize
```

This will list all the fine-grained password policies along with `Name`, `Precedence`, and the targets.

Pass-the-hash attacks

If a client needs to authenticate into a server successfully, the client needs to prove their identity. This is done by using a username and password. The client needs to present its username and password to the authentication server, and it will verify the identity. There are legacy protocols and systems that send this information in cleartext, even in an open network. Telnet is a good example of this. If someone is listening to traffic (packet capturing) on a Telnet session, they can easily capture a password as it is transmitted in cleartext.

Modern authentication protocols are well aware of these types of threats and use different technologies to encrypt credentials or create cryptographic hashes for identity verification. The **cryptographic hash** means a password string is transformed into a fixed-length digest using an algorithm.

Earlier in *AD authentication* section, we saw how Kerberos authentication works using hash values. When we use hash values, the authentication server compares the hash value submitted by the client with the hash value for the user password that is stored in its database. In the Windows environment, these password hashes are stored in three different places:

- The **Security Account Manager** (**SAM**) database
- **Local Security Authority Subsystem Service** (**LSASS**)
- The AD database

The SAM database stores usernames and **New Technology** (**NT**) hashes in a `%SystemRoot%/system32/config/SAM` file. This contains all the hash values for accounts that are local to the computer. The current version of SAM does not store **LAN Manager** (**LM**) hashes in its database file.

The very first password hash schema introduced by Microsoft was LM. It uses the **Data Encryption Standard** (**DES**) algorithm for hashing. This is a legacy-weak schema, and Microsoft highly recommends not using it. It doesn't support passwords larger than 15 ASCII characters, or passwords that are not case-sensitive. However, any new operating system released after Windows Vista supports the **Advanced Encryption Standard** (**AES**) algorithm for hashing.

Compared to the cleartext password, for an attacker, it is almost impossible to figure out the password based on the hash. Even if they are able to do it, it will take a lot of computing power and time. But, if they can find the hash value instead of retrieving the password, the hash value can be used to initiate a connection with the server on behalf of the original owner of the hash. This sounds easy, but in practice, it is still very difficult as these authentication protocols have their own mechanisms to prevent attackers from using someone else's hash value. If you consider Kerberos, it uses timestamps along with requests and responses to verify the authenticity of hashes. **New Technology** (**LT**), **New Technology LAN Manager** (**NTLM**) v1, and NTLM v2 also use a similar challenge-response mechanism to authenticate without revealing the password.

However, even hash values are not transmitted over directly. LSASS stores credentials in memory on behalf of users with active sessions. LSASS can store credentials in multiple forms, such as an NT hash, an LM hash, and Kerberos tickets. This is required in order to maintain active sessions and perform future authentications faster. This will clear up during the reboot, but it can be enough for the attacker to retrieve a hash value and use it to compromise the entire identity infrastructure. Microsoft introduced many features and techniques to protect the AD environment from pass-the-hash attacks, and in this section, we are going to look into them in detail.

The Protected Users security group

The Protected Users security group was introduced with Windows Server 2012 R2 and continued in Windows Server 2016. This group was developed to provide highly privileged accounts with better protection from credential theft attacks. Members of this group have non-configurable protection applied. In order to use the Protected Users group, **Primary Domain Controller** (**PDC**) should be running with a minimum of Windows Server 2012 R2 and the client computers should be running with a minimum of Windows 8.1 or Windows 2012 R2.

If a member of this group logs in to Windows 8.1, Windows Server 2012 R2, Windows 10, or Windows Server 2016, then we can expect the following:

- Members of this group cannot use NTLM, digest authentication, or CredSSP for authentication. Plain-text passwords are not cached. So, any of the devices using these protocols will fail to authenticate to the domain.
- Kerberos's long-term keys are not cached. For accounts in this group, the Kerberos protocol verifies authentication at each request (the TGT acquired at logon).
- Sign-in is offline. A cached verifier is not created at sign-in.

For the Protected Users group feature, it is *not* a must to have a domain or forest functional level running on Windows Server 2012 R2 or higher (Windows Server 2008 is the minimum because Kerberos needs to use AES). The only requirement is to run the PDC emulator's **Flexible Single-Master Operations** (**FSMO**) role in the Windows Server 2012 R2 domain controller.

 If required, after the Protected Users group object is replicated to all the domain controllers, the PDC emulator role can be transferred to a domain controller running a lower Windows Server version.

If the AD environment uses Windows Server 2012 R2 or Windows Server 2016 domain functional levels, it provides additional protections with Protected User groups, such as the following:

- No NTLM authentication.
- No DES or RC4 encryption in Kerberos, pre-authentication.
- No delegation using the unconstrained or constrained method.
- No Kerberos TGT is valid for more than 4 hours.

 Service accounts and computers cannot be members of the Protected Users' security group. These accounts can be protected using different features, such as policy silos, which we will discuss later in *Authentication policies and authentication policy silos* section.

To start with, we can review the `Protected Users` security group using the following command:

```
Get-ADGroup -Identity "Protected Users"
```

The following screenshot shows the output for the preceding command:

```
PS C:\Users\Administrator> Get-ADGroup -Identity "Protected Users"

DistinguishedName : CN=Protected Users,CN=Users,DC=rebeladmin,DC=com
GroupCategory     : Security
GroupScope        : Global
Name              : Protected Users
ObjectClass       : group
ObjectGUID        : 795da445-8143-41bf-93d5-e6cbc1aff863
SamAccountName    : Protected Users
SID               : S-1-5-21-4041220333-1835452706-552999228-525
```

We can add users to the `Protected Users` group using ADAC, ADUC MMC, and PowerShell. This group is located in the default `Users` container in AD.

In here, we are going to add the user account of `Adam` to the `Protected Users` group using the following command:

```
Get-ADGroup -Identity "Protected Users" | Add-ADGroupMember -Members
"CN=Adam,CN=Users,DC=rebeladmin,DC=com"
```

The first part of the command retrieves the group and the second part adds the `Adam` user account to it.

After the user is added to the group, we can verify their group membership by using the following command:

```
Get-ADGroupMember -Identity "Protected Users"
```

In order to test this, we are going to use a tool called **mimikatz** (`https://github.com/gentilkiwi/mimikatz/blob/master/README.md`), which can be used to perform experiments with Windows security.

I logged in to a computer as the user `liam`, and he is not part of the `Protected Users` group. When I list keys from LSASS for users, I can see Liam's NTLM hash clearly:

```
Authentication Id : 0 ; 3059384 (00000000:002eaeb8)
Session           : Interactive from 3
User Name         : liam
Domain            : REBELADMIN
Logon Server      : REBEL-PDC-01
Logon Time        : 15/04/2017 08:35:20
SID               : S-1-5-21-4041220333-1835452706-552999228-1230
        msv :
         [00010000] CredentialKeys
         * NTLM     : 947e1646ca81470d18fdb6d976ba8d6a
         * SHA1     :aabc44618a0645c/ddd29ca5/f95bacc318/1b6
         [00000003] Primary
         * Username : liam
         * Domain   : REBELADMIN
         * NTLM     : 947e1646ca81470d18fdb6d976ba8d6a
         * SHA1     : aabc44618a0645c7ddd29ca57f95bacc3f1871b6
        tspkg :
        wdigest :
         * Username : liam
         * Domain   : REBELADMIN
         * Password : (null)
        kerberos :
         * Username : liam
         * Domain   : REBELADMIN.COM
         * Password : (null)
        ssp :
        credman :
```

When I do the same thing for the user `adam`, who is a member of the `Protected Users` group, I cannot see the NTLM hash stored in the LSASS memory because members who are in the protected group do not use NTLM and don't save any credentials in the cache:

```
Authentication Id : 0 ; 3580277 (00000000:0036a175)
Session           : Interactive from 4
User Name         : adam
Domain            : REBELADMIN
Logon Server      : REBEL-PDC-01
Logon Time        : 15/04/2017 08:52:06
SID               : S-1-5-21-4041220333-1835452706-552999228-1229
        msv :
         [00010000] CredentialKeys
         * RootKey  : fc7b034be210b04c20921a5811dc1165fe4a6dcfddde33b3f939d2b41981b789
         * DPAPI    : c3ebcfb3a1e4b912d6ef928d8bd25c46
        tspkg :
        wdigest :
         * Username : adam
         * Domain   : REBELADMIN
         * Password : (null)
        kerberos :
         * Username : adam
         * Domain   : REBELADMIN.COM
         * Password : (null)
        ssp :
        credman :
```

The *Protected Users security group* was first introduced with Windows Server 2012 R2. It has built-in capabilities to protect privileged accounts from credential theft attacks. In this section, we learned about the technology behind the *Protected Users security group*. We also learned about the configuration of this security feature. In the next section, we are going to look into another built-in security feature, which we can use to prevent the leakage of credentials over unsecured remote desktop connections.

Restricted admin mode for RDP

In a typical identity infrastructure attack, the first target is usually a regular user account or an endpoint. This is because highly privileged accounts and critical systems have advanced protection compared to end user devices. In most environments, these systems and accounts are constantly monitored and there is a high possibility that engineers recognize unauthorized login attempts or unusual behavior quickly. A typical end user account does not have the privileges or capabilities to do much damage, but a privileged account does. Once an attacker completes a successful initial breach, the next thing they are looking to do is to get their hands on the privileged account.

If they start to mess around in an endpoint by doing things such as deleting files, increase CPU/ram usage, and damaging applications, then the end user will contact the IT department for help. IT department engineers are usually members of Enterprise Admins, Domain Admins, or at least a local administrator group of the endpoint. In order to log in and troubleshoot, they have to use their privileged accounts. If the attackers are running programs for password harvesting on the system, then these privileged accounts' credentials will be revealed.

In the previous section, we discussed how we can prevent credential hashes from being stored in LSASS. LSASS memory stores credentials when they do any of the following:

- Log in to a computer locally or using RDP.
- Run an application or a task using the **Run As** option.
- Run a Windows service on the computer with the service account.
- Run a scheduled task or a batch job on the computer.
- Run a task on the local computer using remote tools (system scans and installations).

RDP is the most commonly used method by engineers to access computers remotely. When a user connects to a system using RDP, it sends credentials to the remote computer in the form of cleartext. This is a security issue if the remote computer is already compromised. Microsoft introduced the *restricted admin mode for RDP* with Windows Server 2012 R2. When this mode is used for RDP, it will not send credentials to the remote computer. Once the user is logged in via the restricted RDP session, they cannot connect to other resources such as a shared network. Also, any users can't jump into other systems using RDP. This feature is also available in Windows Server 2016.

This mode can be used with Windows 7, Windows 8, Windows 8.1, Windows 10, Windows Server 2008 R2, Windows Server 2012, Windows Server 2012 R2, and Windows Server 2016.

By default, this mode is not enabled. Before you use it, it needs to be enabled in the target system. This can be done using the registry edit process:

1. Log in to the target computer or server as the administrator.
2. Click on the Start menu, click on **Run**, type `regedit`, and then click on **OK**.
3. In **Registry Editor**, browse to `HKEY_LOCAL_MACHINE\System\CurrentControlSet\Control\Lsa`.
4. Create the following registry key:

```
Name: DisableRestrictedAdmin
Type: REG_DWORD
Value: 0
```

The following screenshot illustrates the preceding step:

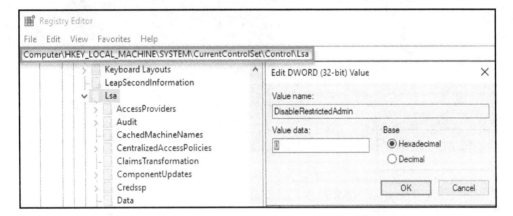

Once this is done, we can connect to the target computer using the restricted admin mode for RDP. In order to do that, the remote desktop client needs to run with the restricted mode. This can be done by running the `mstsc /restrictedadmin` command:

In order to test this feature, we will connect to a Windows 10 member PC using the restricted RDP mode. The user account belongs to Peter, and he is a member of the Domain Admin group:

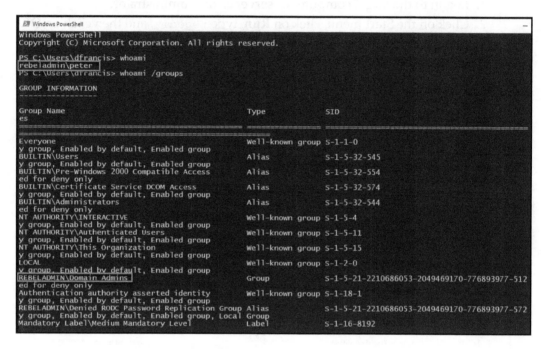

Now, when we try to access another computer hard drive, it prompts with an **Access is denied** error. The user account is a Domain Admin, and it should not prevent access. This is due to the restricted RDP mode, as it cannot be used to access other resources through the same session:

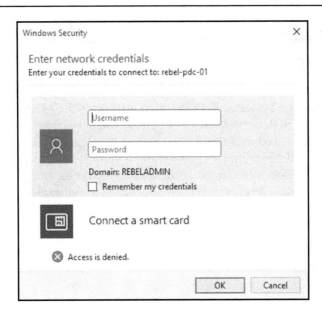

Similarly, I tried to add the domain controller to the **Server Manager** on the remote computer. It issued an **Access denied** error as well:

This feature minimizes the risk of highly privileged accounts being compromised.

The restricted RDP mode can be disabled by changing the value of the `DisableRestrictedAdmin` registry key to `1`.

Authentication policies and authentication policy silos

A rule of thumb in pass-the-hash attack protection is to prevent trusted users from appearing on untrusted systems. Rebeladmin Corp. uses the MS SQL farm to host its database. During the SQL Server setup, engineers use service accounts. It is obvious that these SQL service accounts should be used only with SQL Server. If the accounts appear on a receptionist's computer, something is definitely wrong. With Windows Server 2012 R2, Microsoft introduced authentication policies and policy silos that can be used to limit the use of highly privileged accounts to only selected systems.

Authentication policies

Authentication policies can be used to specify the Kerberos protocol TGT validity period and access control conditions to restrict user sign-on.

Authentication policy silos

Authentication policy silos are similar to containers where we can assign user accounts, computer accounts, and service accounts. Then, these accounts can be managed by the authentication policies.

This feature requires the following prerequisites:

- All domain controllers in the domain must be based on Windows Server 2012 R2, Windows Server 2016, or Windows Server 2019.
- The domain's functional level must be Windows Server 2012 R2 or higher.
- Domain controllers must be configured to support DAC.
- Windows 8, Windows 8.1, Windows 10, Windows Server 2012, Windows Server 2012 R2, Windows Server 2016, and Windows Server 2019 domain members must be configured to support **Dynamic Access Control** (**DAC**).

Creating authentication policies

Before we create policies, we need to enable DAC support for domain controllers and devices. DAC allows administrators to apply access control permissions and restrictions based on rules that can include the characteristics of the resources.

To enable DAC for domain controllers, perform the following steps:

1. Go to the **Group Policy Management** MMC.
2. Edit **Default Domain Controllers Policy**.
3. Go to **Computer Configuration** | **Policies** | **Administrative Templates** | **System** | **KDC**.
4. Click on **Enabled** to enable **KDC support for claims, compound authentication and Kerberos armoring**.
5. Under the options, select **Always provide claims** and click on **OK**. This will ensure that it always returns claims for accounts and supports the RFC behavior to advertise **Flexible Authentication Secure Tunneling** (**FAST**):

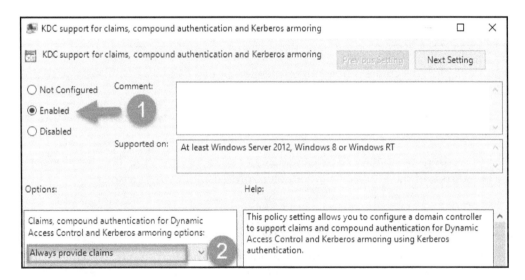

To enable DAC for computers, perform the following steps:

1. Go to the **Group Policy Management** MMC.
2. Edit **Default Domain Policy**.

3. Go to **Computer Configuration** | **Policies** | **Administrative Templates** | **System** | **Kerberos**.

4. Click on **Enabled** in **Kerberos client support for claims, compound authentication and Kerberos armoring**.

5. Once this is done, we can create a new authentication policy using the `New-ADAuthenticationPolicy` cmdlet. This can also be created using ADAC:

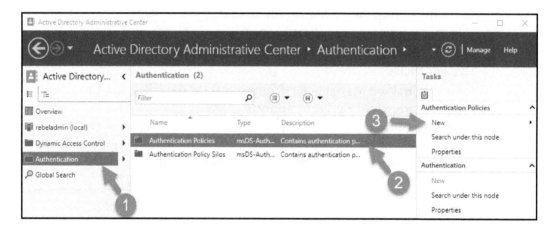

As an example, let's create a new authentication policy called `AP_1hr_TGT` with a TGT lifetime of 60 minutes:

```
New-ADAuthenticationPolicy -Name "AP_1hr_TGT" -UserTGTLifetimeMins 60
-Enforce
```

In the preceding command, `-UserTGTLifetimeMins` defines the TGT lifetime for user accounts and the `-Enforce` parameter enforces policy restrictions.

Creating authentication policy silos

Now that we have created the authentication policy, the next step is to create a new authentication policy silo. My requirement is to create a policy silo to prevent the user account of `Peter` from accessing `REBEL-PC01`.

Policy silos can be created using ADAC or the `New-ADAuthenticationPolicySilo` PowerShell cmdlet:

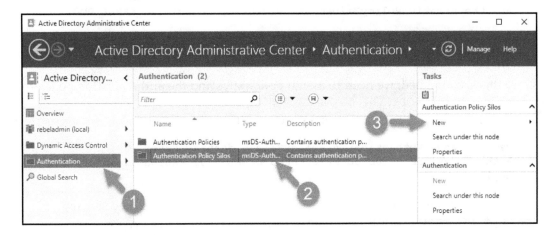

In this demo, let's create a new authentication policy silo called `Restricted_REBEL_PC01`:

```
New-ADAuthenticationPolicySilo –Name Restricted_REBEL_PC01 –
UserAuthenticationPolicy AP_1hr_TGT –ComputerAuthenticationPolicy
AP_1hr_TGT –ServiceAuthenticationPolicy AP_1hr_TGT –Enforce
```

In the preceding command, `-UserAuthenticationPolicy`, `-ComputerAuthenticationPolicy`, and `-ServiceAuthenticationPolicy` refer to the authentication policies that will be attached to the policy silo. Here, we are only using one policy, but if needed, the policy silo can be attached to multiple authentication policies that cover the user, computer, and service classes.

The next step is to add the related objects to the policy silo as permitted accounts. In my demo, this is the user account of `Peter` and the computer called `REBEL-PC01`.

We can add these objects to the policy silos using the `Grant-ADAuthenticationPolicySiloAccess` PowerShell cmdlet:

```
Grant-ADAuthenticationPolicySiloAccess –Identity Restricted_REBEL_PC01
–Account Peter
```

The preceding command adds the user account of `Peter` to the `Restricted_REBEL_PC01` policy silo as a permitted account.

We also can combine it with a filter and then add the result to the policy silo:

```
Get-ADComputer -Filter 'Name -like "REBEL-PC01"' | Grant-
ADAuthenticationPolicySiloAccess -Identity Restricted_REBEL_PC01
```

In the preceding command, we search for the computer object and then pass the result to the policy silo.

Once this is completed, we need to assign policy silos and the authentication policy to Peter and REBEL-PC01. This can be done using Set-ADAccountAuthenticationPolicySilo:

```
Set-ADAccountAuthenticationPolicySilo -Identity Peter -
AuthenticationPolicySilo Restricted_REBEL_PC01 -AuthenticationPolicy
AP_1hr_TGT
```

The preceding command assigns the Restricted_REBEL_PC01 policy silo and the AP_1hr_TGT authentication policy to the user account of Peter.

These commands can also be attached to filters:

```
Get-ADComputer -Filter 'Name -like "REBEL-PC01"' | Set-
ADAccountAuthenticationPolicySilo -AuthenticationPolicySilo
Restricted_REBEL_PC01 -AuthenticationPolicy AP_1hr_TGT
```

The preceding command filters for the REBEL-PC01 AD computer object and then assigns both the authentication policy and the policy silo.

The last step of the configuration is to define the access control condition for the AP_1hr_TGT authentication policy. This defines the condition of the device or host from which users log in. The condition for my demo will use the user's policy silo value:

```
Set-ADAuthenticationPolicy -Identity AP_1hr_TGT -
UserAllowedToAuthenticateFrom
"O:SYG:SYD:(XA;OICI;CR;;;WD;(@USER.ad://ext/AuthenticationSilo ==
`"Restricted_REBEL_PC01`"))"
```

In the preceding command, the condition is passed as an **Security Descriptor Definition Language (SDDL)** string. You can find more information about this SDDL string at https://blogs.technet.microsoft.com/askds/2008/04/18/the-security-descriptor-definition-language-of-love-part-1/.

This can also be modified by using the authentication policy properties window in ADAC:

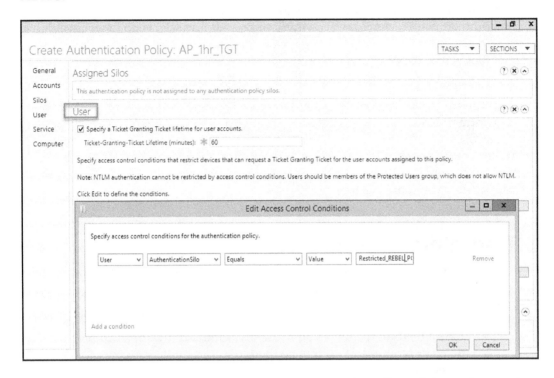

This finishes the configuration of the authentication policy silo and the authentication policy. Authentication policies and authentication policy silos provide greater flexibility in protecting privileged accounts on critical systems.

JIT administration and JEA

In the previous sections, we learned about features that were introduced by Microsoft to prevent pass-the-hash attacks. These types of attacks are still used by attackers in identity infrastructure attacks, so it's important to prevent these attacks whenever and wherever possible. But is this going to secure our identity infrastructures 100%? Software vendors, including Microsoft, release new products, features, security updates, and patches to protect systems, infrastructures, and workloads from various types of threats.

All these companies spend lots of money annually on research and development to protect their software, solutions, and customers from emerging threats. However, we still see constant news about identity infrastructure security breaches. As I see it, this is not a problem with technology. The myth of zero-day attacks is no longer valid. With all these technologies, we fight against human adversaries. If the method they used earlier is not working anymore, they will find another way to get in. We cannot close all the doors; we need to expect a breach anytime.

JIT and JEA are two different approaches to identity infrastructure security. In any identity infrastructure attack, adversaries are after one common thing. In order to gain control of the infrastructure, they need to gain access to *privileged accounts*. This is what they are going after. JIT and JEA are about managing privileges effectively within the identity infrastructure. They limit what adversaries can do in the identity infrastructure, even there is a breach.

JIT administration

In Chapter 2, *Active Directory Domain Services 2016*, we learned about JIT in detail and we discussed how AD DS 2016 features help to do it. Therefore, we are not going to look at it in detail again in this chapter, but I'd like to list a few important facts:

- JIT administration allows you to assign administrative privileges to users whenever required. With this method, user accounts do not need to be members of privileged groups permanently.
- Privileges are time-based. Privileged group memberships have TTL, and once they exceed the allocated time, members will automatically be removed from groups.
- A bastion forest (the administrative forest) introduces to your existing infrastructure in order to manage privileges. This forest can be run on Windows Server 2016 or the Windows Server 2012 R2 forest functional level.
- Minimal changes are required in the existing AD forest. They are not required for the domain functional level or the forest functional level upgrade.
- Microsoft Identity Manager 2016 is part of the solution. It is responsible for managing the bastion forest, managing group memberships, creating workflows, and producing reports.
- One bastion forest can manage privileges for multiple forests.

- Users can make requests for privileges, and they are handled according to the policies in place. It can be either a manual or an auto-approval process.
- All the incidents are recorded and can be included in a report.
- The solution can be integrated with existing helpdesk systems or with CMS, by using REST APIs.

Apart from these facts, AD DS 2016 supports time-based group memberships. This feature can be used to provide JIT administration.

JEA

JEA was first released in 2014, and it was the first approach toward JIT administration. JEA allows you to provide role-based privileges instead of full administrative privileges. As an example, the Rebeladmin Corp. IT team runs a set of PowerShell scripts every month to generate reports about the monthly resource usage of its private cloud. In order to do that, a member of the IT team logs in to a server monthly and runs these scripts. The individuals who run these reports are Domain Admins, as they need to have administrative privileges to do so. But these users do not need Domain Admin privileges for their day-to-day helpdesk tasks. Using JEA, we can assign just enough privileges to run these scripts from specific hosts instead of providing Domain Admin privileges. This is a fully PowerShell-based solution. It can be used with anything that can be managed via PowerShell.

Microsoft AD DS already has some features that can be used to limit administrative permissions, such as role-based administration and delegated control. However, these are still open to certain security risks:

- First-line support engineers are involved with basic troubleshooting only. Log analysis, executing basic troubleshooting commands, and restarting services are some of their most common activities. They are not responsible for system- or service-level changes. But most of the time, they have Domain Admin, Enterprise Admin, or local administrator privileges.
- Software vendors and application support engineers need to be able to access their systems in order to do installations, upgrades, patching, or provide support. Their access requirements are not permanent and their activities are limited to a few servers. However, most of the time, these accounts end up as Domain or Enterprise Admins as it's easy for them to carry out the required tasks. With these permissions, nothing prevents them from accessing other critical systems or data.

- Built-in delegation control capabilities are limited. They cannot be used to limit users and delegate permissions to hosts.
- Some service accounts need to have local administrator privileges in order to run certain service-related tasks, at least. However, these tasks are application-specific. How can we guarantee that these service accounts aren't being used to change system settings or to run other services in the system?

When using JEA, keep these points in mind:

- Users only have permissions that are required for running the tasks they are assigned to.
- Users cannot copy the same permission to other users in the same system.
- If user A is allowed to run task B on computer C, then they cannot run task B on computer D, even if it's the same task with the same privilege requirements.
- Detail logging provides visibility of the activities in the environment.

JEA is implemented as PowerShell session endpoints. It includes the following files:

- **PowerShell session configuration file**: This allows you to map users to the endpoint. We can map users and groups to specific management roles. We can also configure global settings such as virtual accounts and transcription policies. The PowerShell session configuration file is system-specific, so configuration settings can be applied on a per-machine basis.
- **Role capability files**: These files specify which actions can be performed by users. These can be tasks such as running a script, running certain cmdlets, and running a program. These tasks can be grouped into roles and shared with other users. As an example, tasks performed by first-line engineers can be grouped into one role and shared with all the first-line engineers.

One of the disadvantages of JEA is that it is limited to PowerShell and is not compatible with typical GUI-based tasks and functions.

JEA implementation will be covered in `Chapter 16`, *Advanced AD Management with PowerShell*.

Azure AD PIM

So far, we have learned about protecting identities in the on-premises AD environment. But in a hybrid environment, identities exist in the cloud as well. These identities are mostly synced from the on-premises AD environment using Azure AD Connect. Azure AD also has cloud-only accounts. In a hybrid environment, we also need to consider protecting the identities in the cloud. Azure AD is a managed service, so we cannot apply the same features we have used in the on-premises AD environment. Also, the challenges are different. In a hybrid environment, identities appear in various cloud services such as **Software as a service (SaaS)**, **Platform as a service (PaaS)**, **Infrastructure as a service (IaaS)**. Therefore, the potential for attacks is larger compared to an on-premises-only environment. In this section, we are going to learn about some services and features that we can use to protect identities in a hybrid environment.

As we have discussed many times, in an identity attack, adversaries are after privileged accounts as they are the keys to the kingdom. By protecting privileged accounts, we can limit the damage even if there is a security breach. In any infrastructure, we have different types of administrators, including domain administrators, local administrators, and service administrators, but in a hybrid environment, we also have cloud administrators. This brings us to the following questions:

- Do you have full control over these accounts and their permissions?
- Are you aware of their activities when using these permissions?
- How do you know if it hasn't been compromised already?

A solution is to revoke these administrator privileges. Yes, it will work, but how much additional work would we have to do to restore this permission when needed? And also, how practical it is? This also has a social impact. If you walked down to your users and told them that you're going to revoke their admin privileges, how would they respond? Users still need privileged access to their applications and services in order to set up applications and services, manage, and troubleshoot.

Azure AD PIM allows us to manage, control, and monitor privileged access to applications and services such as Azure AD, Office 365, and SaaS apps. This is mostly an automated process (depending on whether automatic approval or manual approval rules are involved) but more importantly, we have the required permissions whenever they are needed.

PIM has the following key features:

- **JIT administration**: You can assign privilege access on demand for a period of time. For example, user A can be an Office 365 administrator from 11:00 a.m. to 12:00 p.m. Once the time is up, the system will revoke the administrator privileges automatically.
- **Approval required**: Approval is required for the privilege to access permissions. This can be done via an automatic or manual approval process.
- **Multi-factor authentication**: We can add multi-factor authentication to the role activation process in order to add an extra layer of security.
- **Notifications**: Approvers will get email notifications when a user requests permission. The user will also receive notifications when the request has been processed.
- **Accountability**: Approvers have records of **who** has privileges and **why** they have them.
- **Revoke permissions**: Approvers can revoke the given permissions at any time.
- **Audit history**: All the requests and activities will be recorded. These records can be used for auditing purposes.

License requirements

In order to use Azure AD PIM, we need one of the following paid licenses:

- Azure AD Premium P2
- **Enterprise Mobility and Security (EMS) E5**
- Microsoft 365 M5

Implementation guidelines

Before we look into PIM configuration, there are certain things we need to consider:

- **Access Audit**: Before we start protecting, we need to know what we are protecting. The only way we can do this is via a proper audit. Azure AD has almost 35 different directory roles. Each of these roles has a different level of privileges. We can review the group memberships and their activities manually, but this takes time. If tasks are manual, and if they take time, then most administrators probably won't do them more regularly. By using **Azure PIM access reviews**, we can review the access and activities of members in privileged groups and adjust their memberships accordingly. **PIM access review** is fully automated so we can schedule it to run more frequently.

In access reviews, we should consider doing the following:

- Identify users with administrative role memberships.
- Identify how frequently they use these privileges. There can be users who have been a member of an administrative group but, don't use those permissions actively. Companies can set up policies to handle these kinds of non-used access permissions.
- Monitor activities of privileged users. Azure AD roles have predefined levels of privileges. How do we know if members of these roles are only doing what they're supposed to do? By using access reviews, we can track down their activities and make sure they do not misuse their privileges.
- Justification. There should be a valid reason for a user to have privileged access. If there is no record, then based on access review findings, we can further investigate and find why this user needs privileged access.
- Map privilege roles to responsibilities. In Azure AD, there are almost 35 different types of privileged roles. In an organization, there are many different job roles. Each of these different job role has their own responsibilities. These responsibilities define what they can do and can't do with IT systems. Access reviews help us to map these privileged roles with job responsibilities. This helps to maintain some sort of standards when assigning privileged access permissions.

I have written a step-by-step guide explaining how to enable PIM access reviews. You can follow the guide using http://www.rebeladmin.com/2019/02/step-step-guide-review-privileged-accounts-using-azure-pim/.

- **Multi-Factor Authentication (MFA) for users**: MFA is no longer an optional security feature; it is the standard for modern authentications. If your organization is still not using MFA, it is time to think about using it. You can use Azure MFA or any other third-party solution to provide multi-factor authentication to users. If the cost is a problem, at least start using MFA for users with privileged access. There are two ways in which we can enforce MFA:

  - **During the sign-in process**: This is common for any user who has MFA enforced. When the user authenticates via Azure AD, they will be verified using MFA. Security in the sign-in process can improve further by using Azure AD conditional access policies.

  - **When activating privileged role permission via Azure AD PIM**: We also can force users to go through MFA when they activate their privilege role memberships. If the user has not already been verified using MFA (during the sign-in process), PIM will force them to do so.

- **Approver groups**: Once PIM is in place, users have to request to have privileged access enabled. If it is a manual approval process, these requests should be forwarded to individuals or groups for processing. A best practice is to create a security group and use it as the approver group. It is best to use a group of approvers rather than individuals because anyone in the group can process requests. The following are the approver's responsibilities:

  - Validate privileged access requests.
  - Check whether the justification matches with the business and operation requirements.
  - Audit user activities to verify whether users are doing what they are supposed to do.
  - Revoke permissions in the event of a suspicious act or permission misuse.
  - Perform periodic access audits and reviews to improve the PIM setup.

- **Protect on-premises privileged accounts**: In a hybrid environment, privileged access accounts also exist in on-premises systems. It is equally important to protect on-premises privilege accounts too. These accounts can include local administrators, domain administrators, enterprise administrators, storage administrators, and application administrators. The protection of on-premises privileged accounts requires quite a bit of planning and investment. You can use a Microsoft product such as **Microsoft Identity Manager** (**MIM**) or a third-party product such as Centrify to do this.

Implementation

I have already written several blog posts explaining how to configure Azure AD PIM. Please follow those to implement Azure AD PIM in your environments:

- *Step-by-Step Guide to Azure AD Privileged Identity Management – Part 1*: `http://www.rebeladmin.com/2016/07/step-step-guide-azure-ad-privileged-identity-management-part-1/`
- *Step-By-Step guide to Azure AD Privileged Identity Management – Part 2*: `http://www.rebeladmin.com/2016/08/step-step-guide-azure-ad-privileged-identity-management-part-2/`
- *Step-By-Step guide to set up temporally privileged access using Azure AD Privileged Identity Management*: `http://www.rebeladmin.com/2018/09/step-step-guide-setup-temporally-privilege-access-using-azure-ad-privileged-identity-management/`
- *Step-By-Step guide: Privileged access management in Office 365*: `http://www.rebeladmin.com/2019/04/step-step-guide-privileged-access-management-office-365/`

AIP

So far in this chapter, we have talked about protecting identities. While this is the most valuable thing in the infrastructure, it is not the only valuable thing. In `Chapter 1`, *Active Directory Fundamentals*, we looked at how data is becoming the new oil. Some data types have a higher value than others, and these high-value data types are confidential/sensitive for a person, group, company, organization, or country. Adversaries are after identities because compromised identity infrastructure allows them to access different types of data. Identity and access permissions decide what sort of data a person should have access to.

As an example, a director of a company has more access to confidential data about the company than a receptionist does. The protection of sensitive/confidential data not only depends on the protection of identity infrastructure, but it also depends on people.

Rebeladmin Inc. is a managed service provider. It has a sales team with 10 representatives. Das is a member of the sales team. Everyone in the sales team has access to a file share. Access to the file share is managed via NTFS permissions. There is an Excel file in the file share, which contains records of every potential *sales lead* the team is working on. Just like all other team members, Das also has access to it. Data in this Excel file is very sensitive for business. One of Das' friends is also working for a managed service provider, and Das wants to share this file with his friend. As he has access to the file, nothing is going to prevent him from emailing it to his friend or copying it to a USB drive. In this example, Das doesn't have any privileged access as he is not an IT administrator. He didn't have to hack into someone else's account or system to get this data. In this context, he was able to do huge damage to the company. So how we can protect sensitive data?

AIP is a cloud-based solution that helps to identify and protect sensitive data in a cloud or hybrid environment. AIP uses *labels* to classify data. Once data has been classified, we can control the flow using policies.

Data classification

Before we protect data, we need to understand what sort of data we need to protect and where it is located. AIP uses *labels* to classify data.

My daughter Salena is in Year 2 now. She loves to read. From time to time, I take her to the library to pick up books for her. When she selects books, she mostly looks at the title of the book and the *label* on it. This *label* is nothing but a color code. This color code references Oxford reading levels. Each level has its own color:

Age 4–5	Age 5–6	Age 6 – 7
		Reading at school
		School Year: 2
Reading at school	**Reading at school**	Band: Turquoise	Level: 7
School Year: Reception	School Year: 1	Band: Purple	Level: 8
Band: Lilac	Level: 1	Band: Blue	Level: 4	Band: Gold	Level: 9
Band: Pink	Level: 1+	Band: Green	Level: 5	Band: White	Level: 10
Band: Red	Level: 2	Band: Orange	Level: 6	Band: Lime	Level: 11
Band: Yellow	Level: 3		
Reading at home	**Reading at home**	**Reading at home**
Read with Oxford: Stage 2	*Read with Oxford:* Stage 3 & Stage 4	*Read with Oxford:* Stage 4, Stage 5 & Stage 6
eBook library: eBooks for 4–5 year olds	eBook library: eBooks for 5–6 year olds	eBook library: eBooks for 6–7 year olds

She knows her level and the color code for it. So without going through the content, she can easily find the books that match her reading level. In addition, the children's section of the library is a bit messy, since kids do not return books to the correct shelves. However, even when these books are on the wrong shelves, thanks to the labels, she can still recognize the right books. Data classifications and labels in AIP work in a similar way. In AIP, we can create labels and use them to categorize/group data. Once labels are created, we can apply them to data using manual or automatic methods. In manual methods, we have to go to the document and label it according to the relevant classification:

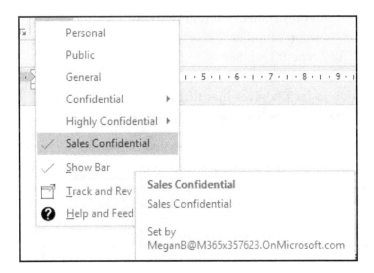

When it comes to the automatic method, AIP allows us to perform classification based on custom conditions or predefined information types, such as the following:

- Canadian Bank Account Number
- Canadian Driver's License Number
- Canadian Health Service Number
- Canadian Passport Number
- Canadian **Personal Health Identification Number** (PHIN)
- Canadian Social Insurance Number
- Chilean Identity Card Number
- Chinese Resident Identity Card Number
- Credit Card Number
- EU Debit Card Number
- EU Driver's License Number
- EU National Identification Number
- EU Passport Number
- EU Social Security Number or Equivalent ID
- EU Tax Identification Number
- UK Driver's License Number
- UK Electoral Roll Number
- UK National Health Service Number
- UK **National Insurance Number** (NINO)
- US/UK Passport Number
- US Bank Account Number
- US Driver's License Number
- US **Individual Taxpayer Identification Number** (ITIN)
- US **Social Security Number** (SSN)

The following example shows how the automated classification rule labels documents based on their content:

I have already written few blog posts about classification. You can access them by using the following links:

- *Step-by-Step Guide: Protect confidential data using AIP*: `http://www.rebeladmin.com/2018/12/step-step-guide-protect-confidential-data-using-azure-information-protection/`
- *Step-by-Step Guide: Automatic Data Classification via AIP*: `http://www.rebeladmin.com/2018/12/step-step-guide-automatic-data-classification-via-azure-information-protection/`

Azure Rights Management Services (Azure RMS)

AIP uses Azure RMS as its protection technology. Azure RMS is a cloud-based service that uses identity, encryption, and authorization policies to protect sensitive data across different types of devices (such as PC, laptop, tablet, and mobile). It can protect data once it leaves the company premises as well, and it can protect data stored in the cloud as well as on-premises.

Azure RMS is capable of the following:

- **Support Office 365 and on-premises services through connectors**: Azure RMS works seamlessly with Office 365. It can also protect data on on-premises services such as Exchange Server, SharePoint, and Windows server. This works through the connectors.
- **Support a wide range of devices**: This is not a Windows-only service. It works with Windows PC and laptops, Windows phones, macOS computers, iOS devices, and Android devices.
- **Support many security standards and compliances**: Azure RMS supports the following security standards:
    - FIPS 140-2
    - ISO/IEC 27001:2013
    - SOC 2 SSAE 16/ISAE 3402 attestations
    - HIPAA BAA
    - EU Model Clause
    - FedRAMP as part of Azure AD in Office 365 certification, issued FedRAMP Agency Authority to Operate by HHS
    - PCI DSS Level 1

- **No boundaries**: Once protection is applied, it doesn't matter where the file is going to be. It may be in an on-premises server or being used in a completely remote network where the IT team doesn't have control. Either way, protection always stays with the file.
- **Track data**: Azure RMS allows us to monitor the access and usage of protected data even if it is in a completely remote network. By using Azure RMS, we can answer the following questions:
    - Who tried to access the file and when?
    - Were preferred users able to access the file? If so, when?
    - Did preferred users fail to access the file?
    - Were preferred users trying to do anything they were not allowed to do (such as trying to print a document or trying to forward email)?
    - Were any unauthorized persons trying to access data?

If there is any suspicious activity, we can also revoke the permissions remotely.

- **Support a wide range of applications**: By using the AIP client, we can protect different types of data using different types of applications. Azure RMS can protect the following:
    - Any Office files (`.doc`, `.docx`, `.xls`)
    - Generate PDF files via any of the supported applications such as Acrobat Reader, IP Viewer, Foxit Reader, and AIP applications
    - PDF files via any of the following supported applications

Apart from that, AIP SDKs allow people to build their own apps with Azure RMS support.

Azure RMS versus AD RMS

In `Chapter 14`, *Active Directory Rights Management Services*, we learned about AD RMS, so, you may already be thinking about why we can't use AD RMS for data protection as it does almost the same thing. However, there are some significant differences between these two services:

- **By default, it can work with any device and in any network**: Azure RMS is a cloud-based service. It also a managed service. It doesn't need any additional configuration changes to get it working with mobile devices.

By default, it supports different OSes such as Windows, iOS, and Android. AD RMS requires a mobile extension and ADFS to support mobile devices. Also, AD RMS requires additional configurations to support the protection of external data. For Azure RMS, it doesn't matter where the data is. It doesn't need any additional configuration or components to protect data in external networks.

- **Data classification**: Azure RMS helps with classifying data by using labels. It can be a manual classification or an automatic classification process. It helps organizations to protect sensitive data in an effective manner. AD RMS cannot perform data classification and labeling.
- **Implementation**: The AD RMS role can't work on its own. It is dependent on many different server roles, such as ADFS, IIS, AD CS, and AD DS. Therefore, implementation requires planning, skills, and resources. After implementation, all these different roles need to work together to maintain the health of the AD RMS service. On the other hand, Azure RMS is a managed service. We do not need to worry about the underlying architecture or service components. The implementation process is also not complex. It can handle any growth at any time, without any configuration changes.
- **Document tracking and permission revocation**: Using Azure RMS, we can track documents and see when they were accessed, from where they were accessed, and who accessed them. We also can set up email notifications so that when someone accesses the file, we will get an email notification. With document tracking, if we notice anything suspicious, we can go ahead and revoke the access permissions of the suspicious party/parties. AD RMS can't do this. I have written a blog post explaining how we can track documents and revoke access, which you can access via `http://www.rebeladmin.com/2019/01/step-step-guide-track-shared-documents-using-azure-information-protection/`.
- **New features and bug fixes**: Azure RMS is a cloud-based managed service. Therefore, it will have new features, bug fixes, and feature enhancements more frequently. As of writing this, there is no planned feature update for AD RMS.

How does Azure RMS work?

So far, we have talked about AIP and Azure RMS's capabilities. But how do they work? What is the technology behind them? In this section, we are going to look into this in detail.

At a high level, I can explain the Azure RMS document protection process as follows:

- When a user protects a document, Azure RMS encrypts the content of the file and attaches an access policy to it. This policy decides what other users can do with the protected data.
- When other users access the file (after successful Azure AD authentication), Azure RMS decrypts the file and applies an access policy to it.

At a high level, it sounds simple, but let's go through this process in detail so we can learn about the technology behind it.

The best way to understand the technology behind the encryption and decryption process is to go through a scenario. **Andrew**, a Rebeladmin Inc. employee, is sending a document with sensitive data to another employee, **Selena**. He does not want anyone else in the sales team to have it, so he is going to use AIP to protect the document. This is the first time that both users are using this solution:

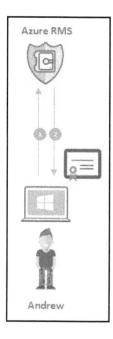

Since this is the first time that **Andrew** and **Selena** are using this AIP, they both need to go through the one-time user environment preparation process:

1. First, **Andrew** installs the AIP client on his PC. This can be downloaded via `https://www.microsoft.com/en-gb/download/details.aspx?id=53018`.

2. Then, he authenticates into the AIP using his Azure AD Account. After successful authentication, the session is redirected to the AIP tenant. Then, it issues a certificate that **Andrew** will use to authenticate into **Azure RMS** in the future. This certificate will be automatically renewed by the AIP client after 31 days. A copy of this certificate is also stored in Azure. If the user changes the device, then **Azure RMS** recreates the certificate using the same keys:

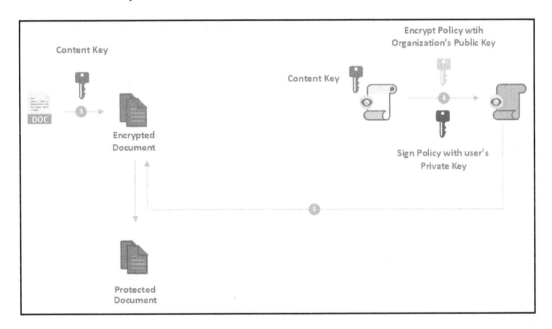

Now, the user environment preparation process is done. The next step is to protect the Word document.

3. **Andrew** goes ahead and requests for the AIP client to protect the document. The AIP client creates a random AES key and encrypts the document content using it. This key is called the **Content Key** and it uses the AES symmetric encryption algorithm. The key length is 128 bits or 256 bits.

4. Then, the AIP client creates a policy that contains the access rights for the recipient **Selena**. This can be done using a policy template, which has already been created by an administrator; otherwise, the user can create an adhoc policy. Once the policy is in place, the system will encrypt the policy and the symmetric content key by using the organization's public key. This key was retrieved by the AIP client during the initial user environment preparation process. Then, the policy and the content key are signed by **Andrew**'s certificate, which was obtained during the same preparation process.

5. In this next step, the AIP client creates a **Protected Document** that includes the encrypted document and the policy that has already been encrypted and signed.

Once the system has created the **Protected Document**, **Andrew** sends it to **Selena** via email:

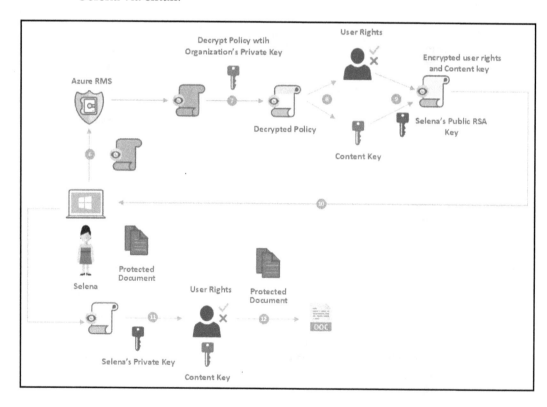

Once **Selena** receives the **Protected Document**, she tries to open it. As this is the first time she has tried to open the **Protected Document**, she needs to complete the user environment preparation process before she can start using AIP.

6. After **Selena** authenticates successfully, the system retrieves the policy and **Andrew**'s certificate from the **Protected Document** and then forwards it to **Azure RMS**.

7. The service decrypts the policy using the **Organization's Public Key**.

8. The **Decrypted Policy** contains **Selena**'s User Rights and **Content Key**. The system evaluates the permissions in order to understand the rights associated with the document.

9. In this step, the **Content Key** re-encrypts using **Selena**'s public RSA key. Then, it is attached to user rights.

10. In this step, the files created in *steps 8* and *9* are delivered to **Selena**'s computer.

11. The AIP client decrypts the **User Key** and the **Content Key** using **Selena's Private Key**, which was retrieved via the initial user environment preparation process. This process reveals the **User Rights** list and the **Content Key**.

12. With the help of the **Content Key**, the AIP client decrypts the encrypted document. The AIP client also passes the right list to the application and application decides what **Selena** can do with the document.

This completes the decryption process and in the end, **Selena** was able to open the **Protected Document**. The previous scenario shows us exactly what is happening behind the scenes when we protect and consume sensitive data using **Azure RMS**.

AIP scanner

In a hybrid cloud environment, data is also saved in on-premises servers. Mostly, it is saved in Windows file shares. Data can also be available in on-premises SharePoint servers. The AIP scanner allows us to discover and apply the same labels defined in AIP policies to data saved in on-premises file shares or SharePoint servers:

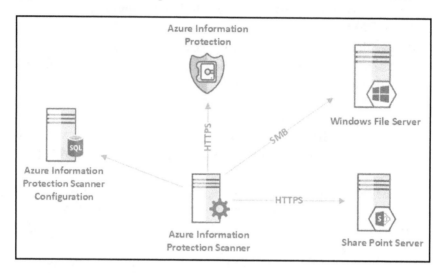

The AIP scanner comes as part of the AIP client. It can be downloaded using `https:/ /www.microsoft.com/en-gb/download/details.aspx?id=53018`. The AIP scanner uses an SQL database to store the scanner configuration. AIP scanner checks with the AIP tenant to protect the same types of files.

The AIP scanner can automatically discover and classify the data in a selected data repository or run in it in discovery mode and report back the findings. Data classification via the AIP scanner is not performed in real time, so you need to decide on how often you want to run the scanner.

 I have written a step-by-step guide that explains the implementation steps of the AIP scanner. You can access it using `http://www. rebeladmin.com/2018/12/step-step-guide-premise-data- protection-via-azure-information-protection-scanner/`.

AIP implementation

AIP implementation is a vast topic that is beyond the scope of this chapter. I have written a series of blog posts covering the implementation of AIP, which you can access by using the following links:

- *Step-by-Step Guide: Protect confidential data using Azure Information Protection,* available at `http://www.rebeladmin.com/2018/12/step-step-guide-protect-confidential-data-using-azure-information-protection/`
- *Step-by-Step Guide: Automatic Data Classification via Azure Information Protection,* available at `http://www.rebeladmin.com/2018/12/step-step-guide-automatic-data-classification-via-azure-information-protection/`
- *Step-by-Step Guide: On-premise Data Protection via Azure Information Protection Scanner*: `http://www.rebeladmin.com/2018/12/step-step-guide-premise-data-protection-via-azure-information-protection-scanner/`
- *Step-by-Step Guide: How to protect confidential emails using Azure Information Protection?*: `http://www.rebeladmin.com/2019/01/step-step-guide-protect-confidential-emails-using-azure-information-protection/`
- *Step-by-Step Guide: How to track shared documents using Azure Information Protection?*: `http://www.rebeladmin.com/2019/01/step-step-guide-track-shared-documents-using-azure-information-protection/`

Summary

AD infrastructure security is a broad topic to cover in one chapter. AD security is not just dependent on AD DS; it is related to every layer of the OSI 7-layer model. At the beginning of the chapter, we learned about Kerberos authentication and what exactly happens behind the scenes when a user tries to access a resource in the AD environment. Then, we moved on to delegated permission control, where we learned about how we can delegate permissions to users, allowing them to only do specific administrative tasks. After that, we moved on to *Pass-the-hash attacks* section, where we learned about pass-the-hash attacks.

Microsoft has introduced new tools and features that can be used to prevent pass-the-hash attacks. The Protected User security group, restricted RDP mode, authentication policies, and authentication policy silos are some of them. In this chapter, we learned about how these tools work and how we can implement them in the AD environment. Then, we moved on to JIT administration and JEA. Both of these technologies can be used to manage privileges in an effective and secure manner.

After that, we learned about how we can protect privileged identities in hybrid or cloud-only environments using Azure AD PIM. In an infrastructure, while identity is the most valuable entity, it is not the only valuable entity. We also need to protect sensitive data in an infrastructure. In the *AIP* section, we also learned about how AIP can be used to protect sensitive data in a hybrid environment.

In the next chapter, we will look into AD management with PowerShell. JEA implementation will also be covered as a part of it.

16
Advanced AD Management with PowerShell

The very first **Active Directory** (**AD**) instance I set up was based on Windows Server 2003. It was a completely different approach from today's AD installations. In Windows Server 2003, there were a lot of prerequisite tasks, such as installing a DNS role, setting up DNS zones, and adding the domain prefix. Even those tasks were directly related to **Active Directory Domain Services** (**AD DS**), and I had to configure them separately prior to running the DCPORMO.exe command. But today, the AD installation process is very straightforward. With basic knowledge and resources, anyone can get the domain controller installed with a few clicks. Microsoft has made server role installations and configurations easy over the years, not just AD DS. The main reason behind all these enhancements was to save time for engineers. Installations, configurations, and repetitive infrastructure tasks take up the majority of an engineer's time. In order to save time on repetitive administrative tasks, people started looking at automation technologies. In times gone by, we used DOS commands, VBScript, and batch files to automate administrative tasks. But there were problems with that. Applications, server roles, and services had limitations on working with these automation technologies. Not every function available in the GUI supported the use of commands or scripts. This lack of support and lack of flexibility was holding engineers back from automating tasks.

To bring automation to the next level, Microsoft promised to release a more flexible, more powerful, more integrated scripting language. PowerShell 1.0 was the answer and it was available to the public from November 2006. During the last decade, there have been a few versions released and it's now at version 5.1 (mainstream). Microsoft also released a separate version of PowerShell called PowerShell Core 6.0 (January 10, 2018). With PowerShell Core, working with macOS and Linux is now supported. As with any other server role, AD DS also fully supports being managed via PowerShell. From the beginning of this book, I have used PowerShell to install, configure, and manage AD DS roles. In this chapter, I will explain how we can use PowerShell to further improve AD DS environment management.

We are also going to look at managing identities in a hybrid environment using Azure AD PowerShell.

The cmdlets and scripts used in this chapter were written and tested in an environment that has the following:

- Windows Server 2016
- An AD domain and forest functional level set to Windows Server 2016
- PowerShell 5.1
- Azure AD Premium P2

Some of these are not supported in an environment that has an older domain, PowerShell version, and forest functional levels.

In this chapter, we will cover the following topics:

- PowerShell scripts and commands that can be used to manage AD objects
- PowerShell scripts and commands that can be used to manage and troubleshoot AD replication
- PowerShell scripts and commands that can be used to manage identities in a hybrid environment using the Azure AD PowerShell module
- An implementation and configuration guide for **Just Enough Administration (JEA)**

AD management with PowerShell – preparation

A PowerShell module includes assemblies, scripts, and functionalities. In order to use the functionalities, we need to import the module. After that, we can call for the contents of the module to manage relevant server roles, services, or features. Before we start AD management with PowerShell, first we need to import the `ActiveDirectory` module.

There are a few ways to do this. These include installing the AD DS server role or by installing **Remote Server Administration Tools (RSAT)**:

- **AD DS server role**:
    1. If we install the AD DS server role using Server Manager, **Active Directory module for Windows PowerShell** is installed as a feature:

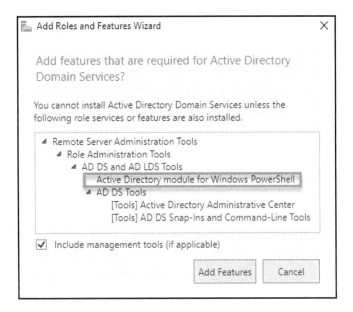

    2. If the AD DS role is installed using PowerShell, we need to include the management tools by using –IncludeManagementTools. Otherwise, by default, it will not install the module:

```
Install-WindowsFeature -Name AD-Domain-Services
-IncludeManagementTools
```

- **Remote Server Administration Tools**:

    1. Even if the server doesn't have the AD DS role installed, the existing domain environment can be managed using the AD DS PowerShell module. The AD PowerShell module is included with RSAT and can be installed using Server Manager or PowerShell.

2. On Server Manager, it can be found by navigating to **Features |
Remote Server Administration Tools | Role Administration
Tools | AD DS and AD LDS Tools | Active Directory module
for PowerShell**, as shown in the following screenshot:

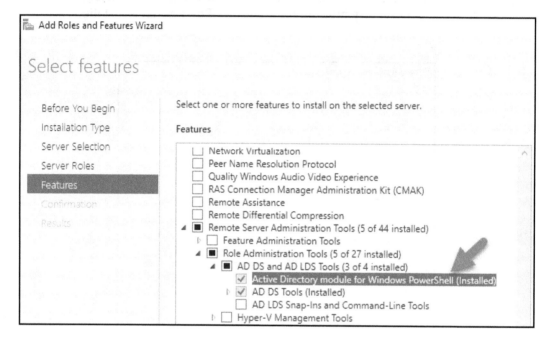

3. It can also be installed using PowerShell:

```
Add-WindowsFeature RSAT-AD-PowerShell
```

 It is also possible to install RSAT on the Windows desktop OS. As an
example, RSAT for Windows 10 can be downloaded from `https://
www.microsoft.com/en-gb/download/details.aspx?id=45520`.

Once the AD DS module is installed, we can list all the commands available under the
module using the following command:

```
Get-Command -Module ActiveDirectory
```

There are about 147 commands under the module. The complete syntax for any
command can be viewed using this command:

```
Get-Command commandname -Syntax
```

As an example, the following command will list the syntax for the `New-ADUser` command:

```
Get-Command New-ADUser -Syntax
```

The following screenshot shows the output for the preceding command:

```
PS C:\Users\Administrator> Get-Command New-ADUser -Syntax

New-ADUser [-Name] <string> [-WhatIf] [-Confirm] [-AccountExpirationDate <datetime>] [-AccountNotDelegated <bool>] [-AccountPassword <securestr
ing>] [-AllowReversiblePasswordEncryption <bool>] [-AuthenticationPolicy <ADAuthenticationPolicy>] [-AuthenticationPolicySilo <ADAuthentication
PolicySilo>] [-AuthType <ADAuthType>] [-CannotChangePassword <bool>] [-Certificates <X509Certificate[]>] [-ChangePasswordAtLogon <bool>] [-City
<string>] [-Company <string>] [-CompoundIdentitySupported <bool>] [-Country <string>] [-Credential <pscredential>] [-Department <string>] [-De
scription <string>] [-DisplayName <string>] [-Division <string>] [-EmailAddress <string>] [-EmployeeID <string>] [-EmployeeNumber <string>] [-E
nabled <bool>] [-Fax <string>] [-GivenName <string>] [-HomeDirectory <string>] [-HomeDrive <string>] [-HomePage <string>] [-HomePhone <string>]
[-Initials <string>] [-Instance <ADUser>] [-KerberosEncryptionType <ADKerberosEncryptionType>] [-LogonWorkstations <string>] [-Manager <ADUser
>] [-MobilePhone <string>] [-Office <string>] [-OfficePhone <string>] [-Organization <string>] [-OtherAttributes <hashtable>] [-OtherName <stri
ng>] [-PassThru] [-PasswordNeverExpires <bool>] [-PasswordNotRequired <bool>] [-Path <string>] [-POBox <string>] [-PostalCode <string>] [-Princ
ipalsAllowedToDelegateToAccount <ADPrincipal[]>] [-ProfilePath <string>] [-SamAccountName <string>] [-ScriptPath <string>] [-Server <string>] [
-ServicePrincipalNames <string[]>] [-SmartcardLogonRequired <bool>] [-State <string>] [-StreetAddress <string>] [-Surname <string>] [-Title <st
ring>] [-TrustedForDelegation <bool>] [-Type <string>] [-UserPrincipalName <string>] [<CommonParameters>]
```

The `Get-Help` command provides help for any command. As an example, the following command provides help for the `New-ADUser` command:

```
Get-Help New-ADUser
```

The following screenshot shows the output for the preceding command:

```
PS C:\Users\Administrator> Get-Help New-ADUser

NAME
    New-ADUser

SYNOPSIS
    Creates a new Active Directory user.

SYNTAX
    New-ADUser [-Name] <String> [-AccountExpirationDate <DateTime>] [-AccountNotDelegated <Boolean>] [-AccountPassword <SecureString>]
    [-AllowReversiblePasswordEncryption <Boolean>] [-AuthenticationPolicy <ADAuthenticationPolicy>] [-AuthenticationPolicySilo
    <ADAuthenticationPolicySilo>] [-AuthType {Negotiate | Basic}] [-CannotChangePassword <Boolean>] [-Certificates <X509Certificate[]>]
    [-ChangePasswordAtLogon <Boolean>] [-City <String>] [-Company <String>] [-CompoundIdentitySupported <Boolean>] [-Country <String>]
    [-Credential <PSCredential>] [-Department <String>] [-Description <String>] [-DisplayName <String>] [-Division <String>] [-EmailAddress
    <String>] [-EmployeeID <String>] [-EmployeeNumber <String>] [-Enabled <Boolean>] [-Fax <String>] [-GivenName <String>] [-HomeDirectory
    <String>] [-HomeDrive <String>] [-HomePage <String>] [-HomePhone <String>] [-Initials <String>] [-Instance <ADUser>]
    [-KerberosEncryptionType {None | DES | RC4 | AES128 | AES256}] [-LogonWorkstations <String>] [-Manager <ADUser>] [-MobilePhone <String>]
    [-Office <String>] [-OfficePhone <String>] [-Organization <String>] [-OtherAttributes <Hashtable>] [-OtherName <String>] [-PassThru]
    [-PasswordNeverExpires <Boolean>] [-PasswordNotRequired <Boolean>] [-Path <String>] [-POBox <String>] [-PostalCode <String>]
    [-PrincipalsAllowedToDelegateToAccount <ADPrincipal[]>] [-ProfilePath <String>] [-SamAccountName <String>] [-ScriptPath <String>]
    [-Server <String>] [-ServicePrincipalNames <String[]>] [-SmartcardLogonRequired <Boolean>] [-State <String>] [-StreetAddress <String>]
    [-Surname <String>] [-Title <String>] [-TrustedForDelegation <Boolean>] [-Type <String>] [-UserPrincipalName <String>] [-Confirm]
    [-WhatIf] [<CommonParameters>]

DESCRIPTION
    The New-ADUser cmdlet creates a new Active Directory user. You can set commonly used user property values by using the cmdlet parameters.

    Property values that are not associated with cmdlet parameters can be set by using the OtherAttributes parameter. When using this
    parameter be sure to place single quotes around the attribute name as in the following example.

    New-ADUser -SamAccountName "glenjohn" -GivenName "Glen" -Surname "John" -DisplayName "Glen John" -Path 'CN=Users,DC=fabrikam,DC=local'
    -OtherAttributes @{'msDS-PhoneticDisplayName'="GlenJohn"}

    You must specify the SAMAccountName parameter to create a user.

    You can use the New-ADUser cmdlet to create different types of user accounts such as iNetOrgPerson accounts. To do this in AD DS, set the
    Type parameter to the LDAP display name for the type of account you want to create. This type can be any class in the Active Directory
    schema that is a subclass of user and that has an object category of person.

    The Path parameter specifies the container or organizational unit (OU) for the new user. When you do not specify the Path parameter, the
    cmdlet creates a user object in the default container for user objects in the domain.

    The following methods explain different ways to create an object by using this cmdlet.

    Method 1: Use the New-ADUser cmdlet, specify the required parameters, and set any additional property values by using the cmdlet
    parameters.
```

We also can view an example for the `New-ADUser` command using this:

```
Get-Help New-ADUser -Example
```

The following screenshot shows the output for the preceding command:

```
PS C:\Users\Administrator> Get-Help New-ADUser -Example

NAME
    New-ADUser

SYNOPSIS
    Creates a new Active Directory user.

    ------------------------ EXAMPLE 1 ------------------------

    C:\PS>New-ADUser GlenJohn -Certificate (new-object System.Security.Cryptography.X509Certificates.X509Certificate -ArgumentList
    "export.cer")

    Description
    -----------

    Create a new user named 'GlenJohn' with a certicate imported from the file "export.cer".
    ------------------------ EXAMPLE 2 ------------------------

    C:\PS>New-ADUser GlenJohn -OtherAttributes @{title="director";mail="glenjohn@fabrikam.com"}

    Description
    -----------

    Create a new user named 'GlenJohn' and set the title and mail properties on the new object.
    ------------------------ EXAMPLE 3 ------------------------

    C:\PS>New-ADUser GlenJohn -Type iNetOrgPerson -Path "DC=AppNC" -server lds.Fabrikam.com:50000

    Description
    -----------

    Create a new inetOrgPerson named 'GlenJohn' on an AD LDS instance.
```

More information on the command can be viewed using this:

```
Get-Help New-ADUser -Detailed
```

Technical information on the command can be viewed using the following:

```
Get-Help New-ADUser -Full
```

Online information about the command can be viewed using this:

```
Get-Help New-ADUser -Online
```

In this section, we learned how to install the Active Directory module for PowerShell. We also learned about the basic functions of the module. Now, let's move on and further explore the Active Directory management capabilities of the module.

AD management commands and scripts

The module has 147 commands, and they can be used in countless different ways to manage the AD environment. In this section, we will look at the capabilities of these commands and see how we can use them to improve AD management.

I'd like to start this section by explaining how we can review the existing configuration of an AD environment. The quick way to review the directory server configuration and capabilities is to use the following command:

```
Get-ADRootDSE
```

This command provides important information, such as forest and domain functional levels, the default naming context, the current time, and the currently logged-in domain controller:

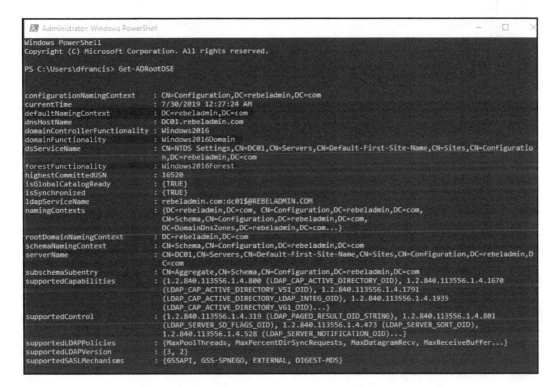

The next step is to find the domain controllers in the domain. We can use the following to list the domain controller name, the IP address, the status of the global catalog server, and the **Flexible Single Master Operation (FSMO)** roles:

```
Get-ADDomainController -Filter * | Select-Object
Name,IPv4Address,IsGlobalCatalog,OperationMasterRoles
```

It is also important to know about the AD site as it explains the physical topology of the AD:

```
Get-ADDomainController -Filter * | Select-Object Name,IPv4Address,Site
```

An AD forest can have multiple domains. The following commands will list the forest names, the domain name, the domain controller, the IP address, and the AD site:

```
$Forestwide = (Get-ADForest).Domains | %{ Get-ADDomainController -
Filter * -Server $_ }
write-output $Forestwide -Filter * | Select-Object
Name,Forest,Domain,IPv4Address,Site
```

If we know the domain name, we can list the domain controllers and **read-only domain controller (RODC)** using the following command:

```
$Domain = Read-Host 'What is your Domain Name ?'
Get-ADDomain -Identity $Domain | select
ReplicaDirectoryServers,ReadOnlyReplicaDirectoryServer
```

With this command, the system will ask the user to input the domain name. Once the user replies, it lists the domain controllers.

In the preceding command, `ReplicaDirectoryServers` represents the read and write domain controllers, and `ReadOnlyReplicaDirectoryServer` represents the read-only domain controllers.

Replication

Data replication is crucial for a healthy AD environment. For a given domain controller, we can find its inbound replication partners using this:

```
Get-ADReplicationPartnerMetadata -Target REBEL-SRV01.rebeladmin.com
```

The preceding command provides a detailed description of the replication health of the given domain controller, including the last successful replication, replication partition, server, and so on.

We can list all the inbound replication partners for the given domain using the following command:

```
Get-ADReplicationPartnerMetadata -Target "rebeladmin.com" -Scope
Domain
```

In the preceding command, the scope is defined as the domain. This can be changed to the forest to get a list of the inbound partners in the forest. The output is based on the default partition. If needed, the partition can be changed using –Partition to configuration or schema partition. It will list the relevant inbound partners for the selected partition.

The associated replication failures for a site, forest, domain, and domain controller can be found using the Get-ADReplicationFailure cmdlet:

```
Get-ADReplicationFailure -Target REBEL-SRV01.rebeladmin.com
```

The preceding command will list the replication failures for the given domain controller.

Replication failures for the domain can be found using this:

```
Get-ADReplicationFailure -Target rebeladmin.com -Scope Domain
```

Replication failures for the forest can be found using the following command:

```
Get-ADReplicationFailure -Target rebeladmin.com -Scope Forest
```

Replication failures for the site can be found using the following command:

```
Get-ADReplicationFailure -Target LondonSite -Scope Site
```

In the preceding command, LondonSite can be replaced with a relevant site name.

Using both Get-ADReplicationPartnerMetadata and Get-ADReplicationFailure, I have created the following PowerShell script to generate a replication health report against a specific domain controller.

The first part of the script is used to define the objects that we'll use throughout the script:

```
## Active Directory Domain Controller Replication Status##
$domaincontroller = Read-Host 'What is your Domain Controller?'
## Define Objects ##
$report = New-Object PSObject -Property @{
ReplicationPartners = $null
LastReplication = $null
```

```
FailureCount = $null
FailureType = $null
FirstFailure = $null
}
```

In the preceding script, I have given an option for the engineer to specify the name of the domain controller:

$domaincontroller = Read-Host 'What is your Domain Controller?'

In the next part of the script, I am collecting the following data, which describes the replication connection status with the other domain controllers:

- Replication partner (ReplicationPartners)
- Last successful replication (LastReplication)

```
## Replication Partners ##
$report.ReplicationPartners = (Get-
ADReplicationPartnerMetadata -Target
$domaincontroller).Partner
$report.LastReplication = (Get-ADReplicationPartnerMetadata -
Target $domaincontroller).LastReplicationSuccess
```

Then, I also gather the following data, which helps engineers to troubleshoot replication issues, if any exist:

- AD replication failure count (FailureCount)
- AD replication failure type (FailureType)
- AD replication failure first recorded time (FirstFailure)

```
## Replication Faliures ~##
$report.FailureCount = (Get-ADReplicationFailure -Target
$domaincontroller).FailureCount
$report.FailureType = (Get-ADReplicationFailure -Target
$domaincontroller).FailureType
$report.FirstFailure = (Get-ADReplicationFailure -Target
$domaincontroller).FirstFailureTime
```

The last part of the script formats the output of the collected data:

```
## Format Output ##
$report | select
ReplicationPartners,LastReplication,FirstFailure,FailureCount,FailureT
ype | Out-GridView
```

Following screenshot shows the output of the preceding script.

 The aforementioned script is displayed in an easy way for readers to understand. When it is used in PowerShell, make sure to prevent extra line spaces.

Further to AD replication topologies, there are two types of replication:

- **Intra-site**: Replication between domain controllers in the same AD site
- **Inter-site**: Replication between domain controllers in different AD sites

We can review AD replication site objects using the `Get-ADReplicationSite` cmdlet. The following command returns all the AD replication sites in the AD forest:

```
Get-ADReplicationSite -Filter *
```

We can review AD replication site links on the AD forest using the following command:

```
Get-ADReplicationSiteLink -Filter *
```

In site links, the most important information is to know the site cost and the replication schedule. This allows us to understand the replication topology and expected delays in replication.

The following command lists all the replication site links, which includes the `CanadaSite` along with the site link name, link cost, and replication frequency:

```
Get-ADReplicationSiteLink -Filter {SitesIncluded -eq "CanadaSite"} |
Format-Table Name,Cost,ReplicationFrequencyInMinutes -AutoSize
```

A site link bridge can be used to bundle two or more site links and enable transitivity between site links.

Site link bridge information can be retrieved using the following command:

```
Get-ADReplicationSiteLinkBridge -Filter *
```

An AD sites uses multiple IP subnets that are assigned to sites for its operations. It is important to associate these subnets with AD sites so that domain controllers know which computer is located at which site.

The following command will list all the subnets in the forest in a table with the subnet name and AD site:

```
Get-ADReplicationSubnet -Filter * | Format-Table Name,Site -AutoSize
```

Bridgehead servers operate as the primary communication point to handle the replication data that comes in and goes out of the AD site.

We can list all the preferred bridgehead servers in a domain:

```
$BHservers = ([adsi]"LDAP://CN=IP,CN=Inter-Site
Transports,CN=Sites,CN=Configuration,DC=rebeladmin,DC=com").bridgehead
ServerListBL
$BHservers | Out-GridView
```

In the preceding command, the `bridgeheadServerListBL` attribute value is retrieved via the ADSI connection.

Information about the replication topology helps engineers in many ways, especially if engineers are troubleshooting Active Directory replication issues or performing an Active Directory audit. By using the preceding commands, I have created the following script to gather Active Directory replication topology data in one go.

As usual, the first part of the script is dedicated to defining objects:

```
## Script to gather information about Replication Topology ##
## Define Objects ##
$replreport = New-Object PSObject -Property @{
Domain = $null
}
```

Before we move on to the replication, it is good to collect the Active Directory domain information. This is important if an organization is using multiple domains as we can easily separate the reports:

```
## Find Domain Information ##
$replreport.Domain = (Get-ADDomain).DNSroot
```

I have used the next section of the script to list the Active Directory sites:

```
## List down the AD sites in the Domain ##
$a = (Get-ADReplicationSite -Filter *)
Write-Host "########" $replreport.Domain "Domain AD Sites" "########"
$a | Format-Table Description,Name -AutoSize
```

Then, I am going to collect data about the Active Directory replication site link and the Active Directory replication site link bridge by using the following:

```
## List down Replication Site link Information ##
$b = (Get-ADReplicationSiteLink -Filter *)
Write-Host "########" $replreport.Domain "Domain AD Replication
SiteLink Information" "########"
$b | Format-Table Name,Cost,ReplicationFrequencyInMinutes -AutoSize
## List down SiteLink Bridge Information ##
$c = (Get-ADReplicationSiteLinkBridge -Filter *)
Write-Host "########" $replreport.Domain "Domain AD SiteLink Bridge
Information" "########"
$c | select Name,SiteLinksIncluded | Format-List
```

In a computer network, there can be multiple IP subnets. These subnets need to be assigned correctly to Active Directory sites. This way, Active Directory domain controller computers know which site they belong to. This also has a direct impact on Active Directory replication. In the next section, we are going to collect Active Directory subnet information and the preferred bridge head servers for the domain:

```
## List down Subnet Information ##
$d = (Get-ADReplicationSubnet -Filter * | select Name,Site)
Write-Host "########" $replreport.Domain "Domain Subnet Information"
"########"
$d | Format-Table Name,Site -AutoSize
## List down Prefered BridgeHead Servers ##
$e = ([adsi]"LDAP://CN=IP,CN=Inter-Site
Transports,CN=Sites,CN=Configuration,DC=rebeladmin,DC=com").bridgehead
ServerListBL
Write-Host "########" $replreport.Domain "Domain Prefered BridgeHead
Servers" "########"
$e
## End of the Script ##
```

 The aforementioned script is displayed in a way that's easy for readers to understand. When it is used in PowerShell, make sure to prevent extra line spaces.

In the preceding script, we need to replace the ADSI connection with the relevant domain DN:

```
$e = ([adsi]"LDAP://CN=IP,CN=Inter-Site
Transports,CN=Sites,CN=Configuration,DC=rebeladmin,DC=com")
```

Replicating a specific object

Once an object is added to a domain controller, it needs to be replicated to all other domain controllers. Otherwise, users will face issues during login using AD integrated applications and services. The replication is dependent on many different factors, such as the replication schedule and intra-site connectivity. Sometimes, however, we need to force the replication that is required to force replication between domain controllers:

```
## Replicate Object to From Domain Controller to Another ##
$myobject = Read-Host 'What is your AD Object Includes ?'
$sourcedc = Read-Host 'What is the Source DC ?'
$destinationdc = Read-Host 'What is the Destination DC ?'
$passobject = (Get-ADObject -Filter {Name -Like $myobject})
Sync-ADObject -object $passobject -source $sourcedc -destination
$destinationdc
Write-Host "Given Object Replicated to" $destinationdc
```

The preceding script will ask a few questions:

- **Name of object**: This need not be a **distinguished name** (DN). All that is needed is that text be included in the object name field.
- **Source DC**: The hostname of the source DC.
- **Destination DC**: The hostname of the destination DC.

Once the relevant information is provided, the object will be forcibly replicated:

```
PS C:\Windows\system32> ## Replicate Objects to Domain Controllers ##
$myobject = Read-Host 'What is your AD Object Includes ?'
$sourcedc = Read-Host 'What is the Source DC ?'
$destinationdc = Read-Host 'What is the Destination DC ?'
$passobject = (Get-ADObject -Filter {Name -Like $myobject})
Sync-ADObject -object $passobject -source $sourcedc -destination $destinationdc
Write-Host "Given Object Replicated to" $destinationdc
What is your AD Object Includes ?: Adam
What is the Source DC ?: REBEL-PDC-01
What is the Destination DC ?: REBEL-SRV01
Given Object Replicated to REBEL-SRV01

PS C:\Windows\system32>          What is your AD Object Includes ?: Adam
                                 What is your AD Object Includes ?: Adam
```

In this section of the chapter, we learned how the Active Directory module for PowerShell can be used to review the topology of an Active Directory environment. We also learned how we can audit, troubleshoot, and manage Active Directory replication using PowerShell. In the next section, we are going to look into Active Directory object management.

Users and Groups

In this section, let's look at PowerShell commands and scripts that we can use to manage AD users and groups.

Last logon time

On certain occasions, we are required to find when a user successfully logs on to a domain. This can be for audit purposes or for troubleshooting purposes:

```
$username = Read-Host 'What is the User account you looking for ?'
    $dcs = Get-ADDomainController -Filter {Name -like "*"}
        foreach($dc in $dcs)
    {
    $hostname = $dc.HostName
    $user = Get-ADUser $userName -Server $hostname -Properties
lastLogon
    $lngexpires = $user.lastLogon
    if (-not ($lngexpires)) {$lngexpires = 0 }
    If (($lngexpires -eq 0) -or ($lngexpires -gt
[DateTime]::MaxValue.Ticks))
    {
      $LastLogon = "User Never Logged In"
    }
     Else
    {
      $Date = [DateTime]$lngexpires
      $LastLogon = $Date.AddYears(1600).ToLocalTime()
    }
  }
  Write-Host $username "last logged on at:" $LastLogon
```

The preceding script will ask for the username of the account and, once it is provided, the system will search for the lastLogon attribute value on all available domain controllers. If it cannot be found, it will return User Never Logged In or, if found, it will return the last logon timestamp.

Last login date report

Periodic housekeeping in AD is required for integrity. There may be user objects that have not been used for years. If we can create a report along with the last login dates, we can use it as a reference to clean up objects:

```
## Script For Filter user with Last logon Time ##
$htmlformat = "<style>BODY{background-color:LightBlue;}</style>"
Get-ADUser -Filter * -Properties "LastLogonDate" | sort-object -
property lastlogondate -descending | Select-Object Name,LastLogonDate
| ConvertTo-HTML -head $htmlformat -body "<H2>AD Accounts Last Login
Date</H2>"| Out-File C:\lastlogon.html
Invoke-Expression C:\lastlogon.html
```

This script creates an HTML report that includes all the user accounts with their last logon date timestamps:

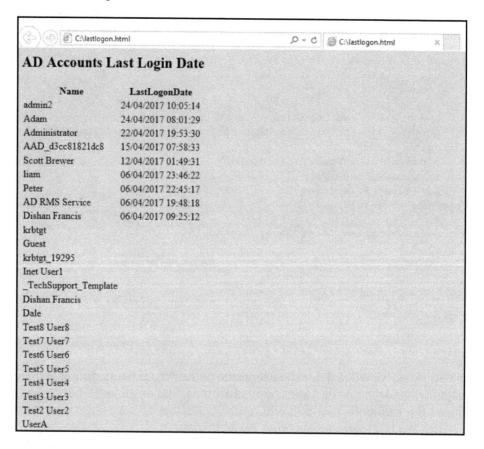

Login failures report

It is important to know about failed attempts to log in to the DC, not just the successful attempts. These can be a result of potentially malicious activity.

The following script will create a report to indicate the login failures on a given domain controller:

```
## Report for DC login Failures ##
$failedevent = $null
$Date= Get-date
$dc = Read-Host 'What is the Domain Controller ?'
$Report= "C:\auditreport.html"
$HTML=@"
<title>Failed Login Report for $dc</title>
<style>
BODY{background-color :LightBlue}
</style>
"@
 $failedevent = Get-Eventlog security -Computer $dc -InstanceId 4625 -
After (Get-Date).AddDays(-7) |
 Select TimeGenerated,ReplacementStrings |
 % {
 New-Object PSObject -Property @{
 SourceComputer = $_.ReplacementStrings[13]
 UserName = $_.ReplacementStrings[5]
 SourceIPAddress = $_.ReplacementStrings[19]
 Date = $_.TimeGenerated
 }
 }
 $failedevent | ConvertTo-Html -Property
SourceComputer,UserName,SourceIPAddress,Date -head $HTML -body
"<H2>Failed Login Report for $dc</H2>"|
 Out-File $Report
 Invoke-Expression C:\auditreport.html
```

The aforementioned script is displayed in a way that's easy for readers to understand. When it is used in PowerShell, make sure to prevent extra line spaces.

When you run the preceding script, it will ask for the name of the domain controller that you wish to run this report against. Then, in the background, it will search for event 4625 in the event viewer and then list the following data in a report:

- The source computer
- The username
- The source IP address
- The event time

The following screenshot shows the failed report for **REBEL-PDC-01**:

C:\auditreport.html   🔍 ▾ ℃   Failed Login Report for REB... ✕

Failed Login Report for REBEL-PDC-01

SourceComputer	UserName	SourceIPAddress	Date
REBEL-PDC-01	administrator	127.0.0.1	24/04/2017 10:54:01
REBEL-PDC-01	administrator	127.0.0.1	24/04/2017 08:25:42
REBEL-PDC-01	administrator	127.0.0.1	24/04/2017 07:57:15
-	REBEL-SRV01$	-	23/04/2017 14:02:29
-	REBEL-SRV01$	-	23/04/2017 13:34:50
-		-	23/04/2017 13:33:47
-	REBEL-SRV01$	192.168.0.131	23/04/2017 11:25:14
-		192.168.0.131	23/04/2017 09:55:37
REBEL-PDC-01	administrator	127.0.0.1	22/04/2017 20:24:35
REBEL-PDC-01	administrator	127.0.0.1	22/04/2017 19:53:26
REBEL-PDC-01	administrator	127.0.0.1	22/04/2017 18:05:24
REBEL-PDC-01	administrator	127.0.0.1	22/04/2017 13:17:39
REBEL-PDC-01	administrator	192.168.0.105	22/04/2017 11:10:22
REBEL-PDC-01	administrator	192.168.0.105	22/04/2017 11:08:22
REBEL-PDC-01	administrator	127.0.0.1	22/04/2017 11:07:39
REBEL-PDC-01	administrator	192.168.0.105	22/04/2017 11:06:21
REBEL-PDC-01	administrator	192.168.0.105	22/04/2017 11:04:21

Finding the locked-out account

If password policies are defined, accounts with a large number of login failures will be locked out. Locked-out accounts in an AD environment can be found using the following command:

```
Search-ADAccount -Lockedout | Select name,samAccountName,Lockedout
```

If any of those in the list need to be unlocked, we can use the `Unlock-ADAccount` cmdlet to unlock an account.

For an individual account, perform the following command:

```
Unlock-ADAccount tuser4
```

For all the accounts on the list, perform the following command:

```
Search-ADAccount -Lockedout | Unlock-ADAccount
```

Password expire report

Issues due to expired passwords are a common support call type for helpdesks. The following script can generate a report about expiring passwords:

```
## Password Expire Report ##
$passwordreport = $null
$dc = (Get-ADDomain | Select DNSRoot).DNSRoot
$Report= "C:\passwordreport.html"
$HTML=@"
<title>Password Expire Report For $dc</title>
<style>
BODY{background-color :LightBlue}
</style>
"@
$passwordreport = Get-ADUser -filter * -Properties
"SamAccountName","pwdLastSet","msDS-UserPasswordExpiryTimeComputed" |
Select-Object -Property "SamAccountName",@{Name="Last Password
Change";Expression={[datetime]::FromFileTime($_."pwdLastSet")}},@{Name
="Next Password Change";Expression={[datetime]::FromFileTime($_."msDS-
UserPasswordExpiryTimeComputed")}}
$passwordreport | ConvertTo-Html -Property "SamAccountName","Last
Password Change","Next Password Change"-head $HTML -body "<H2>Password
Expire Report For $dc</H2>"|
Out-File $Report
Invoke-Expression C:\passwordreport.html
```

The aforementioned script is displayed in a way that's easy for readers to understand. When it is used in PowerShell, make sure to prevent extra line spaces.

This script will search for the attribute values for `SamAccountName`, `pwdLastSet`, and `msDS-UserPasswordExpiryTimeComputed` in every user object. Then, they will be presented in an HTML report:

	C:\passwordreport.html	𝒫 ▾ 𝒞	Password Expire Report For ... ✕

Password Expire Report For rebeladmin.com

SamAccountName	Last Password Change	Next Password Change
Administrator	22/04/2017 11:10:28	22/05/2017 11:10:28
Guest	01/01/1601 00:00:00	
DefaultAccount	01/01/1601 00:00:00	
krbtgt	28/01/2017 18:38:17	29/01/2017 18:38:17
UserA	01/01/1601 00:00:00	01/01/1601 00:00:00
tuser2	11/02/2017 17:08:10	12/02/2017 17:08:10
tuser3	11/02/2017 17:08:10	12/02/2017 17:08:10
tuser4	11/02/2017 17:08:10	12/02/2017 17:08:10
tuser5	11/02/2017 17:08:10	12/02/2017 17:08:10
tuser6	11/02/2017 17:08:10	12/02/2017 17:08:10
tuser7	11/02/2017 17:08:10	12/02/2017 17:08:10
tuser8	11/02/2017 17:08:10	12/02/2017 17:08:10
tuser9	11/02/2017 17:08:11	12/02/2017 17:08:11
dfrancis	12/04/2017 01:53:51	13/04/2017 01:53:51
dfrancis2	15/02/2017 22:12:01	16/02/2017 22:12:01
techtemplate	15/02/2017 23:15:49	16/02/2017 23:15:49
sbrewer	12/04/2017 01:12:21	13/04/2017 01:12:21
inetuser1	18/02/2017 00:38:02	19/02/2017 00:38:02

TIP All these reports can run as scheduled jobs and were developed to be sent over as an email every week or month. This saves administrators' time and also prevents mistakes that can occur with manual tasks.

JEA

In the previous chapter, I explained how JEA can work in an infrastructure to secure the privileges associated with domain accounts. In a nutshell, we can create JEA endpoints and assign them to roles. Users do not need to have permissions such as domain admin or enterprise admin to run these. Users can use these endpoints with their regular AD user accounts. However, in the backend JEA, commands are executed using a JEA local administrator account. These login details need not be known by end users, and their passwords are reset automatically on a daily basis.

As promised in the previous chapter, let's now look at how to get JEA installed and configured.

In order to install JEA, first log in to the server from a user that has local administrator privileges, and open PowerShell:

```
Install-Module xJEA
```

Once it is installed, we can confirm it using the following command:

```
Find-Module -Name xJEA | fl
```

JEA configuration

Now that we have the JEA module installed, the next step is to prepare the environment to use JEA. This can be done using a script that comes with the JEA module. It is located at C:\Program Files\WindowsPowerShell\Modules\xJea\0.2.16.6\Examples\SetupJEA.ps 1.

This script will do the following:

- Remove all existing endpoints from the computer
- Configure the DSC **Local Configuration Manager** (**LCM**) to apply changes and then check every 30 minutes to make sure the configuration has not been altered
- Enable the debug mode

```
Configuration SetupJea
{
  Import-DscResource -module xjea Node localhost
  {
    xJeaEndPoint CleanAll
    {
      Name    = 'CleanALL'
      CleanAll = $true
    }
    LocalConfigurationManager
    {
      RefreshFrequencyMins = 30
      ConfigurationMode    = "ApplyAndAutoCorrect"
      DebugMode            = "ForceModuleImport"
      #This disables provider caching
    }
  }
}
SetupJea -OutputPath C:\JeaDemo
Set-DscLocalConfigurationManager -Path C:\JeaDemo -Verbose
Start-DscConfiguration -Path c:\JeaDemo -Wait -Verbose
#EOF
```

The aforementioned script is displayed in a way that's easy for readers to understand. When it is used in PowerShell, make sure to prevent extra line spaces.

In order to run the script, move to the C:\Program Files\WindowsPowerShell\ Modules\xJea\0.2.16.6\Examples\ folder and run .\SetupJEA.ps1, as shown in the following screenshot:

```
Administrator: Windows PowerShell                                          —    □    ×
Windows PowerShell
Copyright (C) Microsoft Corporation. All rights reserved.

PS C:\Users\dfrancis> cd "C:\Program Files\WindowsPowerShell\Modules\xJea\0.2.16.6\Examples"
PS C:\Program Files\WindowsPowerShell\Modules\xJea\0.2.16.6\Examples> .\SetupJea.ps1


    Directory: C:\JeaDemo


Mode                LastWriteTime         Length Name
----                -------------         ------ ----
-a----        7/30/2019  12:43 AM           1944 localhost.mof
-a----        7/30/2019  12:43 AM           1148 localhost.meta.mof
VERBOSE: Performing the operation "Start-DscConfiguration: SendMetaConfigurationApply" on target
"MSFT_DSCLocalConfigurationManager".
VERBOSE: Perform operation 'Invoke CimMethod' with following parameters, ''methodName' =
SendMetaConfigurationApply,'className' = MSFT_DSCLocalConfigurationManager,'namespaceName' =
root/Microsoft/Windows/DesiredStateConfiguration'.
VERBOSE: An LCM method call arrived from computer DC01 with user sid S-1-5-21-2210686053-2049469170-776893977-500.
VERBOSE: [DC01]: LCM:  [ Start  Set      ]
VERBOSE: [DC01]: LCM:  [ Start  Resource ] [MSFT_DSCMetaConfiguration]
VERBOSE: [DC01]: LCM:  [ Start  Set      ] [MSFT_DSCMetaConfiguration]
VERBOSE: [DC01]: LCM:  [ End    Set      ] [MSFT_DSCMetaConfiguration]  in 0.0770 seconds.
VERBOSE: [DC01]: LCM:  [ End    Resource ] [MSFT_DSCMetaConfiguration]
VERBOSE: [DC01]: LCM:  [ End    Set      ]
VERBOSE: [DC01]: LCM:  [ End    Set      ]  in  0.1250 seconds.
VERBOSE: Operation 'Invoke CimMethod' complete.
VERBOSE: Set-DscLocalConfigurationManager finished in 0.346 seconds.
VERBOSE: Perform operation 'Invoke CimMethod' with following parameters, ''methodName' =
SendConfigurationApply,'className' = MSFT_DSCLocalConfigurationManager,'namespaceName' =
root/Microsoft/Windows/DesiredStateConfiguration'.
VERBOSE: An LCM method call arrived from computer DC01 with user sid S-1-5-21-2210686053-2049469170-776893977-500.
VERBOSE: [DC01]: LCM:  [ Start  Set      ]
VERBOSE: [DC01]:                            [DSCEngine] Importing the module C:\Program
Files\WindowsPowerShell\Modules\xJea\0.2.16.6\DscResources\MSFT_xJeaEndpoint\MSFT_xJeaEndpoint.psm1 in force mode.
VERBOSE: [DC01]: LCM:  [ Start  Resource ] [[xJeaEndPoint]CleanAll]
VERBOSE: [DC01]: LCM:  [ Start  Test     ] [[xJeaEndPoint]CleanAll]
VERBOSE: [DC01]:                            [[xJeaEndPoint]CleanAll] Importing the module MSFT_xJeaEndpoint in force
mode.
VERBOSE: [DC01]:                            [[xJeaEndPoint]CleanAll] 0:43:15 Start Test [EndPoint]CleanALL
VERBOSE: [DC01]:                            [[xJeaEndPoint]CleanAll] 0:43:15 Done  Test [EndPoint]CleanALL
VERBOSE: [DC01]: LCM:  [ End    Test     ] [[xJeaEndPoint]CleanAll]  in 0.0780 seconds.
VERBOSE: [DC01]: LCM:  [ Start  Set      ] [[xJeaEndPoint]CleanAll]
VERBOSE: [DC01]:                            [[xJeaEndPoint]CleanAll] Importing the module MSFT_xJeaEndpoint in force
mode.
VERBOSE: [DC01]:                            [[xJeaEndPoint]CleanAll] 0:43:15 Start Set [EndPoint]CleanALL
VERBOSE: [DC01]:                            [[xJeaEndPoint]CleanAll] Remove [JeaEndpoints]        *
VERBOSE: [DC01]:                            [[xJeaEndPoint]CleanAll] Remove [PSEndPoint]
```

Now we have completed the installation and the initial configuration.

Testing

JEA comes with three demo endpoint configurations, which we can use as references to create an endpoint. These demo files are also located at `C:\ProgramFiles\WindowsPowerShell\Modules\xJea\0.2.16.6\Examples` and `Demo1.ps1`, which include the following:

```
cls configuration Demo1
{
   Import-DscResource -module xjea
   xJeaToolKit Process
```

```
      {
         Name        = 'Process'
         CommandSpecs = @"Name,Parameter,ValidateSet,ValidatePattern Get-
Process
         Get-Service Stop-Process,Name,calc;notepad
         Restart-Service,Name,,^A"@
      }
      xJeaEndPoint Demo1EP
      {
         Name                  = 'Demo1EP'
         Toolkit               = 'Process'
         SecurityDescriptorSddl =
           'O:NSG:BAD:P(A;;GX;;;WD)S:P(AU;FA;GA;;;WD)(AU;SA;GXGW;;;WD)'
         DependsOn             = '[xJeaToolKit]Process'
      }
   }
}
Demo1 -OutputPath C:\JeaDemo

Start-DscConfiguration -Path C:\JeaDemo -ComputerName localhost -
Verbose -wait -debug -ErrorAction SilentlyContinue -ErrorVariable
errors
if($errors | ? FullyQualifiedErrorId -ne 'HRESULT 0x803381fa')
{
    $errors | Write-Error
}

start-sleep -Seconds 30 #Wait for WINRM to restart

$s = New-PSSession -cn . -ConfigurationName Demo1EP
Invoke-command $s {get-command} |out-string
Invoke-Command $s {get-command stop-process -Syntax}
# Enter-pssession $s
Remove-PSSession $s
#EOF
```

 The aforementioned script is displayed in a way that's easy for readers to understand. When it is used in PowerShell, make sure to prevent extra line spaces.

As per the endpoint configuration, users are allowed to use only the following cmdlets:

- Get-Process
- Get-Service

- `Stop-Process,Name,calc;notepad`
- `Restart-Service,Name,^A`

The preceding `Stop-Process` cmdlet can only be used to stop calculator and notepad processes. But it allows you to use the `Restart-Service`, `Get-Process`, and `Get-Service` cmdlets without limitation.

In order to deploy the endpoint, we can use `.\Demo1.ps1`.

Once it's successfully executed, we can verify the new PowerShell session configuration using this:

`Get-PSSessionConfiguration`

The following screenshot shows the output for the preceding command:

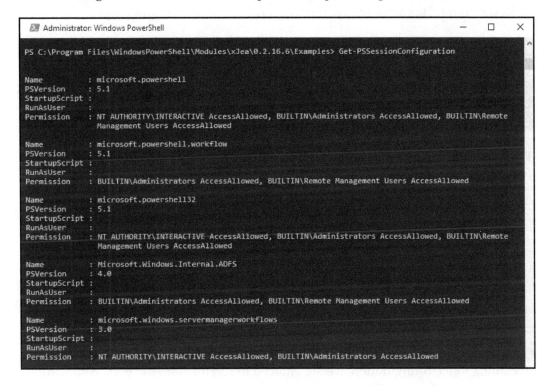

The next step is to connect to a new endpoint. This can be done using the following command:

```
Enter-PSSession –ComputerName localhost –ConfigurationName demo1ep
```

In the preceding command, `–ConfigurationName` defines the endpoint name.

As soon as we run the command, the system is connected to the endpoint and changes the path to `C:\Users\JSA-Demo1EP\Documents`:

```
PS C:\Windows\system32> Enter-PSSession-ComputerName localhost –ConfigurationName demo1ep
[localhost]: PS C:\Users\JSA-Demo1EP\Documents>
```

This user is set up as part of the installation process by JEA. It is the PowerShell session account. This account is part of the local administrator group too:

```
PS C:\Windows\system32> get-localuser

Name               Enabled Description
----               ------- -----------
Administrator      True    Built-in account for administering the computer/domain
DefaultAccount     False   A user account managed by the system.
demo               True
Guest              False   Built-in account for guest access to the computer/domain
JeaSchTaskAccount  True    This is a special Jea account to run the ResetJeaSessionAccountPasswords Scheduled task
JSA-Demo1EP        True    PowerShell Session Acount
```

The following screenshot confirms the members of the local `Administrators` security group:

```
PS C:\Windows\system32> Get-LocalGroupMember -Group "Administrators"

ObjectClass Name                          PrincipalSource
----------- ----                          ---------------
User        REBELADMIN\adam               ActiveDirectory
User        REBELADMIN\Administrator      ActiveDirectory
Group       REBELADMIN\Domain Admins      ActiveDirectory
User        REBEL-CA1\Administrator       Local
User        REBEL-CA1\demo                Local
User        REBEL-CA1\JeaSchTaskAccount   Local
User        REBEL-CA1\JSA-Demo1EP         Local
```

Once the session is connected, we can test it with an allowed command first. According to the configuration, we are allowed to run the `Get-Service` command without any limits:

```
PS C:\Windows\system32> Enter-PSSession -ComputerName localhost -ConfigurationName demo1ep
[localhost]: PS C:\Users\JSA-Demo1EP\Documents> get-service

Status    Name                 DisplayName
------    ----                 -----------
Stopped   AJRouter             AllJoyn Router Service
Stopped   ALG                  Application Layer Gateway Service
Running   AppHostSvc           Application Host Helper Service
Stopped   AppIDSvc             Application Identity
Running   Appinfo              Application Information
Stopped   AppMgmt              Application Management
Stopped   AppReadiness         App Readiness
Stopped   AppVClient           Microsoft App-V Client
Stopped   AppXSvc              AppX Deployment Service (AppXSVC)
Stopped   AudioEndpointBu...   Windows Audio Endpoint Builder
Stopped   Audiosrv             Windows Audio
Stopped   AxInstSV             ActiveX Installer (AxInstSV)
Running   BFE                  Base Filtering Engine
Stopped   BITS                 Background Intelligent Transfer Ser...
Running   BrokerInfrastru...   Background Tasks Infrastructure Ser...
Stopped   Browser              Computer Browser
Stopped   bthserv              Bluetooth Support Service
Running   CDPSvc               Connected Devices Platform Service
Running   CDPUserSvc_32e3f2    CDPUserSvc_32e3f2
Running   CertPropSvc          Certificate Propagation
Running   CertSvc              Active Directory Certificate Services
Stopped   ClipSVC              Client License Service (ClipSVC)
Stopped   COMSysApp            COM+ System Application
Running   CoreMessagingRe...   CoreMessaging
Running   CryptSvc             Cryptographic Services
Stopped   CscService           Offline Files
Running   DcomLaunch           DCOM Server Process Launcher
Stopped   DcpSvc               DataCollectionPublishingService
Stopped   defragsvc            Optimize drives
Stopped   DeviceAssociati...   Device Association Service
Stopped   DeviceInstall        Device Install Service
Stopped   DevQueryBroker       DevQuery Background Discovery Broker
Running   Dhcp                 DHCP Client
Stopped   diagnosticshub....   Microsoft (R) Diagnostics Hub Stand...
Running   DiagTrack            Connected User Experiences and Tele...
Stopped   DmEnrollmentSvc      Device Management Enrollment Service
Stopped   dmwappushservice     dmwappushsvc
Running   Dnscache             DNS Client
Stopped   dot3svc              Wired AutoConfig
Running   DPS                  Diagnostic Policy Service
Stopped   DsmSvc               Device Setup Manager
```

The user I logged in to this computer is a local administrator. So, I have enough privileges to restart the computer using the `Restart-Computer` cmdlet. But when I use the command through the endpoint, it should not allow me to do so according to the endpoint configuration:

```
[localhost]: PS C:\Users\JSA-Demo1EP\Documents> restart-computer
The term 'Restart-Computer' is not recognized as the name of a cmdlet, function, script file, or operable program.
Check the spelling of the name, or if a path was included, verify that the path is correct and try again.
    + CategoryInfo          : ObjectNotFound: (Restart-Computer:String) [], CommandNotFoundException
    + FullyQualifiedErrorId : CommandNotFoundException

[localhost]: PS C:\Users\JSA-Demo1EP\Documents> _
```

As we can see in the preceding screenshot, it is working as expected. Users are allowed to use only the command permitted by the endpoint configuration. This configuration won't be valid for another computer unless the same endpoint configuration is used.

The `Demo2.ps1` endpoint configuration is focused on the file server administrator:

```
cls
configuration Demo2
{
  Import-DscResource -module xjea

  xJeaToolKit SMBGet
  {
    Name = 'SMBGet'
    CommandSpecs = @"
Module,Name,Parameter,ValidateSet,ValidatePattern
    SMBShare,get-* "@
  }
  xJeaEndPoint Demo2EP
  {
    Name = 'Demo2EP'
    Toolkit = 'SMBGet'
    SecurityDescriptorSddl =
'O:NSG:BAD:P(A;;GX;;;WD)S:P(AU;FA;GA;;;WD)
    (AU;SA;GXGW;;;WD)'
    DependsOn = '[xJeaToolKit]SMBGet'
  }
}

Demo2 -OutputPath C:\JeaDemo
Start-DscConfiguration -Path C:\JeaDemo -ComputerName localhost -
Verbose ` -wait -debug -ErrorAction SilentlyContinue -ErrorVariable
errors
if($errors | ? FullyQualifiedErrorId -ne 'HRESULT 0x803381fa')
{
 $errors | Write-Error
}

start-sleep -Seconds 30 #Wait for WINRM to restart

$s = New-PSSession -cn . -ConfigurationName Demo2EP
Invoke-command $s {get-command} |out-string
# Enter-pssession $s

Remove-PSSession $s
#EOF
```

The aforementioned script is displayed in a way that's easy for readers to understand. When it is used in PowerShell, make sure to prevent extra line spaces.

As per the preceding script, the system will allow you to use the following cmdlets list without restriction:

- SMBShare
- get-*

The following screenshot shows the output for the Get-PSSessionConfiguration command.

We can connect to the second endpoint using the following command:

```
Enter-PSSession –ComputerName localhost –ConfigurationName demo2ep
```

Once connected, Get-Command lists all the available commands in the endpoint:

```
PS C:\Windows\system32> Enter-PSSession -ComputerName localhost -ConfigurationName demo2ep
[localhost]: PS C:\Users\JSA-Demo2EP\Documents> get-command

CommandType     Name                                    Version    Source
-----------     ----                                    -------    ------
Function        A:
Function        B:
Function        C:
Function        cd..
Function        cd\
Function        Clear-Host
Function        D:
Function        E:
Function        F:
Function        format-list                             0.0        SafeProxy
Function        format-table                            0.0        SafeProxy
Function        G:
Function        Get-SmbBandwidthLimit                   0.0        SMBGet-Toolkit
Function        Get-SmbClientConfiguration              0.0        SMBGet-Toolkit
Function        Get-SmbClientNetworkInterface           0.0        SMBGet-Toolkit
Function        Get-SmbConnection                       0.0        SMBGet-Toolkit
Function        Get-SmbDelegation                       0.0        SMBGet-Toolkit
Function        Get-SmbMapping                          0.0        SMBGet-Toolkit
Function        Get-SmbMultichannelConnection           0.0        SMBGet-Toolkit
Function        Get-SmbMultichannelConstraint           0.0        SMBGet-Toolkit
Function        Get-SmbOpenFile                         0.0        SMBGet-Toolkit
Function        Get-SmbServerConfiguration              0.0        SMBGet-Toolkit
Function        Get-SmbServerNetworkInterface           0.0        SMBGet-Toolkit
Function        Get-SmbSession                          0.0        SMBGet-Toolkit
Function        Get-SmbShare                            0.0        SMBGet-Toolkit
Function        Get-SmbShareAccess                      0.0        SMBGet-Toolkit
Function        Get-Verb
Function        Group-Object                            0.0        SafeProxy
Function        H:
Function        help
Function        I:
Function        ImportSystemModules
Function        J:
Function        K:
Function        L:
Function        M:
Function        mkdir
Function        more
Function        N:
Function        O:
Function        oss
Function        P:
```

As expected, it is allowing us to run only the allowed cmdlets. In this test, we have used the `Get-SMBshare` cmdlet, which is allowed, and `Restart-Computer`, which isn't:

```
[localhost]: PS C:\Users\JSA-Demo2EP\Documents> get-smbshare

Name        ScopeName Path                                     Description
----        --------- ----                                     -----------
ADMIN$      *         C:\Windows                               Remote Admin
C$          *         C:\                                      Default share
CertEnroll  *         C:\Windows\system32\CertSrv\CertEnroll   Active Directory Certificate Services share
IPC$        *                                                  Remote IPC

[localhost]: PS C:\Users\JSA-Demo2EP\Documents> restart-computer
The term 'Restart-Computer' is not recognized as the name of a cmdlet, function, script file, or operable program.
Check the spelling of the name, or if a path was included, verify that the path is correct and try again.
    + CategoryInfo          : ObjectNotFound: (Restart-Computer:String) [], CommandNotFoundException
    + FullyQualifiedErrorId : CommandNotFoundException

[localhost]: PS C:\Users\JSA-Demo2EP\Documents> _
```

`Demo3.ps1` provides the endpoint to manage and navigate through the filesystem:

```
cls configuration Demo3
{
   Import-DscResource -module xjea
   xJeaToolKit FileSystem
   {
     Name = 'FileSystem'
     CommandSpecs = @"
Module,name,Parameter,ValidateSet,ValidatePattern,
       Get-ChildItem,Get-Item,Copy-Item,Move-Item,Rename-Item,
       Remove-Item,Copy-ItemProperty,Clear-ItemProperty,Move-
ItemProperty,
       New-ItemProperty,Remove-ItemProperty,Rename-ItemProperty,Set-
ItemProperty,
       Get-Location,Pop-Location,Push-Location,Set-Location,Convert-
Path,
       Join-Path,Resolve-Path,Split-Path,Test-Path,Get-PSDrive,New-
PSDrive,
       out-file "@
     Ensure = 'Present'
   }

   xJeaEndPoint Demo3EP
   {
     Name = 'Demo3EP'
     ToolKit = 'FileSystem'
     Ensure = 'Present'
     DependsOn = '[xJeaToolKit]FileSystem'
   }
}
```

```
Demo3 -OutputPath C:\JeaDemo

Start-DscConfiguration -Path C:JeaDemo -ComputerName localhost -
Verbose ` -wait -debug -ErrorAction SilentlyContinue -ErrorVariable
errors
if($errors | ? FullyQualifiedErrorId -ne 'HRESULT 0x803381fa')
{
 $errors | Write-Error
}

start-sleep -Seconds 30 #Wait for WINRM to restart
# This endpoint allows you to navigate the filesystem but not see
# the CONTENTS of any of the files
$s = New-PSSession -cn . -ConfigurationName Demo3EP
Invoke-command $s {dir 'C:\Program
Files\Jea\Activity\ActivityLog.csv'}
Invoke-Command $s {get-content ` 'C:Program
FilesJeaActivityActivityLog.csv'}
# Enter-pssession $s

Remove-PSSession $s
#EOF
```

 The aforementioned script is displayed in a way that's easy for readers to understand. When it is used in PowerShell, make sure to prevent extra line spaces.

This endpoint configuration allows you to use the following cmdlets:

- Get-ChildItem
- Get-Item
- Copy-Item
- Move-Item
- Rename-Item
- Remove-Item
- Copy-ItemProperty
- Clear-ItemProperty
- Move-ItemProperty
- New-ItemProperty
- Remove-ItemProperty

- `Rename-ItemProperty`
- `Set-ItemProperty`
- `Get-Location`
- `Pop-Location`
- `Push-Location`
- `Set-Location`
- `Convert-Path`
- `Join-Path`
- `Resolve-Path`
- `Split-Path`
- `Test-Path`
- `Get-PSDrive`
- `New-PSDrive`
- `out-file`

This explains how we can use JEA endpoints to limit the use of privileges to specific tasks. These demo scripts can be used to build your own configuration. There are lots of examples that you can find on GitHub. You can access the JEA GitHub page using `https://github.com/PowerShell/JEA`.

So far in this chapter, we have learned about how we can use the Active Directory module for PowerShell to manage an Active Directory environment. However, when it comes to a hybrid environment, we can't use the same module to manage Azure AD. We have to use the Azure Active Directory PowerShell module to manage Azure AD objects (cloud-only and synced objects). In the next section of the chapter, we are going to explore the Azure Active Directory PowerShell module and its capabilities.

Azure Active Directory PowerShell

Similar to on-premises Active Directory, we also can use PowerShell to manage Azure Active Directory. Let's see why we should use PowerShell to manage Azure Active Directory:

- **Early bird access to features**: Microsoft keeps releasing new features, bug fixes, updates, and feature enhancements more frequently to Azure AD services than on-premises Active Directory.

Microsoft releases new features to the public in two stages. In the first stage, it is released as a preview version. This is not recommended for use in production, but IT professionals can use it for testing and provide feedback to Microsoft. At this stage, the feature can have many updates and, most of the time, it will take some time to update the GUI accordingly. Some of these changes will not be available on the GUI until general release. But if we are using PowerShell, we do not have to wait. We can have early access to features as soon as it is released.

- **Faster response**: The Azure Active Directory portal has many different windows, wizards, forms to configure and manage users, groups, roles, and associated features. The GUI makes it easy to do things, but it takes time. As an example, if you add a user account using the Azure AD portal, you have to go to four sub-windows at least. But PowerShell allows us to do it using one window and a few lines of commands.
- **Granular control**: The Azure AD portal visualizes the data and configuration of the service using different windows. However, it may not always show what we want. As an example, let's assume we are looking for a specific value in two user accounts. If we use the GUI, we need to go to a few different windows to gather this information. But using a PowerShell command or script, we will be able to gather the same information in one window. This is really helpful when troubleshooting.
- **Microsoft Graph integration**: Microsoft Graph provides a unified programmability model to access a vast amount of data in Microsoft 365, Azure Active Directory, Enterprise Mobility Suite, Windows 10, and so on. As part of it, the Azure AD PowerShell for Graph module allows you to retrieve data, update directory configurations, add/update/remove objects, and configure features via Microsoft Graph.

In this chapter, I will be using the Azure Active Directory PowerShell for Graph module to manage an Azure AD hybrid environment.

Installation

The Azure Active Directory PowerShell for Graph module comes as two versions. The public preview version is the most recent, but it is not recommended for use in production. The installation steps for this version can be found at `https://www.powershellgallery.com/packages/AzureADPreview`.

The general availability version is the stable, recommended version for production environments. It can be installed on any computer that runs Windows Server 2008 R2 or above with the latest updates. Microsoft .NET Framework 4.5 or above is also required.

Once the prerequisites are in place, perform the following steps:

1. Log in to the computer you have selected for the Azure Active Directory PowerShell for Graph module.
2. Launch the PowerShell console as an administrator.
3. Run the `Install-Module -Name AzureAD` command. Answer `Yes` if it is a required repository update:

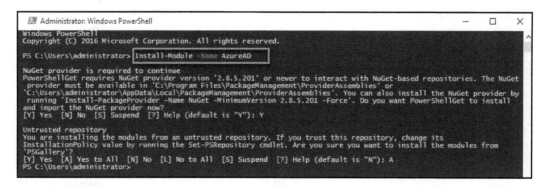

4. After installation, we can verify the module installation using `Get-Module AzureAD`.
5. After successfully installing the module, run `Connect-AzureAD` to initiate a connection to the Azure AD tenant.
6. Then, it will prompt you with a login window. Use Azure AD global administrator account details to connect.

Now we have the Azure Active Directory PowerShell for Graph module installed. Let's see how we can manage an Azure AD hybrid environment using this module.

General commands

We can start by listing all the available commands under the Azure AD module, which can be done by using the following:

```
Get-Command -module AzureAD
```

We can view the full syntax for a command by using the `Get-Help` command. As an example, we can view the full syntax for the `Get-AzureADUser` command using the following:

```
Get-Help Get-AzureADUser
```

We can verify the status of Azure AD domains using the following command:

```
Get-AzureADDomain | fl
```

The preceding command helps to identify the domain verification status by referring to the value of the `IsVerified` attribute.

If you are using a custom domain in Azure AD, we need to verify ownership of the domain using DNS records. If it is not verified, we can retrieve the required DNS records by using the following command:

```
Get-AzureADDomainVerificationDnsRecord -Name
M365x562652.onmicrosoft.com | fl
```

In the preceding example, `M365x562652.onmicrosoft.com` represents the domain name:

```
PS C:\Users\administrator> Get-AzureADDomainVerificationDnsRecord -Name M365x562652.onmicrosoft.com | fl

DnsRecordId      : aceff52c-06a5-447f-ac5f-256ad243cc5c
IsOptional       : False
Label            : M365x562652.onmicrosoft.com
RecordType       : Txt
SupportedService : Email
Ttl              : 3600
Text             : MS=

DnsRecordId      : 5fbde38c-0865-497f-82b1-126f596bcee9
IsOptional       : False
Label            : M365x562652.onmicrosoft.com
RecordType       : Mx
SupportedService : Email
Ttl              : 3600
MailExchange     : .msv1.invalid
Preference       : 32767
```

We can view the details of the Azure AD tenant by using the following:

```
Get-AzureADTenantDetail | fl
```

In a hybrid environment, the health of on-premises AD sync is crucial. We can view the time of the last directory sync by using the following command:

```
Get-AzureADTenantDetail | select CompanyLastDirSyncTime
```

Managing users

We can view the user account details for a known account using the following:

```
Get-AzureADUser -ObjectId AdeleV@M365x562652.OnMicrosoft.com | fl
```

In the preceding command, `AdeleV@M365x562652.OnMicrosoft.com` represents the UPN of the user.

We also can use user attributes to find user account details:

```
Get-AzureADUser -Filter "startswith(GivenName,'Adele')"
```

The preceding command will filter Azure AD users with `GivenName` as `Adele`.

We can also filter users based on a specific attribute value:

```
Get-AzureADUser -Filter "GivenName eq 'Adele'"
```

The preceding command will search for the exact user with the given name value `Adele`.

In my demo environment, I'd like to see a list of disabled accounts. I can do this using the following command:

```
Get-AzureADUser -All $true -Filter 'accountEnabled eq false'
```

We can modify the output of the filtered data further:

```
Get-AzureADUser -All $true -Filter 'accountEnabled eq false' | select
DisplayName,UserPrincipalName,Department
```

The preceding command will display the value of the `DisplayName`, `UserPrincipalName`, and `Department` attributes of the filtered accounts.

In a hybrid environment, we can filter accounts that are synced from on-premises AD by using the following:

```
Get-AzureADUser -All $true -Filter 'DirSyncEnabled eq true'
```

In the preceding command, the value of the `DirSyncEnabled` attribute defines whether it's a cloud-only account or a synced account.

We also can check the last sync value for the synced accounts:

```
Get-AzureADUser  -All $true -Filter 'DirSyncEnabled eq true' | select
DisplayName,UserPrincipalName,LastDirSyncTime
```

In the preceding command, the `LastDirSyncTime` value defines the last sync time of the object.

We can also export the output to a CSV file using the `Export-CSV` command:

```
Get-AzureADUser  -All $true -Filter 'DirSyncEnabled eq true' | select
DisplayName,UserPrincipalName,LastDirSyncTime | Export-CSV -Path
.\syncaccount.csv
```

The `ImmutableID` value of a user account is used to map an Azure AD user object to an on-premises user object. `ImmutableID` does have a relationship with on-premises user accounts' `ObjectGUID`. We can use this to identify cloud-only users. If it is a cloud-only user, the `ImmutableID` value should be `null`:

```
Get-AzureADUser -All $true | where-Object {$_.ImmutableId -eq $null}
```

The preceding command returns a list of all the cloud-only accounts. We can export the required attribute values to CSV by using the following:

```
Get-AzureADUser -All $true | where-Object {$_.ImmutableId -eq $null} |
select DisplayName,UserPrincipalName | Export-CSV -Path
.\cloudaccount.csv
```

Another important thing related to accounts is licences. If we are going to use Azure AD's premium features, we need to have relevant licenses assigned. By default, a user only has Azure AD free version features.

To view licenses associated with a user account, we can use the following command:

```
Get-AzureADUserLicenseDetail -ObjectId
MeganB@M365x562652.OnMicrosoft.com | fl
```

The preceding command will return the licenses associated with the user `MeganB@M365x562652.OnMicrosoft.com`.

We also can view the subscribed SKUs using the following command:

```
Get-AzureADSubscribedSku | fl
```

The preceding command lists all the details about licenses that are associated with the tenant. But, mostly, we only need to know how many licenses have been used and how many licenses are available. We can do this using the following command:

```
Get-AzureADSubscribedSku | select SkuPartNumber,ConsumedUnits -
ExpandProperty PrepaidUnits
```

In the preceding example, the `SkuPartNumber` value represents the license part number. The value of the enabled field represents the number of purchased licenses. `ConsumedUnits` represents the number of consumed licenses.

Let's move on and see how we can assign a new license to a user.

In my environment, I have a user who synced from on-premises Azure AD who doesn't have a license assigned:

```
Get-AzureADUserLicenseDetail -ObjectId
ADJellison@M365x562652.onmicrosoft.com | fl
```

The following screenshot displays the output of the preceding command:

```
C:\Users\administrator> Get-AzureADUserLicenseDetail -ObjectId ADJellison@M365x562652.onmicrosoft.com | fl
C:\Users\administrator> _
```

As a first step, let's create objects to use in the license assignment process:

```
$newlicence = New-Object -TypeName
Microsoft.Open.AzureAD.Model.AssignedLicense
$newlicenceadd = New-Object -TypeName
Microsoft.Open.AzureAD.Model.AssignedLicenses
```

Then, we need to find the `SkuId` of the licenses.

I am going to assign the `ENTERPRISEPREMIUM` license to the user:

```
$newlicence.SkuId = (Get-AzureADSubscribedSku | Where-Object -Property
SkuPartNumber -Value "ENTERPRISEPREMIUM" -EQ).SkuId
```

Then, we need to assign the licenses to the object:

```
$newlicenceadd.AddLicenses = $newlicence
```

Now, we can go ahead and assign the license to the user:

```
Set-AzureADUserLicense -ObjectId
"ADJellison@M365x562652.onmicrosoft.com" -AssignedLicenses
$newlicenceadd
```

The preceding command assigns `ENTERPRISEPREMIUM` licenses to the user `ADJellison@M365x562652.onmicrosoft.com`:

```
PS C:\Users\administrator> Get-AzureADUserLicenseDetail -ObjectId ADJellison@M365x562652.onmicrosoft.com | fl

ObjectId      : irYR8iuwxkSAxcx9WXUe7mAn38eBLPdOtXhbU5K1cd8
ServicePlans  : {class ServicePlanInfo {
                    AppliesTo: Company
                    ProvisioningStatus: PendingProvisioning
                    ServicePlanId: 4a51bca5-1eff-43f5-878c-177680f191af
                    ServicePlanName: WHITEBOARD_PLAN3
                }
                , class ServicePlanInfo {
                    AppliesTo: Company
                    ProvisioningStatus: Success
                    ServicePlanId: efb0351d-3b08-4503-993d-383af8de41e3
                    ServicePlanName: MIP_S_CLP2
                }
                , class ServicePlanInfo {
                    AppliesTo: Company
                    ProvisioningStatus: Success
                    ServicePlanId: 5136a095-5cf0-4aff-bec3-e84448b38ea5
                    ServicePlanName: MIP_S_CLP1
                }
                , class ServicePlanInfo {
                    AppliesTo: Company
                    ProvisioningStatus: Success
                    ServicePlanId: 33c4f319-9bdd-48d6-9c4d-410b750a4a5a
                    ServicePlanName: MYANALYTICS_P2
                }
                ...}
SkuId         : c7df2760-2c81-4ef7-b578-5b5392b571df
SkuPartNumber : ENTERPRISEPREMIUM
```

 It is a must to set the `UsageLocation` value for users who sync from on-premises AD before assigning licenses. We can do this using `Set-AzureADUser -ObjectId ADJellison@M365x562652.onmicrosoft.com -UsageLocation "US"`.

We can remove the licenses assigned using the following command:

```
$licenseB = New-Object -TypeName
Microsoft.Open.AzureAD.Model.AssignedLicenses
$licenseB.RemoveLicenses =  (Get-AzureADSubscribedSku | Where-Object
{$_.SkuPartNumber -eq 'ENTERPRISEPREMIUM'}).SkuId
Set-AzureADUserLicense -ObjectId
"ADJellison@M365x562652.onmicrosoft.com" -AssignedLicenses $licenseB
```

Using the preceding commands, I have created a script to do the following:

- Search for users who synced from on-premises AD.
- Of those users, select the users who don't have Azure AD licenses assigned.
- Set the `UsageLocation` value for selected users.
- Assign Azure AD licenses to selected users.

```
#######Script to Assign Licences to Synced Users from On-Permises
AD############
Import-Module AzureAD
Connect-AzureAD
###Filter Synced Users who doesn't have licence assigned######
$ADusers = Get-AzureADUser -All $true -Filter 'DirSyncEnabled eq
true'
$notlicenced = Get-AzureADUser -All $true | Where-Object
{$ADusers.AssignedLicenses -ne $null} | select ObjectId | Out-File
-FilePath C:\users.txt
#####Set UsageLocation value to sync users#########
(Get-Content "C:\users.txt" | select-object -skip 3) | ForEach {
Set-AzureADUser -ObjectId $_ -UsageLocation "US" }
#####Set User Licecnes############
$newlicence = New-Object -TypeName
Microsoft.Open.AzureAD.Model.AssignedLicense
$newlicenceadd = New-Object -TypeName
Microsoft.Open.AzureAD.Model.AssignedLicenses
$newlicence.SkuId = (Get-
AzureADSubscribedSku | Where-Object -Property SkuPartNumber -Value
"ENTERPRISEPREMIUM" -EQ).SkuId
$newlicenceadd.AddLicenses = $newlicence
(Get-Content "C:\users.txt" | select-object -skip 3) | ForEach {
Set-AzureADUserLicense -ObjectId $_ -AssignedLicenses
$newlicenceadd }
```

In a hybrid environment, users are mainly created through on-premises Active Directory, but there are occasions when we need to add cloud-only accounts. This is mainly for cloud management tasks.

We can create a new user by using the following command:

```
$Userpassword = New-Object -TypeName
Microsoft.Open.AzureAD.Model.PasswordProfile
$Userpassword.Password = "London@1234"
New-AzureADUser -DisplayName "Andrew Xavier" -PasswordProfile
$Userpassword -UserPrincipalName
"Andrew.Xavier@M365x562652.onmicrosoft.com" -AccountEnabled $true -
MailNickName "AndrewXavier"
```

In the preceding command, `-PasswordProfile` is used to define the password profile for the new user account. `-MailNickName` defines the value for the user's mail nickname. In the preceding example, add a new user account, `Andrew.Xavier@M365x562652.onmicrosoft.com`, with the password `London@1234`.

We also can create multiple user accounts using CSV files. In the following example, I am using a CSV file to create users. The CSV file contains the following:

```
UserPrincipalName, DisplayName,MailNickName
DishanM@M365x562652.onmicrosoft.com, Dishan Melroy,DishanMel
JackM@M365x562652.onmicrosoft.com,Jack May,JackMay
RicahrdP@M365x562652.onmicrosoft.com,Richard Parker,RichardPar
```

Then, I can create these new users using the following:

```
$Userpassword = New-Object -TypeName
Microsoft.Open.AzureAD.Model.PasswordProfile
$Userpassword.Password = "London@1234"
Import-Csv -Path C:\newuser.csv | foreach {New-AzureADUser -
UserPrincipalName $_.UserPrincipalName -DisplayName $_.DisplayName -
MailNickName $_.MailNickName -PasswordProfile $Userpassword -
AccountEnabled $true}
```

By using the preceding commands, I have created a script to do the following:

- Create new user accounts using a CSV file
- Set `UsageLocation` for new user accounts
- Assign ENTERPRISEPREMIUM licenses to users

```
########A Script to create new users and assign Azure AD
licences######
Import-Module AzureAD
Connect-AzureAD
###########Create New Users using CSV ##################
$Userpassword = New-Object -TypeName
Microsoft.Open.AzureAD.Model.PasswordProfile
$Userpassword.Password = "London@1234"
Import-Csv -Path C:\newuser.csv | foreach {New-AzureADUser -
UserPrincipalName $_.UserPrincipalName -DisplayName $_.DisplayName
-MailNickName $_.MailNickName -PasswordProfile $Userpassword -
UsageLocation "US" -AccountEnabled $true} | select ObjectId | Out-
File -FilePath C:\users.txt
##########Assign Licences#################
$newlicence = New-Object -TypeName
Microsoft.Open.AzureAD.Model.AssignedLicense
```

```
$newlicenceadd = New-Object -TypeName
Microsoft.Open.AzureAD.Model.AssignedLicenses
$newlicence.SkuId = (Get-AzureADSubscribedSku | Where-Object -
Property SkuPartNumber -Value "ENTERPRISEPREMIUM" -EQ).SkuId
$newlicenceadd.AddLicenses = $newlicence
(Get-Content "C:\users.txt" | select-object -skip 3) | ForEach {
Set-AzureADUserLicense -ObjectId $_ -AssignedLicenses
$newlicenceadd }
```

To remove an Azure AD user, we can use the following:

```
Remove-AzureADUser -ObjectId "JDAllen@M365x562652.onmicrosoft.com"
```

We can combine it with a user search using the following command:

```
Get-AzureADUser -Filter "startswith(DisplayName,'Dishan')" | Remove-
AzureADUser
```

The preceding command will search for user accounts that have a `DisplayName` that starts with `Dishan`. If there are any, the second part of the command will remove them.

Managing groups

Azure AD groups also work similarly to on-premises AD groups. They can be used to manage permissions in an effective manner. In a hybrid environment, there will be cloud-only groups as well as synced groups from the on-premises AD environment. In this section, we are going to look into group management using the Azure Active Directory PowerShell for Graph module.

Let's start with listing groups. We can search for a group using the following command:

```
Get-AzureADGroup -SearchString "sg"
```

In the preceding command, `SearchString` is used to define the search criteria. The preceding example will list any groups containing `sg` in the `DisplayName` field:

```
PS C:\Users\administrator> Get-AzureADGroup -SearchString "sg"

ObjectId                              DisplayName              Description
--------                              -----------              -----------
93291438-be19-472e-a1d6-9b178b7ac619  sg-Engineering           All engineering personnel
2a11d5ee-8383-44d1-9fbd-85cb4dcc2d5a  sg-Executive             All executives
38bd48e7-e37c-48c9-bae4-7f00949529a0  sg-Finance               All finance personnel
c93737dd-0e77-4325-8d5e-6524d8baedff  sg-HR                    All HR personnel
c00fc3df-a395-48fb-a620-05d64384fa3e  sg-IT                    All IT personnel
f7ca523a-3a17-4755-aea9-5c723e8d9c6a  sg-Legal                 All legal executives
73115583-7ce1-4890-8b96-40bc257e0186  sg-Operations            All operations personnel
0636227c-0a03-4584-a72d-52e5479c2aad  sg-Retail                All retail Users
6a232560-7a59-413c-8f2b-60ecda3b21cb  sg-Sales and Marketing   All marketing personnel
```

In the search result, we can see the `ObjectId` for the group. Once we know the `ObjectId`, we can see the details of the group using the following command:

```
Get-AzureADGroup -ObjectId 93291438-be19-472e-a1d6-9b178b7ac619 | fl
```

In a hybrid environment, there will be security groups that have synced from the on-premises Active Directory. We can filter these groups using the following:

```
Get-AzureADGroup -Filter 'DirSyncEnabled eq true' | select
ObjectId,DisplayName,LastDirSyncTime
```

In the preceding example, the `LastDirSyncTime` column displays the last successful sync time of the group.

We can filter cloud-only groups using the following command:

```
Get-AzureADGroup -All $true | where-Object
{$_.OnPremisesSecurityIdentifier -eq $null}
```

In the preceding command, we are using the `OnPremisesSecurityIdentifier` attribute to filter the groups. This attribute only has value if it is synced from on-premises AD.

We can view group memberships by using the following:

```
Get-AzureADGroupMember -ObjectId 2a11d5ee-8383-44d1-9fbd-85cb4dcc2d5a
```

In the preceding command, we are using `ObjectId` to uniquely identify the group.

We can add members to the group using the `Add-AzureADGroupMember` cmdlet:

```
Add-AzureADGroupMember -ObjectId 2a11d5ee-8383-44d1-9fbd-85cb4dcc2d5a
-RefObjectId a6aeced9-909e-4684-8712-d0f242451338
```

In the preceding command, the `ObjectId` value represents the group, and the `RefObjectId` value represents the user.

We can remove a member from the group by using the following command:

```
Remove-AzureADGroupMember -ObjectId
2a11d5ee-8383-44d1-9fbd-85cb4dcc2d5a -MemberId
a6aeced9-909e-4684-8712-d0f242451338
```

In the preceding command, the `ObjectId` value represents the group, and the `MemberId` value represents the user's `ObjectId`.

We can also combine the `Add-AzureADGroupMember` cmdlet with the `Get-AzureADUser` cmdlet to add bulk users to a group.

In the following script, I used the `Get-AzureADUser` cmdlet to search for users in `Marketing Department`, and then used `Add-AzureADGroupMember` to add those users to `Sales Group` as members:

```
#######Script to Add Multiple users to Security Group#############
Import-Module AzureAD
Connect-AzureAD
##### Search for users in Marketing Department ##########
Get-AzureADUser -All $true -Filter "Department eq 'Marketing'" |
select ObjectId | Out-File -FilePath C:\salesusers.txt
#####Add Users to Sales Group#########
(Get-Content "C:\salesusers.txt" | select-object -skip 3) | ForEach {
Add-AzureADGroupMember -ObjectId f9f51d29-e093-4e57-ad79-2fc5ae3517db
-RefObjectId $_ }
```

In a hybrid environment, security groups are mainly synced from on-premises AD. But there can be requirements for cloud-only groups as well. We can create a cloud-only group by using the following:

```
New-AzureADGroup -DisplayName "REBELADMIN Sales Team" -MailEnabled
$false -MailNickName "salesteam" -SecurityEnabled $true
```

The following screenshot displays the output of the preceding command:

```
PS C:\Users\administrator> New-AzureADGroup -DisplayName "REBELADMIN Sales Team" -MailEnabled $false -MailNickName
steam" -SecurityEnabled $true

ObjectId                              DisplayName            Description
--------                              -----------            -----------
7592b555-343d-4f73-a6f1-2270d7cf014f REBELADMIN Sales Team
```

The preceding command creates a security group called REBELADMIN Sales Team. This group is not a mail-enabled group.

We can remove an Azure AD group using the following command:

Remove-AzureADGroup –ObjectId 7592b555-343d-4f73-a6f1-2270d7cf014f

In the preceding command, the ObjectId value defines the group.

Apart from security groups, Azure AD also has predefined administrative roles, which can be used to assign access permissions to Azure AD and other cloud services. There are more than 35 predefined administrative roles. Each role has its own set of permissions. More details about these roles can be found at https://docs. microsoft.com/en-us/azure/active-directory/users-groups-roles/directory-assign-admin-roles.

We can list all the administrative roles using the following:

Get-AzureADDirectoryRoleTemplate

By default, only a few administrative roles are enabled. We can list these roles using the following:

Get-AzureADDirectoryRole

 Here, the company administrator directory role represents the Azure AD global administrators.

We can enable the administrative role using the following:

Enable-AzureADDirectoryRole –RoleTemplateId e6d1a23a-da11-4be4-9570-befc86d067a7

In the preceding command, the `RoleTemplateId` value represents the administrative role.

We can assign the administrative role to a user by using the following command:

```
Add-AzureADDirectoryRoleMember -ObjectId
b63c1671-625a-4a80-8bae-6487423909ca -RefObjectId 581c7265-
c8cc-493b-9686-771b2f10a77e
```

In the preceding command, the `ObjectId` value represents the administrative role. `RefObjectId` is the object ID value of the user.

We can list members of the administrative role using the following:

```
Get-AzureADDirectoryRoleMember -ObjectId 36b9ac02-9dfc-402a-8d44-
ba2d8995dc06
```

In the preceding command, `ObjectId` represents the administrative role.

We can remove a member from the role using the following command:

```
Remove-AzureADDirectoryRoleMember -ObjectId 36b9ac02-9dfc-402a-8d44-
ba2d8995dc06 -MemberId 165ebcb7-f07d-42d2-a52e-90f44e71e4a1
```

In the preceding command, `MemberId` is equal to the user's object ID value.

This marks the end of this section. There are lots of cmdlets that can still be used to manage Azure AD, but here I explained the cmdlets that will be required for day-to-day operations.

Summary

PowerShell has become the most powerful script language for Windows systems. PowerShell is very useful for systems management, but can also be an incredibly powerful tool for managing AD infrastructures. Throughout the book, I have used PowerShell for AD configuration and management. Furthermore, I have shared different commands and scripts that can be used to manage an AD environment efficiently. Toward the end of the chapter, you learned how to implement JEA and how it can be used to protect privileges in an AD environment. We also learned how to manage Azure AD using the Azure Active Directory PowerShell for Graph module. In the next chapter, we will look at Azure AD and learn how to manage identities in a hybrid environment.

17
Azure Active Directory Hybrid Setup

Back in 2006, I was working with a large Canadian managed-hosting service provider. At that time, there was huge demand for hosting dedicated servers. Hardware, bandwidth, and management all came at a high cost. However, things started to change with the rise of virtualization: it was able to bring the hosting costs down. I still remember that there were all sorts of discussions, arguments, articles, and summits where people were bringing the pros and cons of virtualization to the table. As with any technology, in the beginning, there were issues, but virtualization technologies developed rapidly and brought businesses to a point that they can't look away from.

For us, it was the same: business-wise, we were safe with dedicated server hosting. We were making good profits. But with virtualization, customers were able to bring racks of dedicated servers into a few hypervisor hosts. Then, the businesses in the hosting field started to find new ways of making money with virtualized technologies. This was the beginning of the cloud era. However, what I want to emphasize is similar to the technological shift from dedicated servers to virtualization: the majority of today's infrastructures are going through a very interesting phase of moving workloads from on-premises infrastructure to the public cloud. When Microsoft Azure was released, the technology world was deluged with all sorts of discussions again. Most of the points were related to data security, compliance, reliability, and cost.

Over the past few years, Microsoft has been addressing all those concerns and challenges, and it came to the point where organizations could not stay away from it anymore for the following reasons:

- The cloud pricing model (only pay for the resources you use) and operational model can bring down long-term infrastructure operation and maintenance costs.
- Software vendors started replacing their products with cloud-based versions and discontinued support for on-premises versions.
- Microsoft products have equivalent cloud versions on-premises, and new features will only be available in the cloud versions. Also, the cloud versions have more frequent updates and bug fixes compared to on-premises versions.
- It removed dependencies (such as network connectivity, VPN, and firewall configuration) for mobile workers and provided seamless access to workloads from anywhere.
- The cloud adopts new technology changes more quickly compared to on-premises infrastructures.
- A robust cloud infrastructure setup provides **high availability** (**HA**) for workloads, which may not be possible to achieve on-premises.

When an organization adopts cloud technologies, it's not easy to bring each and every workload to the public cloud at once. There are limitations for applications that still require some workloads to run on-premises. Even though workloads operate from two technologies, the user identities for the organization would stay the same. Azure **Active Directory** (**AD**) helps to extend the on-premises identity infrastructure to Azure Cloud and use the same on-premises identities to authenticate with the application and services, regardless of where they are running from.

In this chapter, we will look at the following topics:

- How to integrate Azure AD with the on-premises AD
- Password hash synchronization
- Azure AD pass-through authentication
- Azure AD seamless **Single Sign-On** (**SSO**)
- A step-by-step guide to integrating an on-premises AD environment with Azure AD

Integrating Azure AD with on-premises AD

In `Chapter 1`, *Active Directory Fundamentals*, I explained what Azure AD is and what its characteristics are. We also looked into different versions of Azure AD and the differences in their features. Throughout this book, we've learned about the features and management of Azure AD in a hybrid environment. Now, it is time to talk about the integration of Azure AD with on-premises AD.

Based on experience and best practices, I would like to propose the following steps to consider for integrating Azure AD:

1. Evaluating the present business requirements
2. Evaluating an organization's infrastructure road map
3. Evaluating the security requirements
4. Selecting the Azure AD version
5. Deciding on the sign-in method
6. Implementation

Evaluating the present business requirements

There can be one or many reasons why a business is looking to extend their on-premises AD to Azure AD. Let's look into some of the most common reasons:

- **Use of Software-as-a-Service (SaaS) applications**: This is one of the most common reasons for an organization to start using the Azure AD hybrid model. With the rise of the cloud era, lots of software vendors started to move into the SaaS market. Most of these solutions are now available through Microsoft Azure. Due to this availability, less management, scalability, and cost, most organizations do not hesitate to move into SaaS applications. Every SaaS application requires authentication to handle access permissions. By extending on-premises AD to Azure AD, users become able to use their existing domain logins to authenticate SaaS applications. I think we all agree that Microsoft Office 365 is the most commonly used SaaS, and that it is the beginning of the hybrid identity journey for most organizations.

- **Cloud migration**: When an organization is moving their workloads to Azure, they will be using one or a few of the following methods:

  - **Rehost**: This is also called the lift-and-shift method. This method doesn't require code changes or architecture changes. It is the easiest method for moving workloads from on-premises to the cloud. As an example, let's assume an organization is using a web application that is hosted in a server running on-premises. If we need to move anything to the cloud, we can simply create a similar VM using Azure **Infrastructure as a Service** (**IaaS**), and migrate the application and its data across. However, if the organization is using on-premises AD, it is more likely that their workloads use domain authentication. Therefore, by introducing an Azure AD hybrid setup, we can add new servers to the same domain and use the same identities to authenticate into services.

  - **Refactor**: This method requires changes to the application design or architecture. With this migration method, applications and other services will get benefits from the cloud SaaS and **Platform-as-a-Service** (**PaaS**) offerings. The migration of on-premises Microsoft Exchange to Office 365 is a good example for this method. Instead of migrating exchange applications, an organization can migrate into feature-rich Office 365 solutions and start using the cloud's benefits. If the organization needs to maintain the same domain authentication with these new solutions, they have to use Azure AD with on-premises AD integration.

  - **Re-architecture**: This process will provide a modern touch to applications and services. The whole point of this method is to optimize applications and services to support the cloud's scalability, resilience, and HA. As an example, RebelAdmin Corp. is running an online store. They are currently using a few hosted web servers and MS SQL database servers in order to provide HA. When it comes to the cloud, instead of using the same architecture, they can migrate the application to Azure containers or scale sets. MS SQL clusters can also be replaced by the Azure SQL database in order to provide HA and scalability to applications. This will also give them the opportunity to upgrade the identity element of the application.

As an example, instead of using our AD username and password, by using Azure AD B2C, we can allow consumers to use their already existing social accounts such as Microsoft, Gmail, and Facebook accounts to log in to applications. However, not every application or service will support the re-architecture method. Therefore, organizations will have to use this method along with a rehost or refactor migration method.

- **Rebuild**: This method requires a complete restructuring of applications and services. No applications will be migrated to the cloud from on-premises. This is mainly due to the limitations and drawbacks of applications that cannot be improved by cloud migration; therefore, the only option is to start over and build a solution with modern cloud-native technologies. This also applies to identity management. There are many differences between on-premises AD and Azure AD. Azure AD is not the cloud version of AD. Nothing prevents organizations from putting more pressure on Azure AD capabilities, applications, or other infrastructure components. It isn't easy to completely cut over on-premises AD and start over with Azure AD without having a huge impact on entire identity infrastructure; therefore, it is safer to start with hybrid mode and then plan the cut over.

As we can see, every cloud migration method has a role to play with identities, and it is easy and convenient to start with Azure AD on-premises integration.

- **Features**: Azure AD is a managed service. It receives feature updates and bug fixes more frequently than on-premises solutions. In Chapter 1, *Active Directory Fundamentals*, I explained most of the features that Azure AD has. Most of these features also support work in hybrid environments; therefore, if an organization is looking to use Azure AD features with minimum infrastructure changes, on-premises AD integration is the place to start.

Apart from analyzing the main requirements, we can use the following questions to evaluate requirements further:

- What is the immediate business requirement for using Azure AD?
- Will this requirement affect everyone in the company? If not, which set of users this will apply to? (As an example, if a company has a group of businesses, which company or business unit will this requirement apply to?)
- How soon should the requirement be addressed?
- Is the business aware of the identity infrastructure changes that are required to achieve the business requirements?
- What is the available budget?
- Is the business aware of the other benefits of using Azure AD, apart from authentication (features such as identity protection, data protection, and auditing)?
- Are the business' legal and compliance requirements satisfied by the required changes?
- Does the business have the required resources (skills) to do the implementation and management? If not, how can the organization get it (training, outsourcing)?
- Was the risk analysis for Azure AD integration done?

The answers to the previous questions will help engineers understand the requirements from a business point of view, as well as decide on the next course of action before going further with the planning and implementation processes.

Evaluating an organization's infrastructure road map

In the previous section, we talked about why an organization may use an Azure AD hybrid setup. Moving from an on-premises service to a cloud service is a big decision for an organization; therefore, if it is not planned properly from an early stage, it can be hard to change things after implementation. In order to provide any IT solution, as engineers, we should not only consider the current state of the requirement: we also need to know the upcoming changes or future plans for the company infrastructure as it may have an impact on the solution that you have in mind. This is important as it helps engineers to provide future-proof solutions. RebelAdmin Corp. has an initial requirement to move from on-premises exchange services to Office 365.

However, RebelAdmin Corp. has already decided to move their application and services completely to Azure Cloud by 2020. So, if an engineer just considers the immediate requirements, they can simply finish the project by integrating the on-premises AD with the Azure AD free version that comes with Office 365; but by knowing the business' plans for cloud migration, they can also consider the following, apart from Office 365 migration:

- Decide how to protect identities and data with future infrastructure changes.
- Use a suitable Azure AD version in order to use advanced identity and data protection features.
- Try to use cloud-only identities for new users.
- Start provisioning VMs and applications in the cloud for new business requirements. Integrate these with Azure AD (domain-joined, SSO).
- Educate users on how to use Azure AD features effectively, such as Azure MFA, password-less authentication, and self-service password reset.

We can use the following questions to evaluate the infrastructure road map:

1. What is the company's cloud strategy?
2. Is there any other plan to use Azure services in the future? If so, which services is the company looking to use?
3. If the answer is yes for the previous question, what is the time frame for that?
4. Are there any potential technical challenges that can have an impact on the company's cloud journey?
5. Are there any risks that can have an impact on moving to cloud services?
6. Were any feasibility studies done in order to evaluate the use of cloud services?

The answers to the previous questions will help you determine the company's future in the cloud. Most of the time, it is best to gather answers for these questions from a business' decision makers. We can't make decisions that are purely based on road maps as it is more of a long-term plan for businesses, but it will help engineers to design future-proof solutions. This can help also engineers bring some of the projects forward.

Evaluating the security requirements

Azure AD comes with lot of features and services that can be used to protect identities in cloud-only or hybrid environments against modern threats. Since it is a managed service, these features and services have been continuously improved according to trends. Each and every security feature or service is not needed for every Azure AD environment. We can on decide the security requirements based on the following points:

- **Nature of the business**: Identity protection and data protection is important for every infrastructure; however, some businesses require advanced protection due to the sensitivity of the data they process, compliance requirements, and legal requirements. As an example, a financial institute will require advanced protection compared to a college due to differences in the sensitivity of data.

- **Skills**: Even if you have advanced security features and services, if you do not know how to use them appropriately, they will not provide the expected benefits. Also, the configuration and regular maintenance of some of these features and services requires knowledge. As an example, Azure information protection requires skills to set up appropriate policies and labels in order to get the benefits of data classification. These policies and labels will be different from business to business.

- **Cost**: The security features and services we can use will be impacted by which Azure AD version businesses can afford. There are five different Azure AD versions available to choose from. For more details, visit https://azure.microsoft.com/en-gb/pricing/details/active-directory/.

- **Compatibility**: Some of the Azure AD security features require a compatible device or environment in order to work. As an example, Azure AD password-less authentication (http://www.rebeladmin.com/2018/09/step-step-guide-azure-ad-password-less-authentication-public-preview/) only works with Windows 10 Azure AD join devices. If the existing environment is not compatible with Azure AD security features, either the organization will have to invest in bringing it to a compatible level or hold the implementation until they get there.

- **Resources**: If we only apply a security feature or enable a service, we can't expect the environment to be 100% protected. We are fighting against human adversaries who change their tactics all the time. In order to stay one step ahead, we need to regularly evaluate the service configuration in place, evaluate collected logs, and keep eye on alerts. All of this requires manpower and skills. If the organization is struggling with resources, it will not provide the expected results.

Over the years, I have written many articles about Azure AD-related security features. I have listed some of those:

- *Step-by-Step Guide to Azure AD Privileged Identity Management – Part 1*: http://www.rebeladmin.com/2016/07/step-step-guide-azure-ad-privileged-identity-management-part-1/
- *Step-by-Step Guide to Azure AD Privileged Identity Management – Part 2*: http://www.rebeladmin.com/2016/08/step-step-guide-azure-ad-privileged-identity-management-part-2/
- *Step-by-Step guide to setup temporally privilege access using Azure AD Privileged Identity Management*: http://www.rebeladmin.com/2018/09/step-step-guide-setup-temporally-privilege-access-using-azure-ad-privileged-identity-management/
- *Step-by-Step Guide: Privileged access management in Office 365*: http://www.rebeladmin.com/2019/04/step-step-guide-privileged-access-management-office-365/
- *Step-by-Step Guide: Protect confidential data using Azure information Protection*: http://www.rebeladmin.com/2018/12/step-step-guide-protect-confidential-data-using-azure-information-protection/
- *Step-by-Step Guide: Automatic Data Classification via Azure Information Protection*: http://www.rebeladmin.com/2018/12/step-step-guide-automatic-data-classification-via-azure-information-protection/
- *Step-by-Step Guide: On-premise Data Protection via Azure Information Protection Scanner*: http://www.rebeladmin.com/2018/12/step-step-guide-premise-data-protection-via-azure-information-protection-scanner/
- *Step-by-Step Guide: How to protect confidential emails using Azure information protection?*: http://www.rebeladmin.com/2019/01/step-step-guide-protect-confidential-emails-using-azure-information-protection/

- *Step-by-Step Guide: How to track shared documents using Azure information Protection?*: http://www.rebeladmin.com/2019/01/step-step-guide-track-shared-documents-using-azure-information-protection/

- *Step-by-Step Guide to Azure AD Password-less Authentication (public-preview)*: http://www.rebeladmin.com/2018/09/step-step-guide-azure-ad-password-less-authentication-public-preview/

- *Step-by-Step Guide: Using Microsoft Authenticator app (Public preview) to reset Azure AD user password*: http://www.rebeladmin.com/2019/02/step-step-guide-using-microsoft-authenticator-app-public-preview-reset-azure-ad-user-password/

- *Azure AD Self-Service password reset for Windows 7/8.1 Devices*: http://www.rebeladmin.com/2018/10/azure-ad-self-service-password-reset-windows-7-8-1-devices/

- *Conditional Access Policies with Azure Active Directory*: http://www.rebeladmin.com/2017/07/conditional-access-policies-azure-active-directory/

- *Conditional Access with Azure AD B2B*: http://www.rebeladmin.com/2018/11/conditional-access-azure-ad-b2b/

- *Step-by-Step guide to control data access using Azure Cloud app security (based on content type)*: http://www.rebeladmin.com/2018/09/step-step-guide-control-data-access-using-azure-cloud-app-security-based-content-type/

- *Step-by-Step guide to manage Impossible travel activity alert using Azure Cloud app security*: http://www.rebeladmin.com/2018/09/step-step-guide-manage-impossible-travel-activity-alert-using-azure-cloud-app-security/

- *Step-by-Step guide to block data download using Azure Cloud App security*: http://www.rebeladmin.com/2018/09/step-step-guide-block-data-download-using-azure-cloud-app-security/

Selecting the Azure AD version

Azure AD has five different editions. Azure AD free edition is the default edition for any Azure and Office 365 subscription. Basic and Premium versions are available through the Microsoft Enterprise Agreement, the Open Volume License program, and the Cloud Solution Providers program. Microsoft EMS E3 and E5 licenses also come with Azure AD Premium editions. More information about these editions can be found at https://docs.microsoft.com/en-us/azure/active-directory/fundamentals/active-directory-get-started-premium.

Deciding on a sign-in method

In this section, we are going to evaluate different Azure AD sign-in options for the hybrid environments. The sign-in options for the hybrid environment are managed only through the **Azure AD Connect** configuration. These sign-in methods can simply be grouped into two categories:

1. **Authentication takes place against Azure AD**: In this category, cloud users and synced on-premises users will be directly authenticated via Azure AD. No authentication request will pass to on-premises AD for processing when users access Azure services.
2. **Authentication takes place against on-premises AD**: Under this category, if synced on-premises users try to authenticate into Azure services, it will be processed by on-premises AD.

Password hash synchronization

This is the most commonly used method to allow on-premises AD users to authenticate into Azure services via Azure AD using their existing on-premises AD passwords. It is easy to implement as it is an extension of the Azure AD Connect directory synchronization. It doesn't require any other additional components to be installed on-premises other than Azure AD Connect. It is also recommended that you use this as a backup sign-in method, even if you decided to use a federation or pass-through sign-in method.

When I talk to customers or engineers, on many occasions, I find that people think password hash synchronization uses clear text passwords; however, this is completely wrong. On-premises AD doesn't use clear text passwords either; it stores passwords in the form of hash values. Hash values are generated by using a one-way mathematical function against an actual user password. Even if someone has access to a hash value, it isn't possible to a create cleartext password out of it. Hash values can't be used as passwords to authenticate in AD either. So, how it can be insecure?

After password hash synchronization is enabled, Azure AD Connect retrieves the password hash values that are stored in on-premises AD. Before hash values are synced over to Azure AD, Azure AD Connect will further encrypt them using an advanced hashing algorithm. Once this data is synced to Azure AD, it can't be presented back to on-premises AD and be used to perform a successful authentication.

Let's go ahead and see how password hash synchronization works in a hybrid environment:

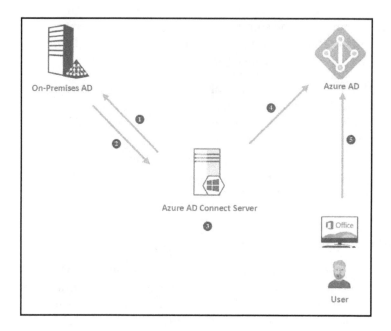

The following steps summaries the flow of password hash synchronization in hybrid environment.

1. In the previous environment, **Azure AD** is configured to perform password hash synchronization. First, **Azure AD Connect Server** is requesting password hash values stored in **on-premises AD** server. This is done by using the **Microsoft Directory Replication Service (MS-DRS)** remote replication protocol, which is standard for inter-**Domain Controller (DC)** replication. Azure AD Connect uses the service account that is used during the configuration to retrieve the password hashes. Hashes stored in AD are in the **message digest 4 (MD4)** algorithm format (http:// practicalcryptography.com/hashes/md4-hash/).

2. Then, DC encrypts the MD4 hash values using a secure key. This key is the MD5 hash value of the **Remote Procedure Call (RPC)** session key and salt. Salt is providing additional security by adding random characters to the hash. Once the encryption is completed, the system sends the encrypted hash values to the synchronization agent via RPC. On-premises DC also sends the salt to the synchronization agent via the inter DC replication protocol.

3. Once the synchronization agent receives the encrypted hash, it uses the `MD5CryptoServiceProvider` class and salt to decrypt the hash envelope and retrieve the original hash values. Then, the synchronization agent converts a 16 byte hash into a 64 byte hash. After that, the synchronization agent adds a further 10-byte salt as extra protection for the original hash. This salt value is unique for each **User**. The synchronization agent then uses the original MD4 value and salt value in the **Password-Based Key Derivation Function 2 (PBKDF2)** (`https://www.ietf.org/rfc/rfc2898.txt`). This process will generate a **Hash-Based Message Authentication Code (HMAC)** by using the **Secure Hash Algorithm 256-bit (SHA256)** hash function.

4. Here, the synchronization agent takes the 32-byte hash, per user salt, and SHA256 iteration. It then transfers this to **Azure AD** over the **Secure Sockets Layer (SSL)**.

5. When a **User** tries to authenticate into **Azure AD** with their on-premises password, the system will use the same method and generate a hash value for the provided password and compare it with the one saved in **Azure AD**. If both hashes match **Azure AD** will accept user authentication.

With password hash synchronization, we also need to consider following:

- Once Azure AD Connect is configured, password hash synchronization runs every two minutes. This schedule can't be changed.
- We can't enable/disable password hash synchronization for only certain users (unless it is controlled in the AD sync scope).
- Password changes will not affect already authenticated sessions.
- Password hash synchronization is not going to enable SSO. Users have to re-authenticate to Azure AD, and even log in using the domain computer.
- Password hash synchronization is only for AD user objects.
- Even if someone has access to the SHA256 hash of a user, it can't be used for on-premises AD authentication as the original MD4 hash was never transmitted to Azure AD.
- It is recommended to use password hash synchronization as a backup authentication method if you are using federation authentication or pass-through authentication.

Federation with Azure AD

Federation trusts between domains allow organizations to manage their own identities within their own environments. Azure AD also supports federation with on-premises AD. When a federation trust is in place, users can log in to Azure AD using the same on-premises AD passwords. With this method, on-premises users will always be authenticating via on-premises AD. We can use **AD Federation Services (AD FS)** or PingFederate to create federation trusts between Azure AD and on-premises AD.

More information about AD FS configuration for Azure AD can be found at `https://docs.microsoft.com/en-us/azure/active-directory/hybrid/how-to-connect-fed-whatis`.

More information about PingFederate configuration for Azure AD can be found at `https://docs.pingidentity.com/bundle/O365IG20_sm_integrationGuide/page/O365IG_c_integrationGuide.html`.

Pass-through authentication

To create federation trusts between Azure AD and on-premises AD, quite a bit of work is involved. We need additional servers, SSL certificates, licenses, HA solution, firewall changes, and advanced configurations. But Azure AD pass-through authentication allows organizations to do on-premises only user authentication with minimum changes being made to the environment. It uses an agent (`https://aka.ms/getauthagent`) that can be installed on any Windows server. By using pass-through authentication, users can do the following:

- Authenticate into Azure AD and on-premises AD using the same password.
- Authentication for on-premises users will always be processed through on-premises AD.
- Pass-through authentication feature comes as a part of Azure AD Connect. We don't need to pay anything to use this authentication method.
- Pass-through authentication agents are lightweight and can install it with other applications. Multiple agents can be installed in multiple servers for HA purposes. No additional configuration is required to enable HA; it is just a matter of getting an agent installed.

- It is recommended to use at least three pass-through authentication agents in an environment.
- Pass-through authentication agents only make outbound connections to Azure AD via TCP port 443. Therefore, there is no requirement to place agents in a **demilitarized zone (DMZ)**. Mostly, this will not require firewall changes at all as most environments allow outgoing TCP 443 traffic.
- Pass-through authentication agents and Azure AD use certificate-based authentication for communication. This certificate will be renewed automatically.
- This works well with Azure MFA and conditional access policies.
- This supports multi-forest environments as long as there is a valid trust and name suffix routing in place.

Let's go ahead and see how pass-through authentication works:

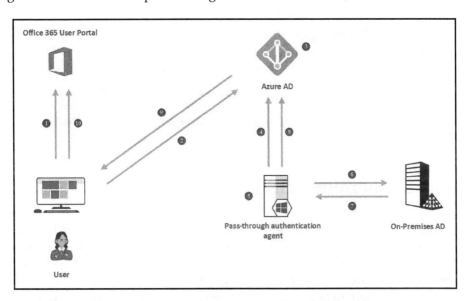

In this example, **User** is trying to access **Office 365 User Portal**. They have pass-through authentication enabled:

1. **User** is accessing `https://www.office.com` using the browser installed on their computer.
2. In order to authenticate, **User** is directed to the Azure AD sign-in page. **User** then types the username and password and clicks on the **Sign in** button.

3. **Azure AD** receives the sign-in request and encrypts the password using the public key of the **Pass-through authentication agent**. This is retrieved from the Azure SQL database for the tenant. Azure AD then places the encrypted password in the service bus queue where the system will hold it until the **Pass-through authentication agent** retrieves it.

4. An on-premises **Pass-through authentication agent** retrieves the username and encrypted password from the service bus queue (using an outbound connection). This is done via a pre-established connection.

5. The **Pass-through authentication agent** decrypts the password using its private key.

6. The **Pass-through authentication agent** validates the username and password information with on-premises AD using the Win32 LogonUser API. It is the same API used by AD FS in the federated sign-in method.

7. The **On-premises AD** evaluates the request and issues a response. It can be a success, failure, password-expire, or account lockout.

8. The **Pass-through authentication agent** passes the response back to **Azure AD**.

9. **Azure AD** evaluates the response and passes it back to the **User**.

10. If the response was successful, the **User** is allowed to access the application.

Later in this chapter, we will look into the configuration of the pass-through authentication feature.

Azure AD Seamless SSO

So far, we have learned about three different methods that we can use to integrate on-premises AD with Azure AD. This also allows on-premises users to use their existing domain usernames and passwords in order to authenticate into Azure AD integrated services. However, even though users can use the same username and passwords, when they access Azure AD integrated services from a corporate device (domain member), they still have to authenticate via the sign-in page. Azure AD Seamless SSO allows users to access Azure AD integrated services via corporate devices without re-authentication. Azure AD Seamless SSO can be used with the password hash synchronization and pass-through authentication methods. However, its use is not supported by the federated authentication method:

- The Azure AD Seamless SSO feature can be enabled via Azure AD Connect, so it doesn't require any additional components in its environment.
- This is a free feature. We don't need to pay anything for it.

- Azure AD Seamless SSO only works in domain-joined devices (no need to use Azure AD join).
- If a SSO process has failed for any reason, the user can still authenticate using their username and password.
- It is supported to work with browser-based web applications and Office 365 clients with app versions 16.0.8730 and higher.
- Azure AD Seamless SSO accepts usernames as values associated with the **User Principal Name** (**UPN**) attribute or the Azure AD Connect **Alternate ID** attribute.
- Azure AD Seamless SSO uses the **security identifier** claim in the Kerberos ticket to find the relevant user object in Azure AD.
- Once Azure AD Seamless SSO is enabled, if an application can forward `domain_hint` (OpenID Connect) or the `whr` (SAML) parameter to identify the tenant, and the `login_hint` (OpenID Connect) parameter to identify the user, we can log in to Azure AD without typing usernames. This is also possible if the application uses a unique URL and is able to pass the domain info or tenant info.
- Once the user is logged in via SSO, if required, the user can still sign out and log in as a different user at any time.

Let's go ahead and see how Azure AD Seamless SSO works during the authentication process:

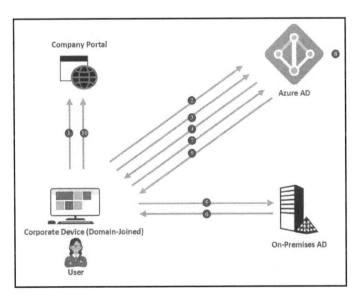

In this example, **User** is trying to access their **Company Portal** using a **Domain-Joined** computer. This is a hybrid setup, and the company already has Azure AD Seamless SSO enabled via Azure AD Connect:

1. **User** types `https://www.office.com` into the browser installed on the corporate device and presses *Enter*.
2. **User** is redirected to the **Azure AD** sign-in page.
3. The web application is not passing any domain info or tenant info, so **User** is typing their username into the **Azure AD** sign-in page.
4. **Azure AD** challenges the browser via a `401` unauthorized response to provide a valid Kerberos ticket.
5. The browser in the computer then requests a Kerberos ticket for the `AZUREADSSOACC` computer account. This account is created in on-premises AD when Azure AD Connect is first configured for Azure AD Seamless SSO. This object represents the **Azure AD**.
6. **On-Premises AD** responds with the Kerberos ticket for the `AZUREADSSOACC` computer account. This is encrypted with the computer account's secret.
7. The browser responds back to **Azure AD** with the encrypted Kerberos ticket.
8. **Azure AD** decrypts the Kerberos key using its decryption key. This key was shared with **Azure AD** when Azure AD Seamless SSO was first enabled on Azure AD Connect.
9. If it is a valid ticket, **Azure AD** returns a token to the browser by accepting access.
10. **User** successfully logs into **Company Portal** without typing in the password again.

Later in this chapter, I will be sharing the configuration steps for Azure AD Seamless SSO.

Synchronization between on-premises AD and Azure AD Managed Domain

Azure AD Managed Domain is not a cloud version of on-premises AD, but it is supported by AD functions such as Kerberos/**NT LAN Manager** (**NTLM**) authentication, domain join, and **Lightweight Directory Access Protocol** (**LDAP**) queries. Azure AD Managed Domain is not running any DCs that we can **Remote Desktop Protocol** (**RDP**) or connect to using any other method. As tenants, we only have limited control over the Azure AD Managed Domain services. So far, we have learned how authentication works in a hybrid cloud environment.

In an Azure AD hybrid environment, two different identity platforms are going to work together and provide the same authentication experience to users, regardless of which environment they are located in. This is only possible through directory synchronization between two identity systems. Therefore, let's go ahead and see how synchronization works in a hybrid environment:

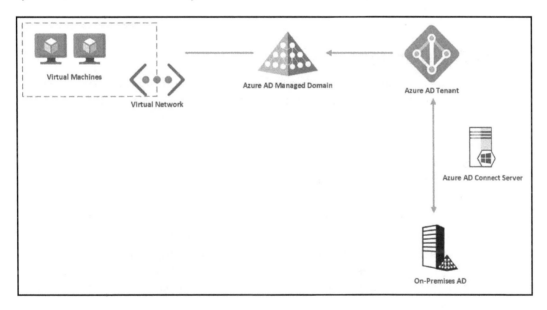

The preceding diagram demonstrates the high-level Azure AD hybrid topology.

1. In a hybrid environment, **Azure AD Connect Server** is responsible for syncing an on-premises user's UPN, **Security Identifiers** (**SIDs**), and group memberships to **Azure AD Tenant**.
2. **Azure AD Connect Server** can also be used to sync password hashes if required.

3. **Azure AD Connect Server** can also be used to define the user sign-in method to the directory (federated, pass-through authentication, and SSO).

4. Group polices, **System Volume** (**SYSVOL**) content, computer objects, OU, and SidHistory attributes will not sync from **On-Premises AD** to **Azure AD Managed Domain**.

5. Data synced from **On-Premises AD** to **Azure AD Tenant** will be synchronized to the **Azure AD Managed Domain**.

6. This synchronization between the **Azure AD Tenant** and the **Azure AD Managed Domain** will be automatic, and we can't change this schedule. Once a change is made in the **On-Premises AD**, it can take up to 30 minutes to sync back to the **Azure AD Managed Domain**.

7. The sync from **Azure AD Tenant** to **Azure AD Managed Domain** is one-way.

8. **Azure AD Managed Domain** will be attached to a virtual network. Any VM in this virtual network will be able to join the **Azure AD Managed Domain**.

Azure AD Connect

Azure AD Connect is the service that's responsible for integrating on-premises AD with Azure AD Tenant. Azure AD Connect replaces the previous versions of **Windows Azure AD Sync** (**DirSync**) and Azure AD sync components. Azure AD Connect has the following features:

- **Synchronization services**: This service checks whether Azure AD has the same identities as on-premises AD. If it doesn't, it will create the relevant objects in Azure AD.

- **Password hash synchronization**: Azure AD Connect can sync password hashes for on-premises AD users to the Azure AD Tenant.

- **Federation service**: Azure AD Connect can be configured to authenticate via an on-premises AD FS or Ping Identity federation service. This is used by organizations that use domain join SSO, third-party MFA, smart cards, and so on.

- **Pass-through authentication**: When this feature is enabled, on-premises users will always be authenticated via on-premises AD. This will be done via the authentication agent and it doesn't require additional servers and complex configurations such as AD FS farms.

- **Monitoring**: Azure AD Connect Health monitors the health of Azure AD Connect and its components. These stats can be viewed using the Azure portal.

Azure AD Connect deployment topology

Azure AD Connect uses two different topologies to support on-premises AD deployments. However, there are certain limitations and unsupported configurations that we need to consider, which are as follows:

- **Single AD forest-single Azure AD**: This is the most commonly used deployment topology. When a user has a single AD forest, it can be synced to one Azure AD Tenant. Even if it has multiple domains, it still can be used with one AD Tenant. The Azure AD Connect express setup only supports this topology. However, at any given time, only one Azure AD Connect server can sync data to the Azure AD Tenant. For HA, staging server support is available, which will be explained later in this section.
- **Multiple AD forest-single Azure AD**: Some organizations have multiple AD forests for various reasons. Azure AD supports syncing identities from all the forests into one Azure AD Tenant. Each AD forest can have multiple domains as well. The AD Connect server should be able to reach all the forests, but this doesn't mean it needs to have AD trust between forests. The Azure AD Connect server can be placed in a perimeter network and then be allowed access to different forests from there. A rule of thumb in this model is to represent a user only once in Azure AD. If a user exists in multiple forests, it can be handled in two ways:
  - We can set the forest to match the user's identity using the mail attribute. If Microsoft Exchange is available in one or more forests, it may also have an on-premises **Global Address List Synchronization** (**GALSync**) solution. GALSync is a solution that is used to share exchange mail objects between multiple forests. This will allow us to represent each user object as a contact in other forests. If a user has a mailbox in one forest, it will be joined with the contacts in the other forests.
  - If users are in an account resource forest topology that has an extended AD schema with Exchange and Lync, they will be matched using the `objectSid` and `sExchangeMasterAccountSid` attributes.

These options can be selected during the AD Connect configuration. There is no support for having multiple AD Connect servers in each forest syncing to one Azure AD Tenant.

Staging the server

By design, it isn't possible to have multiple Azure AD Connect servers sync the same directory data to the same Azure AD Tenant. However, Azure AD Connect supports maintaining a second server in staging mode, which is ideal for HA. A server in staging mode reads data from all connected directories but will not sync it to the Azure AD Tenant. It runs sync jobs as a normal Azure AD Connect server, so in the case of a disaster, it already has the latest data.

In the event of a primary server failure, we can use the Azure AD Connect wizard to fail over to the staging server. This method can be used to replace the existing AD Connect server. We can make all the relevant changes in staging mode, and when everything is ready, we can fail over to the newly implemented server. Maintaining multiple staging servers in an infrastructure is also supported.

Before installing the AD Connect server, we need to check whether the existing environment meets the following requirements. They can be found at `https://docs.microsoft.com/en-gb/azure/active-directory/hybrid/how-to-connect-install-prerequisites`:

- The AD forest functional level must be Windows Server 2003 or later.
- If you plan to use the password writeback feature, then the DCs must be on Windows Server 2008 (with the latest SP) or later. If your DCs are on 2008 (pre-R2), then you must also apply the `KB2386717` hotfix.
- The DC used by Azure AD must be writable. Using a **Read-Only Domain Controller** (**RODC**) is not supported, and Azure AD Connect does not follow any write redirects.
- There is no support for using on-premises forests/domains using **Single Label Domains** (**SLDs**).
- There is no support for using on-premises forests/domains using dotted NetBIOS names (names with a period in them).
- Azure AD Connect cannot be installed on Small Business Server or Windows Server Essentials. The server must use Windows Server Standard or better.

- The Azure AD Connect server must have the full GUI installed. There is no support for installing it on Server Core.

- Azure AD Connect must be installed on Windows Server 2008 R2 or later. This server may be a DC or a member server when you're using express settings. If you use custom settings, then the server can also be standalone and does not have to be joined to a domain.

- If you install Azure AD Connect on Windows Server 2008 R2, then make sure to apply the latest hotfixes from Windows Update. The installation cannot be started with an unpatched server.

- If you plan to use the password synchronization feature, then the Azure AD Connect server must be on Windows Server 2008 R2 SP1 or later.

- If you plan to use a group-managed service account, then the Azure AD Connect server must be on Windows Server 2012 or later.

- The Azure AD Connect server must have .NET Framework 4.5.1 or later and Microsoft PowerShell 4.0 or later installed.

- If AD FS is being deployed, the servers where AD FS or Web Application Proxy are installed must be Windows Server 2012 R2 or later. Windows remote management must be enabled on these servers for remote installation.

- If AD FS is being deployed, you need SSL certificates.

- If AD FS is being deployed, then you need to configure name resolution.

- If your global administrators have MFA enabled, then the `https://secure.aadcdn.microsoftonline-p.com` URL must be in the trusted sites list. You are prompted to add this site to the trusted sites list when you are prompted for an MFA challenge and it has not been added before. You can use Internet Explorer to add it to your trusted sites.

- Azure AD Connect requires a SQL Server database to store identity data. By default, SQL Server 2012 Express LocalDB (a light version of SQL Server Express) is installed. SQL Server Express has a 10 GB size limit that allows you to manage approximately 100,000 objects. If you need to manage a higher volume of directory objects, you need to point the installation wizard to a different installation of SQL Server.

- If you use a different SQL Server version, then these requirements apply:
    - Azure AD Connect supports all flavors of Microsoft SQL Server from SQL Server 2008 (with the latest service pack) to SQL Server 2016. Microsoft Azure SQL Database is not supported as a database.

- You must use a case-insensitive SQL collation. These collations are identified as having _CI_ in their name. There is no support for using case-sensitive collation, which is identified by _CS_ in the name.
- You can only have one sync engine per SQL instance. There is no support for sharing a SQL instance with **Forefront Identity Manager (FIM)/Microsoft Identity Manager (MIM)** Sync, DirSync, or Azure AD Sync.

Step-by-step guide to integrating an on-premises AD environment with Azure AD

Before we start with the integration process, we need the following:

- **Valid Azure subscription**: We need to have a valid Azure subscription. It can be a pay-as-you-go subscription or a partner subscription. You can also get a free Azure demo account with £150 in credit. More information can be found at https://azure.microsoft.com/en-gb/offers/ms-azr-0044p/.
- **Global administrator account**: In order to set up Azure AD, you need to log in to Azure with an account that has global administrator account privileges.
- **Access to domain DNS**: If you are going to add a custom domain name, as part of the process, you need to verify the ownership of the domain name. This is done by using a DNS record. Therefore, engineers need to have access to DNS servers. This is important if you are using a public domain name (.com, .org, or .net).
- **Enterprise administrator account**: In order to set up and configure Azure AD Connect, the engineers need to be members of the enterprise administrator group in the on-premises AD setup.

- **Connectivity**: The server running Azure AD Connect needs to have connectivity to Azure services. If your DCs do not have direct access to the internet prior to deployment, firewall rules need to be modified to allow the Azure service access on recommended ports.

More information about ports can be found at `https://docs.microsoft.com/en-us/azure/active-directory/connect/active-directory-aadconnect-ports`. The service URL and IP range information can be found at `https://support.office.com/en-gb/article/Office-365-URLs-and-IP-address-ranges-8548a211-3fe7-47cb-abb1-355ea5aa88a2?ui=en-USrs=en-GBad=GB`.

Once the aforementioned prerequisites are ready, we can move on to the implementation process. In this demo, I am going to cover the following:

- Creating a virtual network
- Creating an Azure AD instance
- Adding DNS server details to the virtual network
- Creating an AAD DC administrator group
- Creating a global administrator account for Azure AD Connect
- Setting up Azure AD Connect:
    - Enabling pass-through authentication
    - Enabling Azure AD Seamless SSO
- Enabling synchronization of NTLM and Kerberos credential hashes to Azure AD

Creating a virtual network

Azure AD and other workloads should use the same virtual network so that they can be operated under the same managed domain. If you already have a subscription and have your virtual network set up, this step can be skipped:

1. Log in to Azure portal as a global administrator (`https://portal.azure.com`).

2. Click on **Virtual networks** from the left-hand navigation panel. Then, click on **+ Add**:

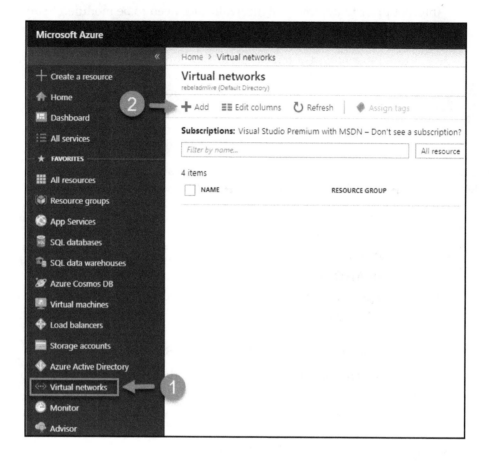

3. In the wizard, provide the following details:
   - **Name**: Provide a name for the virtual network. In this demo, I am using REBELVMNet as my virtual network name.
   - **Address space**: This defines the **Classless Inter-Domain Routing (CIDR)** notation of the IP address range for the virtual network. Always use a large subnet for this as we can create a different subnetwork under this. In my demo, I am using 10.1.0.0/16 as the address space.
   - **Resource group**: Select or create a resource group for the virtual network. In my demo, I am using new resource group for this called REBELDC.

- **Location**: Select a location for the virtual network. Please note that we need to use the same location for the managed domain.
- **Subnet Name**: Here, we need to define a name for the subnet. I have used `REBEL-VN01`.
- **Subnet Address range**: We can define a subnet using this option. Azure AD Managed Domain will also use this subnet. In my demo, I am using `10.1.0.0/24` as the address range.

Once the preceding details have been provided, click **Create** to proceed with the virtual network deployment:

4. Once the deployment has completed, we will be able to see the newly created virtual network in a portal:

Setting up Azure AD Managed Domain

The next step of the configuration process is to set up an Azure AD managed domain.

1. In order to do that, log in to Azure portal (`https://portal.azure.com`) as a global administrator.
2. Go to **All Services | Azure AD Domain Services**.
3. Click on **Create Azure AD Domain Services**:

4. This will open up a wizard. Type in **DNS domain name** for the service. It is recommended that you use the default tenant domain name in the beginning as, we can add a custom domain later on, if required. Also, select the **Resource group** we created in the previous step:

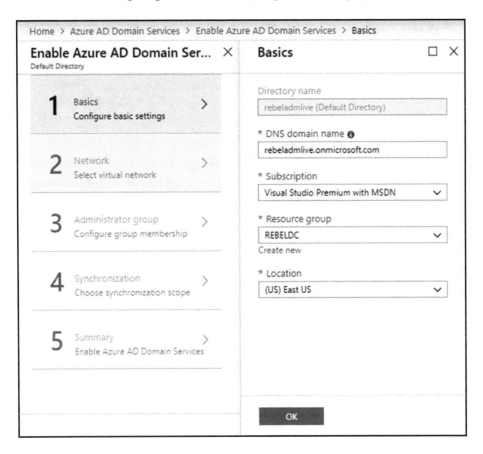

5. In the next window, select the virtual network and subnet we created in the previous section. If needed, we can also create a new virtual network and subnet on this page:

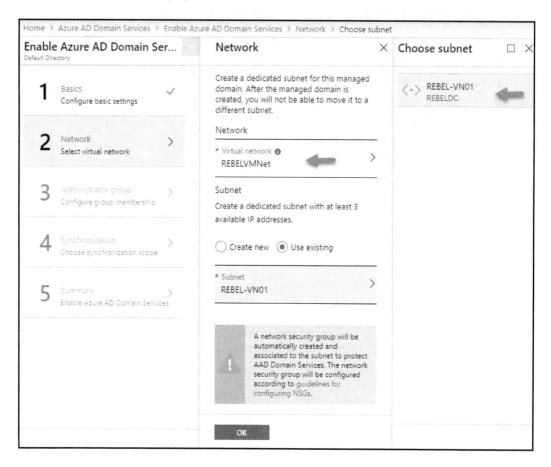

6. In the next window, we can manage the members of the default **AAD DC Administrators** group. Members of the **AAD DC Administrators** group have administrative privileges over the managed domain:

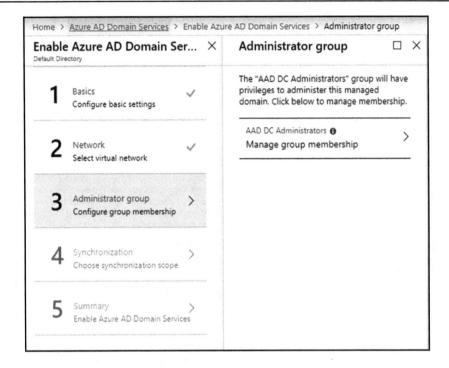

We can add new members using **Add members** option.

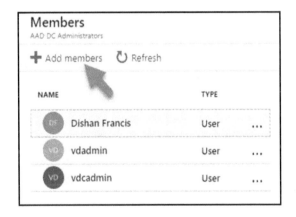

7. On the next page, we can define the **Synchronization scope** from Azure AD Tenant. In my demo, I will keep the default and sync as **All** users and groups:

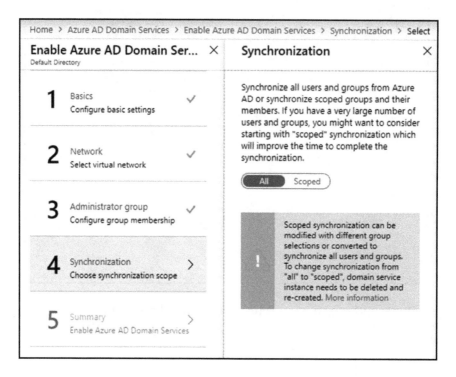

8. On the **Summary** page, review the configuration settings and click **OK** to complete the setup process:

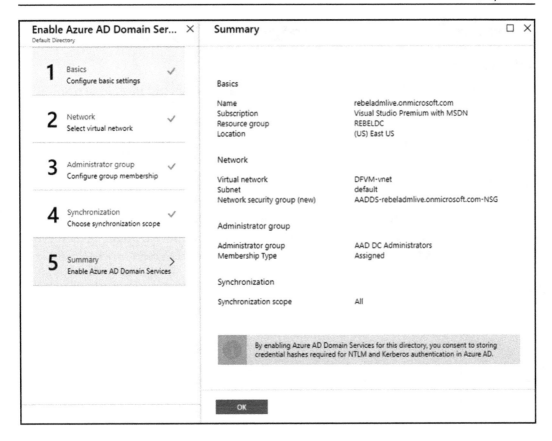

It will take around 30 minutes to complete the setup process. Once it is completed, we will be able to see the managed domain under the **Azure AD Domain Services** page:

Adding DNS server details to the virtual network

If we need to add a VM to this managed domain, the VM should be able to resolve the DNS name of the managed domain. This is done via a DNS server that belongs to the managed domain. We need to add this DNS server to the virtual network so that we can add VMs to the managed domain at a later time.

To do this, perform the following steps:

1. Go to **All Services | Azure AD Domain Services**.
2. Click on the managed domain we just created.
3. On the next page, click on **Configure**, which is under **Update DNS server settings for your virtual network**. This will add DNS servers to the relevant virtual network:

4. Once the DNS update process has completed, we will be able to see the records under the relevant virtual network's DNS settings:

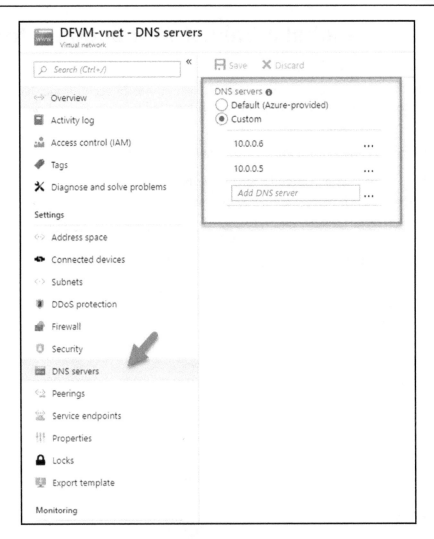

Creating a global administrator account for Azure AD Connect

During the Azure AD Connect configuration, we require an account that has global administrator privileges (in Azure). It is recommended to use a separate account for this.

In order to create a user account, perform the following steps:

1. Click on **Azure Active Directory** in the Azure portal.
2. Click on **All users** | **+ New user**:

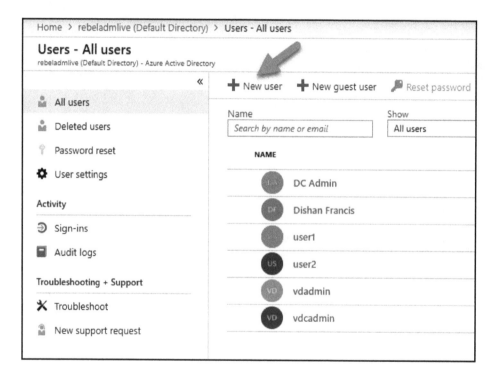

3. Then, type the account name and username in the relevant fields. After that, click on **Directory role** and make sure that you select **Global administrator**:

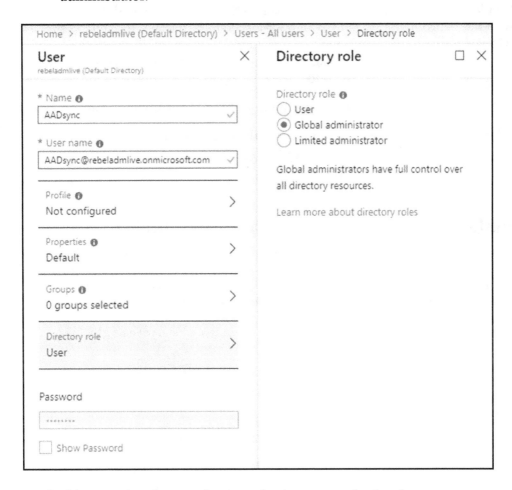

4. After creating the user, log in to the Azure portal using the new account details and make sure that the account is in a working state before using it for AD Sync.

5. Also, make sure that this account is a member of the **AAD DC Administrators** group. This will provide administrative privileges to the managed domain.

Setting up Azure AD Connect

In my demo environment, I have an on-premises DC running. It is operating in the Windows Server 2016 domain and forest functional levels. I would like to integrate it with the Azure AD Managed Domain we just created. In my setup, the on-premises AD uses the same domain name as the managed domain. In the production environment, you can use the **Custom domain name** option and register the domain under Azure AD before going into the Azure AD Connect configuration.

With the Azure AD Connect configuration, I would like to do following:

- Sync all the users and groups to the Azure AD Tenant
- Configure pass-through authentication
- Configure Azure AD Seamless SSO

Installing the pass-through authentication agent

Before we move into Azure AD Connect, we need to install the pass-through authentication agent. It is recommended to install the pass-through authentication agent on the same server as Azure AD Connect. In a production environment, it is recommended to install this agent in at least three servers:

1. Log in to Azure portal (`https://portal.azure.com`) as a global administrator.
2. Click on **Azure Active Directory** | **Azure AD Connect** | **Pass-through authentication**:

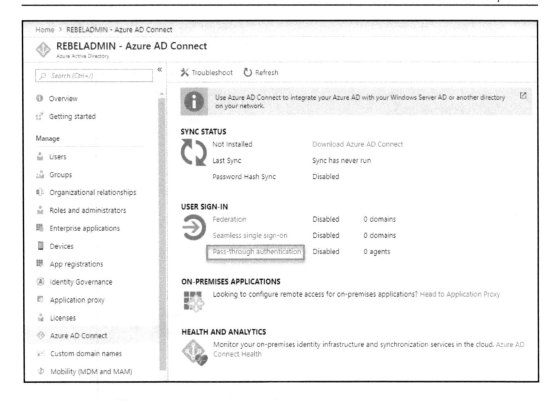

3. Click on **Download** to download the file.

4. Once the `.exe` file has been downloaded, move to the server where it is going to be installed.

5. Then, double-click on the file and proceed with the installation:

6. During the installation process, it will prompt for authentication. Use the global administrator user account we just created:

7. Once it is installed successfully, we will be able to see it under **Azure Active Directory** | **Azure AD Connect** | **Pass-through authentication**:

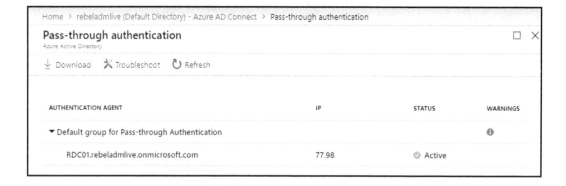

Azure AD Connect configuration

Now, we have everything ready so that we can go ahead with the Azure AD Connect installation and configuration:

1. Log in to the on-premises server as a domain administrator.
2. Download the latest version of Azure AD Connect from `https://www.microsoft.com/en-us/download/details.aspx?id=47594`.
3. Run the `.msi` file as an administrator.
4. On the first page, accept the license terms and click on **Continue**.
5. On the next page, select the **Customize** configuration option:

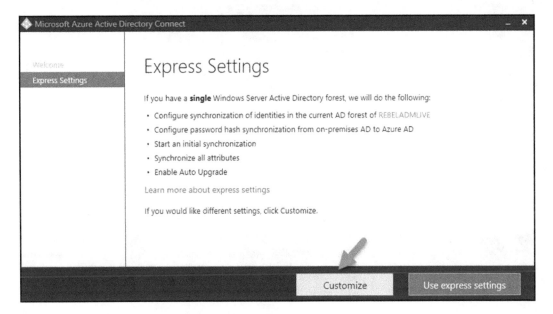

6. On the next page, keep the default selection and click on **Install**.
7. On the user sign-in page, select **Pass-through authentication** and **Single sign-on**, and then click **Next** to proceed. This will enable pass-through authentication for the directory:

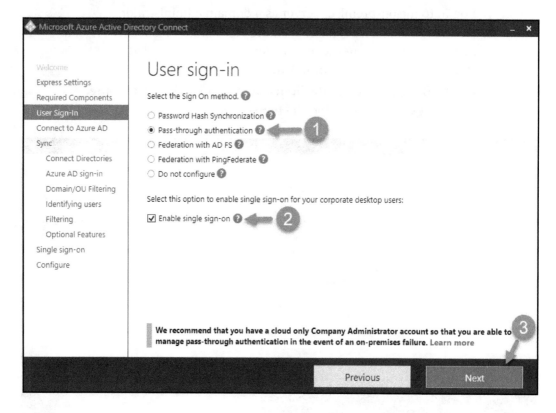

8. On the next page, log in to the user Azure AD global admin account we created in order to connect to Azure AD. After login validation, click on **Next** to continue.

9. On the **Connect Directories** page, provide an on-premises domain admin account and select **FOREST**.

10. For the next few pages, I kept the selections as their default values as I would like to sync all the user objects to Azure AD.

11. On the **Optional Features** page, I am selecting **Password hash synchronization** to work as the backup sign-in option if pass-through authentication doesn't work:

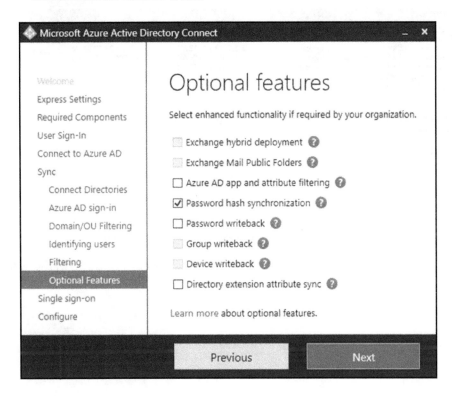

12. Then, on the **Enable single sign-on page**, provide the domain admin credentials.

13. This will complete the configuration process of AD Connect. On the next page, click on **Install**.

14. After completing the installation, go to **Synchronizations Service** in programs and view the sync progress:

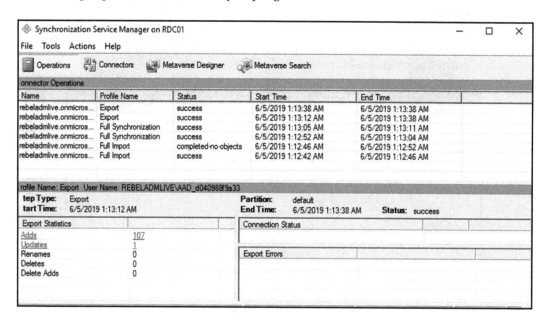

15. After a few minutes, we should be able to see synced users in the Azure AD Tenant under **Azure Active Directory | Users**:

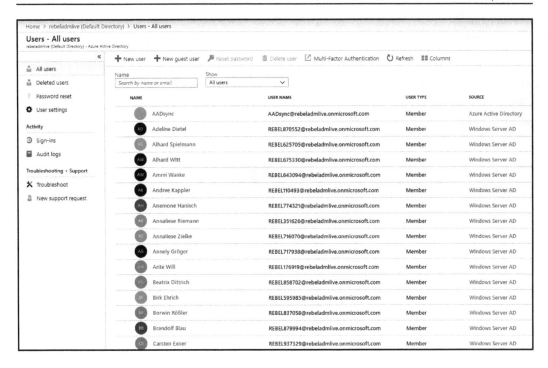

Syncing NTLM and Kerberos credential hashes to Azure AD

Azure AD Connect does not synchronize NTLM and Kerberos credential hashes to Azure AD by default. To use AD domain services, we need to configure Azure AD Connect so that it synchronizes the credential hashes that are required for NTLM and Kerberos authentication. To do that, we need to run the following PowerShell script:

```
$adConnector = "<CASE SENSITIVE AD CONNECTOR NAME>"
$azureadConnector = "<CASE SENSITIVE AZURE AD CONNECTOR NAME>"
Import-Module adsync
$c = Get-ADSyncConnector -Name $adConnector
$p = New-Object
Microsoft.IdentityManagement.PowerShell.ObjectModel.ConfigurationParam
ter "Microsoft.Synchronize.ForceFullPasswordSync", String,
ConnectorGlobal, $null, $null, $null
$p.Value = 1
$c.GlobalParameters.Remove($p.Name)
$c.GlobalParameters.Add($p)
$c = Add-ADSyncConnector -Connector $c
Set-ADSyncAADPasswordSyncConfiguration -SourceConnector $adConnector -
```

```
TargetConnector $azureadConnector -Enable $false
Set-ADSyncAADPasswordSyncConfiguration -SourceConnector $adConnector -
TargetConnector $azureadConnector -Enable $true
```

We can find the AD Connector and Azure AD Connector names under **Start** | **Synchronization Service** | **Connectors**:

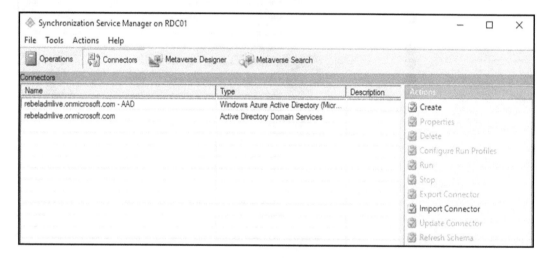

This completes the configuration part of the Azure AD hybrid setup. Depending on the size of the directory, it can take up to 30 minutes to complete the sync process. Once the process is completed, users can authenticate into Azure AD using their on-premises usernames and passwords.

Summary

Azure AD is a Microsoft-managed, cloud-based, and multi-tenant directory service. It can be used in a cloud-only infrastructure or in a hybrid infrastructure. When used in a hybrid infrastructure, it allows us to use the same identities so that we can work with resources on-premises and in the cloud. It extends local AD infrastructure functionalities to the cloud.

In this chapter, we learned what an Azure AD Domain Service is and what its capabilities are. We also looked into the different types of sign-in options that we can use in a hybrid setup, including password hash synchronizations, pass-through authentication, and SSO. After that, we looked at a step-by-step guide for integrating our on-premises directory service with Azure AD. In this chapter, I was only able to demonstrate a very limited number of features and capabilities of Azure AD. For more Azure AD-related topics, refer to my blog at www.rebeladmin.com.

In the next chapter, we will look at AD auditing and monitoring, which is crucial for maintaining a healthy AD infrastructure.

18

Active Directory Audit and Monitoring

The **National Institute of Standards and Technology** (**NIST**) cybersecurity framework (`https://www.nist.gov/cyberframework`) is based on three main things: protect, detect, and respond. All these components are connected to one another. When we implement a system, we first need to understand what to protect and how to protect it. So far in this book, I've explained the importance of an identity infrastructure and how and what we can do to protect it from emerging threats. Based on that, we can build a protected identity infrastructure, but we should understand that we can't close all the doors. We need to expect a breach at any time. But when it happens, we should have a system in place to detect it and notify us. This allows us to respond to the situation quickly and to minimize damage. In order to detect similar incidents, it is important to have proper systems and processes in place. This is where auditing and monitoring comes in. These help us to ensure that the protected system we built is operating as expected; and, if there is any unexpected or unnatural behavior, it's recorded and reported. These findings will help engineers to act proactively and prevent breaches.

Before I use the London Underground service, I always check the **Transport for London** (**TFL**) website to see the status of the tube line services. This is a service provided by TFL to make sure its users are planning their journey properly to avoid delays. The system TFL has in place to monitor the line status gives us two benefits. As a service provider, TFL can detect the problem and start to address it immediately. At the same time, some filtered information is passed to the public that will be important for planning their journey.

Similarly, auditing and monitoring are not only to enable engineers to find problems. They also should provide filtered, structured information to different parties in the business that are important for their roles and responsibilities. As an example, the IT manager would like to know the overall domain service availability over the last month. But it is not important for him to know each and every event that happened in the system during the last 30 days, although this can be important for the IT engineers.

In auditing and monitoring, we also need to identify what to monitor and what is to be reported. Knowing each and every thing that happens in the system is good, but at the same time, unless it has been analyzed and prioritized, it will not deliver any benefit to engineers in detecting the issues properly. Therefore, we need systems to audit and monitor the correct stuff and present it in a useful way.

In this chapter, we will look at the following:

- Monitoring **Active Directory** (**AD**) Domain Service-related events and logs
- Advanced auditing for AD infrastructure
- Using Microsoft **Advanced Threat Analytics** (**ATA**) to monitor identity infrastructure threats
- AD monitoring with Azure Monitor
- Azure AD Connect Health

Auditing and monitoring AD using in-built Windows tools and techniques

Microsoft does have in-built features and tools to monitor and audit AD environments. In this section, we are going to review these features and tools.

Windows Event Viewer

As an engineer, I am sure you are well aware of Windows Event Viewer. It is a built-in tool that can be used to view and filter event logs on a local or remote computer. Events in there are generated by the operating system, services, server roles, and applications. This is the most commonly used tool in Windows systems for auditing and troubleshooting purposes.

We also can write custom events to event logs. This is useful if you plan to run a script or action based on a particular event ID. This can be done by using the `Write-Eventlog` cmdlet.

As shown in the following screenshot, Windows **Event Viewer (Local)** has four different categories to group event logs:

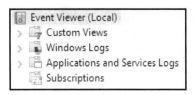

Custom views

Event Viewer allows the creation of **Custom Views** based on event level, time, log type, source type, event ID, task category, keywords, users, or computers. Event Viewer catches thousands of different events. Using **Custom Views**, we can filter events and access the information we need. All these custom-made views will be listed under the **Custom Views** section. It also has predefined custom views.

These predefined custom views are based on the server roles. When **Active Directory Domain Services** roles are added, it also creates a custom view in the event log to group all the **Active Directory Domain Services**-related events, as shown in the following screenshot:

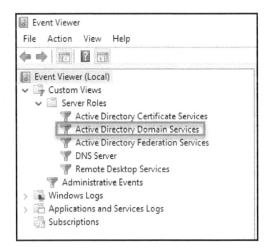

Windows Logs

The **Windows Logs** section includes five Windows log files. These mostly contain OS-related events:

- **Application log**: This log contains the events collected from various applications running on the system. It can be from Microsoft or any other application.
- **Security log**: This log includes events such as successful and failed system login attempts. Engineers can specify which security events need to be recorded using audit policies.
- **Setup log**: This includes events related to application setup and adding/removing server roles.
- **System log**: This log includes events related to Windows system components. As an example, an event related to automatic service start failure will be listed under this log.
- **Forwarded Events**: Using Event Viewer, we can connect to another remote computer and view the events. However, it may be required to watch for specific events from multiple sources. As an example, let's assume we need to collect events with ID `4321` from three computers. Using the **Subscriptions** event, we can collect only those events and forward them under the **Forwarded Events** log.

 Forwarded Events is the default location to push subscribed events. However, if needed, these events can also be forwarded to other log files.

Applications and Services Logs

The **Application and Services Logs** category was introduced after Windows Server 2008. This stores the events related to applications and their components. Most of the events listed under here are more suited for application developers to debugging and application-level troubleshooting.

This category has four log types:

- **Admin**: Events listed in this log are understandable by end users and IT professionals. This information can be used for basic application troubleshooting. Most of these log entries will include instructions or links to knowledge-base articles from the application vendor.
- **Operational**: Operational events include information about configuration changes or status changes of an application/service. These events are useful for application diagnosis.
- **Analytic**: This log is by default hidden and disabled. This is usually enabled during the application or service diagnosis process as this generates a high volume of events.
- **Debug**: This is purely used for troubleshooting purposes by application developers and vendors. Similar to the **Analytic** log, it is, by default, hidden and disabled.

Subscriptions

This category lists down the event subscriptions created with remote computers. Here, we can create/edit/disable event subscriptions, check the runtime status, and forcibly run subscription jobs.

When we open up an event, it gives different levels of information, such as the following:

- A general description about the problem
- The log file name
- The event source to indicate where it came from
- The event ID number
- The level of the error (critical, information, or warning)
- The username of the error owner
- Links to TechNet, KB, or other sources to get more information about the event
- The time of the event
- Hostname of the source computer

Active Directory Domain Service event logs

Apart from the events under the **Windows Logs** category, Active Directory Domain Services and related service events can be found under the following logs. These are located under the **Applications and Services Logs** category:

- Active Directory Web Services
- DFS Replication
- Directory Service
- DNS Server
- File Replication Service (only if using FRS)

Active Directory Domain Service log files

Apart from events, Active Directory Domain Service and related services have other system log files that record data about service install/uninstall, performance, service errors/failures, and so on. These log files can be used for auditing, troubleshooting, or debugging purposes.

The default location for these log files is `%SystemRoot%\Debug`:

- `DCPromo.log`: This log file is created during the AD promotion process. It will also record events during the demotion process. This log will contain events such as the following:
    - Active Directory Domain Service configuration settings
    - Information about schema preparation
    - Information about directory partition creation/modifications
    - Information about data replication
    - Service configuration status
    - Information about creating Active Directory databases and the `SYSVOL` directory

- DCPromoUI.log: This log file can be considered as a progress report for the Active Directory Domain Service promotion/demotion process. It starts the logging process as soon as the Active Directory Domain Service configuration wizard opens, and ends when it completes the installation successfully (until reboot request accept) or when it is aborted due to errors. This includes the results of each and every act of the system during the service installation and removal process. This log includes useful information, such as the following:
  - A timestamp for when the installation or removal process started
  - Detailed results of each validation test
  - The name of the domain controller used for the initial replication
  - A list of directory partitions that were replicated
  - The number of objects replicated in each and every partition
  - Configuration summary
  - Information about registry key changes related to configuration
- DFSR.log: This log file includes events related to DFS replication. This can be used for SYSVOL replication troubleshooting and the debugging process (if SYSVOL uses DFS replication).

 After Windows Server 2008, AD uses DFS replication by default, but if domain controllers have been introduced to a Windows Server 2003 environment, it will use FRS by default.

AD audit

The only way to identify potential security threats and security breaches in infrastructure is through continuous monitoring and auditing. When it comes to auditing, the Windows system itself provides advanced auditing capabilities to identify such security issues. However, by default, only certain types of actions are audited. These auditing settings are handled by Windows audit policies.

Here, we are only going to look at advanced security audit policies, which were first introduced with Windows Server 2008 R2.

There are 10 categories of events we can audit in a Windows system:

- System events
- Logon/logoff events
- Object access events
- Privilege use events
- Detailed tracking events
- Policy change events
- Account management events
- **Directory service** (**DS**) access events
- Account logon events
- Global object access auditing

Each and every event category also has subcategories.

Legacy Windows auditing provides nine categories and each category also has subcategories. These are located under **Computer Configuration** | **Windows Settings** | **Security Settings** | **Local Policies** | **Audit Policies**. Also, categories and subcategories can be listed using `auditpol /get /category:\*`. Advanced security audit policies provide 53 options to tune up the auditing requirements, and you can collect more granular-level information about your infrastructure events than by legacy auditing.

Auditing on these categories can be enabled using group policies. These are located under **Computer Configuration** | **Windows Settings** | **Security Settings** | **Advanced Audit Policy Configuration** | **Audit Policies**, as shown in the following screenshot:

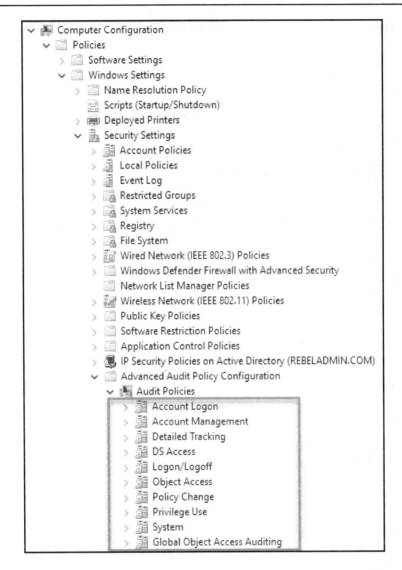

All these categories can collect a lot of system and service events related to AD infrastructure activities. But in this section, we are only going to focus on the **DS Access** events category and its subcategories. It audits events related to AD objects access and AD object modification. Also, the settings under this category only apply to domain controllers.

The **DS Access** events category includes four subcategories:

- **Audit Directory Service Access**
- **Audit Directory Service Changes**
- **Audit Directory Service Replication**
- **Audit Detailed Directory Service Replication**

Audit Directory Service Access

This category records events when an AD DS object is accessed. This will only work if the **system access control list** (**SACL**) is configured and the relevant objects have been added. This is similar to directory service access in legacy auditing.

SACL allows engineers to log access attempts to secured objects. SACL can generate audit records when an access attempt fails, when it succeeds, or both.

When auditing is enabled under this category, the following event can be found under security logs:

Event ID	Event message
4662	An operation was performed on an object

Audit Directory Service Changes

This category records events related to AD DS object changes, such as the following:

- Create
- Delete
- Modify
- Move
- Undelete

When an object value is changed, it records the old value and the new value it was changed into. Again, the event will only be generated for the entries listed under SACL. Once auditing is enabled, the following events can be found under security logs:

Event ID	Event message
5136	A directory service object was modified.
5137	A directory service object was created.
5138	A directory service object was undeleted.
5139	A directory service object was moved.
5141	A directory service object was deleted.

Audit Directory Service Replication

This category logs events when replication between two domain controllers begins and ends. When auditing is enabled, we will be able to find the following events in the logs:

Event ID	Event message
4932	Synchronization of a replica of an AD naming context has begun.
4933	Synchronization of a replica of an AD naming context has ended.

Audit Detailed Directory Service Replication

This category records detailed information about data replicated between domain controllers. Once auditing is enabled, it will generate a high volume of events and will be useful for troubleshooting replication issues. It will log the following types of events:

Event ID	Event message
4928	An AD replica source naming context was established.
4929	An AD replica source naming context was removed.
4930	An AD replica source naming context was modified.
4931	An AD replica destination naming context was modified.
4934	Attributes of an AD object were replicated.
4935	Replication failure start.
4936	Replication failure end.
4937	A lingering object was removed from a replica.

Demonstration

In this section, let's go ahead and see how we can use in-built Windows monitoring and audit capabilities. In order to do these configurations, you need to have domain administrator or enterprise administrator privileges.

Reviewing events

Event Viewer can simply be opened by running `eventvwr.msc`. The same MMC can also be used to connect to a remote computer using the **Connect to Another Computer...** option, as highlighted in the following screenshot:

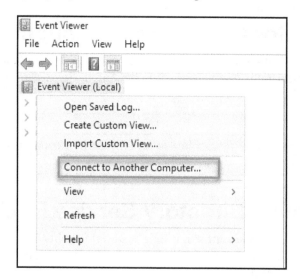

We can simplify this by creating server groups in **Server Manager**. Server groups allow us to group systems running similar server roles or acting as part of a distributed system.

Before we go ahead and create server groups, we need to take note of the following information:

1. We need an account that has administrator privileges for all the member servers to create server groups and use server groups.

2. We must enable **Windows Remote Management** (**WinRM**); after Windows Server 2012, WinRM is enabled by default. The existing WinRM configuration can be reviewed using the PowerShell command `winrm get winrm/config`. If it's not enabled, we can enable it using the `winrm quickconfig` command.

3. Even if we are logged in as a domain administrator or enterprise administrator, by default, it is not allowed to collect events from remote computers. In order to do that, we need to add a collector computer account (the server where the server group is created) to the `Event Log Readers` group. This is a built-in local group. Members of this group can read event logs from the local machine. We can add a computer account to the group using the following command:

```
Add-ADGroupMember -identity 'Event Log Readers'
-members REBELNET-PDC01$
```

REBELNET-PDC01 can be replaced with the collector computer account.

4. In order to create a server group, go to **Server Manager** from the dashboard and select **Create a server group**, as shown in the following screenshot:

5. In the new window, we can provide a name for the group and add members to the group. It provides different methods to select from in order to search for the members, as shown in the following screenshot:

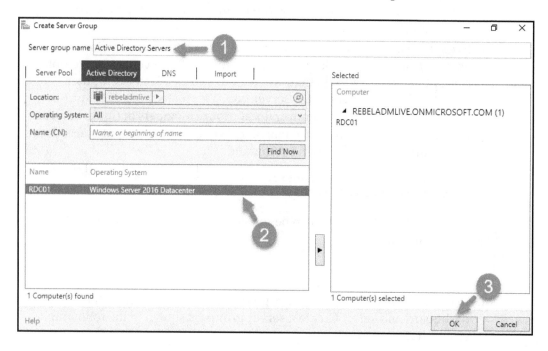

6. Once a group is created, you can access it using the left-hand panel in the **Server Manager**. Inside the group window, there is a separate section called **EVENTS**. When we navigate through each member, it will show us events related to each member in the events window, as shown in the following screenshot:

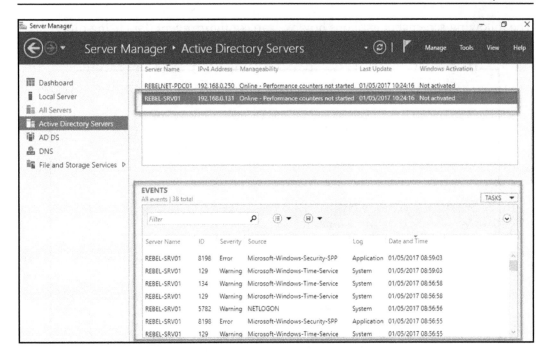

We can configure the event data and modify it as follows:

- Event severity levels
- Event time frames
- Event log files where the data will be gathered, as shown in the following screenshot:

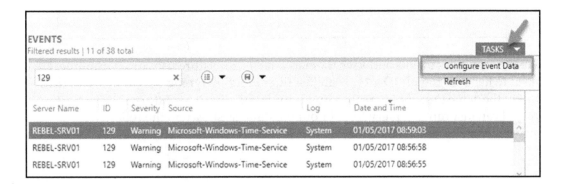

The following screenshot explains how we can configure event data using different options:

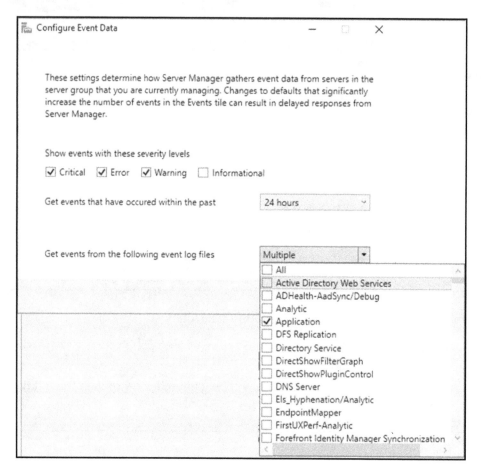

We also can filter events and save them as a query for future use. As an example, I need to list events with **ID** 129. I can just filter it out by typing 129 in the filter field. But at the same time, I can create a query for it and save it for future use. So, next time, I can just run the query to filter out the data, as shown in the following screenshot:

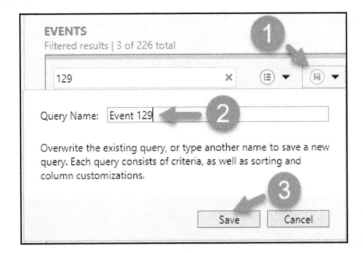

The following screenshot shows how once the query is created, it can be accessed whenever needed:

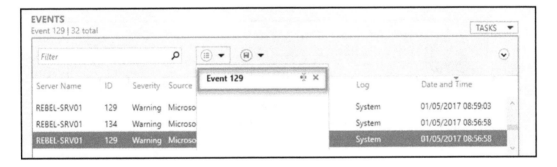

Setting up event subscriptions

Event Viewer contains lots of different event entries. There can be several thousand events per day. Even if every event provides some useful information, we do not need to go through each and every one when we are troubleshooting a particular application or performing a service audit. There are specific events relevant to each server role, application, service, and system component. On some occasions, when we audit or troubleshoot, we need to review events on multiple computers. Event Viewer only allows us to connect to one computer at a given time. It can be a local computer or remote computer. Event subscriptions allow us to collect event logs from remote computers and review them on one console.

Before we configure event subscriptions, we need to perform the following steps:

1. Enable WinRM.
2. Add a collector computer account to the `Event Log Readers` group.

Configuration steps for the aforementioned tasks are explained in the previous section.

Once the prerequisites are fulfilled, follow these steps:

1. Log in to the Collector server.
2. Open Event Viewer and go to **Actions | Create Subscription.**
3. In the new window, enter the following details:

   - **Subscription name**: The name of the subscription job
   - **Destination log**: The log file where collected events should appear. By default, it is the **Forwarded Events** log file. We can select any log file available in the drop-down menu, as shown in the following screenshot:

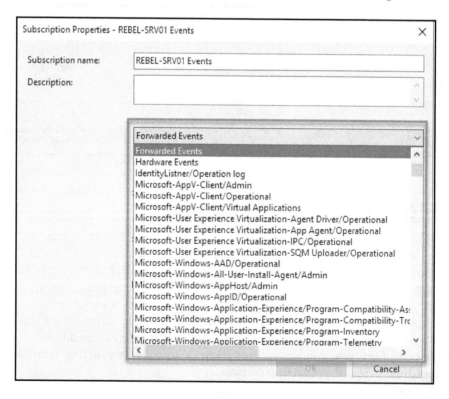

- **Collector initiated**: We can list the source computers here. It is not a one-to-one connection. It can be any number of computers, as shown in the following screenshot:

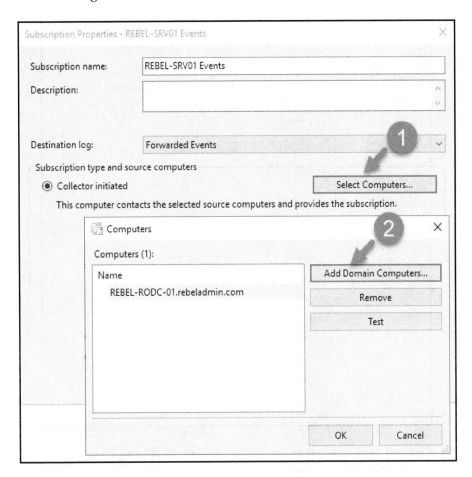

- **Source computer initiated**: This allows you to define a subscription without defining the event source computers. Then, the source computers will be defined using a group policy setting located at **Computer Configuration | Policies | Administrative Templates | Windows Components | Event Forwarding | Configure Target Subscription Manager**.
  In there, the collector should be added in the
  `Server=http://<eventcollector`
  `FQDN>:5985/wsman/SubscriptionManager/WEC,Refresh=10` format.

- **Event to collect**: Using this option, we can define which events are to be selected from the source computers. It is similar to a typical event filter window, as can be seen in the following screenshot:

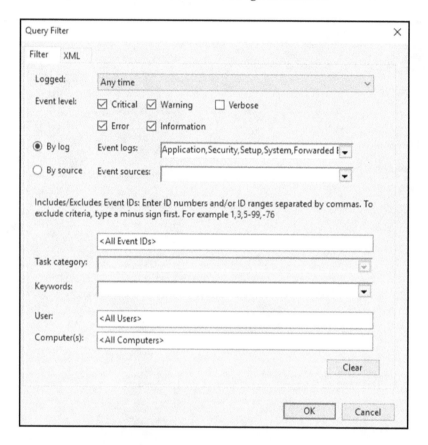

- **Change user account or configure advanced settings**: In this option, we can define a separate account that can be used by a collector to extract events from source computers. It also gives us options to optimize the event delivery settings. This is important if large number of events have been collected. An example can be seen in the following screenshot:

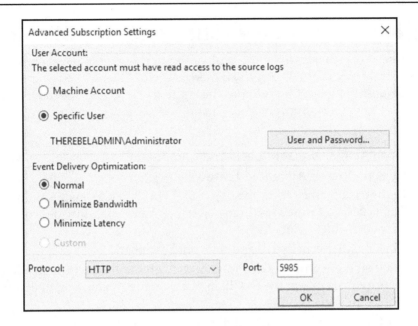

Security event logs from domain controllers

In order to collect security logs from remote domain controllers, we need to add a
network service account to the channel access permissions of the security event log.
This is because the WinRM service is running under the network service account.
This can be done by running the following code:

```
wevtutil sl security
/ca:'O:BAG:SYD:(A;;0xf0005;;;SY)(A;;0x5;;;BA)(A;;0x1;;;S-1-5-32-573)(A
;;0x1;;;S-1-5-20)'
```

O:BAG:SYD:(A;;0xf0005;;;SY)(A;;0x5;;;BA)(A;;0x1;;;S-1-5-32-573)(A;
;0x1;;;S-1-5-20) contains READ permission settings for network service
account (A;;0x1;;;). In the preceding code, the SID value for the network service
account is (S-1-5-20), and the channel access value is
(O:BAG:SYD:(A;;0xf0005;;;SY)(A;;0x5;;;BA)(A;;0x1;;;S-1-5-32-573)).
Once all this is done, after a few minutes, we can see the **Forwarded Events.**

Enabling advanced security audit policies

As we have seen previously, for successful auditing, we need to have a SACL configured for the relevant AD objects. If there is no SACL entry, no events will be generated against that object. In order to configure the SACL, we need Domain Admin or Enterprise Admin privileges. To add a SACL entry, perform the following steps:

1. Open **Active Directory Users and Computers**.
2. Click on **View** | **Advanced Features**.
3. Right-click on the OU or the object that you'd like to enable auditing for. Then click on **Properties**. In my example, I am using the root container, as I wish to enable it globally.
4. Click on the **Security** tab and then on **Advanced**.
5. Click on the **Auditing** tab and then click on the **Add** button to add a new security principle to the SACL. In our scenario, I am using **Everyone** as I'd like to audit everything.
6. For the **Type**, I have selected the **Success** event type. Also, I've applied it to **This object and all descendant objects**, as can be seen in the following screenshot:

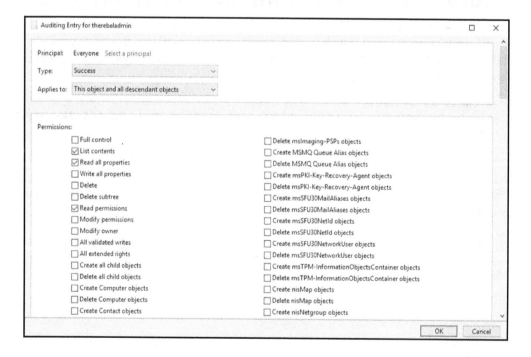

Once the SACL entries are in place, we can enable advanced audit policy configuration. In order to do that, perform the following steps:

1. Go to **Group Policy Management**.
2. In the MMC, expand the **Domain Controllers OU**.
3. Right-click on **Default Domain Controller Policy** and select **Edit**.
4. Then navigate to **Computer Configuration | Policies | Windows Settings | Security Settings | Advanced Audit Policy Configuration | Audit Policies**.
5. In there, we can find all 10 audit categories. In this demo, we are only going to enable audit categories under **DS Access**.
6. Navigate to **DS Access** and double-click on the **Subcategory** entry. To enable auditing, select **Configure the following audit events** and then select the events you'd like to audit. It's recommended to audit both **Success** and **Failure**, as shown in the following screenshot:

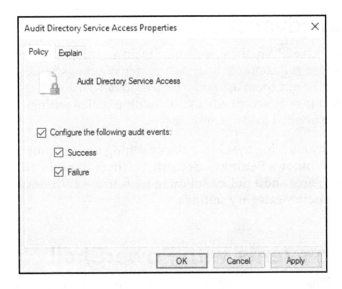

I have repeated the same configuration for the rest of the audit categories, as shown in the following screenshot:

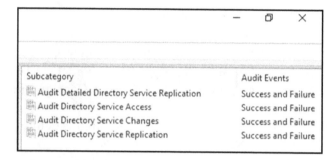

Once the group policy is applied successfully, it will start to log new events according to the audit policy.

Enforcing advanced auditing

Before Windows Server 2008, there were nine main auditing categories and subcategories. Those still continue to appear under Windows Server 2016. It is recommended not to mix them up, and only use advanced auditing instead. We can enforce the system to only accept advanced auditing policy settings if legacy audit policy settings are applied to the same category.

This can be done by enabling the Group Policy setting under **Computer Configuration | Windows Settings | Security Settings | Local Policies | Security Options | Audit: Force audit policy subcategory settings (Windows Vista or later) to override audit policy category settings**.

Reviewing events with PowerShell

We also can use PowerShell commands to review event logs or filter events from local and remote computers without any additional service configurations. `Get-EventLog` is the primary cmdlet we can use for this task, as shown in the following example:

```
Get-EventLog -List
```

The previous command will list the details about the log files in your local system, including the log file name, max log file size, and number of entries, as shown in the following example:

```
Get-EventLog -LogName 'Directory Service' | fl
```

The previous command will list all the events under the Directory Service log file. We can also limit the number of events we need to list. As an example, if we only need to list the latest 5 events from the Directory Service log file, we can use the following command:

```
Get-EventLog -Newest 5 -LogName 'Directory Service'
```

We can further filter it down by listing events according to entry type, as shown in the following example:

```
Get-EventLog -Newest 5 -LogName 'Directory Service' -EntryType Error
```

The previous command will list the first 5 errors in the Directory Service log file. We also can add a time limit to filter events further, as follows:

```
Get-EventLog -Newest 5 -LogName 'Directory Service' -EntryType Error
-After (Get-Date).AddDays(-1)
```

The previous command will list the events with error type Error within the last 24 hours under the Directory Service log. We can also get the events from remote computers as follows:

```
Get-EventLog -Newest 5 -LogName 'Directory Service' -ComputerName
'REBEL-SRV01' | fl -Property *
```

The previous command will list the first 5 log entries in the Directory Service log file from the REBEL-SRV01 remote computer, as shown in the following screenshot:

We can also extract events from several computers simultaneously, as follows:

```
Get-EventLog -Newest 5 -LogName 'Directory Service' -ComputerName
"localhost", "REBEL-SRV01"
```

The previous command will list the log entries from the local computer and the REBEL-SRV01 remote computer. When it comes to filtering, we can further filter events using the event source, as follows:

```
Get-EventLog -LogName 'Directory Service' -Source "NTDS KCC"
```

The previous command will list the events with the source NTDS KCC. It also allows us to search for the specific event IDs, as shown in the following example:

```
Get-EventLog -LogName 'Directory Service' | where {$_.eventID -eq
1000}
```

The previous command will list the events with eventID as 1000.

There is a recommended list of events that we need to audit periodically to identify potential issues in an AD environment. The complete list is available for review at https://docs.microsoft. com/en-gb/windows-server/identity/ad-ds/plan/appendix-1-- events-to-monitor.

Microsoft ATA

Once there is an identity infrastructure breach, sometimes it can take a long time to detect, for the following reasons:

- We fight against human adversaries, and they keep changing their tactics for attacks so they cannot be detected by traditional perimeter defense solutions.
- Existing security solutions require time and knowledge to set up, fine-tune, and maintain.
- Going through a large number of logs and reports to identify risks and issues is not practical, as engineers could miss important events.
- Most of the existing security solutions are for preventing attackers at the perimeter level. They do not have a way to detect the attackers once they have successfully logged into the infrastructure.

Microsoft built AD and has maintained it for more than 20 years now. Many engineers are working daily on the product to make further improvements. Every day, they are dealing with tickets regarding AD infrastructure-related issues, including security. They also have Azure AD that people use via open networks. So, if anyone knows the ins and outs of identity infrastructure security threats, it must be Microsoft. Based on this vast amount of data and knowledge about identity infrastructure threats, Microsoft keeps introducing new tools and services to protect on-premises, cloud-only and hybrid identity infrastructures. Microsoft ATA is also one of those tools, that provides a simple, fast, and accurate way of detecting identity infrastructure threats at an early stage by identifying suspicious user and device activity with built-in intelligence. It also provides clear information in the form of email alerts and timeline view, a web interface.

What is Microsoft ATA?

Microsoft ATA is an on-premises platform to help us protect our identity infrastructure from advanced targeted attacks by automatically analyzing, learning, and identifying normal and abnormal behavior (from users, devices, and resources). It also uses deep packet analysis technology, and data from additional data sources such as Events, to detect threats in real time.

ATA benefits

- **Minimum configuration**: ATA has the required security intelligence built in. Therefore, there's no need for rule or policy setup to detect security threats. The configuration itself is straightforward. Ongoing maintenance is also minimal.
- **Easy alerts**: With ATA, there are no more reports and logs to analyze. The system itself does all the data analysis and informs us about critical alerts, either as email alerts or in the form of an attack timeline in the web interface. If you've worked with products such as **System Center Operation Manager (SCOM)**, you may know how sensitive alerting can distract you from the real issues. ATA minimizes false alarms and lets people know exactly what they want to know.

- **Equipped with knowledge to identify rising threats in the industry**: The Microsoft security graph is continually empowered by various data sources that allow it to identify security issues in identity infrastructures as they arise. These findings will be used by ATA, and it guarantees faster detection than traditional security tools.
- **Mobility support**: ATA does not care whether devices and users are connected from an internal or external network; if there is authentication and authorization involved, it treats all connections equally. There is no configuration change required to monitor connections from external networks.

What threats does ATA detect?

The following types of threats can be detected by ATA:

- Reconnaissance using account enumeration
- Net Session enumeration
- Reconnaissance using DNS
- Reconnaissance using DS enumeration
- Brute-force attacks
- Sensitive accounts exposed in plaintext authentication
- Services exposing accounts in plaintext authentication
- Suspicious honeytoken account activities
- Unusual protocol implementation
- Malicious data protection through a private information request
- Abnormal behavior
- Pass-the-ticket attacks
- Pass-the-hash attacks
- Overpass-the-hash attacks
- MS14-068 exploits
- MS11-013 exploits
- Skeleton key malware
- Golden tickets
- Remote execution
- Malicious replication requests

ATA components

There are three components involved in the ATA deployment:

- The ATA Center
- The ATA Gateway
- The ATA Lightweight Gateway

The ATA Center

This is the main component of the ATA deployment. The ATA Center does the following things:

- Configuration of the ATA Gateway.
- Gathers parsed traffic from ATA Gateways and ATA Lightweight Gateways.
- Detects suspicious activities.
- Runs ATA behavioral machine learning algorithms to detect abnormal behavior.
- Runs various deterministic algorithms to detect advanced attacks based on the attack kill chain.
- Users can use the web console to view the attack timeline, configuration settings, and notifications.
- Configures email notification settings.

The ATA Center is recommended to be installed on a separate server. One ATA Center is recommended for one forest. Cross-forest configuration is not supported.

The ATA Gateway

The ATA Gateway is a separate server that monitors domain controller traffic using port mirroring. Port-mirroring settings depend on the virtualization solution you use. If it's physical, it requires switch-level changes.

The ATA Lightweight Gateway

The ATA Lightweight Gateway component can be directly installed on domain controllers to monitor AD traffic without the need for port mirroring. This is the quickest way to get ATA up and running. However, it will increase the resource requirements of the domain controllers.

Both gateways do the following things:

- Capture and inspect domain controller network traffic.
- Receive Windows events from different data sources, such as **Security information and event management (SIEM)**, syslog servers, and **Windows Event Forwarding (WEF)**.
- Retrieve data about users and computers from the AD domain.
- Perform resolution of network entities (users, groups, and computers).
- Transfer the relevant data to the ATA Center.

ATA deployment

ATA deployment supports three topologies:

- **ATA Gateway only**: In this mode, AD traffic is only captured by the ATA Gateway. All the domain controllers pass the traffic to the gateway via port mirroring.
- **ATA Lightweight Gateway only**: In this mode, it only uses Lightweight Gateways. This component needs to be installed on each and every domain controller.
- **ATA Gateway and ATA Lightweight Gateway mixed mode**: In this mode, both Gateway types will be used. But one domain controller should only use one Gateway component.

ATA deployment prerequisites

The following prerequisites are needed before starting on an ATA deployment:

- The latest ATA installation files.
- Valid ATA licenses.
- Domain administrator or enterprise administrator accounts to install both the ATA Center and ATA Gateway.

- An account with read access to all the objects in AD.
- The ATA Center needs a minimum of Windows Server 2012 R2 with the latest updates. At least 4 GB RAM and 2 CPU cores are recommended.
- The ATA Center needs to have an additional IP address for the console.
- The ATA Lightweight Gateway needs a minimum of Windows Server 2012 R2 with latest updates. At least 6 GB RAM and 2 CPU cores are recommended.
- SSL certificates to be used by the ATA Gateway and ATA Center. For easy installation, it is still permitted to use self-signed certificates that can be replaced later with public SSL or certificates issued by internal CA.

Demonstration

In this section, I am going to demonstrate how to install Microsoft ATA. In the demonstration environment, we'll do the following:

- Domain and forest functional levels are set to Windows Server 2016.
- Only the ATA Lightweight Gateway will be used. Every domain controller will have a gateway installed.
- The ATA Center and ATA Lightweight Gateway will be installed on Windows Server 2016 systems.

Installing the ATA Center

The ATA Center can be deployed using the following steps:

1. Log in to the server as a domain and or enterprise administrator.
2. Run Microsoft ATA Center's `setup.exe` file.
3. In the first window, select the relevant language and click on **Next**.
4. Accept the license terms and click on **Next** to continue.
5. Then it asks how we'd like to know about updates. It is recommended to use Microsoft Update for that. Choose the option **Use Microsoft Update when I check for updates** and then click on **Next**.

6. Then in the next window, we can define the application's **Installation Path**, **Database Data Path** (ATA uses MongoDB), **Center Service IP Address: Port**, **Center Service SSL Certificate**, and **Console IP Address**. After these changes, click on **Install** to begin the installation, as shown in the following screenshot:

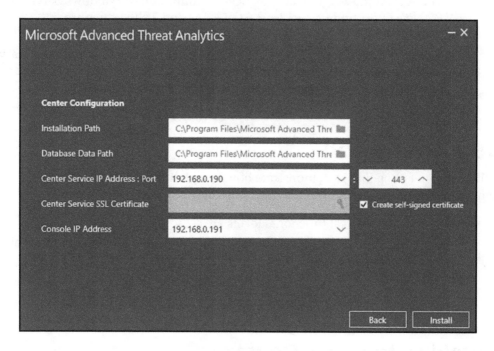

7. Once the installation has finished, it will give you the option to launch the ATA Center.
8. After launching the ATA Center, log in to it using the account used to install it. It will be the default ATA administrator account. In the system, you can later add additional administrator accounts.
9. As soon as you log in, it gives you a window to provide account and domain information to connect to AD. This user account works as a typical service account. No additional permission is needed (except read permission for all AD objects). Once account details are entered, click on the **Test connection** option to verify the connection and then click on **Save**, as shown in the following screenshot:

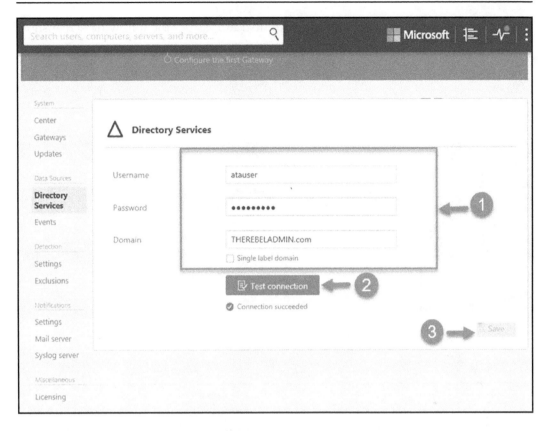

10. This completes the initial ATA Center configuration—the next step is to get the ATA Lightweight Gateway installed.

Installing the ATA Lightweight Gateway

The ATA Lightweight Gateway installation is straightforward. We can install it using the following steps:

1. Log in to the domain controller as a domain administrator or enterprise administrator.
2. Launch IE and connect to the ATA Center URL.

3. Log in to the ATA Center as administrator, as per the following screenshot:

4. When you log in for the first time, it provides the following page. Click on **Download gateway setup and install the first Gateway**, as illustrated by the arrow in the following screenshot:

5. Then it gives you the option to **Download Gateway Setup** files. Click on the button to begin, as shown by the arrow in the following screenshot:

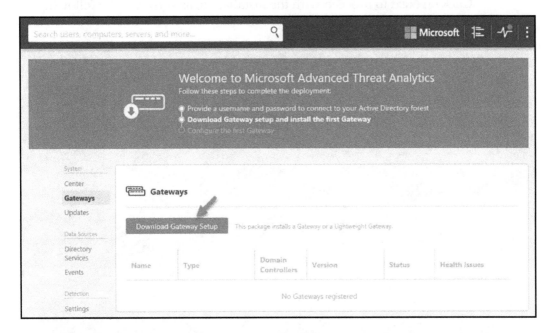

6. After the download completes, extract the ZIP file and run the Microsoft ATA Gateway Setup.exe file.

7. On the initial window, select the relevant language and click on **Next** to continue.

8. In the next window, it will give you a confirmation about **Gateway deployment type**. By default, it detects the type as **Lightweight Gateway**. Click on **Next** to proceed with the installation, as shown in the following screenshot:

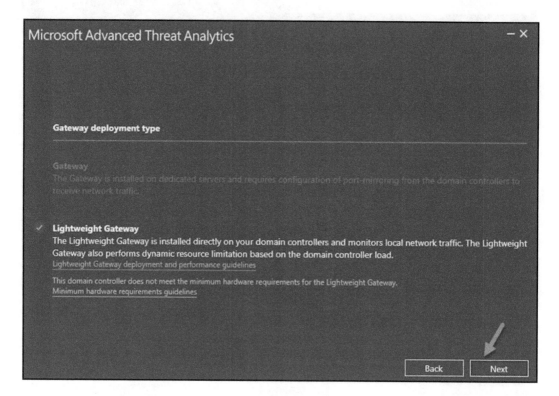

9. In the next window, we can specify the **Installation Path**, **Gateway Service SSL Certificate** information, and account details to register the Gateway with the ATA Center. This account should be a member of the ATA `administrator` group. After you type in the data, click on **Install** to begin the installation, as shown in the following screenshot:

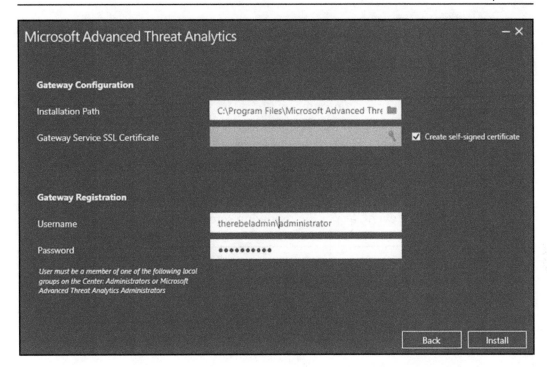

10. Once installation is completed, we can see the new Gateway successfully connected with the ATA Center, as shown in the following screenshot:

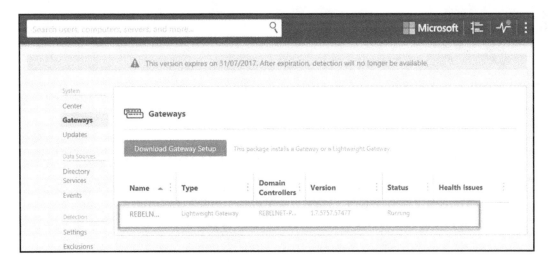

This completes the initial ATA deployment—it's ready to rock.

ATA testing

The easiest way to test the ATA functions is to simulate a DNS reconnaissance type attack, as follows:

1. Log in to a domain computer.
2. Open Command Prompt, type `nslookup – REBELNET-PDC01.therebeladmin.com`, and press *Enter*. The server name can be replaced by any domain controller **fully qualified domain name (FQDN)**.
3. Then type `ls live.com`.
4. Then log in to the ATA Center and check the timeline. There, we can see the detected event, as per the following screenshot:

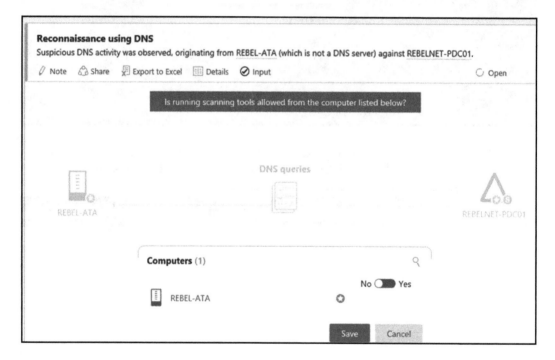

5. It provides a detailed explanation about the issue in a way that engineers can easily understand. These events also can be exported as a Microsoft Excel file.

6. ATA also allows us to send events as email alerts. This configuration can be done using **ATA Center** | **Configuration** | **Mail Server Settings and Notification Settings**, as shown in the following screenshot:

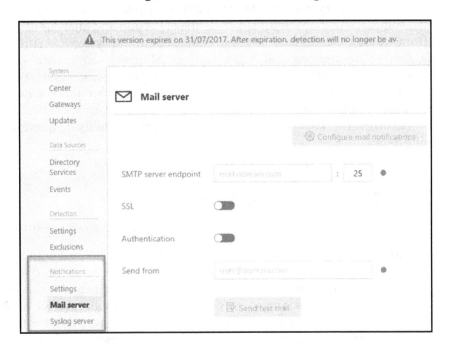

As we can see, the installation and configuration process of ATA is straightforward. But the benefits it provides are extraordinary. This product only reports about growing threats in an AD environment. Fixes and prevention from these reported threats are still dependent on the engineer's skills.

Azure Monitor

So far, we have learned about the tools that we can use to monitor the on-premises AD environment. Microsoft also has solutions to monitor other applications and systems. Microsoft SCOM is a great example of this. It can be used to monitor Windows applications, services, operating system, hardware, and network devices. If you have ever used a systems center product, you may already know how complex it is to configure, use, and maintain. SCOM can also monitor the health of the AD environment. It is a good tool, but I do not think it fits the purpose of monitoring modern infrastructures.

Microsoft has realized this already, and has introduced Azure Monitor to provide a comprehensive solution to collect, analyze, and present application, services, and system data collected from on-premises and cloud environments. This was previously known as the Microsoft **Operations Management Suite** (**OMS**). This is a completely cloud-based solution. Azure Monitor supports the collection and analysis of metrics and logs from various sources such as applications, operating systems, Azure Resources, Azure Subscriptions, and Azure Tenants. **Metrics** are numerical values described as a particular state of a service, system, or application at a given time. As an example, the status (that is, up or down) of a service at a given time is a metric. It is specific and easy to analyze. Metrics are mostly used with performance data. **Logs** contain data from events. This type of data needs to be analyzed using queries to filter specific data.

The benefits of Azure Monitor

Azure Monitor includes the following advantages that increase its values further:

- **Minimal configuration and maintenance**: If you've worked with SCOM before, you may know how many different components we need to configure, such as management servers, SQL servers, gateway servers, certificate authorities, and so on. But with Azure Monitor, all we need is a subscription and the initial configuration of monitoring agents or the gateway; there are no more complex maintenance routings either.

- It is **scalable**: Latest records from Microsoft show Azure Monitor is already being used by more than 50,000 customers. More than 20 PB of data has been collected and more than 188 million queries have been run in a week. With cloud-based solutions, we no longer need to worry about resources when expanding. The subscription is based on the features and the amount of data you upload. You do not need to pay for computing power. I am sure Microsoft is nowhere near running out of resources!

- **Integration with SCOM**: Azure Monitor fully supports integration with SCOM. It allows engineers to specify which systems and data should be analyzed by Azure Monitor. It also allows us to perform smooth migration from SCOM to Azure Monitor in stages. In an integrated environment, SCOM works in a similar way to a gateway, and Azure Monitor performs queries through SCOM. Azure Monitor and SCOM both use the same monitoring agent (Microsoft Monitoring Agent) and therefore, the client-side configuration is at a minimum.

Some Azure Monitor components, such as the network performance monitor, WireData 2.0, and Service Map, require additional agent files, system changes, and a direct connection with Azure Monitor.

- **Frequent feature updates**: Microsoft releases a new System Center version every four years. But Azure Monitor updates regularly and new services come more often. It allows Microsoft to address industry requirements quickly.
- **Dashboards**: One of the great features of Azure Monitor is the rich data visualization. SCOM is more of an alert-based monitoring system and there are very limited data visualization capabilities. Data visualization helps engineers to access relevant data quickly. Azure Monitor contains lots of pre-built tiles to visualize collected and analyzed data. It also allows us to create custom tiles based on our own queries. The dashboard can represent metrics and log data.
- **Views**: Views are used to visualize log data. We can create our own views to display specific data for an application, system, or service, based on queries. If required, views also can be added to the dashboard.

Azure Monitor in a hybrid environment

In a hybrid environment, we can integrate on-premises systems with Azure Monitor using the following three methods:

- **Log analytics agent**: The agent needs to be installed on each and every system, and it will directly connect to Azure Monitor to upload the data and run queries. The system talks to Azure Monitor via port 443.
- **SCOM**: If you already have SCOM installed and configured in your infrastructure, you can send data through the Log Analytics gateway. More information about integration is available via `https://docs.microsoft.com/en-us/azure/azure-monitor/platform/om-agents`.
- **Log analytics gateway**: Nowadays, Azure Monitor supports collecting data and running queries via its own gateway. This works in a similar way to SCOM gateways. Not all systems need to have a direct connection to Azure Monitor, and the Log Analytics gateway will collect and upload relevant data from its infrastructure. More information about the Log Analytics gateway can be found at `https://docs.microsoft.com/en-us/azure/azure-monitor/platform/gateway`.

What benefits will it have for AD?

In a SCOM environment, we can monitor AD components and services using the relevant management packs. These collect a great amount of data. However, to identify potential issues, engineers need to analyze this collected data. Azure Monitor provides two solution packs that collect data from an AD environment and analyze it for you. After analyzing, they will visualize it in a user-friendly way. They also provide insight into how to fix the detected problems, as well as providing guidelines on how to improve the environment's performance, security, and high availability, as follows:

- **AD Health Check**: This solution will analyze the risk and health of AD environments at regular intervals. It provides a list of recommendations to improve your existing AD infrastructure.
- **AD Replication Status**: This solution analyzes the replication status of your AD environment.

Demonstration

In this section, we are going to learn how we can monitor an AD environment using Azure Monitor. Before we start, we need the following elements:

- A **valid Azure Monitor subscription**: Azure Monitor has different levels of subscription. Which is more appropriate depends on the amount of data uploaded and your data retention policies. More info about pricing is available at https://azure.microsoft.com/en-gb/services/monitor/.
- A **direct connection to Azure Monitor**: In this demo, I am going to use direct Azure Monitor integration via the Log Analytics agent.
- A **domain administrator account**: In order to install the agent on the domain controllers, we need to have domain administrator privileges.

Enabling Azure Monitor AD solutions

The first step of the configuration is to enable AD modules in Azure Monitor. We can enable it using the following steps:

1. Log in to the Azure portal using https://portal.azure.com.
2. Then click on **Monitor**, as shown in the following screenshot:

Before we use Azure Monitor, you need to have a valid Log Analytics workspace environment. This is where you define the subscription details. In this demo, I assume you already have a valid workspace setup.

3. In the new window, click on **More**, as shown in the following screenshot:

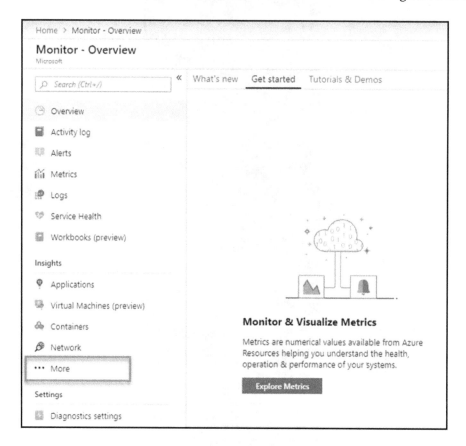

4. Then, in the new window, click on **+ Add**.
5. It will list all the available solutions. Search for **Active Directory Health Check**.
6. It will load the solution page. Click on **Create** to add the solution to Azure Monitor, as shown in the following screenshot:

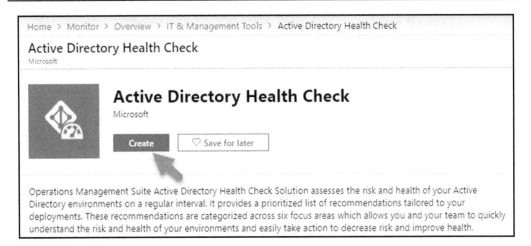

7. Follow the same steps and add the **AD Replication Status** solution, as shown in the following screenshot:

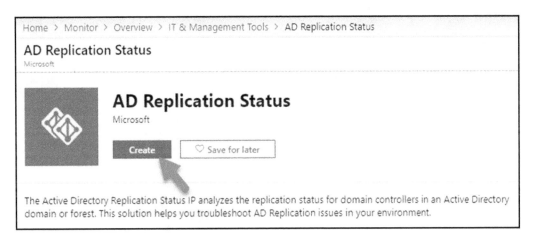

Installing Log Analytics agents

The next step of the configuration is to install the analytics agents on the domain controllers and get them connected to Azure Monitor. This is done in the following way:

1. Log in to the domain controller as domain administrator.
2. Log in to the Azure portal.

3. Go to **All Services**, then search for **Log Analytics workspaces**.
4. Click on the relevant workspace from the list.
5. Then go to **Advanced Settings**, as shown in the following screenshot:

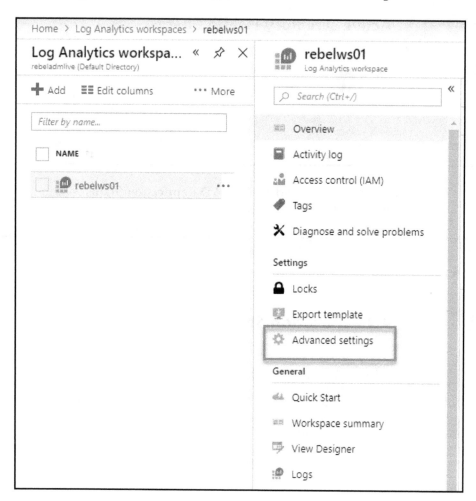

6. Then go to **Windows Servers** and click on **Download Windows Agent (64 bit)** to get the agent. Also, note down the **WORKSPACE ID** and **PRIMARY KEY**, as it is needed during the agent installation, as shown in the following screenshot:

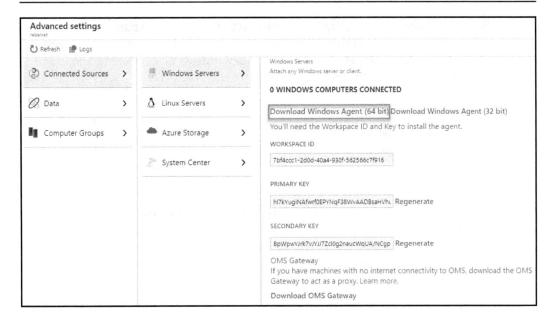

7. Once the agent is downloaded, run it as an administrator. In the **Agent Setup Options** window, select the **Connect the agent to Azure Log Analytics (OMS)** option and click **Next**, as shown in the following screenshot:

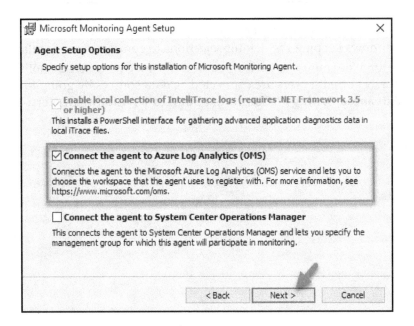

8. In next window, provide the **Workspace ID** and **Workspace Key**. Also, select the relevant **Azure Cloud**. If you are behind a proxy, you will also need to define the proxy settings in this window. Once you are all done, click on **Next**, as shown in the following screenshot:

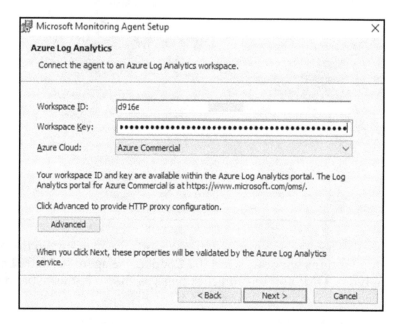

9. This completes the agent configuration—go through the following windows keeping the default selections to complete the installation.

10. After a few minutes, we can see from the following screenshot that the newly added servers are connected as data sources by going to **Advanced Settings** | **Connected Sources** | **Windows Servers**:

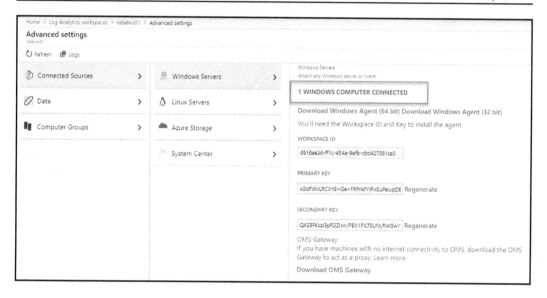

Viewing analyzed data

By performing the following steps, we can access data collected and analyzed by the AD solutions we added:

1. After a few minutes, Azure Monitor will start to collect data and visualize the findings.
2. To view the data, log in to the Azure portal and go to **Monitor**, click on **More** in the **Insights** section.

3. There we can find the tiles related to the solutions we added. When we click on the tiles, it will bring up the analyzed data, as shown in the following screenshot:

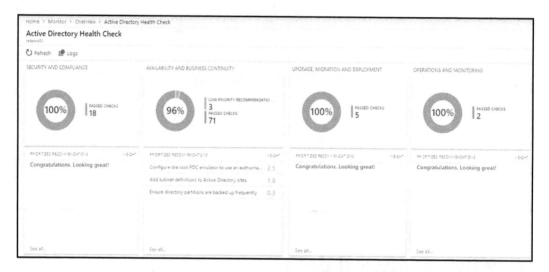

4. As I explained before, it doesn't just display errors; it also provides a **RECOMMENDATION** on how to fix existing issues, as shown in the following screenshot:

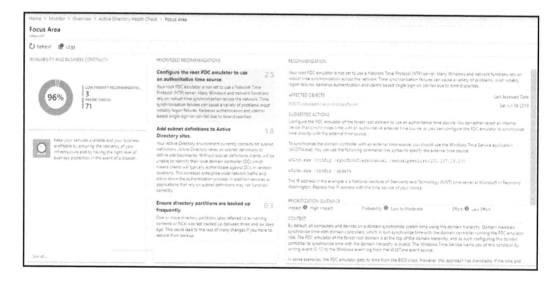

I hope you now have a basic knowledge of how to use Azure Monitor to monitor an AD environment. There are a lot of things we can do with Azure Monitor, and it's difficult to cover all those capabilities in a short chapter. I highly encourage you to go through the available Azure Monitor documentation (`https://docs.microsoft.com/en-us/azure/azure-monitor/`) to get the best out of it.

Azure AD Connect Health

In the previous chapter, we learned what Azure AD Connect is and how it works in a hybrid Azure AD environment. Azure AD Connect is responsible for synchronization between Azure AD and on-premises AD. Therefore, it is important to monitor the health of the Azure AD Connect service to make sure it is running as expected. In computer infrastructure, only one Azure AD Connect instance can be active at a given time, so more pressure is on the health of the service. The Azure AD Connect service is a Windows service, so there are many tools such as SCOM and Azure Monitor, for monitor the status of the service. But even if the service is up and running, it doesn't mean synchronization is healthy.

Azure AD Connect Health is a service that comes with Azure AD Premium to monitor the health of Azure AD Connect. Azure AD Connect Health can monitor the following types of sync errors:

- Duplicate attributes
- Data mismatches
- Data validation failures
- Large attributes
- Federated domain changes
- Existing admin role conflicts
- Other errors (which are not categorized)

Azure AD Connect Health insights are gathered via health agents. There are three types of agents used by Azure AD Connect Health:

- **Azure AD Connect (sync):** This is installed as part of Azure AD Connect. This agent will gather information related to Azure AD Connect, such as service status, synchronization rules, service name, last sync time, sync errors, and alerts.

- **Azure AD Connect Health Agent for Active Directory Federation Services (AD FS)**: This agent can gather additional data to monitor the health of Azure AD Connect in a federated environment. This agent will gather information such as the total number of requests processed by AD FS, requests based on relaying party trust, authentication methods used by requests, alerts, failed requests, and so on.
- **Azure AD Connect Health Agent for Active Directory Domain Services (AD DS)**: This agent can gather additional data from an on-premises AD environment which will provide additional insights to detect underlying directory issues in a hybrid environment. This agent gathers information, such as: AD topology, forest and domain functional levels, **Flexible Single Master Operation** (**FSMO**) role holders, replication status, number of processed authentication requests, and so on.

Prerequisites

We need the following prerequisites to use Azure AD Connect Health:

- An Azure AD Premium subscription.
- Relevant Azure AD Connect Health agents installed on target computers.
- Outgoing TCP 443 to Azure endpoints from the target servers.
- PowerShell 4.0 or above, installed on the target computers.
- **Federal Information Processing Standards** (**FIPS**) should be disabled.

Demonstration

In this section, we are going to look at Azure AD Connect Health in action. In my demonstration environment, I have the latest version of Azure AD Connect installed. Azure AD Connect Health (sync) comes as a part of it, as shown in the following screenshot:

Application Management	Processes in...		Manual
AppX Deployment Service (AppXSVC)	Provides inf...		Manual
Auto Time Zone Updater	Automatica...		Disabled
Azure AD Connect Health Sync Insights Service	Azure AD C...	Running	Automatic (D...
Azure AD Connect Health Sync Monitoring Service	Azure AD C...	Running	Automatic (D...
Background Intelligent Transfer Service	Transfers fil...		Manual
Background Tasks Infrastructure Service	Windows in...	Running	Automatic

But I'd like to install **Azure AD Connect Health Agent for AD DS** to gather additional insights from my on-premises AD environment. In order to do that, perform the following steps:

1. Log in to a target computer as domain administrator/enterprise administrator.
2. Go to the Azure portal using `https://portal.azure.com` and log in as global administrator.
3. Then go to **Azure Active Directory** | **Azure AD Connect** and click on **Azure AD Connect Health**, as shown in the following screenshot:

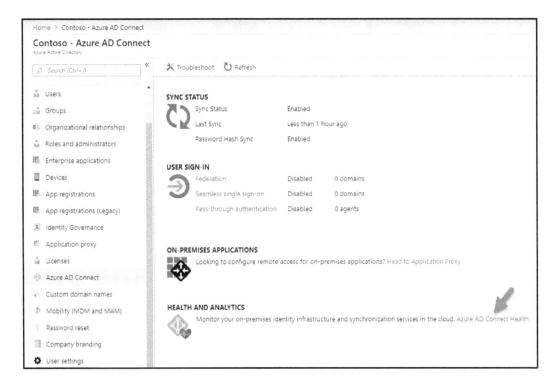

4. In the new window, click on **Download Azure AD Connect Health Agent for AD DS**, as shown in the following screenshot:

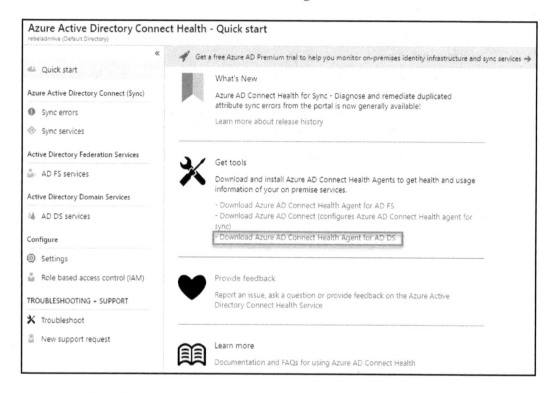

5. Once the download is completed, run the ADHealthAddsAgentSetup.exe as administrator.

6. Complete the installation, and then sign in using the global administrator account in login window, as shown in the following screenshot:

7. Let the system complete the agent registration, as shown in the following screenshot:

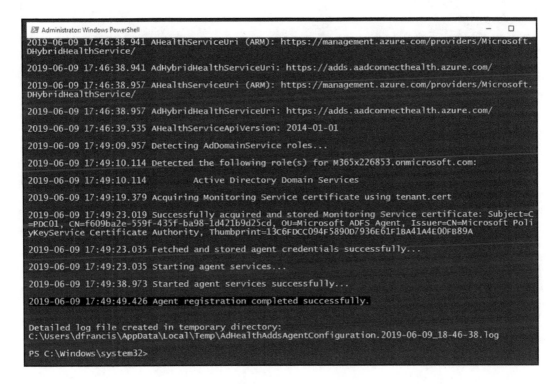

If a proxy is in place, we have to import the proxy settings from Internet Explorer by running `Set-AzureAdConnectHealthProxySettings -ImportFromInternetSettings`.

Once registration is completed, it can take a few hours to display the collected data.

8. Once agents start reporting, we can view **Azure Active Directory Connect (Sync)** data under **Sync errors** and **Sync services**, as shown in the following screenshot:

The landing page shows the high level health status of Azure AD connect.

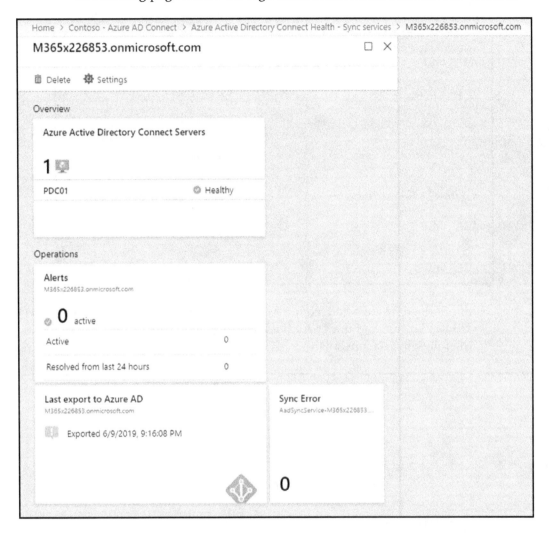

Under error pages, we can see the details descriptions of events.

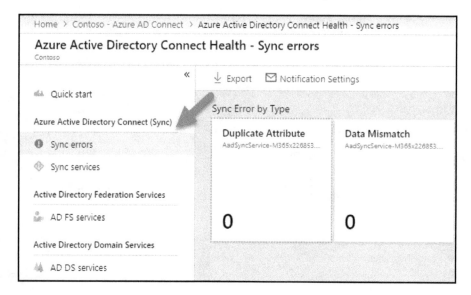

9. Similarly, data collected from the **Azure AD Connect Health Agent for AD DS** can be accessed under **Active Directory Domain Services**, as shown in the following screenshots:

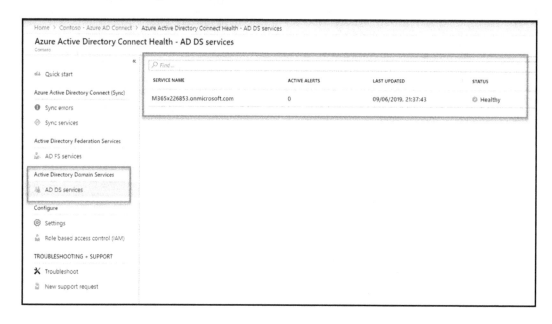

Landing page shows the overall health of replication.

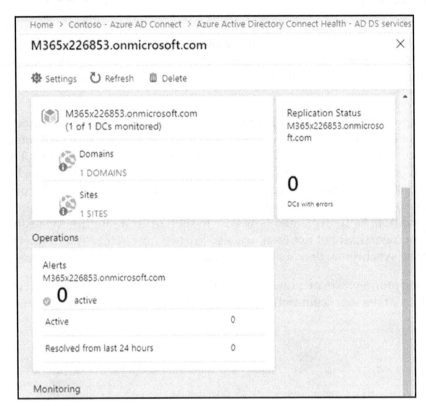

Azure AD Connect Health is mainly focused on monitoring the health of directory synchronization. Additional insights collected from AD FS and AD DS agents mainly help to troubleshoot directory synchronization health issues. However, healthy synchronization doesn't mean we are running a healthy Azure AD hybrid environment. This can only be ensured by monitoring identity infrastructure security threats. Microsoft has different services that can monitor identity infrastructure threats. Azure Security Center and Azure Sentinel are good examples of this. I highly recommend that you look into these solutions to further improve the overall health of your identity infrastructure.

Summary

Continuous monitoring and auditing is a must for an identity infrastructure to identify potential security threats and maintain a healthy environment. There are a lot of tools and methods out there to do this, but the success of these solutions depends on the accuracy of detection, the way it presents data, and how it helps in identifying the root cause.

In this chapter, we started by looking at Windows' in-built tools and methods t can be used to monitor and audit AD environments. First, we started with GUI tools and then moved to PowerShell-based auditing. Then we looked at Microsoft ATA and how it can help to identify security threats in the infrastructure that cannot be detected using traditional tools and methods. Later, we looked at the Microsoft Cloud-based advanced monitoring and log analytics solution, Azure Monitor. Using a demonstration, I also explained how we can set it up and monitor the health of the AD environment. Last but not least, we also learned how Azure AD Connect Health can help the synchronization health of the Azure AD hybrid environment.

After a long journey, we are now reaching the end of this book. In the final chapter, we will look at the most common AD-related issues and how we can fix those.

19
Active Directory Troubleshooting

Like any other IT engineer, I deal with the burden of broken systems from time to time. In the last 15 years of my career, I have spent long and sleepless nights fixing systems. I've spent days in cold data centers. I've missed long-awaited holidays. Even if we do not like it, as engineers, we spend most of our time *fixing* something. As with any other system, **Active Directory** (**AD**) environments can have problems. Some of them have direct business impacts and some don't.

In order to troubleshoot an issue and find a solution, we first need to have relevant knowledge about the application or the service. You do not need to be a master of everything but you should at least have enough knowledge to begin the troubleshooting process. Then, we need to collect the relevant data that can help us to understand the situation. This can be in the form of logs, events, screenshots, or discussions. The next stage is to analyze the collected data and try to find a solution.

I have been involved in many interviews over the past few years. As a part of interviews, I always provide a description of an issue to the candidate and ask what they would do to fix it. But I always say that I do not need an exact answer. All I care about is the starting point of the troubleshooting process and the approach they would take to find a solution.

To become a good troubleshooter, the starting point of the troubleshooting process is crucial. When we are troubleshooting a problem, we may have a lot of information from logs, users, and monitoring systems to process. Also, based on the impact, we will have pressure from the business end too. So, engineers have to deal with all these factors and still choose the correct approach. In this chapter, we are going to look at the most common errors that can occur in an on-premises Active Directory environment and what steps we can take to troubleshoot/fix those. The issues will be categorized under the following topics:

- Troubleshooting **Active Directory Domain Services (AD DS)** replication issues
- Troubleshooting Group Policy issues
- Troubleshooting replication issues
- **Distributed File System (DFS)** replication issues
- Troubleshooting AD DS database issues

Troubleshooting AD DS replication issues

An AD environment with replication issues is a disaster; it can cause all sorts of problems. AD uses a multi-master database. A change made on one domain controller should be advertised to other domain controllers to maintain consistency. The two types of replication in an AD environment are as follows:

- **Intra-site replication**: Replication between domain controllers in the same AD site
- **Inter-site replication**: Replication between domain controllers in different AD sites

In Chapter 11, *Active Directory Services*, we looked at exactly how both types of replication work. I encourage you to refer to it and refresh your memory before we proceed.

There is no smoke without fire. When there are replication issues, we can see the following symptoms in the infrastructure:

- New user accounts experience authentication issues with their systems and applications.
- Once a password is updated, user accounts get locked out frequently.
- After a password is reset, AD-integrated applications fail to authenticate users.
- When an object attribute value is modified, not every domain controller can see it.
- When a new Group Policy is created, it only applies to a part of the target objects.
- When there is a Group Policy change, it doesn't apply to the target object group, or it only applies to a part of the group.
- When an AD object is removed using one domain controller, it still appears on other domain controllers.
- DNS name resolution issues.

Identifying replication issues

In the preceding section, I listed some common symptoms of replication issues. However, these are not only symptoms of replication issues. When we have a fever, it could be just a cold or part of another disease. If it does not go away with paracetamol, then we need to go for further diagnosis to find the problem. When you walk into a GP's, they collect some reports and evidence before they come to a conclusion. Likewise, once we see the aforementioned symptoms, we need to collect data and evidence, which can help us to find the root cause. There are a few tools and methods we can use for that.

Event Viewer

Event Viewer is the most commonly used tool to gather information about any application or service-related issue. AD replication issues will also log certain events in Event Viewer. Some of those will help us to identify the root cause directly and some will only provide insights that we will need to follow with additional troubleshooting steps:

Event ID	Event description	Possible issues
2087, 2088	AD could not resolve the following DNS hostname of the source domain controller to an IP address. This error prevents additions, deletions, and changes in AD DS from replicating between one or more domain controllers in the forest. Security groups, Group Policy, users, computers, and their passwords will be inconsistent between domain controllers until this error is resolved, potentially affecting login authentication and access to network resources.	• The source domain controller is in shutdown status or non-responsive status. • There is a network-layer communication issue between the source and destination domain controllers. • Due to a hardware or software failure, the source domain controller cannot be brought online. In such a situation, a metadata cleanup is required and we need to remove the relevant entries forcibly from AD. • There are DNS-related issues preventing name resolution.
1844	The local domain controller could not connect with the following domain controller, which is hosting the following directory partition to resolve distinguished names.	• The source domain controller is in shutdown status or non-responsive status. • There is a network-layer communication issue between the source and destination domain controllers. • Domain controller service resource records (**SRV**) are not registered with the DNS server. • It's recommended to test the DNS name resolution and see whether the domain controller name can be resolved properly. • It's recommended to try forcible replication of the directory partition using `repadmin /replicate` to confirm whether it's a temporary issue or not.

4013	The DNS server is waiting for AD DS to signal that the initial synchronization of the directory has been completed. The DNS service cannot start until the initial synchronization is complete because critical DNS data might not yet be replicated onto this domain controller. If events in the AD DS event log indicate that there is a problem with DNS name resolution, then consider adding the IP address of another DNS server for this domain to the DNS server list in the **Internet Protocol (IP)** properties of this computer. This event will be logged every two minutes until AD DS has signaled that the initial synchronization has successfully completed.	• The domain controller is using the wrong IP range or VLAN, which prevents communication with the replication partner. • A network-layer communication issue between hosts. • DNS name resolution issues.
1925	The attempt to establish a replication link for the following writable directory partition failed.	• A network-layer communication issue between hosts. • DNS name resolution issues. • The source domain controller is in shutdown status or non-responsive status. • Check the maximum TCP packet size (you can use the `ping` command with the `-f -l` parameters) and verify compatibility with devices and network configuration.

1311	The **Knowledge Consistency Checker** (**KCC**) has detected problems with the following directory partition. **Directory partition**: %1. There is insufficient site connectivity information for the KCC to create a spanning tree replication topology. Or, one or more directory servers with this directory partition are unable to replicate the directory partition information. This is probably due to inaccessible directory servers.	• There are network communication issues between AD sites. • Verify that the domain controllers that host the identified directory partition are accessible using `dcdiag /test:connectivity`.
8524	The DSA operation is unable to proceed because of a DNS lookup failure.	• Due to hardware or software failure, the source domain controller cannot be brought online. In such a situation, a metadata cleanup is required. • DNS name resolution issues. • Verify that the A and CNAME records exist for the source domain controller.
8456, 8457	The operation failed because AD could not transfer the remaining data in the directory partition (`<directory partition DN path>`) to the domain controller (`<destination DC>`). The source server is currently rejecting replication requests.	• The **Directory System Agent** (**DSA**) is not writable. Check the relevant registry keys at `KLM\System\CurrentControlSet\Services\NTDS\Parameters`. • Insufficient disk space. • The Netlogon service has crashed or is in a paused status in the source.

8453	Replication access was denied.	• The `UserAccountControl` attribute on the destination domain controller computer account is missing. It is either the `SERVER_TRUST_ACCOUNT` `TRUSTED_FOR_DELEGATION` flag. • The default permissions of Active Directory partitions have been altered. • The destination domain controller is a **Read-Only Domain Controller (RODC)** and ADPREP/RODCPREP wasn't executed. Or, the enterprise RODC group does not have directory change replication permissions for the partition that is failing to replicate. • Trust relationships are no longer valid. • There is a time difference between the domain controllers that exceeds the maximum time skew allowed.
1722	The RPC server is unavailable.	• System resource limitation. • IP stack issue. • DNS service issues. • Network routing issues. • Relevant TCP ports are blocked by a firewall or application.
1127	AD could not replicate the directory partition (`<DN path of failing partition>`) from the remote domain controller (`<fully qualified computer name of helper DC>`). While accessing the hard disk, a disk operation failed, even after retries.	• An application or corrupted system component is preventing AD from writing data to a hard disk. • Hard disk faults. • Firmware issues related to disk controllers.
1645	`AD_TERM` did not perform an authenticated **Remote Procedure Call (RPC)** to another directory server because the desired **Service Principal Name (SPN)** for the destination directory server is not registered on the **Key Distribution Center (KDC)** domain controller that resolves the SPN. Destination directory server: %1 SPN: %2	This can be due to a recent change to the domain controller, such as domain promotion or demotion. Force replication using `repadmin /syncall` and check the registered SPN values.

System Center Operation Manager (SCOM)

SCOM can be used to proactively and reactively monitor the health of AD DS and related components. We need the relevant management packs to do it. The latest management packs for AD DS are available at `https://www.microsoft.com/en-us/download/details.aspx?id=54525`. If you're running SCOM 2016/2019, then you do not need to install this manually. Once domain controllers are added to the monitoring, the system will scan and recommend which management packs to install. Once the relevant management packs are in place, they can identify issues related to the following:

- Replication
- **Lightweight Directory Access Protocol (LDAP)**
- The domain controller locator
- Trusts
- The Netlogon service
- **File Replication Service (FRS)**
- DFS Replication
- The Intersite Messaging service
- The Windows Time service
- **Active Directory Web Services (AD WS)**
- **Active Directory Management Gateway Service (AD MGS)**
- KDC

Also, SCOM can monitor service availability, collect key performance data, and provide reports.

The findings from management packs will be notified in the form of alerts. We can also automate some of the recovery tasks by binding alerts to runbooks via System Center Orchestrator.

Azure Monitor

In the previous chapter, we discussed in detail how we can use Azure Monitor to monitor the health of an AD environment. Azure Monitor has a separate solution called **AD Replication Status**, which is capable of the following:

- Identifying AD replication errors between domains or forests
- Prioritizing errors that need to be fixed in order to avoid lingering objects

- Providing guidelines to fix replication issues
- Allowing replication data to be exported to source or destination domain controllers, or even for offline analysis

Troubleshooting replication issues

There are certain Windows cmdlets and utilities that we can use for replication issue troubleshooting purposes. Among these, `Repadmin.exe` is the most commonly used Microsoft utility to troubleshoot AD replication issues. It is available in servers that have the AD DS or AD LDS role installed. It is also part of the **Remote Server Administration Tools** (**RSAT**). It is recommended to run this utility as a Domain Admin or Enterprise Admin. However, it is also possible to delegate permissions to only review and manage replication.

 Microsoft also has a great little utility called **Active Directory Replication Status Tool** (**ADREPLSTATUS**), which allows us to review the replication status of an AD environment. We can download it via `https://www.microsoft.com/en-gb/download/details.aspx?id=30005`.

The following list contains the commands supported by `repadmin`:

Command	Description
`repadmin /kcc`	Forces the KCC on targeted domain controllers to immediately recalculate the inbound replication topology.
`repadmin /prp`	Allows an administrator to view or modify the password replication policy for RODCs.
`repadmin /queue`	Displays inbound replication requests that the domain controller must issue in order to become consistent with its source replication partners.
`repadmin /replicate`	Triggers the immediate replication of the specified directory partition to a domain controller.
`repadmin /replsingleobj`	Replicates a single object between any two domain controllers that have common directory partitions.
`repadmin /replsummary`	Quickly and concisely summarizes the replication state and relative health of a forest.

`repadmin /rodcpwdrepl`	Triggers the replication of passwords for specific users from the source domain controller to one or more RODC.
`repadmin /showattr`	Displays the attributes of an object.
`repadmin /showobjmeta`	Displays the replication metadata for a specified object stored in AD, such as attribute ID, version number, originating and local **Update Sequence Numbers** (**USNs**), and the originating server's **Globally Unique Identifier** (**GUID**), datestamp, and timestamp.
`repadmin /showrepl`	Displays the replication status of the last attempted inbound replication on AD partitions.
`repadmin /showutdvec`	Displays the highest committed USN that the targeted domain controller shows as committed for itself and its transitive partners.
`repadmin /syncall`	Synchronizes a specified domain controller with all replication partners.

Let's see some of these commands in action.

As listed in the preceding table, we can use `repadmin/replsummary` to summarize the following command of the replication status for all domain controllers based on the replication destination:

```
repadmin /replsummary /bydest
```

The following command summarizes the replication status for all domain controllers based on the replication source:

```
repadmin /replsummary /bysrc
```

The following command shows the replication partners for REBEL-SRV01.therebeladmin.com and the status of the last sync attempt:

```
repadmin /showrepl REBEL-SRV01.therebeladmin.com
```

The following command lists the replication partners that have replication errors (the last sync attempt failed):

```
repadmin /showrepl /errorsonly
```

We also can view the results in CSV format:

```
repadmin /showrepl /csv
```

The following command initiates domain directory partition synchronization with all replication partners of REBEL-SRV01:

```
repadmin /syncall REBEL-SRV01 dc=therebeladmin,dc=com
```

It also reports whether there were any issues during sync.

The following command shows whether there are any unprocessed inbound replication requests. If the system keeps sending queue requests, then it can be due to a high number of AD changes, system resource issues, or too many replication partners:

```
repadmin /queue
```

The following command lists the changes that are not replicated between the REBELNET-PDC01 and REBEL-SRV01 servers:

```
repadmin /showchanges REBELNET-PDC01 d3f89917-5fff-40a8-scc2-
b148b60d9309 dc=therebeladmin,dc=com
```

In here, REBEL-SRV01 is the source server and it is listed with the object's GUID.

The following command initiates immediate directory partition replication from REBELNET-PDC01 to REBEL-SRV01:

```
repadmin /replicate REBEL-SRV01 REBELNET-PDC01 dc=therebeladmin,dc=com
```

Apart from repadmin, there are certain PowerShell cmdlets that we can use to troubleshoot replication issues. The Get-ADReplicationFailure cmdlet is one that can collect information about replication failures.

The following command collects information about replication failures associated with REBEL-SRV01:

```
Get-ADReplicationFailure -Target REBEL-SRV01
```

This can also be done with multiple servers:

```
Get-ADReplicationFailure -Target REBEL-SRV01,REBELNET-PDC01
```

Furthermore, we can target all the domain controllers in the domain:

```
Get-ADReplicationFailure -Target "therebeladmin.com" -Scope Domain
```

Or we can target all the domain controllers in the entire forest:

```
Get-ADReplicationFailure -Target " therebeladmin.com" -Scope Forest
```

The `Get-ADReplicationConnection` cmdlet can list replication partner details for the given domain controller:

```
Get-ADReplicationConnection -Filter *
```

The preceding command lists all replication connections for the domain controller you logged in to.

We also can filter replication connections based on attributes. The following command lists replication connections with the `REBEL-SRV01` destination server:

```
Get-ADReplicationConnection -Filter {ReplicateToDirectoryServer -eq
"REBEL-SRV01"}
```

We also can force objects to sync between domain controllers. The following command will sync the `adam` user object from `REBEL-SRV01` to `REBELNET-PDC01`:

```
Sync-ADObject -object "adam" -source REBEL-SRV01 -destination
REBELNET-PDC01
```

In `Chapter 16`, *Advanced AD Management with PowerShell*, I shared some scripts we can use with AD replication troubleshooting. I also explained some other PowerShell cmdlets that we can use for troubleshooting and information gathering.

Lingering objects

Let's assume a domain controller has been disconnected from the AD environment and stayed offline for more than the value specified as the tombstone lifetime attribute. Then, it was reconnected to the replication topology again. The objects that were deleted from AD during the time it was offline will remain as lingering objects in it.

When the object was deleted using one domain controller, it was replicated to other domain controllers as a tombstone object. It contains a few attribute values but it cannot be used for active operations. It remains in the domain controllers until it reaches the time specified by the tombstone lifetime value. Then, the tombstone object will be permanently deleted from the directory. The tombstone time value is a forest-wide setting and depends on the OS that is running. For OSes after Windows Server 2003, the default tombstone value is 180 days.

A problem occurs when the domain controller with a lingering object is involved with an outbound replication. In such a situation, one of the following can happen:

- If the destination domain controller has **strict replication consistency** enabled, then it will halt the inbound replication from that particular domain controller.
- If the destination domain controller has **strict replication consistency** disabled, then it will request a full replica and will reintroduce it to the directory.

Events `1388`, `1988`, and `2042` suggest lingering objects in the AD infrastructure:

Event ID	Event description
1388	Another domain controller has attempted to replicate an object that is not present in the local AD DS database into this domain controller. The object may have been deleted and already garbage collected (a tombstone lifetime or more has passed since the object was deleted) on this domain controller. The attribute set included in the update request is not sufficient to create the object. The object will be re-requested with a full attribute set and re-created on this domain controller. The source domain controller (transport-specific network address) is `xxxxxxxxxxxxxxxxxxx._msdcs.contoso.com` Object: `CN=xxxx,CN=xxx,DC=xxxx,DC=xxx` Object GUID: `xxxxxxxxxxxxx` Directory partition: `DC=xxxx,DC=xx` Destination highest property USN: `xxxxxx`.
1988	AD DS replication encountered the existence of objects in the following partition that have been deleted from the local domain controller's AD DS database. Not all direct or transitive replication partners are replicated in the deletion before the number of days in the tombstone lifetime have passed. Objects that have been deleted and garbage collected from an AD DS partition, but still exist in the writable partitions of other DCs in the same domain or read-only partitions of global catalog servers in other domains in the forest, are known as **lingering objects**. This event is being logged because the source domain controller contains a lingering object that does not exist in the local domain controller's AD DS database. This replication attempt has been blocked. The best solution to this problem is to identify and remove all lingering objects in the forest. The source domain controller (transport-specific network address) is `xxxxxxxxxxxxxx._msdcs.contoso.com` Object: `CN=xxxxxx,CN=xxxxx,DC=xxxxxx,DC=xxx` Object GUID: `xxxxxxxxxxxx`.

2042	It has been too long since this machine last replicated with the named source machine. The time between replications with this source has exceeded the tombstone lifetime. Replication has been stopped with this source. The reason why replication is not allowed to continue is that the two machine's views of deleted objects may now be different. The source machine may still have copies of objects that have been deleted (and garbage collected) on this machine. If they were allowed to replicate, then the source machines might return objects that have already been deleted. Time of last successful replication: `<date>` `<time>`. Invocation ID of source: `<Invocation ID>`. Name of source: `<GUID>._msdcs.<domain>`. Tombstone lifetime (days): `<TSL number in days>`. The replication operation has failed.

Strict replication consistency

This setting is controlled by a registry key. After Windows Server 2003, by default, this setting is enabled. The key can be found under `HKEY_LOCAL_MACHINE\SYSTEM\CurrentControlSet\Services\NTDS\Parameters`:

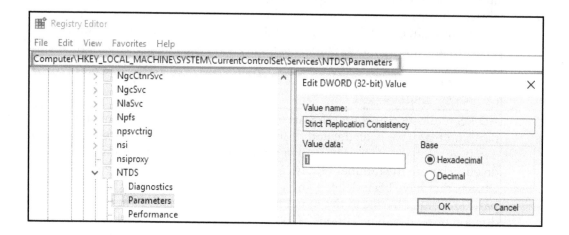

Removing lingering objects

Lingering objects can be removed using the following command:

```
repadmin /removelingeringobjects <faulty DC name> <reference DC GUID>
<directory partition>
```

In the preceding command, `faulty DC name` represents the domain controller that contains lingering objects, `reference DC GUID` is the GUID of a domain controller that contains an up-to-date database that can be used as a reference, and `directory partition` is the directory partition where lingering objects are contained.

Issues involving DFS Replication

After Windows Server 2003, FRS is no longer used for SYSVOL replication. It has been replaced by DFS. But, if you are upgrading AD DS from an older version, then the older version will still be in use and migration from FRS to DFS is required. We have covered this in `Chapter 11`, *Active Directory Services*.

The `SYSVOL` folder in a domain controller includes the domain's public files, such as Group Policy files, batch files, and login scripts. Healthy replication of SYSVOL is required to maintain a functional AD environment. When there are SYSVOL replication issues, you may experience issues such as the following:

- New/updated group policies are applied partially or not applied at all
- Group policies are applied to part of the target object group
- Login scripts are not running

The following events in the event viewer, under the `DFS Replication log` and `System log` files, help us to recognize DFS Replication issues:

Event ID	Event description
4612	The DFS Replication service initialized SYSVOL at the `C:\Windows\SYSVOL\domain` local path and is waiting to perform the initial replication. The replicated folder will remain in the initial synchronization state until it has replicated with its partner, `<FQDN>`. If the server was in the process of being promoted to a domain controller, then the domain controller will not advertise and function as a domain controller until this issue is resolved. This can occur if the specified partner is also in the initial synchronization state, or if sharing violations are encountered on this server or the sync partner. If this event occurred during the migration of SYSVOL from FRS to DFS Replication, then changes will not replicate out until this issue is resolved. This can cause the `SYSVOL` folder on this server to become out of sync with other domain controllers.

2213	The DFS Replication service stopped replication on volume `C:`. This occurs when a DFSR JET database is not shut down cleanly and **Auto Recovery** is disabled. To resolve this issue, back up the files in the affected replicated folders, and then use the `ResumeReplication` WMI method to resume replication. The recovery steps are as follows: • Back up the files in all replicated folders on the volume. Failure to do so may result in data loss due to unexpected conflict resolution during the recovery of the replicated folders. • To resume the replication for this volume, use the `ResumeReplication` WMI method of the `DfsrVolumeConfig` class. For example, from an elevated Command Prompt, type the following command: `wmic /namespace:\\root\microsoftdfs path dfsrVolumeConfig where volumeGuid="xxxxxxxx" call ResumeReplication`.
5002	The DFS Replication service encountered an error communicating with the <FQDN> partner for the Domain System Volume replication group.
5008	The DFS Replication service failed to communicate with the <FQDN> partner for the Home-Replication replication group. This error can occur if the host is unreachable, or if the DFS Replication service is not running on the server.
5014	The DFS Replication service is stopping communication with the <FQDN> partner for the Domain System Volume replication group due to an error. The service will retry the connection periodically.
1096	The processing of a Group Policy failed. Windows could not apply the registry-based policy settings for the <Object GUID> Group Policy object. Group Policy settings will not be resolved until this event is resolved. View the event details for more information on the filename and path that caused the failure.
4012	The DFS Replication service stopped replication on the replicated folder at the `c:\xxx` local path. It has been disconnected from other partners for 70 days, which is longer than the `MaxOfflineTimeInDays` parameter. Because of this, DFS replication considers this data to be stale, and will replace it with data from other members of the replication group during the next replication. DFS Replication will move the stale files to the local `Conflict` folder. No user action is required.

Troubleshooting

When there is a SYSVOL replication issue, we can carry out the following troubleshooting steps to rectify the issue.

Verifying the connection

Check whether the problematic SYSVOL folder can reach other domain controllers. A simple ping can verify the connectivity between nodes. Also, try to access the replication partner shares using `\\domaincontroller` (network path). Verify that replication partners are also in a healthy state. DFS Replication requires specific TCP and UDP ports. Make sure the following TCP and UDP ports are allowed via hardware/software firewalls:

Service name	TCP	UDP
NetBIOS name service	137	137
NetBIOS datagram service	-	138
NetBIOS session service	139	-
Remote Procedure Call (RPC)	135	-
Server Message Block Protocol (**SMB protocol**)	445	445
Lightweight Directory Access Protocol (**LDAP**)	389	389

In some organizations, engineers use antivirus and malware protection on domain controllers with settings made for desktop computers. On many occasions, I have seen that the DFS process has been blocked by endpoint protection solutions. Therefore, if such a solution is in place, then make sure you follow the guidelines provided by Microsoft and exclude the relevant files and processes. These guidelines can be found at `https://support.microsoft.com/en-us/help/822158/virus-scanning-recommendations-for-enterprise-computers-that-are-running-currently-supported-versions-of-windows`.

SYSVOL share status

We need to verify whether the SYSVOL share exists on the domain controllers. This is one of the basic troubleshooting steps. This can be done by running the following command on a domain controller:

```
For /f %s IN ('dsquery server -o rdn') do @echo %s && @(net view \\%s
| find "SYSVOL") & echo
```

This will list down the servers and the SYSVOL shares that are available:

```
C:\Windows\system32>For /f %s IN ('dsquery server -o rdn') do @echo %s && @(net view \\%s | find "SYSVOL") & echo
REBELNET-PDC01
SYSVOL         Disk              Logon server share
ECHO is on.
REBEL-SRV01
SYSVOL         Disk              Logon server share
ECHO is on.
```

DFS Replication Status

As part of the troubleshooting process, we need to verify the DFS Replication Status. The status of the DFS replication can be determined based on the status code.

Status codes for DFS are as follows:

- 0: Uninitialized
- 1: Initialized
- 2: Initial synchronization
- 3: Auto-recovery
- 4: Normal
- 5: In error state
- 6: Disabled
- 7: Unknown

In order to review the status, we can use the following command:

```
For /f %r IN ('dsquery server -o rdn') do @echo %i && @wmic /node:"%r"
/namespace:\\root\microsoftdfs path dfsrreplicatedfolderinfo WHERE
replicatedfoldername='SYSVOL share' get replicatedfoldername,state
```

Once we run the preceding command, the output is as follows:

```
C:\Windows\system32>For /f %r IN ('dsquery server -o rdn') do @echo %i && @wmic /node:"%r" /namespace:\\root\microsoftdfs pat
h dfsrreplicatedfolderinfo WHERE replicatedfoldername='SYSVOL share' get replicatedfoldername,state
%i
ReplicatedFolderName  State
SYSVOL Share          4

%i
ReplicatedFolderName  State
SYSVOL Share          4
```

DFSR crash due to the dirty shutdown of the domain controller (event ID 2213)

This is one of the more common DFSR errors; it happens when a domain controller crashes. This can be fixed by using the existing command listed for event ID 2213. It will resume replication in the volume.

In the following command, the `volumeGuid` value needs to be replaced with the relevant value from your environment:

```
wmic /namespace:\\root\microsoftdfs path dfsrVolumeConfig where
volumeGuid="xxxxxxxx" call ResumeReplication
```

> The relevant `volumeGuid` value can be found under the event ID 2213 description.

If this doesn't solve the issue, then we will have to do an authoritative or non-authoritative restore, which will be explained later, in the *Authoritative DFS Replication* and *Non-Authoritative DFS Replication* section.

Content Freshness

With Windows Server 2008, Microsoft introduced a setting called **Content Freshness protection** to protect DFS shares from stale data. DFS also use a multi-master database similar to AD. It also has a tombstone time limit similar to AD: 60 days by default. So, if there is no replication beyond that time and by re-enabling replication in a DFS member, can create stale data. This is similar to lingering objects in AD. To prevent this, we can define a value for `MaxOfflineTimeInDays`. If the number of days since the last successful DFS Replication is more than the `MaxOfflineTimeInDays` value, then it will prevent the replication. In such a situation, you will be able to see event 4012. After Windows Server 2012, this feature is enabled by default and the initial value is set to 60 days.

We can check this value using the following:

```
For /f %m IN ('dsquery server -o rdn') do @echo %m && @wmic /node:"%m"
/namespace:\\root\microsoftdfs path DfsrMachineConfig get
MaxOfflineTimeInDays
```

The only way to recover from this is to use non-authoritative or authoritative recovery for DFS.

Non-authoritative DFS Replication

In most situations, only one or a few domain controllers (less than 50%) have replication issues at a given time. In such situations, we can issue a non-authoritative replication request so the system will replicate the SYSVOL from the **Primary Domain Controller** (**PDC**). In order to perform non-authoritative replication, follow these steps:

1. First, we need to back up the existing SYSVOL. This can be done by copying the SYSVOL folder from the domain controller that has DFS Replication issues to a secure location.
2. Log in to the domain controller as Domain Admin/Enterprise Admin.
3. Launch the ADSIEDIT.MSC tool and connect to Default naming context:

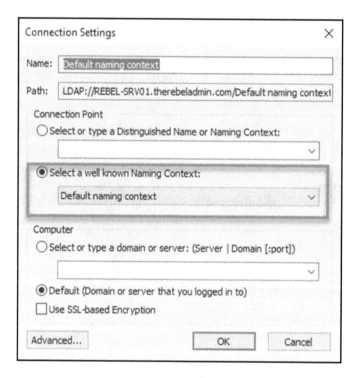

4. Browse to `DC=domain,DC=local` | `OU=Domain Controllers` | `CN=(DC NAME)` | `CN=DFSR-LocalSettings` | `Domain System Volume` | `SYSVOL Subscription`.

5. Change the value of the **msDFSR-Enabled** attribute to **False**:

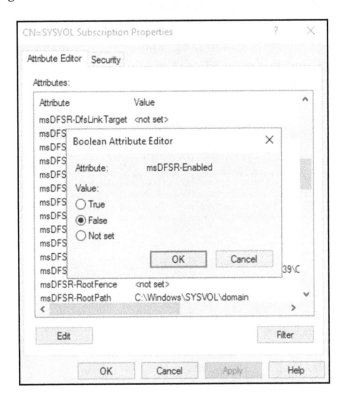

6. Force AD replication using the following command:

   `repadmin /syncall /AdP`

7. Run the following command to install the DFS management tools (unless this is already installed):

   `Add-WindowsFeature RSAT-DFS-Mgmt-Con`

8. Run the following command to update the DFRS global state:

   `dfsrdiag PollAD`

9. Search for event `4114` to confirm that SYSVOL replication is disabled:

```
Get-EventLog -Log "DFS Replication" | where {$_.eventID -eq
4114} | fl
```

10. Change the attribute value of **msDFSR-Enabled** back to **True** (*step 5*).
11. Force AD replication, as in *step 6*.
12. Update the DFRS global state by running the command in *step 8*.
13. Search for events `4614` and `4604` to confirm successful non-authoritative synchronization:

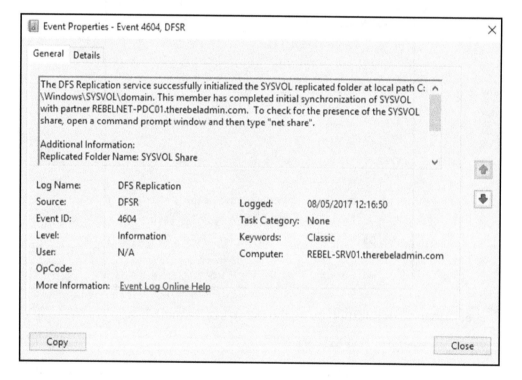

 All the commands should be run from the domain controllers that are set as non-authoritative. It's only recommended that you use this in cases where less than 50% of domain controllers have DFS Replication issues.

Authoritative DFS Replication

In the previous section, only a selected number of domain controllers were involved with forceful replication from the PDC. But there are situations where we need to recover SYSVOL from a backup and then forcefully replicate it to all other domain controllers. This is also the recommended recovery option when more than 50% of domain controllers are experiencing DFS Replication issues. In order to initiate authoritative DFS Replication, follow these steps:

1. Log in to the PDC FSMO role holder as Domain Administrator or Enterprise Administrator.
2. Stop **DFS Replication Service** (this is recommended on all the domain controllers).
3. Launch the `ADSIEDIT.MSC` tool and connect to `Default naming context`.
4. Browse to `DC=domain,DC=local` | `OU=Domain Controllers` | `CN=(DC NAME)` | `CN=DFSR-LocalSettings` | `Domain System Volume` | `SYSVOL Subscription`.
5. Update the given attributes' values as follows:

   - **msDFSR-Enabled** as **False**.
   - **msDFSR-options** as `1`:

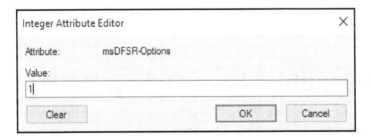

6. Modify the **msDFSR-Enabled** attribute as **False** on all other domain controllers.
7. Force AD replication using the following:

   ```
   repadmin /syncall /AdP
   ```

8. Start the DFS Replication service on the PDC.
9. Search for event `4114` to verify that SYSVOL replication is disabled.
10. Modify the **msDFSR-Enabled** value to **True**, which was set in *step 5*.
11. Force AD replication using the following:

    ```
    repadmin /syncall /AdP
    ```

12. Run the following command to update the DFRS global state:

    ```
    dfsrdiag PollAD
    ```

13. Search for event `4602` and verify successful SYSVOL replication.
14. Start the DFS service on all other domain controllers.
15. Search for event `4114` to verify that SYSVOL replication is disabled.
16. Modify the **msDFSR-Enabled** value to **True**, which was set in *step 6*. This needs to be done on all domain controllers.
17. Run the following command to update the DFRS global state:

    ```
    dfsrdiag PollAD
    ```

18. Search for events `4614` and `4604` to confirm successful authoritative synchronization.

This completes the authoritative synchronization process. During this process, no one can use SYSVOL. But in a non-authoritative process, only DCs with DFS issues will be affected.

How to troubleshoot Group Policy issues

Group Policy troubleshooting is one of the most painful and time-consuming events for most IT engineers. The reason is that there are so many reasons for Group Policy issues. In the following table, I have listed some of the most common reasons for Group Policy issues:

Reason	Description
Replication issues	AD and SYSVOL replication-related errors are the most common reason for Group Policy issues. In the *Identifying replication issues* section of this chapter, we looked into possible replication issues that can occur in an AD environment and how we can recover from those.

Poor design	Using group policies in the infrastructure is like eating curd with a two-edged sword. By design, it should be spot on, but continuous reviewing is also required to maintain it. In `Chapter 10`, *Managing Group Policies*, we learned about how we can design a Group Policy infrastructure properly.
Connectivity issues	If users/devices do not have a stable connection with domain controllers, then this also creates Group Policy-related issues. This is mostly not a problem for periodic disconnection as Group Policy refreshes every 90 minutes.
Loopback processing	Loopback processing settings can create a lot of hassle if you do not use the modes properly. My recommendation is to use the *replace* mode whenever possible.
Group Policy permissions	If a user is having issues with applying certain group policies, then you should always check whether the user has **Read** and **Apply Group Policy** permissions under Group Policy delegation.
Security filtering	Group policies can target individual users, groups, or devices using security filtering. If a particular user or group is having issues with applying specific group policies, then it's better to check whether the particular user or groups are being targeted.
WMI filters	WMI filters are also used by group policies for granular targeting. These filters use system-specific settings such as OS version and architecture. If WMI filtering is in place, then make sure the rules are updated according to target changes.
Inheritance	Group policies, by default, allow inheritance, and it is important to control them wherever necessary. Block inheritance action prevents us from applying unnecessary Group Policy settings, which can result in a longer Group Policy processing time and operation-related issues. We can review inheritance using the **Group Policy Inheritance** tab. Based on the applying order system will also decide which one is the winning Group Policy (if the same setting is used by multiple group policies).

Troubleshooting

Apart from issue-specific troubleshooting steps, there are some common tools and methods we can use to troubleshoot Group Policy-related issues. In this section, we will look at some of these.

Forcing Group Policy processing

This is the most common starting point for any Group Policy-related troubleshooting. Once we log in to a system, it refreshes group policies every 90 minutes. But, if required, we can forcefully process the group policies using the following command:

```
gpupdate /force
```

If a Group Policy change is related to a user setting, then we need to log off and log back in. If it's a computer setting, then the system needs to reboot after running the command.

Resultant Set of Policy (RSoP)

In a system, RSoP can be used to extract details about the group policies that are already applied, and also the policy settings that are planned. RSoP also helps us determine which policy is the winning policy and in which order the policies have been applied.

RSoP has two modes. In planning mode, we can simulate the effect of policy settings that we would like to apply to a computer and user. In logging mode, it reports existing policy settings for a computer and the user that is currently logged on.

RSoP and the command-line based tool, GPRESULT, both do the same work. However, after Vista, Microsoft recommended using GPRESULT instead of RSoP.msc as GPRESULT doesn't show all the Group Policy settings. For example, Group Policy preferences are not shown.

GPRESULT

This is a command-line utility that can be used to display RSoP information for users and computers. It can be used either locally or remotely.

The following command provides RSoP summary data for the currently logged-in user. This is similar to the RSOP.msc default run in logging mode:

```
Gpresult /r
```

Once we run the preceding command, its output is as follows:

```
PS C:\Users\Administrator> gpresult /r

Microsoft (R) Windows (R) Operating System Group Policy Result tool v2.0
© 2016 Microsoft Corporation. All rights reserved.

Created on 09/05/2017 at 09:49:13


RSOP data for THEREBELADMIN\Administrator on REBELNET-PDC01 : Logging Mode
---------------------------------------------------------------------------

OS Configuration:              Primary Domain Controller
OS Version:                    10.0.14393
Site Name:                     Default-First-Site-Name
Roaming Profile:               N/A
Local Profile:                 C:\Users\Administrator
Connected over a slow link?:   No


COMPUTER SETTINGS
----------------
    CN=REBELNET-PDC01,OU=Domain Controllers,DC=therebeladmin,DC=com
    Last time Group Policy was applied: 09/05/2017 at 09:44:13
    Group Policy was applied from:     REBELNET-PDC01.therebeladmin.com
    Group Policy slow link threshold:  500 kbps
    Domain Name:                       THEREBELADMIN
    Domain Type:                       Windows 2008 or later

    Applied Group Policy Objects
    ----------------------------
        Default Domain Controllers Policy
        Default Domain Policy

    The following GPOs were not applied because they were filtered out
    ------------------------------------------------------------------
        Local Group Policy
            Filtering:  Not Applied (Empty)

    The computer is a part of the following security groups
    -------------------------------------------------------
        BUILTIN\Administrators
        Everyone
        BUILTIN\Pre-Windows 2000 Compatible Access
        BUILTIN\Users
        Windows Authorization Access Group
        NT AUTHORITY\NETWORK
        NT AUTHORITY\Authenticated Users
        This Organization
        REBELNET-PDC01$
        Domain Controllers
        NT AUTHORITY\ENTERPRISE DOMAIN CONTROLLERS
        Authentication authority asserted identity
        Denied RODC Password Replication Group
        System Mandatory Level
```

The preceding command lists the summary data for the user and computer configurations. We also can scope it out to user configurations using the following command:

```
gpresult /r /scope:user
```

We can also scope `gpresult` output to computer configurations using the following command:

> **gpresult /r /scope:computer**

We can also run `gpresult` by targeting a remote system:

> **gpresult /s REBEL-SRV01 /r**

In the preceding command, `/s` specifies the remote computer name. The preceding command uses the same account details of the user who is running the command:

```
PS C:\Users\Administrator> gpresult /s REBEL-SRV01 /r

Microsoft (R) Windows (R) Operating System Group Policy Result tool v2.0
© 2016 Microsoft Corporation. All rights reserved.

Created on 09/05/2017 at 10:04:35

RSOP data for THEREBELADMIN\Administrator on REBEL-SRV01 : Logging Mode
---------------------------------------------------------------------

OS Configuration:          Additional/Backup Domain Controller
OS Version:                10.0.14393
Site Name:                 Default-First-Site-Name
Roaming Profile:           N/A
Local Profile:             C:\Users\administrator.THEREBELADMIN
Connected over a slow link?: Yes


COMPUTER SETTINGS
-----------------

    Last time Group Policy was applied: 09/05/2017 at 10:01:18
    Group Policy was applied from:      REBEL-SRV01.therebeladmin.com
    Group Policy slow link threshold:   500 kbps
    Domain Name:                        THEREBELADMIN
    Domain Type:                        Windows 2008 or later
```

We can also run it by specifying user account details:

> **gpresult /s REBEL-SRV01 /u therebeladmin\R540328 /p 1Qaz2Wsx /r**

The preceding command uses the `therebeladmin\R540328` user account with its password specified with the `/p` parameter.

We also can export the result as an HTML report. This is really useful for troubleshooting:

```
gpresult /h r01.html
```

The preceding command runs RSoP summary data for the currently logged-in system and saves it as an HTML report:

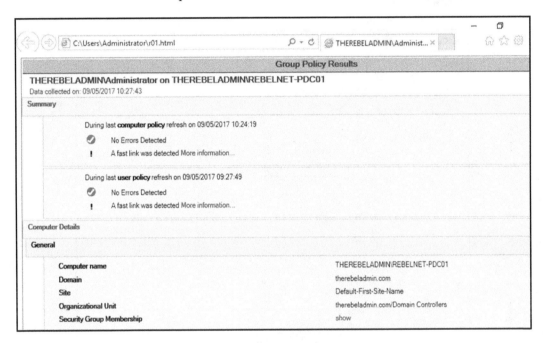

Group Policy Results Wizard

This is a tool that we can access via **Group Policy Management MMC**. This does the same thing as GPRESULT, but, instead of the command line, it uses a GUI. This allows us to access the results via the same console that is used to manage group policies. It is useful for troubleshooting as you do not need to move between different interfaces.

In order to access this, follow these steps:

1. Launch **Group Policy Management** (you can use the domain controller or any other system that has relevant management tools installed).
2. Right-click on the **Group Policy Results** container in the left-hand panel. Then, click on **Group Policy Result Wizard...** from the list, as shown in the following screenshot:

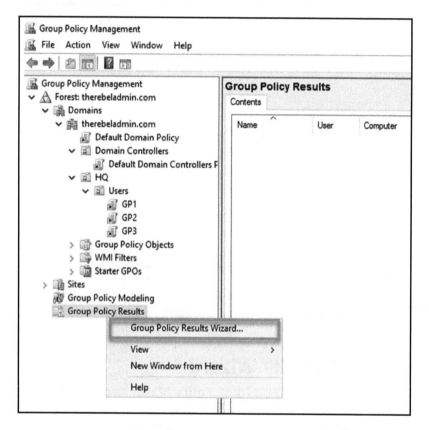

3. This opens up a new wizard. Click on **Next** to continue.
4. Then, the wizard asks us to specify which system it should use as the target. It can be a local system or any remote system. Once you have made your selection, click on **Next** to proceed:

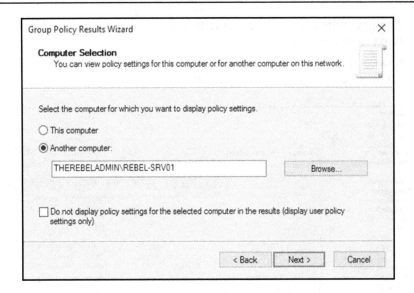

5. Then, it asks us to specify the user to display policy settings. The list only shows the users who are already logged in to the system and have permissions to read Group Policy result data. If we only want to see the computer policy settings, then we can select the option to not display user settings. Once you have made your selection, click on **Next** to continue:

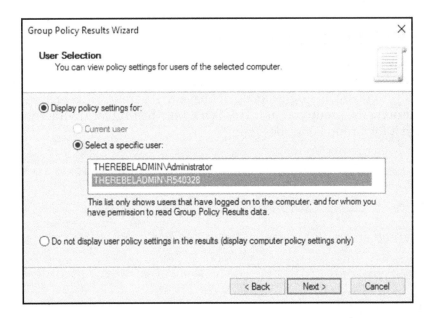

6. The next window provides us with a summary of the selection. Click on **Next** to run the job.

7. Once it is completed, we can see the report in the MMC. If required, the same query can be run at any time:

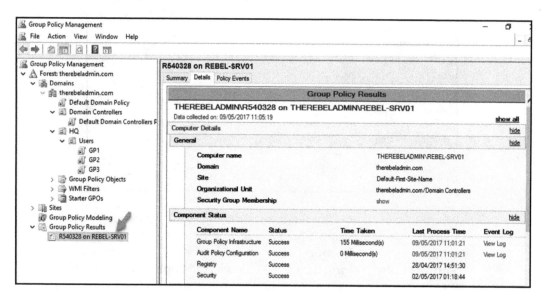

Group Policy Modeling Wizard

When we looked at the *Resultant Set of Policy (RSoP)* section, we learned about how RSoP has two modes. Planning mode allows us to simulate Group Policy processing without really applying it. Engineers do not have to log in to different systems to see how they process the group policies. This is not only helpful for troubleshooting; we can also use it for Group Policy designing.

In order to use **Group Policy Modeling Wizard**, follow these steps:

1. Launch **Group Policy Management** (you can use the domain controller or any other system that has the relevant management tools installed).

2. Right-click on the **Group Policy Modeling** container in the left-hand panel. Then, click on **Group Policy Modeling Wizard...** from the list:

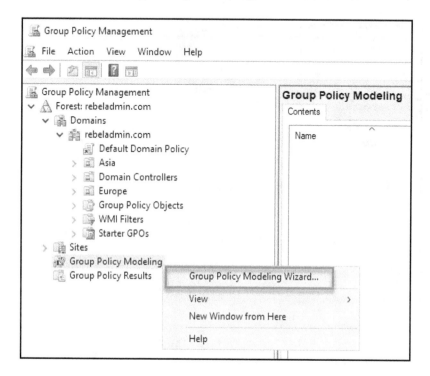

3. On the initial wizard page, click on **Next** to continue with the configuration.

4. In the new window, the wizard asks us to select the domain controller it should use for the simulation. It is recommended that you use a domain controller in the same AD site. Once you've made your selection, click on **Next** to continue.

5. On the user and computer selection page, we can select which user and device should be used in the simulation job. It can be based on an individual entry or at the container level. Once you've made your selection, click on **Next** to proceed:

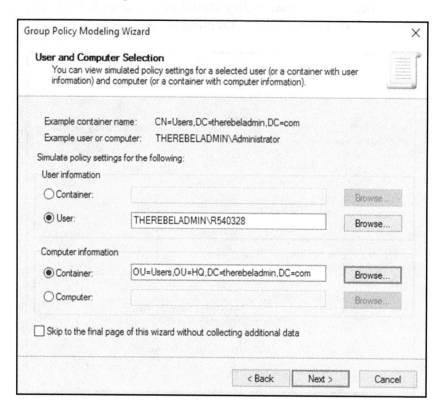

6. In **Advanced Simulation Options**, if required, we can select the **Slow network connection** and **Loopback processing** mode configuration options. We can also define the site that should be used for the simulation:

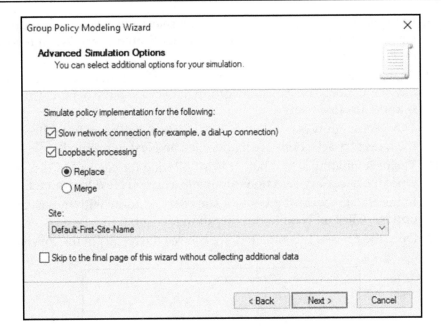

7. In the next window, if needed, we can select an alternative AD path to simulate changes to the network location of the selected user and computer. In this demo, I am using the defaults:

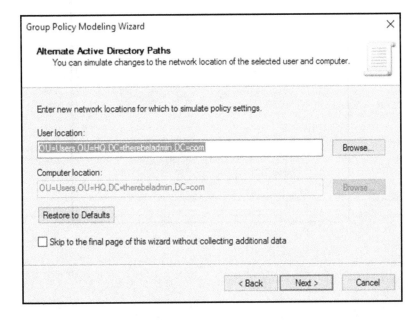

8. In the next window, if required, we can select a user security group to simulate. The default group will be **authenticated users**. When ready, click on **Next** to proceed.

9. Then, it asks whether we need to define the computer security group for our simulation. You can add a group here or keep the default group, which is **authenticated users**.

10. The next window asks whether WMI filtering for users is required. Once the necessary selections are made, click on **Next** to proceed.

11. The next window asks whether WMI filtering for computers is required. Once the necessary selections are made, click on **Next** to proceed.

12. In the end, the wizard gives us a summary window with the selected options. Click on **Next** to run the simulation job.

13. Once the process is completed, we can see the results in the console:

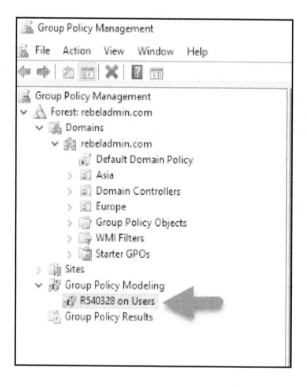

14. We also can rerun the simulation query at any time:

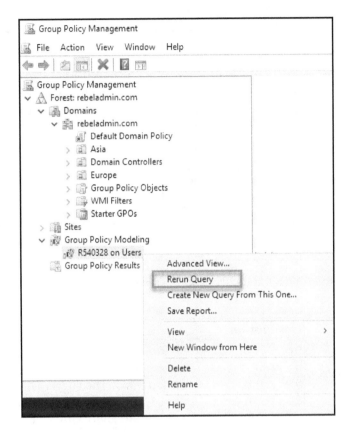

How to troubleshoot AD DS database-related issues

AD maintains a multi-master database. Like any other database, there can be problems such as data corruption, crashes, and data loss. In my entire career, I still haven't come across a situation where a full database recovery was required in a production environment. The reason for this is that an AD DS database keeps replicating to other available domain controllers and it is very rare for all the available domain controllers to crash at the same time and lose data. Unlike other AD issues, there aren't many options for AD DS database troubleshooting.

In the following table, I have listed a few reasons for AD DS database-related issues:

Issue	Description
Hardware failure	The AD database is located in `C:\Windows\NTDS`. This path can be changed, but it cannot be hosted on separate systems. If there is any hardware failure, then we will lose the database along with the domain controller. If there are multiple domain controllers, then recovery is not required as we can simply introduce a new domain controller. If it's an FSMO role holder, then it is still possible to seize roles from any working domain controller and make it the new FSMO role holder.
Software failures	AD runs on top of Windows. System software or any related service corruption can put the AD database in an unusable status. This can also be caused by viruses or malware attacks.
Unexpected shutdown	Unexpected shutdowns can also corrupt an AD database.

In order to prevent AD DS database-related issues, we can take the following precautions:

Option	Description
Back up the AD DS database	In `Chapter 11`, *Active Directory Services*, we looked at AD backup options. There are many tools out there on the market that can be used to back up AD. The success of a backup or disaster recovery solution depends on how quickly and easily it can bring the system back to a working state.
Maintain additional domain controllers	It is not recommended for you to have just one domain controller, even if it's covered with a disaster recovery solution. Each AD site should at least maintain two domain controllers. This is the fastest way to recover from any type of AD DS disaster. If any domain controller becomes unusable, then the other available domain controllers can continue operations with minimal interruptions.
Change the AD DS database and log path	The default location of the AD DS database file and the log files is `C:\Windows\NTDS`. It is recommended that you change the path to a different drive. It can protect database files from OS-level corruption. In `Chapter 11`, *Active Directory Services*, we learned about how we can change the default path.

Defragmentation	Like any other database system, AD DS databases can also have data fragmentation. There are two types of data defragmentation. AD database uses online defragmentation, and it runs every 12 hours automatically. However, after a large number of object cleanups or a large configuration change, it is recommended that you initiate offline defragmentation. The complete process was explained in Chapter 11, *Active Directory Services*.

Integrity checking to detect low-level database corruption

By running an integrity check, we can identify binary-level database corruption. This comes as part of the Ntdsutil tool, which is used for AD database maintenance. This goes through every byte of the database file. The integrity command also checks whether the correct headers exist in the database itself and whether all the tables are functioning and consistent. This process also runs as part of Active **Directory Service Restore Mode (DRSM)**.

This check needs to be run with the **Windows NT Directory Services (NTDS)** service off.

In order to run an integrity check, use the following steps:

1. Log in to the domain controller as Domain/Enterprise Admin.
2. Open PowerShell as an administrator.
3. Stop the NTDS service using net stop ntds.
4. Type the following:

```
ntdsutil
activate instance ntds
files
integrity
```

The output is as follows:

```
file maintenance: integrity
Doing Integrity Check for db: C:\Windows\NTDS\ntds.dit.

Checking database integrity.

                  Scanning  Status (% complete)

     0    10   20   30   40   50   60   70   80   90  100
     |----|----|----|----|----|----|----|----|----|----|
     ..................................................

Integrity check successful.

It is recommended you run semantic database analysis
to ensure semantic database consistency as well.
```

5. To exit from the utility, type `quit`.

6. It is also recommended that you run `semantic database analysis` to confirm the consistency of AD database contents. In order to do this, enter the following:

   ```
   ntdsutil
   activate instance ntds
   semantic database analysis
   go
   ```

   The output is as follows:

```
C:\Windows\system32\ntdsutil.exe: semantic database analysis
semantic checker: go
Fixup mode is turned off
......Done.


Writing summary into log file dsdit.dmp.0
SDs scanned:             117
Records scanned:        4456
Processing records..Done. Elapsed time 1 seconds.

semantic checker: _
```

7. If any integrity issues are detected, then you can type `go fixup` to fix the errors.

8. After the process is completed, type `net start ntds` to start the NTDS service.

AD database recovery

If there is database corruption that cannot be soft recovered (using the preceding method and the `ntdsutil` recovery command), then you need to recover it from a backup. In order to recover an AD database using a system-state-based backup, we need to use DSRM. The relevant recovery steps using DSRM was explained in `Chapter 11`, *Active Directory Services*.

As I mentioned before, AD database issues are very rare in AD environments. If there are any, then you can probably recover from the situation using other options, rather than restoring Active Directory from a backup. This should be the last resort in the troubleshooting process.

Summary

As with any other IT system, AD components can also face issues that can impact their operations. This can be due to many reasons, such as poor design, the result of a management task, hardware or software issues, and resource issues. No one is expected to know how to fix each and every AD-related issue. The most important thing is the starting point of the troubleshooting process and the engineer's approach to finding the solution. This chapter showed you how to troubleshoot the most common AD infrastructure issues with the correct approach.

We started the chapter with AD replication issues. We looked into different scenarios that can cause replication issues and how we can recover from them. Then, we looked into Group Policy-related issues and how to troubleshoot them using Windows' built-in utilities. We also learned about AD DS database-related issues and the approaches we can take to prevent such disasters.

We need to understand that, over the past couple of years, the identity requirements for businesses have dramatically changed. Organizations are moving to cloud-driven identity management such as Azure AD due to many reasons, which we looked at in detail in `Chapter 1`, *Active Directory Fundamentals*. On-premises AD has become a medium that merges traditional authentication and authorization with modern cloud-driven authentication and authorization. Therefore, I added more content about how identity works in a hybrid environment and how we can reap the benefits of Azure AD-centric features in this book. I believe it is more relevant to engineers than only focusing on on-premises AD. If we need to address modern authentication requirements, such as protecting our identities and data from emerging threats, then we need to adopt new technologies and approaches that fit the purpose. I believe this is the same thought Microsoft has about on-premises AD.

Learning never ends for IT engineers. Even I am learning new things still. As IT engineers, continuous research and practice are a must to keep ourselves relevant. Identity management is a skill set that is always in high demand. The products and methods used with identity management can change, but the core concepts about authentication and authorization will remain the same. With regard to the new things you learned from this book, put them into practice. Do not believe them just because they are in the book; try them yourself and understand them. Keep your eyes and ears open for rising identity infrastructure threats and protect your identities as it is key to your environment.

Your feedback is greatly appreciated. Please feel free to send your feedback to `rebeladm@live.com`. I also encourage you to follow me on my blog, `www.rebeladmin.com`, and on Twitter, `@rebeladm`, as I am constantly sharing AD-related content. Thank you for purchasing this book and I wish you all success, happiness, and joy in your life.

Other Books You May Enjoy

If you enjoyed this book, you may be interested in these other books by Packt:

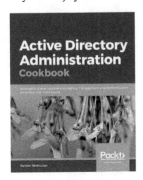

Active Directory Administration Cookbook
Sander Berkouwer

ISBN: 978-1-78980-698-4

- Manage new Active Directory features, such as the Recycle Bin, group Managed Service Accounts, and fine-grained password policies
- Work with Active Directory from the command line and use Windows PowerShell to automate tasks
- Create and remove forests, domains, and trusts
- Create groups, modify group scope and type, and manage memberships
- Delegate control, view and modify permissions
- Optimize Active Directory and Azure AD in terms of security

Mastering Windows Group Policy
Jordan Krause

ISBN: 978-1-78934-739-5

- Become familiar with the Group Policy Management Console
- Create, link, and filter new policies
- Secure your users and devices using Group Policy
- Maintain and troubleshoot Group Policy
- Administer Group Policy via PowerShell
- Control your Active Directory environment efficiently with Group Policy settings

Leave a review - let other readers know what you think

Please share your thoughts on this book with others by leaving a review on the site that you bought it from. If you purchased the book from Amazon, please leave us an honest review on this book's Amazon page. This is vital so that other potential readers can see and use your unbiased opinion to make purchasing decisions, we can understand what our customers think about our products, and our authors can see your feedback on the title that they have worked with Packt to create. It will only take a few minutes of your time, but is valuable to other potential customers, our authors, and Packt. Thank you!

Index

G

geographical model
  about 266, 267, 268
  advantages 268
  disadvantages 268
Global Address List Synchronization
  (GALSync) 615
global catalog server
  about 27
  considerations 103
  placement 103, 104
globally unique identifier (GUID) 31, 33
Globally Unique Identifier (GUID) 284, 454,
  712
good time server (GTIMESERV) 70
GPRESULT 728, 729, 730, 731
Group Managed Service Accounts (gMSAs)
  about 244, 246, 430
  requisites 245
  using 229
group policies, AD environment
  local policies 288
  non-local policies 288
group policies
  administration tasks, automating 281
  benefits 280
  flexible targeting 281, 282
  no modifications, to target 282
  standards, maintaining 280
  users, preventing from changing system
    settings 281
Group Policy capabilities 282, 283
Group Policy container (GPC)
  about 284, 285, 286
  computer configuration 285
  user configuration 285
Group Policy issues
  troubleshooting 726, 727
Group Policy Management 291
Group Policy Management Console (GPMC)
  295
Group Policy Management MMC 731
Group Policy Modeling Wizard 734, 736, 737,
  738, 739
Group Policy objects (GPO)

about 75, 142, 282, 283
  Group Policy container (GPC) 284, 285
  Group Policy template (GPT) 286, 287
Group Policy Results Wizard 731, 732, 733,
  734
Group Policy template (GPT) 286, 287
Group Policy, levels in AD environment
  domain 288
  Organization units (OUs) 288
  site 288
Group Policy
  administrative templates 300, 301
  best practices 319, 320, 321
  conflicts 294, 295, 296, 297
  filtering 301, 302
  inheritance 291, 292, 293
  mapping 297, 298, 299
  preferences 311, 312, 313, 314
  processing 287, 288, 289, 291
  status 297, 298, 299
group scope
  about 248, 249
  Domain Local groups 248
  Global groups 248
  Universal group 249
group
  about 247
  converting 249
  distribution groups 248
  security groups 247
  setting up 250, 251, 252

H

hierarchical naming structure
  about 118, 119, 120, 121
  considerations 120, 121
high availability (HA) 596
High Watermark Vector (HWMV) table 356
hybrid Azure AD join devices
  about 74, 75
  supportive operating systems, Windows
    current devices 75
  supportive operating systems, Windows
    down-level devices 76
hybrid Azure AD join method 74

CPSIA information can be obtained
at www.ICGtesting.com
Printed in the USA
JSHW050500180822
29426JS00002B/15